Economic Organizations and Social Systems

ECONOMIC ORGANIZATIONS AND SOCIAL SYSTEMS

Robert A. Solo

Ann Arbor
THE UNIVERSITY OF MICHIGAN PRESS

Copyright © by the University of Michigan 2000
First published by The Bobbs-Merrill Company, Inc. 1967
All rights reserved
Published in the United States of America by
The University of Michigan Press
Manufactured in the United States of America
♾ Printed on acid-free paper

2003   2002   2001   2000   4   3   2   1

A CIP catalog record for this book is available from the British Library.

Library of Congress Cataloguing-in-Publication Data applied for

ISBN 0-472-09723-7 (cloth: alk. paper)
ISBN 0-472-06723-0 (pbk.: alk. paper)

Preface to the Second Edition

This will be about paradigms.

Thomas Kuhn's *Structure of Scientific Revolutions* taught us that each of the sciences normally operates within the tightly bounded framework of its "paradigm" and all that falls outside the paradigm is excluded or ignored. The most interesting and significant works that I encountered during a long career as an economist, like Joseph Schumpeter's *Capitalism, Socialism and Democracy,* or Kenneth Boulding's *A Reconstruction of Economics, The Image,* and *Ecodynamics,* and my own work as well, all fall outside the economics paradigm. For that reason, rich as they might be in observation and insight, they were never made part of, nor could they contribute to, the evolution of an economic science. Their thought was not among its building blocks, nor was it incorporated into a teaching curriculum so that it might be carried on though the generations.

What happens to books like these? They are read, praised, enjoyed for a season. They are worked over in a handful of graduate seminars, then, relegated to lists of recommended reading, they begin their drift into oblivion.

Aside from the "normal science" done within the paradigm, there may occur the rare event Kuhn calls "revolutionary science" that shatters and reaches beyond the scope of an existing paradigm to create another that might better comprehend some universe of concern.

Each year there are many, perhaps millions of students being indoctrinated with the established economics paradigm, which is to say that an image of economic reality is being inculcated in their minds through which they will thenceforth view reality, organize observation, and form opinion. Suppose we had good reason to believe that this inculcated image is wrong and should be replaced. How to do it? How to revolutionize the established paradigm and replace it? That is the problem with which we are here concerned.

What do we know about the process of scientific revolutions? We know that once established, the paradigm is highly resistant to change. We know that, by the record, this resistance to change goes far deeper in economics than in physics. Thus while the realities of the physical universe do not change, during the nineteenth and twentieth centuries there were a number of great scientific revolutions in physics. While during those same two centuries there were revolutionary transformations of economic realities, the established economic paradigm remained intact.

I will propose, discuss, argue for a change of the neoclassical paradigm. But the conventional wisdom holds that the economic paradigm cannot be changed through reasoned discourse and that nothing can open the way to its replacement short of economic catastrophe. That may be true. Certainly I know of no instance where a paradigm in any science has been transformed through deliberated design and reasoned debate. On the other hand I know of no organized effort to transform an established science paradigm through deliberated design and reasoned debate. We can try, can't we?

Let me tell you of this coincidence. In mid-July 1999, when the University of Michigan Press decided to reissue my *Economic Organizations and Social Systems,* I had just emerged from a long period of scholarly hibernation to attend a conference of the Society for Advancement of Socio-Economics (SASE) being held at the University of Wisconsin at Madison. Circulating among and speaking with colleagues there, I was reinforced in my impression that a degree of dissatisfaction with the adequacy of the neoclassical paradigm coexists with the sense of a need to supplement, transform, or replace it and hence that the time may be ripe to achieve such change through deliberated design and reasoned discourse.

There is this old political dictum: "You can't beat someone (no matter what you think of that someone) with no one." That is the trouble with the SASE-type attack on the established paradigm. They are fighting something with nothing, save a high-flown statement of aspirations and values. Replace the existing paradigm, but with what? For meaningful discourse *and for a rational choice* what is needed is a clear and concrete alternative to the established paradigm, even if only as a basis of discussion. It is here that *Economic Organizations and Social Systems,* first published in 1967, comes into the picture.

I can never complain about the initial reception of that book. It was enthusiastically received and praised by reviews across the whole ideological spectrum. It had its day in the sun, for which I am eternally grateful. And then? Like those other books conceived and written outside the economics paradigm, it too faded into oblivion. But the difference is this. *Economic Organizations and Social Systems* envisages and lays out a new and very different social science. It was written to provide a paradigm that would encompass the essentials of traditional economics but go far beyond its scope, bringing the cognitive and the cultural, the historical, the psychological, and the political into play. Can *Economic Organizations and Social Systems* be considered as the founding format and teaching text for a new economics to replace the established neoclassical economic paradigm?

In his lead review of *Economic Organizations and Social Systems* in *Science* Kenneth Boulding named the book "A Social Science for All of Society."

This is an important work, a milestone in the long and difficult road towards the development of an adequate theory of the dynamics of the world social system or sociosphere as I have sometimes called it.

In his review in the *Economic Journal* G. C. Allen wrote:

With this massive book Professor Solo has lifted the study of economic organization to a new plane of discourse. Although his approach is primarily that of the economist, he has examined his subject "in the round" and with great skill has synthesized the results of relevant work in other social sciences. In particular he makes it clear, in every stage of his exposition, that an understanding of any form of economic organization is incomplete or even impossible without a grasp of the social system within which it operates.

Later G. C. Allen's rejoinder to John Kenneth Galbraith's Reith Lectures was published as an occasional paper by the (British) Institute for Economic Affairs. Professor Allen closes that paper with these words: "For those who view Professor Galbraith's confident assertions with misgiving, Professor Solo may be commended as a guide in whom we can place trust." I like that sentiment, and I consider this good advice. Put your trust in Bob Solo.

Apologies to those who find it unseemly for an author to cite reviews favorable to his work, but I know no better way to induce you to take this book seriously, to read it thoughtfully, and with high expectations.

It is our position in a nutshell that, in spite of its great strengths and transcendent values, the neoclassical paradigm is unsuited for our time. Too often as a mode of thought it blinds us to pregnant realities and offers no conceptual grasp of phenomena of critical importance in the universe of our concern. That universe is of immense complexity and the rife confusions concerning it attest to our failure and to the inadequacy of our paradigm. To bring light and understanding to that universe is surely our responsibility (who else's?) and for that we need another approach, a different mode of thought, a widened scope, but working still from a common base and within a shared framework. In other words, we need a new paradigm. I know that *Economic Organizations and Social Systems* can, and I hope it will, play a role in the creation of that new paradigm.

Because it is no mere statement of aspiration, but is put forward as a concrete alternative to the neoclassical paradigm, this book provides a basis for contrast, for comparison, for reasoned evaluation by you, and you, and you, in the choice of this versus that. Hence, let us hope, the debate begins here!

The book is in your hands, yours to judge. In the rest of this preface, I will try to highlight some elements in the proposed transformation of the neoclassical paradigm.

Consider the post-Keynesian micro-macro model conceived in the Samuelson mode as two views of the same economy. The macro was of the economy as an aggregated whole. The micro supposedly viewed the internal operations of that same economy.

I am forever amazed that for all these years the macroeconomists and the microeconomists, teachers and taught, never recognized that the micro and the macro were absolutely incompatible. These two were not and never could be aspects of the same economy. The micro needed free moving and flexible prices; it could not operate without them. The macro demanded and could not operate without fixed, "rigid," inflexible prices.

Micro and macro are in fact two distinct and different forms of economic organization that may coexist as variants in a market system. The micro refers to a "decentralized market-directed" form with the U.S. farm sector as an analogue.

The macro is what I call the "organizational market-negotiating" form of economic organization, with its analogue in the corporate industrial sector of the U.S. economy, where price is determined as a function of corporate policy. Neither Keynes or the Keynesians ever (at least overtly) recognized that their single economy combined the separate operations of two different and quite incompatible forms of organization, nor did they deal with the fundamental contradiction this implied.

Another word on the organizational market-negotiating form of economic organization that John R. Commons called "the negotiational, organizational, political economy."[1] Commons saw that the massive modern corporate enterprise can possibly be understood as a community, as a government or quasi government, but not as an autonomous, self-interested, greed-driven individual. That, however, is precisely how the neoclassical economist understands it, for the neoclassical paradigm can accommodate no other sort of decision-making entity. Paradoxically, rather than bringing in the skills of other disciplines to comprehend the behavior of the corporate organizational entity, neoclassical economics has, with its theory of rational choice (as a function of the self-interested profit-maximizing choice of the autonomous individual), invaded the other disciplines, infiltrated the judiciary, and distorted the law.[2]

Economic Organization and Social Systems, in its analysis of the "organizational market-negotiating" form of economic organization, conceives of and proposes a theory of *organizational choice*. In so doing it opens a field for socioeconomic explorations seeking to comprehend this restless, evasive political cum organizational entity now in a state of rapid transition, at this moment of writing teetering atop the Wall Street bull market, exploding in buyout and takeover and the endless merging of the already-many-times merged, operating within a system where one witnesses the massive export of manufacturing capacities, the demise of the trade union, the virtual disappearance of public regulation and control, and the onrush towards globalization.

There are thus many forms of economic organization, including those that do not operate through markets (e.g., political economies, household economies, and institutional economies such as academia) and multi-organizational forms where the character of the mix is of vital importance (e.g., compare the character and role of the political and private linkage in the operation of the American agricultural economy with that linkage in the operation of the military-industrial complex). All of these are at least touched upon in *Economic Organizations and*

Social Systems but always and primarily to provide conceptual grasp and to develop a mode of analytic approach rather than to say the final and definitive word.

This then is the First Lesson. There is no "the economy." There is no single economic "essence" that explains it all. There are only different ways of organizing the production and distribution of goods and services, each with its own operating logic, motivational forces and control mechanisms, values, defects, vulnerabilities, and potentials.

The first part of this book is devoted to the comparative analysis and evaluation of three selected forms of economic organization, again with the aim of developing a general approach to the analysis of any form of economic organization. The three selected for in-depth analysis and comparative evaluation are: (1) decentralized market-direction; (2) organizational market-negotiation; and (3) centralized political-direction with its analogue in the operation of the former Soviet Union.

The three are compared and evaluated by reference to:

1. *efficiency,*
2. *motivating force* and *control mechanisms,*
3. *justice* or *injustice* in the distribution of income, and
4. the *social environment* they provide.

Hence a Second Lesson: that the different forms of economic organization should be subject to the rigorous contrast and comparative evaluation absent in neoclassical economics.

There is also a criterion, left out of the list, that is of supreme importance in our time, namely the capacity for technological development. That capacity is the root of technological advance and hence of higher economic productivity and economic growth. It is the prime determinant of power among the nations and of a nation's ability to provide its people with a bountiful life. It is society's sole protection against the inevitable shrinkage and despoliation of the natural resource base. Neoclassical economics has said nothing and has nothing to say concerning the capacity for technological development. There is no place within its tight boundaries to explore and explain the diverse processes of technological advance and its elements of invention, innovation, systemic research, and the flow of information. To explain the rise or decline of productivity neoclassical economics has relied on the alleged effect of changing resource ratios, for example, of labor and land (in Malthus) and of capital and labor for the rest.

Economic Organizations and Social Systems focuses on the capacity for technological development as a critical element in any system of economic progress. It first disposes of neoclassical explanations of productivity change[3] and proposes a theory and an economics of technological development as an element in systems of economic progress. It articulates a brief review of the operation of such systems in the different phases of human history from Neolithic ages to the Organizational Revolution. The book then proceeds to the comparative analysis and evaluation of technological development and advance in the three selected forms of economic organization. Whatever the ultimate value of all this, I can claim at least to have offered a conceptual grasp of and an analytic approach to immensely important economic phenomena.

In the second part of the book, our focus shifts from a study of the individual forms of economic organization to an analysis of the agglomeration of such forms that compose the national, in this case the U.S., economy. Within this national economy we define and differentiate between an enterprise economy, a political economy, a household economy, and an institutional economy, demonstrating that the national economy itself is a system where its political, enterprise, institutional, and household components interact and interdepend, and where the viability and strength of each component is a function of its relation with the others. Compare, for example, the vast peasant economies of South America, Asia, and Africa with the farm economy of the United States. All alike operate as decentralized price-directed forms of economic organization. The former are poverty-ridden and underdeveloped, while the latter is technically advanced and has been, by the measure of performance, the strongest sector of the U.S. economy. In our international trading accounts, it remains the primary source of U.S. trade surplus. Our agricultural economy is as strong as it is only because of its links to and interaction with the U.S. political economy, the institutional economy, and the corporate industrial sector in the enterprise economy. These have been the source of virtually all of its technological advances. They have served to stabilize an impossibly volatile market and have provided its physical infrastructure.

Still more is needed to explain economic (indeed all human) behavior than the mode and manner in which such activities are organized. The third part of *Economic Organization and Social Systems* concentrates on the character of knowledge, on the modes of thought, on prevailing values, on ideologies, and on the icons of tradition as variables in relation to economic behavior and events.

In the first part of the book, "centralized political-direction" as a form of economic organization was studied in depth, stipulating its structural strengths and weaknesses and emphasizing ideological dedication at its motivational core. In this third part, we view the operation of centralized political-direction in the context of Russian-*cum*-Soviet culture and cognition, as part of an immense event, the Russian Revolution where we observe the formation, nature, and tragic path of a revolutionary elite, the cruel and stormy process of an economic development that ultimately established an industrial capacity in the Soviet Union that enabled the Soviets to withstand the most devastating blows of the Wehrmacht and come back from an industry transported to the Urals, to defeat and destroy the German armies and to conquer Germany. The defeat of Hitler was essentially a Soviet victory. And then with its devastated land turned by war into a virtual desert, and without an iota of help from the outside, the Soviet Union recreated a viable society, a strong economy, and a military capability that raised it to the status of a superpower.

For many years the Russian people lived, worked, and fought in an atmosphere of fear and religious fervor (for communism is a religion) under the ruthless tyranny of Josef Stalin. Khrushchev with his bluff commonality liberated them from that tyranny and its accompanying mythos and fanaticism. And then there arose the question as to whether or not Communist Russia could survive as a secular socialist state. The answer came some four decades later (long after this book was written) with the abandonment of Soviet Communism. This was followed by the creation of a Russian capitalism under the instruction of American economists following a blueprint of the neoclassical paradigm which quickly led to virtual economic collapse.

The third part of the book examines other instances or problems requiring fundamental economic and social change, for example, underdevelopment in the Third World and the revolutionary transformation that development requires, with culture and cognition at the heart of the matter. In dealing with such problems a viable economics would take into account, or turn to, or itself assimilate, the concepts and skills of behavioral science.

In our approach to the phenomenon and problem of development we postulate the cognitive-cultural basis for the post–World War II international preoccupation with underdevelopment and international assistance on that score. We tentatively propose the need for a revolutionary elite to spearhead the process of economic development and outline the knowledge, policies, and strategies they might require in order to achieve their revolution. And we offer two case studies, one of relative success and one of failure in the revolution of economic development

All this should underline our paradigm not as a promise of completing things, but one of opening doors.

Though wide-ranging, the book is an integral work. Each part requires and follows from that which preceded it, with an eye to the socioeconomic whole.

NOTES

1. Many years ago when I read philosophy at the London School of Economics as the first graduate student there of Professor Karl Popper, my mentor one day said to me "You cannot learn from others. You must start from the beginning always, and think it through for yourself." He observed what is for me at once a blessing and a curse. It means my work is never systematically and consciously based on someone else's teaching or theories and is always, in that sense, original and my own. But it also means that I am bound to miss so

much that is relevant to my concerns and even anticipates my own work. I have never read Commons, and it is only now in reading John E. Elliot's chapter "The Institutional School of Political Economy" in the book *What Is Political Economy?* edited by David Whynes that I observe and reflect on how very close to some of my own thinking were the arguments of John R. Commons. My apologies to Commons. My apologies to the Institutionalists.

2. Also see my "Inter-Enterprise Conspiracy and the Theory of the Firm." *Journal of Business of the University of Chicago* (April 1961).

3. In his review of my book in *Science,* Kenneth Boulding wrote "[H]e demolishes in a few pages almost 200 years of capital theory, apparently with a single firecracker but with astonishing thoroughness. . . . He does a similar . . . [demolition] of Malthusianism."

REFERENCES

Allen, G. C. 1969. "Review of *Economic Organizations and Social Systems.*" *Economic Journal* 79 (313): 124–26.

———. 1967. "Economic Fact and Fantasy: A Rejoinder to Galbraith's Reith Lectures." Occasional paper, Institute of Economic Affairs, London.

Boulding, Kenneth. 1978. *Ecodynamics: A New Theory of Societal Evolution.* Beverly Hills: Sage Publications.

———. 1956. *The Image: Knowledge in Life and Society.* Ann Arbor: University of Michigan Press.

———. 1956. *A Reconstruction of Economics.* New York: Wiley.

Elliott, John E. "The Institutionalist School of Political Economy." In *What Is Political Economy? Eight Perspectives,* edited by David K. Whynes. Oxford: Blackwell.

Kuhn, Thomas. 1962. *The Structure of Scientific Revolutions.* Chicago: University of Chicago Press.

Schumpeter, Joseph A. 1942. *Capitalism, Socialism, and Democracy.* New York: Harper and Brothers.

Solo, Robert A. 1974. *The Political Authority and the Market System.* Cincinnati: South-Western.

———. 1961. "Intra-Enterprise Conspiracy and the Theory of the Firm." *Journal of Business* 34 (2): 153–66.

———. 1954. "Research and Development in the Synthetic Rubber Industry." *Quarterly Journal of Economics* 68 (1): 61–82.

Preface

If the questioner were to ask: How would *you* comprehend an actual economy? or compare different economies? or confront problems (such as those of economic development) where the capacity to mobilize energies and to act as a coherent social force is at issue? This book would be my answer. The gist of what the book attempts is best conveyed by briefly outlining what it does.

Part I treats of three alternative forms for the organization of economic activities: through the choices of individuals in competitive markets, through the plans of political authorities, and through the negotiated market relationships of autonomous groups, e.g., of "big business" corporations or trade unions. These are among the important building blocks of actual economies. They also might be considered as the ideal types in the conventional approach to the comparative analysis of economic systems.

First, these three forms of economic organization are contrasted for their efficiency, their stability, the costs of their institutional prerequisites, and their capacity to achieve some desired or "just" distribution of income.

Second, the three forms of economic organization are contrasted for their capacity to generate technical advance and higher productivity. To do this, a theory of economic progress is proposed.

Finally, the three forms of economic organization are contrasted as social environments, ways of life that generate particular attitudes and values among their participants.

Part II treats of the national economy conceived as a peculiar complex of interacting forms of economic organization. In broad strokes the structure of the American national economy is drawn, and American economic policy is interpreted as the consequence and response to the problems particular to each of its constituent forms as well as to the tensions and incongruities that arise out of their interaction. The American national economy is divided into four basic sectors: the enterprise economy, the political economy, the institutional economy, and the household economy. Each is studied in turn. Each has its particular *modus operandi.*

The enterprise economy, characterized by profit-oriented entities producing for sale on the market, is subdivided into constituent forms of economic organization. Each form of economic organization is examined for its efficiency, stability, and capacity to generate technical advance in the light of a historical experience of problem and crisis, and the respond-ing formulation of public policy.

The political economy includes those activities of government related to the organization of production and consumption. Particular attention is given to the problems, policies, and policy potentialities for the organi-zation of Research and Development as a function of the American political economy.

The institutional economy includes schools, hospitals, research founda-tions, universities, and churches, where activities are organized around a commitment to core values. Problems and policies in the organization of higher education and "basic" research (with educated manpower and "fundamental" science as outputs) are examined as belonging to the institutional economy.

The household economy includes the production and/or consumption of goods and services by and for families or family-like groups; our con-cern is with the role of this economy in the organization of consumption in the United States.

Finally, in Part II, the problems and policy responses consequent upon the interaction of coexisting but incongruent forms of economic organi-zation are examined (with the difficulty of maintaining full employment *and* stable prices in the United States taken as one example).

Part III, which might be read independently of the other two parts, focuses on the economic development of low-productivity societies. Con-ceiving the central issue as an incapacity for coherent social action, a framework is proposed for the integral conception of society and for the exploration of the constituent elements of social activity.

A number of hypotheses are ventured; their logical implications are developed and "tested" against historical cases. Thus, by reference to the "industrial revolution" and to the "organizational revolution," the process of development is conceived as a continuous transformation of the system of cognition. The role of elites in the development revolution is hypothe-sized, and the hypothesis is developed and tested by reference to the Communist revolution in Russia. The cultural and cognitive preconditions of development are proposed and are examined by reference to the experiences of Mexico and Puerto Rico. The problems and possibilities of organizing cognition as an instrument of development are examined by reference to the concrete functions of science-based activities and science-trained manpower. The attitudes of nations, the universal rise in mass expectations, the problems and costs of cultural transition are con-sidered as the context of development. Finally, some implications for aid policy in the United States are suggested.

This book tries to make a new beginning. It is not systematically and consciously based on someone else's teaching or theories; nevertheless, it brings to bear the influence of many from whom I have learned and who have shaped my approach. The reader will readily discern those influences.

The book itself was a long time in the making. In the summer of 1958, an experimental course given at the University of Michigan at Ann Arbor was based on an embryo version. The theory of economic progress developed in Part I and the chapters relating to the organization of Research and Development owe much to my work at the National Planning Association in 1961–63 where Gerhard Colm is Chief Economist. In the analysis of economic development, I have drawn upon my experience with the Economic Development Administration in Puerto Rico during 1959–61, and with the O.E.C.D. in Paris in 1964, where I studied the use of scientific resources in technical assistance programs. A portion of Part III was covered in my lecture series at the Sorbonne given in 1964–65 at the invitation of Professor Francois Perroux. The book was completed at Princeton, where I have been most generously supported by my mentor, Professor Fritz Machlup.

I acknowledge gratefully the help and support of my wife throughout, and I thank William Wooldridge, who copy-edited the manuscript, for his effort and interest.

ROBERT A. SOLO

Contents

Part I: Forms of Economic Organization

1. Three Forms of Economic Organization   3
The Decentralized Market-Directed Form of Economic
   Organization   4
The Centralized Politically Directed Form of Economic
   Organization   7
The Organizational Market-Negotiated Form   12
The Task Ahead   15

2. A Theory of Organizational Choice   17
Choice and Action Through Autonomous Organizations   17
Authoritative vs. Composite Choice: A Political Analogy   22
Variations in the Structure of Organizational Choice   29
Summary   33

3. Decentralized Market-Direction and Resource Allocation   34
Motivation   34
Recruitment of an Elite   35
Institutional Costs   38
Sensitivity to Stimuli   40
Distortion Through External Economies and Diseconomies   42
Instabilities   45
Uncertainties   47
The Organization of Consumption   50
Justice in the Distribution of Income   53
Implications of Reform   55
Summary   56

4. Centralized Political-Direction and Resource Allocation   58
Modus operandi   58
Motivation and Recruitment   58
Institutional Costs   60
Sensitivity to Stimuli   62

Distortion Through Externality and Through Exclusion   64
Instabilities   66
Uncertainties   66
The Organization of Consumption   67
Justice in the Distribution of Income   69
Summary   70

5. Organizational Market-Negotiation and Resource Allocation   72
   Modus operandi   72
   Motivation and Recruitment   74
   Institutional Costs   76
   Sensitivity to Stimuli   78
   Distortion Through Externalization, Through Exclusion, and
        Through Arbitrary Power   79
   Instabilities   84
   Uncertainties   85
   The Organization of Consumption   85
   Justice in the Distribution of Income   86
   Summary   87

6. Economic Progress as a Social Function   88

7. The Insignificance of Capital Accumulation   91

8. The Economics of Transformation   101
   Transformation to Higher Processes   101
   The Costs of Transformation   103
   The Strategy of Transformation   106
   Summary   110

9. Economic Progress as a System   111
   Three Forms of Economic Choice   111
   Transformation and Innovation   113
   Invention: Setting the Goal of Transformation   114
   Communication: Linking Science-Invention-Innovation-Transfor-
        mation   118
   Summary: The System of Economic Progress   120

10. The Changing System of Economic Progress   122
    Economic Progress in Traditional Societies   122
    Economic Progress in the Era of Individualism   124
    Economic Progress in the Age of Organization   128
    Summary   129

11. Population and Progress: A Footnote 131

12. Decentralized Market-Direction and the Organization of
    Economic Progress 135
    The Capacity for Invention 135
    Investment in Science, Invention, Innovation 138
    The Dissemination of Invention and the Speed of Transformation 141
    A Test of the Hypothesis 144
    Summary 146

13. Centralized Political-Direction and the Organization of Economic
    Progress 148
    The Capacity for Invention 148
    Investment in Science, Invention, Innovation 150
    The Spread of Invention and the Speed of Transformation 153
    Summary 158

14. The Economy of Autonomous Organization and Economic Progress 160
    The Capacity for Invention 160
    Investment in Science, Invention, Innovation 161
    The Spread of Invention and the Speed of Transformation 163
    The Role of Government 166
    Summary 168

15. Economic Organization as a Social Environment 170

16. Decentralized Market-Direction as a Social Environment 175
    Economic Organization as a Way of Life 175
    Impact on Social Values and on Human Character 177
    Compatibility with Other Social and Political Institutions 180
    Summary 184

17. Centralized Political-Direction as a Social Environment 186
    Economic Organization as a Way of Life 186
    Impact on Social Values and on Human Character 189
    Compatibility with Other Social Institutions 193
    Summary 194

18. The Economy of Autonomous Organizations as a Social
    Environment 196
    The Economy as a Way of Life 196
    Impact on Social Values and on Human Character 198
    Compatibility with Other Social Institutions 201
    Summary 202

Part II: The National Economy

19. The Analysis of a National Economy   205

20. The Enterprise Economy   207

21. Problems and Policies in Organizing Production and Distribution
        in the Enterprise Economy   218

22. Problems and Policies in Organizing Economic Progress in the
        Enterprise Economy   244

23. The Political Economy   265
        The Organization of Consumption   265
        The Organization of Production   270

24. Research and Development and the American Political Economy   277

25. The Institutional Economy   302

26. The Crisis in Western Education   308

27. The Organization of Academic Science   322

28. The Household Economy   337

29. The Halfway House   343

Part III: Social Systems and Economic Development

30. Functional, Cognitive, and Cultural Systems   357

31. Economic Revolution as a Revolution in Cognition   376

32. The Revolutionary Leadership   385

33. Economic Revolution in Russia   394

34. The Cultural-Cognitive Basis for Economic Development   416
        The Cognitive Base   416
        Organizing Science as an Instrument of Development   419
        The Cultural Base   431

35. Development that Failed: The Case of Mexico   438
    A Review of Mexican History   438
    The Barriers to Mexican Development   453

36. The World Environment of Economic Development   462

37. Economic Development in Puerto Rico   471

38. Policy and Strategy   479
    A Revolutionary Leadership   479
    A Revolutionary Cognition   480
    Education for Economic Revolution   482
    Sharing the Gains of Development   487

Index   489

PART I

FORMS OF ECONOMIC ORGANIZATION

Chapter 1

Three Forms of Economic Organization

The Economy as a Combination of Decision-Taking Systems. Edward Mason, at the United Nations Conference on the Application of Science and Technology for the Benefit of the Less Developed Economies, spoke of the "critical importance" of determining "what decisions should be centrally made, considering the institutional structure of society, and what should be left to subordinate units, whether public or private . . . centralization versus decentralization is a fundamental problem in all economies seeking development, whether socialist or capitalist. . . . An efficient information and communications system, capable management and effective incentives all depend on an optimal relation between centralized and decentralized authority . . . the problem exists for all." [1]

Mason is right as far as he goes. The question of whether, where, and to what extent authority should be centralized is a problem for all private and public organizations. Every economy, whether labeled "socialist" or "capitalist," has evolved as a complex of both centralized and decentralized decision-taking forms.

Nevertheless, in order to explain the comparative operations and performances, strengths and weaknesses of different national economies, it does not suffice to admit the admixture of centralized and decentralized choice. It is not enough to say, as Mason does, that centralized and decentralized choice is "conditioned by the institutional structure and stage of development of a society," or that the choice between centralizing or decentralizing authority is to be made "considering the institutional structure of a society." In fact, the "institutional structure" is part and parcel with the locus of decision-taking. Inevitably, we are dealing not only with centralization and decentralization, but also with these as elements of integral decision-taking, action-generating systems. Small entrepreneurs in a competitive market and the many shareholders of a great corporation both signify decentralized choice, but they are component parts of radically different forms for generating and controlling economic activities. The key to effective analysis is not that every actual economy exhibits both centralized and decentralized choice, but is rather that every actual economy is composed of a number of different forms of economic

[1] Edward S. Mason, "Some Aspects of the Strategy of Development Planning: Centralization vs. Decentralization," Agenda Item H, Geneva, November 8, 1962.

3

organization, and that social choice is between different forms of economic organization of which a degree of centralization and the locus of authority are elements.

Part I will examine three forms of economic organization. These, combined with still other forms of economic organization, of which there are many, may compose the constituent parts of actual economies. The three forms of economic organization to be studied here will be called (1) Decentralized Market-Directed, (2) Centralized Politically Directed, (3) Organizational Market-Negotiated.

Our objective is *not* to judge between them, nor to suggest any one as the ideal. We suppose rather that in adapting to a variety of needs and circumstances, every society requires a combination of these and/or other forms of organization—which may be more or less optimal in terms of those needs and circumstances. Our purpose is to delineate the prerequisites for the operation of each, and to specify the quite different limitations, dangers, and potential values inherent in each.

THE DECENTRALIZED MARKET-DIRECTED FORM
OF ECONOMIC ORGANIZATION

This form of economic organization is to be associated with the classical or neoclassical model of the competitive market economy. It is the essential model not only of Alfred Marshall, but also of Hicks and (if the equivocal rigidities that he introduced are excluded) also that of Keynes. Its extreme and most simplified form is in the Theory of Pure Competition. It has its practical analogue in the production and marketing of agricultural staples in Western economies. Its essential institutional parameters and the manner in which it is supposed to operate are, or should be, sufficiently familiar that they need not be developed in detail here.

Market Price as the Regulator. In this form of organization, the essential regulator of all economic activities is market price. The nature of the man-to-man relationship in production and in distribution is the relationship of exchange. Economic decision-making involves a number of independent individual choices so large that no one dominates, and all are dominated by the free movement of price.

Individuals bargain together. They bargain as laborers who have services to sell, as consumers who have goods to buy, as savers who have money to lend. They bargain as owners with property to rent, and as entrepreneurs who have resources to acquire and commodities to offer. Out of this universe of bidding, buying, borrowing, emerges *price*. Price is the automatic, double reflex—of the availability of resources, and of the intensity of demand. Guided by price, savers save, borrowers borrow, producers produce, consumers consume, workers work. Under the direction of price, resources are allocated, goods are produced, products and services are distributed, investments are made, and income is shared.

Production is organized through the agency of the firm. The firm is the personal instrument of the profit-seeking entrepreneur who would maximize his private gain by manipulating inputs to minimize costs and by manipulating outputs to maximize the market value of his product.

Price provides an index of real resource scarcities. It reflects every change in resource availability and every change in consumer evaluation, so that the scarcer the resource, the higher it registers on the scale of costs. The entrepreneur adjusts inputs so as to minimize costs because it pays him to do so and because competition requires that he must, reducing the use of what is deemed relatively scarce and substituting what is deemed relatively plentiful. By this action the entrepreneur maximizes for society the output values to be derived from the available resources.

Price provides a schedule of output priorities, indicating the relative intensity of wants of those who have the wherewithal to buy and the will to consume. Adjusting outputs to that schedule of priorities because it pays him to do so and because, under competition, he must, the entrepreneur shapes output to meet the consumer's desires.

Prices change under the shifting winds of demand. The consequent windfall gains and windfall losses are necessary parts of the system's functioning. Windfalls provide the bait and the beating that shape resources to the flux of consumer values.

In this system where price is the universal governor of all activities, who sets price? The question is asked only to emphasize that, in this form of economic organization, the question is meaningless. No one sets price, nor is price set. It moves freely in automatic response to the innumerable individual choices of those who participate in the bargaining process.

Institutional Prerequisites: Markets, Money, Contract. For this form of economic organization, there must be markets: local markets, regional markets, world markets, linking together all stages of production and consumption, so that services can be offered, goods displayed, bids brought together, prices publicized, merchandise cleared, decisions integrated. The market is the first and central prerequisite.

In complex markets, money, that generalized claim on all goods, is necessary. Money is the ultimate credit instrument. Nevertheless, it is but one of the species of this genus, and, like the others, it is required by (and is partially a creation of) the developed market function.

The exchange economy requires the extension of the market bargain through time. Commitments must be projected into the far future: commitments to work, to manage, to borrow, to lend, to repay, to buy, to deliver. Such arrangements and commitments, arrived at through market bargain, require *contract*. Implicit in a system of contract are the means (1) of defining precisely those arrangements which have been or which, legitimately, might be entered into, (2) of resolving conflicts in the interpretation of commitments and obligations, and (3) of enforcing those commitments under the law. Contract is another major institutional prerequisite for this form of economic organization.

Property as the Locus of Power. Every form of economic organization must have loci of economic power; power over men, over resources, over commodities, power over consumption, power to organize, to control, to discipline. In this instance, the economic power has its locus in ownership, in property; property is a form of power inherent in objects rather than in persons or office. By acquiring objects or claims upon objects of market value, power is accumulated. Those in possession of property acquire sets of rights and prerogatives that are guaranteed by society. These rights and prerogatives, defined and limited by law, are subject to change and, in fact, are constantly changing. A piece of land is owned, but for instance, the rights and prerogatives inherent in the fact of ownership vary with changes in the laws of zoning or taxation.

Not only the specificity and revocability of the prerogatives and rights inhering in ownership, but also the dispersion of property limit this property power. The power of an entrepreneur to impose wages or prices is limited by the competitive demands and offerings of other entrepreneurs who also have the power to offer wages and to sell goods. It is, indeed, necessary for the proper functioning of this form of economic organization that there be no concentration of the property power in the hands of one individual or aggregation by arrangement among many sufficient to enable a buyer to go beyond the power to sell or to buy at a price, to the greater power of fixing or influencing deliberately the price at which he sells or buys. For if such a power should be allowed to exist, to that extent price would no longer serve its function as index of scarcities, as barometer of wants, and as guide to the optimal flow of resources. And those who possessed the power might use it arbitrarily to deprive others of the prerogatives and values implicit in what they possess.

It is, therefore, a prerequisite of this system that there be a sufficiently large number of buyers and sellers at every level of production and exchange as to prevent any one from significantly influencing price through his power to purchase or to offer for sale. Under this form of economic organization, in other words, the economic power must be very widely dispersed and hence the controls over production and consumption highly decentralized.

Property has another important characteristic. It offers as an option, the power over production, or the privileges and pleasures of consumption. On both counts, property is desired and sought after. Other types of power do not have this double aspect. The policeman has power, but his power is not legitimately convertible into the rights of consumption.

The Peripheral Role of Government. Government intervention in the economy is constrained by the general persuasion that the market is the ideal regulator of economic activities and that government intervention is dangerous. It suffices for government to maintain the viability of property and of contract as the institutional requisites of the exchange economy, and, perhaps, actively to oppose monopoly.

Summary. A form of economic organization has been described with the following characteristics:

1. Economic decisions are made by individuals. Individual decision-makers are related through the crossties of exchange. Production and distribution follow the dictate of a free-functioning price.

2. Economic power, vested in the claims of ownership or property, is infinitely dispersed and is competitively exercised.

3. The instruments of collective or government action are used only to protect and support the central institutions of the market, and to maintain the required dispersion of the economic power.

Since its salient characteristic is decentralized market power taking its direction from an autonomously functioning market price, this form of economic organization is called here "decentralized market-directed."

THE CENTRALIZED POLITICALLY DIRECTED FORM

OF ECONOMIC ORGANIZATION

In this second form of economic organization it is the *plan*, rather than the free movement of market prices, that is decisive in the control of economic activities. The plan implies complex anticipations concerning future events and complex directives concerning future activities.

Centralization. The English Marxist, Maurice Dobb, maintains that:

. . . the essence of economic planning lies in the fact that decisions which in a capitalist society are diffused among numerous units are embodied in a single complex decision which constitutes the plan. Decisions about price and output and about investment in the renewal or extension of capital equipment are taken, no longer automatically according to profit-motivation—the motive of maximizing profits in a given market situation—but integrally according to the dictates of social policy.[2]

[2] Maurice Dobb, *Soviet Economic Development Since 1917* (London: Routledge & Kegan Paul, Ltd., 1948), p. 29.

F. A. von Hayek, who stands at the opposite end of the ideological spectrum, identifies socialism-collectivism as:

. . . a central direction of all economic activities according to a single plan, laying down how the resources of a society should be consciously directed to serve particular ends in a definite way.[3]

Regardless of the degree to which the specifics of economic activities in fact are planned in a particular society (and surely there are an endless number of possible combinations and permutations of planning and non-planning), wherever planning does exist, and in so far as the specifics of economic activity are in fact planned, then decision-making must be centralized. Many individuals may contribute to and assist in the process of economic planning, but the end product of that process is an integral decision emanating from a single locus of authority. Centralization is the common denominator of all forms of planning. Mason accordingly affirms:

Economic planning implies some substantial degree of centralized decision making. This is true whether planning is undertaken for a firm, a municipality, a region, or for the whole economy. The plans for any of these units may be more or less comprehensive, but they are necessarily centrally determined. It is not possible to talk about decentralized planning.[4]

Total Planning in a Closed Economy. Different sorts of activities can be planned. For example, the plan might apply to production, covering the choice and priority of output goals, the selection of the techniques to be used in production, the allocation of available resources, the organization of inputs in the fabrication of end products. The plan may apply to an effort to generate invention and innovation through research and development, covering the setting of R & D goals, the selection of R & D projects, the allocation of scientists and other resources between selected goals and projects, and the practical application of the information created through R & D. The plan may apply to distribution, covering the sharing of end products between households. It might cover the distribution of productive resources between production for consumption, investment intended to expand or to restructure industry, research and development intended to create new techniques or products, and education or training intended to improve the quality of the working force. The plan may apply to consumption, determining the table of output priorities, and the way in which end products are to be put to use.

Since our purpose is to explore the implications of planning as a technique of activation and control, planning will be considered as a means of

[3] Fredrick August von Hayek, *The Road to Serfdom* (Chicago: University of Chicago Press, 1944), p. 35.
[4] Mason, p. 29.

organizing the whole range of associated economic functions: production, invention, innovation, distribution, and consumption. It will be assumed, in other words, that planning is the control technique for a closed economy.

In actual economies plan-based organizations and other forms of organization coexist, even within the same operating entity, for example, within the same firm. Thus, for a given company, one line of output, say components for space vehicles, may be wholly a function of centralized planning, while another line of output, say automobiles, might be geared to the free play of demand on a competitive market.

In addition, some forms of economic organization will combine planning and other techniques of activation and control. The large industrial corporation may plan its highly complex internal operations, while externally it is subjected to the play of competitive market forces. The plan itself may provide for spheres of unplanned choice and activity within the general scope of its operation, with the specific delegation of discretionary responsibilities. Moreover, whenever complex and dynamic activities are planned, there will be occasions when spontaneous and unstructured choice must occur. Maurice Dobb, writing about the system of planning in the Soviet Union, said:

In practice, however, it will be impossible for a plan to embody decisions about everything. Its preoccupation will necessarily be with the main contours of the economic process. The filling out of these main contours with detail, the adaptation of general directives to the special qualities of a particular situation, which the most long-sighted planner located at the center cannot possibly bring within his focus, must inevitably be decentralized. A plan has to be constructed on the basis of information that can be expressed in generalized form; and the decisions it embraces have to be capable of expression in precise terms. Yet, there will necessarily be much in the economic situation that defies any such precise description, or which has not yet reached the stage of digestion in experience where it can be easily described in verbal terms at all. The actual "feel" of the situation by men standing close to events is here essential to any realistic decision. In the adaptation of a plan to a rapidly changing situation this can be seen to be of special importance. If not in major degree, at least in very large degree the success of any system of economic planning will depend on the character of the personnel near the periphery of economic decision, and on the capacity of the system to provide an adequate motivation for those peripheral decisions to be efficiently taken and implemented.[5]

Here, since our objective is simply to explore its implications as a technique, it will not be necessary to take into account either the discretionary decision-making that is sometimes built into a plan or the spontaneous action and unstructured choice that occurs at its periphery.

[5] Dobb, pp. 29–30.

Planning Under Political-Direction. There are various plan-based forms of economic organization. Activities may be controlled through the plans of a large company or a voluntary association of individuals or businesses. Even when the plan is under the aegis of government, as in France, to a considerable degree it may simply provide guidelines for the voluntary choices of private agencies. Such economic planning constitutes other forms of economic organization than that which is to be examined here.

Here it will be supposed that the planning authority is also the political authority; that planning is a function of government. Not only does the political authority plan; it also imposes, enforces, and supervises the execution of the plan, and it is responsible for the achievement of the plan. It may choose the means it considers expedient and morally acceptable to mobilize the energies and to stimulate the talents of the community and to control operations—but behind that choice stands the ultimate coercive power of the State. The limits upon the power of the planning authority are precisely the limits upon the power of political authority. The economy is, in this sense, politically directed. Therefore the form of economic organization to be examined is termed "centralized politically directed."

In the economy of decentralized market-direction, government stands apart, serving only to support the institutions of the competitive market. In the economy of market-negotiating organizations, to be described subsequently, the government participates in economic activities. But here, with centralized political-direction, the polity and the economy merge into one. The economy is a branch of government; it is one of the agencies of collective choice and political action.

A Résumé of the Planning Process. The planned organization of production and distribution requires that data relevant to centralized choice be collected and transmitted to the decision-making center. This would include information on alternative techniques to produce particular outputs, on resources required for alternative techniques, on the location and availability of resources; information on public needs and private tastes relative to the formulation of output goals; and ongoing information on current operations and on the success or failure of schemes and agencies, so that plans could be appropriately revised, agencies reorganized, bottlenecks broken, and the interdependent flow of outputs kept in steady gear.

Based on this information, a table of priorities must be formulated. Taking the availability of resources and techniques into account, alternative output configurations would be deduced as possible or potential; and these would be matched against the table of priorities. That possible output configuration that seemed best to match production goals would be selected. The trick is to know what you have, where you have it, what you can make of it, and what is most wanted. The complex decision as to what is to be done with what is available—which is the *plan*—must be translated into action. This requires that leadership be selected, that efforts be mobilized, that operations be supervised, that income be distributed. For that, a system of incentive, motivation, supervision, recruitment, and distribution is necessary.

The first task of the plan is to organize the use of given resources and techniques. Except that through time, resources and the technical capacity to use resources cannot be understood as "given." New minerals can be discovered. New knowledge can be acquired. New techniques can be invented. Labor can be trained to higher levels of efficiency. Growth also can be planned.

Key Role of the Planning Elite. Centralized political-direction must have its planning authority; the plan must have its planners. Upon those who exercise the planning authority, who conceive, who design, who implement and supervise and enforce the plan, must rest an enormous responsibility and an enormous power. It is not only for them to decide upon the allocation of resources and the distribution of income shares, and to design and organize the processes of production, invention, and innovation. It is for them to recruit economic leadership and, indeed, to select their own successors. The role of the planning elite is vital inasmuch as planning is used as the instrument of economic control.

Planning is complex and may engage the efforts of considerable numbers. Nevertheless those responsible for the plan, who exercise the ultimate decisions with respect to it, must be very few in comparison to the rest of the working community. More than in any other form of economic organization, centralized political-direction concentrates economic responsibility and power. Correspondingly, the competence and motivation of those few and their dedication to common goals and the degree to which they possess common values is decisive for economic achievement.

The Planning Elite and the Community. Of key importance also in the economy of centralized political-direction is the nature of the relationship between those responsible for the design and enforcement of the plan and the community at large, who follow the directives of the plan. The problems and instabilities of political relationships carry over into the economic sphere.

The capacity for economic achievement under centralized political-direction must in great part depend on the degree of convergence between the motivations and values of the planning elite and the interests, aspirations, and values of the community at large. The popular attitude toward the exercise of the political authority and the capacity for disciplined acceptance of the directives of authority are also crucial. The costs of supervision, the response to incentives, the effectiveness of communication between the planning center and operations at the periphery, all depend on this relationship between authority and those who work under its directive.

Summary. In the centralized politically directed form of economic organization, economic control is exercised as a function of government. The essential choices are made by a political agency representing the State.

That complex decision which distributes resource inputs and product outputs and which designs and organizes the processes of production, including the production of new knowledge and new technology, constitutes the *plan*. It is the essence of the plan that a few decide for the many; and that the activities of the many are carried on under the directives of the few. Consequently, the capacity of the system for achievement will depend upon the competence and the dedication of a controlling elite (and hence on the belief or faith that guides that elite and binds it together); and on the relationships of responsibility and identification between those who control and those who are controlled.

Centralized direction requires a complex apparatus for gathering the data basic to its decisions, for formulating alternatives, for enabling the feedback necessary in order that processes and expectations can be adapted to changing circumstances, for the supervision of operations, for the recruitment of leadership, for the training of technicians, for motivating participants, for generating invention, innovation, and (hence) economic growth.

THE ORGANIZATIONAL MARKET-NEGOTIATED FORM

The Three Forms Compared. Two forms of economic organization have now been described. A third remains.

In the decentralized market-directed form, individuals, as free agents on the market, sought their own ends in the manner of their own choosing. Within an all-embracing system of exchange, many self-interested efforts were guided by the free movement of price.

Under the centralized politically directed form, economic decision-making becomes part of the process of collective choice, and the diversity of relevant activities are coordinated through the instrumentality of the plan.

Now an economic form is conceived where decision-making is neither by individuals acting independently nor by the collectivity acting through its instruments of political choice. Rather, action is organized primarily through autonomous organization. The key agencies of economic control are voluntary associations, profit-oriented, countervailing and counter-vailed against, negotiating together and existing in a context of negotiated relationships. Goods and services are produced and are offered for sale, but the market is not master. Activities are not controlled by a free-moving price. Rather price is decided as a matter of policy, or is agreed upon by counterbalancing powers. This organizational market-negotiated form of economic organization has its analogue in the big business or corporate enterprise sector of the American (or any comparable Western) economy.

Characteristics of the Organizational Market-Negotiated Form. Some of the characteristics of this organizational market-negotiated form may briefly be specified.

1. Production is organized by large corporations in which thousands of individuals in varying capacities associate voluntarily for purposes of mutual gain. That part of labor which is not highly specialized or man-agerial negotiates its working conditions and wages through trade unions.

2. Consumption of end products is partly by decentralized individual choice and partly through collectivized choice of government.

3. Corporation and trade union in the organization of production are poised between the collective power of government and a universe of infinitely decentralized choice. Collective power and individual decision are not simply marginal but, in a particular way, are components of the system.

4. The market is not the mastering mechanism. It is a forum for nego-tiations, a showcase for display, an area for maneuver by entities that find their analogue in rival nations. The struggle of each to survive, to main-tain position, to grow, and to "win" is real and of many dimensions, but rarely does competition erupt in the mutual catastrophe of "price war." Price does not automatically reflect resource availability and end-product demand, but signifies rather corporation or trade union policy, or a nego-tiated relationship between autonomous powers. It cannot be assumed that price is an index of real scarcity. Nevertheless, as a determinant of costs, price guides the planning of purchases, inputs, and consumption.

5. Not every autonomous organization, but only those that have the sale of goods or services as their primary objective belong to this form of economic organization. Universities, schools, foundations, and consumer cooperatives, for example, are voluntary associations that produce impor-tant goods and services, but are not oriented primarily toward the sale of goods and services.

6. In the organizational economy individuals do not relate as subjects of a common political authority, nor as self-interested bargainers each on

his own. They relate together as colleagues, as superior and subordinate, as bargaining agents and representatives of interests that are not specifically their own.

7. Power for the individual resides in his position within, or in his relationship to an economic organization. There are different paths to power. One is up through the managerial hierarchy. Another is via finance and the ownership of equity shares, inasmuch as this provides entree into the policy-making machinery. Legal ownership per se, in the possession of equity shares, does not ordinarily convey any significant degree of economic power.

8. The large modern corporation has grown beyond the control capacities of any single individual or of any colleagued group. Its action cannot be explained as the choice of the individual making decisions on his own, and can only be partly explained as the decisions or plans of those in authority. Chapter 2 will examine the nature of choice and the rationale of action by large autonomous organizations.

The Role of the Individual. In this form of economy, the decision as to what to buy and how to use what is bought, is made, for the most part, by the self-interested individual or private household. The consumer is independent but not sovereign. His choice is deliberately bounded by the prices that are fixed and the products that are offered. Through advertising, his tastes and demands are shaped by the companies who seek his patronage.

The Role of Government. In the economy of autonomous organization, the government has a flexible role. It is both coparticipant and mediator.

It assumes responsibility for articulating as a consumer on the market those social values which cannot be expressed adequately by the decentralized choices of individual consumers. It undertakes to satisfy the collective needs (vis à vis those of the private individual) by procuring and organizing the consumption of goods and services produced by private corporations—thus governments purchase and direct the use of space vehicles and military hardware.

The government undertakes to influence or to regulate the policies of autonomous organizations. It may do this by acting directly on the determinants of organizational planning, for example, through tariffs or subsidies, through changes in the pattern of taxation, through monetary measures intended to alter the rate of interest or through fiscal measures intended to affect consumer demand. Or, the government may regulate organizational policies by legal directive or influence organizational policy by moral suasion.

Where conflicts arise between important autonomous organizations, such as between industrial corporations and trade unions, the government may act as umpire or as mediator and may enter directly into negotiating the terms of settlement.

Hence, while the government is not the nexus of decision and responsibility (as it is under centralized political-direction), it can, nevertheless, exercise broad and significant controls over the autonomous agencies without endangering the integrity of the system.

Summary. In the organizational market-negotiated form of economic organization, the active agencies of production and distribution are large corporations and trade unions. Terms of trade are negotiated, or come to an equilibrium through a balancing of power or are imposed as a matter of policy. Individuals participate in organizations voluntarily, for the purpose of mutual gain—relating together as associates, or as superior and subordinates, or as agents for interests not specifically their own. Power resides in in-group status and is exercised as authority.

The government participates as sovereign among the quasi-sovereignties, king in the midst of his barons. Among its tasks is to arbitrate and mediate between the autonomous powers, to enforce the economic peace of the realm, and to protect the individual within and vis à vis the organization.

THE TASK AHEAD

Efficiency and Justice. Essential characteristics of three forms for the organization of economic activities, have now been broadly described. These three are important building blocks for the modern economy. In analyzing them an approach will have been developed for the study of other forms as well.

Next we will study the values and defects of each of these three forms, first considered as instruments for the *efficient* organization of production and consumption and as instruments for a *just* division of what has been produced. Before attempting this evaluation, the nature of choice and the rationale of action-taking by the large autonomous organization needs to be examined.

Response Through Organizations. In the economy of decentralized market-direction, action is generated through the self-interested decisions of individuals, choosing within the moving parameters of price. In the centralized politically directed economy, action is generated under the direction of political authority, following the prescripts of a plan. But surely there are many actual activities and events, in the economic sphere and elsewhere, that cannot be explained or understood either as deriving from the hard-backed wholly self-interested choices of individuals deciding each on his own, nor as a consequence of systematized planning. Individuals do associate into groups, and a direction of activity can arise from that association which is in no sense the emanation of a plan. It may represent a moving consensus, a balancing and interaction of pressures and interests. "Democracy" as a political system, for example, represents a technique of group choice and control which is neither that of decentralized decision-making nor that of centralized planning.

Presumably this species of unstructured choice-making or action-taking by groups is uniquely important in the organizational market-negotiated economy where the key agencies are voluntary autonomous associations. It is this category of choice or response, which has the rationale neither of the single individual nor of the public authority, that needs to be better understood.

Chapter 2

A Theory of Organizational Choice

A Key Action-Taking Agency. A most significant fact in recent economic history has been the displacement from the center stage of Western
capitalism of the economy of price-directed, decentralized decision-
making by the economy of autonomous organizations. This has altered
not only the locus and breadth of control, but also the nature of control.
The enormous enlargement of enterprise has not meant that the choice of
a single individual (or a single body of men) necessarily controls more,
but rather that the process of choice itself has basically changed. This
chapter will take a first step in seeking to explain this new order of organizational decision-making and action-taking. Indeed, the terms "decision-
making" or "choice" (though, perforce, we shall use them) may be misleading, for they imply that the pattern of organizational activity must be
the conscious, purposeful design of an individual or of a group of individuals. This need not be the case. Our real objective is to comprehend
the dynamic of power within the autonomous organization and to understand how this power is manifested in action, direction, and policy.

Organizational vs. Entrepreneurial Choice. Before attempting to suggest what organizational choice is, it must be made clear (which is much
easier) what it is not. It is not the self-interested, free-wheeling choice
of the individual on his own. It is not to be understood by analogy, nor
compared to the self-interest made manifest in the owner-management
of small enterprise. Why not? Partly because an individual, or any
number of individuals operating from a single vantage point lack the
capacity to comprehend and hence to control the complexity and the
magnitude of the whole range of activities encompassed by such an organization as the modern corporation. Thousands participate voluntarily
as shareholders, officials, managers, experts—each possessing some measure of independent power. Authority is (and must be) dispersed to
permit on-the-spot response to local circumstances of geography, technology, or markets.

The organizational enterprise, moreover, generally performs not a few
but a very large number of technical operations. Each operation may be
carried to a point of great complexity and may be based on the mastery of

highly recondite bodies of knowledge—particularly when, through research and development, the enterprise couples itself to the explosive advances of science. Such operations require experts.

The proliferation of experts is not caused only by the greater diversity and higher complexity of activities carried on by a single enterprise. The scale of operations makes it possible to subdivide management into specialties and thereby to reap the benefits of a greater division of labor. What in the "firm" was the domain of a single entrepreneurial jack-of-all-choices becomes in the organizational enterprise the separate provinces of "personnel management," "operations research," "public relations," "investment analysis," etc., etc. The expert and the specialized group become self-contained, shielded from external surveillance and direction by the very incapacity of the uninitiated to comprehend their activities, to master their language, or to evaluate their work.

The diversity, complexity, and sheer size of organizational enterprise and the many self-contained spheres of expertise within it will preclude effective control or comprehensive choice by an individual or by any number of persons acting from a single vantage point. Hence choice and policy for the autonomous organization cannot simply reflect an entrepreneurial will or be explained as the entrepreneurial self-interest made manifest.

The Autonomous Organization as a Community. Prolonged association and a common history give to the autonomous corporation aspects of a community. It becomes important for the values it represents and for the way of life it offers. It takes on its own myths and symbols, its own image, toward which those on the inside and those on the outside have an emotional response—an image, moreover, that becomes both a guide to policy and a magnet that repels some while drawing others into its orbit.

Nevertheless, if the autonomous corporation is to be understood as a society, it must be understood as a society of a special sort, where participation is transitory, where commitment is partial and voluntary, where members are bound together by shared expectations of individual gains.

The Autonomous Organization as a Government. The autonomous organization can be understood in important respects by analogy to government. In these autonomous organizations, as in political governments, power inheres in authority. There are grades and levels of authority. There is usually some structured form of collective choice, such as the "votes" of stockholders in the selection of a board of directors.

There are also decisive differences between the autonomous organization and political government. The autonomous organization is not "sovereign." No coercive power exists to give its directives the weight of command. With participants free to affiliate or disaffiliate, tied together only by the coincidence of their self-interest, power cannot be intersheaved into fixed hierarchies nor can the ranks be disciplined to unquestioning response. The voluntary nature of association precludes control by a single interest just as it does by a single individual. The autonomous organization, morever, cannot act as a closed system. Although large and complex, the political and economic parameters within which it operates are, nevertheless, highly restrictive. Its dominant values are set through political action, the law, and externally formed public opinion. Its production goals and output priorities are simply anticipations of and responses to the market demands of households and of government. In sum, the autonomous organization has neither sufficient sanctions nor breadth of control to make possible an equivalent to "planning" under centralized political-direction.

The autonomous organization exists by permission of the community. It is a voluntary association. Its cement is the participants' expectation of mutual gain. It can operate only within the constraints of regulation and law, and of profit and loss. Only if it continues to be profitable can it continue to enlist participation.

The political agency exists not by permission but by command of the community. It is not voluntary but imperative. It does not depend on, nor do its powers derive from, the desire of individuals to associate for personal and mutual gain. Rather it draws its power from a broad allegiance to an idea and from a general sense of need. Its powers may be exercised to the ultimate limits of coercion. Because the power of the political agency is intrinsically so great, it is generally exercised only under rigid procedural constraints; but within the external limitations imposed by law and market circumstance, the internal exercise of power in the autonomous organization is relatively flexible and free.

The autonomous organization uses its limited power freely and flexibly within the constraints of profit and loss. In contrast, the political organization exercises unlimited power, generally under narrow procedural restraints.

Opinions from the Inside. Consider the views of two old hands at the business of business organization. Crawford Greenwalt, then President of E. I. du Pont de Nemours & Co., in his 1958 McKinsey Foundation lecture at Columbia University, observed that

Over the past fifty years the proprietorship has mostly vanished, its place taken by the vast, anonymous corporation. Government, educational institutions, and labor unions have all outgrown the control capacities of the single gifted individual. . . . The conviction seems to be that progress in any field requires the creation of an organization. . . . Any organization represents a cross section of society. . . . Grouped together the weakness of one is compensated by the strength in another. . . . Whatever individual dispositions may be present, it is the average, the composite which must prevail.[1]

And Roger Blough, then President of the United States Steel Corporation, similarly described the process of decision-making and action-taking in large corporate enterprise.

The process of reaching understanding within the single group . . . by a group of individuals working together as a corporation is accomplished in much the same way as it is in any other free and voluntary association—whether that association be a local lodge, a committee to arrange a church supper, or even a group of small boys deciding how to play a game of sandlot baseball. As I think back on it, it seems to me that either men or boys reach agreement in much the same fashion, by face to face discussion, presenting their points of view and reaching agreement on the basis of mutual understanding. . . .

Each person in the group has an influence which is related to his role, his capacities, his experience, his judgments and his persuasive abilities. He in turn is influenced by the attitudes and viewpoints of others in the group. A particular individual may have considerable influence within a certain segment of the group but his influence will be lessened with respect to those who are removed from him in their activities. Naturally the larger the productive group, not only the greater the communication problems but also the greater the available means of communication . . . communication like decision-making is a process constantly going on within the many smaller groups that compose a large unit. . . .

By mutual consent the span of an individual's relationships will cover mostly those matters—and the people concerned—about which he is considered competent. This . . . sheds light on the problem of authority . . . *Who makes the decisions?* is a frequent question. In a voluntary association, be it a corporation or any other, those in the group must and do reach understandings. And through the same process these understandings are changed from time to time.[2]

Individual Choice Within Organizations. Individuals possess power in organizations and they exercise that power qua individuals. They will, in part, use their power for at least three distinguishable and frequently conflicting purposes.

1. Power will be used to achieve functional objectives, that is, to "get the job done." Such choice is never unequivocal. Functional objectives are many and diverse, and the "job to be done" varies with the vantage point of the viewer.

[1] *Business Week* (paraphrased), May 10, 1958, pp. 47–50.
[2] Roger Blough, *Free Men and the Corporation* (New York: McGraw-Hill, 1959), pp. 23–24.

2. Power will be used for the sake of the organization as such: to maintain its internal balances and equilibria, to ease the tensions and to facilitate the relationships of those who participate in its activities, to follow its codes and routines which can, sometimes, come to have the intrinsic values of ritual. The perennial (and perhaps proper) concern of bureaucracy is not with what is to be done, but with how it is to be done. The first commandment is to keep the papers moving.

3. Power will be used by individuals (or factions) who possess it to promote their advantage, to advance their status, to augment their authority vis à vis the advantage, the status, and the authority of other individuals or factions in the same organization.

Authoritative Choice and Composite Choice. Aside from the manner of the exercise of power possessed by individuals in an organization, the policy or line of action chosen by an organization will proceed from two different sorts of choice.

1. *Authoritative Choice,* made by an individual or by a group of individuals in authority *for* the group.

2. *Composite Choice,* made *by* (or through) the group itself, in the sense that the very process of choice embodies the diverse interests, drives, and opinions of the group's members. In some cases, this process is formally structured—for example, through a voting machinery—while in other cases, the process occurs through an unstructured interplay of diverse interests and opinions.

Authoritative choice is not at all the same as individual choice. In the decentralized market, the free-wheeling entrepreneur must answer to no one but himself and to no other interest than his own. He decides and he acts without the need to explain or to rationalize. He decides directly, from impulse, from careful calculus, or from the instinctual reckoning of benefit, risk, and cost. The guidelines of his choice are in his "guts," his tastes, proclivities, prejudices, experience. But those in authority, who decide for a group, are "responsible" to those who support their authority. To some greater or less degree, they are answerable for their choice and for its consequences, and hence their choice is geared to that which can be explained, rationalized, justified. Moreover, the exercise of authority must be "acceptable"—which sets critical though highly variable limits on its exercise. The confines of acceptability and the imperative of responsibility must shape the authoritative choice.

Composite choice emerging from the balance of interacting pressures needs no rationalization. It may be entirely inarticulate, manifested not in what the group decides but on what it becomes.

A political analogy will serve to illustrate this difference between the authoritative and the composite choice.

AUTHORITATIVE VS. COMPOSITE CHOICE: A POLITICAL ANALOGY

Authoritative Choice by the Court, Composite Choice by Congress.
Considered as an agency of government, the Supreme Court of the
United States is very small. Each of its nine members exercises an independent authority and assumes individual responsibility for his decisions.
Protected by life tenure and by an immense prestige, the members of the
Court are relatively free to exercise their power in a manner which they
conceive to be consistent with their obligations. The nature of his task
obliges each Justice to systematize his thinking, grounding it in premises
he is prepared to defend. In his decisions, he tends to follow the logical
imperatives of those premises. The exercise of the authority of the Court
thereby derives from the ethical premises of the Justices and from their
conception of reality, in a word, from their *social philosophy*. But if the
Court is shielded from the tug and pull of political pressures, it is plunged
into the currents of contemporary thought. The philosophy of the Court,
after all, is that of a group of representative intellectuals shaped by the
same influences that mold the ideas of their contemporaries. Before the
universe of his peers the Judge, in each of his decisions, will plead his case.
It is to be expected that the social philosophy of the Court would characterize the norm of the time. The acceptability of the Court's decisions
rests on, in the last analysis, their concurrence with the norms of social
thought.

The Legislative and the Executive branches of the American government, on the other hand, are large organizations made infinitely larger by
their "responsibility," or their relationship to and dependence on the
community as a whole through continuing elections and by their interaction with other organizational entities such as political parties, trade
unions, manufacturers' associations, farm bureaus, etc. Not only the Congressmen and Senators and their advisors, and the President and his staff
and his Cabinet, and the officials and the experts—but also the political
machines back at home, also business and labor and the farmer and their
representatives, and the vast conglomerate of special interests: all these in
a real and active sense, partake and participate in legislative and executive decision-making.

Embodied in the direction provided by Congress and the Executive is a
diversity of needs and interests, which may be conflicting or harmonious
or neutral in respect to each other. Power is dispersed and power relationships are in flux. There is compromise and there is gaming. It is hard to
discover where things begin or to know how or whether they have ended.
There is a ceaseless grouping and regrouping in the counterpoise of strategy. The power, favor, and place of individuals shuffle and shift in a
turning kaleidoscope. Skillfully the leader rides the tide and the tide

dictates the direction. What emerges from this conflux of the diverse and disassociated is not the rational derivative of a philosophy, but the outcome of counter-balancing pressures.

The contrast, then, between the Supreme Court and the Executive and Congressional branches is between government through authoritative choice and government through composite choice. The first involves the shared outlooks and beliefs that link the exercise of authority to its acceptance. The second reflects a balance of pressures.

Values and Defects of the Forms of Choice. The value of composite choice is that it *represents*. It embodies the complexity of the elements that compose a real universe. It reacts to the needs, it adapts to the circumstances of that universe. It is flexible, yet resistant. It is expedient. Such are its virtues. Its vices are also the vices of expediency. It is meandering, aimless, and, in terms of any given purpose, wasteful. It reacts to crises but does not anticipate them. It must be jarred into motion.

The personal exercise of authority implies a choice that is independent and isolated. Independent decision—isolated choice: these are two sides of the same coin. Inasmuch as those who rule by authority interact with and depend upon those whom they rule, their authority is diluted, and it is the composite choice that emerges. But though authority means power exercised independently by an individual, it does not imply simple self-seeking. Authoritative choice is answerable, and it answers by reference to a code, an outlook, a philosophy, an ethic presumed to link ruler to ruled.

The value of independently exercised authority, incorporating as it can the vision and learning of the individual, is its capacity for purposeful, rational, and consistent policy. Its weakness is in the perennial inability of the individual to grasp the social whole. The individual masters a philosophy, but philosophy simplifies and excludes. Urgent needs and critical problems may fall outside its purview. And when a dominant outlook is fixed in the face of rapid historical change, then reality will more and more escape its net.

The decisions of the Supreme Court, then, are characterized by the exercise of individual authority where choice expresses a social philosophy; whereas in Congress and in the Executive, policy emerges through the expedient balance of pressures. This, of course, oversimplifies. Differences between these branches of government are far from absolute. The individual qua individual may at a crucial point impose the choice of authority within the organizational flux. Nor are the Justices of the Supreme Court completely detached from the larger community. Expediency and compromise will, to some degree, be reflected in their decisions. Nevertheless the contrast is real and suffices to explain in large part the contrasting roles in history of the Supreme Court and of the other two agencies of Federal Government.

Hypothesis to Be Tested. Authoritative and composite choice have been conceived as component elements in the dynamic of organization. The Supreme Court and the Legislative and Executive branches of the federal government have been offered as examples of each. This hypothesis can be tested by (1) predicting the kind of differences to be expected between the policies of agencies where composite and where authoritative choice is characteristic and (2) matching predicted differences with historical fact.

Barring the pressure of crisis, but given a divergence between the dominant social philosophy and the existing political and social institutions, we would expect the Supreme Court (reacting by reference to the dominant social philosophy) to take the lead in social reform. And when there was the pressure of social crisis, although the dominant social philosophy was more or less in accord with existing institutions, we would expect Congress and the Executive (reacting in response to pressure and expediency) to lead in social reform. Consider, then, what has occurred.

The Dominant Philosophy. During the eighteenth century there evolved a system of thought which became dominant in Western Europe and, particularly, in the United States. It is a system of thought associated with Adam Smith, with the *Federalist*, later with Mill, Spencer, Bentham, Alfred Marshall.

With respect to political organization, it stood against traditional (mainly feudal) dispersions of political power and the correlary privileges of an hereditary aristocracy. It stood for democracy, for equality under a single law, for rational uniform administration, and for a strong national sovereign, that is, for political centralism.

With respect to economic organization, it stood against mercantilism and all forms of state paternalism or special privilege. It stood for laissez-faire, for the free play of competitive forces on the market.

It wished to protect the uncoerced choice of the individual from the "arbitrariness" of majorities and from the vested powers of authorities. For this purpose, it held political rights and property rights inviolable. It saw a perpetual threat to these rights in the powers of government and, hence, believed that the collective power must be precisely bounded and carefully checked.

These were central elements in the social philosophy that was dominant in the United States, at least through the mid-1930s. It was adhered to by Presidents, by Congressmen, and by citizens-at-large. During this whole period, indeed, no other system of thought existed as a significant alternative. And, of course, it dominated the thought of the Justices of the Supreme Court.

Centralization of National Power. The first great question that faced the American Republic was whether a loose confederation of sovereign states should be unified and integrated into a single national power. On the side of decentralization was tradition, the inertia of established institutions, and vested economic interests as well, while on the side of centralization was the prevailing ideal; expediency on the one side, and philosophy on the other. The trend toward unification was led, indeed, was forced, by the decisions of the American Supreme Court, until the issue was finally settled by the Civil War. During this first half-century of political development, the Supreme Court (as would follow from our hypothesis) instigated and stood at the forefront of social change.

Impact of Industrialization. By the mid-nineteenth century, to a remarkable degree, the premises of representative democracy, of political centralism, and of laissez-faire liberalism had become incorporated into the social and political and economic institutions of the United States. It was now no longer the task of the philosopher to spearhead reform, but to man the ramparts and maintain the proverbial "eternal vigilance." Meanwhile the rapid industrialization of the economy was fundamentally recasting economic and social conditions.

Industrialization meant many things. The wealth and power of the community enormously increased. Economic, technical, and social relationships became more interdependent and complex: life lost its former simplicity and the individual no longer possessed a single-handed mastery over his environment. Extremes of wealth and poverty coexisted, castles on the hill and slums in industrial valley. A new factory proletariat clamored for redress of their miseries. Business crisis followed business crisis; the swings between boom and bust were unprecedented and growing.

Industrial strife, rural desperation, the stunted humanity of the sweat shops and the mills, the exploitation of women and children, crisis upon crisis, depression and mass unemployment, income inequalities that eroded the basis of political democracy: these were problems that could neither be blinked nor resolved without radical intervention by government. But the established social philosophy, the system of thought accepted by Congressman, Senator, President, by citizen-at-large, and by Justice of the Supreme Court, stood against such intervention, denied the need for it, brandished its dangers and evils.

On the one side, the idea and ideal opposed intervention, and on the other the pressure of crisis, of specific need, of expediency encouraged it. As our hypothesis would lead us to anticipate, the composite choice of the Congress and Executive was at the forefront of reform, and the authoritative choice of the Supreme Court stood, foursquare, against it.

The Court as a Barrier to Public Intervention. Crisis and the clamor of those who considered themselves subject to inequities generated pressure for government intervention. The pressure was expressed in the laws of the Congress and the actions of the Executive. For nearly a century those laws and actions were repeatedly struck down by the Supreme Court in protecting property rights and in restraining the collective power. Efforts to protect fugitive slaves, to safeguard women workers, to eliminate child labor, to impose an income tax, to fix minimum wages and maximum hours, to regulate public utilities effectively along with the whole "New Deal" program and, in fact, every significant attempt at social amelioration foundered on the conservatism of the Supreme Court. The Court had exchanged roles with Congress and Executive. Now the Congress and Executive led the trend of reform, and the Court fought it. Why so?

The composite choice of Congress and the Executive responded to the requisites of expediency whatever the philosophical predilections of their membership. But the Justices of the Court, exercising their vested authority in isolation and independence, followed the guidelines of the accepted philosophy. Reform advanced through Congress and the Executive as the product of expediency, as the piecemeal response to specific need, special pressure, immediate problem—and always the amelioration, the reform, was conceived as an exception to the rule. The Supreme Court blocked such reform because the Supreme Court followed the rule; the will of the Court prevailed because there was no other rule to invoke. The community by-and-large accepted the premises of the Court, and, accepting its premises, its conclusions were inescapable. Choice by authority errs when doctrine is in error; when doctrine is in error, then the composite choice through organization, with its random response to crisis and pressure, is nearer a rational adjustment to circumstances.

Social Outlook Changes. The crucial turning came in the late 1930s. The world depression, drowning generations in poverty, pounded "waves of the future" against the walls and dykes of Western societies; the future belonged to a Hitler, or a Mussolini, or a Stalin, whose economies were fully employed and whose systems seemed strong and growing. The crisis, starkly outside the compass of the accepted philosophy, was so enormous, so overwhelming, so nearly fatal that it struck at the very roots of the accepted way of thought. Before it, the Court had to break its rule, and for the Court that meant no mere yielding to expediency. In their exercise of authority, the consistency and integrity of their intellectual system was the very essence of choice. Hence, breaking the old rule necessitated finding a new one; a new rationalization must be wrought; a new theory had to be built. And not only for the Court. This was the time of general intellectual realignment. The whole generation broke away from the traditional point of view as from fetters and chain. The late 1930s was a period not only of social catastrophe and of widening spheres of public intervention, but also a time when established notions crumbled and a new philosophy of society began to emerge. This is exemplified by the economics of John Maynard Keynes. Many heretics, of course, had disclaimed or rebelled against classical economics before. But Keynes was not a heretic, not a nay-sayer, not a malcontent and rebel shouting defiance to the Establishment from outside the gates. Rather the economics of Keynes represents a shift in the norm, and therein lies its significance.

A New System of Social Thought? There remain those who regard the uncontrolled bargaining by individuals in the marketplace as the ultimate in human relationships and consider government (like Satan in the medieval cosmology) as a perpetual enemy, a necessary evil against which good must be forever on guard. Laissez-faire liberalism has not vanished. Old philosophies never die, and this one is firmly fossilized in higher pedagogy. It reverberates in the sanctums of the University of Chicago, and is impatiently proclaimed by the addicts of Ayn Rand. It echoes in the naïveté of Eisenhower and in the nostalgia and bombast of Barry Goldwater. But it is no longer at the center. It is no longer characteristic. It no longer dominates either the point of view of the Supreme Court or the attitudes of the intellectual community at large.

But if the old has been pushed aside, it is not easy to define what has taken its place. The social philosophy destined to dominate our epoch evidently is still in flux and evolution. Yet something of its character can perhaps be discerned. Like the outlook that preceded it, the emerging philosophy asserts the value of the individual, but not the individual conceived as an irreducible repository of tastes and desires that must be accepted as the final arbiter of social value; rather, the individual conceived as the bearer of a potential. The focus shifts from protecting rights to extending opportunities, from providing for the uninhibited expression of personal tastes to creating the environment most favorable for individual fulfillment.

Men agree that the individual on his own is not the master of his environment, but that his environment must be adapted or controlled through the action of large organizations. The most important and powerful of these organizations is the government. Government no longer appears as the enemy but as the indispensable instrument; rather than protecting the individual against government, constraints serve to ensure that the powers and agencies of government are used for the sake of the individual.

Given that a new and very different social philosophy has emerged, even though we cannot clearly delimit it, one which, as yet, has not fully permeated social activities and institutions: then the contrasting roles of the Supreme Court and of the Congress and the Executive since the 1940s can be explained.

The Postwar Reversal of Roles. The postwar Supreme Court of the United States has spearheaded the trend of social change. It has been the very harbinger of social reform in great issues and in a host of smaller ones. It took the initiative in the two major social reforms of the postwar period—racial "desegregation," insistence upon equality between the races, and "reapportionment," equalization of the electoral value of the urban and the rural vote.

The Supreme Court today is the most progressive agency of the American government. Yesterday it was the most conservative. Today the source and harbinger of change, for nearly a century prior to the 1940s it was the prime guardian of status. This reversal can be explained by reference to the difference between the composite and the authoritative choice.

Since World War II, there have been few crises or conflicts sufficient to press Congress or the Executive towards significant *internal* reform. Although grandiose plans have been shuffled in and out of the political decks, during these decades no basic internal reform has originated with the Congress or with the President. Business has been prosperous enough, stable enough. Recessions, unemployment, inflation, delinquency and crime, bad as they are, have not been bad enough to shake the governmental organization into the turmoil of experiment and innovation. The dominant philosophy, it is true, has changed, but whatever seemed philosophically desirable, nothing (with the possible exception of Russia's Sputnik) has stung so sharply as to spur Congress and Executive to undertake, on its own, significant internal reform. Philosophy aside, the Executive and Congress have not moved because they have not had to move; they have not been kicked into action. Ideas are never enough to stir the agencies of composite choice from their inertia. But with the Supreme Court it was different.

The rulings of the Court that have led to major social reform have come not as a response to pressure and crisis, but as a consequence of belief. The Justices were called upon to rule, and they laid down a rule consistent with an ethos and philosophy becoming dominant in their time. And if their ruling, rooted in the new outlook, required basic change, then basic change it was. Once the accepted system of social thought, brought to bear by the Court's decisions, barred internal reform; now it spurs it. This has been not by personal design or individual proclivity, but the consequence of a new ethic and outlook, one belonging not only to the Court but also to the community of thinking men.

VARIATIONS IN THE STRUCTURE OF ORGANIZATIONAL CHOICE

Choice in Autonomous Organizations Exemplified. The interaction of the different forms of choice in the activities of the autonomous organization can be illustrated through a hypothetical wage bargain between a trade union and an industrial corporation.

Consider, for example, the wage and salary structure of Corporation X. The mechanics, steam fitters, and sweepers working for the company are as much a part of its operation and organization as are the engineers, economists, managers, research scientists, vice presidents. For all alike, work conditions, prerogatives and status, security guarantees, wages, are of personal and of group concern; the determination of what these are to be is a matter of group decision. Yet while the steam fitters, mechanics and sweepers "bargain" through a trade union on these matters, the others do not. Why is this? Partly it is a matter of chance and history. But also, in part, it is because the participation of the "others" is more truly voluntary; they are less bound, less subject to coercion; they can disassociate more easily and their individual departure would make a bigger dent in the "company" interest. And they are or might become "insiders," able to manipulate the powers of organization to their own advantage and to participate directly in the structured formulation of policy. In any case those less secure, more vulnerable, furthest removed from personal power and responsibility, associate voluntarily in a second group for the purpose of furthering their interests within the first. Thus each year, the representatives of "labor" meet with the representatives of "management" to arrive at some decision respecting the prerogatives, protections, and wages for sweepers, mechanics, and steam fitters in Company X.

But whom and what interest do the trade union representatives represent? What concerns and points of view do they bring into this process of decision-making? They are certainly answerable for more than the interest of the sweepers, mechanics, and steam fitters in this one company. They may represent the interests of workers in other competitive corporations, in other parts of the company, and in other industries. They may represent the interests of certain of the unemployed, or those who might be brought back into employment, or who might be forced out of jobs. They will certainly represent the interests of the trade union qua organization, which must collect dues, pay salaries, increase membership, overcome rivals, survive, and grow. Nor is it impossible that they will be responsive to their self-interest as individuals, ambitious to make a name or even to "cash in" on their vested powers.

The trade union representative at the bargaining table exercises a vested authority. He decides *for* the union, for the membership. He possesses authority. But the exercise of that authority must be accepted. For example, he turns down a settlement and calls for a strike. The membership may refuse to strike, or, if they go on strike, they may refuse the long-drawn sacrifice which would make the strike effective. Or the trade union official may come to terms, sign a contract, and agree to a no-strike pledge. The membership may strike nevertheless. The negotiator has the authority to decide, but his decision, to be effective, must be acceptable and hence must rest on premises and values professed by those for whom he bargains. Moreover, the effective exercise of the negotiator's authority requires that his decisions be acceptable to a group far more extensive than his immediate clientele. The strike may or may not be supported by other unions in the plant, by other unions serving the plant, or by potential strike-breakers. The union negotiator, moreover, has a job. What happens to his present job and to his career opportunities depends on the trade union hierarchy, on his colleagues, on those who might hire him elsewhere—in other unions, in government, or in industry. Or perhaps his position depends on the union electorate and on the union's political machine, in which case the negotiator must take account of their reaction to his decision. Can he afford to affront the powers that are or might be? Is he giving the means to rivals or enemies to brand him betrayer, or fool, or lackey? How will his friends, in whose opinions he sees his own worth mirrored, regard his decision? To all of these, he is in some sense answerable. Because he must be ready to explain and justify, he is likely, in the exercise of his authority, to choose a position that can be explained, justified by precedents, by accepted standards, by general notions of "the workers' interest," the "union's needs," the "labor movement," the "national welfare." The union negotiator in the exercise of his authority is therefore likely to express a philosophy acceptable to a particular community at a particular time.

Choice by the union negotiator is a choice by a vested authority. But in the union hall, when the strike vote is taken, the choice is of another order. There conflicting interests interact and balance. Old grudges weigh against new anticipations. Accumulating grievances against company or against union are measured against habitual loyalties and instinctive cautions. Out of these composite ingredients is fabricated—choice.

On the other side of the table from the union negotiators are the representatives of "management." But what is management? What do its representatives represent? Like their union counterparts, they too possess a vested authority. Like their union counterparts, they too are answerable for their choice, but to a different (though related and overlapping) community. Their authority also must be exercised within the boundaries of the acceptable: what is acceptable to the powers of their own organization, acceptable to the companies that must follow any wage and subsequent price changes, acceptable to customer and consumer, and to all those upon whom the "company" in some sense depends.

They speak for the shareholder's interest, though neither they nor their superiors need be significant shareholders, and even though shareholders have neither cognizance of the issues nor control over their decisions. They represent the shareholder because that is the right and proper thing to do, applauded in the circles they esteem, a matter of mores, not of self-interest. They will represent the "pure" company concern to reinvest earnings and to grow—for they are identified and they identify themselves with the power and prestige of the company. They will take into account the effect that "defeat" or "victory" might have upon their reputations in the industry. They will be sensitive to the firmness in the handshake of their peers and to mutterings at the country club. Had they courage? Did they defy? Were they unreasonable? They will not be immune to the gripes of the consumers, editorials against inflation, young wives' tales about the rises in the price of things. They will be tough or yielding depending upon their conception of trade unionism and the labor movement, of the values of free enterprise, of the prerogatives allegedly necessary for authority.

In their demands and in their decisions, the representatives both of "the workers" and of "management" will be influenced by anticipations of public reaction to a strike and its consequences and by the possibilities of governmental intervention. Public opinion and governmental intervention, in turn, will depend on a complex of pervasive stereotypes: money-bags and trade union gangsterism, labor's cross and the consumer's frustration, the inalienable right to run your own business and rich men riding in Cadillacs earned by poor men's sweat. In this fashion, values, interests, and conceptions held by those far outside the negotiating organizations are drawn into wage bargaining. Both authoritative and composite choice will have had a part in the outcome.

The Two Cultures. Sir Charles Snow has argued that modern society contains not one culture, but two, the literary and the scientific. These are alleged to represent not merely the mastery of different kinds of information, but also a difference in the cast of thought. A dialogue between the two is rare and difficult.

There is another, perhaps more fundamental, dichotomy in the culture of organizations, between those whose capacities and skills gear into composite choice and those habituated to the authoritative decision—the one sensitized to the subtle currents of opinion, bending in the flux of transitory alliances, sniffing the winds of antagonism, moving in the constant recombination of powers; the other working within a firm framework of purpose and prerogative, assigned and assigning clear-cut cubicles of resources and responsibilities, rationally and systematically shaping action to the requirements of the task. One rides the rapids and the other makes bridges. These two also cannot converse.

Choice in Alternative Forms of Economic Organization. Three components of choice have been postulated.

1. The individualized choice, with no point of reference beyond the experience, opinion, observation, and values, the self-calculus and impulse of the individual acting on his own.

2. The authoritative choice, by individuals with the vested power to decide for others. Acceptability by and answerability to those others are its points of reference.

3. The composite choice, without points of reference, emerging from the free interaction of diverse interests.

All of these components are to be found in any of the forms of economic organization. Yet, it may be ventured, their relative importance will be predictably different in the three forms of economic organization analyzed here.

In the decentralized market-directed economy, individualized choice will, of course, prevail, but the other components of choice will still be significant. Everyone cannot be an entrepreneur, no matter how decentralized the market; the coercive power and authority vested in the boss is not inconsiderable. Composite choice is peripheral, covert; yet, during those epochs dominated by an economy of price-direction, the half-articulated, loosely institutionalized association of "class" produced composite choices of the greatest significance for marketplace, factory, union hall, and courtroom.

Under centralized political-direction the mode of choice will be authoritative: choice by planners answerable to the Party or to the electorate, and hence to the community's dominant values and conventions or to the outlook and philosophy of the elite. In turn, choice by organizers, managers, supervisors, and bureaucrats will be made authoritatively by reference to the goals and specifications laid down in the plan. Nevertheless, though these operating choices characteristically will be authoritative, the underlying goals and values themselves will change, evolve, and emerge through a process of composite choice.

Classical economists conceived of choice in the individual pursuit of self-interest. They were justified since this was the kind of choice characteristic of the decentralized market-directed form of economic organization that they observed and explained. The Marxist, on the other hand, conceived of choice as a reflex of class interests. This implies choices made by reference to a dominant social philosophy that is acceptable to leaders and to the led. And indeed, for a revolutionary movement, or in centralized economic planning, this is the essential form of choice. The classical economist emphasized individualized choice, and the Marxist emphasized authoritative choice. Both were right in terms of the form of economic organization, and the problems that were their particular concern.

In the economy of negotiating organizations, based on the flux and loose interaction of independent entities, requiring the lures that cement voluntary association, the composite choice will be characteristic.

SUMMARY

In the economy of autonomous organizations, control over activity resides in group and not in individual choice. Group choice would have at least two components: the authoritative decision, made by an individual for the group, and the composite choice, made in the aggregation or balance of forces or in the expression of a consensus. Authoritative choice though made by an individual is not the same as individualized choice. Authoritative choice is answerable, and hence is shaped by the outlook and ethos of those to whom an answer should be made. It must be within the range of the acceptable for those upon whom it is imposed. The values of authoritative choice are the values of human rationality. Its weakness lies in the narrowness and rigidity of doctrine.

Composite choice arises through the balancing of diverse pressures. The value of composite choice is that it reflects actual needs. It is responsive, expedient, flexible. Its weaknesses are the weaknesses of expediency. It is without foresight, without hindsight, without insight.

The configurations of choice will vary between alternative forms of economic organization. The individualized is predominant but not universal in the decentralized price-directed economy; the authoritative is characteristic in the centralized politically directed economy; the composite prevails in the organizational market-negotiated economy.

Chapter 3

Decentralized Market-Direction and Resource Allocation

MOTIVATION

Spontaneous, Automatic Motivation to Efficiency. Those who work, manage, and decide in the decentralized market-directed economy can expect to gain more for themselves through producing what is wanted at a minimum cost, and through avoiding waste. Hence self-interest motivates the effort to perform efficiently. This is not necessarily so in the other forms of economic organization.

In the decentralized market-directed economy, property and the market link individual self-interest to the economizing intent. By working hard and efficiently, by administering hard and efficiently, by delivering what consumers want where and when they want it, the producer augments his possessions and the power and the prestige that derive from possession. If self-interest in gain is basic, then a most basic, and perhaps a most base human motivation is harnessed to the wheel. In no other form of organization is the relationship between self-interest and the economizing intent so close and so unequivocable. In neither of the other two forms of organization is the motivation to efficiency spontaneous and automatic. Here alone no incentive scheme needs to be designed, imposed, administered, and supervised. The system moves on its own, driven by powerful and pervasive forces that rise from the bottom and never slacken.

Limitations. It is certainly conceivable that more effective systems of motivation could be designed than the spontaneous mechanism of the decentralized market. The analytic mind dissecting the psychology of the human object can devise baits and beatings that drive men more effectively than they can be driven in the ordinary course of independent bargaining. This is so for many reasons:

1. Under market-direction, a whole range of potential motivation, from terror to love, is left untapped.

2. The motivational bait, under decentralized market-direction, is the acquisition of property. But the very acquisition of property reduces the motivational force for further acquisition. As wealth accumulates, a given

34

income-bait becomes cumulatively a less effective incentive. Hence an incentive system based on the free-wheeling quest after possession contains seeds of its own debility.[1]

3. Under decentralized market-direction, a very substantial share of total income will take forms that can have no positive value in motivating efficiency. These include (*a*) windfall gains and losses, (*b*) the inheritance of property, and (*c*) rents which arise as incident to possession. Besides preempting income from use as a bait to motivate effort, the very existence of substantial flows of such nonincentive income weakens those psychological links in the individual's consciousness between efforts and rewards which motivate his choice and action.

RECRUITMENT OF AN ELITE

Recruitment Automatic, By Relevant Criteria. The efficiency of any form of economic organization depends not only on the motivation of decision-makers, but also on the individual quality and personal capacities of those decision-makers. It is, therefore, important to question the system of recruiting economic leadership implicit in any form of economic organization—the system, that is, of selecting those who are to perform the control functions.

In the decentralized market-directed economy, recruitment, like motivation, is linked through markets to the quest for and possession of property. The individual works in order to own. Through owning more, his managerial-organizational powers are extended. The individual increases his ownership through greater effort, shrewder insight, better anticipation, sharper speculation, bolder innovation, by pushing costs lower, by devising products that appeal to the tastes of consumers—thus proving his capacities through the hard testing ground of the competitive market. Having thus established his capacity to economize, or to manage, or to organize, or to innovate, a larger quantity of resources are, as a consequence, drawn under his control. So long as his superiority is manifest, his command over resources will continue to grow, and more and more power in economic decision will be concentrated in his hands. When the magnitude of his control becomes so complex that others less encumbered are able to beat him at the game, his power will cease to grow. When his energies slacken and his personal capacities decline, then

---

[1] It could be argued that this is desirable since the appropriate allocation of a man's time between work and leisure would shift toward leisure at higher levels of income. For society, however, this would be true only where the increase in income is general and proportionate. Otherwise, there need be no relationship between the slackening of the individual inclination and the intensity of the social need, since the economizing effort of the individual relates always to satisfying more than his own consumption wants.

others, more able, will move forward to displace him from the seat of decision-making. The market selects, weeds out, and replaces; it matches capacities to the magnitude and complexity of the managerial task.

Clearly this form of recruitment has great value. It is spontaneous, automatic. It does not have to be designed and imposed from above. It requires no supervision and needs no planners. It is incorruptible.

It offers a method of objective testing. The proving ground is open. The terms of the competition are set. The mechanism is no respecter of persons.

Market-direction bases the selection of economic leadership on relevant criteria. Those capacities that the market tests are those which the operation of the market economy requires and, as the requisites of the organizational task change, the capacities that the market will test for will change correspondingly. The civil servant, too, may be tested, and objectively tested, but it does not follow that that for which he is tested will relate to that which he will, in the exercise of control, be required to do. China for many centuries was ruled by scholarly gentlemen, recruited through an enormously elaborate and difficult system of testing. But the tests emphasized mastery of ancient custom and traditional lore and brought into power men whose capacities and inclinations were quite the opposite of what was required for the tasks of national survival in the modern world.

Spontaneity, objectivity, and relevance: these are great values in the recruitment of economic leadership. Unfortunately, they are values that can only be partially realized in the decentralized market-directed economy. Distorting elements also inhere.

Utilizing Leadership Talents Brings Threat of Monopoly. The objective of recruitment is to select those most qualified for economic leadership and to make the best possible use of their scarce talents. This would suggest that where there is managerial and leadership ability of a very high order, correspondingly more complex and more extensive operations should be concentrated within the sphere of its control. In this form of economic organization, however, control over operations can be concentrated in the hands of the most qualified and able leadership only within narrow limits if the integrity of market-direction is to be maintained. Where, under competition, the most able accumulate property and power and extend their control over operations, they thereby tend also to acquire the monopoly power to direct price rather than to be directed by it. Such monopoly power subverts the integrity of decentralized market-direction. This suggests that without continuing social intervention the decentralized market-directed economy may not be dynamically stable. Nature offers an analogy:

If the pine forests are to survive in the Southern United States they must be cut down approximately in every generation; otherwise oaks and hickories grow up in the shade of the pines and eventually displace them. In the shadeless cutover forest, however, the oak and hickory seedlings do not survive and the young pines flourish.[2]

Monopoly grows in the shade of the increased concentration that arises through intense and effective competition. Competition, then, can renew itself only if there is a periodic pruning and cutting down of the cumulative powers that rise out of its own processes. But the cutting down and pruning limit the utilization of leadership abilities, and threaten the motivation to compete and grow.

Thus the automatic pressure toward the realization of economies would concentrate power, when there are economies in its concentration. If managerial-organizational abilities of highest caliber are rare, then the system, in the efficient allocation of that human resource, will cumulatively augment the economic powers of those who possess such abilities. At some point this concentration becomes incompatible with the requirements of effective market-direction. Optimum recruitment conflicts with the operational prerequisites of the system. On the other hand, the regular pruning and destruction of competitively acquired monopoly power strikes at those expectations that are the system's motivational force.

Property-Based Nepotism and Barriers of Class. The selection of an economic leadership under decentralized market-direction takes place through the accumulation of property. The prerogatives of property imply not only the exercise of the powers of control, but also the power to train others to the exercise of that power, to share that power, to pass that power on through gift or inheritance. Property rights are personal rights and the obligations of property are identical to the personal or familial obligations of those who possess it. Through property, the obligations of personal friendship and family duty are carried into the realm of production and distribution. Nepotism becomes institutionalized, morally sanctified. Subjective criteria, wholly removed from the question of merit or relative ability or competence, are interjected into the process of leadership-selection. This property power to offer family and friend training in the skills and knowledge that are required for economic leadership and to favor them with first access to opportunity can be so important that it creates a cumulative barrier of class that prevents the majority of the population from reaching the first rung of the recruitment ladder.

Malrecruitment Through Windfalls and Inherited Wealth. The decision-making power is not only vested, under decentralized market-direction, in those who have proven themselves by the competitive test. It is also

2 Kenneth Ewart Boulding, *The Organizational Revolution* (New York: Harper & Row, 1953), p. xxvi.

distributed and redistributed haphazardly and continuously through windfall gains and losses. As a result the selection of economic leadership is in part a matter of random chance. For this reason there must be a substantial and ineradicable margin of incompetents among those who achieve positions of power.

Recruitment is further distorted by the advantages in the acquisition of power that derive cumulatively from the possession of power. Property and the power over resources increase not only through the test of contribution, but as a sheer function of the magnitude of possession. If the larger firms can out-compete all the others because of the technological advantages of size, then that initial size advantage fosters further growth and carries those in possession to greater possession without respect to their intrinsic abilities or relative contribution. Certain opportunities, including those innovations that are probably the primary source of big increments of gain, can only be realized by those with substantial resources already at their disposal. Only those already in possession can take what many may see. Gain is a creature of gain; to those who have, it is given.

In the competitive struggle itself, the criteria of selection are not always the most relevant ones. Power may be acquired through skill at prudently imitating the pace setter, but the socially optimum exercise of that power would require not prudent imitation but pace-setting. Skill in fraud, deceit, bluff, and legal maneuver also yield the gains of power and leadership. Exigencies of survival at the lower rungs of the competitive struggle may weed out all save the narrow visioned, the petty, the cautious, the grasping, so that none can rise but those who have proven *not* to have the qualities of daring and imagination required for the socially optimum exercise of power at the higher echelons of control. The skilled speculator acquires the power to organize badly. The skilled organizer acquires the power to speculate badly. Ideally, recruitment should be a race that the swiftest win. The decentralized market economy is a race where all can enter and where swiftness matters. These are considerable virtues. But it is not a fair race, nor a race where only swiftness counts.

INSTITUTIONAL COSTS

Divergence from the Technically-Optimum Size. If, in the decentralized market economy, price is to act as the barometer of scarcity and as the effective mechanism for directing the flow of resources, it is necessary that the share of each producer, distributor, or consumer does not exceed a small fraction of output of the market in which he is competing. This means that the unit of production, distribution, or consumption must be very small in relation to the size of the market. The technically optimum scale of operations need not be correspondingly small. Indeed, events suggest that the technically efficient operation is frequently much larger than is permissible for effective price competition.

This divergence of the technical from the organizational optima can be a source of both ideological and practical dilemma. Under the free competition of the decentralized market, the size of enterprise adapts automatically to the economies of scale and creates thereby operations of a size that is not compatible with price competition. To abort this tendency would deny the community positive technological gains and would restrict "economic freedom." But, left alone, these loci of concentration would use their monopoly power to expand even further. Against them would be created offsetting business and labor concentrations, not as a matter of technical advantage but of bargaining necessity in a chain of response and counter-response that could transform the entire structure of economic organization.

Adjudication and the Enforcement of Contract. The market-directed economy requires a virtually infinite dispersion of decision-making. This is achieved through the institution of private property, including property rights in one's labor. Since this property power must be employed in a wide range of circumstances in ways that cannot be precisely forseen, its implicit rights are, necessarily, loosely defined, flexible, and expandable. The exercise of the multiplicity of prerogatives that inhere in property will cause conflicts in claims, and these conflicts must be adjudicated. In the exercise of the property power, independent decision-makers relate and combine in complex, time-extended arrangements that require contract. Contracts must be made; and they must be enforced. The rights and prerogatives of the parties involved must be protected. In the light of changing circumstance, the terms of contract must be interpreted continually. All this constitutes an enormous and difficult task.

To the degree that decision-making is decentralized, arrangements that interlock and coordinate activities cannot be made uniform. To the degree that decision-makers are independent, adjudication cannot be simplified into administration. Each decision-maker is himself an independent variable in the formulation and enforcement of contractual arrangements. For each, the control of his property constitutes a particular orbit of power, with conflicts-of-powers possible at any point on its periphery. As a consequence of the dispersion of independent decision-making, the adjudication of claims, the settlement of conflicts, and formulation and enforcement of interindividual arrangements becomes correspondingly complex and costly.

The great bulk of the time and effort and energies of the lawyers, the courts, and the agencies of law enforcement in Western capitalism is an institutional cost of decentralized economic decision-making. Every year a considerable proportion of the highest intellectual talent is drawn into tasks of the civil law, making and enforcing contracts and negotiating property rights and damages—tasks that must increase in difficulty and complexity to the extent that choice is decentralized. These adjudicatory tasks of the law impose no corresponding drain on the human resource, say, in Soviet Russia, where economic choice is more predominantly centralized.

There are other important institutional costs that inhere in the exchange transaction itself. These are the energies, talents, and time devoured in higgling and haggling, in waiting and demonstrating, in bluffing and persuading. Included also are the costs of moving goods and commodities, or claims upon those goods and commodities, not from place to place as a technical requirement, but from ownership to ownership, from organization to organization, as a function of exchange. These costs are a multiple of the number of individual exchange transactions in the processes of producing and distributing and must increase as a consequence of greater decentralization. In the market-directed form of economic organization, they are likely to be formidable.

SENSITIVITY TO STIMULI

Adjustment-Time as a Criterion of Efficiency. Traditional economics conceives an equilibrium position as the one where decision-makers and action-takers have fully adjusted to a certain set of circumstances. This conception implies that forms of organization should be evaluated and compared through the contrast of their equilibria. When the system finally comes to rest, how closely will it approximate the ideal? The question, however, should be not only, how near to perfection is the full and final adjustment, but also, how rapidly can readjustments take place?

In every actual economy, the parameters of choice and action are constantly changing; and every actual economy, therefore, is perpetually readjusting. The evaluation of a form of economic organization then, should not be based simply on its capacity for final (or timeless) adjustment, but also on its capacity to respond swiftly to new stimuli to choice and action, and, in the rapid flux of events, to keep its actual resource allocations close to the equilibrium pattern.

Two Stimuli to Choice and Change. At issue is the sensitivity of decision-makers and the swiftness with which they can respond to that which stimulates change. In fact, the stimuli to choice or action may be of different sorts; the relative sensitivity and capacity for response of particular forms of economic organization will vary depending on the stimuli in question.

There is the stimulus to choice and action that is encountered as part of the production or the distribution activity. For example: a consumer asks for an item that is not in stock; a worker expresses a grievance; a shipment of damaged goods is received; a salesman offers a new factory site at a bargain price. Such stimuli, received through the experience of operations, will be termed "local and specific."

There are, on the other hand, stimuli to choice and action that are not specifically encountered in the locale of production or distribution and that need have no direct or indirect relation to any particular operation, but that, nevertheless, change the context of rational choice or the opportunities and potentialities for action. For example: a new device is invented; an oceanographic survey discovers mineral deposits underseas; the tariffs in a neighboring country are changed. Such stimuli to choice and action that affect the general context of economic choice, although they have no relation to existing operations and are unlikely to be encountered in the specifics of production and distribution, are termed here "general and diffused."

These two categories, "local and specific" and "general and diffused" can claim neither precisely to define nor fully to include all the stimuli to economic change. They do serve to illustrate the relationship between forms of economic organization, and the sorts of stimuli to which decision-makers are in fact subjected.

Response to Local Stimuli Optimized. Presumably, the rapidity with which the given decision-maker will respond to a change in the parameters of choice will depend on the length and complexity of the line of communication that transmits knowledge of the change to the point of decision and that retransmits decision to the point of action. Where the process of transmission between fact and act is more direct and less encumbered, the agency of choice and action will be correspondingly more sensitive and responsive to the stimulus to change. Longer and more complex lines of communication, a greater number of individuals through whom knowledge must be relayed before it can be acted upon, less opportunity for a direct confrontation between the decision-maker and the facts or circumstances that provide the stimulus to change: all these factors must reduce the sensitivity and dampen the response to the changing parameters of choice.

Decentralized market-direction brings decision-making into the closest possible proximity to operations. In this form of economic organization, decision-making is inseparable from the experience of production and distribution. Correspondingly, change in the "local and specific" parameters of choice will be easily, completely, and rapidly communicated to decision-makers, and, on that account, adjustive response will be rapid and flexible. It would, therefore, be the rule that decentralized market-direction is more sensitive to stimuli to change and adjusts more rapidly than any other form of economic organization when the changing parameters are local and specific. When, however, the changing parameters are general and diffused, the degree of decentralization is probably a handicap, as will be shown in the next chapter.

DISTORTION THROUGH EXTERNAL ECONOMIES
AND DISECONOMIES

The Invisible Hand Spells External Economies. One of the most cogent arguments of classical economics in favor of the decentralized market-directed economy is summed up in Adam Smith's conception of the "invisible hand." This conception maintains that while individuals in the market strive only for their personal gain, in so doing they bring benefits to others as well. The individual preempts only a part of his economic contribution. Others share in his contribution as he does in theirs. Hence, self-striving contributes to the well-being of others, and each has a self-interest in the self-striving of all. Those benefits, brought about as a result of an individual's effort, which accrue not to that individual but to others (and which Adam Smith considered the bounty of the "invisible hand"), are *external economies*. The benefits that the decision-maker preempts for himself are *internal economies*.

Suppose an American company opens a copper mine in Canada. Who benefits? This is the sort of question being asked today not only by Canadians, but by all of those who at once seek and fear investment from abroad.

To open a territory for mining, docks, harbors, and roads must be built, rivers dredged, electricity and telecommunications brought in, health hazards eliminated, all of which would benefit all the individuals and organizations carrying on or wanting to carry on activities in the area. Landowners will benefit from higher sales and rental values. Suppliers of equipment to the company, builders of homes for company personnel, merchants serving the company and its employees will benefit. Increased manpower demand will cause wages to rise in the territory; hence, labor will benefit. The output of the mine, presumably, will lower the world price for copper, thereby benefiting consumers throughout the world. The Governments of Canada and the United States will benefit from taxing the profits of the mine. All such benefits are external economies. The residual which remains with the company is an internal economy. The external economies are extremely important to society, but only the anticipation of internal economies will influence the company's choice.

Costs Unpaid by Those Who Incurred Them: External Diseconomies. Not all actions taken and decisions made in an economy yield benefits. Some result in damages, sacrifices, and costs of all sorts. These costs are paid, but not necessarily by the agency whose decisions and actions brought them about. The costs that that agency pays are internal diseconomies. The costs incurred through its actions for which it does not pay are external diseconomies.

Suppose the owner of the only factory in a small town considers closing down the plant and shifting its operations elsewhere. In his rational profit-maximizing choice, he takes into account the cost of transporting or replacing his machinery, of building a new factory, and of recruiting and retraining a new work force. He takes these costs into account because he has to pay them. But he will not be motivated by profit considerations to base his decision on the costs, also consequent upon his choice, that the existing labor force must bear in their search for new jobs, in their retraining, in the forced sale of their homes and in migrating to a new place of employment. These costs or diseconomies are external. They may be consequent upon his choice, but since they are not paid by him, he leaves them out of the balance that determines his decision. The decision-maker measures internal economies against internal diseconomies, benefits he receives against costs he pays. External economies and diseconomies have no place in his calculation.

Distorted Choice. That which externalizes costs or benefits introduces irrationality into the process of economic choice. The more the effects of decision-making are externalized, the further the operative criteria of choice will be removed from the scale of real costs and benefits. On that account, the greater will be the deviation between the optimal and the equilibrium patterns of resource distribution.

It does not matter whether external economies over-balance external diseconomies. It is externality, malevolent or benevolent, that introduces the discrepancy between those criteria that control individual decisions and those relevant to a maximum contribution to the social product.

The Cause: Fragmentation of Responsibility and of Power. Because of human fallibilities and because the future is hazed with uncertainty, decision-makers, under all circumstances and in any form of economic organization, will fail to consider some of the costs and benefits that are consequent upon their choice and action. Externality, however, refers only to those sacrifices and benefits which *cannot* be taken into account because (1) no decision-maker has the responsibility to take these sacrifices and benefits into account, and/or because (2) there does not exist the power to control relevant relationships and effects. The meaning of "responsibility" varies between one form of economic organization and another. The nature and motivational basis of the responsibility of the captain for his ship, the policeman for his beat, the foreman for his shop, and the farmer for his land are all quite different. Under decentralized market-direction, lines of responsibility and power are drawn by the ownership of property or by contract, and the crux of responsibility is self-interest in private gain.

Under any form of power and under any system of responsibility, the more that control is divided and responsibility fragmented among independent decision-makers, (1) the larger must be the proportion of the total effects of choice and action for which no rational accounting can be made as a basis for control, and (2) the greater must be the number of relationships between *independent* entities whose effects *ipso facto* fall outside rational control, since, if the relationships between entities are to be controlled, the entities themselves must be controlled, and, to that extent, will cease to be independent.

For example, when the farmer owns the land both on the hill and in the vale, he plants a forest cover on the slopes to protect the soil below from erosion. But when the valley is owned by one set of farmers, and the hill is owned by a different set (with "responsibility" thus fragmented), hill farmers will plant crops on the slopes, and will take no account of (having no responsibility for) the consequent losses through erosion that occur in the valley. Or, again, the purchase, ownership, and use of automobiles and the location of factories and homes are related as component parts of an integral (transportation) function. Inasmuch as the decisions respecting these component elements are made by numerous, independent decision-makers, that functional relationship must remain external to rational accounting and control.

In sum, the externalization of effects and the exclusion of relationships from the possibility of rational accounting and control are consequences of divided power and of fragmented responsibility. These in turn are functions of decentralization. The more that power and responsibility are decentralized, the larger must be the margin of incurred benefits and sacrifices that necessarily are left out of account in choice, and the greater the number of relationships that cannot be subjected to any rational control.

Externality Maximized by Decentralized Market-Direction. Under decentralized market-direction, key decisions are made independently by a very large number of small owners. Responsibility and power are firmly based on property and self-interest, but for each decision-agency the area of responsibility and the range of power is very small. Relative to the universe of economic activities and effects, responsibility is more fragmented, power is more dispersed, and the sum of relationships between independent decision-makers is greater for this form of economic organization than for any of the others studied here. An authority cannot be superimposed to control or restructure relationships between these agencies of choice without compromising the integrity of the system. Hence, the margin of external economies and diseconomies will be larger and the consequent distortions in resource allocation and in other aspects of economic choice will be greater in this than in the alternative forms of economic organization.

INSTABILITIES

Instabilities Exogenous to Form of Economic Organization. There are instabilities in economic activity and discontinuities in economic relationships that might occur in any form of economic organization, brought about perhaps by the forces of nature, in floods, in droughts, in earthquakes, or by changes in taste or in social priorities, or by new inventions or discoveries, or even simply by the termination of the working lives of those in whom economic responsibilities are vested. Such discontinuities, since they are extraneous to the form of organization, will concern us only inasmuch as they are manifested in a particular and characteristic way in different forms of economic organization. Our concern, rather, is with those instabilities that are consequences of the form of economic organization itself.

The Necessary Costs of Horizontal Price Instability. Decentralized market-direction requires the free and discontinuous movement of prices in order to guide the allocation and to coordinate the utilization of resources. When consumer demand for commodity A increases at the expense of commodity B, then, in this form of economic organization, a proper allocation of resources requires that the change in consumer preference be reflected in the relative rise in the price of one good and in the relative decline in the price of the other. Price movements are the characteristic responses to discontinuities extraneous to the operation of the economy itself, as change in consumer tastes or alterations in the relative availability of resources. Such extraneous discontinuities might be differently expressed and differently adjusted to in other forms of economic organization.

Price change that serves to guide the allocation of resources under decentralized market-direction implies instability in particular prices relative to each other, but not an instability in the price level. In order to perform their proper role, prices need only shift along the horizontal, with the rise in some being offset by declines in others. The level of prices need not be affected.

Because there is no power in the economy to resist the pressure to change price in response to alterations in supply and demand and since, indeed, free horizontal price change is essential to the mechanism of adjustment, these horizontal movements in price must be more frequent and more extreme in the decentralized market-directed economy than in the other forms of economic organization. Horizontal price change creates social problems and has a social cost; nevertheless, it has a functional justification under decentralized market-direction.

Functionless Instabilities of the Price Level. While price movements along the horizontal are necessary under decentralized market-direction, vertical movements of the whole price level, that is, not the rise in the price of A relative to the price of B but the rise or fall in the price of A and B simultaneously, have no such functional value. Those upward and downward movements of the price level, called inflation and deflation, neither guide the allocation nor coordinate the utilization of resources nor serve any other useful purpose. Yet the tendency to extreme vertical price instability inheres in the decentralized market-directed economy as a consequence of the dispersion of the independent power to purchase, save, and consume.

Just as individual prices rise or fall in fluid and automatic response to a rise or fall in consumer demand, prices generally will rise or fall with a rise or fall in the total expenditures on goods and services. Since total expenditure is the sum of expenditures of a virtually infinite number of individuals, each deciding on his own how much to consume, to invest, or to save, and with no decision-maker able to take into account the impact on the price level of his own small choice, there is no means in this form of economic organization of keeping total expenditures stable or of holding them to any socially desired level. Except through external intervention, which, in controlling aggregate expenditure, might change the essential character of the system, vertical price instability is inevitable.

Price Level Stability Through Stability of Aggregate Expenditure. At any point in time, total expenditures determine not only the price level, but also the total of all incomes. If price levels are to remain constant, then an amount exactly equivalent to that which is being received as current income must be respent on goods and services. Current total income must continuously equal current spending intentions. But why, in the decentralized market economy, should this ever occur? Total expenditures are the sum of decisions by a very large number of independent individuals and agencies. Each can decide to spend less than his (its) income, that is, to save, and many through accumulation or credit can decide to spend more than their income. Spending and saving, then, will follow shifting individual inclinations, wants, and anticipations. Individuals will spend more or less than their current incomes, thereby causing aggregate expenditure and the price level to rise or to fall.

A vertical rise in prices stimulates speculative purchases, which accelerates the further upward movement of spending and prices. The vertical fall in price, conversely, stimulates the speculative withholding of current purchases and accelerates the downward movement of spending and of prices.

Under the circumstances of free-moving, market-determined prices and a dispersion of the independent power to consume, save, and invest, the wonder is that under decentralized market-direction there could be any check to rapid cumulative movements of price between zero and infinity. Theorists differ on this question and they disagree as to whether the general level of employment would *also* be unstable under such a system. These questions have never been tested. In historical instances, vertical movements of price have been stabilized through government intervention and have been checked by those other intermingled forms of economic organization that are resistant to change in price. It is clear, however, that severe vertical price instability has been peculiarly a problem whenever conditions approximating decentralized market-direction obtain.

Vertical price instability has heavy social costs. It is subversive of forward planning. It weakens all contractual relationships. In its extreme movements it can destroy the long standing expectations of social classes, with possible profound and dangerous repercussions on political attitudes. The great purposeless waves of windfall loss and gain brought about through vertical price instability visit a blind injustice upon the population. By this random favor and random ruin motivation and recruitment are distorted.

Vertical price instability introduces another dimension of uncertainty into economic choice. *Uncertainty*, as a problem in the decentralized market-directed economy, will be dealt with in the following section.

UNCERTAINTIES

Source of Distorted Choice. Under any form of economic organization, rational choice must be based on what is known or anticipated concerning the present and future availability of resources and concerning the present and future priority of outputs or intensity of demand. Inasmuch as future resource availabilities and future output demands cannot be foreseen, or can be anticipated only imperfectly and partially, to that degree the data required for the efficient allocation of resources will be lacking. Decision-makers will err. Their plans will be based on the wrong assumptions. Uncertain in their expectations, they will hesitate and fail to act when action is called for. Whatever limits the foresight of the decision-maker, whatever increases his uncertainty will, under any form of organization, reduce efficiency.

Uncertainties Exogenous to Form of Economic Organization. There are elements relevant to economic choice that escape prediction and elude foresight under any form of economic organization. Techniques are changing. Inventions and scientific discoveries are on the horizon, beyond the shores of present conception. Natural resource availabilities can change with the discoveries of mineral deposits. Natural catastrophe can upset the balance of need and production. Wants change in the perpetual contrariness of personal tastes. Social priorities change with each new political crisis. Under any form of economic organization, these elements of the unforeseen and the imperfectly foreseeable perpetually disturb and distort decision-making.

There are also causes of uncertainty, barriers to foresight and anticipation, that are built into forms of economic organization. It is the "internal uncertainties" particular to the given form of economic organization that are of concern here.

Uncertainty a Consequence of Decentralized, Independent Choice. Under decentralized market-direction, as in every form of economic organization, rational choice requires the anticipation of change in the availability of resources, in consumer preference, and in social need. But, in addition, as a consequence of the form of economic organization itself, decentralized market-direction requires that each decision-maker anticipate the responses of all those other independent decision-makers who supply his goods, or who buy his products, or who compete with him on the market. Rational choice depends not only on his knowledge of objective circumstances whose future effects are common for all. Also and in addition, his choice will depend on his expectation of what others will think and anticipate regarding those changes in objective circumstances and regarding each other's expectations and anticipations. His rational choice must take into account not only anticipated changes in objective circumstances, but also a universe of cross-related anticipations, expectations, and responses of the other independent decision-makers whose activities are related to his own.

Take for example the case of Jones, whose problem is to design a plant to produce certain types and quantities of machine fittings for the next several years. What information is relevant to his choice? He might try to anticipate the future pattern of consumer wants, and the new techniques which are in the offing. Such anticipation would be appropriate under any form of economic organization. But if he is producing in a decentralized market-directed economy there are additional problems of anticipation and additional uncertainties. The sale of machine fittings will not depend directly on end-product needs, but on the plans of those manufacturers who buy machine fittings in order to equip themselves to produce end products they think consumers will want. Hence, in order to foresee the demand for his product, Jones would have to anticipate the reequipment and expansion plans of end-product manufacturers made in anticipation of their end-product sales. Jones, moreover, has competitors. They, like himself, will be developing products and building inventories in anticipation of manufacturer's demands. Jones' future sales will depend also on the price and product offerings of his competitors. Similarly, the costs of alternative materials for which Jones might design his new plant will depend on the competitive demand for materials and on the production and expansion plans of suppliers of those materials, which also will be based on webs of horizontal and vertical expectations and anticipations similarly geared to the expectations and anticipations of many independent decision-makers.

Uncertainty Maximized Under Decentralized Market-Direction. The business entity in the decentralized market economy charts its course by reference not only to the objective parameters of social need, technical potentiality, and physical environment, but also necessarily by reference to the independent anticipations of many others, including their anticipations of anticipations and their response to responses. No matter how sure the decision-maker is about the shape of the former, about the latter he is perpetually in doubt. This uncertainty is internal in the sense that it is generated by the operation of the economy itself. The degree of internal uncertainty will depend on the number of interdependent decisions being made independently of each other. Each additional independent decision-maker extends the range of the half-knowns, the unknowns, and the unknowables that plague the task of choice for all.

Uncertainties internal to the form of economic organization are a function of dispersed economic power and of decentralized decision-making. Such uncertainty must be greater in the decentralized market-directed economy than in the other forms of economic organization studied here. To those of price instability are added the internally-generated uncertainties consequent upon the need to anticipate the anticipations of independent decision-makers. As a result, in the decentralized market-directed economy the task of long-range investment planning or any choice requiring foresight becomes a formidable one indeed.

When the degree of decentralization approximates that of "pure competition," as it does in many agricultural markets, rational anticipatory planning becomes virtually impossible. The degree of internal uncertainty has then increased beyond the point where the individual decision-maker can even attempt to see into the future. He reacts only to the market price of the instant, waiting like a blind beast to be led by bait or driven by beating to the trough or to the slaughter. In his response to changing circumstances, he jumps too high or he falls too low, cracking his head or bruising his bottom, but is never able to stand straight and walk forward in reasonable anticipation of what lies ahead. This perpetual flux between the error of too little and the error of too much is shown in the marked peaks and valleys of output and the contrasting valleys and peaks of price, statistically recorded as "livestock cycles" and "crop cycles" and generalized in the Cobweb Theorem. The cost of this virtual elimination of anticipatory planning lies not merely in the discomfiture of the decision-maker, but also in the implicit waste and malallocation of resources: every adjustment to changed circumstances must proceed from the experience of failure and the effect of malallocation on price. The economy must move like a blindfolded driver who finds his way by bumping his car into obstacles.

There is a twilight zone on this side of pure competition where many independent decision-makers remain and where price is more or less fluid, yet where it is possible, in spite of the deep and pervasive uncertainties, to see and to anticipate vague configurations of the future. Here society must entrust its economic destiny to the entrepreneur, conceived by Frank Knight as a creature of intuition and hunches, more sure-footed than the rest when walking in shadows, too bold or too blind to be paralyzed by the knowledge of all he does not know. For making the best of the uncertainties that the system itself creates, he receives a considerable share (defined by Knight as "profit") of the national income. Such profits are a social cost of internal uncertainties.

The energies and skills of the entrepreneur and of the speculator required to deal with internal uncertainty are costs of the system that creates these uncertainties. Society must pay also for the inescapable margin of error and waste, difficulty and delay that is greater proportionately as knowledge is inadequate and anticipations are blurred and obscured.

Whatever the remedies and palliatives applied, internal uncertainties are likely to remain a basic problem and a peculiar deficiency of decentralized market-direction.

THE ORGANIZATION OF CONSUMPTION

Organization of Consumption and Procurement. Consumption, like production, is a complex social function that may be variously organized. The three economic forms studied here are employed also in organizing consumption. Consumption is sometimes organized through centralized political-direction, as, for example, in the government use of rockets and missiles for space exploration. Consumption is sometimes organized through autonomous, market-negotiating organizations, such as the consumer cooperatives that are of great importance in particular countries in Western Europe. And consumption is often organized by decentralized market-directed choice of individuals. A particular good may be produced through one form of economic organization and consumed through quite another. End products produced and used by government are often produced by great autonomous market-negotiating corporations or by small firms. Conversely, goods or services produced by state-directed enterprise may be purchased and consumed by individuals, small firms, or large companies.

Analogies to the Organization of Production. There are advantages in organizing consumption akin to those in organizing production through decentralized market choice, such as the spontaneous drive toward efficiency and the capacity for rapid flexible adjustment to the "localized" stimuli of personal preferences and tastes. Similarly the disadvantages in organizing production are encountered again in organizing consumption through this form of economy, such as the institutional costs of catering to numerous decision-makers, the limits upon technically optimum size for the agency of consumption, the exclusion of inter-individual relationships from the scope of control, the fragmentation of responsibility for the effects of the consumption choice, and the internal generation of uncertainty. These advantages and disadvantages of consumption through decentralized market-direction will be briefly discussed.

Under decentralized market-direction there is a strong spontaneous motivation to procure and consume efficiently. The individual purchasing on his own account on the market has a direct and immediate self-interest in maximizing, according to his own scale of preferences, the benefits to be derived from the goods and services made available to him.

Complex institutional arrangements are necessary in order to "sell" and to "distribute" to a mass of independent decision-makers, which would not be needed if the consumption decision was centralized. Selling to a great number of independent consumers requires a corresponding extension of the services of display, demonstration, information, credit, etc. Such arrangements are costly and constitute a cost intrinsic to this form of economic organization.

The decision as what, whether, and how to consume may require such complex information, skilled analysis and extensive study (for example, in the decision whether to use or how to use a new medicine) that the costs of individual choice become prohibitive. Consumption and procurement are also technologies with overhead elements and indivisibilities that may require, for efficiency, a larger agency for decision-taking than is compatible with decentralized market-direction.

The organization of consumption by individuals who are themselves the consumers makes possible the immediate and direct expression of individual preferences in response to direct market offerings. On the other hand, under this form of choice there is likely to be a relatively slow and difficult response to "general and diffused" stimuli, for example, information respecting new potential uses for outputs.

Decentralized consumption fragments responsibility for the effects of consumption decisions and increases the number of those relationships between independent consuming agencies that fall outside the range of choice and control. For both reasons, decentralized market-directed consumption will maximize the external economies and diseconomies, and the distortions of procurement and consumption due to externalization.

Individuals consuming on private account are also members of groups and of a society. They are concerned to participate in determining the pattern of procurement and the organization of consumption to satisfy the goals of the groups to which they belong and of their society. This cannot be done through individual choices in the market. The aggregated choice of individuals each deciding independently is not the same as group choice or social choice since it cannot take into account and choose with respect to the relationships between individuals. Similarly the value of organizing consumption through the decentralized choice of individual consumers is limited by the fragmentation of responsibility consequent upon such decentralization. The procurement and consumption of education, for example, is generally considered to bring important benefits to others than the individual receiving the education. In other words there are important external economies of education which are left out of account in the rational decision of the individual as to whether to procure an education for himself or, in proxy, for his child. For this reason, in nearly every advanced society, the decision as to the procurement and organization of the educational services emanates from the political center or from groups and institutions, rather than from the free choices of individual consumers on the decentralized market.

There are uncertainties generated through the decentralization of the consumption choice, and whenever the effects of procurement or consumption extend into the future, those uncertainties are bound to plague decision-makers and to limit the possibilities of an informed and rational judgment. The decision to procure a specialized education as, say, an electronics engineer would presumably rest on an assessment of technological trends and the probable future need for electronic engineers. When many independent decision-makers are involved in this choice then there is also and additionally the need for each to anticipate the intentions of a host of others in their educational procurement plans. Sufficient information concerning the "objective circumstances" of technical trends and future needs may be available, but about the related plans and intentions of other decision-makers, there is an ineradicable uncertainty.

JUSTICE IN THE DISTRIBUTION OF INCOME

The Economy as an Instrument to Achieve Social Values. Three forms of economic organization will be analyzed as instruments for achieving (1) efficiency in the allocation and use of resources, (2) economic progress, (3) a desirable way of life, and (4) distributive justice.

The acceptance of these, or indeed of any social goals whatsoever is necessarily based on value judgments. Value judgments inherently cannot be established by "scientific" prediction and testing or by logical demonstration. We would postulate simply that these goals are accepted by many and hence are related to actual political choice and policy. Aside from their acceptability, it is sometimes necessary to clarify the precise meaning of the terms and the values that are in fact at issue. The meaning of "efficiency," for example, may be sufficiently unequivocal not to need belaboring. Not so with distributive justice. This may mean a number of quite different things.

Equality as the Criterion of Just Distribution. Two standards of "just distribution" will be considered here. One is that of equality in income shares. Under this criterion the ideal distribution of income would be for every member of the community, whether they were young or old, whether they contributed greatly or did not work at all, to receive exactly equal income; or perhaps with their share adjusted for certain peculiar needs. Such income equality might be accepted as intrinsically good or it might be justified by its relation to other values. For example neoclassical "welfare" economics held the equalization of income to be a good thing because it "maximized the sum of satisfactions" of the community as a whole. The argument was that the less a man has, the more satisfaction he will derive from additional increments of income. Hence total satisfactions could always be increased by shifting income from the relatively rich (to whom a unit of consumption means less) to the relatively poor (to whom a unit of consumption means more), until the point of equal distribution is reached. For a number of years this argument has been unfashionable. And indeed it does require an intuitive judgment as to the comparability of the "satisfactions" felt by individuals at given levels of consumption. For those who consider that there are no more than random differences in the capacity of individuals for enjoyment, the argument will continue to be persuasive. Alternatively it might be argued that the equal distribution of income would be conducive to personal dignity, to mutuality in the relationships of man to man, that it expresses a human solidarity and compassion, or that it provides a solid base for political democracy. For any or all of these reasons, some will take the equal distribution of income as a social goal. It will be considered here as one possible measure of distributive justice.

Equity as the Criterion of Just Distribution. Equality assumes that every man receives an exactly equal share. Equity assumes that every man receives a reward according to his contribution. Under equality, those who work hard and give much receive the same as those who work little and give little. Under equity those who give more, get more. Equity conveys the notion of a social contract in which society is bound to reward a man in proportion to what he contributes to society. Undoubtedly for many, equity rather than equality is the appropriate criterion for income distribution. It will be used here as a second possible measure of distributive justice.

Tempered Inequality. The decentralized market economy requires the concentration of private wealth for the launching of innovation and for the control of enterprise. It requires the pressure of loss and the promise of extraordinary profit to keep the system in motion. Hence, even an approximate equality in the distribution of income is not compatible with the concentrations of power needed for its functioning, with its system of incentives, with its means of recruitment, or with the windfalls that guide the movement of resources.

Nevertheless this form of organization sets important limits on the possible extent of income inequality. It positively requires a wide dispersion of property. It excludes those claims on income shares based on the rights of caste, on political power, on brute coercive force or on monopoly advantage. It is also possible through State intervention to remove or limit some of the income inequalities that arise spontaneously through its functioning, as in the redistribution of incomes received from rents and inheritance, without hampering the operation of the economy.

Partially Realized Equity. The distribution of income generated through decentralized market-direction does imply a positive relationship between income received and contribution made. Something is gotten for something given, and *ceteris paribus* where greater effort and greater skill produce a greater contribution, income will be greater too.

Nevertheless the possibility of achieving an equitable distribution of income is limited. There are sources of "inequity" built into this form of economic organization. Among these, for example, are the gains that arise through prior accumulation and from inherited wealth, or through windfall profits, or through the competitive game where the winner takes all though the margin of his superiority is ever so slight. In any case the pattern of income distribution that appears to arise spontaneously in the decentralized market economy is far from equitable. If one considers it equitable that men should be rewarded in proportion to what they have the will, ability, and strength to contribute, then presumably the distribution of income would approximate the "normal" distribution of energy and intelligence among the population. Nothing of the sort happens. In all the studies of income distribution in more or less market-directed economies, from those made by Vilfredo Pareto in the nineteenth century onward, distribution is always skewed in favor of concentrated wealth. The man of average ability receives less than the average income. The bulk of total income accrues to a few.

IMPLICATIONS OF REFORM

This and the following chapters seek to develop the peculiar values and inherent weaknesses and defects of three forms of economic organization without attempting to say what should be done about these defects and weaknesses. Clearly in each instance measures might be taken to ameliorate or to offset them. Book Two will describe the way public policy has been designed in the United States to offset weaknesses and defects inherent in particular forms of economic organization. Now, to illustrate the sort of judgments that are implicit in such measures of amelioration and reform, consider some of the possible policies of government that might counteract the sources of distortion and inequity in the decentralized market economy: (1) the break-up of monopolies, (2) the redistribution of income toward a greater equality or in accord with some other criterion of justice, (3) the limitation or elimination of inheritance, (4) the extension of free education and other measures intended to equalize opportunity, (5) public regulation or public intervention to offset externalized costs and benefits, (6) monetary, fiscal, or other measures designed to control aggregate expenditure as an offset to vertical price instability, (7) the stabilization of price expectations by guaranteed forward pricing.

Any of these measures, indeed the very extension of the powers of government and its intervention in economic control may be considered a threat to the integrity of decentralized market-direction. And surely the possibilities of amelioration are limited by the operational requirements of a system. Windfall loss and gain are necessary to decentralized market-direction. So is income inequality. So is price instability. So is the independence of individual producers and consumers. So is private property. The very nature of the property institution introduces paternal obligation and other economically irrelevant criteria into the recruitment of economic leadership. Taxation or regulation that circumscribes the rights of property, eliminates windfalls, or equalizes incomes is liable to distort the allocations choice, or to weaken economic incentive. In any case, through modifying, counterbalancing, and reforming this (or any other) system, a different form of economic organization tends to evolve with its own particular strengths and weaknesses.

For decentralized market-direction, as for other forms of economic organization, it is possible to devise offsets to characteristic defects. There are always dangers that in so doing some of the values of the system will also be lost. Out of such structural change, new forms of economic organization emerge with a new set of weaknesses and strengths.

SUMMARY

The decentralized market-directed form of economic organization affords a system for the recruitment of economic leadership and for the provision of incentives to work and to economize that is crude but effective. It possesses the virtue of spontaneity.

In the decentralized market-directed economy the self-interested individual works hard, avoids waste, and organizes efficiently in order to acquire property. In so doing he raises output and adds to the general welfare, while furthering his own ambitions and raising his own consumption.

Extraordinary effort or extraordinary ability leading to an extraordinary contribution is likely to result in an extraordinary return. The consequent acquisition of property expands the decision-making scope of those who have thus proven their competence in economic organization. In this manner the competitive market, with a rough justice, weighs out certain rewards by the measure of contribution, provides powerful, spontaneous and universal incentives to efficiency, and recruits leadership on the basis of proven and relevant capacities.

There are also crudities and sources of distortion. Property institutionalizes nepotism and favors the development of class barriers against the recruitment of the most able from below. Windfalls and the advantages of possession permit the acquisition of property, without reference to the leadership capacities of those to whom the property and its implicit power accrue. Accumulations of wealth lessen the incentive-value of increments of income, thereby debilitating motivation among those who have acquired economic power. And the competitive advantages of accumulation, leading to further accumulation, subvert competition and generate loci of monopoly.

The system has high institutional costs in maintaining contract, in the adjudication of property conflicts, in the higgling and haggling, bargaining and exchange, and in the information and demonstration and display required to "sell" a mass of small independent buyers.

Effective decentralization of choice limits the scale of technical operation. The technical optimum will sometimes require that the agency of production or of consumption be larger than that which is compatible with market competition.

The decentralized market-directed economy is the most sensitive and most responsive to the local stimuli to choice and change encountered in the processes of production and sale, and particularly to the preferences of individual consumers. It is relatively unresponsive when stimuli to choice and change are "general and diffused." It offers no means of expressing or integrating group goals or social priorities that take into account relations between independent decision-makers in the organization of production and consumption.

Among the three forms of economic organization to be studied here, decentralized market-direction displays the greatest fragmentation of responsibilities for the effects of choice and excludes the largest number of relationships between *independent* decision-makers from rational accounting or control. Hence the margin of costs and benefits that are external to any rational calculus or choice and the consequent distortions caused by such externality, will be greatest in the decentralized market-directed economy.

The decentralized market economy is subject to boundless horizontal and vertical price instabilities. This is so because it operates through the uncontrolled and fluid movements of price and since it offers no means of gearing the aggregated individual decisions to spend or save to the production plans and output-potential of the economy. Horizontal price instability is costly but necessary in the operation of this economy. Vertical price instability (inflation and deflation) is functionless but inherent.

Uncertainty about the data of economic choice distorts plans and forestalls action. Internal uncertainties, generated by the operations of the economy itself, are greater in the decentralized market economy than in the others; such uncertainties are a consequence of vertical price instability and the need to anticipate expectations and counterexpectations of innumerable independent decision-makers.

The decentralized market-directed economy cannot attain an "equal" or "equitable" distribution of income. Substantial inequalities are prerequisite for its functioning, and the spontaneous operations of this form of the economy appear to generate quite extreme concentrations of wealth, so that distribution does not approximate the normal distribution of effort and ability. Nevertheless, a certain significant relationship between effort, contribution, and reward is maintained, and the possibilities of exploitation through monopoly, coercion, or political prerogative are excluded.

Chapter 4

Centralized Political-Direction and Resource Allocation

Antithesis of Market-Direction. We may proceed more rapidly in the analysis of centralized political-direction than was possible in the preceding chapter since most of the terms of reference have now been defined and explained, and since centralized political-direction can generally be understood as the direct antithesis of decentralized market-direction. The strengths and the weaknesses of one are almost exactly the converse of the weaknesses and strengths of the other.

The strengths of a form of economic organization cannot be added up and totaled and the weaknesses subtracted so that one system can be shown to have a greater net value than another. A choice (if there is to be one) requires intuitive judgment, which will particularly depend on one's assessment of human potentialities and fallibilities.

The Plan. In the decentralized market economy, resources were organized through the competitive reaction of independent decision-makers in response to the free movements of price. In the centralized politically directed economy, which is now about to be examined as an instrument for the allocation of resources, the instrument of organization is the *plan*, made by a group of planners and imposed under the sanctions of the State.

MOTIVATION AND RECRUITMENT

Need to Plan Motivation and Recruitment. In the decentralized market there is a motivation to operate efficiently, a motivation that is spontaneous, automatic, and powerful. Similarly, decentralized market-direction recruits economic leadership spontaneously and automatically. It raises men to positions of economic power through the testing of capacities relevant to the exercise of that power. But also it is subject to certain cumulative distortions, with nepotism built firmly into its processes of selection.

Under centralized political-direction, neither economic motivation nor recruitment is spontaneous. Motivation and recruitment must be planned, and the plan must be imposed and controlled. There is, however, no limit on the potential effectiveness of such a plan. The decentralized market relies on crude self-interest in possession as its motive force. But, conceivably, when incentives are planned, not only self-interest but the whole range of human drives—from love and idealism to hate and fear—could be harnessed to the wheels of economic activity. Conceivably under planned recruitment economic leadership might be selected by testing only relevant abilities, with criteria shaped to the task at hand and with the favors of birth or whims of chance eliminated.

It is conceivable, in other words, that the system of incentive and of recruitment planned and imposed under centralized political-direction could be fairer and more effective than it could possibly be under decentralized market-direction, or indeed, under any other form of economic organization. It is also conceivable that recruitment and incentives planned and imposed under centralized political-direction could be completely ineffective and monstrously perverse. Which then? The best or the worst? That will depend on the competence and motivation of the planners. The crucial issue is in recruiting those who will recruit, and in motivating those who will plan the system of motivation.

Recruiting the Recruiters. To stand responsible for an economic plan is a task for a few. Call those few the planning *elite*. It is possible that this elite could dev~~ ~~ p a system of punishment and reward that would mobilize everymaи s self-interest in the efficient performance of his assigned task. But what will motivate the elite to do so? If they follow their self-interest in personal gain only, the mechanism of control will be riven with internecine strife, and planning will be an instrument for the exploitation of the many by the few. The planner may mobilize the self-interest of others, but for himself self-interest in personal gain will not suffice. He must be dedicated to general goals if general goals are to be served by the plan.

Dedication Required. If the centralized politically directed economy is to function effectively, the ruling elite, or at least some sufficient part of it, must be motivated by some concern that transcends self-seeking. There must be at least a significant minority dedicated to an ideal beyond themselves.

The effective operation of the centralized politically directed economy requires the exercise of authority by a dedicated elite—not only dedicated, but dedicated and disciplined in a common belief. Planning may move in different directions, and there is no absolute criteria to guide economic choice. If it is to work together, the ruling elite must be united in the singleness of its purpose. It must share a doctrine. How else could the disputations be settled and the many oriented toward a single goal?

While it is not necessary that the mass of the population shares in their dedication, it will greatly facilitate the functioning of the system if the mass acknowledges the truth propounded by this elite, accepts its faith, respects its dedication. In their relationship to the rest of the community, the planners exercise what was described in Chapter 2 as the *authoritative choice*. The choice will be accepted if the authority is accepted, and the authority is accepted inasmuch as it derives from premises and a point of view (a doctrine, a philosophy, a belief, a religion) that is shared by rulers and ruled, by those who plan and those who are planned for.

Faith, Philosophy, Dogma at the Core. Religion or philosophy or doctrine, or whatever one terms the outlook and belief that unites, is uniquely important to the economy of centralized political-direction. Such has been, in fact, the ultimate motivating and directing force of every centralized society. And, since the devil as well as God may be worshipped, the main issue may not be the effectiveness of the system but the belief and doctrine at its core.

Every religion has its orthodoxy. And every philosophy or doctrine that serves to discipline many to a common goal has an aspect of the fixed and immutable. In any faith held in common, in every vision that draws the diversity of private inclinations into a focal dedication, there must be an element of dogma. At bottom is that which is the word because it is the word. The common dedication, the demand for complete allegiance is necessarily based on belief, on faith, and rooted in the nonrational.

INSTITUTIONAL COSTS

Costs in Planning and Administering the Plan. Just as the costs of the institutions required for exchange and contract are specific to decentralized market-direction, the costs requisite to the plan and its supervision and control are specific to centralized political-direction. What alternatively the market could decide without intervention becomes the enormously complex task of the planner. And the plan must be transmitted to operating agencies. Central directives, once given, must be enforced. The plan in operation must be supervised, its functioning watched, its defects observed, and its failures noted. This information must be fed back to the decision center so that the plan can be reconsidered and modified. These complex arrangements for the formulation, transmission, supervision, adaptation, and implementation of the plan, require the use of resources aside from and in addition to those resources used in the processes of production and distribution.

The costs of formulating the plan would grow as some multiple of the numbers of variables implicit in choice. Those variables would include the priority of outputs, the quality, potential uses, location, and relative availability of resources, alternative processes, criteria for the selection of management, and alternative systems of incentive and supervision. Administering the plan would require the scheduling of outputs where each must be dovetailed with a set of inputs, the promotion of invention and the selection of inventions, the organization of innovation, the incorporation of new techniques into the matrix of operations.

The costs of control and of supervision will depend also on the relationship between the planning elite and the working community, and on the degree to which the acceptance of the authority and the habits of social discipline are ingrained in the culture.

Costs in Maintaining the Faith. Since unifying faith, philosophy, and religion are primary requirements for centralized political-direction, providing it with its adhesive and driving force, particular attention must be given to preserving the faith, to propagating the religion, to reformulating the doctrine. If the philosophy is to continue to unify and if the faith is to continue to capture the dedication of succeeding generations, then that philosophy must evolve and that faith must be reinterpreted in the light of accumulating experience and in the face of new needs and circumstances.

This will require indoctrination and perhaps proselytization. There must be precedent and dogma, but also the continual interpretation and reinterpretation of precedent and dogma, and the ordering and classification of interpretation as a criterion of choice and as a guide to the perplexed. Deviation and heresy must be confronted. For all this there are complex institutional requirements—and costs. And there may be costs also of iconography, of ritual, perhaps of inquisition.

Necessary Deviation from Technically-Optimum Scale. It was shown earlier that in the decentralized market-directed economy, the technical optimum might require larger scale operations with consequent concentration of economic control than is compatible with price competition. Hence the technical optimum would sometimes be larger than that which is required for a proper functioning of the decentralized, competitive market. With centralized political-direction, exactly the converse is true.

Where economic choice is centralized and politically directed, large numbers of separate and integral operating units are not an organizational requirement. The centralized system depends not on effective competition, but on effective administration, not on keeping prices flexible, but on keeping participants disciplined. Operations must be so organized as to ease supervision, to facilitate the enforcement of directives, and to accommodate the gathering of data and its transmission from loci of operations to the planning center. Administration, supervision, and transmission are likely to require, for their effective, low-cost performance, that operations be grouped in very large agencies of production and distribution. The technically preferred form and scale of operations need not be the same as that which best would serve the needs of administration, supervision, and the transmission of information under centralized planning. Planning and administration will be facilitated by standardizing, integrating and amalgamating the diverse operating components that are to be controlled. Hence the scale of operations preferred on technical grounds is likely to be smaller than that which would best serve the organizational needs of centralized-direction. This divergence between organizational effectiveness and technical efficiency will be especially significant and costly when the political authority is widely opposed and resisted for this resistance spills over in the sphere of economic activity, and therefore the police must be relied upon as an instrument of economic control. Thus Stalin collectivized agriculture in order to control and discipline the farmer more effectively—regardless of the impact on operating efficiency.

SENSITIVITY TO STIMULI

The Transmission Distance Between Points of Stimulus and of Response. Economic decision-making involves the stimulus (the facts, the events, the rumors, the new orders received, the prices bid, the claim made, the patent given, the resource discovered, the rule breached) and the response (the order, the sale, the purchase, the adjustment, the dismissal). Between stimulus and response there is necessarily a process of transmission: the transmission of stimulus to the decision-making center and the transmission of response back to the instruments of action. This process of stimulus and its transmission into decision, of response and its transmission into action, takes place in virtually all organizations, including the complex organization of the human physiology.

Every step in the process of transmitting stimulus or response from person to person, from group to group, is costly, requires time and effort, is a source of uncertainty and error. In order to minimize these costs, uncertainties and errors, data to be transmitted will be simplified with some relevant elements excluded. Suppose, for example, that I am a banker making a character loan (one based upon a trust in the borrower's integrity) to my neighbor Samuel Klein. I know Sam. I have watched him work. I have listened to him talk. I've seen how he acts with his wife and family and with those who work with him. I know something about his health and his capacity to survive adversity. On the basis of this total impression, I make my judgment and grant or refuse the loan. But suppose that instead of making the loan directly, I am a subordinate in a large financial organization, and that the power to make loans is not left in my hands. Rather it is for me to appraise Klein, record my impression, and transmit the information to a superior who will decide whether to make the loan to this man or to others who had been interviewed by different agents. My report must follow a standard form so that it can easily be compared with the reports on the other applicants, making possible a judgment between petitioners by one who has neither seen nor spoken with any of them personally. It takes time and effort to write my report. It takes time and effort to read it. These are costs of transmission. I am liable to err in the facts as I recorded them, and my boss is liable to misinterpret what I have written. Such errors and misinterpretation and the maljudgments to which they lead are also costs of transmission. Further, the report can only partly convey my total impression of Klein's character. This elimination of elements relevant to the evaluation is another cost of transmission. The more extended the transmission chain, the more complex the transmission process, that is, the longer the "distance" of transmission, the greater will be the consequent expenditures, distortions, and exclusions.

Transmission-Distance Between Local Stimuli and Centralized Choice. Generally, centralization removes decision-making from contact with or proximity to operations. In a small retail proprietorship, for example, the stimuli encountered by the owner-manager in his hourly contact with his customers—their complaints, their wants, their tastes, their expectations— become the basis of his decision, with nothing intervening between stimulus, response, and action. But if the same shop had been a store in a large chain, the manager might be obliged to transmit certain of these encountered facts through channels to some distant locus of decision-making. When the stimulus is encountered at the point of operations and the appropriate response is some change in operations, centralization appears to lengthen, complicate, and raise the cost of transmission to and from the point of decision. With respect to local and specific stimuli, the losses from transmission would seem greatest under full centralization, since then the distances from the point of operation to the locus of decision-making would be maximized. But there is another side to the coin.

Transmission-Distance Between Diffused Stimuli and Centralized Choice. The stimulus to the reorganization of processes, or to an extension of operations, or to an alteration in the pattern of resource allocation may come from elsewhere than that locale of operations where response must be made. It may derive, for example, from the financial market, from the turns of political policy, from the twisting skeins of international relationships, from the discovery of natural resources, from the potentialities of the findings of science, from technological developments and adaptations made anywhere. Where stimuli are thus diffused or removed from the locus of responsive action, centralization of decision-making is likely to simplify and facilitate rather than lengthen and complicate the process of transmission. For centralization, in detaching decision-making from the locale of operations, gives to it a greater spatial and intellectual mobility. Decision-making may focus on the critical stimulus to change, acclimating itself for the maximum sensitivity and more rapid response. The decision-maker detached from the locale of operation may approach the source, observe on the spot, and acquire the special expertness needed for evaluation. On the other hand, when decision-making is decentralized and fixed at the locale of operations, distant from changes that are relevant to choice, the realization of those changes and their significance for choice filters slowly, imperfectly, subject to all the distortions of ad hoc transmission.

Centralized Choice and the Stimuli to General Change. The costs of the process of stimulus and response depend not only on the complexity and length of the line of transmission, but also on the number of choices required for a given effect (the number of times that a given information must be examined and a choice made in order for the full response to that information to occur). Where the same information is relevant to a number of operating activities, decentralization would require that it be re-examined, re-evaluated, and responded to by numerous independent decision-makers. Centralization can reduce this duplication. The possibility of eliminating a significant number of duplicative decisions will depend on the degree to which stimuli and the conditions relevant to operations are uniform and the indicated response is general.

Thus when variable conditions require a unique response for each local operation, and when stimulus and response converge at the point of operations, decentralized market-direction offers the great advantage of shortened lines of transmission. But, when, for a number of operations, conditions and stimuli to change are uniform or when the stimulus to change is distant from the locale of operations, then the balance of advantage lies with centralized political-direction.

DISTORTION THROUGH EXTERNALITY AND THROUGH EXCLUSION

Externalities Eliminated. External economies and diseconomies and their consequent distortions are caused by the fragmentation of responsibility for the effects of action and choice, and by the exclusion from the possibility of deliberate control of relationships between decision-making entities.

To the extent that control is centralized, all costs or benefits and all relationships between action-taking entities come within the rationale of choice. Responsibility for the effects of choice is not fragmented and no relationship between economic entities is beyond the scope of control.

Every detectable benefit and detriment consequent upon choice conceivably may be included in the central balance of accounts. On this ground, the perfect allocation of resources can be more nearly approached through centralized political-direction than in any of the other forms of organization considered here.

The minimization of externality is a great advantage and constitutes a powerful argument in favor of centralization. And indeed, in nearly all actual national economies the allocations choice has tended to devolve to the political center in areas such as education and pure scientific research where externality is of special significance.

Relevant Data Excluded. There is, however, a source of distortion in centralized choice equivalent, perhaps, to that of externality in decentralized choice. Centralized, which is to say, concentrated decision-making ipso facto means that a larger body of data must be brought within the cognition of fewer decision-makers. Planning ultimately requires the exercise of choice by an individual. Thousands of men may gather the data and prepare tables of account. Great machines may record, categorize, summarize, and compute. Hundreds of experts may hover near, ready to advise. But at the end of the line, the individual must try to comprehend the elements relevant to the particular decision—and decide. Choice may proceed from the consensus of many planners, but then each one individually must comprehend the elements proper to the decision, before himself deciding what course of action he would support.

As more activities are included within its orbit, as the relevant body of data grows, the tasks of centralized choice become more complex. But the mental scope of the decision-maker is not expanded correspondingly. The capacity of the individual to comprehend remains unchanged.

With increased centralization, a vaster, more complex universe must be comprehended. Elements will escape consideration because the complexity of the whole requires that some of the parts elude one man's grasp. As the scope of variables encompassed by an integral decision is extended, as the variables increase and the complexity grows, the margin of elements likely to escape the individual's powers of comprehension grows also. Inasmuch as centralization widens the compass of the integral decision, it becomes necessary to *exclude* a larger number of relevant elements from consideration to bring the universe of variables within the individual's decision-making competence. Hence the "exclusion" of relevant information increases as a function of centralization.

Simplification Excludes. It may be contended in rebuttal that the data of choice will be simplified to facilitate the complexities of decision-making at the center. But simplification nearly always involves exclusion. Simplification is generally through exclusion of the less significant. Take an example from that classic of centralized decision-making, the army. Corporal Ackley's squad consists of Privates Moses, Chewning, McNee, and Stedman. Each of these men has a special character, peculiar competencies, a kind of endurance, a state of tension, a unique set of proclivities and weaknesses relevant to combat performance or to support roles. But to those at the apex of military planning, these are four X's and a Y, four pfc's and one noncom, along with a million others, each reduced to an average quality and a standard expectation. Inescapably, relevant elements are excluded from calculation and plan.

In contrast to externalization, exclusion is itself a matter of choice. The decision-maker can decide what ought to be excluded on grounds of its relative insignificance to his objectives. Rationality can be exercised in the separation of the more from the less relevant.

Techniques, moreover, might be devised for simplification and selection, for analysis, and even for decision-making that extend the range of variables readily encompassed by a centralized choice, thereby reducing the distortions consequent upon exclusion. Thus the computer is an instrument that extends the variables that can be manipulated for centralized choice.

INSTABILITIES

Internally Stable. Changes in social priorities, consumer preferences, resource availabilities, or in the conditions of the natural environment will introduce discontinuity and will limit predictability under centralized political-direction as in any other form of economic organization. But centralized political-direction will not generate functionless instabilities in vertical movements of price or employment. Centralized political-direction is internally stable. This constitutes a great advantage in its favor in contrast to the two other forms of economic organization studied here.

Spill-Over of Political Instabilities. Such political instabilities as there are must be made manifest in any form of economic organization that is politically directed. Change in political leadership, defeat of a political party, the shift in party line, the reinterpretation of doctrine are events that would be without impact in the economy of decentralized market-direction. Under centralized political-direction they could convulse the economy. The extent to which the economy would be destabilized by such change would depend not on the form of economic but on the form of political organization, and on the prevailing cultural discontinuities that find political expression.

UNCERTAINTIES

Internal Uncertainties Eliminated. Under decentralized market-direction, components of related economic processes are organized as separate, independent decision-making agencies. Although the activities of these agencies are interdependent, each must chart its course of action without knowing the anticipations, intentions, and plans of the others. Thus decentralized decision-making generates pervasive and costly uncertainties. The centralization of choice eliminates the necessity for internal uncertainty. Under centralized political-direction, the different component activities related in processes of production and distribution are geared together through a single plan. And, given the effectiveness of the plan, each component activity operates in full knowledge of the intentions and objectives of each of the others. The elimination of uncertainty internal to the operation of the economy is uniquely a potentiality of centralized direction.

Spill-Over of Political Uncertainties. On the other hand, when economic processes are politically directed, political uncertainties are liable to spill over into the economizing choice. When the direction of an economy is through an integral plan, there need be no uncertainty as to present or future activities of the agents and agencies under centralized direction. But uncertainty might well be inescapable as to the political directives under which the plan would be formulated or implemented. The planner who is certain about his capacity to control the components of an economic process may be uncertain about the tenure of his position of control. Such uncertainty may preclude anticipatory planning. The government program in the United States of aid in economic development is a case in point. That program has been under multiple investigation, with its leadership in flux, tossed by the whims of the public mood and the demands of diplomacy. The objective of aid has been perpetually frustrated by the uncertainties of political directive. Such uncertainty, too, can paralyze choice.

THE ORGANIZATION OF CONSUMPTION

The Consumer Dethroned. In the decentralized market the consumer holds the whip hand. But when the economy is centralized, decisive control is located elsewhere. The weight that is to be given to consumer tastes and preferences must be determined by political authority.

The political authority may want to satisfy the consumer. Various techniques such as polling individuals on the order of their preferences or setting output priorities by reference to the market prices of goods previously produced may be used in order to do so. Nevertheless, the price-directed market will always be a more effective means of *registering* the individual preferences of consumers than can be the case with any form of centrally determined priorities, because competition offers the agency of production no alternative except a direct response to consumer demands, and because the decentralized price-directed market is without the costs and distortions implicit in a long line of transmission from consumer to planner.

All Values Accountable. The decentralized market choice can only express consumer preferences. Yet the members of the community have interests and values relevant to the disposition of the economic product other than those arising from their roles as private consumers. They have a compassionate concern for the needs and deprivations of others. They identify themselves with groups of all sorts and with the common goals of those groups. They want international stability and national security. They would seek for changes in the social, political, or natural environment. All of these, requiring expenditure of goods and services, are also claimants upon the economic product. Decentralized market-direction takes only the individual preferences of the private consumer into account. Centralized political-direction, conceivably, can take into account all those goals and values that are relevant to the consumption choice.

In actual economies where the consumption choice is predominantly through decentralized market-direction, those values that transcend consumer interests are served through the occasional intervention of the State and by voluntary associations, such as charities, religious orders, benevolent associations. Under those circumstances, the activities of the voluntary associations are likely to be haphazard and the intervention of the State a point-by-point response to crisis. Only consumer wants are continuously recorded and systematically responded to. It is, indeed, only through some centralized political-direction of consumption that an instrument could be created that would systematically weigh and balance the whole continuum of social values of which consumer satisfactions are a considerable part, in the determination of output priorities.

Under any circumstances, it would be extremely difficult to render commensurable and to weigh and rationally to choose between the whole range of social values. But under centralized political-direction, the form of economic organization would be no bar to the task. Conceivably any and all social values could be regularly and systematically taken into account in setting the scale of output priorities.

Uncertainties and Externalities Eliminatable. In important respects, moreover, even consumer values may be more efficiently registered and properly weighed under the centralized than under the decentralized system of choice. For, with the choice of consumers as with that of producers, there are uncertainties and externalizations which exact a toll in distorted choice. And for consumers like producers, these costly uncertainties and externalizations may be minimized through centralization.

Bias Against Individual vis à vis Collective Values. By a bias in the system for the determination of output priorities is meant a tendency to favor one set of goals and considerations, not because they are rated higher in the accepted scale of values, but as a consequence of the special form of decision-making involved. The decentralized market-directed economy has a strong bias toward the wants of the consumer qua individual because it cannot accommodate itself to other levels of need or to the goals of groups. The centralized politically directed economy has the reverse bias, favoring collective goals and those values that reflect the needs of groups rather than persons. The nature of his job and of the ambition that took him to it tends to lead the dedicated planner to identify himself with some image of the collective whole, with Society, with Nation, even with Humanity, but not with the multitude of self-contained particularities that compose any of these. And the self-interest of the planner is specifically in the requisites of organization, with the ease with which things run and with the facility with which they can be controlled, with the collectivity rather than with the tastes and whimsies of the individuals who compose it. The General identifies himself with the Glory of the Army rather than with the sweat or salvation of the millions of individuals who live and die in its ranks. The General's self-interest lies in the smartness of the parade (for the parade is seen, and the parade reflects well or ill upon his leadership) rather than with the bunions of the soldiers who march. While what individuals qua individuals value is not excluded from consideration, the self-interest of the planner and his self-identification under political centralization would bias his choice in other directions.

JUSTICE IN THE DISTRIBUTION OF INCOME

A Policy Matter. In the centralized politically directed form of economic organization, policy replaces the autonomous dispensations of the market in the sharing-up of the national product. No particular pattern of income distribution inheres in the economy of political-direction. The distribution of income will depend on the goals of political choice and on the efficiency and incorruptibility of political authority.

Equality or equity can be approached deliberately. No haphazard distribution of income need thwart these goals. Inequalities that are required to motivate effort could conflict with moral objectives. It would then be possible to separate those differential payments that are required as a means of inducing some desired behavior from that portion of national income that can be distributed without reference to functional considerations, and rationally to weigh the benefits of greater output through the use of such differential payments against the sacrifice in distributive justice.

Whether or not it can ever be fully achieved, an ideal distribution of income (whatever that ideal might be) can be more closely approximated in centralized political-direction than in any other form of economic organization. More than under any alternative form, it is possible to distribute income according to moral criteria. Whatever the standard of justice, it is possible for the distribution of income to be more perfectly just under the economy of political centralization than under any other.

It is also possible under politically directed centralization for income to be distributed with a greater injustice, with a more absolute inequality, with a more complete exploitation of man by man, than under any other form of economic organization. With the decentralized market economy, a median way is assured. With centralized political-direction, either extreme is possible. With market-direction, a degree of inequality is inevitable, a degree of injustice must be the rule. With political-direction, full equality could be approached and injustice might be eliminated. With market-direction, there is always an element of rough justice, while under centralized political-direction, the possibilities of exploitation are without limit. The one advances on a path that is imperfect but tolerable. The other follows a way that may be the highest and most perfect or the lowest and most degrading. This contrast suggests the essential difference between these two forms of economic organization.

SUMMARY

In most respects the instrument of centralized political-direction is directly the antithesis of that of decentralized market-direction.

Centralization minimizes as decentralization maximizes, the externalization of the economies and diseconomies of choice. The greater the centralization of choice, on the other hand, the larger the proportion of relevant information that must be excluded from consideration in order to render the immensely complex data of choice amenable to integral planning.

Centralization minimizes those uncertainties that are internal to the operation of the form of economic organization. On the other hand, under centralized political-direction, political uncertainty will have the maximum spill-over into the economic choice.

The economy of centralized direction is internally stable, though it is peculiarly susceptible to the infiltration of political instabilities.

Centralization is more responsive to the goals of the community, while decentralization is more sensitive to the wants of the individual consumer.

Where the stimulus to choice and action is localized in operations, decentralization lowers the costs of transmission. Conversely, when the stimulus to decision is distant from the locale of operations, the costs of transmission will be less under centralized political-direction. Centralization makes possible the elimination of duplication in decision-making, which will be of particular importance where the operations to which decisions relate are uniform.

The operating entities of centralized political-direction will tend to be larger than the technical optimum, while the units of operation required for a sufficiently competitive decentralized market will often be smaller than the technical optimum.

Centralized political-direction dispenses with the institutional costs of higgling and haggling, of hedging and speculating, of exchange, of contractual arrangements and the adjudication of property disputes, all of which are required for decentralized market-direction. On the other hand, a complex apparatus for planning and for supervising and enforcing the plan is needed. The apparatus of enforcement would be more or less costly depending upon the degree to which the goals and authority of planners are popularly accepted. A complex apparatus will probably also be required to propagate, to adapt, and to interpret the faith at the core of the system.

The essential difference between centralized political-direction and decentralized market-direction is highlighted in the contrasting organization of income distribution, of the recruitment of economic leadership, and of motivation. In each case, decentralized market-direction depends simply on the spontaneous interaction of many self-interests, while centralized political-direction is an instrument of reason, or of unreason. With centralized political-direction the government confronts an immensely complex task, and how well it handles that task (and it could conceivably be done superbly or abominably) will depend upon the competence and the motivation of those who are charged with performing it, and upon the response of those on whom authority is exercised.

The centralized politically directed economy concentrates the economic power in the hands of a few, and, if this economic power is exercised wisely and for the commonweal, then those who exercise such power must be wise and dedicated to the commonweal. And, if that dedicated elite is to act in harmony and unison, they must have a unifying ideal, a shared faith, a common belief. Can such an elite be expected? And what can be expected of such an elite? Where there is total dedication, will there also burn the fires of fanaticism? Will the common belief become the fetters of orthodoxy?

Chapter 5

Organizational Market-Negotiation and Resource Allocation

MODUS OPERANDI

A Hybrid Form. The economy of autonomous organizations is a hybrid form that combines characteristics of both centralized political-direction and of decentralized market-direction. It retains the diluted strengths and weakness of the others, while in the manner of hybrids, it possesses virtues and vices that are peculiarly its own.

In this economy the primary agency of action and choice is the large corporate enterprise, a voluntary association of a size and complexity that transcends the control powers of the individual. Decision-making and action-taking are predominantly through "composite" choice, as Chapter 2 explained, in contrast to the individualized choice in the decentralized market economy and to authoritative choice under centralized political-direction.

The external relationships of corporate enterprise are shaped in a number of distinctly different sorts of markets. There are markets for the mass sale of products and services to individual consumers, where consumption is organized by households. There are markets where materials and intermediary products are sold to other business corporations on negotiated terms. There are markets where the sale of goods and services is to government, and consumption is organized under political-direction. There are markets for shares and debentures where arrangements are partially negotiated through intermediary organizations, but final purchase is made in a decentralized market by individual investors.

Internal Relationships Policy-Determined. Relationships between those who participate within the corporate entity are determined as a matter of company policy. The politics of this determination is highly variable. Property rights such as equity shares may be an important ploy in internal strategies. Unstructured internal negotiations are continuous, and periodic structured negotiations with trade unions are significant. Corporate policy and the structure of interpersonal relationships in the corporation are influenced by the prevailing culture and by the "image" and tradition particular to a company, by the imperatives of the law and the pressure or influence of government.

The activity that falls within corporate control can and to a significant extent will be centrally planned. The degree of planning is optional. Many agencies of the corporation will "run themselves" in the autonomous response to the buffeting of the market. Ordinarily there will be some independent decision-taking by departments, divisions, or subsidiaries.

The Market Test of Policy and Plan. The corporation may plan its activities and structure its internal relationships as a matter of policy in somewhat the same way as under centralized political-direction. But the plan and the policy of each corporate entity is continuously submitted to the market test. Through that test, the plan and policy will survive or will be forced to change, or, with the elimination of the corporate entity, will be eliminated. The struggle for survival of the fittest is between these large autonomous groups rather than between individuals. The question of "fittest for what?" remains.

Survival and growth do not require the maximization of net profits in the sense of a residual for equity holders. But survival and growth do require that costs be covered and that funds be made available for expansion.

Divers paths lead toward that objective. It is generally an advantage to avoid waste and to operate efficiently (not always—with government cost-plus-fee contracts, the converse may hold). It is generally an advantage to expand sales volume, which may require advertising and promotion, or the offering of new, different, and possibly better products, or even the offering of price reductions. It is always advantageous to widen the margin between the price of goods sold and their production costs. This may be done by forcing down costs or by raising prices. Whether prices can be raised without an undue loss in the volume of sales depends on whether or not negotiated or tacit arrangements can be made for "competitors" to act in concert. The relationship between corporate entities is somewhat akin to the relationship between rival and allied states, with diplomacy probing for avenues of mutual advantage, with spying and sabotage on the "dirty" side; and behind the diplomacy, the threat and occasionally the use of coercion in the form of patent infringement, harassment in the courts, infiltration into equity holdings, or selective price-cutting.

In sum, the corporate entity must stand the market test for its survival but the market does not necessarily test efficiency or comparative contribution.

Equivocal Motivation, Arbitrary Power. That its leadership may be motivated to further the interests of the corporation is not to say that their economic power will be exercised to promote efficiency or otherwise to serve the goals of social welfare. In order to promote the survival and growth of the corporation or trade union, various strategies may rationally be followed. Some of these are, and some are not, in accord with the public interest. To the leadership of the autonomous organization operating within the boundaries of profit and loss and of law and convention, a wide range of choice is open. Its choice between alternatives will critically affect the public interest.

In the other forms of economic organization, a built-in mechanism might be relied upon to bring the exercise of economic power into accord with what variously could be considered the public interest. Under decentralized market-direction choice was tightly bound to a particular course of action by the force of price competition and that course of action could be considered as generally consistent with particular social values. Under centralized political-direction, economic authority is answerable to the representatives of the body politic and, in that way, the exercise of economic power is directly related to the pursuit of communal goals. But the large autonomous corporation is neither answerable to the community for its action nor bound by competition to lines of action considered a priori to approximate the public interest. In this sense, the power of the autonomous organization is arbitrary, and the motivation of its leadership, in relation to economic welfare, is equivocal.

Government as Participant. In the economy of centralized political-direction, government is the locus of economic choice. In the economy of decentralized market-direction, government is passive. In the economy of autonomous negotiating organizations, government is neither aloof nor does it control. Rather it participates. It exercises residual responsibilities. It does what private enterprise cannot or will not do. It fills gaps. It arbitrates disputes. It influences the formulation of organizational policy. It provides a counterweight to the arbitrary power of the autonomous organization.

MOTIVATION AND RECRUITMENT

Planned Recruitment, Planned Incentives. With respect to the recruitment of leadership and the design of incentives, the organizational price-negotiated economy is comparable to the economy of centralized political-direction. Recruitment to positions of leadership is not spontaneous. The relationship between effort and reward must be planned. Individuals work and are raised to leadership under imposed systems of incentive and promotion or at the discretion of the higher echelons. For the individual, the way up or the way down the rungs of economic status might be quite the same as they would be under centralized political-direction. The farmer under decentralized market-direction was tested by the market throughout. He "got ahead" because he bought shrewdly, because he produced cheaply, or because the shifting tides of demand threw good fortune in his direction. His affluence did not depend on his personality, his politics, his religion, his color. Not so with his son, an executive with the telephone company or the steel company or the oil company or in any great corporate enterprise. His son is chosen for the job by others and he will "go up" because they like him, or because they do not fear him, because he "fits," because he is a good member of the team, because of his seniority, because he is tactful, diplomatic, and a good hand at company politics, or because he has passed the tests and satisfied the demands of an objective system of selection and promotion which others have chosen to impose.

The Market Test. Within the autonomous organization the individual works in the context of an imposed system. His recruitment, his promotion, his incentives are all subject to its design. That system can be so planned that the self-interest of participants is geared into furthering the efficiency of operations and the growth and prosperity of the organization. Whether in fact the system is so designed depends on the competency of the planners and the motivations of those who wield power. What will motivate them?

The design and control of a system of centralized political-direction must depend on the idealism of an elite at its apex. On the other hand, the design and control of autonomous organizations need not rely on this dedication beyond self-interest. In the economy of autonomous organization, self-interest in material gain can spontaneously motivate efficiency on the part of those who exercise control—but this self-interest must be based on an "enlightened realization" (or a deluded notion) of an identity in the interest of the company and of the individual who exercises power within it.

The Need for Enlightened Partisanship. The cold calculation of self-interest can hardly lead the individual to suppose that whatever he does to make the organization prosper will protect his own security and promote his own gain. The relationships of self-interest of those who lead or participate in corporate operations and the long-run growth and the survival of the organization, are likely to be so complex and distant that the individual will not perceive them directly, but will accept them (if he does accept them) as a matter of faith. The possibility of benefiting one's self or one's faction at the expense of others within the organization is always more clearly and immediately visible. The organizational economy requires for its effective operation that those who exercise power have a loyalty to organization and a sense of the team, and that these be built into the prevailing values.

Simple greed can fuel the engine of decentralized market-direction. Political centralization must rely on the dedication of an elite. The organizational economy requires at least an "enlightened" (or deluded) partisanship that identifies the interest of decision-makers with the survival and growth of the organization.

INSTITUTIONAL COSTS

No Necessary Deviation from Technically-Optimum Scale. The size of the operating entity required for price competition under market-direction is likely to be smaller than the technical optimum. The size of the operating entity required to facilitate centralized planning and control under an economy of political-direction is likely to be larger than the technical optimum. Only the organizational market-negotiated form creates no inherent conflict between the technical optimum and the requisites of the economy.

The absence of inherent conflict between the technical optimum and the requisites of the economy of autonomous, market-negotiating organization does not mean that the technical optimum must evolve. Forms of competition between organizations, possibly decisive in determining the scale of operations, may be irrelevant or detrimental to the social weal. The normative form and scale of operations, rather than being the technically most efficient, might be that which would convey a maximum pricing power, or which would give the greatest advertising advantages, or which would be most amenable to the convenience of public officials in their procurement of (say) weapons, or which simply would enable corporate entities to cancel out the bargaining or advertising advantages of one another.

The single corporate enterprise is organized to perform a diversity of tasks. Each of these tasks might best be performed under a quite different form and scale of operations. Suppose for example, that an enterprise performed tasks A and B, and task A could be performed most efficiently when the operating organization was small, while task B could be performed most efficiently when the scale of operations was very large. Under these conditions, any operating size for the organization as a whole would sacrifice advantages in the performance of task A or B or both. Indeed, it is entirely conceivable that a small organization performing A efficiently, at a sacrifice of B, could compete on equal terms with a large organization that realizes economies of scale with respect to B, but sacrifices efficiency in A.

Where a large complex of tasks and systems are involved, as is normally the case with corporate enterprise, it might be expected that an industry in competitive equilibrium would contain a wide diversity in the scale and form of its constituent organizations, with each enterprise realizing a different combination of particular advantages and corollary disadvantages. This may be a very good thing in a dynamic society, providing a wider range of potential avenues of development. Further, the variously sized and shaped operating entities might complement each other in the services they together render. For example, it may well be generally true that to support research and development, and to spearhead innovation to higher levels of technology a far larger operating organization is required than that needed for highest efficiency at a given level of technology. Where this is the case, the few giants of the industry may open the way to technological advance, gaining special benefits for themselves thereby, while a large number of smaller but more efficient producing units would follow in their wake.

This suggests a unique value for the market-negotiated economy: namely, the evolution, through experiment, of new and superior forms of operating organizations, including the evolutionary development of complex industrial systems combining different forms and sizes of operating organizations.

Institutional Cost of Advertising. Advertising, of the sort that seeks to influence consumers' tastes and preferences, to shape opinion and to develop attitudes toward (and a public image of) a business enterprise, is peculiarly an institutional cost of the organizational market-negotiating economy. Under the circumstances of this form of organization, some advertising has a social value in offsetting the tendency of consumers, untempted by a lowering of prices, to oversave. Though sometimes justified under the circumstances, the circumstances are a consequence of the form of organization, unnecessary under alternative forms. Even under the conditions of the price-negotiated market, a substantial part of the expenditures on promotion and advertising will have no socially viable function. The net result of such expenditures may merely be to maintain the relative share of the market at approximately what it would have been without any advertising, for example in the competition between brand-name cigarettes.

Values Distorted. Advertising constitutes an arbitrary exercise of a significant power to shape habits, attitudes and tastes. Those who here reshape consumer values, and thus influence the culture, can neither pretend to an interest in maximum consumer satisfaction or in the harmonies of community life or in the moral rectitude of the people, nor claim any concern with or insight into those deeper needs of men that the individual by himself might have difficulty in realizing or formulating. The advertisers acquire an incidental and dangerous power over the press and the other media of mass communication. These costs and dangers are peculiar to the organizational economy.

Institutional Costs of Plan and of Market Place. The economy of organization combines in itself some of the institutions and consequently some of the institutional costs of centralized political-direction and decentralized market-direction. In the organizational economy, however, these costs are generally of a lower order of magnitude.

For the coordination and control of intracorporate operations, there are costs of planning, administration, and supervision. In the resolution of property claims and in the enforcement of contract, there are costs of adjudication and enforcement. In dealing with market instabilities, there are the costs of hedging and speculation. There are also costs of bargaining and exchange. Current costs of exchange and bargaining would be relatively much less than in the decentralized price-directed market. But the bargaining process in the economy of autonomous organizations can have a dangerously explosive quality, for which there is no counterpart in other forms of economic organization.

Bargainers are sometimes so large and powerful that stalemates or conflicts can paralyze the economy. For example, in the decentralized market, wage-bargaining between management and labor is constant, and there are constantly wastes due to disputes, work stoppages and negotiations. Among the multitude of independent operators a number of firms are always involved in some conflict or dispute with a consequent drain on resources and a restriction of total output. But there is never a threat to the functioning of the economy itself. With corporate enterprise, instead of constant bargaining and negotiation the bargain is periodic and for the entire sector. A few men in a few days settle for an extended period of time what might have consumed thousands of hours and created perpetual uncertainty, if bargaining were individual by individual or firm by firm. But an unresolved wage dispute in the corporate economy can bring the entire industry to a halt, thereby threatening even the essentials of living. For this reason, government is obliged to assume the roles of mediator and arbitrator in the conflict of giants.

SENSITIVITY TO STIMULI

Elements of Planning and Market-Direction. The cost of transmitting and responding to localized stimuli (encountered in the processes of production and distribution) is a function of the "distance" between the locale of operation and the locus of decision. In the economy of autonomous organization, this "distance" is less than under centralized political-direction and greater than under decentralized market-direction. Hence the transmission costs and capacity for quick response to localized stimuli for the economy of autonomous organization will be intermediate: less responsive with 'higher transmission costs than decentralized market-direction and the opposite for centralized political-direction.

Where stimuli to choice are diffused and distant from the point where a response must be made, then the ease of transmission is greatest and the costs of response least where the power to mobilize resources and to take action in the light of new circumstances is not tied to any locale of operation nor identified with a particular process or operation, but is flexible and mobile. In responding to diffused and distant stimuli, decentralized market-direction is at a comparative disadvantage. The decision-making, action-taking power in centralized political-direction, detached from the specifics of operation, can be more mobile and flexible than in any other form. In the economy of autonomous organization, the power to mobilize resources freely and rapidly in response to diffused and distant stimuli is less than it is under centralized political-direction. The economy of autonomous organization, however, has the peculiar advantage of combining a considerable detached and mobile power with a capacity for response through a range of independent initiatives.

Where operations and conditions of application are uniform and the indicated response is general, centralization will minimize the costs of choice by reducing duplicative evaluations. Conversely, the extreme decentralization of the market-directed economy will maximize such costs. The economy of autonomous organization stands midway between the other two.

DISTORTION THROUGH EXTERNALIZATION, THROUGH EXCLUSION,
AND THROUGH ARBITRARY POWER

Externalities Fewer than with Decentralized Market-Direction. The costs of externalization for the economy of autonomous organization fall between those of centralized political-direction and decentralized market-direction. Externalization remains, but there is neither the degree of fragmented responsibility nor the number of relationships between components of related processes outside the scope of control as exist under decentralized market-direction. Compared to the firm in the decentralized market, the large corporation is better able to capture a share of the benefits of its actions and is more liable to bear the costs of its decisions. This is so since a far broader range of activities fall within the orbit of its control, since it is not bound to pass on the gains of its cost-saving innovations in reduced prices, and since it has the mobile technical and financial power to capitalize on a wide range of opportunities.

The sources of support for scientific research in the United States suggest the relative capacity of the three forms of economic organization to "internalize" the effects of choice. Benefits of research are characteristically diffused and vulnerable to externalization. Therefore, in the United States small firms undertake virtually no research at all, except under contract. Large corporations undertake a substantial amount of *applied* research where benefits are relatively more subject to anticipation and recapture. So-called fundamental research, where effects are most diffuse and contribution is most subject to externalization, must be supported by the government. Only centralized choice is of sufficient scope to take the contribution of the latter into practical account.

Data-Exclusion Less than with Centralized Political-Direction. The greater the mass of data that must be processed for choice and the more complex the sets of activities made subject to control, the larger must be the margin of relevant data excluded from consideration to accommodate the inherently limited capacity of the individual as planner or decision-maker. Because the sphere of activities subordinated to an integral control is greatest in the centralized form, the margin of excluded data will be the greatest there also. Conversely, such exclusion will be least in the decentralized market economy. In the economy of negotiated organization, where the complex of activity under unitary control is smaller than in the economy of centralized political-direction and larger than in the economy of decentralized price-direction, the rate of exclusion will fall between these two.

Distortion Through Arbitrary Exercise of Power. Price competition in the decentralized market obliges the individual to follow a particular line of action. In that line of action the system finds its justification. For example, the decision-maker does not choose the price at which he sells his goods. He is forced by the system to sell at a price that approximates his marginal costs. Normal "equilibrium" price approximates his lowest average costs, not as a matter of anyone's volition but as a consequence of the operation of the system. In the economy of autonomous organization, on the contrary, the decision-maker *chooses*. The company selects the price at which it sells its goods or services. It is highly unlikely that this price policy, which is part of a complex strategy of action, will be made by reference to marginal costs or to lowest average costs at optimal levels of output.

Within a significant range, covering many critical options, the corporation has the power to decide at what price to offer its goods and services. Price need not fall when demand declines. Price may rise in the face of static or declining demand and increasing productivity. Price, in a word, ceases to be an index of relative scarcity. Yet the price of what is sold constitutes the cost of what is purchased and hence, inasmuch as there are motivations to use resources efficiently internally, price continues to guide the allocation of resources. Allocations made by reference to prices that do not in fact provide a measure of relative scarcities must result in waste and maldistribution.

In the decentralized market the decision-maker has no power to set price. Under centralized political-direction, the decision-maker has full power, but also full responsibility. In the economy of autonomous organization the decision-maker has a considerable discretionary power, without commensurate responsibility. Distortion arises, not so much from the inability to take effects of choice and action into account, but rather because of the limited and equivocal responsibilities of those who exercise the discretionary power. Power without commensurate responsibility, that is, *arbitrary* power, is a crucial problem and peculiarly a source of distortion in the economy of autonomous organizations. The importance of policy made at the discretion of the autonomous organization is illustrated below in two concrete instances recently experienced in the United States.

The Pivotal Importance of Corporation Policy: the Example of Wages and Prices in Steel. In 1962, when negotiations started between the steel unions and the representatives of the steel industry, it was widely feared that a wage rise would force an increase in steel prices, and that this would set in motion a new upward spiraling of the general price level. Therefore the President of the United States and his advisors proposed that the unions limit their wage demands to an amount roughly approximating the rise in productivity. Thus, it was supposed, a "cost-push" increase in the price of steel products would be avoided. The unions agreed. The wage contract was signed. Shortly thereafter the United States Steel Company, the "price leader" in the industry, announced a substantial increase in steel prices. Other companies quickly followed suit.

Under decentralized market-direction a rise in prices would signal that demand was in excess of what could be produced at the old price. Rising prices would have followed (and would have provided an index of) the increased scarcity of real resources. Scarcity had nothing to do with the rise in the price of steel. The industry could have profitably doubled its output under the old prices. And even at the old prices, increasing quantities of foreign steel had been entering American ports at discount levels. At the old levels, steel production was in the neighborhood of 50 percent of capacity and, in spite of that, the United States Steel Company was making a comfortable profit.

What United States Steel did, it did as a matter of policy. It might just as well (as a matter of policy) have lowered its prices. It justified itself on the grounds that it needed higher profits to "modernize" its plant. There are other ways, of course, to finance plant modernization than through raising prices, presumably at the expense of sales volume. A greater share of current profits, for example, could have been reinvested rather than be distributed as dividends. Or new shares could be offered on the market, or funds could have been borrowed.

Nevertheless United States Steel chose the path of higher prices, without recognizing any responsibility for the effects of that choice in stimulating a whole new wave of price-wage increases throughout the economy. The President of the United States and his advisors exerted intense but informal pressure on the steel producers, and succeeded in persuading one company, Inland Steel, to refuse to follow the price leader. For that reason, United States Steel's price policy was frustrated, and the concerted effort to raise steel prices collapsed, at least for a time.

From the foregoing, the following should be noted: (1) the broad discretionary choice open to the autonomous organization in its economic policy; (2) the pivotal importance of that policy to the economy as a whole; (3) the lack of any mechanism built into the economy to hold the policies of autonomous organization in line with the public interest; (4) the ad hoc *participation* of government in the formulation of the policies of the autonomous organization as a means of bringing autonomous choice into closer accord with the public interest.

Bell Labs and the Transistor Technology: A Second Example. Bell Laboratories, research and development arm of American Telephone and Telegraph, would seem as of this writing, to be the most successful nongovernmental research organization in the world. Semiconductors and transistors are among its brain children. Indeed, its complete outperformance of the research of other corporate enterprise suggests that each great corporate organization must be understood as a unique entity with highly particular traditions, motivating objectives and policy-making structures.

By the end of World War II, through its patent holdings and its research and operating know-how, Bell dominated the emerging electronics industry, particularly with respect to semiconductors and transistors. Given this situation, various options were open to Bell—and to the American Government. In fact, among different government agencies diametrically opposed positions were taken.

The Department of Defense would have imposed tight security wraps upon the new transistor semiconductor technology, allowing information concerning that technology only to its own contractors, and building a second wall of military secrecy around the barriers of proprietary control that were there already. The Department of Justice and a group of anti-trusters in the United States Senate wanted to force Bell to turn its patent holdings over to the public domain. At the turn of the 1950s an antitrust suit was instituted partly for that purpose.

Under these external pressures and through the play of equally diverse internal forces, Bell launched a uniquely activist policy. It fought the Pentagon's inclination to secure the new technology within the bounds of military secrecy, even though that could have perpetuated Bell's monopoly. It decided not simply to make its patents available, but vigorously to promote their international dissemination and utilization. Taking the position that patents are a poor means to convey technical information, Bell prepared a complete and elaborately illustrated research guide and engineering manual, explaining and bringing up to date the transistor and semiconductor science and technology. This was to be called "Mother Bell's Cook Book." Bell then gave an extended seminar. Any company willing to make a (reimbursable) $25,000 advance royalty payment on the patents they might want to use was invited. Company representatives from the United States, Europe, and Japan attended. At that seminar and subsequently, Bell used its full scientific and engineering prowess to unfold the industrial potentialities of its discoveries. Licensing agreements were negotiated without constraint. A network of patent licenses was created, with Bell at the center of a worldwide system for the exchange of research information and patent rights. Bell became thus the prime mover, and is now the nexus of allegedly the "fastest growing big business in the world."

Bell's policy turned out to be to the company's advantage. It also turned out to be of immeasurable importance in advancing the defense posture and the growth potential of the United States. In this case, the policy chosen by the autonomous organization was entirely in accord with the general interest. But Bell's policy could have been quite different. With equal rationale, it might have sought to keep to itself the use of the technology that its own research had created. In fact no other major business organization in the United States (and, perhaps, in the world) has adopted a policy with respect to its research findings which approximates Bell's. The usual objective of the industrial corporation is not to disseminate or to promote the most general use of its research findings, but is precisely the opposite.

Government Offsets to the Arbitrary Power of the Autonomous Organization. In the economy of autonomous organization, by pressure, influence, or the force of the law, government may participate in the formulation of corporate policy. This can offset the dangers inherent in the arbitrary powers of the autonomous organization only to a limited extent, for government action must always be *ad hoc* and occasional. It must wait for trouble to come. It mends leaks but it builds no roofs. It is on the treadmill of expediency. In the economy of autonomous organization, government mingles the roles of preacher and policeman, promoter, handyman, fixer, and patcher.

INSTABILITIES

Employment and Production Instabilities. In contrast to decentralized market-direction where prices are unstable and employment is stable, there is relative price stability but extreme instability of employment and production in the economy of autonomous organization. In this economy there is no control of the level of aggregate expenditure. Consumption and saving decisions remain a function of decentralized choice. And the effects of corporate investments on the level of total expenditure are generally too diffused to be taken into account by the corporate decision-maker. The levels of aggregate spending therefore vary as much as they would under decentralized market-direction.

The difference will be this. In the decentralized market, price moves freely, in automatic response to changes in the level of spending. A higher level of aggregate spending will raise the level of prices, and a drop in spending will cause a fall in prices. Extreme price instability is the consequence. But in the economy of autonomous organization, price is not an automatic reflex of spending, but is a function of organizational policy. In the economy of organization, the price of labor is fixed by the trade unions as a matter of policy, and the price of goods and services are fixed by business enterprise as a matter of policy. Policy, generally, tries to hold prices and wages fast in the face of a decline in aggregate demand. Less spending, with prices the same, must result in less purchased, less produced, and fewer employed. A change in aggregate demand shows itself as price instability in decentralized market-direction and as instability in production and employment in the economy of autonomous organization.

Task of Maintaining Full Employment. When, in the economy of autonomous organization, aggregate expenditure falls below the level necessary to maintain full employment, the government may, through monetary or fiscal measures, add to the stream of spending. But the government's efforts to increase aggregate expenditure sufficiently to achieve full employment at a given price level can be frustrated by a corporate policy of raising prices and a trade union policy of raising wages. And indeed, government measures to increase total expenditures provide an environment favorable to higher wage policies by trade unions and higher price policies by business corporations. Hence the achievement of full employment would probably require that government control aggregate expenditures and participate in the formulation of trade union wage policy and of company price policy.

UNCERTAINTIES

Uncertainties Less than for Decentralized Market-Direction. Under decentralized market-direction those uncertainties arising out of the inability to foresee the actions, anticipations, and intentions of other decision-makers in the economy are so great that they preclude anticipatory planning. In the economy of autonomous organizations, the number of independent decision-makers is so reduced that it becomes possible to anticipate many specific responses. Economic activities that would have been independently controlled in the decentralized market are brought within the scope of the company plan. There are fewer independent decision-makers whose responses need to be anticipated. Fewer independent agencies lead to intercompany accommodations, wage contracts, standardized costing practice, and pricing conventions, which further stabilize interorganizational relationships. The power to influence consumers through advertising brings consumption more within the producer's control. Thereby end-product demand is made more predictable. Those uncertainties that were the consequence of decentralized market-direction will thus be significantly reduced. In the economy of autonomous organization, a considerable anticipatory planning is feasible. Nevertheless, as compared to centralized planning, costly internal uncertainties remain.

Spill-Over of Uncertainty from Governmental and Organizational Politics. While centralized political-direction can eliminate uncertainties internal to the operation of the economy, the distortions consequent upon political uncertainties will be maximized. In contrast, the market-directed economy (where internal uncertainties generated through economic operations are maximized) is insulated from political uncertainty. In the economy of negotiating organizations, where government influences or participates in organizational choice, the uncertainties of governmental behavior are of intermediary importance, but, in this economy, to the uncertainties of governmental politics must be added those uncertainties arising from intraorganizational politics.

THE ORGANIZATION OF CONSUMPTION

The Influence of the Autonomous Organization on Public and Private Consumption. In this model of an organizational, market-negotiating economy it is supposed that consumption will be organized either by the private household or by the government. This does not mean, however, that the organization of consumption is the same as it would be under decentralized market-direction or under centralized political-direction. What is distinctive is the bilateral relationship of the large corporation as producer-seller, to the household consumer in the one instance and to the government consumer in the other.

While decentralized purchasing by households offers an immediate and direct expression of consumer preferences, those preferences are shaped by corporate advertising. To some degree, consumer values become the synthetic product of the autonomous organization.

When primarily engaged in sales to government, the great corporations become themselves a force in the formation of public policy. Where complex technologies are involved, as in the purchase and use of weapons or missiles, the organization of procurement and consumption must rely on knowledge acquired in the organization of production. Since autonomous organizations become the repositories of that technical know-how, they tend also to be integrated into the processes of political-direction. This infiltration of the corporate power into government procurement brings some of the capacity for diversified initiative and some of the dangers of arbitrary, irresponsible power, which characterizes the economy of autonomous organization, into the political-direction of consumption.

JUSTICE IN THE DISTRIBUTION OF INCOME

Intermediary Scope for Policy Choice. A certain proportion of the income that an economy generates may be redistributed without reducing efficiency in the operation of the economy. Among the three forms of organization examined here, this "detachable" proportion of income available for redistribution is likely to be smallest in the economy of decentralized market-direction, where incentive cannot be planned and where windfall gains and losses, price variability, and intergal property rights are necessary to the functioning of the economy. The proportion of income available for redistribution is largest in the economy of centralized political-direction where incentives can be planned and where windfalls and the prerogatives of property are not required for the operation of the system.

In the economy of autonomous organizations, in contrast to that of decentralized market-direction, the allocations choice will respond to the signal of relatively slight variations in *anticipated* profits. Because of this greater capacity for anticipatory planning, fewer or smaller windfalls are required. Private property has a role, but a subordinate one, in the organization of production, and hence its prerogatives need not be held so sacrosant as under decentralized market-direction. Within the autonomous organization itself, incentives can be planned so as to minimize the costs required to motivate effort. For these reasons the share of the economic output subject to discretionary choice or available for a policy-based redistribution in the economy of autonomous organization would be intermediary between that available under centralized political-direction and under decentralized market-direction.

SUMMARY

The organizational market-directed economy is a hybrid that combines the planning of complex operations with the force of market interactions. Activities are planned, but plans and planner must survive the market test. The significance of that testing is equivocal, since survival and growth may be based on capacities unrelated to efficiency or to other economically desirable criteria.

In the balancing of advantages and disadvantages, the economy of autonomous organization stands somewhere between centralized political-direction and decentralized market-direction in respect to (1) internal uncertainties, (2) externalization, (3) exclusions, (4) sensitivity and response to stimuli, and (5) the income available for redistribution as a matter of social policy.

The economy of autonomous organization incorporates some of the institutions and institutional costs of centralized planning and of market-direction. Peculiar to its operation is the cost of advertising as a means of shaping consumers' tastes. This institution of mass advertising is not only costly in itself, but it is also liable to have unwonted effects on cultural values and on political choice.

Price instability, in this form of organization, is a consequence of the variabilities of corporation and trade union policy. Conflicts between trade unions and business corporations can be explosively destabilizing to the economy at large. Variations in aggregate spending will be manifested in extreme instabilities of employment and production.

The policy-making power of the autonomous organization is neither accountable to the community at large nor held in close proximity to the public weal by the force of market competition. In order to bring that policy into conformity with the public interest, government is obliged variously to influence or to participate in the critical economic choices of autonomous organizations.

The role of government in this form of economic organization is necessarily equivocal and expedient. It has the residual responsibility of filling the gaps, of doing what the economy of private organization leaves undone. It does not plan, but influences plans. It arbitrates and pacifies. It acts in point-by-point response to crisis.

Chapter 6

Economic Progress as a Social Function

The Need for a Theory of Economic Progress. Hitherto, this book has been concerned with studying three forms of economic organization as instruments for "efficient" resource allocation and for "just" income distribution. Now another relationship will be at issue: the connection between the form of economic organization and the rate of economic progress. However, before a form of organization can be evaluated as an instrument of economic progress, we must specify what is meant by economic progress and what its determinants are. There is needed, in other words, a theory of economic progress. In the next six chapters a theory or at least the outlines of a theory of economic progress will be proposed. Then, in the conceptual frame of that theory, the three forms of economic organization will be studied and evaluated.

The Meaning of Economic Progress. We are not obliged to consider progress in its broadly humanistic sense, but merely *economic* progress, where measures and meanings are less equivocal. *The measure and meaning of economic progress is in higher productivity,* that is, in the ability to produce with the same input of labor-time new goods, other goods, more goods than before. Whether it is better to have more than less, even though the "more" consists of weapons, or of idle time and empty display, or of wearisome luxury or hectic diversion, is not a matter on which we need pass judgment. Economic progress need not make life better, but it does, at least, release men from bonds of physical necessity and enables them more freely to play the fool and the monster as well as the other roles of the human repertoire.

Economic Progress and Economic Growth—Not Identical. Economic progress, as the term is used here, is related but not identical to economic growth. Economic growth means the increase in the real value of the GNP (Gross National Product) for a given national economy. Growth is also affected by changes in the size of the population, so that growth may occur (given an increase in population size) while output per man declines. This sort of growth would have no relation to economic progress understood as the source of any sort of human betterment. Growth is also affected by the capacity of an economy to make full and efficient use of its resources. Higher productivity may be reflected not in larger national output but in greater involuntary unemployment. The failure of an economy to avail itself of the increased capacity to produce, which is the consequence of economic progress, is of great importance for economic welfare. It is, however, a failure in the task of making full and efficient use of resources—which was the subject of analysis in the immediately preceding chapters—rather than in the correlary but different task of advancing the technology of production.

Productivity, the Measure of Economic Progress. The measure of economic progress is the change in productivity, the change, that is, in the real value of the product output of a representative unit of resource input. If we may take natural resources as given and disregard variations in the intensity of effort, then the measure of progress is the change in the value of output per man-hour of labor. The place of "capital" in this relationship will be discussed later.

For the sake of what is to follow, this relationship between output and labor inputs can be simply illustrated. Any agricultural output requires that a farmer work on a farm and that he use certain tools, materials, and services. Hence, there are involved, one output—Y—and three types of labor input. There is the labor of the farmer (and his helpers) on the farm; call that E. There is the labor required to make the tools that the farmer uses and wears out in producing Y; call that T. There is the labor input in providing the farmer with the seeds, materials, aids, and services that he utilizes in raising his crop of Y; call this R. Suppose that in order to produce 300 Y, the farmer has to "put in" 100 units of labor (E), and uses up tools embodying 60 units of labor (T) and requires other materials and services embodying 40 units of labor (R). This could be stated, with Y output as a function of the three labor inputs as follows:

$$300 \text{ Y} \quad \text{F} \quad (100 \text{ E}, 60 \text{ T}, 40 \text{ R})$$

The productivity ratio is 1:1.5, with one labor input associated with 1.5 product outputs. If account were taken *only* of the farmer's work, then the ratio would be 1:3 with one labor input associated with 3 product outputs. Clearly, this would be misleading. A change in organization might reduce the labor inputs of E as a ratio of product outputs, but if the reduction in E were more than offset by increases in T or R, then productivity would have been reduced, not raised thereby. Any change that reduces E, T, or R inputs without causing offsetting increases in the others, will raise productivity. For example, if a farmer with a tractor raised three times as much wheat as a farmer with a horse and plow, this still need not count as an increase in productivity unless there is no offsetting increase in the labor inputs required for the maintenance and replacement of the tractor over those required for the maintenance and replacement of the horse.

Causes of Productivity Change. The following four variables have most often been used to account for changes in productivity:

1. The quantity of *physical capital* or the fund of producers durables. Productivity supposedly rises when more physical capital becomes available, per unit of labor.

2. The size of the *population.* Productivity supposedly declines, as population is greater with respect to the natural resources available to that population.

3. The acquired *mastery* over natural and social phenomena, existing as a potential in society's fund of scientific knowledge, inventions, achieved techniques, and recorded experience.

4. The assimilation or *embodiment* of this mastery over social and physical phenomena, in the skills and knowledge of individuals, in social and political institutions, in tools, equipment, and instruments, in technological products and processes.

The theory of economic progress, which will be developed in the following chapters, will take account only of the last two variables. Capital accumulation will be excluded as a determinant of economic progress for reasons that are explained in the next chapter. The relationship between population size and economic progress will be separately examined in Chapter 11.

Chapter 7

The Insignificance of Capital Accumulation

The Theory of Capital Accumulation Rejected. For a long time economic growth has been regarded as a self-evident consequence of capital accumulation. Many still so consider it. This explanation of growth, however, and the very conception of capital as it has been developed and understood in economics is rejected here. What follows explains why.

These controversial and significant issues are nevertheless a digression. Not every reader will wish to enter into their complexities. The theory of capital accumulation need not be disestablished among those who have never accepted it. Nor is a rejection of the old theory a necessary precondition to accepting the usefulness of the alternative explanation of economic progress, which will be proposed in subsequent chapters. If the reader chooses to skip this chapter, he will not therefore be less able to follow what lies ahead.

Classical and neoclassical economics primarily explain the rise of per capita output as a consequence of capital accumulation. In this tradition, Mrs. Joan Robinson's production functions are differentiated only by different levels of capital accumulation. And Mr. Roy Harrod maps out his paths of growth via accumulation of capital (by way of consumption propensities, the interest rate, and investment). In recent years Mr. Harrod has conceded that other things relevant to growth may fall within the cognizance of "political economy," but he nevertheless sternly relegates all but capital accumulation to a limbo beyond the pale of "economic theory." [1]

There are reasons, which will be developed immediately below, for dispensing with the notion of capital entirely in the analysis of economic progress. It will be shown that the capital accumulation-productivity relationship has failed the test of empirical verification; that there are fundamental difficulties in measuring any capital quantum that could be considered an independent determinant of growth; that there appear to be contradictions between the logical consequences of the capital-productivity postulate and the implications of other popular theorems of economics, and contradictions also between the pattern of events congruous with capital theory and those that are commonly observed. Finally the a

[1] Roy Harrod, "Second Essay in Dynamic Development," *The Economic Journal* (June 1960), pp. 277–278.

priori argument, always the mainstay of the theory, fails logically and also fails to survive a confrontation with the facts.

Theory Fails the Empirical Test. If the theory of capital accumulation "worked," then a strong statistical relationship should exist between observed increases in per capita output and observed increases in the accumulation of capital. In 1956 Professor Moses Abramovitz published a study of this relationship, which had long been postulated, but not before tested. He correlated output per capita and capital per capita in the United States since 1870, a period covering the major phases of American industrialization.[2] His attempt was to measure the significance of capital accumulation. Much to his chagrin he found it had no significance. Even including as capital (sic) the capitalized value of land and of other rents, he found that a mere 14.5 percent increase in per capita output could be explained by a correlary increase in capital per capita, whereas a 250 percent increase in per capita output had to be otherwise accounted for. A more recent study, taking into account the effect of rising productivity on the costs of capital, found that there had been an absolute *decrease* in capital per capita during this whole period of industrialization in the United States.[3] Other studies covering the same period and dealing with the same question, by Solow [4] and by Massel,[5] confirmed that no significant relationship existed between capital per capita and output per capita. Through this extended period of American development, capital per capita has remained virtually constant while productivity skyrocketed. The theory failed the test of empirical verification. It didn't work. It proved without predictive value.

Capital Not Measurable as a Variable Independent of Productivity Change. Those inclined to oppose the findings of Abramovitz and the others will possibly question the adequacy of the measures of capital used. They have the right to do so, since an adequate measure for the capital quantum is yet to be devised. In the words of Mrs. Joan Robinson:

In a world where unexpected events occur which alter values, the points of view of the man of deeds, making investment decisions about the future, and of the man of words making observations about the past, are irreconcilable,

[2] "Resource and Output Trends in the United States since 1870," *American Economic Review, Proceedings* (May 1956), p. 5. Published also by the National Bureau of Economic Research as *Occasional Paper No. 52.*
[3] Luigi Passinetti, "On Concepts and Measures of Changes in Productivity," *The Review of Economics and Statistics,* Vol. 41 (August 1959), p. 270.
[4] R. Solow, "Technical Change and the Aggregate Production Function," *The Review of Economics and Statistics,* Vol. 39 (August 1957), pp. 312–320.
[5] B. F. Massel, "Capital Formation and Technological Change in United States Manufacturing," *The Review of Economics and Statistics,* Vol. 42 (May 1960), pp. 182–188.

and all we can do is botch up some conventional method of measuring capital that will satisfy neither of them.[6]

Capital is a quantity of producer durables existing at a particular time. One capital quantum might be compared with another theoretically by measuring the real resource (ultimately labor) inputs embodied in each; if one embodied twice the input of real resources, it would constitute twice the capital. Real resource inputs, however, are extremely heterogeneous, and, for sake of comparison, must ordinarily be resolved into some money equivalent. Furthermore, account must be taken of the degree to which a capital item has lost value through use or with the passage of time. In practice, therefore, capital is measured either by its market value or by the net investment (initial expenditure minus depreciation) that it embodies. Neither one of these measures of capital is independent of productivity change. What changes productivity will, to a significant degree, determine the market value and/or the net investment attributed to particular capital items. A change in technique that succeeds (and to the degree that it succeeds) in increasing per capita output in a particular sector will thereby raise the quasi-rents and, hence, the market value of certain producer durables. Such a change will also lower both the market price and, by accelerating depreciation through obsolescence, the net investment value of a different set of capital items. This dynamic causes "standard" depreciation to vary in different industries depending upon the pace of technological change (and rate of technological advance) characteristic of particular industries. If the pace of technological advance accelerates, standard depreciation eventually adjusts, and measured capital shrinks. It is circular to measure capital where the measured quantity of capital varies as a function of productivity change, and to attempt, at the same time, to explain productivity change as a function of the capital thus measured. The inability to break out of this circle is another reason, though of itself not a compelling one, to dispense with the concept of capital in the analysis of growth.

Contradictions of Theory and Fact. According to classical theory, the accumulation of capital has a double function. It raises per capita output and it lowers the rate of profit. If the theory holds, where productivity increases as a consequence of capital accumulation, there should be a corolary decline in profits (and interest). In an equilibrium situation, indeed, the rate of return on capital would have to decline to induce any net investment or capital accumulation whatsoever. Instead, one commonly observes investment, profits, and productivity rising together.

Further, it has been the argument of those who propounded the "stag-

6 Joan Robinson, "The Production Function and the Theory of Capital," *The Review of Economic Studies*, Vol. 21, p. 90.

nation thesis" that, in recent decades at least, investment has been "capital saving." In order to explain the growing severity of the problem of unemployment, they postulated less capital per worker. To explain the simultaneous increase in productivity, they (or others) postulated more capital per worker. One or both postulates had to be wrong.

The A Priori Argument Restated. In the Ricardian conception, production takes place through the combinations of three more or less substitutable inputs: land, labor, and capital. It is regarded as axiomatic that increments of any one, with the others held constant, will yield (generally diminishing) additions to output. Capital is understood not as mere financial assets, but as the stock of machines and other producer durables.

Marxists argued that capital was not an independent factor that made its own contribution and was rightfully entitled to its own reward. Rather capital was a frozen form of labor and, hence, the return on capital was rightfully labor's.

To counter this argument, the classical apologists sought for a meritorious sacrifice, which was necessary for the accumulation of capital, but which was not subsumable under the "efforts of labor." They found it in "abstinence." Further, to justify payment for "abstinence," it had to be shown that there was some point to the continual increase of capital stocks. Böhm-Bawerk's particular contribution was to "prove" that there was a general technological value in the continual accumulation of "frozen labor" through abstinence.

Böhm-Bawerk's argument had two prongs: (1) that higher per capita output requires methods of production that are more "roundabout," and (2) that more roundabout methods require more physical capital. In order to consider this argument, it is necessary first to discover, if possible, some unequivocal meaning for "capital" and for "roundaboutness."

Capital, an Immobilized Resource. Capital, as this term is used in economics or national accounting, is not an index of the number of tools, or of the complexity of tools, or of their weight and size. It is not a measure of the resource inputs embodied in the tools and in the equipment *used up in* the production of goods and services. On the contrary, capital is the measure of the resource inputs that a particular technology requires, but requires to be *withheld* from the nexus of production. Capital is not to be found in the resources used, but in those relegated to a permanent state of nonuse by a particular technology.

The making of wooden crates might serve as an example. Nails are driven into the boards to hold the boxes together. These nails are not capital, since they are used in the product output. Suppose that irregularities in the demand for types of boxes and uncertainties in the procurement of nails should make it necessary to hold in stock an average of twenty barrels of nails of various sizes. The nails in this stock would be capital because this approximate quantity, necessary to operations, must permanently be withheld from use in the production of boxes. If growing inefficiencies of procurement should make it necessary to increase the quantity of nails held in bins and warehouses, then capital ipso facto would be greater, that is, it would be necessary to withhold a larger quantity of resources from current use. On the other hand, if by standardization of crates, by procurement efficiencies, or by ironing out the irregularities of demand, the required nail inventories could be reduced, then capital would be less, that is, the given organization and technology of production would require that fewer resources be withheld from use.

Another example might be a factory building with an anticipated life of twenty years. Each year 1/20th of the building is used up (depreciated) in current output. If the building is currently replaced as it wears out, then 19/20th of the resource inputs contained by the structure are permanently withheld from use. That 19/20th is capital. Supposing that by using less expensive methods and less lasting materials, both the life expectancy and the cost of the building are halved, annual depreciation and replacements remaining the same. There is now the same current cost of replacement and the same annual value of service (shelter) rendered, but the value of resources tied up in the building has been reduced by 50 percent. Capital is less by half. The same shelter might eventually be provided by one of the collapsible plastic shells currently under development, which are erected and held firm by the pressure of conditioned air, and are replaced, say, every year. Then the tying up of resources in the form of a factory building would be virtually dispensed with. Capital would be eliminated. The difference between the structure with the 20-year life, the 10-year life, the one-year life, is a difference in divisibility: divisibility in the performance of a service. In the first instance shelter cannot be provided for one year (or for one hour) without providing it for 20 years, and in the second without providing it for 10 years. In the third instance, shelter can be provided year by year.

Capital, then, consists of the resources that a particular organization and technology of production and distribution require be withheld from use as production inputs. Capital is to be found in the frozen margin of resource inputs between use (depreciation) and replacement. This margin of immobilized inputs is a function of the indivisibilities of a particular technology or of the inefficiencies of a particular organization. Now consider whether this capital quantum is a prerequisite to more "roundabout" production, and whether greater roundaboutness leads to higher per capita output.

Two Meanings for Roundaboutness. Roundaboutness would seem to have two possible meanings, that of *lengthiness* and that of *indirectness*. Lengthiness would refer simply to the averaged time span between inputs and end-product output, where that time span is a technological or organizational necessity. This time span is *not* a function of the number of phases or steps to a process of production unless these are necessarily sequential. In a Robinson Crusoe economy, of course, all steps and phases of production are necessarily sequential, for they must be performed by a single, indivisible resource. Crusoe must first make his tool, then use it, then sharpen it, then again use it, then replace it. But in a world of divisible resource inputs, the using, maintaining, and replacing of tools goes on simultaneously. New phases or steps may mean a mere rearrangement of the pattern of inputs carried on concurrently, with no increase in lengthiness. It must be clear, furthermore, that lengthiness has to refer to the time between input and output points of a "going process," but not to the time required to put into operation a new process. The time required to set up a process or the difference in time required to organize alternative processes is certainly an important consideration in business choice, but it is something quite other than lengthiness. Particularly it would be fallacious to compare, as a measure of relative roundaboutness, the input to output time span of a going process with the time required to set up alternative processes. Indeed, a considerable time may be required to reorganize a process *in order* to reduce its lengthiness.

The second possible meaning of roundaboutness is in the degree of "directness," the more "indirect" meaning the more roundabout. Consider, for example, the difference in "roundaboutness" in hand-knitting and machine-knitting a sweater. Measuring the time span between the input of labor and wool and the output of the garment, the hand-knit process is far lengthier. Nevertheless the Böhm-Bawerkian would say that the hand-knit process was less roundabout. If he avoided the trap of supposing that the machine-knit process was more roundabout *because* it was more capitalistic (in which case roundaboutness would cease to be an independent term, and, being merely synonymous with capitalistic, could no longer pretend to explain *why* capitalistic methods are allegedly more productive), he would be obliged to propose that the machine-knitting was more productive because it was more indirect. By "more indirect" he could only mean that a larger proportion of the inputs embodied in the finished product were of depreciated machinery in the case of machine-knitting than in the case of hand-knitting. The notion of indirectness requires that production be divided into a primary phase and secondary phases, the primary phase being restricted to the ultimate fabrication, and the secondary phases to the supply of tools, materials, and services to those engaged in the primary phase. The arbitrariness of this division is such that, operationally, the notion of indirectness is probably hopeless. If however, the primary phase—sowing the seed, sawing the wood, plowing the field, knitting the garment—could be adequately identified, then the labor inputs of the primary phase would be called direct inputs. The labor and other resource inputs used to supply all the aids and services, and tools and materials required for use by those engaged in the primary phase would be called indirect inputs. Production for a particular end-product output would be more roundabout when the ratio of indirect to direct inputs was higher. Indirect inputs may take many forms, for instance, tools currently produced and used, the replacement values of depreciated equipment, fertilizers, catalysts, statistical services, planning services, etc.

There are then these two possible meanings for roundabout production: lengthiness (averaged time span between resource inputs and end-product output) and indirectness (the ratio of indirect to direct inputs). Between these two there is no necessary connection. A more indirect process may be adopted in order to reduce lengthiness, say, the use of a catalyst designed to accelerate fermentation. Given these possible meanings of roundaboutness, the following questions must be asked. Do more roundabout processes (considered first as lengthier, then as more indirect) require more capital? Are roundabout processes more productive?

No Increase in Productivity Through Lengthy-Roundaboutness. There is indeed a connection between the more lengthy process and capital requirements. Lengthiness, like other indivisibilities, does immobilize resources and hence requires more capitalistic production. If a whiskey must be aged not for five but for ten years, then implicitly for a given output, a larger stock of resources will be immobilized in the form of insufficiently aged liquor. Since lengthiness is not the only source of indivisibility, an alternative, less lengthy process may, for other reasons, be more capital-using. The lifespan of (and the capital immobilized in) factory buildings has no relationship to the shortness or lengthiness of the processes carried on within their walls.

But if there is some logical connection between lengthiness per se and capital accumulation, is there any relationship of technological or organizational necessity between lengthiness and productivity? Keynes answered that question in one of his most significant obiter dicta.

It is true that some lengthy or roundabout processes are physically efficient. But so are some short processes. Lengthy processes are not physically efficient because they are long. Some, probably most, lengthy processes would be physically very inefficient, for there are such things as spoiling or wasting with time. . . .

[Explaining that the premium paid for use of capital is not an index of its contribution to productivity, but an offset to the inconvenience of its accumulation.] Moreover there are all sorts of reasons why various kinds of services and facilities are scarce and therefore expensive relative to the quantity of labor involved. For example, smelly processes command a higher reward, because people will not undertake them otherwise. So do risky processes. But we do not devise a productivity theory of smelly or risky processes as such. In short, not all labor is accomplished in equally agreeable attendant circumstance; and conditions of equilibrium require that articles produced in less agreeable attendant circumstances (characterized by smelliness, risk, or the lapse of time) must be kept sufficiently scarce to command a higher reward.[7]

In what he says, Keynes is certainly right. Lengthiness has no intrinsic technological worth. It is simply costly and undesirable. Inasmuch as the means can be found to reduce lengthiness, the particular process becomes *ipso facto* more efficient. The "open sesame" of productivity and the path of growth are certainly not to be found in greater lengthiness. The lengthy-roundaboutness relation to productivity fails as a matter of logic and of fact.

Productivity Not Determined by Indirect-Roundaboutness. Taking roundaboutness to mean a more indirect organization of production, there is still no relationship of technological necessity between greater roundaboutness and higher productivity. It may be historically true that more primitive processes are very direct, simply because such processes are developed in an economy where specialization is minimal. A high degree of indirectness in the organization of inputs can take place only where specialization is the general rule, and specialization can be the general rule only in an advanced form of economic organization, either a developed market economy with its accoutrements of credit and contract or under effective centralized planning. In an advance from a primitive economy where specialization is virtually impossible to one where it may be commonplace, there is bound to be an increase in the indirectness of inputs. But the increase in productivity that will arise through such a transition will be the consequence not of a more indirect organization of inputs per se, but of all the advantages of a more rational organization and a higher technology.

In an advanced society, however, variations in the ratio of direct to indirect inputs are neutral with respect to costs. For the achievement of greater productivity, there must be less input per unit of output. From a given technology, a new process may be developed that reduces *indirect* inputs per unit of output (in which case productivity rises through the use of less "roundabout" production), or a new process may evolve that reduces *direct* inputs per unit of output (in which case productivity rises

[7] *The General Theory of Employment. Interest and Money* (New York: Harcourt, Brace & World, 1936), pp. 214–215.

through the use of more "roundabout" production). There are two paths, and technology is advancing on them both simultaneously: along which the advance is most rapid is surely a matter of chance.

With roundaboutness understood as the degree to which inputs are indirect, there is not only no link of technical necessity between greater roundaboutness and higher productivity, but also there is none between roundaboutness and the level of capital accumulation. It is, of course, conceivable that between alternative processes the more roundabout would also be the more capitalistic. The converse is equally conceivable. This is obviously so, since indirect inputs can indefinitely increase relative to direct without any reference whatsoever to the possession or use of producer durables, for example, through the greater use of such services as forecasting, market analysis, advertising, or through the use of material aids such as fertilizers, catalysts, preservatives, etc. But it could be true also where indirect inputs are solely in the form of depreciation of producer durables since the annual rate of depreciation replacement has no necessary connection to the magnitude of resources immobilized as capital. It is likely, for example, that irrigation with dams and dykes would require a heavy immobilization of resources in those structures, with small annual depreciation-replacement expenditures, whereas irrigation with pumps and hoses would require a smaller quantum of resources tied up as producer's durables but a large annual depreciation-replacement expenditure—hence a high ratio of indirect inputs per unit of output. Farming with irrigation by dams and dykes would be more capital accumulative and less roundabout, while farming with irrigation by pumps and hoses would be less capital accumulative and more roundabout. Another example might be the contrast between a transport system based on aircraft and one based on the use of railroads.

Another story of Crusoeland must be put on the shelf where good fairy tales belong. There is no relation of logic or fact between roundaboutness and productivity.

Summary. Capital accumulation as an explanation of economic growth is rejected for the following reasons. It has been tested against historical event and has failed the test. It is inconsistent with other aspects of "accepted" theory, and is out of accord with observed relationships between the rate of return, investment, and productivity. The measure of the capital quantum is not independent of the growth it purports to explain. And the a priori argument that capital is necessary for more roundabout processes, and that more roundabout processes are required for higher productivity, is an argument grounded neither in logic nor in evidence. Roundaboutness, understood as the lengthiness of processes, is detrimental to productivity. Roundaboutness, understood as the indirectness of inputs, is neutral with respect to productivity. Nor is there any general relationship of technological necessity between greater or less roundaboutness, measured by the ratio of direct to indirect inputs, and that immobilization of resources prerequisite to a particular technology called capital accumulation.

An alternative approach to the analysis of growth must be developed, an approach that takes into account the real values of investment and the costs of accumulations, but that wholly dispenses with the alleged relationship between roundaboutness, capital, and productivity.

Chapter 8

The Economics of Transformation

TRANSFORMATION TO HIGHER PROCESSES

The Meaning of "Higher Process." Any output, understood even broadly enough to include the whole national product or as narrowly as Farmer Brown's hogs, may be conceived as the product of a particular organization of inputs. This organization of inputs, relevant to a particular output, will be called a *process*. Process will mean the organization of the entire matrix of (variable) inputs that determine a specific output. Hog raising, as a process, for example, will be taken to include not only all the inputs organized by the hog farmer, with the fattened pig as output, but also to include the production of the vitamins to be fed to the pig, the transporting of the feed to the farmer and of the hog to the market, the fabrication of the tools and equipment that are used by the farmer and those who service him. A "higher" process is one where for identical or equivalent outputs there is a lesser real value of inputs. A "higher" process is the corollary of "higher" productivity.

The Transformation of Processes. Productivity was earlier defined by the ratio of the output values to a relevant continuum of inputs. Necessarily, any rise in productivity requires and proceeds from some change in the organization of inputs. There must be, in other words, a transformation of process. This may take place in many different ways. It may come about through a change in the manner in which workmen sit or hold their hands at the workbench. It may be in the alternation of plant layout. It may be in the use of new energy sources, new measuring devices, a more convenient form of notation. It may result from new methods of cost analysis, the use of different fertilizers, new hybrid seeds, insecticides, catalysts, techniques, or tools of any kind. It may be brought about through a better system of communication or transportation, or through the availability of better roads, harbors, subways, airlines, or through the installation of a traffic control system that facilitates the flow of materials and labor. It may be the consequence of a better diet, or of medical advances that improve health and reduce the absenteeism of the work force. It may be in the greater availability and wider use of statistical data, or in the development of better systems of business forecasting. It may arise out of the more effective recruitment of personnel, better job-sorting, and improved management-labor relations. It may result from educational advances and improved literacy. It may come about through the more effective implementation of a government "full employment" policy that brings into use otherwise unutilized resources. (For the economy as a whole, all available resources, including those which are unemployed or "wasted," can be considered as inputs.) It may be the result of more effective antitrust enforcement. Which of this universe of inputs need be included in the analysis of a particular process will depend not only on the specified output to which these inputs relate, but also on the productivity change or transformation that is to be accounted for. Many inputs, especially those of the "infrastructure," are constant over a very broad range of transformations and hence for analytic purposes could most often be disregarded in the explanation of a particular transformation.

A Notation to Describe Economic Progress. Economic progress is here conceived as the transformation of lower into higher processes. This sort of transformation can be illustrated by a simple notation. Suppose there are two processes, P1 and P2, for the output of farm product Y (assuming all inputs to be reducible to equally valued labor units), with E inputs consisting of the labor of the farmer and his helpers, with T inputs consisting of the production or replacement of tools and equipment used up in the production of Y, and with R inputs consisting of the materials and services requisite to E and T inputs.

$$300 \; Y = F \quad P1 \; (100 \; E, \; 60 \; T, \; 40 \; R)$$
$$300 \; Y = F \quad P2 \; (50 \; E, \; 80 \; T, \; 50 \; R)$$

The higher process, obviously, is P2, where the same output of Y requires 20 fewer units of input. Economic progress consists of the movement from P1 to P2, whereby the process for the production Y has, in effect, been transformed. It is not the organization of processes, but their transformation that constitutes economic progress and that is of interest here.

Transformation as a Process Subject to Transformation. Before there can be an advance to a higher process, that process must first exist conceptually. It must first have been put forward as a goal. The creation of transformation goals is a process, indeed the most important of all. Among its inputs are costs of education, of laboratories and scientific equipment, and of the creative labor of research scientists and inventors. The processes of "goal creation," moreover, may themselves be in a continual state of transformation to higher levels.

Similarly, transformation, which is likely to require complex organization and great skill and the expenditure of resources, is also a process that is continuingly subject to upward transformations.

THE COSTS OF TRANSFORMATION

A Function of the "Distance" Between Processes. Given a higher process as a goal, transformation costs are simply the costs of achieving that goal. They are the costs of getting there. Transformation requires many sorts of resource expenditures; for example, the efforts of engineers working in pilot plants to iron out "bugs," or the time and talent needed to plan and to implement a new organization, or the resources used to adapt old machines or to build new tools and equipment, or the efforts of recruiting, assembling, and training labor for changed tasks, or the inefficiencies that are an inevitable cost of acquiring new operating experience. Also, there are the risks of new ventures, the cost of securing trade union and political acquiescence and consumer acceptance, the costs of extending or readapting such social utilities as housing, police and fire protection, gas and electricity, phone and other communication services, transportation facilities. Transformation costs are the once-over costs, the costs not of an operation but of setting up an operation. The cost of transformation is the cost of making a change, and the magnitude of the change will depend as much on the lower (existing) process from which change begins as on the higher process that is the goal. In this sense, the cost of transformation is determined by the "distance" between the higher and the lower processes. For example, the transformation to a new and higher metallurgical process would surely be less costly in the United States than in India, though the goal sought was exactly the same, since the breadth and complexity of the change required in India would be so much greater.

Extreme Uncertainty and Diffusion of Benefits.. Economic rationality would require that the benefits of any transformation be set against its costs, and resources allocated between this and alternative uses in a way that would maximize output values. In this regard all the virtues and defects of a particular form of economic organization, considered as a mechanism of resource allocation, will be brought into play. This particular sphere of choice, however, is marked out from the rest at least in one respect. The possible benefits will be more diffused and the uncertainties will generally be greater than for alternative uses of resources because goal creation and innovation (which can be considered as the initial stage of transformation) plunge always into the unknown and deal always with the unforeseeable.

"Capital," A Partially Recoverable Transformation Cost. Transformation expenditures may variously affect the subsequent paths of development.

In some instances, for example, in the grading of a railway bed, the benefits of transformation expenditures will not go beyond the process they make possible. In other instances, aside from the achievement of the higher process for which it was intended, a particular transformation expenditure may "shorten the distance" and reduce the cost of a wide variety of subsequent transformations, and hence influence the rate and direction of future developments. The inculcation of work habits and of new levels of skill among a selected labor force falls in this second category.

Some transformation expenditures may be partially recoverable at the discretion of those who incurred them, in the event that projected processes fail or when more advanced processes supersede them. This quality of partial recoverability gives to producer durables ("capital") its special significance, indeed its *only peculiar characteristic*, as a growth phenomenon. Consider this.

Some part of producer durables may be recovered if they have junk value, or if they can be shifted to uses other than that for which they were initially intended, or, most important, if they can be used up in current production without being concurrently replaced or maintained. When durables can be so depleted, the normal cost of "replacement inputs" covers the costs of transformation. It is this sort of recoverability that is meant when transformation (variously described) is said to occur through "normal replacement."

Limitations on Transformation Through "Normal Replacement." In fact, the possibility of offsetting the costs of transformation through "normal replacement" is much more limited than might at first appear. Of those producer durables that can be and constantly are being depleted and replaced in a given production process, only a (presumably minor) fraction can be recovered when the intention is to transform the process. For sake of illustration, consider process P2, with a quantity of producer durables D which are used up and replaced at the rate of 80 T (replacement) inputs per 300 units of Y produced.

$$300 \, Y = F \qquad P2 \, (50 \, E, 80 \, T, 50 \, R) \, D$$

With the intention of transforming to P3, it might be supposed that D could be recovered by the continued withholding of the 80 T inputs per output of 300 Y, that is, by allowing equipment to depreciate without concurrent replacements. If D embodied 800 labor inputs, then presumably it could be fully depreciated by producing 3000 units of Y without any replacement inputs. This recovery of 800 labor inputs, of course, would be to some degree offset by the sacrificed opportunities of using the higher process with respect to those 3000 units of Y.

However, when D is understood to be composed of heterogeneous items, the complete recovery of capital in the process of transformation ceases to be conceivable. Suppose that D is composed of heterogeneous items, say, d_1, d_2, d_3, d_4, d_5, each with a different rate of depletion. Suppose that d_1 wears out after the production of 600 Y, d_2 after 900 Y, d_3 after 1200 Y, d_4 after 1500 Y, and d_5 after the production of 1800 Y. When 600 Y have been produced, d_1 is ready for discard but all other durable items are usable, and if further value is to be tapped from the rest of the durable good complex, then d_1 must be replaced. When 900 units of Y have been produced, then d_2 is ready for discard, but all other items are operational and if their value is to be liquidated, then d_2 must be replaced. And so on with the liquidation of the successive durable items leaving the rest of the durable goods unrecovered. Under these circumstances, the components of D cannot be so depleted that a transformation to a higher process can be made without leaving a substantial proportion of the technically recoverable producer durables unrecovered. In view of the great complexity and variability of the durable producer items that characterize manufacturing and other processes, the nonrecoverability of a substantial proportion of these must be postulated as the general case.

Positive and Negative Values of Capital Stocks. The existence of a partially recoverable complex of producer durables can have several possible effects on transformation. (1) Inasmuch as replacement inputs can be used to offset the costs of changeover, the opportunity costs of transformation will be less and transformation will be encouraged. (2) The piecemeal depletion contingent upon heterogeneous sets of durable items will offer a constant temptation to piecemeal transformation as a means of maximizing recovery of capital costs. Piecemeal replacement means that incremental units of equipment replacing worn out sets (c_1 for d_1, c_2 for d_2, c_3 for d_3, etc.) must in each case fit into the existing pattern of operations so that even when c is totally substituted for d, the essential pattern of operations and the nature of the process will remain substantially unaltered. The effect is to shift the focus of creative inquiry to the search for modifications and improvements of existing patterns rather than into the general overhaul of basic relationships, to component development rather than the reconstruction of operating systems. (3) Finally, the attempt to maximize the recovery of producer durables takes time and, on that account, may delay the transformation choice and slow down the process of transformation.

In a dynamic society, the decision to postpone is always liable to become the decision to forego; hence that which tends to delay tends also to forestall. The external economies of transformation are likely to be peculiarly significant. Since each achieved transformation generates new horizons for goal-creation and opens the way to further development, the general postponement of transformation decisions, stretching out their period of incubation, is likely to lower the rate of technical progress and to reduce the annual net increment to the national product. For these reasons, existing capital accumulations may actually slow the rate of transformation and consequently be a drag on growth.

THE STRATEGY OF TRANSFORMATION

The Timing of Transformation. There are reasons to delay transformation besides optimizing the recovery of producer durables. Transformation is itself a process that is subject to rapid transformation, so that it may ordinarily be anticipated that transformation costs will fall rapidly once a particular category of transformations, for example, the transformation from punch cards to computers, has begun. These costs will fall for many possible reasons: because social services and public utilities more favorable to the needs of the transformed processes will have developed under the pressure of cumulating demands, because new techniques for transformation itself will have been discovered during the course of repeated transformations, because accumulating experience with alternative processes will facilitate choice and minimize risk, because a pool of workers experienced in the new processes will become available for hire, because consumer tastes will have become accustomed to new outputs, because, through the greater volume of demands, the production costs and prices of the tools and equipment needed for the higher process will have been reduced. Furthermore, the goals of transformation may in time advance so that sitting out the first round may allow an entrepreneur or corporation to achieve greater gains at yet higher process levels, with no increase in transformation costs. These are the gains to be anticipated through a delayed transformation. There are, on the other hand, gains which are specific to an *early* transformation. Joseph Schumpeter emphasized the price advantage that accrues to first-comers via a profit position of temporary monopoly. Those who transform early, that is, who innovate, might pre-empt a favored position with respect to markets, or to patents, or in access to resources. Early transformation may give to first-comers a competitive advantage that tends to cumulate through its exercise, particularly where competition takes the form of a continuing race for technical supremacy.

These lower costs of "delayed" transformation and the relative benefits of early transformation are not functions of time (as they might appear to be to the small entrepreneur faced with the autonomy of the competitive market) but of the sequence of transformations. The costs of transformation will *not* be lowered by the passage of time, but only by the fact that others have ventured to transform already. The benefits of early transformation also do not so much depend upon the time a transformation comes, but rather require that it precede the transformations of competitors. When there are but fewer competitors who each understand that the issue is not time but their place in the sequence of transformations, then the question becomes not of "how fast" but of "who first." Transformation merges into the strategies of oligopoly. Each may seek to let the others bear the brunt of risk, experiment, and high initial cost while waiting for the appropriate moment to step in and scoop up the major gains. Where each waits for the others to take the first dangerous step, it is perfectly possible that that first step will not be taken at all.

Conflicting Requirements for the Organization of Production and of Transformation. While the organization of production, the organization of transformation, and also the organization of whatever creates the goals for transformations, may all converge on a particular category of outputs (say, steel products), they are, nevertheless, different processes, different tasks, each with its own institutional requisites. Often, however, these very different processes are (and must be) controlled by the same decision-making, action-taking agency. The same firm may be responsible for managing the production of steel products, for introducing new techniques into the production of those products, and for devising the new techniques and products to be introduced. There are advantages in the integration of these tasks. The control capacities and the data relevant to choice for each task derive in part from the same fund of experience. The several tasks must often be done simultaneously, relying upon the same resources. Setting the tasks apart must increase the difficulties of communication and coordination.

There are also disadvantages in their integration. Each task, for its best performance, is likely to require different talents, a different acquired knowledge and skill, different values, and a different technique and scale of organization. The leadership and control organization that is best for one may not be best, indeed, may not do at all, for the others. Where the same agency controls production and transformation, the kind of leadership and the form of control organization that survive the continuing test of efficiency in production might be wholly unsuited for the occasional but vital task of transformation.

The possible divergence between the organizational requisites of production and transformation is suggested by the contentions of neoclassicists against Schumpeter's view that high productivity in the modern economy depends on the gigantic corporation with its extensive power to administer price. Against this, neoclassicists have pointed to two indubitable facts (*a*) that frequently the smaller and middle-sized firms are the low-cost producers of an industry, and (b) that within the great corporation itself, scores or hundreds of plants, factories, shops, and divisions are autonomous operating units that could act as independent agents on the market, with no fragmentation of technological relationships. But these facts do not refute Schumpeter, who is concerned not with the organization of production but with the organization of transformation. The inference may be that the optimum size for the producing unit is not optimum for the transformation task.

Consider, for example, the problems that may arise through the integration of the transformation task and the production task in the same decision-making entity. Suppose that processes (P_3) and (P_4) describe the aggregated output and input sequence for an entire industry, to be written:

$$300 \; Y = F \qquad P_3 \quad (200 \; E, \; 200 \; T, \; 200 \; R) \qquad 800 \; D_3$$
$$500 \; Y = F \qquad P_4 \quad (200 \; E, \; 100 \; T, \; 300 \; R) \qquad 700 \; D_4$$

where Y is the end-product output, E is the labor input in the end-product production, T is labor input in the replacement of tools, equipment, etc., and R is the labor input in the provision of other required goods and services; D is the labor input embodied in the producer durables in use in the processes designated by the subscript. Now suppose that (P_3) is the starting point and that there are no costs in the transformation to (P_4) other than the acquisition of D_4, but that these costs could be offset against D_3 which is wholly recoverable through normal replacement; that is, as units of D_3 wear out in the process of production, instead of the 200 T inputs per 300 Y being used to replace D_3, these inputs could be used to produce D_4, and when D_4 was substituted for D_3, operations could correspondingly be transformed to (P_4). Assuming rational decision-making, intent on maximizing output values, there would seem to be no barrier whatsoever to the eventual transformation to (P_4), via the normal replacement of D_3, as long as only the aggregated input-outputs for the industry as a whole are taken into account. The industry, however, is composed of operating units, of firms. It might be assumed that in these firms resides the whole economic power to organize production or transformation. Suppose, for simplicity's sake, that E, T, and R inputs are combined in the single firm, and that the optimum or competitively permissible size of the operating unit in (P_3) and (P_4) respectively are:

$$3 \; Y = F \qquad P_3 \quad (\; 2 \; E, \; \; 2 \; T, \; \; 2 \; R) \qquad 8 \; D_3$$
$$50 \; Y = F \qquad P_4 \quad (20 \; E, \; 10 \; T, \; 30 \; R) \qquad 70 \; D_4$$

Then no one operating unit could transform itself through normal replacement for it would long have ceased to be able to operate at all at

(P3) before it had acquired D4 requisite to minimal operations at (P4). Where none of the operating units that compose the industry is able to transform itself, then, under our assumptions, the industry must remain untransformed. How likely is it that such a situation might actually exist as a barrier to transformation?

In the peasant economy of rural India, for example, there are large quantities of producer durables in the form of cattle, used as beasts of burden. This stock of durables is constantly being replaced at great cost in labor inputs. In aggregate terms there would seem no reason why replacement should not take the form of the durables required for a higher tractor process. But, as long as the effective unit of operation *and of transformation* is the peasant farm, the task of transformation will be beyond the ken of the agency through which that task must be performed, in part because the tiny operating entity characteristic of the lower bullock-using process (P3) is too small to transform itself through the process of normal replacement into the higher tractor-using process (P4).

Need for a Power to Transform, Detached from Operations. Not only may the operating entity be inappropriately organized for the transformation task, the vested interest and the habits ingrained in the operating entity will often provide the major source of resistance and the bitterest opposition to transformation. Probably every economic system requires some form of mobile economic power, detached from operations and able to deliver an innovationary thrust that will disrupt and dismember the existing organization of processes.

It has often been argued that, in the early stages of economic development, an extreme concentration of private wealth is required for economic progress, since by suppressing consumption, resources are made available for investment. This argument is largely false. There are many other ways of promoting saving. There are other sources of investment than the savings of the developing economy. Besides, very often in developing countries there is an abundance of unemployed or semiemployed resources available on demand, and hence the diversion of resources from consumption through savings is not called for. Whether or not savings are required, aside from and prior to the need for savings, concentrated power is needed in order to massively transform an economy. There must be power, detached from going processes and existing industries, to mobilize and recombine resources from the whole breadth of the economy for a revolutionary reorganization of economic processes. Probably the signal importance of great concentrations of private wealth in the early stages of the industrial revolution was not so much that they induced a higher rate of saving, but rather that they embodied mobile power in support of innovation. Even if savings and initial accumulations of wealth had been greater—but if those accumulations had been widely dispersed rather than concentrated—there still might not have been the power required radically to reorganize resources in a major transformation of the economy.

This does not mean that in developing countries today, great concentrations of private wealth are necessary for transformation, since other ways to mobilize resources are possible. Except by accidents of birth and a peculiar and particular psychology prevailing among the rich, such concentrations need neither augment savings nor support innovations.

Subsequent to the industrial revolution, the free, resource-mobilizing, resource-reorganizing power became institutionalized in investment banks, then in the international security markets. In the modern organizational economy of the West, the great corporation, at once a self-financing, goal-creating, transforming, producing entity, wields a mobile power for radical innovation. In the socialist societies, characterized by centralized political-direction, the requisite mobile power for transforming economic processes is concentrated in the agencies of economic planning.

SUMMARY

Economic progress takes place through the interaction of two sets of activities. The first produces the *goals* for the transformation of processes; the second transforms existing processes. Goal creation and transformation are themselves processes, subject to transformation.

The cost of transformation is a function of the "distance" between an existing process and the transformation goal. The peculiar significance of accumulated capital as a transformation cost is that it may be partially recovered in the advent of subsequent transformations, that is, growth may be financed through "normal replacement." Hence an existing complex of capital goods may lower opportunity costs for subsequent transformations. Capital accumulations, on the other hand, may influence the timing and design of future transformations in a manner detrimental to economic progress.

Frequently power over production and transformation is concentrated in the hands of the one decision-making entity. The optimum performance of these two functions, however, may require quite different skills and abilities, and different forms of organizations.

The fullest realization of growth opportunities requires some mobile loci of economic power, detached from operations, but able radically to reorganize the form of operations. In particular historical instances, this mobile source of power has been the amassed wealth of a few individuals, the great banking houses, the security markets, the large autonomous corporation, and state planning bodies.

Chapter 9

Economic Progress as a System

THREE FORMS OF ECONOMIC CHOICE

The Managerial Choice. Those who control the agencies of production or planning are charged with three different sorts of choice: managerial, engineering, and transformation.

The management choice (as it is conceived here) has to do with variations in the resource inputs and changes in the product mix, within the range allowed by the techniques in operation. A railroad, for example, at any given time embodies a range of techniques for transporting goods and passengers. Within this frame of operating techniques, the railroad management variously distributes the assigned freight among its rolling stock and varies the routes and speeds that its trains will follow. It does this, presumably, in response to the intensity and urgency with which particular goods or services are in demand in various parts of the country, or in response to the relative perishability of the goods that are shipped or to the pattern of competitive demands for freight cars and sidings. Managerial choice, recombining resource inputs and product outputs within the limits determined by techniques in operation, is *not* a component of the system of economic progress. Economic progress implies a widening of the technical limitations on managerial choice.

The Engineering Choice. Nor should it be thought that choice between alternative techniques is invariably a concomitant of economic progress. There is always a range of *established* techniques, known, familiar, practiced, proven, accepted, which can be substituted one for the other in producing the same good or service, or in producing substitutable goods or services. Each of these offers a different set of operating characteristics that will be evaluated on the basis of the circumstances in which it must be employed. One technique is more speedy, another is more reliable. One requires extensive equipment, while another needs expert supervision or the use of special skills. One operates cheaply but permits no variation in resource inputs or product outputs, while in another the operating costs are higher, but the flexibility in resources used and products made is greater. One requires this fuel, another that. Each, presumably, would be preferred under different circumstances, and, as the circumstances change, as the parameters take on a different configura-

111

tion, the one technique is substituted for another. For example, a commodity might be transported by any of several established technical processes: by railroad, by barge, by truck, or by aircraft. Which would be the most economical, and which, therefore, should be rationally preferred, will depend on the parameters of a particular choice. As parameters change, choices will shift from one to another.

Sometimes the choice between established techniques or technical processes is simple and easily resolved, as when any one of us decides to take the trip by railroad because the weather threatens or to take it by air because the weather is fine. Often, however, the choice between established techniques and technical processes is very difficult and replete with risk—particularly when choice is based on the anticipated change in parameters. Consider, for example, the problems in choosing between established atomic power reactor techniques, as described by the Empire State Atomic Development Associates, Inc. (ESADA).[1]

There are many different ways to design an atomic power reactor. Given the many possible combinations of fuel, coolant, and moderator materials, and the even greater number of possible variations in system conditions, an imaginative engineer could probably work out at least 100 basically different reactor concepts. . . . In appraising a power reactor concept, the designer looks for a number of things. He wants a fuel that is cheap to prepare and can withstand radiation effects well enough to be left in the reactor a long time (high fuel "burnup"). He wants a good "neutron economy," meaning efficient use of the neutrons that are generated as fuel is consumed and which are the reactor's life blood. All else equal, he would like a system that can operate at a high temperature so that the heat generated can be efficiently converted to electricity. Similarly, he would like a system that operates at a low pressure and is physically compact (high "power density"), since these characteristics tend to reduce capital costs. He would like to use inexpensive materials of construction —again to keep down capital costs—and, above all, he wants a system that is inherently dependable.

The above ideal characteristics are often at odds with each other. A fuel that is cheap to prepare (measured in dollars per pound) may not withstand either high temperature or high burnup. A structural material that does not wastefully absorb neutrons may not withstand high temperature. A coolant that is excellent in its ability to carry away heat from the reactor may require a high operating pressure.

Because choice between established techniques and processes often requires the special expertise and knowledge associated with professional training as an engineer, the selection, evaluation, and recombination of established techniques will be considered aspects of engineering choice. Neither the managerial choice, which varies resource inputs and product combinations, nor the engineering choice, which decides between estab-

[1] ESADA, 2nd report, February 16, 1962, p. 6.

lished techniques, should be considered as parts of the system of economic progress.

The Transformation Choice. There is the third type of choice, where the process or product-output chosen is not merely preferred under changed conditions, but is considered superior under the same conditions. That is the transformation choice. For example, the decision to ship by barge rather than by railroad because of a change in prevailing conditions is an instance of engineering choice. But when the decision was made to replace the steam-driven locomotive with the diesel locomotive, this was no mere adjustment to operating circumstances. The diesel locomotive was considered superior under circumstances where once the steam locomotive alone would have been preferred. This exemplified the transformation choice.

The transformation choice is the final phase of the system of economic progress.

TRANSFORMATION AND INNOVATION

The Preconditions of Transformation. No matter how desirable a particular transformation might be, it will take place only if there exists an agency of choice and action (a company, a government department, an individual) aware of what is possible and able to reckon benefits and costs. Even then, transformation can only occur if the agent of choice and action has the motivation to transform coupled with power to decide; and, further, only if the resources are available to cover the costs of transformation. These preconditions to transformation need not be met. The "underdeveloped economies" of the world are massive examples of how these preconditions might, for centuries, fail to be met.

Those who have power need have no knowledge. Or, if they have power and knowledge, like the Admirals who demurred when confronted with Billy Mitchell's proposal to replace the big guns of the fleet with the striking force of air power, they may lack the motivation.[2]

[2] Elting Morison has described the resistance to the introduction into use in the Navy of continuous aim firing methods prior to the direct intervention of President Theodore Roosevelt. "The Navy is not only an armed force—it is a society. In the forty years following the Civil War, this society had been forced to accommodate itself to a series of technical changes . . . (which) wrought extraordinary changes in ship design . . . in fleet tactics, and even in naval strategy. To these numerous innovations, producing as they did a spreading disorder throughout a service with heavy commitments to formal organization, the Navy responded with grudging pain. It is wrong to assume, as civilians frequently do, that this blind reaction to technological change springs exclusively from some causeless Bourbon distemper that invades the military mind. There is a sounder and more attractive base. The opposition, where it occurs, of the soldier and the sailor to such change springs from the normal human instinct to protect oneself and more especially one's way of life. Military organizations are societies built around and upon the prevailing weapon

Costs of Transformation and Innovation. The first phase of transformation has a peculiar character. It is a step into the unknown, the proving-out of an hypothesis that may fail entirely and that certainly will entail unforeseeable costs and problems of adaptation and modification. This is the phase of innovation.

But even when innovation has blazed the trail, there are likely to be special risks and problems in transformation. The new process is likely to require different equipment, different skills, relocation, reorganization, and hence retraining and reeducation. Not only the equipment but the operating experience and the managerial competencies of a firm or of a whole industry may be rendered obsolete. The psychological stress may be substantial. The new technique may have been established as superior elsewhere—no matter. For the decision-maker, particularly one ensconced in the obsolete mode of operation, an important uncertainty remains about whether *he* can handle the transformed process and can survive in a position of authority after the transformation has been made.

INVENTION: SETTING THE GOAL OF TRANSFORMATION

Invention, First Phase of the System. Before the decision is made to transform, those higher processes that are the goal of transformation must themselves have been tried and their superiority established; innovation must precede transformation. And before that, what is novel in those processes must have been conceived, must have existed as an idea in a man's mind. It had first to be invented. If the final phase of the system of economic progress is the transformation to higher processes, the first phase is invention.

Invention is understood here broadly to include the novel idea, which widens the range of human vision or choice and adds to the potentialities for rational action, whether it is embodied in a new question, a new conception, a new hypothesis, a new choice, a new form of action. Invention, thus understood, can occur at any level of social activity, in science, in linguistics, in politics, in techniques. And it may or may not be relevant to economic progress.

Invention, an Individual Activity. Invention is a product of the creative mind of an individual. Many can shout in unison and march in step. Thousands can work en masse as a disciplined machine. One can replace another on the assembly line or on the battle line, or in digging up the facts, or in mastering techniques, or in applying information. But only the individual by himself, of himself, within himself can have a new idea. No

---

systems. Intuitively and quite correctly the military man feels that a change in weapons portends a change in the arrangements of his society." From "A Case Study of Innovation," *Engineering and Science Monthly,* Vol. 13, No. 7 (April 1950), pp. 5–11.

one can force another to think a thought that has not yet been thought, nor instruct another concerning the undiscovered, nor indoctrinate him on what is yet to be conceived.

If creativity is uniquely a quality of the individual, then what can the study of society have to do with the process of invention?

Creativity, a Quality of Human Populations. First it must be insisted upon, that while an invention is the act of a unique individual, creativity is a human quality that exists (like every human quality) at least incipiently in every man and among all representative groups of men. The capacity to invent, the capacity to make a creative contribution is a function of human populations, that is, of the numbers of individuals composing any group. If, for example, no inventions (or an insignificant creative contribution) are forthcoming from any substantial population covering a range of representative types, for instance, the peasant population in southern Italy, the working class in France, the native peoples of the Congo, the presumption is not that these groups are characterized by some genetic lack but that social organization has failed to stimulate or to offer an outlet to that group's inherent inventive-creative capacities: the failure is in the social organization. The argument that the magnitude of the creative *potential* is a function of human numbers and that the capacity to capitalize on that creative potential is a function of social organization is one which will reappear in Chapter 11 when the relationship of population size to economic progress will be considered.

Social Organization and the Preconditions of Invention. The question is this: What is the relationship between social organization and the individual's exercise of his creative capacities?

For one thing, the creative man needs a problem. Nothing is found that is not looked for. No problem is solved until it is posed. To creative man, society gives a focus for his inquiry, sometimes directly, in the name of necessity. Out of the floods of the Nile, geometry was created in Egypt. Out of the terrors of war came electronics, synthetics, jet propulsion, atomic power in our time. Sometimes society asks the question through the lure of profit or the promise of reward. The woman's role in the American family and her control over the American purse has something to do with our native outpouring of household gadgets and machines. And when the creative man selects his own problem, he does so by reference to values that prevail in place and time. Shall he concern himself with the number of angels or with the number of electrons that dance at the point of his needle?

The creative man needs more than a focus of inquiry. How far one can go depends on where one begins. What can be acquired depends on what is already possessed. Who would invent the stove knowing nothing of fire? The individual's capacity to advance knowledge depends on his mastery of the known. And his acquisition of this mastery depends to a considerable degree on the institutions of society. Men are educated in the schools and on the job. Education is opened to some and closed to others because the particular forms and institutions of a society are what they are. It is through social organizations that ideas are spread, that the data of experience are gathered, that the cumulus of fact, thought, and theory is systematized and made available.

The creative man needs a dialogue with his peers. He needs stimulus, and sympathy, and sometimes a certain peace. The social environment may permit him neither stimulus nor peace.

The creative man needs time—time to wonder, time to contemplate, time to figure things out. And time costs. Costs must be covered. He needs to experiment. There are many levels of experimentation: testing in the lab, digging beneath the earth, diving under the ocean surface, working on the job, calculating at home with a yellow pad and a sharp pointed pencil. To experiment entails costs, in talent and effort, in time and materials, in errors and failures. These costs must be paid. Whether resources are forthcoming, and the basis upon which they might be forthcoming to defray those costs, depends partly upon the form of economic and social organization.

At issue are not only those supports that condition the creative effort. At issue also is the receptivity of a society to that which is new and runs counter to the established way. Pitted against invention and innovation are habits, inertia, vested interests, and orthodoxies. Social and economic organization will, to a significant extent, determine the form and force of these resistances.

Knowledge as a Parameter of Invention. We narrow the term invention to consider only *practical* inventions, inventions that relate specifically to technical practice and economic progress.

The capacity of the inventive individual to make a technically significant contribution depends partly on his grasp of relevant bodies of knowledge. This might include knowledge concerning technical experience and practice, concerning social and economic institutions, concerning the environment of industrial operations, and concerning the nature of physical phenomena.

Here the problem for social organization is twofold: first, to enable the individual to acquire the mastery he needs over existing relevant bodies of knowledge, and second, to provide for the systematic and progressive development of these bodies of knowledge. Of these, the most highly evolved and perhaps the one most generally relevant to invention is that of "natural science."

Science and Invention. For our purpose, science may be understood as that body of data which describes and seeks tentatively to explain physical phenomena in terms of postulated general relationships. These generalizations of science are subject to test through observation or experiment and, in fact, are constantly being tested, modified, developed, and broadened, generally by highly trained, specialized professionals. To acquire the mastery needed to comprehend the natural sciences and to stay informed with respect to the multitudinous and rapid changes within each of them requires professional training and systematic effort.

It is often alleged that invention today absolutely requires a knowledge of physical "science" and a mastery of its language and method, as if the "old time" inventiveness deriving from more commonplace experience or from ad hoc probing had now exhausted itself. In this view, only the larder of "science" is full; all the other shelves in the cupboard of experience and thought are bare of inventive potentiality.[3]

This is not a new notion. In the sixteenth century Sir Francis Bacon denigrated the invention of printing, of gunpowder, and even of the compass as having been "lighted upon by chance . . . a kind of hunting by scent rather than by science." All that was to be changed by science. "My way of discovering" proclaimed Bacon "performs everything by the surest rules and demonstrations."

But, new or old, this notion of invention as essentially a derivative of science, is not in accord with the facts. For many of the problems that cry out for inventive solutions, the methods and data of science are only of peripheral relevance. Some of the major problems of science itself, such as the effective communication of research data, are essentially organizational. Some of those inventions-innovations of our time that have had the greatest impact on economic progress—for instance, the piggy-back rail carrier, the container ship, and the supermarket—are derived from experience and knowledge that is almost entirely entrepreneurial. Neverthe-

---

[3] For a typical instance, the words of Mr. Earl Stevenson, Chairman of the Board of Arthur D. Little, Inc.:

"I think that the great lesson of the last two decades is that major technological advances are impossible without a deeper understanding of nature. Here I always go back in thought to a very good friend of mine whom I greatly admired and enjoyed in his older years, one of the Stanley brothers, the inventor of the steam-driven automobile. It is simply inconceivable to think of the Stanleys, who never went beyond the eighth grade, trying to perfect a gas turbine.

"They also made a great contribution to photography. They developed the first dry plate. They would have been utterly unable even to understand or approach the problem of technicolor, or of color photography.

"So industry is today trying to exploit nature in ways that are more and more subtle . . . The shift from the inventive approach to basic understanding through scientific research."

From "The Role of Patents in Industrial Progress," *The Patent, Trademark and Copyright Journal of Research and Education*, Vol. 5, Conference Number, 1961, p. 85.

less, as will be shown in the next chapter, to an unprecedented degree in recent decades, the data of science are being accumulated and are being systematically utilized by trained professionals in order to solve problems of technology.

COMMUNICATION: LINKING SCIENCE-INVENTION-INNOVATION-TRANSFORMATION

The Communication of Invention. Except in the special case where the inventor is himself in a position to apply his invention, before a creative contribution can have any impact on the transformation choice, it must be communicated. This is liable to be complex and difficult, even when the invention is made within a given organization and the task is simply to communicate it from one part of that organization to another—for example, from the researchers in the laboratories of an industrial corporation or of a military establishment to those in the firm or in the military hierarchy who are in a position to apply the invention.

Within the military there is official recognition of the need for technical innovation. Military research and development chiefs and civilian advisors emphasize the need for radically new developments. . . . The formal channel by which the ideas of individuals may enter the military is the military screening offices. The major research and development agencies of each of the three services have such offices. . . . The function of these agencies is to receive and screen . . . and to pass on to appropriate technical personnel those ideas which seem to have most merit.

How much innovation goes through this channel? We interviewed 14 men from 7 screening offices which receive from 40 to 2000 ideas a month. The chief question asked of each man was whether he could identify an invention submitted through his office and later used by the military. *In not one case could he do so.*

For this reason we can conclude that as a means of helping the military to use resources of invention . . . these screening offices are virtually a hindrance . . . a wall, rather than a screen. They protect the main body of military R and D from the disturbance of outside inventors and inventions. . . .

In brief, there are significant resources of innovation for which there is an expressed need, and there is a screening organization whose main function is to serve as a buffer against them. . . . The rate of rejection of ideas submitted internally through formal channels is as great as the rate of rejection of ideas submitted from the outside.[4]

The complexity and difficulty of communication will be so much the greater when the task of transmission is not within an organization, but

[4] Donald A. Schon, "Champions for Radical New Inventions," *Harvard Business Review*, March–April 1963, pp. 79–80.

from organization to organization, or from industry to industry, or from economic sector to economic sector, or from national economy to national economy.

Consider, then, the general problem of communication. Each one of us is in great part a universe of activity and thought closed unto itself, only partially and occasionally receptive to the thought or observant of the activity of another. In order that a new idea and its related complex of new or unfamiliar knowledge be communicated even between two individuals, the one must desire to communicate, must have the skill to articulate, and must make the requisite effort. The other must be ready to listen, receptive, able to understand and assimilate. Between the two there must be a common language or at least its rudiments, so that unfamiliar and possibly complex meanings can be conveyed. If there is not the will or the capacity to communicate directly, the new idea or invention might be conveyed through observation of its practice. This requires that the invention be made sufficiently manifest in action, and that there be attentive observers, able to understand and reconstruct.

Mark it well, the communication of new ideas, new conceptions, new understandings, inventions, new ways of doing things, between individuals fixed in their ways and intent upon their separate objectives is difficult and rare. The intent to communicate is the exception rather than the rule; the more common motivation, indeed, is to hide and obscure. Nor need there be a common language. If there is a common language, it is likely to be inadequate for the task of conveying what is intended, for the very novelty of an idea sets it outside the common points of reference by which communication occurs. Even if the inventor wants to communicate and has the language that explains, others need not want to listen nor have the time and will to attend. These are the difficulties of communicating a new idea even between individuals, face to face, man to man. In fact the problem is far more difficult, for the communication of invention is rarely from man to man, from inventor to innovator, from source to destination directly. Rather it is a transmission of an idea "through channels," infiltrating, drifting, passed along through the layers upon layers of organization. Beyond the barriers that separate individual from individual, it must cross those which set apart groups and communities.

Communication also can be understood as a process and a choice. There are motivations to communicate and motivations to withhold. There are circumstances and techniques that facilitate the transmission of invention. There are costs that seriously impede and activities and policies that designedly frustrate the movement of ideas and information, for instance, the security classification on military research or the practices of industrial secrecy.

Communication: Linking Each Phase of the System. The problem of communication has been developed here by reference to the difficulties of linking invention to innovation. Invention cannot become a parameter of innovation unless the knowledge of invention is effectively communicated. Similarly the data of scientific research and other relevant knowledge cannot become the parameters of invention unless they are effectively communicated. Nor can innovation become a parameter of the transformation choice unless the knowledge of technical requisites and results, and of costs and benefits, is communicated. In each case there must be motivation to make information available and/or to seek for it. And there must also exist institutions that provide a capacity to transmit and to comprehend complex information.

SUMMARY: THE SYSTEM OF ECONOMIC PROGRESS

In very broad strokes the constituent elements of a system of economic progress, under any form of economic organization, has been traced.

The starting point of the system is invention. But invention also has its parameters: (1) in the degree to which those who possess creative capacities have been educated to a mastery of techniques or of the data of science, (2) in the pressures of social need and in the lures of industrial opportunity, (3) in the chance to experiment, (4) in the inducements to persevere in the inventive effort, and (5) in the organization and availability of the data of science and of other relevant bodies of information.

Within the framework that feeds the inventive capacity, sets its limits, influences its direction, and provides its outlets, the inventor invents. A new technique, allegedly superior, is conceived and is developed. If the invention is not withheld, but is communicated, and if those with the command over economic resources can understand its implications, can evaluate its worth, and are interested in putting it to use, then the invention becomes a parameter of the innovative decision.

Within his own complex parameters of choice, of which available invention is but one, the innovator innovates. He incorporates the invention, the newly conceived technique or product, into the context of productive operations. He tries it out. He sees whether it works. And if it does, or if, even through failure, it establishes potentialities, it may then become a parameter of the more general economic choice: the choice to transform.

Provided that the value of the innovation has been communicated, and that the decision-maker has been persuaded of its value or has observed its success, and provided the other preconditions of transformation are favorable, then the new technique will replace previously established practice. The result is economic progress. Whether a society will capitalize on the potentialities of such progress depends on a capacity based on socio-political skills and economic organization to put to use what is available for use.

This chapter has been concerned with the components of *any* system of economic progress. But there are different systems for the organization of these components. The chapter that follows will broadly survey the evolution of the systems of economic progress in Western history.

Chapter 10

The Changing System of Economic Progress

ECONOMIC PROGRESS IN TRADITIONAL SOCIETIES

The Transmission of Technology in Traditional Societies. In the traditional society, where the dominant social value is continuity and the primary individual concern is status, techniques and crafts are learned at the workbench or on the farm, not as methods understood but as mysteries practiced. They are acquired by son from father, by apprentice from master, through imitation and observation, by way of the skin, so to speak, into the instincts. The crafts are bits in the great mosaic that constitutes a way of life. They are one with the way of praying, the way of authority, the way of magic, of manners and morals, of ethics and law, of caste and class, all part of a tightly woven cloth where a single strand torn out might unravel and destroy the fabric entirely. In the traditional society, all these are given, not to be rationalized or planned, nor viewed as alternatives open to choice—but to be accepted and lived.

Those societies where the techniques of the craftsman are of the same self-perpetuating nature as the doctrine of the priest are not exceptional. They still prevail in many parts of the world, and there are aspects of every modern society where tradition remains as the organizing principle. Prior to the thirteenth century, except for the brief Hellenic interregnum, where Greek reason flared, flickered, and dimmed, these were the only visible forms of social organization.

Technological Achievement in Traditional Societies. Yet, in the vast spaces of history where technology evidently was fixed into a way of life, and the way of life evidently was fixed as a ritual, and social forms were shored up against all change, there was, nevertheless, change. There were discoveries, inventions, innovations. Some were fundamental, profoundly altering social organization and the scope of individual experience. Fire was mastered. Minerals and metals, copper, brass, bronze, gold, iron, were found and mined, smelted and fabricated The wheel was developed. Stone was quarried, hewed, shaped. The kiln was used to make the brick. The horse, the cow, sheep and oxen, the chicken and the hawk, the dog—were domesticated, trained, bred. The cultivation of crops—agriculture, horticulture—came into being. The ax, the saw, the plane were made. Leather was tanned, dyed and worked. Building techniques evolved and with them the marvelous forms of architecture that raised the temples in Egypt and in Guatemala and the great cathedrals of Europe. For the farm, there came the plow and the harrow and the scythe. For the horse, there was the horseshoe, the saddle, the bridle. For the soldier, there was the spear, the bow, the cross-bow, the armor, the chariot, the catapult, the fortress, and all the strategies of war. There was the ship, capable of crossing oceans and navigating its way between distant points on earth. There was the weaving of cloth, and its dyeing. There was paint and paper. There was the written alphabet. There was arithmetic, geometry, surveying, astronomy. There was the abacus and the calendar. All these came when, ostensibly, there seemed no interest in invention, no opportunity for experiment, no allowance for innovation. Evidently men under all circumstances are driven to try to understand their physical environment, and evidently even ignorant men in tradition-bound societies may be endowed with the insight to understand and with the capability to master their environment.

Civilization after civilization, society after society, has emerged slowly or in a sudden bursting forth. It is curious how ignorant we are of the process through which they achieved their complex social and technological organizations. By the time such societies stood strong and powerful enough to catch the eye of history, the seed had grown into the tree, the bark had thickened and the bud was gone.

> Sans ce bourgeon, qui n'a l'air de rien,
> Qui ne semble rien, tout cela ne serait que du bois mort
> Et le bois mort sera jeté au feu.

By then the beginning and the unfolding were already lost in myth. From wherever it had come, the form of social organization, the way of living, was already set in the iron of tradition. The energies of its people were concentrated on expanding its domain and holding to its heritage. The magic that creates had become the ritual that preserves.

Discovery, as Revelation. If the beginnings of these societies are lost in myth, the myth itself is instructive. It provides a clue of sorts to what did happen. In those myths it is God or the gods who gave to man his law and his techniques. Prometheus, who revealed the secret of technique, did so in his mercy and at his cost. In the myth, the origin of these things belongs to magic, to revelation. And in fact, in actuality, in our day as in theirs, the inventive and creative quality is outside the bounds of logic, and has the quality of magic. And those insights where man's vision leaps through the surfaces of knowledge to true discovery: those insights, now as then, have the aspect of revelation. But to uninstructed man of the prescientific age, with his mystic predispositions and his sense of the supernatural, the experience of an insight that dips down into the unknown and draws up what was not seen before, *was* revelation. Truth spoke, and man heard. If man saw the value of the wheel and the fire, the seed and the harvest, the horse and the sheep, it must have been because God had pointed His finger. Discovery came because the veils had been lifted, and a vision was revealed; but mystic revelation has built-in limits, and follows its own peculiar, descending dialectic.

Once the Word is given, it is never to be denied, contradicted, or transcended. Once it has been given, all that remains is to make the Word manifest. The peak, the hour of truth—is always behind. The descent begins at the instant of revelation. After the prophets come the rabbis; after the Torah comes the Talmud, and the Mishnah, generations drinking upon the Truth without renewing it, interpretation upon interpretation obscuring the first clear vision. After Christ come the apostles, and the disciples, and the fathers, and the Church, and the priests, in descending order. After Aristotle came the academies, the doctors, the schoolmen, the vulgarizers, the scholastics, subordinated to the authority (and finally to the misted memory) of the Greek's conception, for more than a thousand years. After revelation, religion. After discovery, authority. After the premises born of vision, the logic of their fulfillment. The free leap becomes the ritual dance.

Thus in all earlier societies at that stage of advancement and self-awareness where they could, so to speak, explain themselves, the golden age was seen, not in the future but in the distant past. History was conceived as decay, degeneration, and decline. Only in the seventeenth century in Western Europe did the notion of "progress" dawn. The idea of progress as a natural function of historical time belongs entirely to the modern epoch. It was foreign to the conception and foreign to the experience of previous eras. Earlier civilizations had developed in discrete, isolated, unaccountable creative outbursts, that left a residue for ordinary men to gather and use, to worship and fear, to organize and ritualize, to learn and remember. When at last the content of the vessels, passed for so long from hand to hand and generation to generation, was exhausted, or lost its flavor, or was forgotten or soured—then the people dispersed and the civilization withered.

ECONOMIC PROGRESS IN THE ERA OF INDIVIDUALISM

Emergent Individualism. Its genesis is entirely obscure. But in Italy during the thirteenth century the form of a new kind of society could be discerned. It conceived itself as a return to, as a rebirth of, an ancient way; but in fact it contained the germ of perpetual regeneration, the capacity, unprecedented in history, for sustained and cumulative development.

Individualism was its pervasive element. It expressed, it evolved from, and it made manifest the ethic, the capacity for reason, the creativity, the aspiration, the outlook of the self-interested, self-accountable, self-seeking, self-contained individual. It succeeded, at least partially and occasionally, in accommodating the expression of free, individual choice with the prerequisites of social order, and in harnessing the power of unbridled individual ambition and imagination to the cumulative development of societies of unprecedented wealth and power.

The individualism of the age appeared in its philosophy, its art, its politics, its religion, its science, and in its system of economic progress. It is the last two of these that will concern us.

Scientific Inquiry in an Era of Individualism. There has been a craving common to the people of all societies for answers concerning the nature of their environment, concerning the physical context of the individual life: questions of how, of why, of where, of whence. Where did this world of phenomena come from? Why does it follow its ageless patterns? What will happen? When? For those throughout history who have been able to provide acceptable answers to these questions status and homage has been due. On a par with the authority of the temporal powers was the authority of those who possessed the key to the mysteries. In the modern era, in the place of the prophet and oracle, of the priest and the philosopher, stands the scientist as he who explains the cosmos.

And the scientist not only stands in the place where these others once stood, but he occupies that place for somewhat the same reasons that they did; his motivations are not unlike theirs—to possess authority through knowledge, to gain fame, homage, to make an imprint upon time, or to satisfy a hunger for truth and fulfill a capacity for creative insight.

Nor can we suppose that those who created modern science were more or less disinterested, more or less dedicated, more or less insightful or more or less intelligent than those who in another age prophesied, philosophized, or interpreted the law.

That which made science different in this era of individualism was precisely the element of *individualism*. For, in this newly emerged society, the fixed point of all reference and the final arbiter of truth was simply the judgment of the individual. In another time, the controverted issue had to be resolved by reference to the revelation of Christ, to the writings of the Fathers, to the words of Aristotle or Plato, to the law as it had been given to man and to the judges. But now the controversy must be resolved through the choice and reason of the individual, must be resolved, in a sense, by reference to the judgment of any individual who cared to judge. In the new scheme of things it was for the individual to doubt, and for the individual to accept. There was no other arbiter. This perpetual right of every individual to challenge, to doubt, to accept or reject, on his own, generation after generation, constituted the new element.

In the seventeenth century, the Marquis of Halifax observed:

In former times . . . the men in black made learning such a sin in the laity that for fear of offending they made a conscience of being able to read. But now the world is grown saucy, and expecteth reasons, and good ones too, before they give up their own opinions to other men's dictates.[1]

The "method" of the new science evolved as a means of establishing the credibility of the claims and the generalizations made by scientists before the free inquiry of any reasoning individual. For this, it required that the theories of science perpetually be put to the test, that is, required to predict natural or experimentally contrived events. When predictions worked, the generalizations or "general principles" were said to "explain" the event. Whenever predictions failed, theories lost some of their credibility. The "method" of science also recognized the right, indeed, the obligation, of the inquiring individual to challenge those claims to credibility by offering observations and experimental data in refutation of established theories.

Science as an Aristocratic Preoccupation. Scientific inquiry through the mid-nineteenth century was essentially a leisure class occupation, a hobby for the aristocracy, those who had the wherewithal and the time to devote themselves to objectives without monetary value. For them it was a great adventure, a noble game. Those prodigies of science who had not sufficient private incomes to support their pursuits required the patronage of great lords, or sinecures from the State, or the subvention of the Crown. And subsidies were granted to them in the same way and for the same reason that subsidies were given to encourage composers or painters or philosophers, or to support the ballet or the opera.

The marvelously sustained and vastly productive endeavor of that science was without utilitarian pretention. It was without the crass incentives of profit and loss. It did not operate under the rational economic calculus, nor was there price to guide its allocation of resources. Indeed, when the "spirit of enterprise" was pervasive and the practical orientation was supreme, as De Tocqueville observed it in the United States in the early nineteenth century, there was little science or little interest in science.

[1] Christopher Hill, "Emergence of Scientific Method," *The Listener,* June 7, 1962, p. 985.

Technological Achievement Independent of Scientific Advance. The scientific inquiry was organized and was carried on in a universe of values and motivations and social relationships quite removed from that of business enterprise. And during these centuries, the great advances in science and the great progress of technology constituted parallel lines of endeavor, independently generated and with little overlap. The relationship between the knowledge of science and practical invention was tenuous and rare.

. . . before (1860) the facts and theories discovered and invented by scientists contributed little to progress and technological innovation. Despite persistent rumors to the contrary, neither the Greeks, nor Galileo, nor Newton, nor even Black and Lavoisier taught the great technological innovators very much of what they needed to know about nature. Astronomy, dynamics and inorganic chemistry—the principle fields in which these famous men made their most notable contributions—did not prove very relevant to major technological advances.[2]

The Organization of Economic Progress. Economic progress through the mid-nineteenth century was the product of predominantly decentralized market-directed economies—a form of economic organization where individual choice was pre-eminent. Profits were the incentive to invention, to innovation, to transformation. Organizational skills and technological capacities acquired outside of the system of formal education, on the job, in small independent enterprises each with its integral technical operation, supported the evolution of a bourgeois power that eventually became predominant in Western Europe and in the United States.

Invention was based on a technological mastery acquired on the job. The extreme dispersion of independent choice and of technical responsibilities in the firm and on the job created opportunity for experiment and innovation. Every factory and shop could be a kind of laboratory. Any entrepreneur who chose to run the risk and pay the cost could experiment with products and processes, and test his hypothesis at will. The entrepreneur-inventor, the inventive entrepreneur, was characteristic. Out of this came a stream of inventions-innovations, such as the steam engine, the internal combustion engine, the cotton gin, the locomotive, the steamship, the photograph and the moving picture, the automobile, the Bessemer and the open-hearth furnace, the concept and techniques for standardization of parts, textile machinery including the fully automatic power loom, automatic control and feedback devices, such as the flyball governor and the thermostat, the vulcanization of rubber, and an endless

---

[2] Thomas S. Kuhn, from the symposium titled *The Rate and Direction of Inventive Activity* (Princeton, New Jersey: National Bureau of Economic Research, 1962), p. 454.

proliferation of mechanical devices, few of which relied on the data or derived from the concepts and theories of science.

ECONOMIC PROGRESS IN THE AGE OF ORGANIZATION

The Organizational Revolution. At the turn of the twentieth century the individual *qua* individual, deciding and acting on his own, had begun to retreat from center stage. Initiative and choice were shifted from the multiplicity of individuals acting on their own to the organized group. The individual participated through the group and at the behest of the group. The group was sometimes voluntary and autonomous, like the labor union or the great corporate enterprise. The group was sometimes an agency of the political power operating under the sanction and coercive power of the State. But increasingly the individual was submerged in a larger entity.

The large economic organization has by no means wholly superseded the small enterprise, but it has become dominant in the modern economy of Europe and the United States. And this transition from an economy where the individual was essentially a free agent in a competitive market to one where the individual participated through the activities of the great organization has profoundly affected the system of economic progress.

Research and Development in the Economy of Organization. There has evolved in the economy of organization a new technique called Research and Development (R & D), which uses professionals trained in the physical sciences for the creative solution of practical problems and for promoting the advance of technology through the systematic organization of invention and transformation. Science has been integrated into the system of economic progress and, as a consequence, since the turn of the century, the most important new technologies (in chemistry, in electronics, and in synthetic materials) have derived from the concepts and data of science. Coincidently with the emergence of an economy of organization, science-based technologies have become pre-eminent.

The role of Research and Development in the organizational economy may be illustrated by the record of events in the United States. In 1920, R & D expenditures in the United States totaled about $115 million.[3] By 1930 R & D expenditures had increased to about $330 million. By 1940 they had increased to about $690 million. By 1950 they had increased to

[3] Vannevar Bush, *Science, The Endless Frontier* (Washington, D.C.: United States Government Printing Office, 1945), p. 80. Covers R & D expenditures from 1920 to 1940. Subsequent surveys indicate that Bush's estimates were too low and, consequently, they have been adjusted upward in line with later series.

about $3 billion.[4] By 1960 R & D expenditures were running at the rate of $14 billion.[5] By 1964 they were in the neighborhood of $20 billion.

This R & D activity, moreover, is a function of large organizations. For example, in 1959 in the United States, 94 percent of the total R & D performed in industry was by companies with more than 1,000 employees; and 86 percent was performed by companies with more than 5,000 employees. Four companies with 7 percent of the total net sales for manufacturing companies performed 22 percent; twenty companies with 18 percent of the total net sales performed 54 percent. A hundred companies with 41 percent of the total net sales for all manufacturing companies performed 81 percent of the R & D by private companies.[6]

The causes and some of the consequences of this change will be developed later when the three forms of economic organization are evaluated as instruments of economic progress.

SUMMARY

Previously in traditional, prescientific societies discovery and invention occurred evidently in the occasional and sporadic outthrust of genius, which assumed the aspect of revelation, of truth beyond challenge.

The characteristic of European post-Renaissance societies was a free and reasoning individualism, which gave form to the subsequent development of science and of technology. In science there evolved a universal system of independent inquiry, with postulated generalizations open to perpetual test through inferential prediction. The advance of science was matched by unprecedented and cumulative advances in the practical technologies. But, between the rapid progress of science and of technology there was no clear connection. Invention-innovation-transformation were based on the knowledge acquired, and on the independence implicit in the small man-sized firm under the control of an individual entrepreneur.

By the end of the nineteenth century, the economy of large organization had begun to displace the economy of decentralized markets and individualized choice. In the economy of large organizations, inventive-innovative activity could no longer be an occasional function of the en-

[4] U. S. Department of Defense, Research and Development Board, "Research and Development Expenditures in the United States and Cost of Research and Development Performed by Government, Industry, and Colleges and Universities—1941–1952." April 1953.
[5] National Science Foundation, *Reviews of Data on Research and Development*, April 1962, NSF 33 (Washington, D.C.).
[6] National Science Foundation, *Funds For Research and Development in Industry*, 1959, NSF 62-3 (Washington, D.C.), pp. 17–22.

trepreneur. As "Research and Development" it became the specialized task of highly trained professionals.

The emergence of Research and Development as a specialized operation in the economy of large organizations has a number of consequences. Most important is the exploitation of the knowledge and competencies of science for the task of advancing the practical technologies.

Chapter 11

Population and Progress: A Footnote

Population Increase Supposedly A Barrier to Economic Progress. Economic progress has been conceived here as occurring through the development and application of superior techniques. The last five chapters have studied those elements that enter into the determination of the rate of economic progress. However, one variable frequently put forward as having a negative impact on economic progress has not been discussed here: the size of population. All have heard the perennial alarm, sounded by political leaders, journalists, and social scientists alike, that observed or predicted increases in population in particular societies and in world society will abort economic development and turn progress into regress. According to the rationale of this Malthusian prognosis, population increase reduces the amount of land (or other of the fixed or declining resources of nature) available per man, consequently lowers productivity, and in the end destroys the capacity of society to sustain itself.

Malthusian Theory in Open Societies. Before attempting to deal with the logic of theory, a precautionary question may be raised with respect to its application. The Malthusian theory was conceived as applying to a closed society, e.g., to a given set of resources and to a given population, producing for its own consumption. The world as a whole constitutes such a closed society. But can the theory also be applied to population change in specific open societies, in the sense of those that exchange goods and services (or even populations) with other societies? If, for example, the population density of the State of Delaware gives us no concern, since the State of Delaware is open to trade with the plentiful agricultural lands of the American West, need we have Malthusian shivers about Puerto Rico, which is equally and in the same sense open to Western agriculture? England, for example, is an open society; its population has, through trade, access to the lands of Australia, Canada, New Zealand, to the oil of Arabia, to the plantations of Malay, etc. How then, by reference to man/natural resource ratio, would we reckon the impact of an increasing population density in England? And if it is decided that the theory cannot be applied with respect to the increasing population density of England, since England is an open society, then must the theory be equally rejected for Germany? for Japan? for India? We will beg this question, and turn rather to consider the validity of the Malthusian prognosis in the prediction of historical event.

The Failure of Malthusian Theory in the Test of Prediction. This Malthusian notion has the virtue, rare among social hypotheses, of being so framed that it is subject to test through prediction. For a century and a half the theory has been used and is repeatedly being used to predict and to prophesy. For a century and a half its predictions have failed. Events have not followed the path indicated by its premises. For the world, there has been a rapid increase both in population and in per capita output. If one compares country with country, region with region, one finds that there are poor countries which are densely populated and rich countries that are densely populated. There are poor countries that are sparsely populated and rich countries that are sparsely populated. But, over the whole, no inverse correlation appears between densities and per capita outputs; nor does there appear to be any inverse correlation, country by country, between relative rates of population increase and relative rates of economic development.

In spite of this failure in prediction, the a priori logic of the theory is so strong that it continues to be accepted, and policies continue to be based upon it.

Why Prediction Failed. The logic of the Malthusian theory is indeed strong. An increase in population does decrease the per capita availability of natural resources. That disadvantage in production will, presumably, be most clearly felt inasmuch as the population of a given society, for whatever reason, is specifically dependent on a given quantity of land or some other natural resources. Then why has the theory failed in prediction?

The usual explanation of failure is that the decline in productivity caused by increasing population has been offset by an increase in productivity caused by the development and introduction of superior techniques. If this explanation is acceptable, does it validate Malthusian theory, that is, does it validate the proposition that an increase in population of itself is detrimental to economic progress? It would, if we could believe that, great as the increase in productivity has been, it would have been even greater if population had remained stable, and greater still if population had declined. The Malthusian theory, in other words, remains valid if the development and assimilation of superior techniques is exogenous to the magnitude of population. But is it? Or is the capacity to create and to invent also a function of the size of population?

Population as a Pool of Creative Talent. Economists generally have looked upon population as a quantity of work instruments, in effect as numbers of tools. If the number of tools is increased in combination with fixed natural resources, output per tool declines. The Malthusian conclusions followed *if* with respect to the level of productivity, human populations can be understood simply as a number of working instruments, each able to exert a certain energy, each shaped by training for a certain level or type of skill. But it has been shown here that human populations have another relationship to productivity. Increases in productivity from the introduction of superior techniques, have their source, necessarily, in invention; invention arises from the inventive contribution of individuals; numbers of individuals mean numbers of creative men and numbers of potential inventors. The capacity for creative contribution is also a function of human populations. Population is not only a fund of human work instruments, it is also a pool of creative talent. And when population increases this increases not only the quantity of labor-energy and skill that can be put to work in combination with available natural resources. It also increases the pool of creative abilities, and hence the sheer capacities for invention-innovation-transformation.

Consider the anomalies that arise if one should suppose that the capacity for invention is not related to the magnitude of population. This would be quite the same as supposing—indeed, it would precisely be supposing —that recent advances in science, inventions, and technology would have been the same if the state of California and its population were blotted out, or if the United States and its population had been eliminated. Very clearly the level of science and technology would not have been the same without the contributions of these population groups. England, Germany, Russia, the United States, and California describe representative human populations that have contributed and will continue to contribute (as every representative human group can and should contribute) to the world advance of science and technology.

The increase in the size of human population, therefore, seems to have a double function: on the one hand it changes the man/natural resource ratio in a manner detrimental to economic progress, and, on the other hand, it increases the pool of creative talent that is an essential prerequisite for accelerating the rate of scientific advance and technological development. The one effect is negative for economic progress. The other effect can be positive. The two are joint functions of population change. The record of history suggests that the contribution of an incremental population to economic progress can greatly outweigh its detrimental effects through the man/natural resource ratio, *provided social and economic organization realizes upon the creative-inventive potential* of that population. That is a big proviso. There are societies where the creative potential is suffocated, where masses are bound down by ignorance or dogmatic authority to the level of working instruments, of skilled animals and nothing more, and where the power of tradition bars the transformation to higher processes. When such is the case, population increase can only have a negative effect on productivity, and the Malthusian dictum would seem still to hold. Such societies might be well advised to check their increases in population until they have devised the means of realizing the creative potentialities of their own people and of utilizing the technical advances that are universally available.

Population Increase Limiting Investment in Education. Consider a common case. The father is the sole breadwinner of a family in Madrid. He works as a clerk and earns the equivalent of $80 a month, out of which he is obliged to support himself, his wife, and his twelve children. His income is such that he cannot do more than sustain his family, and all of his children are obliged to leave school for work as soon as it is possible for them to find jobs. If he had had a small family of, say, one or two children, he might have been able to support their education, and perhaps to have enabled them not only to make themselves more productive, but also, eventually to make a creative contribution to science and technology. This illustrates a common dilemma in many poor countries, and particularly where the parents are responsible for the children's education. Out of a given level of current income, less will be available to invest in the education of the new generations depending on the size of the oncoming generation. The choice may be between a smaller, better-educated population and a larger less-educated population. This is an important choice. Though it has nothing to do with the Malthusian man/natural resource ratio, it does relate to the capacity of a society to realize the creative potentials of its people and to develop the institutional means for assimilating and utilizing the advances made available by world science and technology.

Chapter 12

Decentralized Market-Direction and the Organization of Economic Progress

In this and the two following chapters, the three economic forms will be compared as instruments for the organization of economic progress.

The characteristics of a particular form of economic organization will sometimes be the same with respect to the efficient utilization of resources as they are to the effective organization of invention, innovation, and transformation. What has been already said, for example, concerning *motivation* in the "managerial" or "engineering" choices (where efficiency is the criterion) in the three forms of economic organization would apply equally to motivation in the choice to innovate or to transform (where progress is the criterion). In the following, we will avoid going over the same ground and will confine ourselves to those characteristics of economic organization that have a peculiarly significant or unique relation to economic progress.

THE CAPACITY FOR INVENTION

The Small Firm as an Instrument for Self-Education. For invention, a first requirement is that the creative individual be educated to a mastery over relevant bodies of knowledge. The nature and extent of that "education" will determine the potential range of invention.

The decision-making, action-taking entity in the decentralized market-directed economy is the firm, small enough to be subject to the full and direct control of the individual entrepreneur. The economy includes a very large number of such firms, each one an instrument of the knowledge and thought and ambitions of an individual. Hence, necessarily, the processes of the economy are broken down into financing-producing-transforming-merchandising-selling integrals, each shaped to the capacities of an individual. Each entity embodies an organization and a technology that an individual can control, and therefore can comprehend as a rational whole, including the parameters relevant to choice, the techniques, and the interaction and interdependence of elements involved in converting inputs into a product. What can be comprehended and controlled by the entrepreneur can also be learned about and com-

135

prehended by others who work for the entrepreneur: learned, that is, through observation and experience on the job, as part of the job.

The man-sized operation of the decentralized market economy spontaneously makes possible self-education on the job, through the job, offering to many the opportunity to acquire a composite knowledge of technique, of operating organization, and of output values relevant to significant invention. The clerk who works in the offices of the United States Steel Company can learn to be a clerk, but he cannot possibly learn the techniques of steel-making, or of labor bargaining, or of product merchandising; he cannot learn the "steel business" through his experience and observations on the job. For that matter neither can the President nor anyone else who works in the company learn the business as a whole from experience and observation at a single functional vantage point. It is probable that the individual cannot learn from his work at a single functional vantage point even the rationale of his own activity, or the significance of his role, or the effects of his assignment. The clerk working for the nineteenth-century iron master could possibly, and sometimes did actually master the steel business as a technological-commercial-administrative whole, in all its facets and opportunities and problems, through his observations and his experience on the job.

The potency of man-sized enterprise as an instrument of technically relevant education is shown by the industrial revolution. In the eighteenth and early nineteenth centuries in England, access to extensive resources and access to formal education were the prerogatives of an aristocracy. Excluded from the public schools and universities, it was through their work in the shop and in the factory that the upstart bourgeoisie got the training they needed and acquired that mastery that enabled them to organize, control, and revolutionize industry, and eventually to raise themselves to a position of political dominance. The modern proletariat could never similarly educate itself and thereby raise itself through experience and observation on the job, in the large industrial corporation.

Motivation to Acquire a Mastery Relevant to Invention. Not only does the decentralized market offer to many the opportunity to acquire mastery over techniques and processes. It also drives individuals to avail themselves of that opportunity. The way up is through independent initiative: the necessary, inevitable upward step is to go into business for yourself. In order to rise, the individual has to learn the business—the whole business. What matters is not to please your superior, or to avoid the enmity of your colleagues. What matters for the ambitious is to learn to run a business, to master the financial, the managerial, the technological, the mercantile, all the circumstances of the market and the tricks of the trade—so that somehow, sometime, you can run a business by yourself.

On the basis of that mastery and his imagination, the individual may invent and through the business skills and property he has acquired, he might find the means to transform. The mastery of operations, as a product of business competition, becomes a basis for independent creative thought with respect to the goals, and to the manner and means of economic progress.

Decentralized Choice Builds in Opportunity to Experiment. Invention requires not only a mastery of relevant knowledge. It requires also the opportunity to experiment with techniques, with products, and with processes. Those whose activities are planned for them cannot, while participating in planned activities, experiment. To experiment implies discretionary choice. Experiment proceeds from the right and power to play a hunch on one's own, to put a new idea in practice, to waste resources, to deviate, to try and to fail. Only those who possess discretionary power, who have the prerogative to use resources independently, can experiment. And in the decentralized market this capacity for discretionary choice, and hence for experiment, is more widely dispersed than in any other form of economic organization. It is the virtue of the decentralized market that it offers the broadest opportunity for experiment within the regular operations of the economy, as a part of the very processes of production and distribution. The resources at the disposition of any one experimenter, the range of relationships subject to his control, and hence the range of his experimental opportunities will be relatively narrow and limited. Nevertheless, every factory and shop and farm is potentially a technical laboratory and pilot plant, open to the imagination and daring of an individual. The decentralized market economy thus opens itself to the creativity of the common man.

The Attitudes of Individualism, and Invention. Economic organization, as a social environment, tends to generate particular sets of personal values which, in turn, relate back to the organization of economic activity. This general relationship between the forms of economic organization, social environment and individual values will be developed in Chapters 15 through 18. Here the feedback of values into the organization of economic progress will briefly be considered.

The decentralized market is a place where each is self-responsible, self-concerned, on his own. It is virtually without the element of group activity or state authority. Survival requires expediency. Success requires toughness, drive, judgment, self-sufficiency. The emphasis is pragmatic. It offers no haven for the theoretical and abstract. It rewards the puritan virtues, and vices. Its environment is of a hardheaded, commercially oriented individualism; among the values it generates are those of independence, initiative, scepticism of authority. And these are surely values that are relevant to the inventive activity, for invention uproots the accepted, the conventional, the authoritative; invention is an act of the independent and personal initiative realizing the unique vision of an individual.

But while these values, generated through the environment of decentralized market-direction, give an impetus to technical invention, they are not congenial to the discipline, the sense of the authoritative, and the capacity for abstraction which characterize the scientific enterprise.

INVESTMENT IN SCIENCE, INVENTION, INNOVATION

Implicit Uncertainties and Diffused Benefits of Scientific Research, Invention, and Innovation. In no other types of economic activity are there such uncertainties, or a comparable propensity for the diffusion of responsibilities and benefits, as in scientific research, inventive effort, and innovation.

Surely, in spite of every effort to exclude them, the unknown and the unknowable infiltrate the margin of every kind of economic choice. But only in these components of the system of progress is the unknown the very target of effort, the essential "raw material" to be worked. Who will say what can be seen where none has looked? How long will it take to solve what has never been solved before? How much will consumers want of what they have not yet tasted? For these questions, uncertainty is the ineluctable core.

It is perpetually uncertain not only when and whether the creative scientific inquiry or the inventive effort will succeed in bringing benefits, but also how well it will succeed, and what benefits it will bring, and to whom those benefits will accrue. The more general or "fundamental" the focus of inquiry, the broader will be the range of potential beneficiaries, and the more subject possible benefits will be to diffusion.

Moreover, nothing is more difficult to "possess" exclusively, nothing easier for others to appropriate, than those ideas and knowledge that are the essential product of creative science and invention. An invention that might be the fruit of a lifetime dedicated and of a fortune invested slips from the possession of its creator at the instant that it is revealed, at the moment that it is stated. To take it, no doors need be pried or locks broken. Because it has been taken, it cannot be proven missing. To steal an invention is a theft of a peculiar sort. In taking it for myself, I do not thereby deprive you of its use. It is indeed only by the rapid and ruthless appropriation of every creative idea that comes into view, and its immediate and unreserved use, that the economy will be transformed to the full limits of its output potential.

Nor is the market innovator easily able to possess for himself the bene-

fits of innovation. The great effort, risk and cost of innovation is essentially the effort, cost, and risk of proving the practical value of an idea.
But, once proven, that "proof" may be accessible to all. The "proof" that is
the true product of innovation, is appropriated by those who took no risks
and incurred no costs. It may well be the general case in the competitive
free for all that the greatest gains accrue not to those who, through
invention and innovation, open the floodgates, but rather to those who are
skilled at riding the tide. Too often those who generate the wave are at
once swallowed by it; those who make the breech are thereby broken.

Bias of Decentralized Choice Against the Diffused and Uncertain. Because decentralization *externalizes* diffused benefits, and because it *multiplies* the costs of intrinsic uncertainties by the number of interrelated but
independent entities, investment under decentralized market-direction
will be biased against forms of investment characterized by a relatively
great uncertainty of return and by a relatively high diffusion of benefits.
Hence decentralization will create a bias against investment in the processes of invention and transformation where return is diffused and uncertain relative to alternative uses of resources.

The logic of this may briefly be recalled. Investment is made because of
expected benefits discounted by uncertainties and risk. From the standpoint of society, the preference between alternative investments should be
according to their relative net benefits to society, discounted by costs
implicit in actual uncertainty and risk. When the decision to invest is
made by independent agencies, their choice will deviate from this norm
if in a systematic way certain sorts of cost or benefit are not accurately
reflected in the decision-maker's balance of accounts.

It was earlier shown that when decisions are made by independent
agencies, the uncertainties that are implicit in an investment will be multiplied by the decentralization of choice. Where there is the need to
anticipate the responses of other decision-makers as a basis for rational
choice, the exogenous or objective uncertainty is multiplied by the number of relevant responses of independent decision-makers. Endogenous
uncertainties afflicting decision-making are a multiple of the exogenous,
objective uncertainties, and the multiplier of uncertainty is higher in direct proportion to the number of independent decision-makers involved.
Therefore, decentralization creates a bias against investment in activities
characterized by a relatively great objective uncertainty. Where social
benefits per unit of expenditure, discounted by those costs of uncertainty
that exist regardless of the form of organization, are exactly equal for
alternative investments, decentralized choice will favor alternatives with
the low-uncertainty component. Decentralized choice, thus, will under-
invest in high-uncertainty alternatives. The more choice is decentralized,

the greater will be this bias and the consequent under-investment in high-uncertainty alternatives.

The benefits of investment may be relatively concentrated, i.e., "focused," or diffused. From the standpoint of society, it does not matter in the choice between alternatives whether benefits are focused or diffused. What matters is the total benefit, focused and diffused, attributable to a particular investment. When the investments are made by independent agencies, diffused benefits will tend to be externalized and left out of account. The greater decentralization, the more the relatively diffused benefits of investment will be externalized and disregarded. Consequently decentralized choice will be biased against investment to the extent that the benefits attributable to such investment are diffused rather than focused. The more that choice is decentralized, the greater will this bias be against investment with a high proportion of diffused benefits.

In the market-directed economy there is a greater decentralization of choice than in alternative forms. Hence there will be the greatest bias against and the least incentive to invest in those activities with a high component of uncertainty and a high ratio of diffused to focused benefits. Research and development, the effort to invent and the intention to innovate, are alike characterized by extreme uncertainties and diffusion of benefits. Correspondingly there will be a greater bias against investment in these activities in decentralized market-direction than with the other forms of economic organization.

Investment in Research and Development Precluded. Among the component phases of the system of economic progress, the elements of *diffusion* of economic benefits and of *uncertainty* with respect to the economic values of results will be greater for scientific studies than for the inventive endeavor, greater for the inventive endeavor than for innovation. This will be so not only because there is a descending order of generality in the end-objective of effort, but also because a practical payoff on the scientific inquiry must be realized through invention, and a practical payoff on invention must be realized through innovation. Added to the intrinsic diffusabilities and uncertainties of the effort to invent are those of the subsequent innovation prerequisite to payoff. And added to the intrinsic diffusabilities and uncertainties of scientific enterprise are those of invention and innovation. The bias of decentralized market-direction will be greatest against investing in the scientific endeavor and nearly as great against investments in long-range programed efforts to invent and to develop new products and techniques, that is, in Research and Development. So formidable is this bias that it might be laid down as a general rule, supported by the evidence of history, that no matter how vast are their economic benefits, there will be no investment in fundamental science or in long-range programs of Research and Development under decentralized market-direction.

Progress and the Capacity to Respond to Technological Opportunity. The capacity for economic progress depends not only on the number of inventions and innovations that are generated, but also on the facility with which the knowledge of invention and innovation are disseminated, on the extent to which such knowledge is used, and on the speed with which processes are transformed.

It is therefore necessary to consider those aspects of the forms of economic organization that facilitate or frustrate the dissemination of information, the exploitation of invention, the speed of transformation.

Patents and Secrecy: Incentive for Invention, Barrier to Dissemination. In order to internalize a greater proportion of the benefits of invention, firms resort spontaneously to secrecy, and wherever property is an essential component of economic control, the law allows certain inventions to be patented. Patent law turns ideas into "industrial property," which cannot be used without consent of the property holder, but which can be bought, sold, or rented.

Under decentralized market-direction, industrial secrecy and the patent system are probably beneficial or even necessary to economic progress. By internalizing the benefits of invention and innovation, patents and industrial secrecy may motivate the investment of resources, including the exertions of the inventor or innovator, in the effort to invent and to promote the sale or licensing of invention and the spread of innovation. Nevertheless, secrecy and patents have heavy social costs.

Industrial secrecy encourages internal policing, spying, and counter-intelligence operations in business enterprise—all of which are detrimental to interpersonal relationships and to efficient organization. It limits investment to the support of those inventions where operations or outputs will not automatically give away the secret. The patent system is immensely complex, costly to administer, and in practice is strongly biased in favor of those whose skills are manipulative and legalistic rather than creative, and of those who have the financial power to last out long litigation.

The patent system supports a concentration of economic control and a magnitude of enterprise beyond the needs of efficiency or of transformation. Every grant of patent, moreover, gives monopoly a foothold from which it can extend itself; monopoly induces the development of other countervailing concentrations; such concentrations threaten the integrity of price-direction in this form of economic organization.

Patents and secrecy simply manifest a motivation built into any property-based market economy: withholding information that might help outsiders (the competition), and narrowly restricting the use of invention to the control powers of a given enterprise. Hence the operation of decentralized market-direction substantially precludes the full dissemination of information and the full utilization of available invention.

Decentralization and the Cost of Acquiring, Evaluating or Adapting Information. In order that they might be embodied in operations or otherwise put into use or taken into account, the invention, the discovery, the new idea, even the proven technique must first be communicated, assimilated, evaluated. Decision-makers must be familiarized with the evolving potentialities for change.

There are grave difficulties in the communication, assimilation, and evaluation of the information produced by science as well as the data of invention and innovation in the economy of decentralized market-direction. Communication has its costs, the costs of notification, of demonstration, of education, of indoctrination. These costs increase as a function of the number of independent decision-makers and of their dispersion through space. With infinite decentralization these costs of transmission are at a maximum.

Suppose, for example, that there should be developed a kind of paint that has to be applied through an unconventional technique, but that, demonstrably, would give better results at lower costs than any substitute in the painting of automobiles and barn doors. Consider the costs of convincing the automakers and the farmers of this fact. Conceivably, a few demonstrations, reaching a few score specialists in a single city would lead to a rapid change in the painting of auto bodies all over the world. But to reach the millions of farmers over the spaces of the earth in order to demonstrate and to convince them would be a monumental task that would be counted as being done quickly if it were accomplished in decades.

Nor is the problem only in the costs of transmitting concept and knowledge to a multitude of widely dispersed independent decision-makers. There are the costs also in the evaluation of that information, the determination of its relevance to particular circumstances, and of its applicability to particular problems.

It was earlier shown that where the stimulus to action was "general" and "distant" from the locale of operations, the costs of transmission will be greater, and the response slower and more costly correspondingly as decision-making is decentralized. As a stimulus to change, the information-output of scientific endeavor and of inventive activity is peculiarly general and peculiarly detached from specific loci of operations. On that account, with respect to information on science, invention, and innovation, the difficulties and costs of transmission, of assimilation, and of response are greater under decentralized market-direction than under the alternative forms of economic organization. This is to say that in the study and evaluation of new techniques and of scientific claims, there are likely to be very large, even unlimited, economies of scale. When dealing with a scientific discovery or mechanical invention, where values are likely to be general and implications universal, a single evaluation would do for a million. (If every doctor were himself called upon to evaluate alternative vaccines!) The more centralized evaluation is, the larger is the absolute expenditure that is justifiable on the procurement of testing mechanisms, on the conduct of experiments designed to evaluate alternative techniques and alternative applications, on the development of special knowledge appropriate to evaluation, and of experts trained in the techniques of evaluation.

When evaluation is centralized, the task may be one for the expert and the professional. Where evaluation is decentralized, as it is under market-direction, evaluation and response to the evolving potentialities of science and technology is a task for the layman, for the entrepreneurial jack-of-all-choice.

Tradition and Convention as Barriers. Under decentralized market-direction, the evaluation of the evolving potentialities for transformation created through the advance of science and through technological invention and development is not a task for the professional but is performed rather by the common man, by great numbers of small entrepreneurs whose responsibilities encompass every aspect of a business activity.

The specialist, exercising his professional judgment within a narrowly confined range, can, for the limited number of variables within that range, study causal relationships, test alternatives, evaluate rationally; but the common man, and in this sense we are all common men, cannot study causal relationships or test alternatives with respect to the whole shifting infinity of variables that converge on all the aspects of business choice. Rather, the man of all choice can rarely choose. Instead he does what is done. He responds as the others respond. He follows the folkways, as indeed he must if he is to find his way through complexities that no individual can resolve by himself. And, in following convention, he is assured at least that when he is wrong, he will be no worse off than his neighbors are.

Folk wisdom evolves very slowly. And tradition, whatever its virtues, is hardly the appropriate criterion by which to evaluate opportunities for change. The more that decision-making is decentralized, and hence the more that the transformation choice is thrust back to the judgment and competencies of the multitude, the more difficult will be those educative processes that are prerequisite to the acceptance and assimilation of change, and the more will the inertia of tradition and custom, of social habit and social mores constitute a barrier to economic progress.

The Minimal Resisting Power of Monopoly and Orthodoxy. In no other form of economic organization is the sheer dissemination of the knowledge prerequisite to innovation and transformation so complex and difficult as it must be in market decentralization. And nowhere else will convention and tradition constitute so powerful a barrier against transformation. On the other hand, certain resistances to transformation that are characteristic of the other two forms of economic organization will be entirely absent or relatively unimportant.

The "monopoly" power and motivation of the large corporation or trade union to prevent the dissemination of invention and to block transformation do not exist as resistance to economic progress in the market-directed economy.

Orthodoxy and dogma, scientific and technological as well as theological and political, have, throughout history, been formidable antagonists of those ideas and inventions that threaten established concepts and positions of authority. When and inasmuch as the new idea is barred by the massed phalanx of antagonized authorities, its chance of survival will be greatest where price and not planners direct. The new idea that runs counter to established theory and official doctrine has its greatest fighting chance in the decentralized economy.

A TEST OF THE HYPOTHESIS

De Tocqueville's Analysis of Progress in a Decentralized Economy. In 1835 Alex de Tocqueville published his great book, *Democracy in America,* giving his impressions of the economy and politics and sociology of the United States during the first half of the nineteenth century. His observations are peculiarly relevant here since the United States economy was, perhaps to a degree unique in history, decentralized and market-directed. His observations, therefore, provide a useful point of reference and possibly a means of testing some of the arguments made in this chapter.

In examining the decentralized market-directed economy of the United States, De Tocqueville did not, of course, intend to contrast it with centralized socialist planning, nor with the economy of autonomous organizations. These latter did not then exist. Rather, he was comparing the economies of hereditary privilege and feudal power in Europe with the "equal conditions" in the competitive market economy of small holders in the United States.

In "The Influence of Democracy on Science and Arts," [1] De Tocqueville observes that the (decentralized price-directed) American economy through the values of individualism it fostered, and through the incentives it offered, engendered a universal impetus toward technical mastery and practical experiment, opening itself in an unparalleled way to the inventive contribution of the common man.

When hereditary wealth, the privileges of rank and the prerogatives of birth have ceased to be, and when every man derives strength from himself alone, it becomes evident that the chief cause of disparity between the fortunes of men is the mind. Whatever tends to invigorate, to extend or to adorn the mind, instantly rises to great value. The utility of knowledge becomes singularly conspicuous, even to the eyes of the multitude: those who have no taste for its charms set store upon its results, and make some effort to acquire it. . . . As soon as the multitude begins to take an interest in the labors of the mind, it finds out that to excel in some of them is a powerful method of acquiring fame, power, wealth. The restless ambition which equality begats instantly takes this direction as it does all others. The number of those who cultivate science, letters and the arts becomes immense. The intellectual world starts into prodigious activity. . . . What is done is often imperfect, but the attempts are innumerable; and although the results of individual effort are commonly very small, the total amount is always very large.

On the other hand, in the American economy, where resources were allocated through the instrumentality of decentralized market choice, no support was given and virtually no effort was made at the level of fundamental science.

It must be acknowledged that among few of the civilized nations of our time have the higher sciences made less progress than in the United States. . . . The mind may, as it appears to me, divide science into three parts. The first comprises the most theoretical principles, and those more abstract notions whose applications are either unknown or very remote. The second is composed of those general truths which still belong to pure theory, but lead nevertheless by a straight and short road to practical results. Methods of application and means of execution make up the third . . . none of them can prosper long, if absolutely cut off from the other two. In America the purely practical part of science is admirably understood and careful attention is paid to the theoretical portion which is immediately requisite to application. On this head the American always displays a clear, free, original and inventive power of mind. But scarcely anyone in the United States devotes himself to the essentially theoretical and abstract portions of human knowledge . . . every new method which leads by a shorter

[1] Alex de Tocqueville, *Democracy in America* (New York: Oxford University Press, 1946), pp. 265–278. All quotations that follow in this chapter will be from these pages. This and the following excerpts from *Democracy in America* are reprinted with the permission of Oxford University Press.

road to wealth, every machine which spares labor, every instrument which facilitates pleasures or augments them, seems to be [for them] the grandest effort of the human intellect. It is chiefly from these motives that a democratic people addicts itself to scientific pursuits. . . . In aristocratic ages, science is more particularly called upon to furnish gratification to the mind; in the democracies, to the body. . . . In vain will some innate propensity raise the mind towards the loftier spheres of the intellect; interest draws it down to the middle zone. There it may develop all its energy and restless activity, there it may engender all its wonders.

De Tocqueville observed also that the universal experience of decentralized activity and independent choice promoted a scepticism of authority and a distrust for abstraction that favored expedient creativity and practical invention but not the discipline of science.

Equality begets in man the desire of judging everything for himself; it gives him in all things a taste for the tangible and the real, a contempt for tradition and for forms. . . . Those who cultivate the sciences among a democractic people are always afraid of losing their way in visionary speculation. They mistrust systems; they adhere closely to the facts and the study of facts with their own senses. As they do not easily defer to the mere name of any fellowman, they are never inclined to rest upon any man's authority. . . . Scientific pursuits then follow a freer and a safer course, but a less lofty one.

Finally, De Tocqueville, anticipating that the circumstances he observed in the United States were bound to become general in Europe as well, foresaw that the support of science must eventually become the responsibility and function of government, i.e., of centralized political-direction.

If those who are called upon to guide the nations of our times clearly discerned from afar these new tendencies, which will soon be irresistible, they would understand that, possessing education and freedom, men living in democratic ages cannot but fail to improve the industrial part of science; and that henceforward all the efforts of the constituted authorities ought to be directed to support the highest branches of learning and to foster the nobler passion for science itself. In the present age the human mind must be coerced into theoretical studies; it runs of its own accord into practical application.

SUMMARY

The spontaneous motivation to invent, to innovate, and to transform inhere in the economy of decentralized market-direction.

There is also a spontaneous and general motivation to acquire technical mastery. For this purpose the job itself, in the small firm under the control of an individual entrepreneur, offers an effective means of self-education. The wide dispersion of decision-making and of independent control over resources correspondingly affords an opportunity for experimentation in and as a part of production and distribution. In thus providing the means to acquire a technical mastery and the opportunity for experiment and innovation, the decentralized market opens the way to the creative contribution of the common man.

The values engendered through the experience of the decentralized market economy, including an independence of thought and a scepticism of authority, support the impetus to practical invention. These values are less congenial to fundamental science.

Because the results of fundamental research and of long range programs of Research and Development are peculiarly uncertain, and because their effects are diffused, and since decentralization multiplies such inherent uncertainty and externalizes such diffused effects, the bias of decentralized market-direction is heavily against investment in support of fundamental science or of long-range programs of applied research.

The costs and difficulties of transferring, evaluating and assimilating the knowledge of scientific discovery and information regarding technical advance will be greater when the economy is decentralized and price-directed than in the alternative forms of economic organization.

Under decentralized market-direction there will be a general incentive to withhold information relevant to transformation and to restrict the use of invention in order to secure the competitive advantage of the agency possessing such information. Restriction will be exercised through industrial secrecy or through the use of patents. The internal security requirements of industrial secrecy and the complex institutions required in order to grant and to enforce patents are inherently costly. Given their use, the social value of available technical information can never be fully exploited. On the other hand, without patents and/or industrial secrecy, the benefits of invention and innovation might be so thoroughly externalized that, in the decentralized market economy, there would no longer be a practical motivation to support efforts to invent or to innovate.

Under decentralization, where the transformation choice is left to the limited knowledge of the common man, the force of convention and social habit will constitute a formidable barrier to economic progress. On the other hand, this form of economic organization minimizes resistance to change from the powers of monopoly and of doctrinaire authority.

Chapter 13

Centralized Political-Direction and the Organization of Economic Progress

Economic progress will not occur spontaneously under centralized political-direction. The required incentives and processes will have to be planned, and the plan will have to be implemented. The rate of progress that is achieved, compared to what is conceivable, as with all other goals of economic activity under centralized political-direction, will depend on the motivation and competence of the planning elite. This motivation and competence will be assumed and the concern of this chapter will be with the values and detriments of the form of economic organization as an instrument of control.

THE CAPACITY FOR INVENTION

No Self-Education on the Job. The creative individual's opportunity to learn will fix the range of his inventive prowess. Under decentralized market-direction, the processes of production and distribution provide an opportunity for self-education through observation and experience on the job. This is so since each one of the multitude of independent agencies of production and distribution contains in itself an integral technology and organization under the control of a single entrepreneur. What is controlled by the individual entrepreneur can be comprehended through experience and observation by others who work with him. In the "one-man enterprise," the enterprising man can acquire a technical and organizational mastery that is relevant to useful, practical invention.

Under centralized political-direction, the operation of the economy does not require that processes be broken up into technical and organizational integrals, each within the scope of a single individual's powers of comprehension and control. Rather the vast activity within the scope of the plan must be blocked out and formed to simplify the tasks of transmitting information and of exercising supervision. Each individual's assignment is but a minute fragment of an enormous whole. The individual cannot observe the operation of that whole from the vantage point of his own work, nor is there any reason to suppose that he will be able either to determine through his work-experience and work-observations the significance of his function or its interrelations with that of others, or in any way to comprehend the rationale of the technology and organization into which his work is joined.

This is not to say that a mastery over science, technology, and organization cannot be acquired under centralized political-direction. It can be, by studies directed specifically toward that objective, but not through experience on the job. To the extent that the scope of enterprise ceases to be man-sized, the value of the work-experience as an instrument of education diminishes. The job itself no longer offers the means of acquiring technological or organizational mastery.

It is an institutional requirement of decentralized market-direction that the operating entity be kept small (man-sized) to insure the integrity of profit motivation and price-directed competition. It is an institutional requirement of centralized political-direction that operations be concentrated to the limit of the technical optimum and beyond for the sake of effective planning and supervision. Through the fragmentation of control into small man-sized operations, the organization of production retains its value as an instrument of education. Through the concentration of operations into systems of vast extent and great complexity, beyond the observational scope of participating individuals, the organization of production loses its value as an instrument of education.

The "university of hard knocks" with learning on the run by watching the boss and doing the job has grave limitations. It also has unique values: emphasis on free initiative, lack of bias against the maverick or the unconventional and the unpolished man, and above all the intrinsic value that it can give to the hours of labor.

Support for Formal Education. Under centralized-direction, the acquisition of any breadth of technical mastery is, perforce, through formal education, through courses in schools or universities, through training programs in the plant, or even through private study . . . but in any case, as an effort and a discipline apart from the work activity. Of course, under decentralized market-direction technical mastery can also be acquired through the institutions of formal education. Under centralized political-direction, however, the support that would rationally be given to formal education would be greater, not only because formal education is an absolute prerequisite for the system's functioning, but also because the benefits of education are highly diffused and would correspondingly be subject to externalization in the decentralized economy.

No Built-in Opportunity for Technical Experiment. In the decentralized economy, entrepreneurship implies the power to experiment. The agencies of production themselves provide the media for probing, venturing, trying-out, testing hypotheses, expressing the vision and creativity of the individual. The workbench is like a laboratory, and the corner of the factory may be converted into a pilot plant. Every enterprise, potentially, is the means whereby change may be ventured, where the hunch can be played, where an idea can be tried out. In the epochs of the decentralized market, many an inventor was educated at the workbench, devised his notion in the environment of production, and tried it out through the enterprise of which he was a part. Experiment, discovery, and innovation alike were aspects of the entrepreneurial function.

No such breadth of opportunity for experiment is necessarily open to the mass of individuals who participate in planned production under centralized-direction. There the organizing principle is a plan, and the plan is the antithesis of experiment. The plan arranges, fixes, gears all the parts together. Experiment disarranges. Experiment is an exercise in the uncertain, a rendezvous with the unknown. But the virtue of the plan is that it is known, that it is clearly, cleanly intermeshed, that it rolls out uncertainties. Under the plan, efforts are mobilized under orders. What is to be produced in one sector requires specified receipts from another, and discretionary experiment would jeopardize the long complex chain of intermeshed and scheduled activities. Hence, in the economy of centralized-direction, free experimentation must be carried on outside of the organization of production; experimental probing, if it is to exist, cannot be integrated freely into the processes of production and distribution but must be a unique function of special institutions created specifically for that purpose.

INVESTMENT IN SCIENCE, INVENTION, INNOVATION

Investment in Science. It has been shown that decentralization externalizes the diffused benefits of economic choice and multiplies the uncertainties inherent in economic activities. Conversely, centralization brings the diffused benefits of choice within the sphere of the decision-maker's responsibility and permits objective uncertainties to be given their intrinsic weight in the balance of costs and gain. The bias built into decentralized market-direction against investment in the processes of economic progress, where uncertainties and the diffusion of effects are extreme, does not exist under centralized political-direction. There is nothing in the centralized politically directed economy that, inherently as a function of the economic organization, would lead to systematic underinvestment in science or in any of the other component phases of the system of economic progress. Because its beneficial effects can more fully be taken into account in this form of economic organization than in any of the others considered here, it follows that, under rational choice, the level of investment in the scientific enterprise and in long-range programs intended to develop new technology would be higher under centralized political-direction than under the alternative forms of economic organization.

It was earlier postulated that centralized political-direction is likely to place more value on social goals, such as those suggested by the terms *national prestige, posterity, strategic power, man, civilization,* and *humanity,* than on the universe of individual tastes, wants, and needs. Emphasis on collective values is another factor that might tend to encourage greater support for scientific enterprise, though not necessarily of a science geared to economic growth.

Systematic Organization of Economic Progress. Under centralized political-direction it becomes possible, indeed, necessary to systematize and to plan the whole process of economic progress, from the inculcation of technical mastery to the transformation of the processes of production and distribution. Individuals cannot educate themselves on the job but must be taught in formal institutions of learning. Individuals cannot experiment independently as a part of their work when that work is assigned under a plan. Rather it is necessary that special facilities, laboratories, and research establishments be provided. Moreover, financial support to education, to fundamental science, and to all the components of the system of economic progress become economically justifiable under the central planner's calculus of costs and gains.

The organization of the process of economic progress under centralized political-direction will therefore contrast sharply with its organization under decentralized market-direction. In the latter, the scientific inquiry is divorced from economic choice and has no link with the objectives of technological change. The processes of technical self-education, experimentation, invention, innovation, and transformation merge and intermingle as incidentals of activity in production and distribution. Under centralized political-direction, on the other hand, scientific and technical education, scientific inquirly, programmed technical invention and development, innovation, and transformation *all* fall within the scope of the economic choice. Investment in support of fundamental science is warranted within the scope of economic choice, and the scientific inquiry is related directly to technological objectives. The phases of progressive economic change are organized systematically, as a separate process, complementary to but distinct from the organization of production and distribution. Under centralized political-direction, and in a more limited way in the economy of autonomous organizations, programed "Research and Development" becomes feasible.

Technically Oriented Science. Centralization of control tends to shift technical education from the farm and the shop to the school and the university, and to shift the task of invention away from the creative entrepreneur to the professional, trained in science, working in the laboratory of a research institution. There are great advantages in this kind of organization for progressive change. It is designed to exploit fully and directly the knowledge of the physical universe. It permits the systematic accumulation of data relevant to technological development and the systematic evolution of inventive and developmental techniques and processes in a way that would not be possible where invention and innovation can take place only through the occasional and ad hoc activity of gifted individuals.

Untapped Creativity of the Common Man. "Research and Development" concentrates the creative task in the hands of a relatively few highly trained individuals who are selected on the basis of their academic performance. Scientists and researchers selected via the university route for their academic excellence certainly will not include all, and need not include many of the creative minds of the community. The way has not yet been found to identify the inventive ability, let alone to grade individuals or to recruit them on the basis of their creative potential. Therefore academic selection will exclude many creative individuals from participation in Research and Development. Nor will there be any place for those who are excluded to make their potential contribution to economic progress within the scope of the planned organization of production and distribution. In this sense, reliance on Research and Development by a trained elite may close the opportunity of the common man to make his creative contribution toward economic progress.

Opening Experimental Opportunity. It is possible that centralized political-direction, attempting to capitalize upon the ingenuity and inventiveness of the man on the job, will provide the institutional means, outside of the planned organization of production and distribution, to motivate and to enable those who are engaged in the ordinary tasks of producing and distributing goods and services to experiment, to invent, and to promote the use of their inventions. Such an attempt in the large American corporation has made the "suggestion box" commonplace. In the socialist economies of Eastern Europe, prizes and elaborate "patent" incentives, which reward the patent owner with a predetermined share of the savings made through the use of their inventions, are used to motivate creative contributions from the working force. Resources and facilities are variously made available for free-time study and experiment. It was reported in 1962 that in the Soviet Union "two thousand laboratories for amateur research were already operating at plants and factories. These are being used by about 30,000 engineers and other employees who like to tinker in their spare time . . . [and are alleged to have] 'potentialities' of making a serious contribution to science." [1]

THE SPREAD OF INVENTION AND THE SPEED OF TRANSFORMATION

The Problem of Dissemination. Of the elements (invention, innovation, transformation) conceived as the component parts of a system for technological advance, none is self-contained. Each depends on an inflow of information and on an external stimulus of ideas. Each must be in some way geared to receive, to comprehend, and to assimilate this inflow. And each requires responses to its achievements in spheres of activity outside of itself.

Invention and innovation take place in response to opportunities that arise out of the conflux of what is wanted and what is possible. Problems or needs provide an outlet, open a market, favorably predispose an audience. New possibilities are suggested through a restructuring of the technical or organizational context of operations. But also, aside from the context of operations and the needs of the market, opportunities for invention and innovation are created through scientific discoveries that permit deeper understanding and greater control of natural phenomena. But neither the needs of the market, the changing boundaries of science, nor the developments of the social infrastructure can serve as a stimulus to invention or innovation unless they reach the ear and sink into the understanding of those who might invent or innovate. Such transmission is always difficult. For some facts and ideas no outlet or instrument of dissemination may be available, while concurrently there is a flood of data, at once so complex and so largely trivial that it is beyond the capacity of any individual or group to assimilate or to sift for its relevancies. Buried in the archives of the patent offices of the world are inventions that will yet be reinvented a thousand times. And piled on the shelves, heaped in the aisles and stored in the cellars of libraries, millions of scientific articles, books, and documents contain data that will surely never reach those to whom such information might serve as a stimulus to invent or to innovate.

Receptivity to Field Experience and to Science. Centralized political-direction divorces the inventive and innovative functions from the processes of production and distribution and requires their consequent professionalization, specialization and concentration in Research and Development. In contrast, decentralized market-direction disperses the inventive, innovative activity so that these become an incident of the organization of production and distribution, and virtually aspects of en-

[1] *New York Times,* April 27, 1962.

trepreneurship. So understood, the two forms of economic organization can be compared as media for the transmission of stimulus and response between the constituent parts of the system of economic progress.

Where the inventive-innovative activity is concentrated and professionalized as Research and Development, it is, thereby, opened and sensitized to the stimuli of *scientific* advance and discovery. The professional researcher is trained in science, habituated to its techniques and methods, familiar with its meanings. His own work may feed back into the cumulative growth of its generalizing theories and experimental data. But while such Research and Development gears easily into the evolving body of science, its "coupling" with the needs and problems of operations and organization at the level of production and distribution is more difficult. Exactly the converse is true where inventive and innovative activities are dispersed in the decentralized market as a function of the entrepreneurial enterprise. Then the experience of operations is always a ready stimulant for the exercise of inventiveness and creative ingenuity, while great difficulty will be encountered in responding to the distant stimulus of new scientific conception and discovery.

Collective Ownership of Information, and Its Optimal Utilization.
"Private property" means that (more or less) sole control over something has been vested in an individual or an agency, to the exclusion of claim or access by any other. Through this institution, authority over a given resource may be divided, possibly into very small and scattered parcels. But does this subdividing of control over a given resource mean of itself that the magnitude or quality or potential contribution of that resource to production will be changed?

An acre of land remains an acre of land, a one-ton machine press remains a one-ton machine press, a man-hour of labor remains a man-hour of labor regardless of whether control is vested in a political center or in an individual's private property. Nor does that resource's technical *potential* contribution to output depend on whether its use is coordinated and controlled by a private owner, a company manager, or a public official. The land in the valley, whether it is the domain of the private landowner, the corporation, or the State, may be tilled by exactly the same cultivator in exactly the same way, and under his harrow and plow it may yield the same crop. The form of control matters, of course, but *not*, it would seem, with regard to potential technical contribution of an existing resource. Whether control over it resides in the one or in the many, the resource, and its potential contribution to output, remains the same. Such has been the assumption.

And the assumption is valid when applied to land or minerals or waterpower, or buildings and equipment, or even to the energies of labor.

Within given boundaries of time, it is conceivable that for any resource the full value and absolute technical potential can be fully exploited through its single, specific, once-and-for-all use—whether under public or private control. The coal can be dug and burned until none remains. The trees of the forest can be cut, logged, sawed, and used up entirely as lumber. The land can be tilled and harvested, and, for the season, no other use can be made of it. The technical possibility of fully utilizing the resource does not depend on whether it is controlled as private property or as a collective possession.

Not so when property is in ideas, in invention, in discovery, in knowledge. Then the consequence of the exclusive, private possession of a resource, as property, is entirely different. Unlike the others, these are resources whose contribution to production is not exhausted through use; on the contrary, their contribution to production is increased without limit through the multiplicity, variety, and continuity of their use. For the resources of knowledge, of invention, of conception, the issue is not whether one private owner *or* another, of whether a private owner *or* a public official would be best equipped to organize their use. Rather the issue for maximizing their potential contribution to production is how to spread their use so that they may be employed by private decision-makers *and* public officials: any and all, simultaneously. If the institution of private property limits access to knowledge, invention, concept, and idea, or if it motivates their restriction, then ipso facto their technical potential for a contribution to production is diminished.

The seasonal contribution to output of a piece of land is exhausted through the activities of the single cultivator. Whether the land belongs to that cultivator or to the community, only one cultivator can use the plot of land. But how many cultivators can use and benefit by the use of a superior technique of crop rotation? Sole possession of the land did not change its value-in-use. But sole possession of the new technique for crop rotation? It does not suffice that the new technique be used efficiently by one user alone. If its output value is fully to be realized, it must be used by many, indeed, by all.

The resources of knowledge are, then, different from the other forms of economic resources in this fundamental respect. The magnitude of their contribution is a function not simply of the efficiency with which they are used, but also of the extent, breadth, and continuity of their use. The value of their contribution cannot be exhausted through use, but increases directly and without limit as a consequence of greater use. Anything that restricts their use irrevocably reduces their potential contribution.

When knowledge, invention, conception, and discovery are treated as property, as pawns in the process of exchange, then necessarily, in the pursuit of private advantage, access to these resources will be limited and their use will be restricted. Such is the dilemma. The institution of property upon which the decentralized market relies to stimulate invention and to promote its application and to induce its efficient use will itself diminish the potential contribution of knowledge and invention. This surely is a disadvantage of the decentralized market economy or of any form of economic organization that treats knowledge and invention as a form of property.

Possibility of Eliminating Duplicative Research. The product of research effort can be conceived as solutions to problems. Unlike the product of any other economic process, increments of the same research output, that is, repetitions of the same solution, are wholly valueless. At the instant it is achieved, the value of a cure for cancer would be infinite; and a day later the value of the same cure, independently arrived at, would have a social value of zero. From this characteristic proceeds a unique danger of waste through duplicative effort. Some duplicative effort is necessary under any form of economic organization inasmuch as communication is imperfect and as scientists must learn by doing. Moreover, some duplication in the sense of taking alternative paths toward the same objective is desirable in probing for a breakthrough. But that duplication which arises because researchers are denied access to available information and are obliged therefore to tread the same paths, to take the same false turns, to perform the same experiments, and to find and withhold what others could use—is waste pure and simple, and waste of irreplaceable creative energies. This waste must occur wherever the universe of knowledge is parceled out as property, and that property is used to further self-interest or competitive advantage.

It is the virtue of centralized political-direction, where knowledge and invention may be considered and used as a collective possession, that there is no intrinsic barrier to the widest dissemination of knowledge, that no built-in motivation necessarily restricts the use of invention. Universal access is then at least conceivable.

Orthodoxy and Doctrine Contra Invention-Innovation. In the decentralized market-directed economy the response to innovation is the response of the mass. Here the grip of the folkways, the rigidity of tradition, the marked-out paths of convention, the indifference and ignorance of Everyman throws up a deep dense barrier against novelty. The entrepreneurial jack-of-all choice can only rely on intuition and convention in the infinitely varied and multifarious decisions of every day.

Centralized-direction removes the function of choice from the domain of the many to the realm of the trained few, where professionals, operating within the narrowed bounds of their expertise, can develop techniques for the rational evaluation of invention and for the informed appraisal of innovation.

The central plan is the work of the expert. The performance of the centralized economy rests ultimately on the dedication of an elite. The expert has his theory. The elite have their faith. But what of the invention and innovation that runs counter to these?

With control centralized, the quick and economical decisions of a few experts can open the way to a general and rapid transformation. But experts also err; indeed they have a chronic propensity to error when faced with fundamental novelty. The weakness of the common man in his evaluation of the potentialities for change is that, in his ignorance, he relies on social habit, and hobbles on the crutch of the folkways. The weakness of the expert is in his orthodoxy, in his attachment to established authority. The expert defends his expertise, his conceptions and his formula and his analytic tools, all acquired with care and at a cost, from the subversion of novelty and from the threat of the transcending vision that might render the lot obsolete.

The centralized politically directed economy appears to require, moreover, the dedication of an elite, and a faith is needed to fuse that dedication into unified movement. A faith will have its doctrine. What of the novel idea that challenges the doctrine? Hell hath no fury like that of the zealot whose faith is threatened.

Ignorance, convention, the inertia of habit are the barriers to progressive change when economic choice is decentralized. The orthodoxy of the expert and the frenzy of the faithful are its enemies under political centralization.

Unlimited but Unwieldy Power to Transform. In the decentralized market the power to innovate and to transform is fragmented and dispersed among a multitude of small private entrepreneurs. This power to innovate and to transform, while very limited, is nevertheless highly concrete and is exercised freely by those in possession without check or accountability.

With centralized political-direction, on the other hand, the power to innovate and transform is of quite unlimited scope, but its means of exercise may be so diffused through the system of political choice that it can be brought into focus only with the greatest difficulty.

Transformation in the decentralized market requires no group or political consensus. It proceeds from the choice of the most daring of the many who possess the decision-making power. On that account, first steps will be taken more readily under market decentralization than under alternative forms of economic organization. By reason of this same fragmentation of power, transformation in the decentralized market can never be achieved at once and for all. Rather it must always be piecemeal, with the zig and the zag of adjustment and of counteradjustment in a game where all the rules are changed by each new throw of the cards. One advance brings a host of responsive changes that in turn require a widening train of change and adaptation. Nor are the elements of the economy necessarily moved nearer to their full and final adjustment thereby. The relationships of social ecology, thrown out of balance, may create problems as severe as the benefits incurred. Consider the impact of the auto on the American economy. Its massive use created a massive need for a new sort of fuel, for facilities for servicing, for criteria for lending and techniques for borrowing. The existence of the autos required the development of roads, brought hotels to Miami and motels over the breadth of the land, caused fumes and speed and many deaths, crowded highways, blocked bridges and choked up streets, and entailed supermarkets, burgeoning suburbs, a crisis in the schools, the financial collapse of urban transit and railroads, and a blight in the center of the great cities. The economy's realization of the potentialities of the auto has brought many great benefits but the process of transformation has been long-drawn, costly, with successive crisis brought on by the unanticipated (and as a consequence of the form of economic organization—unanticipatable) effects of each forward step in innovation.

Under centralized political direction, the costs of these backward and forward adjustments could, conceivably, be eliminated. Transformation could be general, goal-conscious, direct, taking into account all that might rationally be anticipated.

With decentralized decision-making it may be enormously difficult to transform concurrently all the independently controlled but interdependent processes. But under centralized political-direction, where transformations must pass through the cumbersome and complex planning apparatus, it may be correspondingly difficult to effectuate transformation requiring many dissimilar and discrete adjustments.

SUMMARY

What is lacking here as in the other aspects of centralized direction is a spontaneous, self-generating drive to invent, to disseminate invention, to innovate, to transform. Rationale may be clear, but motivation may be lacking. And a system of motivation will be designed only if those who have the power to design it are motivated to do so.

When production and distribution are planned, self-education in technical mastery cannot take place through observation and experience on the job. Under centralized political-direction, the technical mastery needed for invention can be acquired only through formal education. And under centralized direction special institutions must be created to provide an opportunity for the experiment that invention requires. On the other hand, because all benefits would be internalized, economic rationale would induce a larger investment in scientific and technical education and in the provision of special research and experimental facilities than under alternative forms of economic organization.

Investment in scientific education, in scientific research, and in invention and innovation as planned processes following necessity and rationality under centralized political-direction produces "Research and Development," a planned and professionalized system for linking invention and innovation to the physical sciences. No longer merged as under decetralized market-direction with production and distribution, the components of economic progress are organized as distinct processes where the opportunity for technical creativity becomes the prerogative of an expert few.

Invention and transformation under centralized direction are more responsive to scientific advances and less responsive to changed operating conditions than they would be under alternative forms of economic organization.

The value of science depends on the breadth of its diffusion, and the benefits of discovery and invention grow as their applications increase. Only when knowledge is collectively owned is it conceivable that the values of science and invention could be fully realized or that duplicative wastes in research could be eliminated.

Under centralized direction it is possible to transform without the costly zig and zag of piecemeal adjustments. There are important transformations that absolutely require some degree of central direction over a host of separate but related processes. Sometimes transformation must proceed through many discrete adjustments. Where that is the case, centralized political-direction is a cumbersome instrument of transformation.

Under centralized political-direction, the transformation choice can be lifted out of the inertia of folkways. Rather than being left to the intuitive and conventional evaluations of little entrepreneurs on the run, it may be vested in experts who are skilled in scientific measurement and in rational and systematic appraisal. On the other hand, the plan requires experts; political direction requires the dedication of an elite. The dedication of an elite, merged into the faith of the zealot, allied to the doctrine of the expert, may be a barrier against the creative out-thrust and a powerful enemy of many kinds of innovation.

Chapter 14

The Economy of Autonomous Organization and Economic Progress

THE CAPACITY FOR INVENTION

Formal Education and Facilities for Experiment Required. The economy of autonomous organization offers the individual neither the opportunity for experimentation nor for technical self-education through observations on the job as an incident to production and distribution. Rather these twin requisites to economic progress must be especially provided.

This lack of a spontaneous opportunity for technical self-education is a result of the size and complexity of operations, which place technology beyond the observational scope of the participating individual. The lack of opportunity for spontaneous experiment is due to the "planned" pre-assignment of tasks and techniques. Although their cause is the same, these deficiencies are not so clear-cut and complete as they would be under centralized political-direction. Marginal opportunities remain for technical self-education on the job and for spontaneous technical experiment as an incident to production and distribution—for the following reason. The large autonomous organization requires a host of much smaller, often very small, satellites: subcontractors, technical consultants, lawyers, brokers, advertising agencies. Also, a certain number of small competitors find a place in this form of economic organization, as best equipped to navigate in the shallow waters and narrow passages where the great organization cannot venture. Personnel continually move between these satellites and the large organization. The great organization often "buys up" and absorbs smaller related entities. Individuals, sometimes even operating groups, splinter off from the large organization to create small special agencies. Individuals working in these smaller satellites may have the opportunity to make experimental changes on their own initiative. Moreover, the small operation brings a technical and organizational activity, as an integral whole, within the purview of the man on the job. A marginal opportunity is thus provided for technical self-education through job experience, and for spontaneous technical experiment as an aspect of entrepreneurship.

160

INVESTMENT IN SCIENCE, INVENTION, INNOVATION

Basic Science and General Education Unsupported. In contrast to the firm in the decentralized market economy, the large autonomous organization is able to recapture a substantial proportion of the benefits of investment in the component elements of economic progress, since (1) its operations include a larger number of the activities to which the benefits of progress-oriented efforts might accrue, and (2) it controls the terms at which its products are offered for sale and hence is able to retain a substantial share of the cost savings that are the consequence of invention and innovation, rather than passing these on as lower prices, and (3) it has the technical and financial resources to exploit a wide and indefinite range of technical potentialities that Research and Development might create for new industries or novel products. On the other hand, compared to the centralized politically directed economy, the scope of each decision-maker's responsibility remains limited. Correspondingly, externalities remain, and there continues to be a significant bias in the economy of autonomous organization against investment where benefits are diffused and uncertain. In practice this has meant that the large autonomous corporation sometimes finds it economic to invest in Research and Development and even in the training of its employees, where education and R & D relate directly to its particular operating needs or focus on problems and objectives within the scope of its operating responsibilities. It will, on the other hand, hardly ever have an incentive to invest in the development of a system of general technical education, or in the support of scientific inquiry whose objective is to deepen the comprehension of physical phenomena per se. Hence "basic science" and "general education" are not provided by economic choice of the autonomous organization.

Equivocal Support for Research and Development. The decision of the autonomous corporation to invest or not in applied Research and Development is beset not only by uncertainty about whether such investment will actually result in commercially valuable invention and whether it will be able to retain the benefits of such invention. The corporation will have reason to doubt, also, whether it makes "good business sense" to be the radical innovator in an industry or whether radical innovation represents a desirable form of competition from the industry's point of view. The company may take the eminently "reasonable" position that it "pays" to let others bear the costs of research and run the risks of innovation, that only when the value of an innovation has been thoroughly established is the time propitious to hire away the experts, to buy up the patents, and to move in with financial know-how and merchandising skill. Or, quite rationally, it may choose to shun radical innovations altogether in order to preserve amicable intra-industry relationships. In any case the incentive to invest in Research and Development or to exploit the opportunities it offers is never clear-cut. In certain great and prosperous industries dominated by large autonomous corporations, such as the automobile industry in the United States, Research and Development has been most notable by its absence.

The Procurement of Invention. Research and Development by the large corporation has two purposes related to the process of economic progress. It is, first, a source of inventions that the company exploits as innovation or sells or licenses to others. It is, second, a means for searching out, evaluating, and developing inventions that have had their genesis elsewhere, in the research of other corporations or in the inventive activities carried on in coexisting sectors of the world economy: universities, small enterprises, or government agencies, etc.

Both of these functions have social merit. It is of the utmost importance for economic progress in any economy not only that inventions are produced, but also that the decision-making agencies be sensitized to technical opportunities, wherever they happen to arise, and that they be prepared to innovate rapidly on the basis of those opportunities. If Research and Development enables the corporation to do so, it is all to the good.

The Tie to Pure Science. Corporate enterprise will not be motivated to support Research and Development other than that oriented toward problems within the scope of its production activities or interests. Research justified because of its relevance to the commercial interests of the corporation will also yield information, and sometimes insights into the nature of physical phenomena that are of general interest for science. Hence, results may be in that sense "fundamental" though the objectives are practical.

Some of the research carried on by the agencies of the large corporate enterprise will nevertheless be motivated by the desire to achieve "fundamental" results, without reference to the specific problems or commercial objectives of the corporation. Research and Development seeks to exploit any relevant advance in the general body of science. In order to attune the company's R & D activity to current developments in special fields of science, some of the company's researchers may be occasionally allowed to engage in free research in special fields of "pure science." It then becomes their task to bring leads and possibilities for technical exploitation to the attention of their development-oriented colleagues. Furthermore, it is often alleged, in order to bring "high class scientific talent" into corporate research, some limited time for fundamental studies must be allotted as a bonus of sorts to the scientist. Academic achievement, moreover, might yield the company a return in prestige and an advantage in recruiting new talent from universities. Finally, because others are without the capacity to evaluate its highly complex activities, the R & D entity is largely immunized from external judgments or supervision. Hence, like any quasi-autonomous group of colleagues, it will follow some pursuits solely because they are of intrinsic interest to its membership.

THE SPREAD OF INVENTION AND THE SPEED OF TRANSFORMATION

Sequestering Information. Research and Development in the economy of autonomous organization develops knowledge for private purposes, sequesters it as private property, and restricts its use to the service of the company in possession. The effect of this, as Chapter 13 showed, is to reduce the contribution that a given body of knowledge can possibly make to economic progress and to waste resources in duplicated research. In none of the alternative forms will there be a degree of built-in waste and restrictiveness comparable to that in the economy of autonomous organization. The dangers and losses arising from the private ownership of knowledge are less in the economy of decentralized market-direction, for several reasons. The information produced through scientific research is ordinarily without commercial value in the decentralized market economy. If the scientific inquiry is to be carried on at all, it must be carried on outside the sphere of economic choice, for noncommercial objectives. This will probably mean that the level of investment in science will be far below the social optimum, but that the results of scientific inquiry will be fully and freely available as a basis for technical invention. Technical invention itself will be privately possessed, and often will be jealously guarded, but (by definition) ownership in the decentralized market-directed economy can never be concentrated enough to create a roadblock to change, nor to permit control over a broad avenue of technological and industrial development. In the economy of autonomous organization, on the other hand, no functionally required limitations on concentration forestall the accumulation and exclusive exploitation of privately possessed bodies of knowledge. In the economy of autonomous organization, perhaps the predominant share of the scientific resources and research effort available to the entire community will be drawn into the nexus of corporate research. The discovery, invention, or information resulting from that research will be sequestered as private property, which means that a great part of science will be privately controlled and its outputs privately possessed. The private possession of bodies of scientific knowledge implies a significant power to control avenues of technological advance.

What is at stake here is not simply invented products and techniques that are protected by patent or held in secret, but the accumulated scientific knowledge that will serve as the basis for future invention. To illustrate, consider a visit made recently to a certain American pharmaceutical company. The heart of the company's research effort was its file of chemical compounds. It was to this file that the company researchers turn first, rather than to the general scientific literature, and it was on this file that they primarily depend in their work. The files contained the results of the careful analysis and clinical testing for a wide range of animal and sometimes human reactions to 17,000 different compounds. It costs $2000 simply to prepare a compound for the purpose of testing. Hence, this information represented an enormous expenditure of funds and, more important, of research efforts. These files are secret. The rapidly accumulating and extremely expensive masses of data that they contain are available only to a few scientists working in one company. Data that could support the research efforts of ten thousand instead serve the needs of ten. A significant part of the body of science (a subdivision of a field of science) is sealed off and isolated, except for the particular searches of a particular few. Such is the case not only for this pharmaceutical company, but for every large pharmaceutical house and every large chemical company in the United States, Japan, and Western Europe; each has its private corpus of science. The cumulative advantages of those in possession raise continually higher barriers against possible incursion by fresh competition from outside the field.

This waste of effort and talent in duplicative research and the circumvallation of the values of scientific knowledge constitute a major defect of the economy of autonomous negotiating organization.

Competition of R & D Organizations. The strivings of the corporate organization to survive and grow will provide the occasion for competition in Research and Development. Such competition will spur the research effort, and will also stimulate the development of new techniques and organizational forms in research. The market testing of these, presumably, will lead to the evolution of higher R & D processes.

The numbers of independent R & D agencies, and the variety in their forms, will permit an unparalleled diversity in the response of the economy to the stimulus of scientific discovery or to the stimulus of practical need.

The Monopoly Barrier to Innovation. In contrast to the economy of decentralized market-direction, the economy of autonomous organization avoids the inertia and ignorance of the common man by developing expert instruments for the evaluation of invention and for the choice to transform. In contrast to the economy of centralized political-direction, the economy of autonomous organization avoids the inhibiting orthodoxies of the political elite by spreading the evaluation of invention and the transformation choice among numbers of independent agencies. These are considerable advantages. On the other hand, it is peculiarly in the economy of autonomous organization that the monopoly power and interest operate through control over scientific research and through the possession of scientific information and science-based invention. Only in the economy of autonomous organization is economic choice motivated and able systematically to block technological change and to inhibit economic progress in order to maintain or increase a private advantage.

Monopoly may not simply raise the price of what is offered; monopoly may have the power and motivation to block the processes of invention and innovation. Two quite commonplace examples will illustrate how this can occur.

Antitrust proceedings revealed that after I. E. DuPont procured the patent on cellophane from a French inventor, that company then turned its research prowess to developing and patenting a whole range of alternative transparent and waterproof wrappings, not with any notion of using them, but simply in order to block developments that might compete with cellophane.

Before World War II the basic patents for synthetic (buna) rubber were jointly the possession of Standard Oil of New Jersey and the German firm I. G. Farben. The Germans urged that the international rights to the synthetic rubber patents should be sold to the natural rubber cartel, in the expectation that that cartel would pay a high price for the patents, not in order to produce synthetic rubber, but in order to prevent it from ever being produced. Frank Howard, who headed Standard's research effort, relates:

Dr. Herman Schmitz, financial leader of the I. G., told me that one of their directors had conceived the idea that the most money with the least risk could be made out of the Buna development by selling it to the Dutch-British interest who dominated the rubber trade through the International Rubber Regulation Agreement. It was argued that these interests would be willing to buy the synthetic rubber development in order to hold up the price of their natural rubber. I opposed this suggestion at once as a shortsighted plan, probably impractical and in any event out of line with the policies of my company.[1]

Fortunately for American industry and the war effort, Mr. Howard would not accept the German position, but the fact that the sale of the

[1] Frank Howard, *Buna Rubber* (New York: Van Nostrand, 1947), pp. 68–69.

key synthetic rubber patents to the rubber cartel was urged at the highest level of negotiations between two of the world's most powerful industrial organizations suggests the danger implicit in the private possession of scientific knowledge or invention, in the economy of autonomous organization

Built into the economy of autonomous market-negotiating organizations are the strong motivation and the dangerous power to restrain the dissemination of knowledge and the application of invention, and to use research prowess and the possession of patented inventions to block and destroy competitive lines of technological development.

THE ROLE OF GOVERNMENT

Values of Diversity vs. Dangers of Arbitrary Power. The unique value of the economy of market-negotiating organizations with regard to the process of economic progress is in the competitive stimulus to which it subjects Research and Development, and in the flexibility and organizational variations of R & D that it allows. These features provide an opportunity for experiment and innovation in research techniques, and favor the upward transformation of the R & D process itself. But valuable as such competition is, it need not happen. Organizations may choose not to compete. There are always "good business" reasons for one company to let the others pay the costs of R & D and run the risks of innovation, and then to pounce in and follow along paths already broken. It might always appear to make "good business" sense to wait and buy up research results when they occur, if they are successful and if they threaten, rather than investing in the risks and uncertainties of R & D. It is a "good business" argument that those who survive and who thrive are not those best at inventing, but those who are best at cashing in on the invention of others. Because it is "good business" the corporate organization may choose to withhold and wait. If most organizations follow that logic, stagnation is the consequence.

The corporate structure and scale most conducive to efficient production, selling, and merchandising may differ substantially from the scale and structure of organization required for successful Research and Development, and innovation. Hence a complex of mixed structures and sizes of enterprises might evolve, where those with an R & D prowess will spearhead the advance of the industrial technology while the rest follow in their wake, managing resources on the way more efficiently than the innovators could. There need not, however, be any such happy symbiosis; those who are fitted for a breakthrough may be submerged (or never rise) in the face of their more "efficient" competition, or research and innovative prowess may be used to steamroll and absorb those better equipped for the efficient management of resources.

With respect to the use of knowledge, the market incentive in the economy of autonomous organization is dual and antithetical. There is motivation to use knowledge and to disseminate invention, and there is also the motivation to withhold and to restrict the use of knowledge and invention. Whether the corporation promotes or restricts the invention and knowledge it possesses is a matter of corporate policy, and the policy to restrict is as feasible and reasonable as the policy to promote. Society always gains and the particular business entity also *may* gain by freely disseminating and actively promoting the use of its acquired knowledge and know-how, as the previously cited instance of Bell Laboratories and the transistor technology demonstrates. The company may also lose its competitive advantage through such a policy. It may prefer easy sailing on still waters and avoid the unforeseeable effects of releasing the information, discovery, and invention that it possesses, even though these are of no use in its own plans and strategies, choosing not to introduce new unknowns into the competitive game.

Note the singular ambiguity that characterizes every aspect of the economy of autonomous organization in respect to the organization of economic progress. To invest in research, or not; to compete in product innovation, or not; to disseminate research information and to promote the use of invention, or not; different paths are open and decision as to which to take is subject to a multiplicity of considerations and pressures.

Residual Role of Government. In the economy of autonomous organizations, government neither stands aloof from the economy, as it does under decentralized market-direction, nor does it have the primary responsibility in the organization and transformation of the economy as it does under centralized political-direction. Rather the government participates as one force among many. Its responsibilities are residual. It fills the gaps and offsets the peculiarly arbitrary power of autonomous agencies that are neither subject to the imperatives of price competition nor are politically accountable.

In various ways, the government may try to bring the policy and the activities of private corporations into closer accord with the general interest in matters related to research, invention, and transformation.

1. Government may, for this purpose, employ coercive regulation: periodic antitrust attacks in the United States are used to force the dissemination of patents when accumulated portfolio confer an "undue" power to monopolize.

2. Through influence, persuasion, pressure, and the lures of aids and

favors, government may insinuate guidelines into the formulation of company policy. This has been the French approach in promoting research and innovation by private enterprise.

3. The government may, through subsidy or otherwise, (*a*) support selected *forms* of research activity, such as the cooperative industrial research associations in Great Britain, Germany, and France. Such support is sometimes conditional on the free dissemination of the information produced through research, or (*b*) support selected R & D projects, as in the UK "development contract" scheme, offering to share with private companies the financial risks and possible profits on selected research projects.

4. Government may encourage selected innovations, or categories of transformation, through subsidy or otherwise. Supports given for the transformation of facilities for public transportation in the United States, first in canals, then in railroads, then in airlines are examples.

5. The government may make R & D contracts with private companies where the government is the customer for the transformed products or processes, or information, as in the procurement of space vehicles or of information related to public health.

Limited Possibilities of Planning. Government, as an instrument of choice and action in the economy of autonomous organization, is limited by its residual role. It serves to offset corporate policies that are perpetually arbitrary and uncertain, and its own responsibilities are equally equivocal and unsure. In responding to leads and lacks, to initiatives and failures of initiative in the universe of autonomous organization, the government cannot truly *plan* national research, even though it substantially supports the research of autonomous agencies. It cannot, that is, attempt rationally to balance the available resources of scientifically trained manpower against a table of priorities, or exercise foresight in the progressive development of research capacities against anticipated needs and goals. Rather it is bound to the treadmill of expediency, responding to crisis, to sudden external threat, and to occasional popular outcry. In this form of economic organization, the apparatus of government choice and control evolves in response to fragmented demand and to piecemeal crisis. It is likely to be a patchwork of powers without the capacity to take cognizance of general problems and needs, or provide a basis for the formulation of social priorities.

SUMMARY

Unlike decentralized market-direction, the economy of autonomous organization does not provide a spontaneous opportunity for technical self-education and experimentation.

Unlike centralized political-direction, the economy of autonomous organization does not bring the benefits of general education or all the levels of scientific inquiry within the scope of economic choice. There will be some investment by the autonomous enterprise in research and in technical training, but the support for general education and for basic science will be left as a residual task of government.

This form of organization, uniquely, generates spontaneous competition between independent R & D agencies, which provides a stimulus to research performance, and thus leads to the evolution of new R & D techniques and processes.

The research outputs of the R & D of corporate enterprise will be sequestered as private property. Necessarily, this sequestration will significantly limit the potential values for economic progress of such research. Moreover, R & D prowess, coupled with the intent to monopolize, may serve to block avenues of technical advance and to forestall economic progress.

The arbitrary powers of the autonomous enterprise, unrestrained either by price competition or electoral responsibility, make it incumbent upon government to influence corporate policies in respect to research and innovation.

Chapter 15

Economic Organization as a Social Environment

What a Man Makes, Makes a Man. Many years ago, the founder of modern economics, comparing the newly emerging free-market economies with the self-sufficing and isolated producing units of the feudalism of his time, explained the advantage of specialization—which he alleged the free market to enable, by a now famous example. A man who was but occasionally a metalsmith would be doing a creditable job if, when he turned to it, he could make half a hundred pins in the length of a day. But where the market system allowed a man to specialize and to sell the world the product of his labors, then a man could give all of his time to the making of pins and of nothing else, or even, the making not of a pin, but the head of a pin, while another made the body of the pin, and a third joined body and head together. With a man working on the part of a pin, not as an occasional task, but full-time, day-in and day-out, for decades, for the length of a working life, then it could reasonably be expected that not a mere fifty, but thousands of pins would be forthcoming per man-day of work. Thus, was illustrated the marvelous economies and great benefits of the free-market mechanism—for the price of a day's labor, society would have not tens but thousands of pins to consume.

Another wise observer later asked a different question. Granted that by concentrating an individual's labor on making one part of a pin, the output of pins would be greatly increased. But what about the men who did nothing all day but make heads of pins, bodies of pins, join a body and head of a pin together all day. What would a whole life incessantly dedicated to making the heads of pins do to a man? Would he be all of a man? Could there be left a remnant of imagination? What thoughts could he think, what experiences relate? What would it do to the shape of his body? And to the shape of his soul?

When a workman is unceasingly and exclusively engaged in the fabrication of one thing, he ultimately does his work with a singular dexterity; but at the same time he loses the general facility of applying his mind to the direction of his work. He every day becomes more adroit and less industrious; so that it might be said of him that in proportion as the workman improves the man is degraded. What can be expected of a man who has spent twenty years of his life in making heads for pins? And to what can that mighty human intelligence, which has so often stirred the world, be applied in him except it be to

170

investigate the best method of making pins' heads? When a workman has spent a considerable portion of his existence in this manner, his thoughts are forever set upon the object of his daily toil; his body has contracted certain fixed habits, which it can never shake off; in a word, he no longer belongs to himself, but to the calling which he has chosen. It is in vain that laws and manners have been at pains to level all barriers around such a man, and to open to him on every side a thousand different paths to fortune; a theory of manufactures more powerful than manners and laws binds him to a craft, and frequently to a spot, which he cannot leave. . . . In proportion, as the principle of the division of labor is more extensively applied, the workman becomes more weak, more narrow minded, more dependent. The art advances, the artisan recedes.[1]

It may be said that the most important consequence of the social system is society, the most important product of the producing system is the producer—what counts the most is the man who emerges. Therefore, in the comparison of alternative forms of economic organization, it would seem proper to try to take into account not only the prowess of the economy as a producing and self-transforming machine, but also the environment for living that it provides.

Economic Relationships Are Human Relationships. The economy not only delineates activities; it also imposes a structure of relationships between man and man, even between man and nature. Different economic forms, all of which raise, slaughter, and deliver the same chicken to the same consumer's plate, may imply vastly different man-to-man relationships between an independent farmer and the housewife who buys his produce, or between tenant farmers and the feed company officials who contract-out chicken raising at piecework rates, or between manager and employee, or between master and slave, or between collective farmer and the state bureaucrat. The chicken may be equally tough or equally tender; even the costs of breeding, dressing, and transporting the chicken may be the same. Nevertheless, if not to the consumer, certainly to those who participate in production and distribution of the chicken, it matters greatly whether the man-to-man relationship is beween superior and subordinate, or between independent buyer and independent seller, or between lord and serf. It matters to you and to me whether we bargain as equals, whether we agree as partners, or whether one of us gives orders that the other must follow, aside from and independently of the activity in which we are engaged. It matters to us whether in our work we are herded together, or whether we are separate and isolated. It matters whether our position is one of dependence or independence. Regardless of what we make and where and how we make it, the work discipline that

[1] Alex de Tocqueville, *Democracy in America*, pp. 362–363. Adam Smith had the same foreboding.

we are obliged to endure or able to impose matters. Are we baited by the carrot or beaten with the stick? Must we march in step? Do we set our own pace? Do we work out of fear, or from desire? Whom do we suppose to benefit from our efforts? It matters whether we consider ourselves firmly and permanently fixed where we are, whether we dare hope to rise higher, whether we tremble that we may lose our place. It matters greatly whether our work offers an outlet for our talents and our creativity, or whether the chance of such fulfillment is to be tucked away to die in young dreams.

Economic Activity as a Source of Values. Economic organization, because of the forms of activity it requires and the human relationships it imposes, engenders a particular outlook and encourages the development of particular cultural values.

I recall words once said to me as I watched farmers laboriously cultivating steep mountainsides. "The ones who work the soil are honest. You can't bluff the earth. You can't trick it." The salesman, the soldier, the farmer, the servant, the politician, the scientist—each has an outlook and values that are the reflexes of his special experience or derive from the requisites of his task. Similarly, a particular economy ingrains values and an outlook reflecting the common experience and manifesting the general requisites of success or survival in that form of economic organization.

There is in the consciousness what Boulding calls an "image" of the universe of men and things that is relevant to the interests, beliefs, and decisions of the individual. Therein I envisage my role and yours, my purposes, my rights, my place, my worth—and yours, my obligations and yours, what I expect of you and what I expect you to expect of me. And there also are conceived the multifarious interconnections that compose the circuit of cause and consequence. Each has in some sense, a private, peculiar vision. But that which binds is the image we hold in common. Only if (and inasmuch as) we share a vision, do our independent acts mesh harmoniously together, so that I give what is expected and what you do does not disappoint my expectations. The shared image, wherein each conceives his relationship to the whole and his place and function vis-à-vis the others, is the organizing principle of any sort of social system.

The private vision of place and purpose derives from a private experience. The shared image reflects the shared experience—shaped significantly by the form of economic activities and the frame of economic relationships. The individual vision and the shared image are rooted in the minutely familiar, and are formed and sustained by the familiar and commonplace but they cast a distant shadow. As he understands the seen, so man conceives the unseen. He projects what he has learned in the small corner of his existence over the vistas of history and life. The imprint of his economic experience is fixed upon his politics, his religion, his art, his culture. In the ages when men fought and worked in the feudal hierarchy, they made a hierarchy of their Church, and saw hierarchies in heaven with God at the apex of a carefully ordered echelon of lower and higher saints and angels. In the ages of individualism, where each worked for himself, on his own, they sought salvation alone, on their own also, and allowed no intermediaries between the individual and his God.

The form of economic organization shares in shaping the spiritual and aesthetic accomplishments of a civilization. The economic experience shapes the human vision; that vision, coupled with a system of power, expresses itself in cultural achievement.

Interdependence of Social Systems. What his work experience teaches a man to value, to think, to believe, carries over into his behavior in the home, to his vote at the polls, to his religion, to his morals, to his art. A liberal philosophy is incompatible with the integrity of the slavemaster's role. The stratification of political privilege is inseparable from the caste differentiation of economic function. The economy must also be evaluated for its impact on the other elements that compose the social whole, for the other than economic institutions which are its requisites or its consequences.

This relationship works also in reverse. Culture and institutional forms dictate the paths of economic evolution. If values are generated by forms of economic activity, forms of economic activity require particular values for their effective performance or arise as a consequence of these pre-existing values. Collectivism will not work in a context of jealous individualism, and progress under decentralized market choice requires something other than faith, hope, and charity. The successful emergence of new forms of economic organization may require a prior revolution in dominant values.

What here is at issue is the way in which the range of experience attributable to a particular form of economic organization infiltrates the social psychology, outlook, and ethic. Any hypothesis on this score can only be established through observation. Unfortunately, clear-cut proof through observation is hardly possible. Psychological and behaviorial phenomena have been conditioned not by one but simultaneously by a diversity of economic, social, and political forms. Moreover, the body of attitudes and ideas that constitute a culture, with its enormous power of self-perpetuation, is the consequence of an historical experience that antedates existing economic, social, and political activities and institutions.

These complications preclude unequivocally establishing through observation the relationships between a form of economic organization and the components of a social environment. Nevertheless, an impression will be ventured as to the likely consequence of the experience of decentralized market-direction, of centralized political-direction, and of the economy of autonomous organization on value systems and ways of thought and on political organization and social institutions.

Summary. Because it fixes significant man-to-man relationships, because it rests on a peculiar system of power, and because it requires particular forms of activity and striving, economic organization can be evaluated intrinsically as a way of life.

Through the experiences implicit in its operations, through the qualities it rewards, through the types of individual fulfillment and social achievement it permits, the economic organization encourages particular values and attitudes and forges a common outlook. Therefore the economic organization can also be evaluated for its impact on the human character and the social ethic.

Because of its operational prerequisites and because of the values and outlook it engenders, the prevailing form of economic organization will be more or less compatible with other political forms—for example, democratic government and social institutions such as the paternalistic family. Hence an economic organization may be evaluated on the basis of its compatibility with other social forms and institutions that might be looked upon as desirable.

The three chapters which follow will consider decentralized market-direction, centralized political-direction, and the economy of autonomous organization as social environments. Each will be evaluated as a way of life, for its impact on human character and the social ethic, and for its compatibility with certain other social institutions.

Chapter 16

Decentralized Market-Direction as a
Social Environment

ECONOMIC ORGANIZATION AS A WAY OF LIFE

Everyman on His Own. This is the economy of small enterprise. Price is master. The market swallows all striving. Everyman stands alone, on his own, deciding for himself. He is beholden to no other, responsible for no other, and no other man for him. Here, the bargain relates man to man. Men are linked in the antagonism of competition, linked in the interaction of exchange. Seller is competitively poised against seller, buyer against buyer, each straining for self-advantage; buyer and seller, employer and employee are juxtaposed in the thrust and parry, tied together by the tension of the deal. The relationship is competitive, combative, but the combat is the combat of the game.

The Great Game. The essence of this environment is that of an enormous, all-encompassing game, a game of skill and of chance combined. The object of the competition is not to destroy the other, as in the conflict of war, nor to attain a state of dominance, as in the strategy of diplomacy. The object, rather, is to win. Not to vanquish, but to succeed. Each is encircled by threats, readied for a thrust from any side. Motives are not suspect, for the uncompetitive motivation is not expected.

Between man and man there is a kind of equality. Not that they are equal in their skill, or in their luck, or in their possessions, but as players in the game. The rules of the game, such as they are, apply to all equally. Privilege does not attach to persons, but to winnings. Around the gaming table, men stand at a level, each calls his number, makes his bet, and watches the wheel go round. There is the unbitter antagonism of players. Across the bargaining table, men stand at a level, each upon the ground of his own deliberations, and in the calculus of his own advantage makes his bid, fails or succeeds, and engages or disengages at will.

Perpetual Flux. This is a universe of perpetual change, of perpetual chance. There is no let in the game; no break in the pressure. There need be no terror, but there will be tension without end. Skill counts, but so does the luck of the cards. Chance gives and chance snatches away. Every height is under the attack of a thousand climbers. The highest fall; the lowest rise. Always rich-poor, high-low—the ranks are there, but those who compose the ranks are perpetually shifting. None is without fear, and none need be without hope.

The upward and downward social mobility in the fluid economy of decentralized price-direction will create a bond of sorts between rich and poor. The high can be tumbled down, and the poor, in their ambition and hope, identify themselves with the rich. Each sees himself in the other, unless or until nepotism and monopoly have thrown up the barriers of class and have begun the rigidification and transformation of the economy.

The Anonymity of Power. There are no hierarchies and no hierarchs in this form of economic organization. There is no apex of personal power. There are no pedestals from which a few can capture the gaze and imagination of the mass. There are no powerful organizations each with a unique character and image. There are only individuals striving and laboring on the leveled plain, each one for himself by himself. Outlets for achievement and for creative accomplishment are everywhere, and everywhere are petty. Each man makes his own start and ends with the exhaustion of his meager human energies. Any single effort is hardly to be noticed against the outpouring of the whole. Personal fortune and private disaster count for little; one does badly, another does well; one up and another down—what matter. Any man sees any other man without awe, as a winner or a loser like he himself might be. His awe is reserved for the whole, for the system cumulating the infinity of private contributions. No person, but the system, commands respect. It is to the anonymous voice of the market that each must submit.

The Missing Conception of Society. In other forms of economic organization, men are ranged as superior and subordinate in hierarchies. They follow commands that issue from distant heights of power. They are bound together in identifiable groups, or into an organized social whole. Day by day they must work within these groups or within society, for such groups constitute the action-taking, decision-making systems upon which their opportunities depend. Under these conditions the individual cannot do without a viable *conception* of society and of social groups as such, and his every experience impresses upon him the power and significance of these.

Not so in the economy of decentralized market-direction. There the individual has no operational need to conceive of society or of social groups. His economic universe is without hierarchies, without ranks of superior and subordinate, without distant peaks of power. Enough that he knows the tastes of his customers, the vulnerabilities of his rivals and the quirks of his employees; of social groups and of society he need know nothing.

In this universe, the value of activity and effort is in the price they bring. The individual plans, labors, and produces. Thereby, presumably, he benefits others; but he cannot be aware of those benefits and they have nothing to do with his striving. His concern must be and can only be with the price that the results of his efforts yield. For him, the only worth of what he has done or made is the pay-back, and the value of the pay-back is as a means to other ends and gratifications. Philosophers may assure him that what he does maximizes benefits to society. He lacks a conception of society. He knows only the multitudes of competing individuals, and the anonymous power of the market. He is told that what he produces maximizes the utilities of other men. He does not know how, or who, or why, or whether. He stuffs his product into the market's faceless maw and he is paid. That into which he pours his vision and his effort and his hope and his creativity and his days upon days is neutral, without evident purpose—other than the pay or profit that it brings. But if his work is without social purpose, it need not be without intrinsic interest. On the contrary. More than in the alternative forms of economic organization, the tasks of day to day will take the form of problems, within the scope of Everyman, challenging his ingenuity, and rewarding him with the satisfaction of personal achievement.

IMPACT ON SOCIAL VALUES AND ON HUMAN CHARACTER

Man is marvelously adaptive. He assumes the color of his environment, though it is an environment that he would not have chosen. He bends to the needs of survival. He can hardly avoid accepting that which succeeds. He becomes what it pays to become; in the most basic sense, he becomes what he is paid to become. If he fails or rebels, if he will not or cannot adapt—as is sometimes the case—then, in the world of temporal powers he is the more liable to be crushed and trampled under. The way of work, the human relationships in work, the opened paths of ambition—these shape the man. What then does the decentralized market require of him? What does it pay him to become?

Profitable Attitudes. It pays to be aggressive. It pays to push ahead, to know your worth and demand your due, to grab first and to grab hard. If your aggressiveness offends it is no matter. There is no penalty for ruthlessness; and popularity is not the issue.

It pays to try. It pays to hope. Rags to Riches, from Log Cabin to President, is a proper myth and faith for Everyman. Hard work, drive, perseverance are likely to pay. So is thrift. Moderation and temperance that serve to clear the head and conserve the energies are useful. In this world of credit and contract, the confidence of men of property is essential, and hence, honesty (moderated and held in bounds) is a good policy. A tight-fisted creativity, careful not to aim too high, or to go too far too fast, can be a source of considerable reward.

The entrepreneur, the boss, must react and act decisively on a thousand issues round the whole circle of economic choice. He is a jack-of-all-choice. Jack must be nimble, and Jack must be quick. Failure can come suddenly, and opportunity can come suddenly, from anywhere. He must be flexible. He must move fast, but he moves only on the skin of things. He reacts to the circumstances of the instant, to the event and not to that which underlies the event. His experience never confronts him with questions of basic cause or intrinsic purpose. The market yields him no return for comprehending the complexities of the social mechanism, or for a grasp of abstract science or for insight into the guts of phenomena. It pays to be shrewd and pragmatic rather than knowledgeable or contemplative or philosophical or profound.

There is no payoff for pity, piety, generosity, grace, loyalty, or devotion. Eloquence, the genius for intrigue, the charismatic magic of the demagogue are irrelevant here.

Emphasis on Private Choice. As group or social choice is minimized, the strength of the private choice and the sense of private prerogative correspondingly increases; while group or communal choice, outside of the common economic experience, becomes merely an abstract notion, the independent decision constrained only by the "objective" circumstances of the market is commonplace and appears as the natural way of things. The individual practices private choice, acquires skill in it, bends to its imperatives, is indoctrinated into its satisfactions and virtues. Private choice (vis à vis the communal choice) will be valued intrinsically as "freedom." Property, as guarantor and instrument of private choice, comes to be looked upon as a natural and inalienable right.

Individualism and Independence. Above all, the decentralized market economy demands of the individual that he stand alone. It requires that he survive by his own strength. No floor checks his fall and no ceiling blocks his rise. Independent he must be, with the knack and the taste for it: self-reliant, self-responsible, self-concerned, self-instructed. Beginning and end is in the sphere of personal choice and personal responsibility. He is his own prime partisan. Number one, maybe Only One, is himself.

Men are always self-concerned, but self-identification and self-interest may take root in a concept that encloses many others, transcending the personal life. In the decentralized market, the focus of self-interest is narrow, devolving wholly on the gratifications of personal tastes and ambitions. In this form of economic organization, it will be rightly considered that energetic self-seeking and unbridled self-concern, within the constraints of the competitive market, provide the motive force that drives the machine efficiently, that makes the nation strong, that benefits all. The point of view that emerges from the imperatives of the system, the idea, the ideal, the philosophy of individualism, will seem admirable to some. It will strike others with despair. About Individualism, an outlook which he attributed to the "equal conditions" of the decentralized market economy of the United States in the early nineteenth century, De Tocqueville said:

Individualism is a novel expression, to which a novel idea has given birth. Our fathers were only acquainted with egotism. Egotism is a passionate and exaggerated love of self, which leads a man to connect everything with his own person, and to prefer himself to everything in the world. Individualism is a mature and calm feeling which disposes each member of the community to sever himself from the mass of his fellow-creatures; and to draw apart with his family and his friends; so that, after he has thus formed a little circle of his own, he willingly leaves society at large to itself. Egotism originates in blind instinct; indivdualism proceeds from erroneous judgment more than from depraved feelings; it originates as much in the deficiencies of the mind as in the perversity of the heart. Egotism blights the germ of all virtue; individualism at first, only saps the virtues of public life; but in the long run it attacks and destroys all others, and at length is absorbed in downright egotism. Egotism is a vice as old as the world, which does not belong to one form of society more than to another: individualism is of democratic origin, and it threatens to spread in the same ratio as the equality of conditions.[1]

Some will admire the man who emerges from the experience of the system, adapted to its demands: rugged, clear-headed, straightforward, sure-footed. Others will despise him. Cleveland Amory described this dichotomy in two portraits of Commodore Vanderbilt:

In the first portrait he is handsome, hard-headed, bold, brave, virtuous, generous, free-wheeling, constructive—a lovable old empire builder who stands as a paragon of all the old-fashioned virtues of the free-enterprise system. In the second portrait he is a mean, cold, ignorant, truculent, selfish, self-willing, illiterate, ruthless, loveless buccaneer—the original waterer of stock and the autocrat of the directors' table.[2]

In the decentralized market economy, man is shaped as the individual, rugged and alone, independent and aggressive; therein are his virtue and his vice.

[1] Alex de Tocqueville, *Democracy in America*, pp. 310–311.
[2] *The New York Times Book Review*, February 18, 1962, p. 6.

COMPATIBILITY WITH OTHER SOCIAL AND
    POLITICAL INSTITUTIONS

The Diffusion and Interaction of Values. The values that are separately
generated by the economic, political, and social experience cannot be held
apart. The same individual responds to them all, and in him the values
each sphere generates, merge and fuse. What he observes in the market
place, he teaches in the schools and votes at the polls. What is learned at
home or is experienced in the army or at the hands of the police, is
manifested at the workbench or in the trade union. A diversity of experience creates a variegated pattern of values, and it is this whole pattern of
values, this complex of tastes, interests, and competencies, that in turn
influences the operation of the economic organization, the political organization, and the social organization—all three.

The form of economic organization, the form of political organization,
the form of social organization may be more or less compatible, and more
or less antagonistic to each other, since the values fostered through the
operation of the one accelerates and reinforces, or checks and degrades
the operation of another. Hence, a given form of economic organization,
aside from its intrinsic worth, may be valued for the degree to which it
supports or subverts other possible constituents of a society.

As examples of this, consider the compatibility of decentralized market-
direction with (1) political democracy, (2) political freedom, and (3)
Protestantism and nationalism.

Political Democracy. Political democracy may be understood as a government that is effectively answerable to the electorate through periodic
elections, and that includes in its processes of choice a representation of
those different interests and points of view, that, in fact, characterize the
society. Implicit in the *ideal* of political democracy are the norms of
universal suffrage and majority rule.

History gives only an equivocal answer to the question of whether
decentralized market-direction supports or subverts political democracy.
On the one hand, coincident with the rise of Western "capitalism," the
idea of democracy did spread to the ends of the earth and become accepted almost universally as a norm of political behavior. On the other
hand, democracy was born in the slave economies of ancient Greece.
Parliamentary institutions were the creation of feudal aristocracies. And
established "free-enterprise" societies have given rise to dictatorship and
tyranny. On a priori grounds, however, one would suppose that the experience of decentralized market-direction favors conditions of political
democracy.

The habit of independent choice, the ingrained self-reliance developed in the struggle for economic success, will be manifested in political behavior also. The taste for independent choice, cultivated in the economy will incline the individual to assert his views in the political sphere as well; it will sharpen his demand that his goals be furthered and his interests considered through elected representatives.

Democracy demands submission to the will and the rule of a faceless average—the majority. In the market also the individual yields to the impersonal expression of aggregated opinion—to market demand, abstracted from the multiplicity of individual plans, schemes, and exertions. The Consumer (like the majority), a composite of the multitude of visible men, totaled and averaged, is sovereign.

Democracy requires, above all, respect for a process, rather than for persons. And under decentralized market-direction also, the individual, who recognizes and accepts no personal authority, willingly follows the beckoning of price, and submits to the process of exchange.

The habit of the market has its analogue at the polls. The citizen casts his vote to choose between candidates for office. The consumer spends his dollar to choose a product. Economists like to speak of the consumer as voting with his dollar. The producer follows the power of the dollar. The politician follows the power of the vote. As consumer demand is the arbiter of economic values, majority opinion is the democratic criterion of political values.

Political Freedom. Political "freedom" or "liberty" has been variously understood. It sometimes means the converse of the exercise of authority by a government that has not been elected by or does not represent the interest of those who must submit to its rule. This was the kind of liberty that Patrick Henry proposed to have or to die for. So understood, freedom is synonymous with political democracy. It is, in effect, the condition of the electorate in a system of political democracy.

Political freedom can also mean the procedural guarantees that protect the person against the arbitrary exercise of power. In the U.S. Constitution and in the common law, these procedural protections are expressed in the guarantees of "due process." Such is the nature of "freedom" demanded by those who ask for a "government of laws and not of men." Between "freedom" or "liberty" thus understood and the experience of decentralized market-direction, there is no discernable relationship, one way or the other.

Political freedom or liberty, finally, can mean an absence of political constraints upon the choices and activities of individuals. Thus understood, the fewer the political constraints on the activities of the individual, the greater would be his freedom. Conversely, the wider the sphere of collective choice and of governmental responsibility, the less would be "freedom." The values of this kind of "freedom" or "liberty" are controversial, not only at the extreme of a human jungle where political authority would be absent and, hence, "freedom" would be complete, but also in the exercise of the supposedly rock-bottom, ineluctable, inalienable human rights (such as exercise of freedom of speech in the U.S.A., by communists and other minorities considered to be "subversive"), as absolute prerogatives. Nor should it be thought that extending freedom of this sort, that is, diminishing the exercise of public sanction or governmental power, means a lessening of exterior constraint upon the activities of the individual. It may mean rather the substitution of other, and perhaps more onerous constraints. The Federal Employment Practices Act, for example, constrained the employer. But in allowing the employer untrammeled freedom to accept or reject any who apply for a job, constraints are imposed upon the Negro's choice with respect to his work or association.

In any case, adaptation to a decentralized market economy would certainly generate attitudes that favor a reliance on private rather than on communal choice. And these attitudes are likely to be manifested in the defense of such "freedom" against political authority. The powers of private property inherent in the operation of the decentralized market also carry over into social organization, for example, in the perpetuation of the paternalistic family. The possession of property, the outlook of individualism, and the habit of independent and self-responsible choice will reinforce the notion of inalienable rights of private choice and will encourage a general antipathy for public intervention anywhere.

Protestantism and Nationalism. In Bernard Shaw's play, *Saint Joan,* there is a scene where the Earl of Warwick, speaking for the feudal aristocracy, and Peter Cauchon, Bishop of Beauvais, speaking for the medieval Church, discuss the threat of Joan of Arc to the spiritual and to the temporal powers of the time. The Bishop inveighs against Joan for her "monstrous self-conceit of being directly inspired from heaven." Warwick answers:

. . . Remember that there are temporal institutions in the world as well as spiritual ones. I and my peers represent the feudal aristocracy as you represent the Church . . . do you not see how this girl's idea strikes at us?
CAUCHON: How . . . ?
WARWICK: Her idea is that the kings should give their realms to God, and then reign as God's bailiffs. . . . It is a cunning device to supersede the aristocracy, and make the king sole and absolute autocrat. . . . That we cannot suffer. If the peoples' thoughts and hearts were turned to the king and their lords became only the king's servants in their eyes, the king could break us across his knee one by one, and then what should we be but liveried courtiers in his halls? . . .

CAUCHON: . . . I see now that what is in your mind is not that this girl has never once mentioned The Church, and thinks only of God and herself, but that she has never mentioned the peerage, and thinks only of the king and herself.

WARWICK: Quite so. These two ideas of hers are the same idea at bottom. It goes deeply, my lord. It is the protest of the individual soul against the interference of priest or peer between the private man and his God. I should call it Protestantism if I had to find a name for it. . . .

CAUCHON: . . . As a priest I have gained a knowledge of the minds of the common people, and there you will find yet another most danger-ous idea. I can express it only by such phrases as France for the French, England for the English, Italy for the Italians, Spain for the Spanish. . . . When she threatens to drive the English from the soil of France she is undoubtedly thinking of the whole extent of the country in which French is spoken. For her the French-speaking people are what the Holy Scripture describes as a Nation. Call this side of her heresy Nationalism if you will. . . .

WARWICK: Well, if you will burn the Protestant, I will burn the Nationalist.

In the decentralized market economy the individual stands alone, self-responsible, self-reliant, self-seeking. And for those shaped by that experi-ence, it will seem evident that the individual must be himself the arbiter of his private truth and must rely on his own efforts and prayer and awareness in seeking God. Given the outlook of individualism, the notion that the hierarchies of the Church should intervene between the private soul and its God must lose force. With the historic advent of the outlook of individualism, the Church ceased to be understood as an instrument of intercession. It became the place, rather, where the individual turned to the task of spiritual self-examination. In Protestantism, individualism projected itself heavenward.

Similarly the outlook of individualism rendered the feudal political hierarchies obsolete. The self-reliant, self-responsible individual might recognize the sovereign power of the State but not the need for inter-mediaries to stand between that sovereign power and himself. National-ism brushed aside the intercession of the peerage between man and the sovereign power of the State, just as Protestantism had eliminated the intercession of the priest between man and the sovereign power of his Lord.

Nationalism as Super-Individualism. Nationalism did more. It created a new *kind* of community, one not based on the traditional submissions and allegiances of feudalism, nor on the blood heritage of the tribe, nor on adherence to a common faith and doctrine, but rather, and perhaps uniquely in history, on a *felt* affinity among multitudes. Men came to-gether because they felt alike. Each was magnetized toward others who were like himself in appearance, in speech, in religion, in attitudes and values, in tastes, in the stamp of a common history. The patterns in which men found a common national identity are many and varied. Though religion, language, or race may be similar in a nation, the nation is not a community based on religion, race or language except in that these may contribute to the sense of likeness. The individual identifies himself with a group in which he sees himself. The Nation is his mirrored image. And it is on the depth and strength of this sensed alikeness that the cohesiveness of the nation depends.

Decentralized markets, the philosophy of individualism, national states, and the cult of nationalism came at the same juncture of history. In part through the experience of the decentralized market economy, an outlook became dominant in which the rationality of the private man was understood as the sole arbiter of truth, where the private decision was the proper locus of all choice, and where the only meaningful values were the private goals and wants and moral imperatives of the individual on his own. Given this outlook, the only temporal agency which the individual could acknowledge as sovereign was one in which he saw himself reflected. The Nation in the epoch of individualism was the individual by proxy. The idea of nationalism is nothing else than the projection of the peculiar and particular physiognomy of self. It is, for the individual, a means of self-conception; in the Nation he finds his own face. So powerful a force today as, say, Arab nationalism, is quiet empty of social objective or moral imperative, or common law or doctrine, or allegiance to a God or a man or tribe, but is simply a sensed image of self in which millions find their identity. Its importance is an assertion of self-importance. Nor could the idea of Nation have the tremendous emotional impact that it has had unless it had been juxtaposed to other identities, other faces (other nations) in which the individual does not see himself but sees the other. The cult of nationalism projects and fuses the egoisms of a multitude, asserting their uniqueness and particularity vis à vis others.

The experience of the decentralized market thus generates (or reinforces) the outlook of individualism, which asserts the supreme value and ultimate sovereign power of the self-responsible, free individual. Individualism proves incompatible with political and religious hierarchies and finds its collective expression in nationalism, where the Nation, in proxy of the individuals who find their identity in it, asserts absolute sovereignty, admitting no power beyond itself and no interest beyond its own.

SUMMARY

Man is shaped by his experience in the decentralized market as the self-reliant, self-responsible, self-interested individual. The relationship between men lies in the tension of the deal, in the bargain, in the thrust and parry of the game. Relationships are fluid, subject to a perpetual change and a perpetual chance that raises the poor and tumbles down the rich, so that none is without fear and none needs to be without hope.

Individualism is the summarizing value and philosophical nexus reinforced by the experience of the decentralized market-directed form of economic organization. Those who participate in this market know the equality of contestants competing independently in a universe of unending but bounded conflict. Work is unrelated to any purpose outside itself. Efforts are without social purpose, and indeed the notion of social purpose, or of society, or of social groups, as operative entities, is lacking. The joy is in the doing, in winning, and in the winnings. All efforts are bent to succeed, for the sake of success, success in the concrete, specific, saleable. Outlets for creativity are everywhere, and petty everywhere. The individual is small; his efforts among all the efforts are infinitesimal. But the abstract force of the system is overwhelming. The power of the massed whole is overwhelming. The experience of this market fosters no regard for authority or for personages, but fosters respect for the abstract will of the consumer, for the averaged taste, for the system.

Values created by the economic experience, by the political experience, by the social experience amalgamate. This amalgam relates back to (and must be consistent with) the operations of the economic or political or social forms of organization. Values created through the experience of one such form of organization intersect to support or to subvert, the other forms of organization. The capacity for independent economic decision-making, the philosophy that holds that all worth resides in the individual, the habit of submission to a general (consumer) will, the exaltation of the average: all these derivatives of decentralized market-direction gear into and support the processes of democratic government and the notion of personal political liberties.

Individualism, bred of the market experience, impatient with intercession between man and his sovereign on earth or in heaven, created in its own terms a cosmology and a polity in which there was only God and man, only State and citizen, with nothing intervening. The nation-state, moreover, is a political community that found its cohesion as the projected and fused individualism of the multitude writ large.

Chapter 17

Centralized Political-Direction as a Social Environment

ECONOMIC ORGANIZATION AS A WAY OF LIFE

Society as the Locus of Values. Under centralized political-direction, the locus of choice, the focus of concern, and the repository of values is a society, including the interests and activities of all who are within a political domain. Under decentralized market-direction, choice was by the individual; here choice is by the all-encompassing group. In the decentralized market, Everyman stood alone. Here he is merged into the group, bound by it, and his choices are effective only within and as a part of its processes of decision-making and action-taking. He depends absolutely on the directives of others and on the social policy. Society is responsible for him and he is responsible to a society, and for a society.

The Apparatus of Centralized Direction. When a vast complex of activities are planned from the center and directives are transmitted to the far reaches of the economy, then there will be hierarchy, chains of command, chains of responsibility, and chains of answerability.

Between those who formulate the social policy and those who are engaged in the specifics of production and distribution, there will be the substantial echelons who gather, organize, and transmit information, who study and deliberate on phenomena relevant to choice, who formulate plans, who transmit directives, who keep accounts, who coordinate activities. The bureaucracy will constitute a higher proportion of the total labor force and will play a more significant role under centralized political-direction than in the alternative forms of organization. Because the work of the bureaucrat is second, third, or fourth removed from the points of its practical payoff, it is generally impossible to evaluate its real contribution, or to build into the bureaucratic controls an incentive system that effectively relates contribution to reward. When the bureaucracy becomes the judge of its own functional necessity, internecine rivalry and the ambitions of "empire builders" may serve to swell the apparatus into a gigantic and parasitical body. The possibilities of exploiting their positions for private gain or for satisfactions in the exercise of personal tyranny perpetually tempt the petty bureaucrats who act as gatekeepers for the doors and long winding avenues to power and decision. These are problems for any bureaucracy, but they will be relatively the most severe in the economy of centralized political-direction where the bureaucratic apparatus is larger and of greater importance.

Finally, to offset regressive tendencies in the bureaucracy, to check ideological deviation, and to support the implementation of the plan (by using the stick as well as the carrot), centralized political-direction has the capacity to use and will probably require an instrument of supervision and coercion that stands apart from the activities of the bureaucracy and of those engaged in the specifics of production and distribution. The police are also likely to be an instrument of economic control.

Income Equality but Functional Inequality. Conceivably, the distribution of income could be more nearly equal, more "just" (or "unjust" and "unequal") under centralized political-direction than under any alternative forms. But, though the distribution of income may be more equal, the distribution of functional responsibility and power will inherently be less equal under centralized political-direction than in the alternative forms of economic organization studied here. Centralized direction fixes rank upon rank, superior upon subordinate, in an enormous pyramid. The decision-making power devolves upon a few, as, conversely in the economy of decentralized market-direction, it was spread among multitudes.

The Religious Core. Centralized political-direction, for its initial organization and for its continuing development and effectiveness, needs something other than the self-interested ambitions of individuals. There is absolutely required on the part of those who exercise the ultimate power a dedication to a goal beyond the sphere of personal gain. Moreover, if their efforts are not to be dissipated in dissension, and are to result in the evolution of a coherent system and in consistent policy, then dedication must be to the same goal; they must accept the same criteria of evaluation; and, since the choice of means depends not only upon the goal but also upon the conception of the universe of action, they must also share an outlook with respect to the nature of society and of man. They need a common understanding of what is, a common belief in what ought to be, and a common faith in what will be.

The centralized politically directed society, or at least the elite of that society which formulates and stands responsible for the system, must have *religion*: a religion which in the old sense embodies cosmology, morality, and social philosophy—powerful, all-pervading, and at the root of economic choice.

The economy of centralized direction has not only the aspect of a political society, but of a religious society also. And a religious society has its own operational prerequisites.

The Religious Apparatus. A religious society, if we may judge from historical experience, needs its revealed truth as an anchor of its belief, and a doctrine as a guide to all those who are perplexed. It needs its prophets and its saints as examples for the faithful. It is likely to have an iconography and a ritual since these excite the zeal and capture the dedication of the multitudes.

A religion that is to continue must be passed on from generation to generation. This requires indoctrination through teachers, and priests, and through myth, folklore, history, and tradition.

And the living religion, particularly one that serves as a basis for economic choice in the modern world, must have the capacity to incorporate the lessons of experience, to modify itself, to change and evolve with the currents of thought and in the light of the new vistas with which history confronts every society. This process of reinterpretation, adaptation, and change, which would adjust to the new without sacrificing the unifying force of that which is revealed, revered, and accepted, also requires separate and special institutions.

The Nature of the Faith. In examining the centralized politically directed form of economic organization as an instrument for the efficient allocation of resources and for the just distribution of income and for the achievement of economic progress, it is perhaps enough to say that this economy requires a powerful "religious" dedication as its first motivating force. But when one considers this form of economy as a social environment, it is necessary to ask "What religion?" The nature of the faith will be of supreme importance in coloring the way of life. But the nature of the faith is not implicit in the form of economic organization itself.

It follows certainly from the rationale of Marx's thought that the Nazi triumph in Germany was a great and successful *socialist* revolution, since the real controls over the "means of production" passed from the holders of private property exercising choice in the market place to planners who derived their power from and were held responsible to a political society. That the Nazi triumph was in fact *not* a socialist or a communist revolution in spite of essentially the same modalities of production is due to a difference in the nature of the faith that dominated centralized political-direction in the one instance and in the other.

While the system of centralized political-direction requires a religious core, it may be God or the Devil who is worshipped. The nature of the religion rather than the fact of religiosity gives to such a society its values as a social environment.

There is, alas, no simple relationship between the nature of the faith and the environment it produces, nor between the articles of a faith and the values that in fact dominate the faithful, nor between the commands of the prophet and the demands of the church, nor between what is preached and practiced. Carrying the banner of love and gentleness, zealots murder and rape; under the flag of freedom they enslave. The Christian Church triumphed, but how many lived by Christ's teaching? Under the ideal of justice, tyranny is practiced. Yet the acknowledged ideal, though ignored, the preaching that is not practiced, matters if only for providing the standard by which the practice is seen as perverse.

The content of the dominating faith, the nature of the unifying image: these are not given by the form of the economic organization. These derive from elsewhere. But in the politically directed, centralized economy, the substance of the faith and the norms of the religion will be of consummate importance, for there more than elsewhere they will reach into the patterns of day-to-day living.

Derived and Inculcated Values. Under decentralized market-direction, dominant values and outlook will derive spontaneously from the particular pattern of economic experience. Certain values and a particular outlook also will be promoted through the experience of centralized political-direction; however, in centralized political-direction, to a unique degree, values must and will be inculcated deliberately as a matter of policy.

As Chapters 12 and 13 showed, centralized political-direction cannot rely (as the economy of decentralized market-direction might) on technical self-education on the job. It must provide institutions for formal scientific education and for technical training as part and parcel of its economic plan. So also, as a "religious" society, it needs an apparatus of propagation, indoctrination, perhaps of proselytization.

Hence, the instruments for the deliberated inculcation of values are readily at hand. To some extent the values chosen for indoctrination will be dictated by economic necessity and by the requisites of the system. Nevertheless, within the bounds of operational needs, there are wide variations possible in the values which might be inculcated. The choice of those values is not implicit in the form of economic organization per se.

IMPACT ON SOCIAL VALUES AND ON HUMAN CHARACTER

The Environment of Centralized Political-Direction. Centralized political-direction thus provides an environment where choice is collective rather than personal, where emphasis is social rather than individual, where bureaucracy is pre-eminent, and where the police constitute an instrument of economic activation and control. Hierarchy here is more complex and more sharply drawn, and inequalities of function are greater than in the other forms of economic organization. This is, moreover, a religious society, of priests and believers, of doubters and heretics, with its apparatus of exegesis, indoctrination, and propagation. At issue, then, is what impact an environment such as this might have on social values and on human character.

The Sense of Social Purpose. Since this economy acts as a single entity, since it chooses goals as a group qua group, since its parts find meaning and gain significance only in their relationship to the integral operation of the whole, it requires that its elements see themselves as members of the group and acknowledge the group as more than themselves. What unifies will be made sacrosanct. The communality will be emphasized. Communication, community, commonality are prerequisites to effectiveness.

Centralized political-direction could thus maximize the individual's sense of fellowship, of participation in social achievement, of personal immortality through identification with the social whole. Through the operation of the system, individuals may find their way to a true community. Each is offered an outlet for devotion and for dedication. To give rather than to get could become the point and order of every day's efforts. Everyman may find for the years of his strivings (which in any case will be full of pain and pettiness) a high and a rational purpose.

Individual Aggression vs. the Social Furies. In the decentralized economy each man is perpetually involved in the struggle of the business game, where his aggressiveness is cultivated, and where, perhaps, his aggressions are exhausted. With centralized political-direction, men are not plunged in a perpetual and generalized state of conflict. They dwell more in the quietude of the herd. They know the comradeship of the ranks. They rise by seniority, by popularity, by the favor of those above, or through examination. Their aggressiveness is not cultivated, nor is it exhausted. It may be sublimated, or it may be repressed to reappear in the frenzy of hatred against the antigroup, or the outgroup, or against nightmare images painted by the demagogue in the shape of men's hidden fears.

The decentralized market is a kind of jungle with each on his own, where the weak fall and are eaten, where the play of chance raises some high and flings others down. The centralized politically directed economy creates an association where relationships may be ordered by reason and morality, and where the individual is secure in the solidarity of the group. The strength of the whole buoys each of its parts.

The market economy confronts the individual with a universe of ambitions and aggressions, but the politically directed economy confronts the individual with the massive all-encompassing collective power. Under centralization, man may be protected against man and against chance, but he is helpless before the wrath of the group, before its panic and prejudice, before its doctrinal fanaticism, before its tyranny. Decentralized society may be a jungle, but in its coverts an individual can escape the furies of society. Which then is to be preferred, a system that supports the individual with the solidarity of the community, or one where there remains an escape from the social juggernaut?

Command and Submission. Centralized political-direction requires that the multiplicity composing the whole be unified and ordered into an integral organization, responsive to the single directive of a central authority. The vast echelons must whip and turn to the emanation of a central will. This necessitates discipline, the habit of obedience, and the manner of command. For the ranks to be disciplined, rankers must be self-disciplined, able to shape themselves to the rule. They must be adaptable, flexible, able to fit the niches they are given, able to adapt to the comradeship of the instant, accommodating their assigned roles, tasks, and purposes. And those who command must acquire the skills and habits of hard-faced decisiveness, simplicity, and certainty.

Hierarchy requires that the hierarchs be loyal—but the necessary loyalty is not to persons or to friends chosen by the whims of personality or to those linked in the genetic accident of family, but to constituted authority and to the ranks below, loyal to office, to the "stripes"—to the system and its ideology.

Priests, Believers, and Heretics. The centralized politically directed economy is, at core, a religious system, and like every powerful religious system it needs its priests and its believers. The good, the consecrated, the effective priest should be selfless and dedicated. The faithful should be pious, accepting, and loyal.

As in any religious system, there will be doctrine and dogma. The actual or incipient powers of orthodoxy will always be great, and may perhaps fix blinders on Everyman's thought and imagination.

As in any religious system there will be defenses against whatever divides allegiances or casts doubts upon the unifying faith. Independence and self-sufficiency may be suspect. Heresy, schism, and disloyalty will face anathema. To the degree that the group is glorified, the out-group is a subspecies, the ungroup is a purgatory, the antigroup is the very host of Lucifer.

The Capacity for Abstraction. On the leveled plain of individualism, in the universe of decentralized choice (where the operating unit is cut to the size of a single man, where all plans and decisions are within the scope of the one on his own), authority is suspect. Every man judges for himself. No man needs a philosophy to find his way. What is needed is a feel for the particular and a sharp eye for the main chance. Theory is shunned. Abstraction is an affectation. In this environment, there is no language but the vernacular. Truth is in the facts, the everyday facts, the lay experience. Thought seeks the concrete, the expedient, the particular, and the practical.

In the vast pyramidal operating complex of the centralized economy, authority is pre-eminent. Command descends from the peaks of the hierarchy. And beyond the highest hierarchs is the Word itself, interpreted by a consecrated elite. The breadth of the operating entity is beyond the grasp, beyond the scope of any man. Its organization and direction are shared among groups of experts, each with its own hierarchs, and each set apart from the rest by its peculiar knowledge and its special jargon. Authority of the expert, authority of the hierarch, authority of church or party, authority of the plan, authority of doctrine: Everyman must seek for and must learn to accept the word of authority. Thought seeks for the stamp and the sanction of authority.

No man, in the complexity of this universe, can find his way, can make sense of things, can find his place and rationalize his role except through an encompassing philosophy (or through an encompassing dogma). In this universe of experience, abstraction is not indulgence, but is the very essence of any creative action and choice. The image of society is itself an abstraction and so is the faith that unifies and the ideal that directs. A workable conception of the operating organization demands a high level of abstraction.

In the environment of centralization, thought will be more pressed to master abstraction and to acquire dialectical skill. Compared to the decentralized society, thought will be more systematic and less sceptical; learning will be easier, unlearning more difficult. The mind will tread more easily in the high reaches of pure theory, but fumble more often the particular, the practical, the applied. Thought will more readily congeal into complex systems developing cumulatively under the aegis of authority, and authority will throw up a powerful barrier against the challenge of doubt and the thrust of innovation. Philosophy will be more general; common sense more rare.

The Individual and the Social Being. Homo sapiens is a biological, physiological organism, but *Man* is a varied and changing conception. This conception, then, shapes men; their characters mirror it. They make themselves into what they conceive themselves to be. And the image of man derives, in part, from the requisites of society, from the circumstances of the economy. In the decentralized society man was conceived as the individual, a composite of tastes, passions, possessions, and accomplishment. Thus the person understood himself. In the centralized society man is conceived as the member of the group, as its part, its cog, its requisite element. The person understands himself as a social being, functionally part of the group, whose purpose is the purpose of the group, who finds his power, prestige, and accomplishment, in the power, prestige, and accomplishment of the group. In the decentralized society, an individual is responsible, and cannot evade responsibility, within the narrow but clear and stern boundaries of private choice. In the centralized environment, the dedication of the social being may be high and noble, or it may dissolve into a mere yielding, a blind obedience that surrenders all the prerogatives of private judgment.

The politically directed centralized economy makes men obey and believe. Some will be pious, serene. Some will be loyal, obedient in the dignity of belief. Some will be servile. Some will be the creatures of fear.

COMPATIBILITY WITH OTHER SOCIAL INSTITUTIONS

Personal Liberties and Rights. The centralized politically directed economy organizes the whole of the economic process as a political activity and a species of social choice. The scope of political participation is maximized. Independent decision-making is constricted.

It is doubtful that our traditional conception of individual liberties, deriving from the taste for independent decision-making and asserting the rights of the individual against the group, can flourish or long survive in the environment of centralized political-direction. Under politically directed centralization, the very conception of the individual as an independent entity aside from groups, outside or above groups, would seem to lose meaning. The ideal and idea of choice by the individual, responsible to none but himself, becomes anachronistic. On the other hand, the extension of political controls over a vast sphere of activity requires the multiplication of personal guarantees of another sort. Only clear definition and careful enforcement of the hierarchs' prerogatives and responsibilities will keep the organization running well. The nature of power requires an increase in the political guarantees of personal rights. Under decentralized market-direction, the abuse of power is automatically checked by the limitations implicit in property (where economic power has its locus) and by the force of market competition—checks that partially reconcile the private exercise of power to the public weal. Under politically directed centralization, there is no such inherent limitation; therefore if the system is to work effectively, the use and abuse of power must be controlled by rules of law. It is thus likely that the rational evolution of a system of centralized political-direction would lead to the extension of legal guarantees of personal rights and prerogatives beyond what has hitherto been practiced or even conceived. The "liberties" proper to the centralized economy would be quite unrelated to the liberal goals of protecting individual values and individual decision-making against the incursion of collective values and collective decision-making. Rather, their objective would be to facilitate the process of collective choice and action by regulating the relationship between those who participate, and by controlling the use of the authority delegated to those charged with implementing policy.

Representative Democracy. It is finally to be doubted that representative democracy in the politically centralized society could ever have the functional significance and the moral value that it has had in the liberal tradition of decentralized choice. If, as has here been supposed, the effective centralized economy requires a religious core, then majority rule, with its glorification of average values, loses its force as a political criterion. The Goal is not in the tastes of the multitude, the Truth is not in the majority, but rather in the unifying image, in the perpetuated belief, in the revealed doctrine. It is the function of the consecrated elite to fulfill that Truth, to interpret the doctrine, to carry the torches of belief. The good priest may be responsible to his parishioners, and responsible for them, but he does not represent them. He is no mere pollster. He serves his people, but he is not their servant. He is the servant of what he believes is above them all. Hence, in the politically directed economy and the centralized society, good government and bad will be of a different order than in the environment of individualism and in the economy of decentralized choice.

SUMMARY

The environment of centralized political-direction is of an all-encompassing social group that absorbs the strivings of the particular participant, demands his dedication and loyalty, and controls and protects him. Only within the group, through the group, in proxy of the group is there an exercise of personal choice.

The apparatus of the system will be characterized by a massive bureaucracy, by the exercise of the police power as an instrument of economic supervision. The exercise of political control over economic activity will require a hierarchy of command, with loyal hierarchs and disciplined ranks.

If it is to be effective there must be at the core of this system, motivating at least the controlling elite, a common and unifying outlook and a dedication beyond the self-interest of individuals. In this sense, the economy of centralized political-direction will be a "religious" society, with a shared faith as its cohesive and driving force, inseparable from its processes of choice. The religious society requires its priests and its true believers, its rituals, its saints, its prophets, and its institutions for indoctrination and propagation and reinterpretation. The significance of religiosity colors the environment of any centralized politically directed economy; but more important for the environment of social life than the fact of religiosity is the particular nature of the faith, for the sublime and the monstrous are equally admissible. The nature of the faith will be determined by historical forces and circumstances extraneous to the form of economic organization.

Centralized political-direction, more than any alternative form of economic organization, can offer Everyman a sense of social purpose and the experience of community. He is sustained by the strength of society. But he is bound with the rigidities of orthodoxy and is vulnerable to the collective furies.

Rather than on the individual, with his self-reliance and his clear lines of private responsibility, the emphasis is on the social being, disciplined and obedient, conscious of his obligations to the group, subordinating himself to its values, and oblivious of any other choice beyond the collective will, or of any obligation or value or right that is not of the group. The social being is surely a creature of many possible faces, of many possible qualities: dedication, brotherhood, fellowship, patience, loyalty, submissiveness, diplomacy, cunning, orthodoxy, parasitism, megalomania, tyranny, servility.

The experience of centralized political-direction is also likely to have its impact on the systems of cognition and the qualities of thought. In its complexity and extension, the centralized organization cannot be comprehended with the immediacy of concrete individual experience. To understand it and to make headway within it demands an effort of abstraction. Moreover, with power exercised from a distant center and with a "religious" faith as the core of that power, the notion and the experience of authority must be pervasive. These two features, a capacity for abstraction and an emphasis on authority, will stamp the norm of thought.

That notion of freedom which juxtaposes a sacrosanct sphere of individualism against collective choice becomes meaningless here, where all decisions are political. Nor is representative democracy consistent with a system where authority does not represent independent interests but interprets revealed doctrine or expresses the unifying faith. Procedural and legal guarantees that protect the rights and define the relationships of individuals are entirely consistent with this form of organization.

Chapter 18

The Economy of Autonomous Organizations as a Social Environment

THE ECONOMY AS A WAY OF LIFE

Organizational Choice. The economy of autonomous organization requires that individual choice be exercised, private initiatives be taken, and private responses be made through the medium of an organized group. The individual can realize his ambitions only within the group, as part of the group, through the group. His self-identification, perforce, is tied to that of the group. The group on which he depends, however, is not the whole of his society as it is in centralized political-direction, but is, nevertheless, large and complex, requiring an apparatus for making and implementing policy.

"Voluntary" Association. Participation in production and distribution requires that the individual integrate into the activity of and operate through an organized group. But there are many groups in this economy, each autonomous, independent, and competitive. The individual is free to seek an association with any particular group or with a number of groups. He must associate, but he is, to a degree, free to choose his association and free to disassociate or change his affiliation. In that sense association is voluntary. In particular instances, this freedom of choice, however, can be extremely constricted.

Intermediary Qualities. The social environment of autonomous organization incorporates elements of centralized political-direction and of decentralized market-direction. These elements are not always compatible. Consequently, contradictions arise.

While the task of planning and control is not all-inclusive, as it is under centralized political-direction, nevertheless it will be formidable, requiring a large and powerful apparatus. Correspondingly there will exist the conditions and consequences of bureaucracy.

For his livelihood and in his economic activities, the individual depends on the group, and hence he is subject to group biases and conventions and politics to a degree that he could not be under decentralized market-direction. On the other hand, because of the multiplicity of groups among which he may find haven, and because those groups are functionally oriented rather than ideologically directed, the individual is less exposed and less vulnerable to social prejudices or to political bias than he would be under centralized political-direction.

The use of the police power as a means of supervising and controlling the individual in his economic activities is not possible in this economy, nor presumably is it necessary. The competitive struggle of organizations to survive and grow and the self-interest of individuals within the organization give the system its dynamism. But the nature of competition is equivocal, and policies of autonomous agencies may run counter to the social interest. While the individual in his economic activities will not ordinarily be subjected to the coercive supervision of the State, the organizations to which he belongs will be pressured, regulated, and policed under the government's coercive powers.

Although nothing is substituted for the rationale of self-interest as the motor force of the economy, nevertheless there is a highly equivocal relationship between the self-interested choices of individuals within the autonomous organization and the interests of the organization qua organization, or between the rationale of organizational interests and the social interest. For example, the trade union is considered an instrument for maximizing the benefits of the trade unionists, but if the trade union official, following his self-interest, uses his powers and position to benefit himself by taking "kickbacks" from the companies he bargains with, he is considered a criminal, and, if the trade union official considers only the gains to his membership, he is also frowned upon as socially perverse. Such contradictions appear throughout. It is likely that the group will evolve codes of behavior designed to protect its interest qua organization, holding the private drives of participating individuals in check.

The Managerial Elite. The economy of autonomous organization has also its pyramids of power. At the apex of its hierarchies will stand the "managerial elite," functionally oriented experts and technicians, rather than politicians and ideologists. At those heights, however, here as in centralized political-direction, the problems are both technical and political. If the zealot, politician, or party man at the helm of the other system may blunder out of technical incapacity, the managerial elite in the economy of autonomous organization is as likely to lack needed sensitivities and capacities in the realm of politics and social values.

The Shaping of Opinion. The processes through which the ideas, information, knowledge, insights, and creative artistic achievement of individuals or groups are communicated to a public (i.e., publishing, newspapers, television, radio) are controlled here, as are all marketable activities, by large business corporations.

Control of the channels of public communication by a relatively small number of market-oriented autonomous organizations will mean that only a narrow range of political, artistic, literary, or philosophical viewpoints can be expressed, since the number of controlling agencies, each with its particular editorial bias, will be few. The bias of these agencies will reflect the values and prejudices of the leadership of autonomous organizations. Hence the values, views, and interests of this segment of the society will be given a disproportionate emphasis relative to the opinions and interests prevailing elsewhere in the community.

The autonomous organization has, to a significant degree, the *power* to inform public opinion, to develop public taste, to open or to close the channels of artistic creativity. It has the power, without commensurate responsibility. It is not motivated to consider the full impact of its policies.

Its advertising is a powerful instrument for the inculcation of ideas and the propagation of values. But what values? What point of view? Good or bad? Socially desirable or undesirable? The issue does not arise among advertisers or advertising agencies. Nevertheless, advertising may shape society and its values in a way that is clearly pernicious.

IMPACT ON SOCIAL VALUES AND ON HUMAN CHARACTER

The Capacity for Association. In the economy of autonomous organization, the individual must associate. He can only work, he can only be effective in his intended actions, he can only realize his personal ambitions, he can only achieve power and acclaim and material reward through the group (or groups) and as part of the group (or groups). Yet this relationship of the individual to the group is of a very particular kind. It is not passive, based on ties of affection or on a sense of common identity, as that which for example might unite the members of a family or which might relate Catholics, or Jews, or Americans, or Negroes. Rather it is a relationship in action, uniting individuals in the organization of highly complex, functional activities. These are not functional activities carried on under some common moral, or political, or ideological imperative; nor do they imply an adherence to a common purpose; nor, for these reasons, can such an organization operate as an army would, through the techniques of coercion and command, through regularized lines of status and hierarchy and habituated obedience. It is rather an amalgam of private interests voluntarily related for the purpose of mutual gain. For such an organization to operate effectively requires "teamwork." Personal success within it "on the team" requires a capacity to influence rather than to command, requires a sensitivity to the interests of associates, requires initiative without manifest aggression. The circumstances will favor and the success of the system will require the development of the values and skills of "association." The experience of autonomous organization and its imperatives will encourage cultivating this capacity for association and the pleasures of association. The possibility of self-fulfillment through association—will acquire a primary place in the scale of values.

The Company Man. The "company man," shaped to the requirements of autonomous organization, has the skills of association and is dominated by the values of association. He is friendly, a good mixer, pleasant, careful not to incur enmity. He is a conscientious hard-working technician, absorbed in the "pure" problems of technique. He adapts well. He merges easily. He avoids "useless" controversy. In his ideas and opinions, he seeks the safe common ground. He is always attuned to the tides of consensus. He knows when to chime in and when to keep quiet. He associates and he disassociates; fits in, slips out. He is loyal on the job, to the job, to the gang, as long as he is on the job, as long as he is one of the gang. He is enthusiastic, but his enthusiasm like his friendliness is hardly related to (or dependent upon) its object. He has a sense of the team, and he enjoys the shoulder to shoulder striving of the team, as an athlete does. His moral imperative is the code of teamwork.

To compare and contrast the human qualities that are shaped by the experience of decentralized market-direction, of centralized political-direction, and of autonomous organization, one might use an approach and two of the categories developed by David Reisman.

The experience of the decentralized market-economy thrusts the individual into a complete responsibility for himself and for his own. It demands that his choice be self-interested, independent, answerable to no other. The man who emerges from that experience is "inner-directed" searching himself for what is right and wrong, feeling himself the receptacle of values and the final judge of truth.

The experience of centralized political-direction draws the individual into the body of society. He is subordinated by a private dedication or by external coercion to social objectives. He is perpetually confronted with the question of social purpose, continually engaged in the issue of social values and ends. The form of power is political, and the underlying dynamism is religious. The man who emerges from this experience might be called "ideologically directed."

The experience of the economy of autonomous organization imbeds the individual in the group. The individual must find purpose not in the group (for the group qua group is without purpose) but rather in his private self-interest. He is self-interested without being self-responsible. He exists in the group without the values of community. He finds truth and moral right, not in his private philosophy and outlook and in the hard core of his instincts and conscience, as the inner-directed man would, nor does he find these in revealed doctrine, in shared ideology, in a common social purpose, as the ideologically directed man would. Truth and right for him are rather to be sensed in the shifting consensus of his peers, in the workable, in the expedient, in the agreeable, in the conventional. He is perpetually on edge to remain within the bounds of the acceptable. He is sensitive to trends. He swims with the mainstream. He must associate; above all, he must get along with others. He belongs to the category that Reisman called "other directed," adaptable, conforming, agreeable, rootless, with morality attuned to the whispers of group opinion.

The Paths of Thought. The team spirit of the company man is transmuted into a social and political partisanship, a fierce but facile partisanship that shifts easily with each change in the wind of opinion.

Unanchored either in the private integrity and independent thought of the inner-directed, nor in the common faith of the ideologically directed, the company man will seek security in uniformity. He has only others against whom to measure himself; he is secure only in being as they are. And they are secure only in being as he is. Convention rules.

The company man shapes an amorphous group into a complex and effective instrument. He creates a unity out of diversity through his ingenuity, his persuasiveness, his enthusiasm. He knows how to get things done. He is an expert in techniques. He is a master of means. It is the matter of ends and of purpose that must perpetually elude him. And as he is obliged to brush these matters aside in economic activity, he is likely also in his social and political thought to emphasize technique, to focus on the immediate, and to thrust aside questions of cause and purpose. He will be everywhere pragmatic, embarrassed by ontology.

The Empty Middle. The economy of autonomous organization, compared to the ceaseless flux of price-direction and to the extremes possible under political-direction, provides a comparatively stable social environment. It offers the individual a considerable security of association, while permitting him to retain a significant degree of independence in the freedom to associate or disassociate as conscience demands or self-interest beckons. In the very labyrinth of the multifarious components of any autonomous and independent organization, the individual can find some protection against the dictate of society and the prejudice of groups. This form of economy provides the advantages of large-scale operations without saddling participants with ideological dogma. It might with good reason be argued that the economy of autonomous organization maintains the maximum degree of individual choice consistent with modern technology.

The defect of the economy of autonomous organization is the purpose-lessness with which it afflicts those who are of it.

The individual on his own in the roughhouse struggle of the market knew his business, his function, his responsibilities; for his goals, he looked inside himself. Life might be miserable, but life had its meaning. It made sense. Social man, in the environment of political-direction, can also know a place, a significance, a role. He is offered a clear resolution to his doubts, an answer to his uncertainties. He can conceive the goals toward which he works, the purposes to which he is committed. Whether it degrades or exalts, whether he is for it or against it, the whole makes sense.

Not so with the company man. He finds purpose neither in himself nor in his group. He is neither self-responsible nor responsible for his group. He participates without his knowing and without anyone's knowing the why or the where. He spins his threads expertly without understanding the reasons for their coming and without sighting the fabric they weave. He seeks approval, uncertain always of what it is that is to be approved. Association, in this economy, is easy, but men are uneasy. In the absence of purpose, they fall back on compulsion. Neurosis is the environmental characteristic and the occupational hazard.

Self-responsibility has gone, but social responsibility has not replaced it. Individualism is gone, but a secure place in the society of men has not been found. For the company man there is neither that harsh dignity in freedom and the omnipresent creative opportunity which was the virtue of the decentralized economy, nor the outlet for idealism and devotion that is the value of political centralization. Independence fades, community is not yet gained. To "do justly, and to love mercy, and to walk humbly with thy God" is for the man who walks alone. To "love the God of All absolutely, and love thy neighbor as one who is like thyself" is for the man of the social whole. But what creed for the partisan? For the company man, what belief? Between dedication and self-responsibility, the organizational economy strikes the middle—and the middle is empty.

COMPATIBILITY WITH OTHER SOCIAL INSTITUTIONS

Compatibility with Representative Democracy. The habit of independent choice and self-responsibility acquired under decentralized market-direction provides a psychological support for the institutions of representative democracy. This psychological support is not to be derived from the experience of the economy of autonomous organization. Nevertheless, since the rationale of private self-interest remains the only coherent basis of choice, and since the institutions of representative democracy offer the means of compromising and harmonizing the amalgam of private self-interests, representative political democracy would be compatible with the economy of autonomous organization.

The Merging of Political and Economic Organization. The role of government as it was conceived under classical liberalism, aloof and apart from the sphere of economic activity, is not possible in the circumstances of autonomous organization. On the one hand, the arbitrary power of corporate and trade union organizations requires intervention by government as representative of the social interest, while, on the other hand, the choices of those autonomous organizations impinge upon and become constituent elements of social policy. In its relationship to this form of economy, government becomes an organization among organizations, presumably the greatest and most powerful, the most responsible, speaking for the most general interest, but still one among the several, king among the barons. Moreover, the skills and outlook and values of private and public official are so similar that the cross-mobility of personnel between the private and public sphere becomes commonplace. For these reasons governmental and autonomous organizations will tend to overlap, merging the organizational and the public power.

Individual Liberty and the Arbitrary Power of Autonomous Organization. In the economy of autonomous organizations, individual liberty, in the sense of the unimpeded exercise of independent private choice, cannot exist in the sense that it did under decentralized market-direction. Constraints upon individualized choice will be imposed by the policy of autonomous organization and by the requisites of association, rather than by government. It will be essential for government to regulate the arbitrary power of the autonomous organization in order to protect the rights and prerogatives of the individuals who participate within such organizations.

SUMMARY

Individual choice is narrowed, but it survives. The group is powerful, but a multiplicity of groups protects the individual. Technical values of aggregation are realized without the imposition of doctrine or the burden of fanaticism. But purpose is lacking. Life manifests neither the clear hard values of individualism, nor dedication to the goals of community. Instead of self-interest and self-responsibility there is convention; instead of the unifying faith there are the equivocal loyalties of the company man. Communication is commercialized; the Word is standardized and packaged, for sale. Thought is shaped by a habit of fierce and facile partisanship, by the yearning for the comfort of uniformity, by the booming voice of the advertiser, by the pragmatism of the job.

PART II

THE NATIONAL ECONOMY

Chapter 19

The Analysis of a National Economy

The National Economy: A Complex of Organizational Forms. The two economic functions, namely, the production of goods and services and the consumption of goods and services, must be organized in any society. Three forms for the organization of these functions were analyzed in Part I. Those three are, however, by no means the only ones. They and others may be found coexisting and comingled in any national economy.

A national economy—economic functions organized within the sovereignty of a national political power—always consists of some unique combination of organizational forms. Unique combinations imply particular characteristics and peculiar problems. Analysis requires, therefore, that the component forms of organization be identified and studied as the structure of the national economy, and that the interaction of these components, the tensions generated between them, and the controls imposed upon their operations be studied as the dynamics of the national economy. In this way Part II will study the structure and the dynamics of the American national economy. An approach will be developed when possible through the tools put forward in Part I, to the study of any national or regional economy.

Economies and Forms of Economic Organization. We shall use the term *Economy* to connote the organization of economic functions through some identifiable agency (or mechanism) of choice and action that usually serves also for the organization of other than economic functions. "Household," for example, certainly implies a mechanism for organizing economic functions, but many other forms of social activity also center there. Four *Economies* will be studied, always with reference to the structure of the national economy. The four studied will be:

1. The Enterprise Economy
2. The Political Economy
3. The Household Economy
4. The Institutional Economy

The enterprise economy includes those economic functions controlled by privately owned enterprise, from the private shop of the entrepreneur to the massive corporate organization. It is subdivided into the (*a*) decentralized market-directed, (*b*) the organizational market-negotiating, (*c*) the decentralized market-segmented, and (d) the price regulated, public utility forms of economic organization. Models of the first two were developed in Part I. The political economy includes economic functions controlled by government. In the United States, government control is so piecemeal, so sheaved-in with and supplementary to functions of the household, the institutional and the enterprise economies, that, with the possible exception of one special field of activity, planning under centralized political-direction is not conceivable. The household economy covers the organization of those economic functions such as saving, consumption, and do-it-yourself construction, which are controlled by families and individuals by reference to personal values, without the objective of sale or exchange. The institutional economy includes those economic functions controlled by autonomous organizations which are not market or profit oriented. Included, for example, would be the production of "education" and "basic science."

Chapter 20

The Enterprise Economy

Characteristics and Significance of the Enterprise Economy. The enterprise economy includes diverse forms of economic organization, but in every case: (1) the agencies of control (enterprises) produce goods and services for sale on a market; (2) private ownership is a significant (though not the only) source of power and instrument of control; and (3) profits are a significant (though not the only) objective of economic activity.

In the United States the enterprise economy dominates the organization of production, accounting for about 80 percent of the National Income generated through economic activity. In the organization of consumption, the enterprise economy is important in one sense and unimportant in another. One might consider the significance of consumption in its impact on price and on the organization of production—for example, in the power of the buyer in bargaining with the producer or seller. In this sense the enterprise economy is immensely important as a source of demand, conditioning the organization of production, and influencing price, since the great bulk of sales is between enterprise and enterprise along the stages of production and distribution, before an end product is sold and used.

The significant function in the organization of consumption may be understood rather as that of determining the pattern of final outputs and of organizing the utilization of these. In this regard, the enterprise economy in the United States is relatively unimportant. In 1962, for a Gross National Product in the United States of $554 billion, the consumption of $357 billion in goods and services was organized through the expenditures of households, and the consumption of $117 billion in goods and services was organized through the political economy. The $77 billion of domestic investment covers the procurement of producer durables by the enterprise economy. Even this pattern of investment is a derivative of the anticipated end-product demands on the part of households and of the political economy.

Characteristics of Decentralized Market-Direction. The characteristics of decentralized market-direction were developed in Part I. To recapitulate, in this form of economic organization the enterprise serves the purpose and will of an individual entrepreneur, and its operations must be within the scope of his personal cognition and control. The power of the entrepreneur over the activities of his enterprise is based on the prerogatives of ownership. Since ownership of property also conveys the rights of consumption and inheritance, the management of the enterprise merges with the operation of the household and with culturally based obligations to the family. There is a substantial freedom in the movement of resources (manpower, entrepreneurship, and investment) into and out from industry. The numbers of competitors and the conditions of competition are such that no individual producer or producers acting in concert can significantly influence the price of what they sell or buy. Consequently, within limits set by governmental intervention, prices will move autonomously. Output will be proportional to the availability of resources; price will be an equilibrating mechanism between production and demand. Factor income will be a function of the value of its marginal product.

Importance in the United States Economy. In the United States the conditions of decentralized market-direction are roughly met in a part of the construction industry, in forestry and fisheries, in marginal areas of mining and manufacturing, and in a part of trade and services. It is, however, only in American agriculture that these qualifying characteristics can be considered general or dominant.

The American farm is usually subject to the control of a single individual. In 1959, out of a total of 3.7 million farms, some 3.1 million were run by one person or by a family.[1] Out of a total farm work force of 6 million, nearly 5 million worked on such "family farms."

So also, control is primarily based on ownership, and ownership supplies a general motivation to efficiency. In 1959, out of 3.7 million farms, more than 2 million were fully owned, and more than 800,000 were partly owned by their operators. Nearly all the rest were run by tenants, who had motivations to efficiency analogous to those of owners. A mere 21,000 farms were operated by hired managers. Owner-operated farms constituted 70 percent of total farm acreage.[2]

The free movement of resources into and out from the farm sector is indicated by migration statistics. In 1960 and in 1961, there was a *net* outmigration of population from the farm to the city of over a million annually.[3] Nevertheless, while *net* migration has generally been away from the farm, there have always been simultaneous and unchecked movements of population from the city to farm. Between 1941 and 1950,

[1] United States Bureau of the Census, *Statistical Abstract of the United States 1963* (Washington, D.C., 1963), p. 640.
[2] *Ibid.*, p. 622.
[3] *Ibid.*, p. 613.

the average movement of population from city to farm was more than a million annually.[4]

Not the whole of American agriculture conforms to the conditions of decentralized market-direction. For certain crops, sales are predominantly organized through large and powerful "cooperatives," which are beyond the scope of entrepreneurial control. The statistics suggest that there is already an important and rapidly growing part of American agriculture where the farm is no longer a man-sized operation. Farms of 1000 acres and over numbered 100,531 in 1940 and 136,299 in 1959, and these included 364 million acres in 1940 and 551 million in 1959. In 1959 farms of 1000 acres or more covered 49.2 percent of all land in farms and 19.9 percent of all crop land harvested.[5] These farms, which sometimes are highly mechanized, may employ large contingents of hired labor and market "brand-name" products through cooperatives, approaching the conditions of market-negotiating organization.

The significance of American agriculture, and consequently the decentralized market-directed form of economic organization in the enterprise economy, is steadily diminishing and is now relatively small. In 1962 the farm population constituted 7.7 percent of the total U.S. population,[6] and agricultural output added slightly more than 3 percent to the Gross National Product.[7]

Characteristics of Organizational Market-Negotiating Enterprise. The characteristics of the organizational market-negotiating form of economic organization were developed in Part I. To recapitulate, the enterprise is beyond the scope of the individual cognition or of control by a particular group or a single interest. It is rather a voluntary association of diverse interests united in the expectations of mutual gain. Its highly complex internal operations will be controlled, in part, through the instrumentality of the plan. Its internal and external relationships will be fixed as a matter of policy, and the significant variations that are possible in corporate policy suggest a corresponding degree of arbitrary power. The gigantic organizational enterprise is but the solar center of a host of smaller satellite enterprises: contractors and subcontractors, consultants, advertising agencies, public relations agencies, legal advisors, and other special services, as well as smaller competitors suited to manipulation and operation in circumstances too constricted for the giant.

Importance in the United States Economy. It is difficult to demarcate the organizational market-negotiating form in the enterprise economy, partly

4 United States Bureau of the Census, *Historical Statistics of the United States; Colonial Times to 1957* (Washington, D.C., 1960).
5 *Statistical Abstract 1963,* p. 613.
6 *Ibid.,* p. 610.
7 *Ibid.,* p. 321.

because the available statistics can provide no more than rough clues about the structure of internal control and the nature of external power. It is not possible precisely to fix the point at which the magnitude of an enterprise pushes it beyond the scope of individual cognition or control. Nor is the question simply a matter of the magnitude of any measurable business quantum. An enterprise with a thousand employees can be within the control competence of a single manager when that thousand are working on standard machines producing a standard output; but a research firm employing twenty scientists working in a score of different fields might be beyond the capacity of any single individual to direct. Moreover, the organizational enterprise exists not merely as a matter of functional necessity. It is a *mode* of action-taking, a mode of decision-making, a mode of human association. It implies (and it generates) values, habits, and sets of interconnecting expectations and reciprocal obligations.

Once this mode of action infiltrates the culture, it becomes not simply necessary but preferred. Because it is strongly and broadly preferred, it may become necessary where other forms for the organization of choice would have done as well or better in a different cultural climate. Participants will not accept the old fashioned boss; they join the small organization, where one-man control is technically feasible, not as employees but as "associates." The voluntarism and flexibility and team relationships of the autonomous organization come to characterize operations, where tight one-man control would also be feasible. This kind of difference would be exemplified, I think, in a comparison between the enterprise economy in the United States and, say, in France. In the United States, partly because of the necessary size and complexity of particular enterprises, the mode of autonomous organization has permeated the business culture, so that it is to be found dominant even in firms of a size and complexity which, in France, remain the absolute domain of the single entrepreneur.

In any case, the census category "manufacturing" will be designated as that part of the American enterprise economy where the organizational market-negotiating form of economic organization predominates. Clearly, manufacturing enterprise tends to be large, technically complex, and often engaged in a wide diversity of activities.

In 1958, for example, 48.5 percent of the value added and 43.8 percent of the employment in the manufacturing sector was by "establishments" of 500 or more employees. Many such establishments may be included in a single company. In such great industries as motor vehicles and parts, blast furnaces and steel mills, aircraft, radio, newspapers, bread, cotton and woven fabrics, the average employment per company is 5000 or more. Nor is this a sufficient index of the size of dominant enterprise. In 1958 the average employment of the largest four companies in motor vehicles and parts was close to 100,000 per company; in blast furnaces and steel mills about 68,000 per company; and in aircraft in excess of 50,000 per company.[8]

The extent to which sales are concentrated with a few sellers in particular markets suggests the degree to which price and the terms and conditions of exchange can be imposed or must be negotiated, in either case to be determined as a matter of policy. In motor vehicles and parts, in blast furnaces and steel mills, in aircraft, in aircraft engines, in organic chemicals, in tires and inner tubes, in cigarettes, in tin cans and tinware, in tractors, and in synthetic fibers, the largest four companies in 1958 accounted for 50 percent or more of the value of shipments. In petroleum refining, in inorganic chemicals, in flour and meal, in plastic materials, in wire-drawing, and in motors and generators, the largest eight companies accounted for 50 percent or more of the value of shipments. In meat-packing, paper and paperboard mills, radios and related products, canned fruits and vegetables, cotton broad-woven fabrics, pharmaceutical preparations, beer and ale, paper and paperboard products, periodicals, farm machinery (except tractors), and boiler-shop products, the largest 20 companies accounted for 50 percent or more of the value of shipments. In contrast, at the periphery of the manufacturing sector, in structural and ornamental work, plastic products, poultry-dressing plants, ready-mix concrete, machine shops, lithographing, and bottled soft drinks, the largest 20 companies accounted for less than 30 percent of the value of shipments made.

More than observed structural characteristics, the performance of manufacturing enterprise, which will be examined in Chapter 21, serves to establish the dominance of the organizational market-negotiated form in this sector of the American enterprise economy.

Manufacturing, and hence presumably the organizational market-negotiating form of economic organization, are of great importance in the American enterprise economy. In 1962, "manufacturing" added $133 billion, or about 25 percent of the Gross National Product.

Characteristics of Decentralized Market-Segmented Enterprise. The analytic models developed in Part I are applicable to two parts of the American enterprise economy. Important spheres of activity in the enterprise economy and in the other economies as well remain, for which the analysis of Part I does not provide a point of reference. To comprehend the configuration of the American national economy, these also must be covered.

There are a mass of economic activities that share, to an important

[8] Department of Commerce, Bureau of Census, *Concentration Ratios in Manufacturing Industry*, 1958.

extent, the characteristics of decentralized market-direction, and that are significantly related to and are sometimes in transition toward organizational market-negotiation. Characteristically the enterprise is "man-sized," small enough to be within the scope of enterpreneurial control, and the basis of control is ownership. Since profits accrue to ownership, a spontaneous motivation to efficiency is provided, and the selectivity of the market offers an autonomous system of recruitment. The influx and efflux of resources is relatively free. Competitors are relatively numerous. In these respects the conditions of decentralized market-direction are substantially met.

On the other hand, markets, characteristically, are segmented, and the force and continuity of competition is broken by (1) real or fancied differences in the goods and services offered for sale, for example, the skill of a particular doctor or lawyer, the "taste" of the buyer for a particular boutique, the public confidence in a particular "brand name," and by (2) the barriers of time, distance, and imperfect information between enterprises offering similar goods and services for sale. Individual bargaining becomes an important element in the organization of sales. This form of economic organization is termed here *Decentralized Market-Segmented.*

In these segmented but, nevertheless, dynamically interacting markets, price is not wholly controlling. To a significant degree competitive pressures are indirect. Price and, indeed, the forms of competition are not beyond the influence of entrepreneurial choice. That choice will be subject to private inertia and to cultural pressure. Combination and agreement between enterprises to re-enforce a policy choice are always feasible and tempting, but, with numerous self-seekers and the free movement of resources, such policy agreements and coalitions of competitors will be difficult to maintain.

The decentralized market-segmented form of economic organization (as was inferred in Part I) is the proper home of the Knightian entrepreneur whose "profits" are a return on his superior intuitive capacity to sense the responses of the competition and to act more rationally than the rest in the face of uncertainties built into an organization of numerous independent decision-makers. This also (as Part I suggested) is the most appropriate environment for ad hoc invention. The theories of monopolistic competition, imperfect competition, and workable competition, as developed by E. H. Chamberlin, Joan Robinson, J. M. Clarke, and many others, are all specific to the decentralized market-segmented form of economic organization.

There are also activities, which we will not attempt to segregate from the mass of decentralized market-segmented enterprise, that in fact constitute quite a different form of economic organization. These are the decentralized, "man-sized" enterprises which are satellites of the large autonomous organization, as contractors, subcontractors, servicing agencies, and sales agents, operating within constraints of organizational policy. In some instances, such as contract building and truck transport, the dominant organization is not a large corporation but a trade union.

The Importance of Decentralized Market-Segmentation in the United States Economy. Decentralized market-direction would seem roughly characteristic of the census categories of "Wholesale and Retail Trade," "Contract Construction," and "Services."

"Retail Trade" is characteristically carried on by small and numerous enterprises. In 1958 there were 1.8 million retail establishments in the United States. About 70 percent of these were unincorporated proprietorships. More than one out of every eight in the retail trade work force was an active proprietor of an establishment. Large enterprise also has an important place in retailing. Companies owning 11 or more retail stores accounted for 25 percent of total retail sales volume in 1962; and in 1958 the 3,795 establishments (out of a total of 1,646,900) with 100 or more employees accounted for 11 percent of the sales volume.[9]

Numerous enterprises within the scope of the individual's control also characterize "Wholesale Trade." Out of nearly 300,000 establishments, in 1958 40 percent were unincorporated proprietorships or partnerships. Establishments of less than 20 employees accounted for more than half the total payroll, while establishments with 100 employees or more accounted for only 17 percent of the total payroll. Nine percent of the wholesale establishments, accounting for 30 percent of wholesale trade volume, were offices or sales branches of manufacturing enterprise. This fact suggests the degree to which the trade is a satellite of the large market-negotiating organization.[10]

Similarly very large numbers of small enterprises characteristically carry out "Services." For the census category "Selected Services," the 1958 Census of Business shows more active proprietors than establishments. In the work force, the ratio of proprietors to paid employees is 1:3. For example: there were 85,580 hotels with 89,926 proprietors and 502,265 paid employees; 41,332 motels with 45,799 active proprietors and 78,860 paid employees; 67,920 laundries with 70,403 proprietors and 554,493 paid employees; 105,000 barber shops with 111,576 proprietors and 76,183 paid employees; 103,724 auto repair shops with 115,039 proprietors and 170,463 employees.[11]

But, if a proportion of "Retail Trade," "Wholesale Trade," and "Serv-

9 *Statistical Abstract 1963*, p. 822–823.
10 *Ibid.*, pp. 834–838.
11 *Ibid.*, pp. 840–841.

ices" surely must be considered as satellites of the market-negotiating form, there are also certain branches of "manufacturing" that should be counted as decentralized market-segmented. For example, the 1958 Census of Business shows that in "Women's and Misses' Outerwear," there were 9,781 establishments with an average of about 30 employees per establishment; in "Commercial Printing" there were 17,310 establishments with about 16 employees per establishment; in "Cleaning and Toilet Goods" there were 2,654 manufacturing establishments with about 29 employees per establishment; and the 2,086 establishments manufacturing "Jewelry and Silverware" had an average of 20 employees each.[12]

If, as a first and rough approximation, one considers decentralized market-segmented enterprise to include "Retail Trade," "Wholesale Trade," "Contract Construction," and "Services," then this constitutes the most important form of economic organization in the American enterprise economy. In 1962 it accounted for 28 percent of the value added to the GNP and for 40 percent of nonagricultural employment.

Characteristics of Price-Regulated Public Utilities. Not only is the price-regulated public utility a form of economic organization that is not covered by the analysis of Part I, but also it is a form of organization that is perhaps peculiar to the American national economy.

The agency of technical control and of business action is a large, profit-motivated autonomous organization, selling a product or a service on the market. The ownership of equity shares is a significant element in the internal structure of power. In all these respects, there is no difference between this and the organizational market-negotiating form of economic organization.

This category of corporate organization, however, operates as a legal monopoly, under the permission and supervision of some designated agency of government. This agency (usually a state or a federal public utility commission) is responsible for seeing that the prices charged are "fair." Fair price has to come to mean a price that permits profits no greater than are required to provide equity holders with some conventionally acceptable return on their investment. While such price control, supposedly, protects the consumer, the investor is protected by keeping any competitors from poaching upon the company's market.

The "public utility" concept has a long history. For centuries, the common law has held that there are certain lines of production where the technically optimal size is such that if operations are to be efficient, there cannot be sufficient producers to insure effective competition. Hence, efficiency requires monopoly. If monopoly is to be allowed, the consumer must be protected against exploitation by the monopolist. In Europe the

12 *Ibid.,* pp. 776–780.

State took over the so-called natural monopolies: the railroads, the electric power facilities, the telephone facilities. It operated them, presumably, in the public interest. In the United States, technical control and financial responsibility were left with private companies, and the prices charged by these private companies were "regulated" by the Public Utility Commissions.

It was supposed at one time that the natural monopoly properly subject to regulation was clearly distinguishable from the rest of the enterprise economy. But the dichotomy is no longer clear. Today it is in fact hard to see what inherent or necessary differences set the traditional "natural monopolies" apart from other autonomous business organizations. The pressure of competition is hardly greater in the steel industry than it is, say, in urban transit or in electric power, nor is the output of steel any less important to social welfare, nor are the consumers of steel in any less need of protection against the arbitrary exercise of corporate power. This is no more to suggest that regulation should be less for urban transit and electric power, than that regulation should be greater for steel.

The price-regulated public utility poses two fundamental dilemmas. The first involves resistances to effective regulation built into the structure of power. The second involves contradictions inherent in effective regulation.

A small public agency, the Public Utility Commission, whose work is essentially clerical, without policy-making responsibilities, without any technical demands or creative challenge to mold its competencies, is given (1) the power to grant or withhold concessions of great financial value and (2) the task of supervising vital aspects in the operations of technically complex company organizations, while the companies remain the repositories of the financial information and of the technical knowledge required for any effective control or regulation of their operations. The first dilemma is that of a sheep who has been put in charge of wolves. The one who is supposed to control is likely to be controlled. And if, nevertheless, an effective control is achieved, there then arises the second dilemma; for effective regulation subverts the company's motivation to progress and efficiency. When regulation achieves its prescribed objectives, then profits cease to have any value as an incentive to efficiency. When profits begin to rise above the level of "fair return," immediately prices would be reduced, and when profits begin to drop below the level of "fair return," immediately prices would be raised.

Importance in the United States Economy. Included in the category of publicly regulated enterprise in the United States are the telephone and telegraph companies, the electric power companies, the artificial and natural gas companies, natural gas pipelines, radio and television companies, railroads and urban transit companies, and truck, ship, and air

FIGURE 1

The Enterprise Economy

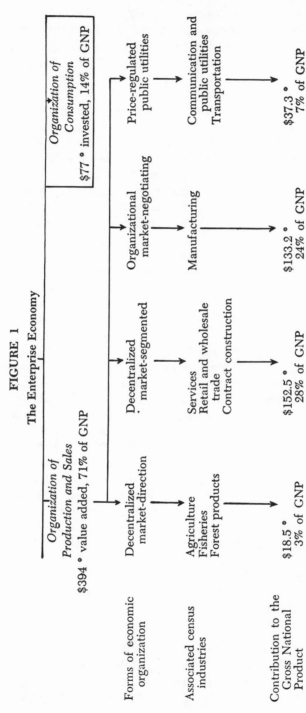

Based on 1962 data.
* In billions.

transportation companies. Not all of these enterprises are regulated in the same way, or under the same rationale. The model of regulation briefly sketched above applies more specifically to the regulation of companies supplying electricity, gas, telephone services, railroad transportation, and urban transit.

During 1962 "Public Utilities and Transportation" and "Communication" added $37 billion, or 7 percent of the GNP.

A Chart of the Enterprise Economy. The United States enterprise economy, property-based, profit-oriented, market-related, is predominant in the organization of production, and is relatively unimportant in the organization of consumption. Its constituent forms of economic organization are (1) decentralized market-direction, (2) organizational market-negotiation, (3) decentralized market-segmented, (4) price-regulated public utilities. The first two could be analyzed by reference to Part I. The last two required that a new framework of analysis be briefly sketched. The relative significance of these four forms of economic organization is suggested in Figure 1. It is to be understood that the available census categories can only be taken as crudely approximate. Certain census categories (mining, finance, insurance, real estate) are so heterogeneous that they are excluded entirely.

Chapter 21

Problems and Policies in Organizing Production and Distribution in the Enterprise Economy

Introduction. This chapter will consider certain problems that have been or are being confronted by the American enterprise economy, and the government policies that have developed in response to these problems. For each of the four forms of economic organization that have been identified here as parts of the American enterprise economy, distinct and different problems have elicited distinct and different government policies.

The relationships between circumstance and problem, between problem and policy, and between policy and circumstance, are dynamic ones. Problems give rise to policy, which, in turn, recreates the circumstance out of which problems arise. For many reasons the economy takes on new configurations. Thus between 1940 and 1963, agricultural employment in the United States decreased from 9.5 million or 20 percent of the civilian labor force to 4.3 million or 6 percent of the civilian labor force. Correspondingly, the significance of autonomous market-negotiating organization has increased and that of decentralized market-direction has diminished.

This chapter will consider those policies and problems of the American enterprise economy involving the *efficient* organization of production and the *equitable* distribution of income. The next chapter will study problems and policies relating to the organization of technical progress in the American enterprise economy.

The Variability of Aggregate Demand. Total end-product expenditures in the national economy equals aggregate demand equals gross national product. Expenditures are of two sorts: those that occur autonomously out of personal and business decisions and those that occur as consequences of government policy.

Autonomous expenditures are the consequences of the decentralized choice of a vast number of individual householders and business firms. Since they are a function of infinitely decentralized choice, aggregate expenditures are highly fluid, and have, for example, varied between $56 billion in 1933 and $554 billion in 1962.

At least during the period between the two world wars, the expenditures of households and of business enterprise tended to lag behind the

218

rise of productivity in the enterprise economy. This period was a critical one for the development of economic policy in the United States, and during it, underlying the random or cyclical movements of autonomous expenditure, there appeared a widening gap between the capacity to produce and the inclination to spend. This growing gap had quite different effects in the constituent parts of the American enterprise economy.

Price Instability: A Problem for Decentralized Market-Direction. Decentralized market-direction responds immediately and automatically to changes in the configuration of spending or to changes in the level of expenditure. When aggregate expenditure rises or falls, and activities are organized under decentralized market-direction, then the price level also must rise or fall. With the autonomous market-negotiating organization, on the other hand, where price is a matter of corporate policy, the price level can be stabilized in the face of change in the level of aggregate demand. The difference is illustrated in Figure 2, where for the period between 1901 and 1940, the price of wheat, exemplifying decentralized market-direction, is contrasted with the price of steel rails, exemplifying organizational market-negotiation.

Movement in the price level under decentralized market-direction can generate cumulative forces which accelerate the rise of rising prices and the fall of falling prices. As a result of the extreme instability of price, expectations and plans can be disappointed and contractual obligations disrupted, with financial crisis and bankruptcies spreading throughout the national economy. Such was the format of the recurrent "panics" in the period before World War I, when decentralized market-direction was a more significant part of the American national economy.

Between the two World Wars, the problem was not only price instability, but also a tendency for the price level of decentralized market-directed outputs to decline, relative to the level of industrial prices, since the autonomous organization could resist the down-pressure of a lagging aggregate demand as the small entrepreneur in the decentralized market could not. As a consequence, the real income of those who participated in decentralized market-directed activity tended to decline also—at least relative to the earnings of others. The farmer's demand was for "price parity" to stablize the real return on his products by keeping the prices of the goods he sold in line with the price of the goods he purchased.

Government Price Guarantees and Output Controls. In the mid-1930s under the New Deal, and thenceforth, the American government guaranteed minimum prices for major agricultural outputs. These minimum prices have been set by a parity formula that relates agricultural products to the general price level. In order to support farm prices, the government has purchased and has stored that portion of agricultural outputs that

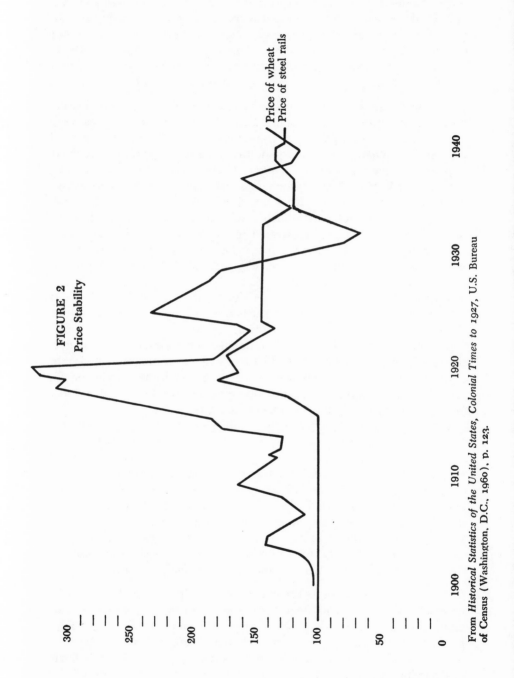

FIGURE 2
Price Stability

Price of wheat
Price of steel rails

From *Historical Statistics of the United States, Colonial Times to 1927*, U.S. Bureau
of Census (Washington, D.C., 1960), p. 123.

cannot be sold to households at or above the guaranteed price level. By paying farmers to withdraw from cultivation some of the land in their possession, the government has sought also to control agricultural output, and thereby to reduce the food surplus that it must purchase and withhold. However, since the input of alternative resources (man hours, fertilizer, equipment) has not been restricted, the control on agricultural outputs has not been successful.

A Composite Form of Economic Organization. A form of economic organization creates problems specific to itself. In response, policies of reform and techniques of amelioration develop. Such policies and techniques may so modify the situation that an essentially new form of economic organization emerges, which, in turn, creates new problems specific to itself. These problems generate new reforms. Decentralized choice exercised within the frame of centralized price supports constitutes a novel form of economic organization in American agriculture. Compared to what existed before, it is an eminently successful innovation. It has led to a rate of technical progress unparalleled in American agriculture. This rate of progress, coupled with price support, has permitted the farmer to prosper. While providing more food at reasonable prices, a great stream of labor has been simultaneously released to add to the nation's industrial output. And the accumulated "surpluses" have been useful in war, in diplomacy, and in technical assistance to developing countries. Those who formulated and supported these agricultural reforms did not foresee the great benefits that were to be their consequence. Those who inaugurated these reforms were merely intent on increasing the farmer's share, and not at all on accelerating the rate of increase of agricultural productivity. The chief merit of this altered form for the organization of agricultural activities is its effectiveness in a system of economic progress.

From the standpoint of efficiency in the use of resources, the new form for organizing production in agriculture has grave weaknesses and raises problems not yet resolved. Goods are produced and withheld from use, denying consumers the benefits of more consumption at lower costs. The use of available land is restricted, with no check upon other resource inputs, thereby distorting the technology of production without effectively limiting output.

Instability of Production and Employment: A Problem of Organizational Market-Negotiating Enterprise. If the autonomous market-negotiating enterprise holds firm on price, it must then absorb the buffetings of demand in its level of output. The sag in aggregate demand will mean less production and lower employment. In contrast, output and employment in decentralized market-direction remain comparatively stable. This is

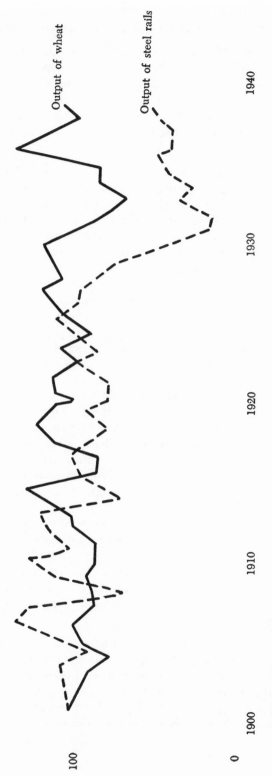

FIGURE 3

Production and Employment Stability

From *Historical Statistics of the United States, Colonial Times to 1957*, U.S. Bureau of Census (Washington, D.C., 1960), p. 123.

illustrated in Figure 3, where the decentralized market-directed production of wheat is contrasted to the organizational market-negotiated production of steel rails in the United States between 1901 and 1940. Figure
4 compares the impact of change in aggregate expenditure (Gross National Product) on employment in decentralized market-directed *agriculture,* on decentralized market-segmented *wholesale and retail trade,* and
on organizational market-negotiating *manufacturing* between 1929 and
1943, a period of depression and recovery in the United States. Organizational market-negotiated employment appears explosively unstable,

FIGURE 4

Impact of Change in Aggregate Expenditure

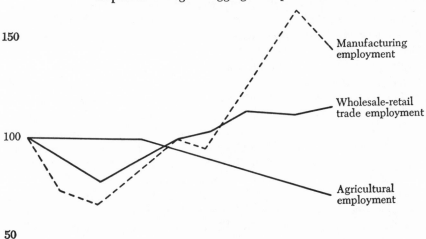

From *Historical Statistics of the United States, Colonial Times to 1957,* U.S. Bureau
of Census (Washington, D.C., 1960), pp. 73, 280.

moving in direct response to variations in aggregate expenditure. Decentralized market-directed *agricultural* employment appears highly stable.
In fact, the net effect of a catastrophic drop in aggregate demand is
temporarily to halt the long-term decline in agricultural employment by
checking the migration from the farm to the city, since in the city there
were no jobs. On the farm, following the rule of decentralized market-
direction, output and employment were a function of the availability of
resources, not of the level of demand. In the decentralized market-
segmented *wholesale and retail trade* where price is only partially resistant to the autonomous force of market demand, and output is only par-

tially determined through satellite relationships with the great firm, employment varied, but not to the same degree as in manufacturing.

From Panic to Depression. In the economy of autonomous enterprise, where price is a matter of corporation policy and when the policy is to hold prices stable, then the lag or sag of aggregate demand relative to a rising output potential results in a decline in production and unemployment, and a reduction in the earnings, and hence in the income of households. The drop in income further reduces aggregate demand, and in turn lowers production and employment. With the widening margins of unused productive capacity, and worsening sales expectations, business investment declines also, further reducing aggregate demand, production, employment, household income, and hence private and business spending intentions. This grinding of the economic mechanism nearly to a halt is the modern phenomenon of *depression,* a response proper to the economy of autonomous market-negotiating organizations. This shift in the nature of the response to instability in aggregate expenditures, from "panic" to depression, is a measure of the emergence of the organizational market-negotiated form as dominant in the American enterprise economy.

The Great Depression of the 1930s constituted virtually a crisis in Western Civilization. It required, under pain of survival, a change in the prevailing outlook in matters of economic control. In order to reconcile the need for government action in offsetting unwanted change in aggregate expenditure, Keynes and his disciples postulated a double-look in economics: the micro and macro. Microeconomics, studying phenomena from the viewpoint of the firm, left the classical conception unchanged. Macroeconomics explained why this universe of decentralized market-directed activities bounced or floated between full and zero employment. While this macro-micro bridge served to rationalize amelioratory political action, the reconciliation between the two conceptions is, in fact, illusory, for Keynesian macroeconomics requires the assumption that prices and wages are set as a matter of organizational policy, and that assumption is not compatible with the decentralized market-direction of micro theory.

Full Employment Policy. In the United States, government has tried to maintain full (or adequate) employment, essentially through influence upon aggregate expenditure. This influence has been exercised partly by modifying the rate of interest and other monetary parameters of business investment. But, in the crux, the Government always has had to rely on its fiscal powers to spend more than it taxes or to tax more than it spends. This is the most, and perhaps the only, effective control measure now at its disposal. Public expectations and political habit now combine to assure that government fiscal policy will not permit the recurrence of a major depression. Nevertheless, government has not succeeded in maintaining full employment in the United States. Significant cyclical variations continue, and there appears to be a widening margin of hard-core unemployed. There are a number of reasons for the limited success or relative failure of full employment policy in the United States.

The objective of government policy is not only to maintain full employment, but also to maintain stable prices, that is, full employment without inflation. This is difficult to do simply through a control on aggregate expenditures, since a change in aggregate expenditure reaches all parts of the enterprise economy, and the parts respond differently. An increase in aggregate expenditure automatically and necessarily will cause price to rise where activity is decentralized and market-directed. Moreover, the increase in aggregate expenditure creates a more optimistic climate, which favors a shift in the policy of autonomous organization in the direction of negotiating or imposing higher wages and prices, regardless of whether or not there is full employment. Hence, each time that government seeks to raise the level of employment through an increase in aggregate expenditure, simultaneously it sets inflationary forces in motion. This has caused it to reverse its policy of raising aggregate expenditure before full employment has been achieved.

Moreover the configuration of demand consequent upon an increase in aggregate expenditure has no necessary relationship to the distribution of unemployment between regions, industries, and levels of skill. Unemployment now tends to be intensively concentrated in particular regions, industries, and in educationally unfavored social groups. The situation mingles the problem of full employment with the correlary problem of intraregional and intraindustry mobility of resources, and poses the task of continually adapting the manpower resource to the changing complex of technical need and economic opportunity.

Natural Resource Conservation: A Problem of Decentralized Market-Direction. A long-standing and continuing problem in the American enterprise economy has been in the uneconomic exploitation of natural resources, to a degree that has sometimes amounted to a senseless and massive destruction. The forests were stripped and burned and not replaced. Denuding the hills led to the erosion of the top soil, the siltation of rivers, the flooding of valleys. Wildlife was annihilated. The great herds of bison were destroyed. In the oil fields, hundreds of wildcatters drilled wells by the thousands, as close together as trees in a forest, each struggling to increase his share of the subsurface pools of oil. This debauching of oil was so rapid that the subterranean pressure of compressed gas that forces the oil to the surface could not be economized but was so dissipated that a large part of the petroleum resource was irrevocably lost.

In the Old South of Virginia, West Virginia, Georgia, and the Carolinas, a marvelously rich soil was mined of its fertility through successive recroppings of cotton and tobacco and through the primitive methods required in order to exploit cheap, ignorant slave labor. When the soil was exhausted, the plantation owner abandoned it, and, lock, stock, and barrel, moved West to repeat the process in the free lands of the frontier, leaving poverty as a heritage for the rural community that remained.

Such destructiveness was endemic in agriculture, forestry, hunting, early prospecting. Not as a matter of coincidence these are all in the domain of decentralized market-direction, where the externalization of costs and benefits is at a maximum. The uneconomic disposition of natural resources has always occurred because individuals were in a position to dispose of natural resources, without being in a position to benefit personally from a decision to conserve, and without being held answerable for the real values that they destroy.

The dissipation of natural resources in the earlier period of American history was a consequence of the pre-eminence of decentralized market-directed choice, and the existence of a large public domain that could not be entirely and simultaneously brought within the scope of individual control as property. The government, committed to *laissez faire,* did not develop the capacity for an over-all reckoning of costs against benefits in disposing of the resources in the public domain. Neither did it afford the means of expressing collective goals in the disposition of resources, like the provision of recreational areas for collective use, the preservation of mineral resources for national security, the maintenance of continuity in community evolution, the protection of the aesthetic values in natural beauty and in wildlife. Such goals could not be expressed by the profit-seeking firm or by the private consumer seeking private gratification through market purchases. Hence they were left entirely out of account.

Conservation Policy. From the beginning of this century, first at the Federal and then at the State level, a government policy of resource conservation developed, in reforestation, in the regulated use of public forests, in the setting aside of reserved territories, in the development of state and national parks, in the protection of wildlife, in the state regulation of oil-depletion rates, in soil reclamation, flood control, and many sorts of public conservation programs. Analagous current problems are air pollution, the pollution of streams, the dissipation of fresh water, and the losses incurred through the use of chemical insecticides, all of which arise also from the externalized efforts of decentralized choice.

Conspiracy in Restraint of Trade: A Problem of Decentralized Market-Segmentation. The common law conceptions of "monopoly" and of "conspiracy in restraint of trade" have been centuries in the making. These conceptions evolved in the frame of certain circumstances of economic organization, and they are valid as concepts and operational as a basis of political action, as long as these circumstances exist: (1) a universe of decentralized decision-making directed by the autonomous forces of the market (2) composed of firms that can increase their profits if they succeed in influencing the movement of price in their own favor, (3) and where there exists the practical possibility of an individual's devising the means or of a group of competitors' conspiring together to control the bidding for a particular item or the output of a particular product, so that by frustrating the normal autonomous forces of market competition, they can thus gain a selfish advantage at the public's expense.

It follows, given these circumstances, that outlawing the devices of the monopolists or breaking up the conspiratorial agreement of the competitors, will restore the rule of competition and the autonomous force of the market.

But notice that in a practical sense, these circumstances exclude: (1) centralized political-direction; (2) decentralized market-direction, inasmuch as outputs are standardized and buyers and sellers are so numerous that no monopoly device can capture supply and no conspiracy can be broad enough effectively to restrain output or to control bidding; and (3) market-negotiating organization, inasmuch as price movements are not autonomous, but are a function of organizational policy.

What remains as subject to the traditional conception of "restraint of trade" and "conspiracy to monopolize" is the decentralized market-segmented part of the enterprise economy. There the autonomous forces of market competition are significant but the discontinuities of demand and the segmentation of control enable these market forces to be occasionally influenced or controlled in favor of particular buyers or sellers. The classical problems of "monopoly" and of "conspiracy in restraint of trade" are specific to decentralized market-segmented enterprise.

Anti-Trust Policy in the United States. For centuries under the common law, those who suffered could seek damages in the courts against monopolists and conspirators in restraint of trade. From the enactment of the Sherman Act in 1890, the United States began to incorporate these concepts into its statutory law, so that they could be enforced (through the Department of Justice and through the Federal Trade Commission) not simply as a private right, but as a public policy. The Sherman Act, the Clayton Act, the Robinson-Patman Act, as these were subsequently interpreted and developed in the Courts, constitute the United States anti-trust policy.

Anti-trust policy in the United States has had no relevance to decentralized market-directed agriculture. Nor has it ever evolved firm guidelines, or clear purpose, or effective regulation, in respect to large autonomous business organization. For the economy of autonomous organization, the value of anti-trust policy has been largely symbolic: it proclaims public approval of competitive attitudes and influences corporate policy in the direction of more aggressive competition.

It is with respect to decentralized market-segmented enterprise that anti-trust policy has been purposeful and effective. With respect to this particular form of economic organization, the law has had two quite separate anti-trust objectives.

The first objective of anti-trust policy has been to outlaw conspiracies and arrangements between independent enterprises intended to fix prices, share bids, control supply, or otherwise to frustrate the force of market competition. Anti-trust policy has been eminently successful in preventing cartels and price agreements from developing in the United States as they did in Europe.

The second objective of anti-trust policy is to preserve the universe of market-segmented decentralized choice as a "way of life" against the incursion of the "bigness" of autonomous organization. This objective is certainly more equivocal than the first, and less explicit in the law. Yet an antagonism to size, to "the curse of bigness" as Justice Brandeis termed it, has certainly been an element in the formulation and enforcement of the anti-trust laws. Particularly the Robinson-Patman Act, which tries to neutralize the bargaining advantage of the large buyer, and the successful prosecution of the A & P food chain, which was marked out for its aggressive competitiveness and its low retail mark-ups, must be thus understood.

The Arbitrary-Discretionary Power of Autonomous Enterprise. The great corporation and trade union have a wide range of discretion in the formulation of policies and in the choice between alternative lines of action. Those outside and many of those within the autonomous agency whose welfare is significantly affected by policies of that agency, will have no role and no representation in the formulation of those policies.

It becomes the task of government to reconcile the discretionary exercise of this arbitrary power with the various interests of those who are affected by it. The public and individual interest must be reconciled with the arbitrary power of the autonomous organizations to influence or to determine (1) distribution of income, (2) the opportunity for employment and promotion, (3) the level of investment, and (4) the form of competition. The public policy response in the United States to the exercise of arbitrary power in the economy of autonomous market-negotiating organizations in these spheres of policy will be briefly described below.

The Power of Autonomous Organization in the Internal Distribution of Income. Nearly the whole of the income generated through decentralized market-direction is related to its mechanism for the control of economic activity. Therefore to interfere with the spontaneous distribution of income under decentralized market-direction risks jeopardizing the effective organization of the economic functions. With organizational market-negotiating enterprise, on the other hand, economic activities are not to a comparable degree controlled through the autonomous market forces of price and of windfall loss and gain. Rather they are planned: and so also the internal distribution of income is planned by the company. There is, within the limits of operational necessity, a considerable proportion of corporate income which can be shared among equity holders, workers, salaried officials, and executives as a matter of company (and trade union) policy without jeopardizing the effective organization of economic activities. What is subject to distribution as a matter of enterprise policy can be significantly redistributed through governmental policy without undermining the operation of this economic form.

Public policy has (1) responded to the existence of a larger margin of income that can be redistributed without jeopardizing the effectiveness of organization in the economy of autonomous enterprise, and (2) reflected a prevailing preference for decentralized business choice as a way of life by developing two radically different systems of taxation in the United States. One applies to the income of the corporation, and the other to the income of small unincorporated enterprise. In the latter only the income received by individual participants is taxed. In the former the income received by individual participants is taxed, and in addition the organizing entity (the corporation) is separately and heavily taxed. When the government procures from autonomous enterprise, it renegotiates contracts as a general practice whenever profits seem to be in excess of a norm. There is and there can be no equivalent practice of "renegotiation" when government procures from firms under conditions of decentralized market-direction or of decentralized market-segmentation.

Government does not only tax (and redistribute) the income of the autonomous enterprise; it also influences and regulates the *internal* distribution of corporate income. Taxes on undistributed profits are a means of stimulating the payment of dividends. Tax exemption on gifts to charitable foundations and educational institutions is a means of encouraging such support. The minimum wage came first, and is most important for the industrial proletariat in the sphere of autonomous organization. And the government's support of industrial trade unionism was intended, in large part, to enhance the ability of industrial labor to demand for itself a larger share in the internal distribution of the income of the autonomous corporation.

The Policy of the Autonomous Organization and Opportunities for the Individual. If the social objective is to overcome prejudice, which bars the offering of equal opportunity to every member of the society for work and for promotion, then decentralized market-direction will not, itself, pose any barrier to this objective. Rather (given decentralized market-direction) those barriers to equal opportunity will tend to arise (and will have to be overcome) in the domain of the power of the family, the police, the court, the school and university, and other social institutions.

A different problem plagues the economy of autonomous organization. There the barriers of prejudice against equality of individual opportunity and liberty of private action can arise in the organization of economic activity itself. Corporate policy of recruitment and promotion will embody and perpetuate the prejudices of groups and even of individuals (like Henry Ford's antisemitic manias). Thus the discretionary choice and arbitrary power in the formulation of corporate policy will determine and may distort the context of opportunity and liberty for the individual. Recruitment and promotion policy of autonomous enterprise is, in turn, subject to influence and regulation by government.

Currently, for example, the recruitment and promotion policies of the large international corporation are peculiarly important for national objectives in assisting the economic and social development of emerging nations. It would appear that prior to World War II the large international corporation with its operations in both advanced countries of Europe and America and in technically backward areas of Africa, the Middle East, Asia, India, and Latin America, characteristically recruited its technical and executive personnel entirely from Western Europe or the United States. Such European or American personnel had the status and lived the lives of colonial officials in foreign enclaves, cut off from the "natives" and offering no employment opportunities to indigenous populations except as cheap unskilled labor.

After World War II, the social climate and political context in which these companies operated changed radically. Colonial empires were dismembered. The protections of the former imperial powers disappeared. The international corporation was confronted by sensitive new nationalisms, and by the determination of former colonies or satellites to be masters in their own homes. Corporate policies have adapted accordingly. The Shell Oil Company, as an example of one of the greatest of the international corporations, reorganized certain of its divisions in the newly independent countries into quasi-autonomous national subsidiaries and has actively sought to recruit talented youth from among indigenous peoples. For this purpose Shell develops local programs of education and training, and sends recruits to Holland or Britain or the United States for higher education. The policy turns out to be profitable, since the new recruits perform as well as the old, and the high bonuses and repatriation allowances are no longer required to induce Americans or Europeans to settle in these territories. But it was no economic calculus that inspired the large international company to restrict its recruitment to the "head-quarters" nations in Western Europe and the United States before the war, and to extend its recruitment to the indigenous peoples after the war. Rather it was a change in external political pressures. Instead of only a colonial elite that shielded them and to whom they were ultimately responsible, newly self-aware societies and sovereign nations had to be accommodated in the formulation of corporation policy.

In the United States also, corporation policy has opened and closed the doors of economic opportunity to particular groups. Prior to World War II, the upper echelons of the great engineering-based corporations were largely the exclusive domain of White Protestant Americans. The Negro was excluded from clerical and supervisory posts and from membership in trade unions. The postwar effort in the United States to break down the barriers of religious and racial discrimination has infiltrated trade union membership policy and corporate policies of recruitment and promotion. This pressure has sometimes taken the force of law, as in the Fair Employment Practices Acts, and in standard clauses in government contracts forbidding discrimination in hiring and promotion.

The Investment Policy of Autonomous Organization. The autonomous enterprise has the power greatly to vary the magnitude and to alter the timing of its investment. Corporate investment will have a "multiplier" effect on household expenditures. The magnitude and timing of the investment decisions of autonomous enterprise may serve to stabilize or profoundly destabilize price and employment. However, the autonomous enterprise, no matter how large and powerful it may be, cannot take into account the effect of its investment decisions in determining the level of the GNP. Because each corporation, by itself, is obliged to formulate its investment policy without taking this important effect into account, it becomes part of the task of government to influence the investment policies of autonomous organization in the interest of price and employment stability. Toward this end, the United States government has offered tax exemptions as an inducement to certain sorts of corporate investment. The French "plan" offers an interesting example of how government can influence the investment policy of autonomous organizations. At the heart of the French planning system is the voluntary coordination of corporate output planning and investment policies. This is done by creating a framework in which each corporation can realize the effect of its decision —as part of an aggregate—on the conditions of demand, and where the need for considerable increases or decreases in aggregate expenditure can consciously be met by sharing many small incremental adjustments. Enlightened self-interest is supplemented by government aids and pressures, and the choice of the autonomous enterprise economy is geared into public expenditure decisions.

Interrelations of Those Within Autonomous Organization. When there is decentralized market-direction, the decision-maker is the self-interested individual, and it is the relationship between independent decision-makers that may be of public concern. But in the economy of autonomous organization, where decision-making is in the composite choice of groups, social concern must be not only with the relationships between decision-making entities, but also with the structure of the relationships between individual and individual *within* the trade union or the corporation. When the individual employer bargained with the individual worker, society's concern with the context of that bargaining relationship sufficed. But when the trade union bargains for the worker, concern must also be with the effectiveness of those institutional relations that insure that the trade union is in fact bargaining *for* the worker, and with those that protect the ordinary trade unionists from abuse by the trade union official. Reform in the direction of (1) imposing on trade union officials limitations of income and authority akin to those imposed on public officials, (2) the progressive development of democratic electoral and internal juridical procedures, and (3) the protection of dissidents and minorities has taken place through internal demands and public pressure, and in slow increments through the Court's interpretation of the law, and recently, in the Landrum-Griffin Act, through government regulation.

Similarly the courts have long been concerned to protect investors and shareholders, and to define their rights and relationships to other powers in the corporate entity. The Security Exchange Commission was created partly to insure the accuracy and adequacy of the information provided to investors and equity holders.

Government support for the development of industrial trade unions has had as its most unequivocal and fully accepted benefit the development of grievance procedures within the large corporation that permit the juridical resolution of conflicts, and the reformulation of relationships between worker and worker (for instance the resolution of conflicting claims of seniority and other promotion credits), between foreman and laborer, between skill and skill, between management and labor.

The National Labor Relations Board and later the Taft-Hartley Act defined the role and rights of the trade unionists and of management in bringing before workers their respective points of view concerning trade union activities and objectives.

The Control of Internal Competition. The large corporate enterprise sometimes includes a number of technically distinct and separately managed entities, organized as subsidiaries, divisions, and branches, etc., whose objectives will be, to some degree, competitive. For example, the divisions or subsidiaries of a distillery corporation, producing different types or brands of whiskey or different liquors, or the different stores of the same chain, or the different branches of the same bank, will, in the normal course of events following the self-interested motivations of their separate managements, compete together, as well as competing with other brand-name liquors, or with the stores of another chain, or with the branches of different banks.

Such interenterprise competition might be considered in the public interest for exactly the same reason that intraenterprise competition is considered to be in the public interest. The government under the anti-trust laws has the right to require intraenterprise competition, for example, to forbid two corporations from imposing a common price policy on independent retail outlets. Can the Government (or should it) similarly have the right to require some degree of interenterprise competition, such as preventing the upper echelon of a corporate management or the financial interests represented on its Board of Directors from imposing lines of common pricing upon the normally competitive retail outlets of that corporation?

Here again, the key fact is that many different policies respecting inter-enterprise competition are reasonably open to corporate choice; here again, it is only government that can conceivably consider whether or not the policy chosen is in line with the public interest or, if it is not, that can act to bring it into accord with the public interest.

Finally, here again the essential problem is how far political direction can go in influencing, delimiting, or regulating corporate policy without unduly hampering the flexibility and authority required for effective, corporate decision-making and action-taking.

In fact, in the so-called Inter-Enterprise Conspiracy decisions,[1] the Supreme Court of the United States ruled that the government had the right under existing law to support internal or interenterprise competition by imposing constraints on corporate policies in this regard. Whatever one thinks of these controversial decisions, they illustrate very well the discretionary-arbitrary power of the autonomous organization and the problems and complexities implicit in bringing that power into accord with the public interest.

Price and Wage Policy. The postwar generation of economists were taught to consider prices and wages in the "big business" sector as rigid, as though rigidity were somehow a built-in quality of the market relationship. And the prices and wages set by negotiating organizations are rigid, as long as it is the policy of those organizations to keep them so in the face of changing costs and demands. Sometimes it is the price or wage policy of

---

[1] General Motors Corp. *vs.* U.S., 121F 2d 376; U.S. *vs.* Yellow Cab Co., 332 U.S. 218, 227 (1947); Kiefer-Stewart *vs.* Joseph E. Seagram and Sons, 340 U.S. 211; Timken Roller Bearing Co. *vs.* U.S., 341 U.S. 593.

the autonomous organization to hold tight—and sometimes it isn't. During the last decades, it has frequently been the policy of trade unions to raise wages, and the policy of corporate enterprise to raise prices, regardless of the movements of cost and demand. Prices and wages were pushed up, periodically, not in any automatic market response, but through the force of accumulating expectations and in the strategy of public relations.

In the formulation and imposition, or in the negotiation of the wage or the price policy of autonomous organization, the United States government has generally played the role of ad hoc arbiter and umpire. In response to repeated crises, it has developed certain procedures, and acquired certain powers, for example, the imposition of a "cooling-off" period and the temporary take-over of industry, used to protect the economy from the disruption of a strike and possibly to protect the consumer from price inflation. During the Kennedy Administration, as a first approximation to a general rule, the Government proposed as a guideline to trade union and corporation policy that wage hikes be limited to the average annual increase in productivity and that prices be kept constant. It undertook to support this proposal through informal pressure.

The Autonomous Organization as a Pressure Group. The autonomous organization not only is acted upon by government; it also acts upon government. It supports politicians and political parties. Sometimes its own policy-making apparatus merges with that of government or with that of a political party. In Great Britain, for example, trade union organization is scarcely distinguishable from that of the Labour Party.

Autonomous organization may dominate political government. That is the meaning, surely, of the "company town" or the "company state." This has been particularly dangerous in the past, when the large international corporation, often with the support of the State Department or of the European foreign office, and with the U.S. Marines or their European equivalents on possible call, confronted governments of small, technically backward and politically immature nations.[2]

This is not to say that the autonomous organization ought not to play a political role. On the contrary, in a representative democracy it is right and proper that it should. It is probably necessary, nevertheless, to avoid any uncertainty about the corporation's permissible role, that the ground rules, like the legal limitation in the United States on the political contribution that can be made by the corporation or trade union, be specified explicitly.

Subversion of the Regulator: A Problem for the Price-Regulated Public Utility. The drama of public utility regulation in the United States has been obscured for the lay public and its elected representatives by techni-

[2] François Perroux, "Grande Firme et Petite Nation," *La Politique de Coopération avec les Pays en Voie Développement,* Paris: Ministère D'Etat Charge de la Reforme Administrative, Rapport de la Commission a'Etude instituée par décret du 12 mars 1963 remis au Government le 18 juillet 1963, Annexes, No. 4, pp. 55–56.

cal and legal complexities. There are two roles in this drama: the Regulator and the Regulated. The Regulator is a public utility commission, characteristically an obscure body of bureaucrats, engaged in essentially routine administration, isolated from other branches and powers of government. The Regulated are private companies, financially powerful, technically complex, each with a privileged monopoly position. The Regulator is charged with protecting the vast unknowing public from the rapacious exercise of monopoly power, and, at the same time, with allowing the company to nibble—just so much and no more—of the fruits of the monopoly it possesses. The regulator weak, the regulated powerful, the prize rich, the circumstances obscuring: the inevitable end of the drama is easy to guess. Those who would control are controlled. The public authority is subverted.

Nearly all of the great public scandals in the United States have arisen in circumstances where technical and financial complexities that obscure issues from public understanding are combined with an administrative body that is charged with protecting the consumer or shielding the public domain from powerful private agencies—in public lands, in public forests, in mineral and oil-drilling concessions, in natural gas, in utility franchises. At the turn of the nineteenth and during the first decades of the twentieth century in the United States, the state and municipal utility franchise was coveted by financially powerful individuals and organizations. The utility franchise for supplying urban transportation, or power or light was the prize, and it could be won by capturing the political machinery and controlling the commissions. Political reformers of the period, Lincoln Steffens for example, explained the general degradation of state and local politics and the endemic corruption of the state and city political machines, as the consequence of this drive to corrupt and control by franchise seekers and franchise possessors.

In fact, the regulating authority was crippled and the control of public utilities was effectively frustrated in the courts. Public utility commissions were obliged under the law to fix rates at a level that would permit and would no more than permit a "fair return" to investors on the value of their investment. But what return was "fair"? And what was the value of the company's investment? On the basis of these questions, the companies went to the courts.

The Supreme Court postulated "reproduction costs" as the operational criterion for fixing the value of the company's investment. Under this criterion the value of the company's investment would be precisely equal to the costs of duplicating the capital equipment that the company had acquired over decades. But how could anyone know the precise costs of duplicating vastly complex and obsolete machines and structures? Such a highly technical determination would always be beyond the administrative competence of the commissions and beyond the juridical competence of the judges. No matter who made them, such estimates could never be unequivocal, and hence they could always be challenged, and regulation could be obstructed by endless legal battles. Whatever its theoretical justifications, the "reproduction cost" criterion eliminated any practical possibility of effective regulation. The alternative "prudent investment" criterion, urged by Justice Brandeis, would count as investment all reasonable monetary expenditures, over and above operating costs, minus standard depreciation. Under "prudent investment," the basis of "fair return" could have been precisely computed within the administrative competence of a public utility commission.

For nearly a century, while "reproduction costs" remained the rule, there could not be, and there was no effective regulation of "fair return." In the mid-1940s, the Supreme Court revoked the "reproduction cost" criterion, and left the commissions virtually a free hand in choosing their own technique for the precise and continuous determination of "fair return." Effective regulation, at last, became feasible—but rarely, if at all, have public utility commissions responded to this opportunity by regulating "fair return" effectively. Perhaps they are too deeply habituated to their marginal role. Perhaps they defer because many utility enterprises are no longer rapacious monopolists in need of regulation, but sick industries in need of help. Perhaps they sense that an effective regulation of profits might introduce more serious problems than it would solve.

Debilitation and Distortion of Managerial Motivation in Regulated Companies. Regulation may lead to the subversion of the public authority. But consider also the effect of regulation on the motivation and mores of the regulated company. When the primary emphasis of corporate leadership is on "getting around" regulation, the interest in lowering costs through efficient management or through the development of new techniques shifts into second place. Moreover, effective regulation threatens not only the profits of monopoly pricing, but also profits that are the consequence of expanded sales or lower costs. It threatens, that is, the motivation to efficiency or progress. Hence motivation is debilitated.

This distortion of motivation and this debilitation of the drives for lower costs built into the organization of price-regulated utilities, helps to explain the holding company swindles of incredible magnitude in railroads and in electrical utilities during the 1920s and 1930s, and to explain also the technical stagnation and widespread bankruptcy in urban transit lines and, until recently, in American railroads.

Structural Change and Institutional Costs. The shift from the conditions of decentralized market-direction toward those of organizational market-negotiation altered the prerequisite institutions and hence the nature of institutional costs. The shift also brought profound differences in the way of life. The nature of this change can be briefly suggested by two sets of statistics. Figure 5 shows occupational change in the United States for selected years between 1900 and 1950.

FIGURE 5
Selected Professions

Year	1900	1910	1920	1930	1940	1950
Population (in millions)	76	92	106	123	132	151
Occupations (in thousands)						
Total	29,030	37,291	42,206	48,686	51,742	58,999
Accountants and Auditors	23	39	118	192	238	390
Architects	11	16	17	28	22	25
Chemists	9	16	28	45	57	77
Dentists	30	40	56	71	71	76
Engineers	38	77	134	217	297	543
Lawyers and Judges	108	115	123	161	182	184
Veterinarians	8	12	13	12	11	14
Purchasing Agents	7	8	18	29	34	65

From *Historical Statistics of the United States, Colonial Times to 1957*, U.S. Bureau of Census (Washington, D.C., 1960).

During the period between 1900 and 1950, population and "occupations" about doubled. Some occupations, those concerned with providing services for individuals or households, architects and dentists, for example, changed in about the same proportion.

It was hypothesized in Part I that a transformation to an economy of organizational market-negotiation would require (a) that a professionalized education acquired through formal studies would have to be substituted for the technical education previously acquired spontaneously in the farm or shop of small, decentralized enterprise, and (b) that for the organization of economic progress, there would have to be a significant increase in science-based Research and Development in place of ad hoc experiment and invention, which was feasible in the economy of small, decentralized enterprise. The data confirm these hypotheses. During these five decades, when population about doubled, engineers, representing formal professionalized training in production and business techniques, increased more than fourteenfold (from 38,000 in 1900 to 543,000 in 1950) and the number of chemists, representing the increase in organized research, increased more than sevenfold (from 9,000 in 1910 to 77,000 in 1950).

It was also hypothesized in Part I, that a transformation to organizational market-negotiation would increase complexities and costs in the planning and control of economic activity. Reflecting this, the numbers of accountants and auditors increased from 23,000 in 1900 to 390,000 in 1950—nearly seventeenfold! Similarly, the more than ninefold increase in purchasing agents (from 7,000 to 65,000) suggests the structural change from the owner's omnicompetence in the man-sized enterprise to the delegated responsibilities in autonomous organization.

It was also hypothesized in Part I that the complexities and costs of legal activity are, in considerable part, a function of decentralized decision-making. It would therefore be expected that a transformation toward organizational market-negotiation would reduce the costs of legal adjudication as an institutional cost of economic organization. Between 1900 and 1950 the increase in the numbers of lawyers and judges was considerably less than the general increase in population or in occupations; correspondingly, the number of lawyers and judges as a ratio of total population or total occupations significantly declined. Similarly, the ratio of veterinarians to population declined, as would be expected in a shift from agriculture and from the use of the horse to the car and tractor.

It was also suggested in Part I that a change from decentralized market-direction to the conditions of the economy of autonomous organization might be expected to restrict the opportunity for the expression of individual opinion, and to dampen the variability of taste. Such a supposition is supported by the fact that in spite of a doubling of population and a great broadening of higher education the number of new books published

FIGURE 6

New Books Published in the United States, 1900–1950

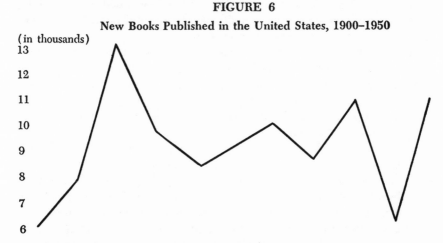

From *Historical Statistics of the United States, Colonial Times to 1957,* U.S. Bureau of Census (Washington, D.C., 1960), p. 499.

each year in the United States between 1900 and 1950 showed no upward trend (see Figure 6).

In Figure 7, the publication of newspapers and periodicals between 1900 and 1954 is shown.

FIGURE 7
Newspapers and Periodicals Published in the United States (1900–1954)

Year	Weekly Newspapers Numbers	Weekly Newspapers Circulation (1000)	Daily Newspapers Numbers	Daily Newspapers Circulation (1000)	Weekly Periodicals Numbers	Weekly Periodicals Circulation (1000)
1900			2226	15,102		
1904	13,513	18,809			1493	17,418
1909	13,903	20,946	2600	24,212	1194	19,877
1921	6,059	20,816	2334	33,742	995	23,090
1931	6,313	16,173	2044	41,294	1066	30,782
1939	6,212	18,295	2040	42,966	1109	55,825
1947	7,705	21,408	1854	53,287	892	69,393
1954	6,249	30,336	1820	56,410	487	82,066

From *Historical Statistics of the United States, Colonial Times to 1957,* U.S. Bureau of Census (Washington, D.C., 1960), p. 500.

For each category of publication there is a great increase in circulation, but a steady decline in the numbers of independent publications. During the half century, the drastic and progressive reduction in the numbers of newspaper and periodical outlets and of new books per reader (and writer) suggests the degree to which the opportunity for the expression of the individual viewpoint has been narrowed and variability in individual taste dampened.

Summary. Diverse forms of economic organization compose the United States enterprise economy. Not one, but a number of distinct sets of economic policies, have been evolved to meet the distinct sets of problems raised by each of these forms.

The American Economy has experienced during the first half of the twentieth century a revolutionary change in the comparative significance of its constituent forms. The economy of autonomous organization has increased; the economy of decentralized enterprise has declined in importance. This change has had its impact on the social environment and on the structure of individual relationships.

The specific operational characteristics of each of the forms of economic organization which together constitute the American enterprise economy, the problems consequent upon these built-in characteristics, and the response of public policy to these problems are recapitulated in Figure 8.

FIGURE 8

Problems and Public Policies in the United States Enterprise Economy

Form of Economic Organization	*Inherent Characteristics*	*Critical Problems*	*Policy Response*
Decentralized market-direction	Extreme vertical price instability in face of variation in aggregate demand	Comparative decline in real farm income	"Parity price" supports for agricultural outputs, through the government purchase of "surplus" food stocks, and through governmental restrictions on the use of farm acreage
	Propensity to externalize the costs and benefits of choice and action	Uneconomic depletion of natural resources, e.g., soil, forests, wildlife, minerals	Public conservation projects, e.g., C.C.C., government soil reclamation, public control and management of forests, regulation in protection of wildlife, national and state parks, and forest and wildlife reservations
Decentralized market-segmented	The feasibility of distorting the force of market competition through price-conspiracy and monopoly devices	Cartels and price agreements	Anti-trust policy, effectively outlawing price agreement and cartel arrangements between independent producers
Organizational market-negotiating	Extreme instability of production and employment in the face of variations in aggregate demand	The modern depression	Fiscal and monetary policy intended to stabilize aggregate expenditures
	Arbitrary power in formulating the policies of the autonomous organization in regard to:		

FIGURE 8 (*Continued*)

Form of Economic Organization	*Inherent Characteristics*	*Critical Problems*	*Policy Response*
	(1) Internal distribution of income		(a) Corporation income tax, surplus profits tax, undistributed profits tax (b) Minimum wages and hour legislation (c) Public support to industrial trade unionism, as a means of promoting "fair shares" through collective bargaining
	(2) Fixing the context of individual opportunity, through policies of recruitment and promotion	Racial and religious discrimination	(a) Fair employment practices acts (b) Fair employment clauses in government contracts
	(3) Choosing a level of investment	Full employment policies	Tax inducements to encourage specified types of investment
	(4) Control of internal relations of participants	(a) Victimization of equity holders and potential investors	Security Exchange Commission
		(b) Anti-union propaganda by employers	National Labor Relations Board to protect right of trade unionist to propagate trade-union position, and later, the Taft-Hartley Act to correct the balance in favor of management's rights

FIGURE 8 (*Continued*)

Form of Economic Organization	Inherent Characteristics	Critical Problems	Policy Response
		(c) Worker discontents	Evolution of union-management grievance procedures, under Government (N.L.R.B.) support
		(d) Nondemocratic procedure, failure to protect minority rights, irresponsibility and corruption in the exercise of authority in trade unions	Court decisions and the Landrum-Griffin Act
	(5) Control of competition between decentralized interenterprise entities	Conflict with government interest in promoting competition	Interenterprise conspiracy decisions of the U.S. Supreme Court
	(6) Control of prices and wages	Wage and price inflation in spite of unemployment and pervasive underutilization of industrial capacity	Ad hoc intervention by the President and government agencies, with "cooling off" periods and occasional "taking over" of plants
		Frustration of full-employment policy	Suggested guidelines for wage-negotiation and corporate price-policy, supported by informal public pressure
	(7) Exercise of pressure on government	Need to fix rules-of-game	Limitation on contribution to political campaigns

FIGURE 8 (Continued)

Form of Economic Organization	Inherent Characteristics	Critical Problems	Policy Response
Price-regulated public utilities	Motivation to subvert the regulating authority	Corruption of the political machine at the state and city level, by the early "franchise seekers"	
		The hobbling of effective regulation by the decision of the Supreme Court imposing "reproduction costs" as criterion for determining "fair-value" of investment	Reversed in the 1940s
	The threat, possibility, or approximation of effective regulation (which would equalize profits regardless of relative efficiency or successful technical innovation) and the consequent effort of management to "get around" regulation	The debilitation of management's interest in expanded sales and lower costs, and the consequent technical stagnation and eventual bankruptcy of "sick" utility industries	
	Emphasis on financial manipulation based on evasion of regulation and monopoly prerogatives	Financial scandals in railroads and electrical utilities	Government control of utility finance and simplification of holding company structure

Chapter 22

Problems and Policies in Organizing Economic Progress in the Enterprise Economy

The last chapter dealt with the organization of production and distribu tion. This chapter will examine problems and policies in the organizatio. of economic progress in the enterprise economy.

Organizing Economic Progress in American Agriculture. The agricultural sector, still of great importance in the American enterprise economy, remains, as far as the motivation and choice of the farmer is concerned, decentralized and market-directed. Given this form of economic organization, it follows: (1) that there will be a widespread technical mastery acquired spontaneously through experience on the farm, and (2) that this technical mastery coupled with the broadly dispersed entrepreneurial prerogative to experiment and to innovate, will favor ad hoc invention. (3) However, it will be extremely difficult for the inventor or innovator to recapture any substantial share of the highly diffused benefits of his invention or innovation, because of the propensity that inheres in decentralized market-direction to externalize the benefits of choice. (4) Given this difficulty of recapturing the benefits of invention and innovation (*a*) the impetus to develop ad hoc invention will be limited, and (*b*) there will be virtually no long-range investment by the farmer in the processes of invention and innovation.

In fact, there has never been any significant investment by farmers in the processes of invention-innovation (Research and Development). There have been a significant number of ad hoc inventions and innovations arising through private motivation, for example, the evolution of "factory" techniques for the production of poultry and in the development of quick-frozen foods. The benefits of these have generally eluded recapture by their inventors or innovators. An important source of progress in American agriculture has been government R & D, e.g., of the Department of Agriculture, and ad hoc inventions-innovations made in other parts of the enterprise economy, e.g., the mechanical harvester.

Scientific Research in Support of Progress in Argiculture. Agriculture, far more than industry, depends on natural process and on the variability of natural conditions: weather, soil nutrients, climate, micro-organisms, insect pests, animal and plant ecology, and biological and chemical processes of germination and growth. To collect information relevant to the understanding of these natural processes requires extended, painstaking, disciplined studies, and "scientific" experiments under carefully controlled conditions—in other words, it requires long-range investment in science. Such investment has not been generated under private motivation in the agricultural sector. Nor has there been any R & D related to agriculture in the other parts of the enterprise economy except on items produced by large corporations and sold to the farmer, for instance, in research on chemical fertilizer and insecticides. For the rest, R & D oriented toward agricultural advance has required government support.

Difficulties in Transmitting Invention and Innovation. Decision-making is highly dispersed in American agriculture. The problems and costs of demonstrating new techniques and processes and persuading decision-makers of their value are multiplied correspondingly. Moreover, because the farmer must be conversant with many practices and processes, rather than having a deep and authoritative knowledge in any one, he will tend to rely on tradition and convention and, for that reason, will resist innovation. And this conservatism will be reinforced by his reliance on the delicate ecological balance of nature.

Hence the small farmer on his own farm, the peasant throughout history has tended to rely on folkways and tradition and to resist technological change. In order to offset this tendency, built into the circumstances of agriculture and the form of decentralized market-direction, political initiative from outside the agricultural sector has been necessary.

Government Organization of Research and of Its Transmission. For about a century, the American government has been engaged in long-range programed scientific research, and in the systematic transmission of scientific information and technical innovation in support of progress in American agriculture. It has done this in a number of ways.

1. *The development of a science infrastructure for agriculture to enable more informed, rational, and sophisticated choices by farmers.* The notion of a physical infrastructure: roads, harbors, bridges, drained swamps and cleared forests, telecommunications, controls against floods, hurricanes, etc., is familiar. So is the notion of a social infrastructure: parks and clubs, police to protect property, law courts to enforce contract, etc. These constitute the context within which choice, by the individual, the group, or society, must be made. Another important part of that context of choice is a science infrastructure. The science infrastructure makes available information from the corpus of science data, and provides science-based capacities to measure, to test, to analyze, to predict. For example, in agriculture, a laboratory that analyzes a soil sample for its structure

and its chemical composition and reports its deficiencies in minerals or organic matter, or a service that identifies an insect pest or a fungal parasite that is attacking a crop and recommends methods for dealing with that pest or parasite, or an organization that has evolved standards and techniques for grading agricultural outputs or for inspecting foods in transit to limit the spread of plant disease or of weeds or of plant parasites, or the organized capacity to predict the weather—all these are parts of the science infrastructure. They are not themselves agricultural techniques or processes, but are rather a part of the framework within which agricultural choice is made and agricultural processes are organized. The framework affects the level of agricultural productivity, and the upward transformation of this framework lifts with it the level of agricultural productivity.

2. *Long-range programed research intended to transform the science infrastructure, and to develop higher agricultural processes.*

3. *Education and training to support agricultural advance.* In order to promote agricultural skills and develop a capacity for sophisticated choice on the part of the farmer, the government supports a system of higher and lower education geared to the needs of the farmer.

4. *An extension service designed to offset the difficulties in the transmission of information related to technical choice and science-based innovations, when decision-making is highly dispersed.* Communication is through direct contacts between county agent and farmer, through publications and radio and television programs, and through farm demonstrations.

The American government has, then, supported progress in the decentralized, market-directed organization of the agricultural sector through the development of a four-pronged apparatus: (1) a science infrastructure including documentation services, soil mapping, soil analysis and pest identification services, inspection and crop protection, weather prediction, etc.; (2) programed Research and Development, with both regional and centralized laboratories and considerable effort devoted to the long-range problems of agriculture; (3) educational institutions, including land-grant colleges established in every state to train agricultural scientists, agricultural engineers, and to give the oncoming generation of practicing farmers a capacity for sophisticated choice vis à vis the offerings of science and of the science-based technologies; and (4) an extension service to act as a disinterested guide and counsel to the farmer. The U. S. extension service is supported or supplemented by the extension services of the states and by such special agencies as the TVA. Through numerous demonstrations and discussions, it helps the farmer to employ the most advanced techniques in dealing with his particular problems, and encourages the continued upward transformation of agricultural processes.

Economic Progress in American Agriculture. In these varied ways for a hundred years the American government has systematically supported the technical advance of agriculture. But this does not mean that agriculture has been uniformly progressive for a full century. On the contrary, the figures suggest that for a great part of this time, the technology of U.S. agriculture was stagnant.

FIGURE 9
Farm Productivity in the United States

Period	Output Per Man-Hour (Annual rate of increase)
Pre-1899	1.1
1899–1909	0.0
1909–1919	0.0
1919–1929	1.2
1929–1937	0.8
1937–1948	3.8
1948–1953	6.2
1950–1958	6.2

Data are from John Kendrick, *Productivity Trends in the United States* (Princeton: Princeton University Press, 1961), p. 152, except for the period 1950–1958, which is derived from *Trends in Output Per Man-Hour in the Private Economy, 1909–1958*, Bureau of Labor Statistics, Washington, D.C.

Figure 9 shows that from before 1899 to the mid-1930s, the value of output per man-hour in agriculture increased very slowly. For whole decades it seems not to have increased at all. But from the mid-1930s onward, progress has been extraordinary. This is a curious phenomenon. A science-based politically directed system to support technological advance in a decentralized market-directed agriculture has been in operation for a century. According to the record, that system worked badly prior to the 1930s: indeed, it seemed hardly to work at all. After the 1930s, it seemed to work extremely well. Why? What had been added at that juncture to complete the system of economic progress and to make it effective?

The Support for Innovation and Transformation in Agriculture. The government organized education, a science infrastructure, and an extension service, to create new potentialities for technical advance and to disseminate the knowledge of these potentialities to the farmer. But a farmer will not transform his processes unless he has the resources available to cover the costs of transformation. Nor is a bankrupt farmer, biding his time to migrate to the town and find a job in the factory, likely to be willing to embark on new technological adventures. Before a decentralized market-directed agriculture would take advantage of the potentialities offered it by science, farming itself had first to offer prospects that would attract the long-sighted plans and efforts of ambitious men. It was these prospects precisely that the New Deal Administration provided from the mid-1930s onward. It offered financial support for basic transformation, for example, through the Rural Electrification Administration and it guaranteed stable prices for farm products. These supplementary measures, which were not specifically related to science, technology, or education, made agriculture a relatively attractive occupation for ambitious men and eventually enabled the farmer to finance innovation and transformation with his own savings. Thus the system of economic progress was completed and made effective.

The Organizational Revolution and Economic Progress. The enormous increase in the absolute size and in the relative importance of the organizational market-negotiating part of the American enterprise economy is often called the "organizational revolution."

Following the postulates of Part I, the organizational revolution would result in: (1) a decline in the opportunities to acquire technical mastery spontaneously through experience on the job; and (2) an increase in the opportunity of the decision-making entity to recapture a greater share of the benefits of investments made in the process of invention-innovation.

As a consequence one might anticipate: (1) an increase in formal education, substituting for education through work experience, as a means of acquiring the technical mastery that is prerequisite to invention; (2) a decline in ad hoc invention based on work experience and on the widespread opportunity to experiment and innovate under entrepreneurial aegis; and (3) an increase in long-range investment in programed invention-innovation by science-trained specialists.

The Organizational Revolution and the Extension of Formal Education. The displacement of large numbers of small, individually controlled businesses by the massive, autonomous enterprise eliminates opportunities for individual self-education on the job and through the job. The rough and tumble of market competition no longer automatically and spontaneously recruits economic leadership. Other more formalized methods must be employed to recruit leadership in the autonomous organization and to train that leadership and inculcate the technical mastery that is a prerequisite to invention and innovation. Technical schools and universities must take the place of the old "college of hard knocks."

Coincidently with organizational revolution in the American enterprise economy, there has been an enormous increase in formal education in the United States. From 1911-1920, to 1951-1953, Americans receiving their Bachelor or first professional degrees increased from 22 per 1000, to 150 per 1000.[1] Between 1910 and 1960, while population doubled, the rate at which Bachelor and first professional degrees were granted increased tenfold. Those degrees that relate specifically to the sort of technical mastery that, under decentralized market-direction, might be acquired spontane-

[1] Dael Wolfle, *America's Resources of Specialized Talent* (New York: Harper & Row, 1954), p. 31.

ously on the job, such as engineering degrees, and those relating to the special needs of organizational control and planning, such as accounting and auditing, increased at an even more phenomenal rate. The number of first degrees in engineering increased from a 1000 granted in 1910 to 37,808 in 1960.[2] The extraordinary growth in the numbers of accountants and auditors was shown earlier in Figure 5 above (p. 237). Between 1900 and 1964, the number of trained engineers and scientists in the United States increased thirtyfold, from 50,000 to 1,500,000.[3]

The relationship we have hypothesized between the organizational revolution and the professionalization of industrial leadership is supported by the fact that, in the American enterprise economy, the massive autonomous organization is the primary employer of professional engineers and scientists.

When in 1959 the United States Department of Labor studied the employment of scientists and engineers in American industry, it immediately eliminated the two million smallest firms from the survey, having established that they employ virtually no engineers or scientists. Of the 47,000 relatively large firms surveyed, the category of the largest, those employing 5000 or more employees, which constituted 1 percent of the total number, employed 52.6 percent of the engineers and scientists in American industry.[4] For these largest firms, the scientists and engineers employed as a ratio of total work-force was double or more the ratio for firms of any other size category.

Research and Development as a Consequence of the Organizational Revolution. Research and Development here means programed, science-based activities, directed toward the transformation of economic (or other) processes. R & D might do this through the invention of new techniques or products, or through the evaluation, procurement, and adaptation of techniques or products invented elsewhere. Or it might occur through improving the science infrastructure, thereby increasing the rationality of engineering and entrepreneurial choice.

There are two preconditions for R & D in the enterprise economy. First, there must be available to industry a sufficient number of scientists and managers sufficiently sophisticated in scientific matters to organize and perform R & D on the one hand, and to comprehend and integrate the research contribution into industrial choice and transformation, on the

---

[2] Recent data from the *Statistical Abstract of the United States 1962.* Earlier data from Wolfle.
[3] National Science Foundation, *Scientific Personnel Resources* (Washington, D.C., 1955), provides data on the size of the community of engineers and scientists, from 1900 to 1954. Later estimates are from the *Statistical Abstract,* or are projections therefrom.
[4] National Science Foundation, *Scientific and Technical Personnel in American Industry* (Washington, D.C., 1960), pp. 60–62.

other. Second, enterprise must be able to recapture as profits a significant share of the benefits of research.

The organizational revolution established these two preconditions. Through the massive extension of formal education, a substantial corps of industrially oriented scientists, science-trained technicians, and managers sophisticated in matters of science was produced. And the large autonomous enterprise, because of the magnitude and variety of its outputs and because of its power to choose and control the terms and conditions of its operations and sales, is able to recapture a sufficient proportion of the benefits to justify its investment in certain kinds of R & D.

Research and Development in the American Enterprise Economy before World War II. As a significant activity, Research and Development is quite new in the American enterprise economy. Prior to World War II, no statistics were gathered concerning it, which suggests its relative unimportance at the time. Figure 10 estimates the expenditures on R & D performed in the American enterprise economy, the American institutional economy (universities, foundations), and the American political economy (government) from 1920 to 1940.

R & D in the enterprise economy before World War II seems to have been almost entirely carried on by large autonomous companies and geared to industrial and consumer markets. R & D as supported or performed by Government was comparatively insignificant, amounting to from 10 to 15 percent of the total. From 1920 to 1940, the rate of expenditure on R & D increased rapidly from .2 to .9 percent of the national income, but the great jump did not come until after the war.

FIGURE 10
Research and Development Expenditures in the United States, 1920–1940 in Five-Year Intervals

Year	R & D in the Enterprise Economy ($ millions)	R & D in the Political Economy ($ millions)	R & D in the Institutional Economy ($ millions)	% Total R & D ($ millions)	Total as a % of National Income (%)
1920	90	16	10	116	.2
1925	158	18	13	199	.3
1930	289	24	20	333	.4
1935	321	25	29	375	.7
1940	571	67	50	690	.9

Estimates for the period were first published by Vannevar Bush in his book *Science, The Endless Frontier* (Washington, D.C.: Government Printing Office, 1945). These estimates have been drastically revised upward to make them commensurable with later surveys of the National Science Foundation. Expenditures on R & D in the Enterprise Economy were deduced by subtracting from total R & D, R & D by the Political Economy which (from 1925–1940) is known, and the estimated R & D expenditures of the Institutional Economy, i.e., of nonprofit industrial research institutes, colleges, and universities.

Research and Development in World War II. The experience of World War II established, irrefutably, the relationship of national power and R & D. First Germany, through its research prowess, leap-frogged the threat of a sea blockade by achieving virtual industrial autonomy, based primarily on the chemical conversion of Silesian brown coal deposits into a range of synthetics. Then the decisive weapon in the naval struggle and in the war in the Pacific turned out to be military aircraft, the product of two decades of R & D competition between military establishments. The Battle of Britain was won and the island spared an invasion as much by the British scientists who developed radar as an effective instrument of defense and attack as by the few brave fliers that Churchill praised. Toward the end, a crippled Germany tried to save itself through the development of the rocket-propelled missile. The United States, combining the genius of refugee scientists from Europe with an unprecedented mobilization of engineering talents, at a cost of perhaps two billion dollars, made the atomic bomb and ushered the world into a new age of war and weaponry.

The Magnitude of Research and Development in the Postwar Economy. During the decades since the end of World War II, there has been a very rapid increase in the expenditures on R & D, both absolutely and as a proportion of national income. From less than half a billion dollars in 1940, R & D expenditures have risen to about 20 billion dollars in 1964. From less than 1 percent of the national income, R & D expenditures in 1964 approached 4 percent of the national income.

During this period, R & D has come to employ more than a third of all engineers and scientists working in industry in the United States, including, presumably, the nation's most highly trained and technically creative manpower.

FIGURE 11
Scientists and Engineers Employed in Industrial Research and Development for Selected Years

Years	*For R & D*	*For All Purposes*	*% R & D Employment as a % of Total Employment*
1954	157,300 *	553,800 *	28.4
1957	222,800 †	728,400 †	30.6
1961	301,000 ‡	814,800 ‡	36.9

* National Science Foundation, *Science and Engineering in American Industry*, NSF 56–16 (Washington, D.C.), p. 68.
† National Science Foundation, *Science and Engineering in American Industry*, NSF 59–50 (Washington, D.C.), p. 53.
‡ U.S. Bureau of Census, *Statistical Abstract of the United States 1963*, p. 547.

The Concentration of Research and Development in Large Enterprise.
The phenomenal increase in R & D in the postwar economy has been
almost entirely within the sphere of large, autonomous enterprise, concentrated within a few industries in the organizational market-negotiating
part of the enterprise economy.

In 1959, of the 17 (census) industries, two performed 50 percent and
four 70 percent of the national R & D.[5] Out of the millions of firms in the
American enterprise economy, only 12,000 did any R & D at all. Of the
total R & D 100 of these companies performed 81 percent; 20 performed
54 percent; 8 performed 33 percent; and 4 performed 22 percent.[6]

The concentration of R & D activity is in orders of magnitude greater
than the concentration of employment or sales volume. In 1957, for example, the 100 largest industrial corporations (ranged in the order of their
sales volume) did 18.5 percent of the total national sales volume and
accounted for 7.8 percent of employment.[7]

Government procurement is a powerful force in promoting this concentration. While four companies performed 13 percent of all company-
financed R & D in 1959, they performed 29 percent of the R & D financed
by the federal government. While the first 20 companies performed 33
percent of company-financed R & D, they performed 68 percent of R & D
financed by government, and so on.

This concentration of R & D is likely to have the following consequences. It will (1) augment and fortify the predominance of a part of
organizational marketing-negotiating enterprise and (2) cause this part of
the economy to operate at a level of scientific sophistication far above that
of the rest. Difference between parts of the economy in their levels of
scientific sophistication checks the cross-flow of personnel, of ideas, of
information, of invention. It causes incongruities to be introduced into an
educational system that tries to cater to the diverse needs and levels of
technical sophistication.

Government Predominance in Postwar Research and Development.
Figure 12 shows the sources of funds for the support of R & D and Basic
Research, and the locus of performance of that R & D or Basic Research
between 1953–1954 and 1961–1962.

The great bulk of R & D in recent decades has been paid for by the
federal government and performed, under contract, by private industry.
Should this activity be considered, then, a function of the American enterprise economy or of the American political economy? We prefer the latter. Hence the analysis of the policies and problems of organizing R & D

[5] National Science Foundation, *Funds for Research and Development in Industry,*
1959, NSF 62–63 (Washington, D.C.).
[6] *Ibid.*
[7] *Statistical Abstract of the United States 1959.*

FIGURE 12

Funds for Total Research and Development and for Basic Research, by Source and by Performance Sector: 1953–1954 to 1961–1962

(In millions of dollars. Includes Alaska and Hawaii, except industry data prior to 1957–1958. Hyphenated time periods indicate that data are for a variety of financial years beginning in the earlier year and ending in the later year. Data refer in general to the natural sciences; however, some funds for psychology and the social sciences could not be eliminated.)

Item and Year	Total	Sources of Funds				Performance of Research and Development by—			
		Federal Government[1]	Industry	Colleges and universities[2]	Other nonprofit institutions[2]	Federal Government	Industry[3]	Colleges and universities[3]	Other nonprofit institutions[3]
Research and Development[4]									
1953–54	5,150	2,740	2,240	130	40	970	3,630	450	100
1954–55	5,620	3,070	2,365	140	45	950	4,070	480	120
1955–56	6,390	3,670	2,510	155	55	1,090	4,640	530	130
1956–57	8,670	5,095	3,325	180	70	1,280	6,600	650	140
1957–58	10,100	6,390	3,450	190	70	1,440	7,730	780	150
1958–59	11,130	7,170	3,680	190	90	1,730	8,360	840	200
1959–60	12,680	8,320	4,060	200	100	1,830	9,610	1,000	240
1960–61 (prel.)	13,890	9,010	4,550	210	120	1,900	10,510	1,200	280
1961–62 (prel.)	14,740	9,650	4,705	230	155	2,090	10,870	1,400	380
Basic Research									
1953–54	432	195	147	62	28	47	151	208	26
1954–55	485	5	5	70	35	55	166	230	34
1955–56	547	5	5	75	38	65	189	250	43
1956–57	694	5	5	90	46	90	253	300	51

FIGURE 12 (*Continued*)

Item and Year	Total	Sources of Funds				Performance of Research and Development by—			
		Federal Government[1]	Industry	Colleges and universities[2]	Other nonprofit institutions[2]	Federal Government	Industry[3]	Colleges and universities[3]	Other nonprofit institutions[3]
1957–58	834	422	249	111	52	111	271	392	60
1958–59	975	524	275	118	58	180	305	420	70
1959–60	1,064	578	275	140	71	147	332	500	85
1960–61 (prel.)	1,256	684	328	161	83	193	388	575	100
1961–62 (prel.)	1,488	849	351	180	108	238	403	695	152

[1] Data on sources of funds are based on reports by the performers.
[2] Includes State and local funds received by these institutions and used for research and development.
[3] Includes expenditures at Federal contract research centers administered by organizations in this sector.
[4] Includes basic research, applied research, and development.
[5] Not available on a comparable basis.

U.S. Bureau of Census, *Statistical Abstract of the United States 1963* (Washington, D.C.: U.S. Government Printing Office, 1963), p. 543.

as an instrument of technical progress in the American economy will be deferred until our discussion of the American political economy in Chapter 25.

Patented Invention Under Organizational Market-Negotiation. The patent system was devised and evolved as a means of stimulating invention and innovation where choice was decentralized and market-directed. In a situation where the diffused benefits of a creative idea are extremely vulnerable to externalization, it tried to help the individual to capture for himself a greater share of the realized benefits of his ad hoc invention: and, above all, to give to the individual the means of profiting by systematically disseminating his invention through its sale or license. The patent device in the circumstances of organizational market-negotiation has other implications.

The patent system is not as necessary in providing a profit motive for invention and innovation under organizational market-negotiating enterprise, as when choice is decentralized and market-directed. With or without the patent system the autonomous organization can "cash in" on Research and Development. Without the patent system, the autonomous organization would continue to invest in R & D (and *perhaps* more than before) as a prerequisite for survival. Some firms in the organizational economy, in electronics for example, claim to disdain patents as not worth the trouble, preferring to cultivate a sheer capacity to outrace their rivals rather than concentrating on building little islands of special advantage, like a runner who concerns himself with his stamina and form rather than the trivialities of handicap. Corporate policies in this regard vary widely.

This is not to say that the patent system is without social value under organizational market-negotiating enterprise. The patent system in this form of economic organization is surely useful in promoting as a profitable activity the systematic exchange through sale and licensing of invention and technical information and, therefore, *possibly* in motivating firms to promote the dissemination of its patents and technical information. Nevertheless the value of patents as a device for motivating inventive effort or investment in this form of economic organization is highly equivocal and there is room for maneuver by government in the control and restructuring of the patent system without detrimental effect on invention and transformation.

The business organization, like the individual inventor, may be motivated by the possibility of selling or licensing a patented invention to reveal and to promote the use of a creative idea which, otherwise, it might try to keep secret. But, on the other hand, the patent system offers corporate enterprise new possibilities for systematically stifling the use of invention and for blocking avenues of innovation. It can, and it does, through deals and purchases as well as through its own research, accumulate patents and associated know-how for the purpose of preventing competitive products and processes from ever developing.

By its sheer power to accumulate patents, a particular enterprise can come to control a field of technology, so that there can be no outlet or market for future invention in that field except to that company or with its consent. Once again the autonomous organization has the arbitrary power to choose between alternative paths, both consistent with its own survival and profit—but with very different effects on economic growth: either to use patents as an instrument to promote the creative idea, or as a means of blocking change and frustrating innovation. Once again, government must intervene in the public interest. Following a precedent that the discovery of an important scientific law cannot be patented because it reserves too broad a field for private control, the Courts have forbidden a company to accumulate patents beyond some (not precisely specified) "critical mass." The Department of Justice has periodically attacked such accumulations (American Telephone and Telegraph Company, International Business Machines, Radio Corporation of America) and has required that blocks of patents be released to the public domain. Hence, there has begun to take form a patent-control policy specific to organizational market-negotiating enterprise.

Sequestering the Data of Science by Autonomous Organizations. In the decentralized market-directed economy, many inventions, patented or not, will be withheld from general use. But the data of science, which is not produced through private investment for commercial purpose, will be universally available. Not so in the economy of autonomous organization. Organizational enterprise produces the data of science for commercial purposes, and sequesters it for private advantage.

The R & D of autonomous enterprise does not initially produce patentable invention. Rather the thrust of privately supported, commercially oriented R & D is systematically to produce, gather, and organize bodies of information as a component of the science infrastructure in order to sharpen managerial choice. R & D produces a base for subsequent invention and a sheer problem-solving instrument of cumulating significance and power. Accumulating bodies of scientific and technical information generated through corporation research amount to privately possessed subbranches of science, which are only occasionally expressed in the patentable solution of technical problems. The sequestering of privately possessed subbranches of science will, one day, constitute a major problem for public policy. The corporation interest dictates holding these accumulating bodies of scientific knowledge perpetually in secret, for the exclusive use of its own research to serve its own competitive advantage.

The public interest requires incorporating these bodies of information into the public domain, to fortify the national science infrastructure and to accelerate the extension and advance of world science. As yet, this problem has not infiltrated public awareness, but it is inevitable eventually that this contradiction between corporation policy of withholding growing bodies of research data and the public interest in accelerating economic growth will lead to crisis and political action. Conceivably the conflict could be resolved through a government commitment to pay for a share of the company's R & D in return for a commitment on the part of the company to release systematically and completely all research data within a fixed period (say, of five years) after the data has been acquired —giving the company not permanent possession, but the advantage of a substantial lead time in the application of its data. A solution of this sort will be complicated by the fact that in such industries as chemicals, pharmaceuticals, and electronics, the effective sphere of competition is international and hence, if one national grouping is not to be disadvantaged relative to the others, an effective system for the periodic release of R & D information might require an international convention.

Ad Hoc Invention in Decentralized Market-Segmented Enterprise. In the decentralized market-segmented part of the economy: (1) it is the prerogative of multitudes of small entrepreneurs to experiment and to innovate; (2) the possibility of acquiring a significant competitive advantage, through variations in the product or service offered, provides a motivation for experiment and innovation; and (3) the individual control of an integral business operation provides the knowledge and technical mastery required for creative manipulation and change. Consequently one might anticipate a mass of petty creative activities in the adaptation and maneuver of the market. And this decentralized market-segmented part of the American enterprise economy has indeed been the primary source of variations in style and design, with product and process variations shading into patentable invention. But, although it may provide the bulk of ad hoc invention, this form of economic organization generates virtually no significant investment in Research and Development for the following reasons. The firm controls too small a part of total sales and output to enable it, through its own production, to capitalize on a substantial proportion of the advantages to the industry, which its invention might bring. The competence of the firm is likely to be too narrow to exploit the range of variable and unpredictable outputs of R & D. The great uncertainties inherent in decentralized choice handicap any form of long-range anticipations and, hence, bias the decision-maker against investment in R and D where benefits are likely to be only distantly anticipated and can only be gradually realized upon. In this form of economic organization, the competitive advantages of the firm are like island dunes on a shifting sea of sand.

In some countries—France, Germany, and particularly Great Britain, where the D.S.I.R. (Department of Scientific and Industrial Research) has been in existence for nearly half a century—government has supported cooperative research associations for decentralized market-segmented enterprise. In general these cooperative research associations have provided a useful component of the science infrastructure but they have rarely produced significant inventions leading to basic industrial transformation, probably because the firms that are members of the research associations have opposed research by their associations that might disturb a competitive balance based on shades of variation in output and services. In the same fashion, in the United States, an effort by the Department of Commerce in 1963 to start a small government-supported research program to promote technical advance in decentralized market-segmented industries (such as building and construction) was killed by the opposition of the very industries that the program was intended to help, because the individual firms of those industries were afraid that research-produced technical change might upset the structure of competitive advantage. This attitude contrasts sharply with that of the farmers in the market-directed organization of agriculture, where outputs are standardized and no competitive balance is threatened by public research supports.

The Brain-Drain from Decentralized Market-Segmented Enterprises. It might be anticipated that a cumulatively greater part of the technically gifted, creative members of oncoming generations would be drawn into the new, prestigious, and challenging opportunities of Research and Development and that, correspondingly, fewer of these would be left to find their way into decentralized market-segmented enterprise. By being drawn into R & D, those who were or who might have been restless, probing industrialists, innovating entrepreneurs, or inventors tinkering in their shops become, instead, engineers on project teams, scientists in laboratories, or research managers.

Patent statistics provide a clue to the extent that talent has been diverted. R & D does produce patented inventions, and the more R & D, the more patented inventions that would be forthcoming. Therefore a great increase in national R & D expenditures per capita, would lead to a corresponding increase in the number of patented inventions, unless the increase in R & D activity diverted inventive efforts from elsewhere in the economy. Figure 13 below suggests that this is precisely what has happened in the United States. It shows that accompanying the enormous increase in R & D expenditures per capita, there has been a steady *decline* in patents-applied-for per capita.

FIGURE 13

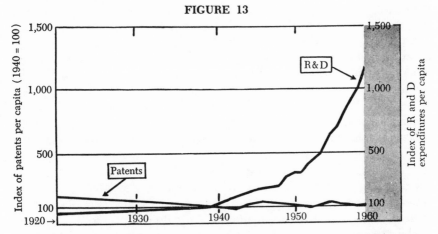

From *Science*, May 12, 1961, pp. 1464–1465. Resident population data from U.S. Bureau of Census, *Statistical Abstract of the United States 1961* (Washington, D.C.: U.S. Government Printing Office, 1961).

Fewer patents-applied-for per capita need not mean a net decline in the technically creative contribution. In fact, the same input of effort and the same output of ideas and devices are bound to result in more patent applications when the creative activity is by private inventors in the decentralized market rather than by R & D teams in large corporate enterprise or in government laboratories. This is so because the individual inventor in the decentralized market must rely more on patent protection than he would if he were a member of a corporation research team, and since the autonomous enterprise can exploit the technical advances generated by its research teams without the necessity of embodying each small step in a patent claim. In other words, incremental R & D adds to the total of *patented* invention but adds fewer patents than would have been added by the same inventive effort in decentralized market-segmented enterprise, and the actual decline in patents per capita suggests the extent of the shift of technically creative activity away from the independent entrepreneurs in the decentralized market to the R & D teams of autonomous enterprise.

This shift of technically creative manpower may partly explain an evident lag in the science sophistication of decentralized enterprise and its relative lack of receptivity to the potentialities offered by new science-based technologies.

Summary. Agriculture, reflecting characteristics that inhere in decentralized market-direction, generates few ad hoc technical inventions and provides no private means or motivation to support programed Research and Development. Great difficulties in the spontaneous diffusion of new information and of technical knowledge are created by the large numbers, spatial dispersion, and isolation of decision-makers. Moreover, the decentralization of decision-making spreads choice among a host of nonspecialists, and the nonspecialist is necessarily conservative with respect to technical change. In response to these problems for progress inherent in decentralized market-direction, the American government has programed R & D to develop new agricultural techniques and processes. It has provided the components of a science infrastructure as a basis for a more rational and informed entrepreneurial choice. It has created institutions for the education of scientific farmers and agricultural scientists. It has developed an extension service that uses direct contacts by agricultural agents, farm demonstrations, and publication and indoctrination through radio and television, in order continuously to educate the farm community to the techniques that have become available and otherwise to promote the upward transformation of agricultural processes.

The American government has thus attempted to generate and to feed the results of research into the farmer's choice for about a century. In spite of this, up until the mid-1930s, the rate of agricultural progress was very slow. The New Deal provided the farmer with the wherewithal to finance technical innovation, and, in guaranteeing a minimum price for farm products, made agriculture an attractive enterprise for ambitious men. The *system* of economic progress, supplying the information-basis for transformation on the one side and providing the financial means and motivation to transform on the other, was completed and made effective. Thereafter, the rate of progress in American agriculture has been phenomenal.

The extraordinary growth in the absolute size and relative importance of autonomous market-negotiating enterprise has been called the "organizational revolution." As a consequence of this revolution, experience in the man-sized firm no longer served, as before, to educate oncoming generations in the technical mastery required for industrial leadership. The rough-and-tumble of market competition no longer served for the recruitment and selection of that leadership. Instead, formal educational institutions were required to select and train an industrial elite. In response to this need, inherent in the economy of autonomous enterprise, there has been an enormous increase in academically trained business professionals. The bulk of the engineers and scientists in American industry are employed by very large corporate enterprise.

The autonomous enterprise was able profitably to invest in substantial Research and Development programs. The extension of formal education provided the prerequisite corps of scientifically trained engineers, industrially oriented scientists, and managers sophisticated in science-related choice. Given large output volume, a capacity to stabilize the terms and conditions of sale, and financial and technical mobility in exploiting a variety of technical potentialities, the autonomous enterprise could recapture a significant part of the benefits of R & D. Hence, from the 1920s, as an aspect of the organizational revolution, investment in R & D rapidly increased. The great postwar increase of R & D has been for space and military purposes performed by autonomous enterprise under contract to Government.

The autonomous enterprise accumulates patents and research data. The corporation has many alternatives in the way it chooses to use or dispose of those patented inventions and accumulated research data. It is government's task, through influence or regulation, to liberalize corporation policy for the dissemination of research data and to encourage the use or aggressive dissemination and licensing of the patented inventions in the corporation's possession. Following a different tack than in the regulation of patents possessed by individuals and small enterprises, the courts have ruled that when patents are accumulated by the large autonomous enterprise beyond the critical power to block an avenue of technological advance, those patent holdings must be dispersed and forced into the public domain. The more critical and fundamental problem raised by the accumulations of research data (constituting subbranches of science) in the well-guarded vaults of autonomous enterprise has yet to be dealt with.

Decentralized market-segmented enterprise is the home of ad hoc invention because there the opportunity to experiment and to innovate is the most widespread, and there it is possible to gain a competitive advantage in the creative variation of techniques and outputs. For that very reason, decentralized market-segmented enterprise, which is itself unable to support investment in R & D, resists the support of government R & D programs and extension services out of fear that such research or service might disturb the delicate and shifting balance of competitive advantage.

Technically creative manpower seems to have moved from decentralized market-segmented enterprise to R & D in autonomous market-negotiating enterprise, causing a decline in the per capita output of patented invention. Decentralized market-segmented enterprise suffers, possibly as a consequence of this shift, a comparative lack of sophistication on the part of its management and technical personnel in matters of science and science-based technique which checks the inflow of advanced technology into characteristically decentralized industry, such as textiles or construction.

Figure 14 recapitulates problems in the organization of economic progress and responses of public policy to those problems in the various parts of the American enterprise economy.

FIGURE 14
Problems and Public Policies in the U.S. Enterprise Economy

Form of Economic Organization	Inherent Characteristics	Critical Problems	Public Responses
Decentralized market-direction	Propensity to externalize benefits of invention and innovation	Failure to generate sufficient ad hoc invention Failure to provide a private means or motivation to support Research and Development programs	Research and Development programs in government and university laboratories and experiment stations, oriented toward the development of superior products and processes for agriculture, and toward the provision of a science infrastructure as a basis for more rational and informed entrepreneurial choice Government price supports and financial aids for farm improvement, to motivate and facilitate transformation
Decentralized market-direction	Decentralization of decision-making and the isolation of the decision-maker	High costs and difficulties in the transmission of scientific and technical information Conservatism of the unspecialized decision-maker, relying on folkway and convention, *contra* the opportunities for science-based innovation	Government extension service to disseminate technical and science information, and to promote the transformation of agricultural processes, through direct contacts with county agent, farm demonstrations, indoctrination through mass media

FIGURE 14 (*Continued*)

Form of Economic Organization	Inherent Characteristics	Critical Problems	Public Responses
Decentralized market-segmented	Small-scale operation, extreme uncertainty. Consequent incapacity to undertake Research and Development	Shift in technical talent to R & D elsewhere, decline in ad hoc invention; lack of science sophistication and consequent inability to capitalize on new opportunities for science-based innovation; "sick industries" lagging in the wake of technical progress in autonomous enterprise	Multi-level, continuous, agricultural education, based on land-grant agricultural colleges, shaped to regional circumstances and needs

Largely abortive attempt by government to provide supporting research and extension, parallel to support in agriculture |
| Organizational market-negotiating | Delegation of specialized tasks under centralized planning in the autonomous enterprise | Incapacity to generate the technical mastery prerequisite to industrial leadership, or to invention, through experience on-the-job, *or to* recruit and select industrial leadership automatically through the rough-and-tumble of market competition | Training, recruitment and selection of industrial leadership, through massive education of professional managers, scientifically trained engineers, and industrially oriented scientists, in universities and technical schools—thereby providing the manpower required for R & D |

FIGURE 14 (*Continued*)

Form of Economic Organization	Characteristics	Problems	Public Responses
Organizational market-negotiating	Arbitrary power in formulating organizational policy	Restrictiveness or liberality, with respect to the dissemination of research data, and the release of patented invention, are equally consistent with the integrity of this form of economic organization. It is of critical importance for the public interest in economic growth, that the corporate entity should choose (or be influenced or forced to choose) the path of liberality	Court decisions holding that patents accumulated by the autonomous enterprise beyond a certain "critical mass," judged as blocking a general avenue of technical advance, could be forced into the public domain

Chapter 23

The Political Economy

The "political economy" includes activities that are integral to the organization of production or consumption, falling within the scope of governmental policy or directive. The political economy in the United States is chiefly important in the organization of consumption.

THE ORGANIZATION OF CONSUMPTION

Consumption for Collective Purposes. At the municipal, county, state, and federal levels, American government procures or produces goods and services and organizes their "end use" for collective purposes, in ways that vary from the provision of parks and roads, to the use of battleships and congressmen, and the attempt to put a man on the moon. It has been argued that when a society goes beyond a certain threshold of "affluence," the values of increments of politically directed consumption for collective purposes will increase relative to increments of consumption organized by households for private purposes. This is so, presumably, because a greater importance then attaches to the improvements in the social environment. Similarly, when a society is at a low level of technical development and has not yet crossed the threshold of industrialization, the collective organization of a relatively high proportion of end-product output under political-direction will be necessary to provide the infrastructure required for development.

Under certain circumstances, increments of collective consumption (or collective investment) are not a diversion from (but may add to) consumption by households. This happens when the increase offsets underemployment or stimulates productivity or provides the infrastructure for development. In other instances, in order to increase politically directed consumption or investment, it is necessary to use resources diverted from consumption by households or from investment by enterprise. Then there will be the question of *either* public investment-consumption *or* private investment-consumption. Certainly there is no formula for determining a priori the proper balance between, say, private consumption of automobiles, and the collective consumption of space vehicles. But surely a more rational policy and a more reasonable balance will be possible inasmuch as the real alternatives are known and systematically contrasted. In fact the real alternatives are not "known"; nor is the information required for rational choice sought concerning, for example, the forms and magnitudes of collective consumption and investment that might occur without diverting resources from household consumption or from business investment. Nor is there any systematic effort in the United States to examine, as alternatives, various collective patterns of consumption vis à vis privately determined patterns.

Consumption Expenditures of American Government. Figure 15 lists the expenditures on consumption of *end products* and *end-services,* including public "investment" in providing components of the infrastructure, at the federal, state, and local levels of government in the United States for a selected year.[1] In this table and those that follow, the attempt is made to differentiate between those expenditures that utilize resources for collective purposes (resource-utilizing), in contrast to those government expenditures that simply transfer the prerogatives of consumption from one nongovernmental agency to another, or that do not consume resources as end products but use them in production.

FIGURE 15
End-Product Expenditures by the Federal Government

	(in billions of dollars)
Department of Defense Military Functions	51.0
Military Assistance	1.5
Atomic Energy	2.8
Defense Related Activities	.6
Conduct of Foreign Affairs	.3
Economic and Financial Aid Programs	2.1
Foreign Information and Exchange	.1
Space Research and Technology	3.6
Agricultural Land and Water Resources	.4
Natural Resources	2.5
Public Housing Programs	.2
Urban Renewal, Community Facilities, and National Capital Region	.5
General Government	2.2
Total Resource-Utilizing Expenditures by the Federal Government	67.8

[1] Figure 15 and those that follow in this chapter are derived from data given in the *Statistical Abstract of the United States 1963.* Federal expenditures are for 1964, state and local expenditures are for 1961, and "social welfare expenditures under public programs" are for 1961. Official statistics do not follow the categories that are used here, and many highly approximate estimates were necessary. Hence the data given in these tables are not intended, and should not be understood as suggesting more than comparative orders of magnitude—which is all that is required for our purposes.

End-Product Expenditures by State and Local Governments *

(in billions of dollars)

Education	1.0
Highways	9.8
Public Welfare	.7
Health	.6
Hospitals	1.5
Police	2.0
Fire Protection	1.1
Natural Resources	1.3
Sewerage	1.8
Housing and Urban Renewal	.9
Local Parks and Recreation	.9
Financial Administration and General Control	2.2
Other	2.9
Total Resource-Utilizing Expenditures by State and Local Governments	26.7

Data seek to exclude those portions of expenditure that are transfers to households, institutions, or private enterprise.

* Expenditures on physical facilities, e.g., school buildings and hospitals, are considered as end-product expenditures, but medical care and education are considered as institutional activities, and expenditures in support of such activities are considered as *transfers* to the institutional economy.

About $95 billion in goods and services are consumed under political-direction, constituting about 22 percent of the national income.

Politically Directed Support of Consumption and Investment. An important part of politically directed expenditures is not for collective consumption, but is intended rather to support consumption or investment by entities outside the political economy. These *transfers* shift the consumption of end products from the taxpayer or, when prices increase as their consequence, from the purchaser, to particular groups, agencies, and individuals in the national economy. These transfers generally imply some degree of public participation in the organization of consumption or investment by the household economy, or the institutional economy or the enterprise economy. Transfer expenditures for the selected year are shown in Figure 16 below.

It would then appear that about $80 billion, or some 18 percent of the national income, are transferred under political-direction.

Income Distribution Under Political-Direction. To some degree transfer expenditures reflect an effort to achieve a distribution of income and property other than that which might occur spontaneously. The most general objective of such "redistribution policy" is the achievement of

FIGURE 16
Transfers in the United States to the Household Economy and to the Enterprise Economy

(billions of dollars)

Federal Government

Farm Income Supports and Production Adjustment	4.4
Support to Airlines	.2
Business Support	.2
Support to Maritime Industry	.2
Payments in Support of Area Redevelopment	.2
Public Assistance and Welfare Services Payments	3.6
Labor and Manpower Support Payments	.2
Compensation Benefits for Veterans	4.3
Interest on Public Debt	10.1
Social Insurance	16.0

State and Local Governments

Public Welfare Payments	4.0
Interest on General Debt	1.8
Interest on Utility Debt	.4
Others	2.0
Social Insurance	6.4
Total Transfers to Household and Business Enterprise Economies	54.0

Transfer to the Institutional Economy
Federal Government

Health Service and Research Support Payments	1.0
Educational Support Payments	1.1
Basic Research Supports	1.0
Payments for Hospital and Medical Care for Veterans	1.2

State and Local Governments

Expenditures in Support of Education	19.6
Expenditures in Support of Hospitals and Medical Care	3.0
Total Transfers to the Institutional Economy	26.9

more equal shares. This objective is more manifest in the pattern of federal taxation than in the flow of transfers. However, public assistance and public welfare payments, shown here as amounting to about $8 billion at the federal, state, and local levels, are intended to raise the consumption of the destitute.

A second objective of transfers is to provide society with security against the debilities of old age and other disabilities. State-local and federal social insurance payments, during the selected year, amounted to more than $20 billion.

A third objective of transfers is to raise the consumption of groups who are considered warranting some special considerations, such as veterans, who received compensation benefits in excess of $4 billion, and farmers, who are considered at a disadvantage in "terms of trade" vis à vis autonomous enterprise. Many other groups in the economy are favored, and support is given to their consumption levels, not only through transfers, but also in other ways. Tariffs favor particular manufacturers and groups of workers. Interest payments on the public debt constitute a massive subsidy to bankers and rentiers. Minimum wages and legislation safeguarding the status of trade unions are intended to bolster the share of labor. The requirement that coastwise shipping be carried on in high-priced United States ship bottoms increases the income of American shipowners at the expense of those who must bear the higher freight costs, etc.

Interest on the Federal Debt: The Price of a Social Tabu. The federal government never has to tax or to borrow in order to "raise money." It is the source of money. It can and continually does create new money. Taxation and borrowing are never necessary to provide the means for public expenditure. The functional significance and the sole value of taxation and of borrowing are as means of controlling private expenditure.

In fact, the federal government sells bonds, that is, borrows, for diametrically opposite reasons. First, under certain circumstances—war, for example—when production is pushed to the limit and the fullest possible reduction of private consumption is desired, then the government borrows in order to reduce private spending further and less painfully than it could through taxation alone. By reducing private spending, public expenditures can be increased without a rise of total expenditure (and, hence, without increasing the pressure on prices). In this case the government borrows to reduce private spending.

But there are also circumstances in which the government's objective in borrowing is not to reduce but to increase the level of total expenditure, private and public expenditures simultaneously, in order to offset economic recession or otherwise to bring idle resources into employment. Then the deliberated public purpose is to inflate, not prices, but the level of aggregate spending. And as a prerequisite to such purposefully inflationary expenditure, government borrows on the assumption that the banks and corporations and insurance companies and rich people who buy the bonds will *not* reduce their investments or their consumption on that account. Such is the rationale of deficit finance.

This is surely paradoxical. A bond is a contract wherein the possessor of the bond is paid to defer the expenditure of "X" dollars. Government enters into this contract with rich individuals and with well-heeled institutions in the fervent hope that the contract will in no way constrain their spending, that they will consume or invest all that they ever intended to consume or invest. Then why enter into a useless contract? Not because government needs to borrow from private sources. It can as well borrow from the central bank, in the United States from the Federal Reserve, with no subsequent obligation to pay interest or to repay capital. In fact, government borrows from private sources simply because the idea of "printing money" sends chills down respectable spines. A great part of the $10 billion of annual interest on the federal debt, which systematically transfers income from the poorer to the richer, from those who are without to those in great possession, is a cost of a social tabu.

The American Government in the Organization of Consumption. The American political economy is thus the instrument for the organization of collective consumption. It also, through transfers and fiscal policy, influences the organization of consumption (and investment) in the household, institutional, and enterprise economies. Either in directly organizing the one or in influencing the other, the tasks and responsibilities of the political economy are residual. Its decisions and policies are ad hoc responses to a multiplicity of expedient goals and to diverse and transitory pressures. Political-direction is decentralized, dispersed among federal, state, and local authorities and fragmented between factions and agencies at each of these various levels of government. With its power decentralized, its responsibilities residual, its policies as the ad hoc response to need and pressures of households, institutions, and enterprises, political-direction in the United States cannot "plan" collective consumption. Nor in the United States is there any general policy which guides the redistribution of income or the modification of undesired consumption patterns under political-direction. Nor is there any systematic balancing of the comparative values of collective consumption vis à vis consumption by households in order to make explicit the alternatives with which society is confronted.

THE ORGANIZATION OF PRODUCTION

Political Participation in the Enterprise Economy. Government may itself direct the organization of production or it may influence, support, or regulate the organization of production in the household, the institutional, or the enterprise economies.

1. *Participation in decentralized market-direction.* Through price supports, through financing of technical transformation, for example, financing the installation of electricity on farms, and through agricultural research and extension services, the political economy gears into the organization of production (and the organization of progress) in American agriculture. These supports all imply a direct and profound involvement of government in planning and transforming the processes of production. Related expenditures would include the following:

	(billions)
Agricultural Land and Water Resources	$ .4
Financing Rural Electrification and Telephones	.3
Agricultural Research and Other Services	.4
Natural Resources (also forests, fisheries)	1.6
Farm Income Supports and Production Adjustment	4.4
Total	$ 7.9

2. *Participation through the support of favored industries or the regulation of those less favored.* By making available subsidies or particular services or facilities, the American political economy acts in support of certain industries considered of peculiar importance in providing elements of the infrastructure, such as water, rail, and air transportation. Some degree of public participation in the organization of production is implied by these subsidies and supports even if only to insure the "proper use" of public aid. Government regulation also bears upon the organization of production, not only when regulation is direct, as it is when commissions fix the rate of return on investment or control public utility rates, but also when the law and its administration shapes the parameters of private choice, as it does through the pure food laws and the antitrust laws. The corporation recently created to control the commercial use of earth satellites has government representatives on the Board of Directors. Participation of that sort has been for a long time practiced in other countries.

Expenditures related to participation in the organization of production, through support to, or regulation of industries in the selected year, was as follows:

	(billions)
Support to Airlines and Aviation	$ .9
Support to Water Transportation and Carriers	.7
Advancement of Business	.6
Regulation of Business	.1
Total	$ 2.3

Political Participation in the Institutional Economy. Fundamental science, educated manpower, and numerous social services that are of great importance intrinsically and as factors of production and elements in the organization of economic progress, are outputs of the institutional economy (to be studied in Chapter 26). In the United States, the institutional economy is not self-sustaining. It relies financially on the political economy, or the household economy, or the enterprise economy. For example, churches and religious institutions are supported by the household economy in the United States. In some other countries support comes from the political economy. Private foundations, funded through the enterprise economy, are increasingly significant in supporting basic research and higher education in the United States and Western Europe. In all of the technically advanced countries of the world, education and basic research rely primarily on transfers from the political economy. Government transfers to the institutional economy in the United States are shown in Figure 17.

FIGURE 17

Transfers to the Institutional Economy

	(billions)
Federal Government	
Health Services and Support of Medical Research	$ 1.0
Support of Education	1.1
Support of Fundamental Research	1.0
Hospital and Medical Care for Veterans	1.2
State and Local Governments	
Support of Education	19.6
Hospitals and Medical Care	3.0
Total	$ 26.9

The magnitude of this support assures that public opinion and political goals will be given weight by the institutional economy. In some cases, political choice shapes the organization of institutional outputs directly. For instance, the support given by federal grants and research contracts largely determines the absolute numbers and the relative distribution of specialists in the various fields of science and in the professions.

Production Organized Under Political-Direction. In a quite limited way, production is organized directly by and within political economy. In some instances its product is sold to households, along with the product of the enterprise economy. In other instances the product is consumed collectively under political-direction. Call the first "market-oriented," and call the second "policy-determined" production in the political economy.

(1) *Market-oriented production in the political economy.* Politically directed production resulting in the output of goods or services for sale is primarily by state and local governments, e.g., in the provision of water supplies, toll roads and bridges, light and power, urban transportation, and the retail distribution of alcoholic beverages. Expenditures on market-directed production in the American political economy are shown in Figure 18.

Expenditures of market-oriented production may, in fact, be somewhat higher than shown here, since expenditures of certain public agencies, the Tennessee Valley Administration, for example, are excluded from government budgets. It can, nevertheless, be assumed that in the neighborhood of $10 billion worth of outputs are produced annually by the American political economy on which some market return is expected. In terms

FIGURE 18

Market-Oriented Expenditures in the American Political Economy

Federal Government	*(billions)*
Atomic Energy (isotopes, power reactors)	$ .8
Financial Service for Rural Housing	.2
Financial Service for Rural Electrification and Telephones	.3
State and Local Governments	
Toll Roads, Bridges	2.0
Water Supply Systems	2.0
Electric Power Systems	1.3
Transit Systems	.7
Gas Supply Systems	.2
Liquor Distributing Systems	1.0
Other	1.0
Total	$ 9.5

of the total of marketed commodities and services, this is a drop in the bucket, a mere .025 of the value added by the enterprise economy. It includes however, about 10 percent of the gas and electricity output, about a third of urban transit, and about a quarter of liquor sales.

The production of outputs for some money return in the American political economy can be variously accounted for. Market return is often merely incidental to the objective of social control or to the support of activities outside of government. For example, low-cost financial servicing for rural electrification is intended to encourage a transformation of agricultural processes. Experimental nuclear reactors or their outputs are sold to promote an awareness on the part of private enterprise about the potentialities of nuclear power. For the five or so billion expended by state and local governments in the operation of utilities and in the distribution of liquor, however, market return is of primary concern. State and local governments have organized these outputs as the lesser of evils, preferring in the one instance public ownership to the ambiguities implicit in regulating private monopolies through public utility commissions, and, in the other, preferring government liquor stores to the aggressive promotion of the morally obnoxious liquor trade by private enterprise. Market-oriented production in the political economy, undertaken to minimize abuse rather than as a means of positive achievement, is hardly likely to be characterized by dynamic management nor any strong motivation toward technical progress. Operations will be organized along political subdivisions with no necessary relationship to technical efficiency or commercial payoff. Market-oriented production under political-direction, organized in fragmentary bits, scattered through and submerged within the universe of private enterprise, seems to combine the disadvantages of several economic forms. Neither the scope nor the concentration of authority is sufficient to permit central planning; nor is there the spontaneous motivation and clear-cut line of responsibility of small privately owned firms in the competitive market; nor is there the administrative and technical flexibility of large autonomous enterprise. On the contrary, decision and action proceed through the complex mechanism of the political bureaucracy, rigidified and bound by the constraints normally imposed upon the exercise of coercive political power. Market-oriented production in the American political economy offers none of the advantages of centralized planning and all of the disadvantages of decentralized choice, for, in fact, choice is highly decentralized. While decentralized choice in the competitive market may be narrow in scope, its responsibilities are concentrated and its objectives are concrete. Decentralized market-oriented choice in the American political economy is narrow in scope, but its responsibilities are diffused and equivocal, and its objectives are uncertain.

(2) *Policy-determined production in the political economy.* Policy-determined outputs produced in the political economy cannot be precisely quantified. Not only are the relevant data lacking, but it is not always possible to draw the line between the politically directed organization of production and the politically directed organization of consumption. When, for example, does a rocket assembled at Huntsville and fired off at Cape Kennedy cease to be politically directed production and become politically directed consumption?

In any case a substantial part of the goods and services collectively consumed are also produced under political-direction. Of these there are two main categories: (1) space-military Research and Development, and (2) goods and services that provide an infrastructure for social activity and economic development. Total expenditures in these two categories (only a *part* of which is produced as well as consumed under political-direction) are shown in Figure 19.

Organizing Production in the American Political Economy. The political economy in the United States is far less important as an instrument for the organization of production than it is for the organization of consumption. Nevertheless, a substantial quantity of goods and services are produced under political-direction. About ten billion dollars worth of such production is sold on the market; an output of probably equivalent value is produced for collective consumption. The important items produced for sale or for collective consumption are (1) utility services, such as gas, electricity, water, and urban transit, produced for sale by some states and municipalities as a preferred alternative to the public regulation of private monopolies, (2) the retail distribution of alcoholic beverages, undertaken by some states as a means of checking the aggressive promotion of

FIGURE 19
Goods Produced Under Political-Direction

(billions)

Federal Government

Space-Military Research and Development

Department of Defense	$ 8.0
Atomic Energy Commission	2.0
Space Research and Technology	4.2
Total	$ 14.2

Infrastructure, Services and Facilities

Postal Service	.6
Area Development and Public Housing	.4
Urban Renewal and Community Facilities	.5
Natural Resources	2.5
Total	4.0

State and Local Governments

Infrastructure, Services and Facilities

Highways	7.8
Public Welfare	.7
Health	.6
Fire Protection	1.1
Sewerage	1.8
Housing and Urban Renewal	.9
Local Parks and Recreation	.9
Natural Resources	1.3
Police	2.0
Total	17.1

morally undesired consumption patterns, (3) the provision of elements of
the infrastructure, such as postal services, roads, streets, parks, bridges,
flood prevention, health protection and sanitation, playgrounds, fire and
police protection, and (4) Research and Development in government
centers for public objectives. Goods and services produced under political-
direction either to be sold for private consumption or for collective consumption constitute only a small fraction of the total of privately consumed or of collectively consumed outputs.

The political authority also participates in the organization of production by the enterprise economy, particularly in agriculture and price-
regulated public utilities, and in the institutional economy, particularly in
the organization of basic research and education. The lines of influence or
control extend through subsidies and price or income supports, through
regulation and the imposition of legal restraints as parameters of private
choice, and through the public production or procurement of auxiliary
services and facilities.

Centralized Political-Direction and the American Political Economy. In
Part I, centralized political-direction was developed as a theory of eco-

nomic organization. Clearly in the American political economy nothing even distantly approximates this model. The "public sector" in the United States is often referred to as though it were that part of the national economy where a centralized plan replaces the decentralized choice of the market. Nothing of the sort occurs. Whatever the values or defects of centralized planning in the organization of production or consumption, those values or defects have no relevance to the state of affairs in the American political economy. In the American political economy, with respect to the organization of production and consumption, decision-making and action-taking are highly decentralized. Given the Constitutional distribution of government powers, it can hardly be otherwise. The economic functions of the American political economy are chiefly residual. They are the "left-over" tasks. The economic functions of the American political economy, moreover, are submerged within the activities and unconstrained choices of households, institutions, and business enterprise. So much is this the case that there can be no general control or central planning for any category of production or consumption, with the single important exception of Research and Development. With respect to R & D the breadth of public control and the locus of public responsibility is such that centralized planning is conceivable; and indeed, a degree of centralized political-direction is necessary for the rational organization of R & D in the United States. Chapter 24 will analyze critically American R & D policy with the framework provided by the model of centralized political-direction.

Chapter 24

Research and Development and the American Political Economy

The Preponderance of Political-Direction. Out of the more than 17 billion dollars spent in the United States on Research and Development in 1963, 12.2 billion was by the federal government. And out of the federal R & D total, 10.9 billion was spent by three government agencies, the Department of Defense (D. O. D.), the National Aeronautics and Space Administration (NASA) and the Atomic Energy Commission (AEC). In other words, about 90 percent of federal R & D expenditures was concentrated on space-military objectives. In addition, some very considerable part of the R & D expenditures by private companies was also directed to space-military objectives (estimated here as 2.5 billion) related to competition for government contracts, or as part of their effort to develop services or components to sell to government agencies or to government contractors. In that year then about 85 percent of the R & D in the United States was done directly or indirectly for or by the federal government, and the great part of such R & D was for space-military purposes. Figure 20 shows the distribution of expenditures between space-military and other sorts of R & D in 1963.

But if the R & D is paid for by the federal government, most of it is performed by private companies. In 1963, 63 percent of federal R & D was performed by private companies under contract.

In the United States, the bulk of Research and Development is for space-military purposes performed by large autonomous enterprises and "procured" under government contract.

The analysis to follow will be based on a study made in 1963. It should be borne in mind that R & D in the political economy is in a state of rapid transformation. Hence, since 1963, in response to the problems described, there have been policy changes that could not be taken into account here. Particularly this is the case with the innovations of the National Aeronautics and Space Administration.

Procurement Agencies. The three major departments of Government procuring R & D are the Department of Defense, the Atomic Energy Commission, and the National Aeronautics and Space Administration. Of these,

FIGURE 20
R & D Expenditures (1963)
(*billions*)

Department of Defense (D.O.D.)	$ 7.1		
Atomic Energy Commission (AEC)	1.4		
National Aeronautics and Space			
Administration (NASA)	2.4		
Total Government Space-Military R & D	—	10.9 }	89% of Government R & D
Total Government R & D		12.2 }	is space-military
Private Space-Military R & D	2.5		
Gov't Space-Military R & D	10.9		
Total Space-Military R & D	—	13.4 }	74% of all U.S. R & D is
Total (Public-Private) R & D		17.35}	space-military
Private Space-Military R & D	2.5		
Total Government R & D	12.2		
R & D Done Directly or Indirectly	—		
for Government		14.7 }	84.5% of all U.S. R & D is
Total (Public-Private) R & D		$ 17.35}	done directly or indirectly
			for Government

Total R & D is from *Reviews of Data on Science Resources,* National Science Foundation, Vol. I, No. 4 (Washington, D.C., May 1965), p. 6. R & D expenditure by government agencies is from *Federal Funds for Research, Development and Other Scientific Activities,* Fiscal years 1962, 1963 and 1964, Volume XII, pp. 110–111, by National Science Foundation, NSF 64–11 (Washington, D.C.).

by far the most important is the D.O.D., accounting for about 60 percent of federal R & D expenditures in 1963 and a higher proportion in earlier years. Characteristically, procurement is done by very numerous agencies making R & D contracts independently within the government departments as part of their functional assignments. In the Department of Defense, these missions are generally strategic, and the procurement of R & D is incidental and subordinate to strategic tasks. The consequent dispersion of procurement responsibility and the degree of decentralization of the procurement choice is indicated below by an abbreviated listing of agencies and missions in the Department of Defense having in 1962 independent responsibility in the procurement of R & D.

Under the Joint Chiefs of Staff, there are ten area commands (the "Continental Army Command," etc.) each with its own "Combat Operation and Research," "Special Weapons Development," "Combat Development Experimental Center." Under the Joint Chiefs also there are the special agencies for "Communication," "Intelligence," "National Security," each with its separate R & D responsibilities. Also under the Joint Chiefs there is the "Atomic Agency" with its research division, including responsibilities for "Damage Assessment," "Radiation," "Blast, Shock," "Medical Research," "Weapons R & D."

At the level of the Joint Chiefs of Staff are the several functional agencies, Army, Navy, Air Force, Defense Supply. Under the Secretary of the Navy, a number of special divisions have peculiar R & D procurement or other R & D responsibilities: namely, "Communications," "Logistics," "Installations," "Materiel," "Controller," "Anti-Submarine Warfare," "Long-Range Objectives." Within the cognizance of the Chief of Naval Operations who is directly responsible to the Secretary of the Navy, are the following special R & D oriented missions: "Strike Warfare," "Atomic Energy," "Anti-Air Warfare," "Ballistics," "Naval Navigation," "Advanced Technology," "Astronautics." Within the cognizance of an Assistant Secretary of the Navy, who is responsible to the Secretary, is the Office of Naval Research (ONR) with direct research and research procurement activities in the "Earth Sciences," "Materiels," "Physical Sciences," "Biological Sciences," "Psychological Sciences," "Underwater Sound," "Arctic Research," and "R & D Applications (undersea, sea, air)." Responsible to the Assistant Secretary also are the various Naval Bureaus: Personnel, Medicine and Surgery, Ships, Weapons, Supplies and Accounts, Yards and Docks, the Marine Corps and also the various operating forces. Each of these is also replete with mission-based R & D responsibilities and activities. The Bureau of Medicine and Surgery has its special departments on "Medical Field Research," "Overseas Research," "Naval Medical Research," and research within the divisions on "Application," "Planning," "Advanced Concepts," "Warfare Systems," "Surveillance"; "Electronics," "Underwater Sound," "Radiological Defense," "Underwater Mine Defense," "Oiler Turban Laboratories," "Naval Materiel," "Nuclear Power," "Nuclear Design," "Nuclear Propulsion." In the Bureau of Naval Weapons, R & D activities or responsibilities reside in the following divisions, "Ship Installations," "ASW," "R & D Engineering," "Plans," "Weapons Analysis," "Aircraft," "Missiles," "Astronautics." This Bureau has cognizance over twenty-five substantial, partially autonomous research and development organizations, such as the Applied Physics Laboratory. R & D responsibilities within the Bureau of Supplies and Accounts reside in the following divisions or missions: "Advanced Logistics," "Equipment," "Float Facilities," "Systems Research," "U. S. Naval Supply." In the Bureau of Yards and Docks, there is the Civil Engineering Laboratory and under the "Office of Research," are the following designated R & D missions, "Atomic Energy," "Mechanical Engineering," "Civil Engineering," "Environmental Engineering." The Marine Corps also includes its Deputy Chief of Staff for Research and Development, and consequently has its own R & D responsibilities.

At the echelon answering directly to the Secretary of the Army, R & D responsibilities reside with the "Comptroller Office," and with the "Logistics," "Operations," "Personnel," and "Research and Development" divisions. The R & D division includes various advisory boards, a liaison system, and branches for "R & D Plans," "R & D Management," and a "Special Weapons" division with sub-branches to deal with "Air Defense," "Atomic Weapons," "Missiles and Space." Sub-branches in "Development" include "Air Mobility," "International," "Electronic," "Communication," "Combat Materiel." Sub-branches in "Research" include "Life Sciences," "Research Support," "Physical Sciences," "Human Factors," "Research Planning," "Earth Sciences." A special chain of command reaches to a complex of "Research Centers." Lower on the control hierarchy, narrowing to the levels of functional responsibility, are the various Army Corps, namely the Medical Corps, the Army Engineers, the Transportation Corps, Chemical Warfare, Ordnance, the Quartermaster Corps, and the Signal Corps. In addition there is the Continental Army Command, the Air Defense Command, the Overseas Army. Each have taken R & D responsibilities. Each is a procurer of R & D. Thus even the Adjutant General has an R & D command, which covers "Systems Development," "Human Factor Research," "Enlisted Evaluation Center." The "Military History" mission has its R & D activities in "Photography" and "Cartography." The Surgeon General has, under its medical command, the following R & D activities: "Operators," "The Pathology Institute," "Nutrition," "Environmental Health," "Medical R & D," "Equipment Development," "Tropical Research," "Environmental Medicine," "Walter Reed Research," "United States Army Prosthetics," "Nuclear Energy." In addition separate research agencies are maintained for study in the "Basic Sciences," "Dental Research," "Neuro-Psychiatry," "Psycho-Psychology," "Surgical," "Preventive." In addition the Surgeon General conducts research at special units in Panama, in Malay, and in Europe. The Army Corps of Engineers includes research units dealing with "Nuclear Power," "Technical Services," "Military Science," "Military Engineering," "Atomic Reactors," "Polar R & D," "Engineering R & D," "Waterways," "Geodesy," "Cold Regions." The Transportation Corps has research and development missions designated as "Aviations," "Materiel," "Combat." The Chemical Corps has R & D missions designated as "Chemical," "Biological," "Nuclear," "Test Evaluation," "Advance Planning." The Ordnance Corps has R & D missions designated as "Artillery," "Vehicle," "Guided Missiles," "Infantry," "Aircraft Systems," "Nuclear and Special Components," "Diamond Ordnance Fuse Research," "Ordnance Research," "Ordnance Technical Intelligence." The Ordnance Missile Command has, of course, great R & D responsibility. The Ordnance Weapons Command carries on special R & D activities including research and testing at three major arsenals. There are, further, the Special Weapon Ammunition Command Arsenal, the Frankford Arsenal, Watervelt Arsenal, and the Aberdeen Proving Grounds. The Quartermaster Corps designates the following R & D missions: "Applications," "Standardization," "Operation Mathematics," "Programs Research Development." Separately designated R & D activities are the "Food and Container Institute," "Field Evaluations," "Airborne Test Activity." Other R & D missions include "Air Delivery Equipment," "Chemistry," "Plastics," "Environmental Protection," "Mechanical Engineering," "Pioneering Research," "Textile and Clothing," "Technical Services." The Army Signal Corps includes specified R & D agencies designated as "Combat," "Communications," "Signal Research," "Missile," "Space," "Avionics," "Surveillance," "Air Defense and Countermeasures." Separate research installations are listed for "Signal Missile Support," "Signal R & D," "Electronic Proving Ground," "Combat Surveillance," "Electronic Research," "Electronic Defense."

Above the functional departments and the Joint Chiefs of Staff the Defense Department itself maintains a large R & D establishment. The following designated missions at the Assistant Secretray of Defense level include R & D activities and responsibilities: "Atomic Defense," "International Security," "Installations-Logistics," "Manpower," "Comptroller," "Armed Forces Policy," "Research and Engineering."

Under the Director of Research and Engineering are the special research missions on "Command and Control," "Space," "Arms Control," "Weapons Evaluation," "Administration and Planning," "International Programs," "Advanced Research Project Agency," "Weapons Systems," "Communications," "Special Projects," "Atomic Warfare," "Biological Warfare," "Chemical Warfare," "Electronics," "Fuels and Materiel," "Maintenance and Engineering," and the "Office of Science" with its multi-missions. Under the Weapons Systems Agency there are the R & D branches on "Air Defense," "Limited Warfare Systems," "Strategic Weapons," "Ranges and Space Ground Support," and the "Office of Aeronautics" and the "Office of Ordnance." Under the Advanced Research Project Agency there are the designated divisions on "Special Programs" and "Programs Management." Under the Programs Management there are the following: "Ballistic Missiles Defense Research," "Ballistic Missile Defense Engineering," "Advanced Propellent Chemistry," "Nuclear Test Direction," "Materiels Science."

This is but a partial and fragmentary listing. It does not mention, for example, the massive R & D for the Air Force. Nevertheless, it suffices to suggest the degree to which choice is decentralized and responsibility for procured R & D is dispersed.

The Mechanism of Procurement. Characteristically, R & D is procured through the submission by private companies of "proposals" related to some projected need of the procurement agencies. Companies propose, in effect, a goal, and a plan, including an estimate of the costs and time required for the attainment of that goal. On the basis of an evaluation and comparison of such proposals by the agency of procurement a contract is awarded.

It must be understood that what is evaluated and procured is not a product but a promise, or rather the expression of an intention and a hope. Between what is promised and what is delivered, between what is intended and what is realized, there is no necessary relationship. This reflects no intent to deceive, but inheres in the nature of the activity. Inasmuch as there is implicit an element of the novel, requiring solutions based on reconceptualization, invention, discovery—in other words, inasmuch as there is to be real research and not merely a complex task of engineering—it is not possible to know *ex ante* the means by which the problems posed will be solved, nor the form of their final resolution; hence, it is not possible to calculate the costs in time and effort that the solutions will require.

Because output cannot be known and costs cannot be calculated beforehand, government R & D contracts undertake to cover the costs actually incurred by the company plus some fee. The fee may be "fixed," but whether "fixed" or variable, it is bound to be set in relationship to the anticipated or experienced magnitude of the operation, that is, the fee will have some positive relationship to costs.

Has Procurement Failed? Has *procurement* as a means of organizing Research and Development in the United States succeeded, or has it failed? To this question, there can be no unequivocal answer. There has been an immense activity, and results have been forthcoming. But no objective standards have been even proposed against which those results might be judged in relation to the efforts. Besides, if it were possible to evaluate results, there are other determinants of success or failure than the form through which R & D has been organized. Nevertheless, there are reasons to suspect that results are less than might reasonably have been expected, and that this failure is a consequence of the form of R & D procurement.

It should be remembered that not the product (which is the consequence of engineering and manufacturing prowess), but rather the new concept, the prototype of what is to be produced, the new technique to be incorporated into production are the outputs of R & D, and the basis on which R & D achievements should be evaluated. In the domain of space, it could be inferred (to judge from the absolute magnitude of the American effort and the relative resources available to the two countries) that the American expenditure in scientific and technical manpower and facilities must have been in toto far greater than that of the Soviets. Yet in space achievement, America lags substantially behind the Russians. This is so in spite of the relatively advanced status of our science and technical capacities.

Moreover, if one compares the achievement of R & D procured from large companies by the space and military agencies (which constitutes the bulk of the national effort) with the part of R & D which has been otherwise organized, it would appear that the latter, though much smaller in terms of money expenditure and inputs of scientific manpower, has far outdistanced "procured" R & D in significant achievement. The electronic computer was developed in a small university research project. The transistor and semiconductor, telestar, and most advances in pharmaceutics and synthetics were developed on private account in private companies. "In-house" R & D carried out within public agencies, *not* that procured from companies under government contract, accounts for the atomic bomb, the atomic submarine, radioisotope technology, the sidewinder missile, as well as the important research achievements of the Department of Agriculture.

Finally, structural weaknesses evident in the system itself suggest a priori the need for reform. The most exhaustive and highest level official study yet made on the subject is the so-called "Bell Report." In it the heads of the major government agencies concerned recognize structural weaknesses and express their dissatisfaction with the performance of the present system of R & D procurement.[1]

Deficiencies of the R & D Procurement System. In traditional procurement, the agencies of government buy goods or services from established industries which are producing and selling in the free market. The major public concern, then, is to see to it that there is no conspiracy to defraud, and no unfair or discriminatory advantage taken of the government buyer. Underlying the rationale of such "procurement" is the assumption that there are dynamic, well-established companies that are, in any case, producing the goods and services that the government needs, that these goods and services are being produced efficiently, and will continue to be produced efficiently. The government has merely to bid and buy.

For the most part, in the past that assumption was in accord with the facts. A dynamic and powerful American enterprise economy was producing for household and business needs, goods and services of the sort that the government wanted. The industries producing "procured" goods and services were kept dynamic and efficient by the competitive interactions of a market that linked profits and growth to low-cost performance and that weeded out the sluggard.

That assumption, essential to the "bid and buy" rationale of government procurement, does not fit the facts for R & D. Here there is no pre-existing industry for which government constitutes merely another customer. There is no autonomous market that, with rough efficacy, weeds out the inefficient and sluggard. There is no automatic relationship between effective, low-cost performance, profits (or profit-seeking) and (hence) survival and growth. On the contrary, with the new R & D industry dependent on "cost plus" procurement the built-in relationship between profits and performance is quite the opposite; the more the padding, the greater the inefficiencies, and the higher the costs—the higher also will be the income, salaries, and profits of the private R & D contractor.

The principal type of contract for research and development work which is made with private industry is a cost-plus-fixed-fee contract. Such contracts have been used in this area because of the inherent difficulty of establishing precise objectives for the work to be done and of making cost estimates ahead of time.

1 *Report to the President on Government Contracting for Research and Development,* G.P.O., Washington, D.C. This report was prepared by the Bureau of the Budget, as a joint statement of the Secretary of Defense, the Administrator of NASA, the Chairman of the Civil Service Commission, the Chairman of the AEC, the Director of the NSF, the Director of the Bureau of the Budget, and the Special Assistant to the President for Science and Technology, and transmitted by the President to the U.S. Senate on May 17, 1962.

At the same time this type of contract has well known disadvantages. It provides little or no incentive for private managers to reduce costs or otherwise increase efficiency. Indeed the cost-plus-fixed-fee contract in combination with strong pressures from Governmental managers to accomplish work on a rapid time schedule probably provides incentives for raising rather than reducing costs.[2]

Government procurement officers should, it is easy to say, award contracts only to efficient low-cost performers. But this would require that these procurement officers evaluate not a product (which in any case does not exist at the time the contract is made) nor a mere proposal, but rather that they evaluate the practices and potentialities of complex organizations, choosing to support some and to eliminate others. In order to determine whether R & D performance is, in fact, efficient and progressive would require (1) continual supervision of R & D activities and (2) judgment at the highest level of technical and scientific sophistication. Such supervision and such evaluation are outside the scope of the traditional system of procurement. The competencies required for such supervision and evaluation are entirely different from the competence of the honest accountant, which is all that is needed for traditional procurement. The task is of a different order.

Traditional procurement was shaped in a situation in which the political economy was peripheral, where motivation depended on and where the impetus to efficiency was produced through competition on a market oriented toward sales to enterprise and to households. With R & D, however, the political economy is central. R & D performers are necessarily agents of the political economy; their survival, their profits, their growth, their existence, depend on government policy and government demands.

But the most striking difference is the reliance of the newer industries almost entirely on Government sales for their business. In 1958, a reasonably representative year, in an older industry, the automotive industry, military sales ranged from 5% for General Motors to 15% for Chrysler. In the same year in the aircraft industry, military sales ranged from a low of 65% for the Beech Aircraft to a high of 99.2% for the Martin Company.

The present situation, therefore, is one in which a large group of economically significant and technologically advanced industries depend for their existence and growth not on the open competitive market of the traditional economic theory, but on sales only to the U. S. Government. And, moreover, companies in these industries have the strongest incentive to seek contracts for research and development work which will give them both the know-how and the preferred position to seek later follow-on contracts.[3]

. . . A number of profound questions affecting the structure of society are raised by our inability to apply the classical distinctions between what is public

[2] *Ibid.*, p. 16.
[3] *Ibid.*, pp. 2–3.

and what is private. For example, should a corporation created to provide services to Government and receiving 100% of its financial support from Government be considered a "public" or "private" agency? In what sense is a business corporation doing nearly 100% of its business with the Government engaged in "free enterprise"? [4]

No matter how efficient or progressive the R & D enterprise is, the company will fail without the patronage of the political economy; conversely, no matter how regressive and inefficient it is, it will prosper and grow if it has the patronage of the political economy. Survival-growth, or failure, depends not on any test in the market, but on government choice. The task is of another order than the "bid and buy" of traditional procurement. To choose the efficient, to weed out the sluggard, to evaluate performance, to build in incentive, are responsibilities of government. The responsibilities are inescapable; but before the political economy will or can meet those responsibilities, it must have a leadership with the *motivation* and, as an even prior requirement, with the *competence* (the high scientific authority and technical capabilities) required to supervise, to evaluate, and to exercise control over a vastly complex activity and over powerful private organizations. To develop such a competence in government is conceived, by the Bell Report, to be the central problem for R & D procurement. "In order for the contracting system to work effectively, the first requirement is for the government to be a sophisticated buyer—that is, to know what it wants and how to get it. Mention has already been made of the requirement this placed on governmental management officials." [5]

The management and control of such programs must be firmly in the hands of full-time Government officials clearly responsible to the President and the Congress. With programs of the size and complexity now common, this requires that the Government have on its staff exceptionally strong and able executives, scientists, and engineers, fully qualified to weigh the views and advice of technical specialists, to make policy decisions concerning the types of work to be undertaken, when, by whom, and at what cost, to supervise the execution of work undertaken, and to evaluate the results. [6]

By and large, we believe it is necessary for the agencies concerned to give increased stress to the need to bring into governmental service as administrators men with scientific or engineering understanding, and during the development of Government career executives, to give many of them the opportunity, through appropriate training and experience, to strengthen their appreciation and understanding of scientific and technical matters. Correspondingly, scientists and engineers should be encouraged and guided to obtain, through appro-

[4] *Ibid.*, p. 4.
[5] *Ibid.*, p. 15.
[6] *Ibid.*, p. vii.

priate training and experience, a broader understanding of management and public policy matters. The average governmental administrator in the years to come will be dealing with issues having larger and larger scientific and technical content, and his training and experience, both before he enters Government service and after he has joined, should reflect this fact.[7]

A capacity must be built into the political economy for the evaluation, or direction, or supervision, or management of R & D. This capacity must be based on the public servant's commitment and on a competence not only to deal with highly complex problems of science and technology but also to act effectively and expeditiously in the context of the immense political bureaucracy. The necessary competence must be sensitized to goals and values that are not commercial, but are social and strategic. It is, therefore, not the same as the competence needed to run successful R & D programs in private enterprise. Hence, it is not a competence that can be bought or borrowed from private industry.

But if such a competence is essential, there are two *special* problems of creating it in the context of the American political economy. First, science is now subordinated to strategy and R & D carried out by the government itself takes place in the unfriendly environment of a military establishment. Second, the existing imbalance in the quality of those who supervise and those who are supervised results in the domination by the industrial contractor of the industrial contractor-government contractee relationship.

The Unfriendly Environment of the Military Establishment. The bulk of the government-supported R & D is managed by (or "procured" through) the military. The military establishment has indubitable qualifications for this task. It has the responsibility for disposing of the weapons and many of the techniques developed through R & D. It is habituated to organizing highly complex, technically sophisticated, and massive operations. It has, moreover, evolved a dedicated leadership motivated by the values of the "service." Nevertheless, the military establishment is, in certain ways, profoundly unsuited to be an instrument of R & D direction.

Consider the task of the military. It must train and maintain millions of men; it must indoctrinate them, inculcate them with skills that range from a brute capacity to survive in jungle wilderness and kill in hand-to-hand combat to the most sophisticated levels of technical mastery. It must

[7] *Ibid.*, p. 9.

procure, store, maintain, and use equipment, materiel, and weapons of unbounded diversity. It is required to augment, mobilize, shift, recombine, concentrate, or disperse this mass of men, equipment, materiel, and weapons in response to all possible configurations of crisis, and to do this with swiftness and precision. In the nonsocialist economies, at least, there is no task of organization that compares to that of military establishments in complexity and difficulty.

For the flexible, rapid reshuffling of forces there must be round pegs for round holes and square pegs for square holes—clearly labeled. The ideal is an organization where millions of men and the whole immense diversity of activities would respond exactly and immediately to the signal of a single decision. To achieve this, even as a distant approximation, there must be discipline, ingrained obedience, the habit of command. For precision's sake, for swift and sure communication, there must be simplification, and uniformity. The proper modal units (the soldier, the officer, squad, ship, mission), so far as possible, are to be rendered autonomous and self-sufficient, yet readily subject to replacement and rearrangement, like building blocks of standard sizes that can be assembled in any number of forms. For this reason operating practice (methods, techniques, materiel, roles, responses) must be specified, simplified, standardized. The specialist of peculiar shape and unique ability is sometimes necessary but always peripheral. The general officer, conditioned to the standard requirements of standard niches, carries the burden of command and decision. The American military establishment (any military establishment) operates "by the book," by prespecification, by doctrine, by command.

Military activities run "by the book," by rules and by regulations; and the book changes, and is intended to change, slowly, organically, through the experience of generations. A military establishment values continuity, requires uniformity, develops standard responses to standing orders. It is built on precedent and status. It operates through command, through obedience, through loyalty, through tradition, through doctrine. It simplifies the premises for action and choice down to the bare bones. It will not tolerate insubordination; it allows no dissent. It enshrines authority. This approach is common to all military establishments; no doubt it is integrally related and probably essential to the performance of the military task. Whatever its values, the military surely is the approach *least* suited for engendering creativity. The skills it develops and the attitudes it encourages are the very antithesis of those needed in order to conduct, comprehend, or inspire creative science and invention. The environment of the military establishment is incompatible with creative R & D and is unattractive to the scientist and the creative engineer. DuBridge contended:

. . . The Government is not getting its money's worth out of many existing military laboratories. Military organization, military customs, practices and rules, military traditions are made for fighting and not for research . . . let's face the facts: a civilian scientist, as a scientist, just doesn't care to take his orders from a Colonel.[8]

This is one important reason why R & D has been in great part contracted out to private companies, rather than being done in government laboratories and arsenals. But the consequent lack of "in-house" R & D (or its suffocation by the unfriendly environment of a military establishment) prevents the development within government of the technical and scientific competence required to control the R & D "procured" on the outside. Moreover, as "military organization, military customs, practices, and rules, military traditions" are incompatible with the effective direction of "in-house" R & D, so also they must be incompatible with the effective evaluation and control of R & D "procured" from enterprise.

Presumably because of these contradictions, important scientific and developmental activities have gradually been separated from the control of the Department of Defense: first, Research and Development related to atomic energy, which was turned over to the Atomic Energy Commission, and second, government support of basic research, which was turned over to the National Science Foundation, and third, space exploration, which became the responsibility of NASA. Control functions also have been exercised by the Office of the Science Advisor to the President. Nevertheless, the bulk of federal R & D remains in the control of the military establishment, and the D. O. D. remains the primary agency of R & D procurement.

The Subordination of Science to Strategy. The planned activity of a military establishment, quite properly, begins with broad lines of strategy, setting available resources against strategic objectives for the short and the longer run. Given this strategy, the component parts of a military establishment are organized into a complex of *missions* (sometimes with broad and general, sometimes with narrow and specific objectives). These mission-oriented components are then charged (within budgetary limits) with procuring what they need to strengthen themselves in their tasks. They procure clothing, lodging, transportation facilities, vehicles, ordnance, and R & D. The diffusion of the control over R & D throughout the entire military establishment is suggested by the lists on pages 278 to 281.

R & D is thus deployed in order to strengthen each of the many separate component parts of the gigantic military organization in the achieve-

[8] *Chemical and Engineering News*, April 6, 1953, pp. 1384–1390.

ment of missions assigned within the frame of a given strategy. It is virtually inconceivable that any significant innovation in military technology could result from R & D organized within a fixed framework of military conceptions in order to support a strategy based upon those conceptions—since those conceptions and that strategy must be based upon a known and familiar technology. Significant technological innovation almost certainly would transcend preconceived strategy, and would be realized only by disrupting established conceptions and established organization. It is, therefore, not surprising that even though the great bulk of the national R & D effort has been controlled through military procurement, none of the R & D thus controlled has yielded significant innovations in military technology. The important military innovations—the atomic bomb, the atomic submarine, the ICBM—have been forced in from the outside in the face of top-to-bottom resistance. On the other hand, billions have been spent in R & D intended to preserve given military organization against the *threat* of a superior, science-based technology: witness the futile efforts of the Air Force to develop Skybolt in order to protect the position of the manned bomber command from the incursions of ballistic missiles.

Has the United States, in its procurement of military R & D, put the cart before the horse? Science has been subordinated to strategy. Should it have been the other way around? Should military organization have been made subordinate to the achievements of research, with military strategy adapting itself in a perpetual effort to exploit the potentialities created through science? And might not a science, which was not so subordinated to military directive, be more likely to produce potentialities for economic progress and social betterment as well as for destruction?

Domination by the Private Contractor. Consider what is likely to happen when (for whatever reason) the Government contract-maker is inadequate to his task, is transitory, temporary, unprofessional. Suppose that he is relatively incompetent in contrast to those with whom he deals. Suppose that he is scientifically and technologically inferior to those from whom he procures R & D. Suppose that he is unable to evaluate the performance of the companies under contract, that he is unable to grapple with the hard problems and essential questions that confront the R & D effort, and that he is unable himself to supply the vision for a creative thrust forward. And suppose (for whatever reason) that the high-powered scientific talents, the top engineers, the creative minds are drawn powerfully and en masse to the ranks of the contract-seekers. Weak and inadequate contract-makers and strong, overriding profit-oriented contract-seekers; what then?

The initiative, surely, would then come not from the contract-makers, but from the ranks of contract-seekers. There would reside the capacity to generate ideas, to formulate, and to evaluate complex plans. The contract-maker would be passive. He would wait to be approached; wait to be pushed; wait to be influenced; wait to be sold on the idea. It is enough that he sits on the money. The others come "a'courting." He watches, reluctant and coy, uncertain under the formidable phalanx of argument and blandishment. He hopes for something authenticated, safe. His motivation, above all, will be to avoid errors so glaring that they will light up his own deficiency.

Nor would the contract-seeker be motivated by the profits he seeks to search the high horizons of science and the vistas of new technology for the paths of greatest promise. He would presumably be motivated, rather, to tell the contract-maker what the latter wants to hear; to give him what he is looking for. His primary effort would be on the *sale* of a promise, and not on the achievement of that promise, for the payoff is for the attractive proposal, not the effective performance.

Between promise and performance the relationship would likely be equivocal, perhaps merely accidental. In any case this relationship between promise and performance would rarely be brought to light (1) because the comparative evaluation of performed R & D requires skills and abilities of the highest order (which in this hypothetical example, the contract-maker does not have), and (2) because it is not in the contract-maker's self-interest to investigate performance and to expose failures which may reflect ill upon his judgment.[9]

The Bell Report, as the most authoritative appraisal of R & D procurement, suggests that this imbalance leading to the domination of government R & D procurement by private contract-seekers is no mere hypothesis but is, in fact, the general case.

The Bell Report on Contractor Domination. It is the position of the Bell Report: (1) That R & D contracting by the government requires, above all, a particular and unique competence in government able to control, to direct, and to evaluate R & D activities. (2) That this competence must be developed within the government itself, particularly through the government's in-house R & D activities.

---

[9] In fact, critical post-mortems of the plentiful R & D failures in the United States are virtually unknown. Projects are abandoned with nothing forthcoming after years and billions of R & D expenditure—and no one asks who or how or why. To paraphrase what J. K. Galbraith once said about foreign aid: There can surely be no feature of present R & D activity that is so unsatisfactory as that by which great public expenditure brings little or no technical progress, and no one gets blamed. Similarly there has been no systematic evaluation of the relationship between promise and performance as a basis for future contract-awards. The Bell Report recommends, however, that procurement should "include previous performance as one element in evaluating different contractors and the desirability of awarding them subsequent contracts." (*Report to the President*, p. 17.)

No matter how heavily the Government relies on private contracting, it should never lose a strong internal competence in research and development. By maintaining such competence it can be sure of being able to make the difficult but extraordinarily important program decisions which rest on scientific and technical judgments. Moreover, the Government's research facilities are a significant source of management personnel.[10]

(3) That this competence is not only inadequate at present, but that it has been and is being eroded by the mass migration of talent to the ranks of the private contract-seeker, where salaries are higher, where the challenge is greater, and where the environment is more conducive to scientific and creative technological achievement.

Finally, we consider that in recent years there has been a serious trend toward eroding the competence of the Government's research and development establishments—in part owing to the keen competition for scarce talent which has come from Government contractors.[11]

The effects of the sharp rise in contracting-out have included the following. First, contractors have often been able to provide a superior working environment for their scientists and engineers—better salaries, better facilities, better administrative support—making contracting operations attractive alternatives to Federal work. Second, it has often seemed that contractors have been given the more significant and more interesting work assignments, leaving missions and static programs which do not attract the best talent. Third, additional burdens have often been placed on Government research establishments to assist in evaluating the work of increasing numbers of contractors and to train and educate less skilled contractor personnel—without adding to the total staff and thus detracting from the direct research work which appeals to the most competent personnel. Fourth, scientists in contracting institutions have often had freedom to move "outside of channels" in the Government hierarchy and to participate in program determination and technical advice at the highest levels—freedom frequently not available to the Government's own scientists. Finally, one of the most serious aspects of the contracting-out process has been that it has provided an alternative to correcting the deficiencies in the Government's own operations.

In consequence, for some time there has been a serious trend toward the reduction of the competence of Government research and development establishments.[12]

The main recommendation of the Bell Report is that the salaries of government scientists and officials be raised as a means of offsetting their migration into contract-seeking enterprise. It is hard to see what difference this could make except as a first step in a new round of salary

---

10 *Report to the President*, pp. 21–22.
11 *Ibid.*, p. ix.
12 *Ibid.*, p. 21.

increases. So long as R & D procurement rests on a system of cost-plus-fee awards (and no other system has been proposed as feasible), contract-seekers will continue to outbid government agencies in the recruitment of top-level scientific and engineering talents in the future, in the same way and for the same reason that they have in the past *unless* the government also controls the salaries that R & D contractors pay. But this carries government deeply into the direct organization of R & D.

The Possibility of Research and Development Planning Under Political-Direction. The weakness implicit in any political direction of economic activities whether through "procurement" or otherwise is that such direction carries neither a spontaneous motivation to efficiency nor any automatic elimination of the ineffective or sluggard. If there is to be a system of incentive and selection, it must be designed and built into the organization of activities. This is true whether R & D is organized in government laboratories or "procured" from private enterprise. Either way, the design and supervision of the system of incentive and selection must be and can only be functions of political direction. This chapter, until now, has examined the problem of developing within the political economy the sheer competence required to evaluate R & D performance and select R & D performers as an elemental prerequisite to any sort of effective political direction.

But if the absence of spontaneous motivation and any automatic means for selecting the fittest is its inherent weakness, on the other hand political-direction offers the potential values of centralized policy-making and planning. Because R & D in the United States is so predominantly a function of political-direction, it is *possible* to formulate nation-wide policies for R & D and to coordinate the parts in relation to the whole. This would be impossible if control were fragmented as the necessary consequence of another form of economic organization.

R & D in the United States could be planned. This is not to say that it will be planned. In fact, the political-direction of R & D in the United States is incredibly fragmented and diffused. The degree of such decentralization was suggested by the partial listing of independent procurement offices in the Department of Defense (pp. 278–281). Added to these are the similarly decentralized task-oriented procurement of the AEC, of NASA, and the other departments of government, all uncoordinated, none concerned with optimizing the values of the science resource as a whole. While this decentralization exists, it is not a matter of organizational necessity. Choice and control could be centralized. Given the nature of R & D, what might be the values of integrated policy-making and planning?

Centralized Choice and Control of R & D. Centralized planning has no evident relevance to the supervision of R & D operations or the evaluation of given R & D outputs. It would, however, permit a rational decision as to the allocation of resources in support of science, and in the deployment of available research scientists, research organizers, and procurement officials. It would be possible, through planning for R & D activity as an integral whole, to develop and impose a *general* system for training and recruitment, for the comparative evaluation of performance, and for incentives to achievement and efficiency. Moreover, through a centralized coordination of choice, directive, and supervision, it is possible to minimize uncertainties regarding correlary outputs, and to minimize the wastes and miscalculations consequent upon those uncertainties. The heralded development of so-called P.E.R.T. is a first attempt at such coordination at the level of the prime contractor, correlating work-in-progress and anticipated fulfillment dates of each of the multiplicity of subcontracted R & D operations concerned with component elements of a weapons system (or of some other complex task or product).

Through centralized control, it is also possible to minimize the "waste" of duplicative research through the fullest possible dissemination of the information outputs of R & D. These are all possible values of integrated policy and centralized choice, and hence they could possibly be realized in the United States where organization of R & D is a function of the political economy. Possibilities indeed—but how far are we from achieving them?

Centralized Planning in the Allocation of Science Manpower. The ultimate resource is manpower. In the enterprise economy, the allocation and deployment of manpower takes place through the medium of competitive markets, more or less in accord with a particular pattern of social priorities. In the political economy, on the contrary, there is no autonomous force that brings the allocation of manpower automatically into accord with *any* pattern of social priorities. Such resources as R & D manpower in the United States, that are within the control of the political economy—will only be allocated in accord with social priorities through the process of political deliberation leading to the formulation of government policy and the implementation of that policy. A rational allocation of science-trained manpower under political-direction would require that its alternative uses be made explicit, and that the marginal values of the alternative uses of such manpower be (in some sense) calculated and set in the balance. Any table of social priorities will be subject to controversy and dispute, and the effort to match resources and priorities will be fraught with difficulty. Nevertheless, there is no other possible way of even approximately optimizing the use of science resources. In fact, no such choice has been made, and no basis for the informed evaluation of alternatives exists. The allocation of science manpower has been, correspondingly, irrational. Each public agency, given its mission, has tried to draw science-trained manpower into its own orbit, without regard to the deprivations it imposed as a consequence on the research of others or on teaching in universities. Congress, of course, calculates money costs. In this instance, budgets have masked rather than revealed the issue. When Congress votes X billions for R & D by NASA and the D.O.D., it knows that it is authorizing the expenditure of a substantial sum, although but a minor fraction of the national income. The money does not indicate the proportion of scientists and engineers who will be drawn into space-military R & D, at the expense of research for other public purposes, of future teaching in the universities, of the economic progress that science-trained talent might otherwise have generated in the enterprise economy.

There are certain issues. What proportion of manpower should be trained in science and prepared for careers in research? What part of such manpower should be pre-empted by the government? What part should be fed back into the university system for teaching and basic research? What part should be left to be employed in private enterprise, or to generate its own employment opportunities in the enterprise economy? How should that science manpower pre-empted by the political economy be allocated between various public objectives? What part of it should be drawn into the public service? All of these issues are actually decided by what government does, but the government has not yet developed means for deciding deliberately, rationally what it should do. The rational discharge of its ongoing functions by the American political economy requires an integral policy and a centralized choice regarding the allocation and deployment of science manpower.

The Impact on Higher Education. Simply as a concrete example of this need for centralized responsibility and an integral plan for the allocation and disposition of science-trained manpower, and of the possible consequence of the lack of such planning, consider some random opinions concerning the impact of government R & D programs on higher education in the United States.

. . . The demands of national defense and the exploding progress of science have brought the Federal Government and the higher education community together in ways and to a degree that would have been unthinkable as little as twenty years ago . . . no major university today could carry on its research program without Federal money. . . Harvard, Yale, and Princeton now get a larger proportion of their operating revenues from Federal funds than do land-grant colleges like Illinois, Kentucky, and Maryland.[13]

[13] Don K. Price, *Science*, Vol. 136 (1962), p. 1099.

At least 80 percent of the institutions of higher education in the United States now receive Federal funds, and Harvard is one of those heavily involved in federal programs.

Government funds tend to concentrate in the relatively few institutions with strong graduate and professional programs in the natural sciences because of the heavy national emphasis on research. A recent study of Federal expenditures for research in 287 institutions shows that 5 institutions received 57 percent of the total, while 20 institutions received 79 percent and 66 received 92 percent.[14]

Government R & D programs affect the universities (1) through the allocation of research funds and research tasks to educational institutions or institutions related to higher education, (2) through the nature of job opportunities for scientific and technical personnel, and (3) through preempting scientists and engineers for research rather than teaching activities.

Major programs with major impact have come about rapidly with consequences only dimly understood. . . research and development funds flow in larger amounts. . . and lead to the concentration of facilities and talented manpower . . . an estimated twenty-five thousand graduate students . . . are employed on sponsored research projects.

. . . It is very doubtful whether the continued concentration of vast resources in the top twenty is in the national interest. In one ten year period (1947-1948 to 1957-1958) the proportion of Federal income of all colleges and universities received by the top twenty institutions rose from 32 to 61 percent and the absolute amount by two hundred and seventy million, while that received by over 17 hundred other institutions declined 85 millions.

. . . Can the trend towards heavy concentration of academic capital be reversed? Can the universities summon the courage to say "no" when confronted with unpalatable loyalty oaths, disclaimer affidavits, and the like? . . . Is the research enterprise choking the teaching enterprise, with possible disastrous consequences? Is the gadgetry of Big Science itself a threat to creativity? These are some of the questions that inevitably loom larger as the pace of the Federal effort quickens.[15]

The decentralized nature of Federal research programs may help the university protect itself against deliberate encroachment, but it makes it all the more difficult to preserve the proper balance . . . among various schools and departments, or within each of them between research and teaching.

[14] Nathan Pusey, *Harvard and the Federal Government* (Cambridge: Harvard University Press, 1961).

[15] Harold L. Enarson, reviewing *The Federal Interest in Higher Education*, by Homer D. Babage, Jr., and Robert M. Rosenzweig (New York: McGraw-Hill, 1962) and *The Effects of Federal Programs on Higher Education*, ed. by Harold Orlans (Brookings Institute, 1962), in *Science*, November 2, 1962, pp. 581–586.

. . . The three greatest threats posed by Federal aid are likely to be in the balance among the several fields of learning; in the balancing between teaching and research; and in the balance within the faculty between those with and those without tenure appointments.

University and Government people alike have been slow to realize the significance of their new relationship. The Government now calls on the universities for achievements that depend on the highest qualities of creativity, but sometimes through purchasing procedures that could destroy the environment in which such qualities flourish. . . Research can be carried on effectively in the long run only if a university maintains its overhead in an intellectual and academic, as well as an administrative, sense. . . . It is not a question of asking the Government for more money, but, rather, of asking it to give its funds with a proper regard for the total function of the university.[16]

But Uncle Sam is a blind giant.

The Federal agencies . . . are mission oriented. They buy research talent, and as prudent buyers they go where the talent is—the big, prestigious universities. Uncle Sam is a "blind giant." If, in buying research, he also helps the university, well and good, but this is incidental. Even in the support of students, the "blind giant" is largely indifferent to the effect of its programs on the institutions themselves. Direct financial aid to students simply exacerbates the problems of institutions already bulging with students and desperately short of facilities and teaching staff.[17]

A Rational Choice Between Research Paths. Given any set of social objectives, there are numerous alternative research paths toward those objectives. For example, suppose the objective is to lower energy costs in industry. This might be done through R & D in the field of nuclear energy, or alternatively in the field of solar energy, or alternatively on any of the fossil fuels and, alternatively, at any of the stages of energy conversion, energy transmission, or energy utilization. And, within each of these areas, numerous alternative projects will be possible. How to judge between these alternatives? Similarly, for any other economic, social, or military objective, many alternative paths of R & D are likely to exist. Given the objective, which path (or paths) should be taken?

A prerequisite to a rational choice between alternative research paths is staking out those paths that are open. Inasmuch as it is possible to do so, their comparative costs, the implicit risk of failure, and the possible benefits proceeding from their success should be calculated. This is very difficult. It is, moreover, an open-ended and unending, task. Projects are the product of the creative imagination, and new research alternatives can be perpetually devised. Each discovery and each technological achieve-

[16] Pusey.
[17] Enarson, pp. 581–586.

ment changes the costs and the pay-off potential of a host of R & D alternatives. For these reasons, perhaps, the deliberate laying out of the alternative research paths open to choice in the political economy is yet to be undertaken in the United States or, evidently, anywhere else in the world.

To formulate and rationally to evaluate alternative R & D paths instead of the present reliance on the initiatives and pressures of self-interested contract-seekers might be a means of reducing the great costs of "brochuremanship with its heavy waste of scarce talent." [18]

Centralizing the *analysis* of R & D alternatives does not imply that the choice of research projects need be centralized. It would mean simply that certain information concerning costs, risks, and potential benefits of alternatives would be made systematically available to decision-makers, whether decision-makers are many or few. On the basis of this information, different decision-making agencies would undoubtedly choose different research paths, in the light of their available resources and of their particular functions and divers objectives. Indeed, the value of centralizing this analysis and performing it once for the ease of many, transcends the national economy and suggests an eventual opportunity for fruitful international collaboration. An American study analyzing the costs, risks, and potential of R & D alternatives having, say, the objective of lower power costs, could be useful to the British, the French, the Russians, the Israelis—though each, on the basis of such information, might program their efforts differently. Similarly, a comparative analysis of R & D alternatives by the British, the French, the Russians, or the Israelis could be useful as a guide to research choice in the United States.

Policy for the Dissemination of R & D Information. The essential product of R & D is information concerning devices, techniques, operating systems, information concerning the data accumulated through tests, and concerning experiments that failed and experiments that succeeded. Only a very small part of the information generated through a given R & D project is likely to be physically embodied in the ultimately produced product or in the technique finally applied.

The information generated in one R & D project may be useful for others. It may suggest other end-products or techniques; it may serve to prevent false starts and duplicative experiments; it may bear on the development of theory; it may fuel scientific revolutions. It is the information produced through R & D, rather than the products used and techniques applied, that constitutes its contribution to the advance of science and technology; or rather that *could* constitute its contribution to science and technology. For the information generated through R & D projects

18 *Report to the President,* p. viii.

can only be incorporated into the body of world science, can only serve to advance technology if and inasmuch as it is effectively transmitted. This process of transmission may be costly and difficult. It will certainly require motivation and skill. It will include not only publication and dissemination, but also selection, synthesis, and promotion.

The public interest in economic progress demands the fullest possible dissemination and the most effective transmission of all the information produced through R & D. There are intrinsic limitations upon the transmission of R & D information in the enterprise economy. The nature and gravity of these were described in Part I. The autonomous profit-seeking business enterprise is not ordinarily motivated to disseminate and reveal, but to withhold and conceal the R & D information it controls. When R & D information is produced within or for the political economy, on the other hand, there is no inherent barrier to its dissemination and transmission. Conceivably universal dissemination could be rationally planned.

There have been significant efforts in the American political economy to disseminate the information embodied in reports from R & D contractors or generated by in-house R & D programs. In 1964, the American government spent $201,225,000 for this purpose.[19] The unusually successful effort of the Atomic Energy Commission in this regard provides an instructive example. The Atomic Energy Commission has (1) actively promoted nuclear physics in the universities and thereby brought the universities into the process of transmission; (2) with great success organized information concerning and promoted the use of radioisotopes in research and industry; (3) at great cost supported the construction and civilian utilization of nuclear power plants, presumably in order to transmit technological know-how evolved within the national laboratories into business cognition and practice; and (4) through its Technical Information Service actively disseminated R & D reports received from the AEC's national laboratories, from its private contractors, or through international exchange agreements from organizations engaged in nuclear research throughout the world. It classifies and abstracts this massive information in *Nuclear Science Abstracts*. Some 90 repository libraries have been established in the United States, and about the same number abroad, where (in 1963) some 47,000 titles on nuclear science and technology were available to the public. Unclassified AEC reports are disseminated automatically to interested agencies and companies, and are offered for sale through the Office of Technical Services of the Department of Commerce. Four journals are sponsored to provide a publication outlet for research in special aspects of the nuclear technology. Scientists with reputations in

[19] National Science Foundation, *Federal Funds for Research, Development, and Other Scientific Activities*, NSF 64–11, Vol. 12 (Washington, D.C.: U.S. Government Printing Office, 1964), p. 159.

their fields are regularly commissioned to prepare studies, synthesizing and bringing up-to-date the research outputs in particular branches of nuclear science or technology, for instance, the "rare earths." The AEC offers convenient access to its classified information to all who possess the appropriate security clearance without any "need to know" limitation.

On the other hand, R & D "procurement" from private companies places peculiar constraints on the disposition and use of R & D information produced for the political economy, so that, on balance, limitations on its dissemination and use are even more onerous than those that are intrinsic to the enterprise economy. Consider the practices of the Department of Defense, which controls the bulk of government-supported R & D activity.

Research and Development Information and the Department of Defense. The Department of Defense, through its vastly diffused procurement agencies, is concerned only with R & D end products: prototype devices and techniques or reports answering particular questions relative to the assigned mission of the agent of procurement. The information incorporated into such end-products constitutes only a minuscule fraction of the information generated by the procured R & D activity, but only this fraction concerns the Department of Defense. The rest, including the nonmilitary use or disposition of patented invention remains the property of the private contractor, and, hence, subject to the constraints inherent in the enterprise economy upon the dissemination of such information.

The disposition of the information produced as "reports" for the Department of Defense by its own research agencies or by private contractors must be understood in the light of a military outlook that treats information acquired at a price as "intelligence." The guiding principle in the disposition of military "intelligence" is to confine it to as few hands, to as few eyes, to as few mouths as possible; to deny access to such information to all but those who have established their "need to know." The military holds that the value of "intelligence" is a function of its secrecy. The canon of science would be exactly the reverse, holding that the value of technical or scientific information, in terms of its contribution to scientific progress or economic advance, increases directly in proportion to the speed and breadth of dissemination. In the Department of Defense, it is not the canon of science but that of "military intelligence" that applies, as a matter of course, to the R & D it procures. The objective of those who control the disposition of R & D information is to minimize the leakage of anything that anyone at anytime might find embarrassing or consider dangerous, or which some enemy might in some way someday find useful. Nothing is balanced against such security considerations, neither the value of dissemination for technical advance in the national economy nor even specifically for technical advance in the military technology among those who produce for the Department of Defense. Consider the consequences.

The Armed Services Technical Information Agency (ASTIA) is the repository for R & D information of the Department of Defense.[20] Reports prepared by R & D contractors for the Department of Defense, however, are only sent to ASTIA at the discretion of the contracting officer or of unspecified powers-that-be in the Pentagon. ASTIA estimated that it receives one out of every ten of the reports prepared by R & D contractors for the Department of Defense. Out of the 300,000 technical reports estimated as the annual output of R & D contractors in 1962, ASTIA received only 30,000. It had a work force capable of processing only half that number. The rest was heaped in limbo outside of anyone's reach or knowledge. Of the 15,000 documents processed, half were declassified and sent to the Office of Technical Services of the Department of Commerce for sale and distribution to the general public. Besides ASTIA there are allegedly "hundreds" of other agencies in the Department of Defense disposing of technical information. High Pentagon officials charged with information policy (when questioned) did not know how many there were, or when they were, or what they did, or how they worked. No one had ever evaluated the possible utilities or relevances of the already vast numbers of technical reports accumulating in the storerooms, vaults, and libraries of the military establishment. No one knew how much there was, or where it was, or how it was handled, or what use it might be. And no one very much cared.

In order to see a classified report held by the Department of Defense, it is not enough to be a scientist working in a government laboratory or an industrial contractor working as a prime contractor for the Department of Defense with the highest possible security clearances. It is necessary also that the scientist or industrial contractor have established his "need to know." Logically, it is impossible to establish the "need to know" new information, since the only way to determine whether or not an item of information is needed is by knowing what it is.

The American political economy therefore not only fails to realize the potentialities for optimizing the transmission of R & D information through centralized direction, but actually superimposes on the constraints of private proprietorship another dense barrier against dissemination and communication.

Summary. Research and Development is predominantly supported by public funds and is oriented toward space-military objectives. Following a

[20] Data that follow were gathered in a study of the "Civilian Application of Military Research and Development" made by the author in 1962.

habit ingrained by history, the government has "procured" its R & D from private contractors. But in this instance, the assumptions of traditional practice that the firms from which the government buys will be kept efficient and progressive through market competition in the enterprise economy fail. For many firms government constitutes the major or even the only customer. Market-interaction therefore cannot be relied upon to motivate efficiency and to select the most able. Rather, it is inescapably the task of the political economy to evaluate performers and performance, to recognize the potentialities of alternative organizations, and to weed out the incompetent. This demands a technical and scientific competence in government of a very high order that is geared also to social values and skilled in the techniques of political action. This is a competence that needs to be created in the American political economy. Two special problems, however, stand in the way of creating it: the leading role of the military establishment whose environment is unfriendly and whose values are incompatible with creative research, and the capacity of the private contractor to outbid the government in the recruitment of first class talent.

Beyond the need in the political economy for a sheer competence to evaluate and to control R & D performance, the fact of political-direction also offers the opportunity to realize some of the advantages of centralized planning. The present organization of R & D, with its broad decentralization of R & D procurement and its general subordination of science to the specifics of strategy, has allowed little scope for the realization of these advantages.

The possible values of centralized R & D planning would be those in minimizing the uncertainties of organizing related R & D projects, in developing general criteria for the comparative evaluation of R & D performance and performers, in developing general systems for the training and recruitment of scientists and research administrators, in minimizing duplicative research, in rationally allocating science manpower between teaching, research, and administration and between the alternative projects, in developing a basis for an informed choice between alternative R & D paths, and in effectively transmitting and in fully utilizing the information outputs of research. At present the American political economy is far from achieving any of these values.

Chapter 25

The Institutional Economy

The organization of production and the disposition of end products by the enterprise economy and by the political economy have been analyzed in the preceding chapters. But clearly there remain outputs of real value, such as the services of housewives, or of a Salvation Army or a Red Cross, or of the churches, or of the universities, or of the foundations engaged in "fundamental" scientific research that are neither products of profit-seeking firms operating through the competitive market nor of processes under the political-direction of government agencies. These also must be explained.

Economists recently have been particularly concerned with "education" and "basic research." References to "investment in education" and to "human capital" have become commonplace. Yet, strangely, economists have apparently not attempted to comprehend the rationale implicit in the production of these outputs—a rationale that can be subsumed under neither market- nor political-direction.

Built-In Values as the Institutional Core. Aside from outputs by individuals or households producing for their own consumption, there remain a number of activities, some highly organized and complex, and some only loosely structured, including education in schools, worship in the churches, "fundamental" scientific research in universities and foundations which constitute what will be called here the "institutional economy." [1]

Consider the difference between the operating entities (or "institutions") that compose the institutional economy and those of the political and enterprise economies. In the political and enterprise economies, activity is organized to serve purposes which are external to the agencies of choice and action. In the enterprise economy the firm or the autonomous corporation follows the dictate of consumer values expressed through the market. In the political economy the agencies or agents of government are guided by social values expressed in the law through the processes of collective choice. But while the guiding values are external to the agencies of action and choice in the enterprise economy and in the political econ-

[1] Some of the concepts introduced in this chapter will be more systematically developed in Part III, where a more definitive terminology will also be proposed.

omy, for the institutional entity, guiding values are internal. Those "values" or subjective criteria by reference to which situations, events, actions, and possibilities are judged to be desirable or undesirable and the goals and purposes that derive from those values are built into the core of the action-taking entity itself.

An institution, as it is to be understood here, is the embodiment and expression of certain values. Those values will be framed in a particular conception of or outlook upon a relevant universe. For example, the natural scientist's essential belief in the desirability of discovery is a value, but to express that value in research requires a conceptual framework covering the nature of phenomena, probability, and the acceptable means of verification. The communist may value an equal distribution of income, communal living, and the triumph of the proletariat. But to express these values in revolutionary action, he needs a conception of society and of group motivation. Hence the values inherent in the institution need a related "system of cognition"[2] for their concrete expression. The values at the core of an institution are not only expressed in an activity. They may also be expressed, embodied, or symbolized in "valued" objects or events. Indeed, the values can be forgotten, and *things* themselves can come to be intrinsically valued: thus the prophet rather than his prophecy, the teacher rather than his teaching, the Cross, the Crucifixion, the Flag, the Revolution, the work of art rather than the sense of beauty.

Embodied in every institution, distinguishing it, giving it its motivation and its direction, are particular core values, some system of cognition in terms of which these values are concretely conceived or expressed, and a number of valued things. All three generate emotional attachments. In practice they are difficult to disentangle.

Institutional Elements in the Enterprise and Political Economies. The difference between the agencies of action and choice in the political and enterprise economies, and in the institutional economy is a difference of degree. The goals and objectives of institutions are influenced and sometimes are determined by external values and powers. University teaching, for instance, may reflect vocational needs in the enterprise economy. Similarly, goal-generating values sometimes inhere in the business enterprise and in the government agency: "property" as a form of power in the enterprise economy builds the values of family continuity and perpetuation into business choice, and "institutionalizes" nepotism in the recruitment of business leadership.

The values of "the service," and a complex of valued things may be built deeply into parts of the political economy. For example, core values

2 To be developed in Part III.

embodied in symbols and in a way of life are so powerful a motivating and goal-generating force in military establishments that these often can better be understood as institutions than as agencies of political-direction.

Requirements for Institutional Effectiveness. There are three determinants of the effectiveness of any institution.

There is, first, the intrinsic quality of the institution's values (and the related system of cognition), their internal consistency, their emotional appeal, and their capacity to provide guidelines and outlets for practical action.

There is, second, the dedication of initiates and participants to these values. In the institutional economy, dedication is the essential motivating force, linking values to action.

There is, third, the compatibility of the core values and their institutional expression with other components of the social structure and with the cultural environment.

Consider, for example, the communist parties in noncommunist countries—institutions in the sense the term is used here. At the Party core there are always particular values ("equality," "justice," "classlessness," "the perfectability of the proletariat"), and a system of cognition ("Marx-Leninism," "dialectical-materialism"), and valued symbols, mythologies, and objects (the Soviet Motherland). This complex has demonstrated a sufficient emotional appeal to enlist dedication and has shown the capacity to provide guidelines and outlets for practical action.

The effectiveness of each Party depends not only on the value complex at its core, but also on the dedication of the communists to those values. This is the motivating force.

Finally, the effectiveness of the Party depends on the compatibility of the complex of core values and the related system of cognition with the other components of the social structure and the cultural environment, for example, on the "revolutionary situation," on the existence of a "disciplined proletariat," and on the strength of antithetical "religions" and "political ideologies."

The effectiveness of the Catholic Church could be similarly analyzed, in different societies and at different periods in history, by reference to the value-complex at its core, to the dedication of its initiates and partisans, and to the compatibility of these with the social and cultural milieu.

The effectiveness of the loosely structured institution of "fundamental research" can be understood in the same terms. Here also there are core values defining private integrity, credibility, objective truth, and the worth of achievement. Here also there is a system of cognition including the conceptions of causality, measurement, and the structure of nature, as well as a set of valued concepts, theories, and accumulated information.

This complex must have the intrinsic power to enlist interest and support and to provide an outlet and guideline for action.

The effectiveness of fundamental science will depend not only on its core values, but on the dedication of its initiates to those values. Only through such "dedication" can these values find expression.

Finally, the success of the endeavor and the survival of the institution will depend on the compatibility of the value-complex with the cultural environment. Compatibility with the milieu would in this instance depend on such things as the resistance of coexistent "religions" and "ideologies" and the degree to which there is conviction external to the institution that fundamental research also, incidentally, serves the goals of the enterprise and political economies. These attitudes will determine the magnitude of the resources made available from external sources for fundamental research.

The Institution as a Way of Life. Given the embodiment of a value-complex at the core of an institution, that value-complex will be expressed by its devotees, not only in achievement or service-directed action, but also as a code of private life and in a manner and pattern of living. The priest, clerks, and initiates of the Church will certainly teach and preach the ethics, doctrines, and vision of things that constitute the value-core of their institution. But bishops, priests, monks, and nuns will also presumably practice what they preach and will express their values in the manner of their lives and in private efforts at self-realization. The participant will often discover the purpose and meaning of the institution in his private realization of its embodied values.

To those on the outside, it will be the "objective" achievements of the institution, its external effects, which will count the most. But for the insider, for the initiates, it is likely that the way of life and the opportunity that the institution provides for the realization of inherent values as part of the way of life will be of primary importance.

In judging the Church, the outsider will weigh the moral guidance it has given, the social effects of its policies, the services and solace that it renders: the insider will count its saints. For the soldier it is not the functional needs of defense or the objectives or costs or consequences of war, but the comradeship in the ranks and the heroism in combat, which count for most. For the scientist engaged in fundamental research, it is not the usefulness of his discoveries, but the exhilaration of learning, the challenge of the search, and the triumph over the unknown and unresolved that impel him to the quest.

The organizations of the political and the enterprise economies (the farm, the great corporation, the government department) will all, in time, take on for those who participate an intrinsic importance as a way of life.

But in the institutional economy, the way of life is not a residual incrustation, not an accidental or incidental reflex of activities that have quite another purpose and justification. In the institutional economy alone, the formulation, perfection, and perpetuation of a way of life as an end in itself, become primary goals of organizational action, eliciting systematic surveillance, continual concern, and conscious transformation. Is he a true scholar? Is he a good communist? Is he a saintly priest? Each question carries a complex (and changing) notion, not of method and achievement, but of a proper way of life.

The Control and Transformation of Institutions. Unlike, say, the Communist Party in the Soviet Union, or the military establishments of Latin America, or the Church in some parts of the world, American institutions are not wholly self-directing nor are they socially dominant. Characteristically, they are subject to political influence or control and are supported by government, enterprises, or households on the basis of the external services they render. Hence, in diverse ways American society has the task of influencing, reshaping, or controlling its institutions by reference to the purposes of government, of enterprise, and of households. And, in order to survive and to preserve or augment their sources of support, institutions are obliged to adapt and to transform themselves in the light of changing circumstances.

The institutional *modus operandi* always raises barriers to both external control and inner transformation:

1. Its built-in complex of values gives the institution as a whole a sacrosanct or diabolic aura that makes the reasoned analysis even of structure and organization appear to be an attack on that which symbolizes good or a defense of that which symbolizes evil.

2. Routines and procedures may take on a ritualistic or symbolic meaning. The whole pattern of activity is absorbed into a valued way of life, and in the defense of that way of life all change is resisted.

3. The different value-base of those who stand within an institution as participants, and of those who stand on the outside but are called upon to support it, makes a true dialogue between the two difficult.

4. Above all it will be difficult to change the complex of values built into an institution in order to satisfy external circumstance and demand, since for initiates that value complex is the very basis for evaluation and the motivation for action. Core values, nevertheless, can and do change through the efforts of participants who are externally indoctrinated or are sensitive to external values and needs.

Education and Basic Research in the United States. Statistics are not available that would permit a ready estimate of the magnitude of the resource inputs in the American institutional economy. Since, however, in the chapters which follow, current problems in the organization of education and basic research will be dealt with, the magnitudes of at least these two institutional outputs can be suggested.

In 1960, more than 500,000 elementary and secondary school teachers [3] and nearly 400,000 faculty members of institutions of higher learning processed some 45 million persons, including more than three million at colleges and universities. Expenditure on elementary and secondary schools exceeded $18 billions, and on institutions of higher learning, $5.5 billion.[4]

Expenditure on basic research in 1963 totaled $1,815 million, of which $840 million was performed in colleges and universities, and $200 million in other nonprofit institutions.[5]

[3] Department of Commerce, Bureau of Census, *U.S. Census of Population 1960*, Vol. 1.
[4] *Statistical Abstract of the United States 1963*, p. 113.
[5] National Science Foundation, *Reviews of Data on Science Resources*, Vol. 1, No. 4 (Washington, D.C., May 1965).

Chapter 26

The Crisis in Western Education

Educated Manpower: A Prime Output of the Institutional Economy. For the economist today, educated manpower is the most important output of the institutional economy. During the past decades the organization of education has been in a state of unprecedented flux and revolutionary change. In nearly every country in the world the lags between outputs and goals or needs is of such magnitude that one can reasonably speak of a world crisis in education. This chapter will examine that crisis in the light of the conception of institutional organization developed in Chapter 25. It is not a survey, but an exploration of the educational crisis, conceived as the throes of an institution adjusting to the changing needs and circumstances of the American and Western European societies.

Academia as an Institution. A college or a university brings together a host of activities. Each of these, for example, teaching in economics or in art, or research in physics or in medicine, will be more directly and concretely related to distant activities diffused through the societies of the world than it will be to others carried on in that same college or university. The instructor teaching in a college classroom is part of an integral process that encompasses the activity in his "discipline," in colleges and universities, in foundations, in learned journals and presses, in professional societies, across the world. It is this integral process, or the cross-related webwork of such processes, rather than the university or college where it is housed, which constitutes the *institution*. We will call this institution "Academia."

What gives the constituent processes of Academia their coherence? their cohesion? What makes the whole thing work? What, for example, is the criterion by which one judges merit? And why would the Dean or the Head of the Department recruit and promote on the basis of merit? And what is the basis for determining what should or should not be taught, of what belongs to this discipline or to that? Whatever the answers are, the answers to these questions must always be made by reference to a built-in complex of values and valued things, and to the dedication of initiates and participants to that built-in value complex. When the process works badly (and we often judge it to work badly) it is because the built-in complex of values is inadequate, obsolete, empty, or (as when the Deans disregard merit and when Heads of Departments favor fawning incompetents) because participants lack a dedication to the values at base.

Custodian of the Scientific and Cultural Heritage. The value imperative of Academia is to preserve and embellish an accumulated body of idea and concept, knowledge and art, that might be called the "scientific and cultural heritage." This heritage is itself a complex of valued things, and implicitly, of values. It is a value complex, moreover, that is set within the context of and must be expressed through systems of cognition that relate to the means and the potentialities for its communication and to its role in human life. The teaching mission is only a derivative of this core of values; it preserves and embellishes them as a heritage of culture and cognition.

Academia as a Way of Life. The philosopher must learn the accumulated ideas of philosophy and in his own way synthesize these in order to teach them. And, being devoted to philosophy, he will philosophize. And, being dedicated to a philosophical approach to life, he will seek to live philosophically. Physics can truly be taught only by the physicist: one who has absorbed the knowledge, techniques, and ethic of the science, and who is absorbed into the problems, quests, and searches of the science. To teach and to know, to show the way to discovery and to discover, to value and to live in terms of what is valued—these are not separable. Academia must not only preserve and embellish the cultural and scientific heritage: as a means and a result of the process, initiates and participants will themselves embody that heritage and will live out its implicit values. Academia is also an intrinsically valued way of life, a way of life replete with ritual, symbol, honors, and accepted patterns of activity. To the academician, the way of life is likely to be of primary importance.

External Demands upon Academia. Academia, everywhere, requires the support of a larger community than itself. To some extent that support is forthcoming because Academia's values and its task of preserving and perpetuating a heritage are accepted as self-sufficient and self-justifying. But the households, enterprises, churches, and governments that are called upon to support Academia have also objectives or values of their own. Consequently, their support to Academia will, more often than not, have a price. Their support will be forthcoming to the degree that Academia comports with their values and secures their objectives. These external demands upon Academia differ among societies; in any society, they change with the passage of time. But when external demands have been long and successfully pressed, they will work their way back into the value complex of the institution, into its "world view," and into its accepted way of life.

External Demands upon Academia in Closed, Class-Structured Societies. Academia is a most venerable institution. It took its initial form and for the great part of its existence evolved in societies that were class-structured, aristocratic, and closed: "class-structured" in the sense of being divided into distinctive populations, each with different cultural characteristics, each largely genetically self-perpetuating, standing in an hierarchical relationship to each other; "aristocratic" in the sense of a concentration of political power in a class which possessed hereditary political status and was considered the possessor of a superior culture; "closed," in the sense that the primary imperative of political organization and the central objective of political activity was to preserve a given structure of social organization and to perpetuate an order of social status. And indeed, while the aristocratic element was of steadily diminishing importance, the countries of Western Europe remained predominantly class-structured, closed societies to the period of the second World War.

Academia served the external demands of the class-structured, closed societies in Western Europe in two ways. It was, first, a means of recruiting and selecting those who were to occupy roles in the power hierarchy. Undoubtedly the exposure to the "heritage" had a useful side-effect in "broadening the mind" and increasing the facility for communication, but what was in fact required was not special training for the performance of a function. Rather, the service of Academia was to *select,* to close the doors of power to the many, and to open them for a few.

In the closed, class-structured society, moreover, it is necessary that those who wield the power, whatever their origin, should have a solidarity of outlook, should share the same values, should identify themselves with the same stream of history and the same continuum of thought. This also Academia helped to achieve. If it did not train men for a function, it prepared them for a position. It gave them a sense of status. Indoctrinated to the same heritage of thought and values, they were linked to their predecessors and to their successors. Amateurs in science, trained in the refinements of a culture, they had the invincible, invisible means of recognizing those who belonged and of excluding intruders from their ranks.

External Demands on Academia in a Liberal, Democratized Society. In the new United States of America, a revolutionary outlook and value (which also existed as a powerful but subordinated force in Europe) took hold and became dominant. The social norm that emerged was socially egalitarian, politically democratic, and economically liberal: "egalitarian" in the absence of structured classes, in a positive emphasis on cultural homogeneity and on creating a breadth of opportunity for individual initiatives; "democratic" in its espousal of the political primacy of the average opinion, of the mass consensus, and of majority rule; "liberal" in favoring a predominantly decentralized market-directed economy, with government playing a merely peripheral role in economic affairs.

In consequence, the United States demanded of Academia efforts to support the homogenization of culture, to raise the average cognition and thereby to develop more "informed" majorities and a more "mature" public opinion, to spread and to equalize opportunity, and to assist in preparing the ordinary man for his ordinary tasks.

And in the United States, education has developed as a means of processing virtually the whole population, including massive education at the college and university level. For the first time, higher education became vocational, producing "scientific" farmers, business administrators, journalists, home economists, etc. The prevailing educational approach, with John Dewey as its prophet, would have ordinary people learn by doing ordinary things, emphasizing social adaptability, supporting the self-confidence and encouraging the initiatives of the average man.

Academia and the Organizational Revolution. The "organizational revolution," shifting the locus of economic choice and action from private entrepreneurs in a decentralized price-directed universe to massive organizations that are either centrally planned and politically directed or autonomous and market-oriented has greatly accelerated since the end of World War II.

1. Governments have assumed a positive responsibility in planning and promoting technological advance and economic growth partly because in an organizational economy, these will not occur spontaneously but must be deliberately organized.

2. As R & D, scientific research has been integrated into the growth process, through centralized political-direction, or at the initiative of the large autonomous enterprise.

3. Experience in the entrepreneurial firm and survival in the competitive market no longer serve spontaneously and automatically to develop economic leadership. Other means must be found to train personnel for highly specialized, science-based functions, and to recruit and select the leadership echelons of large (politically directed or autonomous) organizations.

These changes, and their consequent demands upon Academia, have led to a crisis in education. Because the starting point of change has been very different, the nature of the crisis in Europe and the United States has been very different also.

Academia in Europe: A Crisis in Quantity.. The European commitment to social planning for the promotion of economic growth implies a revolutionary shift of emphasis. The political imperative once was to preserve status and maintain structure, but now is to widen opportunity and organize a perpetual change in chosen directions. The shift is from the closed to the open society.

The commitment to growth necessitates making the fullest use of the human resource, which requires that men be trained to the highest skills that their talent permits, and that their opportunity for initiatives and creative contribution be maximized. This objective is inconsistent with the restrictiveness of a class structure. Hence the pressure is toward a socially egalitarian, democratized society.

The transition from a closed to an open society transcends the commitment to growth and the consequent, massive need for trained manpower. Sometimes seen as the "Americanization" of Europe, the shift from a class-structured society toward a socially egalitarian one was possibly accelerated by the "Yank invasion," and certainly the change brings the structure of modern European society into closer approximation to conditions that have been long established in the United States. American organization is, therefore, often a guideline for European policy, and American experience provides the standards for the expansion and vocationalization of European education.

The pressing problem for Academia in Europe is to change from a system for the selection and indoctrination of few to a system for provoking the ambition and for developing the capacities of the many. The distance which remains to be traversed is suggested by a comparison of European and American education.

The proportion of the college-age group enrolled in colleges and universities in the United States is from seven to ten times as great as it is in Western Europe. For example, Figure 21 shows the total enrollment in higher education, in relation to the population of the corresponding age group, in the United States and in the largest countries of Western Europe in 1959.

FIGURE 21
Comparative Enrollment in Higher Education

Country	Percent of age group enrolled
United States	36.6
France	5.4
United Kingdom	4.1
Germany, F. R.	3.1
Italy	3.6

From Organization of Economic Cooperation and Development, *Resources of Scientific and Technical Personnel in the O.E.C.D. Area* (Paris, 1965).

The problem, moreover, is not only in increasing the number of graduates. It is also one of drawing into the processes of higher education children of working class and peasant origin who have been and who continue to be virtually excluded.

In France, where every level of education is free, and where selection is by objective examination, nevertheless some 95 percent of those entering universities are the children of executives and professionals. The current ratio of university degree earners with parents in the higher professions against those with parents of labor backgrounds was 20 to 1 in Great Britain against 2 to 1 in the United States.[1] Current (1964) O.E.C.D. surveys show that labor families, constituting about half the population, supply only 5.2 percent of the students attending institutions of higher education in West Germany, 5.9 percent in Austria, 5.2 percent in the Netherlands, and 5.5 percent in Switzerland.

Here the problem, which is outside the domain of Academia itself, is (1) to offset the relatively heavy cost of a child's education, including the child's lost opportunity to earn wages and thereby augment the income of peasant or working-class families, (2) to offset those elements that centuries of experience in a closed society have built into the working class culture, de-emphasizing education and individual ambition, and (3) to offset the powerful bias against children of low-literacy family backgrounds that inheres in all known systems for testing intellectual capacity.

Academia in the United States: A Crisis in Quality. The central issues for European education are not of major importance in the United States. In the United States "the number of high school graduates . . . is nearly 80 percent of the age group. . . . Today (1962–1963) we admit to college about 43 percent of the age group; this 43 percent of the age group includes 52 percent of the men and about 36 percent of the women of the age group. . . . With the admission to college of about 50 percent of the age group, we must be approaching our ceiling of capability." [2]

Moreover, in spite of the bias of testing systems against children of low-literacy backgrounds, higher education in the United States draws substantially from all population sectors and from all economic levels.

The problem for Academia in the United States has not, as in Europe, to do with the opening and democratization of society, but rather with the need to produce science-trained specialists in order to integrate science into the processes of progress, and to provide the means of recruiting and training a leadership for the complex tasks of planning and control at

1 Seymour Harris, "Student Financing and Enrollment in Higher Education," paper for O.E.C.D. conference, Paris, 1964.
2 Wallace R. Brode, "Approaching Ceilings in Supply of Scientific Manpower," *Science*, January 24, 1964, pp. 313–324.

FIGURE 22

Parent Occupation in the U.S.	Percent in College	
	Boys	Girls
Profession		
Scientific, nonmedical	65	69
Medical	83	84
Education (noncollege)	61	76
Other	59	75
Business-Supervisory	61	55
Labor		
Skilled	32	24
Unskilled	32	24

From Charles Chester Cole, Jr., *Encouraging Scientific Talent* (New York: College Entrance Examination Board, 1956), p. 147.

the higher levels of government and of autonomous organization. The problem is not quantity and democratization, but quality within the frame of mass education. It is a problem of selecting and training functional elites within a system designed to promote the values of social egalitarianism and political democracy; the conflict of these aims is self-evident.

Academia has never had an easy time of it in the United States. The external demands of class-structured, aristocratic, closed societies were, in fact, more compatible with the objectives that derive from the core values of Academia, and more compatible with the expression of those values as a way of life. The objectives of social equality and political democracy have required Academia to level and equalize. The objectives of a liberal economy have forced Academia to prepare the common man for ordinary tasks. These demands of American society upon Academia posed a pedagogical challenge: yet they were hardly conducive to creative science or to the peaks of cultural achievement, or even to a deep appreciation of science or of the refinements and subtleties of culture. When, in the words of the late Huey Long, the objective is to make "every man a king," royalty loses some of its luster and the making of kingdoms becomes a dubious preoccupation. What America asked of Academia demanded neither tautness nor excellence, but called rather for looseness, permissiveness, and the embracing of mediocrity.

Moreover, the preoccupation with a cultural heritage and the dedication to "pure" science as an end-in-itself were not in accord with the pragmatism, the utilitarian values, the absorption in practical tasks characteristic of emerging America. The status of the professor in the United States was incomparably lower than in Europe. The academician (egghead, longhair) was looked upon with suspicion, sometimes with resentment and contempt. From the School Board in the town to the Board of Trustees at the university, his activities were kept in check by his "practical" betters.

The motivating value complex built into the core of Academia thus conflicted with the social demands and dominant social values of an earlier America. As a consequence, prior to World War II, in spite of the greater numbers deployed in its schools, colleges, and universities and the vastly larger output of its graduates from institutions of higher learning, the United States nevertheless maintained a largely parasitical relationship to Europe, in respect to fundamental science and to all forms of art.

On the other hand, the postwar demand for quality in the United States runs with the grain of Academia's core values. Sputnik, and all the pressures of the cold war, have speeded the process of change. Certainly, in recent decades, there has been an extraordinary transformation in (1) the curriculum, (2) the pressure for student performance, and (3) the upgrading of fundamental science. The same years witnessed an extraordinary concentration of academic prowess and the emergence of a hierarchy of educational institutions that, though serving to select and train needed elites for science-based tasks in an organizational economy, threatens egalitarian values.

Academic Conservatism. Academia is notoriously conservative. It has, for example, been reported that between the inception of a new educational idea or practice and its adoption by a majority of schools and colleges there has typically been a time lag on the order of 25 to 50 years.[3]

That Academia is difficult to move and difficult to change is the necessary consequence of its form of organization. It is not, in its most essential aspect, a decision-taking entity. It has hitherto offered no loci of responsibility where issues can be confronted and where choice can be made. It is rather a group of initiates loosely bound together in an ill-defined complex in which fundamental values mingle and merge with the trivia of valued things and ritualized habit. Values, valued things, and a valued way of life permeate all activity. Nevertheless, Academia can change, and is now changing rapidly.

Change from Within. The force for transformation may come from within Academia itself, sometimes from the dedication of participants to Academia's imperfectly realized values or from their dedication to values and

[3] Paul R. Mort, *Educational Adaptability*, Metropolitan School Study Council, Institute of Administrative Research (New York: Columbia Teachers College, 1953). Paul R. Mort and Donald H. Ross, *Principles of School Administration: A Synthesis of Basic Concepts* (New York: McGraw-Hill, 1957).

goals external to Academia. Initiates of Academia, after all, are also members of a larger society and sometimes are sensitive to its needs. Caught up in the popular enthusiasms, they seek, even as academicians, to contribute to its goals. In Europe, and particularly in France, it is the Young Turks—abruptly brought within the gates by the pressure for educational expansion, dedicated to social goals beyond the academic institution and impatient with the ritual patterns of an ancient way—who press for the reform of academic method and of academic substance. Here and there, there are breakthroughs, for example, the establishment at the School of Mines in Nancy of a system of higher scientific and technical education as a continuous process through the individual's working life.

The way in which academic change does come about, the resistances which it faces, and the motivation on which it relies are illustrated in the case described below of the first major change in the organization and content of the secondary school curriculum ever achieved in the United States.

Revision of the Physics Curriculum: A Case of Change from Within. Since the 1920s there have occurred revolutionary changes in the conceptions and research interests of professional physicists; but the physics taught in the high schools remained as before. Consequently, what the schoolboy learned about physics became quite unrelated to the concepts and theories that dominated the thought and directed the research paths of the scientist. This was an anomalous situation; but who was to alter it? Neither schools nor colleges nor principals nor teachers, individually, could take the step. And there was no means of collective choice. There was no place in the "institution" of Academia where the problem could be confronted as such and a decision could be forced. It could only be proposed through the initiative of dedicated individuals within Academia. It would only be accepted because school principals and teachers were also motivated by a dedication to intrinsic values. Moreover, it required the internal and external dissatisfactions with Academia's performance, rising to a crescendo with the shock of Russia's Sputnik, to trigger the initiative and to weaken the resistance of established ways.

Dedication to Built-In Values as the Motivation to Change. The movement to initiate the curriculum change in physics was initiated by Jerrold R. Zacharias, Professor of Physics at the Massachusetts Institute of Technology, and certain of his colleagues. In the fall of 1956, they called together fifty physicists and teachers, who formed themselves into the Physical Science Study Committee (P.S.S.C.). Professor Zacharias has described the requisites and motivation of the effort.

It must be recognized from the outset that the task of curriculum revision is one of the most difficult of all the tasks upon which the scholar or the research scientist can embark. . . . It requires . . . the highest degree of scholarship and skill. Successful curriculum revisions have been those in which the most eminent men and women have been willing to suspend their own careers over a long period of time. . . . Unsuccessful revisions have been those in which this association has been denied or has been limited.

The involvement of able men and women must be direct, and it must continue through the life of the program. . . . The sole involvement that makes sense is a continuing and deep involvement; and if such an involvement cannot be obtained from the very best men and women available, then there is little point in attempting any program of curriculum revision.[4]

The Process of Curriculum Reform. The physics curriculum revision evolved as a process of transformation, a process that was itself subject to invention, innovation, and transformation and was, in fact, continually being transformed, and a process which, once developed, could be, and was applied to other areas of the school curriculum.

This task of transforming a curriculum includes the following: (1) making a choice between alternative means and ends—

One might wish to provide the student with an intimate knowledge of modern technology, or. . . with the manner in which physics has grown. . . . Both of these were . . . warmly debated. . . . It was decided instead that the course would be directed towards familiarizing the student with . . . the wave-particle duality and the modern concept of the atom. Behind this notion was the view that these two notions lay at the heart of the modern physicist's outlook upon his universe.[5]

(2) designing a course of study including producing a text, films, and other teaching aids, and providing the required laboratory apparatus for illustrative experiments; (3) testing all these in the classroom and feeding back the results of such tests to those responsible for the evaluation and revision of the course—

The test of a curriculum lies in the classroom. . . . they must prove their worth in practice. It must be demonstrated that the student understands and, indeed, employs those elements . . . presented to him. Classroom experimentation with materials, and the provision of a system by means of which classroom experience can be evaluated and fed back into the process of revision are basic requirements. . . . Without such a feedback system, the program wanders blindly . . . and is likely to end with a curriculum which in practice accomplishes no part of what it intended.[6]

[4] Jerrold R. Zacharias and Stephen White, "The Requirements for Major Curriculum Revision," a paper delivered at the United Nations Conference on the Application of Science and Technology for the Benefit of the Less Developed Areas, November 13, 1962, Agenda Item K/95. Reprinted with the permission of the United Nations Publications Board.
[5] *Ibid.*
[6] *Ibid.*

and (4) retraining teachers—

The teacher, if he has been any length of time in the school system, is already familiar with (say) a biology course; he has taught it for years . . . to him it is likely to represent Biology. To be faced with a new course which may be entirely different in spirit and content, and which nonetheless bears the same name and occupies the same position in the school, is somewhat disconcerting. It is also probable that the teacher will not understand it, and will not be able to teach it. Yet, as a practical matter the new course must be taught initially and for many years by exactly such teachers.

Thus, the retraining of teachers becomes an inescapable part of major curriculum revision.[7]

The achievement of the curriculum revision required not only the dedication of those who initiated the movement, but also substantial financial support, supplied in this instance by private foundations. It required the voluntary and extensive cooperation of schools. It required a willingness on the part of teachers to submit themselves to retraining. All this would not have been forthcoming except for the external pressures arising from a general sense of crisis in American education.

The curriculum change in high school physics was a revolutionary achievement, not for itself, but because it introduced the systematic evaluation and purposeful transformation of educational substance and organization. Subsequently there have been a series of other major curriculum revisions in the United States, in other natural sciences, in mathematics, in modern languages—including English—in the social studies, and in several of the humanities. There thus arises the possibility of building into Academia curriculum transformation and teacher retraining as a systematic, continuous process.

The Values and Fallibilities of Educational Decentralization for Curriculum Reform. Part I argued that when power is concentrated and exercised by established authority, orthodoxy is likely to pose an insuperable barrier to radical innovation, and that "the new idea which runs counter to established theory and official doctrine has its greatest fighting chance in the decentralized, competitive economy." The same rule holds for Academia, where power may be concentrated, as it is in France, or highly decentralized, as it is in the United States. Those who represented the pedagogical authority in the United States stood foursquare against curriculum revision and excluded it from teacher training in the "institutions of higher learning."

Institutions of higher education from which the great majority of teachers emerge are, for the most part, intensely conservative and have been resistant to

7 *Ibid.*

curriculum change. As yet, no major program has been devised that would adopt the same approach towards curriculum in teacher-training institutions as . . . is being described in this paper.[8]

That P.S.S.C. was, nevertheless, able to find its way around entrenched pedagogical authority, was due to the extreme decentralization of power in American Academia.

In this regard the United States benefits from the benign anarchy of its educational system. With some 36,000 school districts, and an almost complete absence of any central direction, it becomes possible in the United States to carry on almost any kind of educational experiment—somewhere there is certain to be a school supervisor or principal who will undertake to assist. In countries with a more rigid educational structure, reform can be effectively blocked by the refusal of conservative educational administrators to cooperate in the initial steps of curriculum revision.[9]

But while the curriculum revision thus benefited from the advantages of decentralization, it also suffered from disadvantages for innovation and transformation that inhere in decentralized choice, for example, the high costs of demonstration, the delay in dissemination, the necessity of piecemeal change, and, consequently the impossibility of the simultaneous transformation of the interdependent elements that constitute the integral process of education. For these, centralized control would have been advantageous.

Change from the Outside. Change may be, and in fact is now being imposed upon Academia, under political-direction, as a means of gearing education to particular social goals. So-called "educational planning" has been important in Western European efforts to increase radically the numbers of university graduates and to influence the distribution between specializations and professions in relation to anticipated economic needs.

The core value of Academia is to preserve and to embellish the heritage of science and culture. Those who know science and who have mastered the arts are presumably best able to teach them. Hence Academia's task is functionally related to that of education. But the external needs and demands for teaching may relate to quite other purposes or values than those of Academia. The values of pure science and of the heritage of culture, for example, clearly have little to do with teaching stenography, or hairdressing and, indeed, are only partly related to training in the higher professions. Vocational and professional education, creative art, scientific revolution, the preservation and embellishment of the heritage of culture and knowledge, have each a different value base. Yet they are

8 *Ibid.*
9 *Ibid.*

inextricably interwoven in the activities of schools and universities. This, surely, is a perpetual source of difficulty.

In the light of this confusion of tasks, one might understand Milton Friedman's proposal [10] that public support should not be given to Academia directly but rather should take the form of grants to individuals (as with the G.I. Bill of Rights) who would, henceforth, be able to buy their education where and how they liked. In that way, supposedly, the market would link vocational and professional outputs to economic priorities, and would shape the quality of the educational production to the pattern of consumer preferences.

Inasmuch as the output of Academia can be understood as a product intended to please the taste of the consumer or to be used as a factor of production, Friedman's proposal, which would subordinate education to the price-directed decentralized market, is certainly arguable. But if education is understood not as a means of catering to the customer, but of shaping the citizen, and if Academia is considered also to have the task of preserving, embellishing, and even developing the heritage of culture and science, as ends in themselves, then decentralized market-direction must prove inadequate.

Summary. Academia has been conceived as that "institution" expressing and embellishing the cultural and scientific heritage. But since Academia is also subject to external demands, its form will depend in part on those external demands. In the closed, class-structured societies of Western Europe its external task was to select and condition a small elite for positions of power. In the socially egalitarian, economically liberal society characteristic of an earlier America, the external task of Academia was to equalize opportunity, to homogenize culture, and to prepare the average man for ordinary tasks. In consequence, the United States developed a uniquely job-oriented system of mass education in secondary schools and in colleges and universities.

The "organizational revolution" and the recognition of "economic growth" as the imperative of survival and a primary government responsibility have had consequences for the external demands upon Academia in both Western Europe and in the United States. In Western Europe the pressing problem is radically to increase the numbers of educated manpower, and, more specifically, to educate the intellectually capable members of the labor class. The crisis is one of quantity. In the United States the problem is one of quality. An earlier America's demands that Academia equalize, homogenize, and cater to the work needs of the average man were not compatible with an emphasis on high cultural and scientific

[10] Milton Friedman, "The Role of Government in Education," *Economics and the Public Interest,* Robert A. Solo, ed. (New Jersey: Rutgers University Press, 1955).

achievement. The consequence was academic mediocrity. The organizational economy requires science-based competence of the highest order, and looks to Academia to recruit, select, and train its functional elites.

Academia is profoundly conservative, difficult to move, difficult to change. It is permeated by values, valued things, and ritualized habit, none of which is subject to logical refutation or empirical disproof. Nevertheless Academia does change. Sometimes such change is externally imposed, for example, by government "planners" in the current expansion of educational facilities and the extension of educational opportunity. But when change has to do not with quantity but with quality and content, it generally must work from within.

Chapter 27

The Organization of Academic Science

The Myth of "Basic" Research. Perhaps like all institutions, science is loaded with symbols and myths. The very word is a synonym for "true." In one modern Christian sect, Science is Christian, and Christ is the Scientist. There are modern painters who call their abstractions "scientific." There are modern composers who call their music "scientific." There are modern pastors who call their sermons "scientific." There are Marxists who call their prophecies "scientific." There are serious people who believe that science is the "open sesame" to progress and that, if more money is spent on research, more economic development, growth, prosperity, power, health and all the good things of life must be forthcoming.

It is not ours to strip science of its myths and symbols, except to confront one that is both powerful and pernicious. This is the myth of "basic," also called "pure," also called "fundamental" research. There is a category of research that the National Science Foundation defines, and researchers report as "basic"—that is real enough. The myth is that such research is, in those normative terms—basic, pure, fundamental, in the sense of prior, better, more important, more universal, than research of the other sort. The myth is that basic research comes first, and it is the results of basic researches that then can be "applied." The myth is that the output of basic research is a sort of "capital fund," which is exhausted through practical applications, and, hence, which must be continuously renewed as a prerequisite to solving the practical problems of society. All this is nonsense. It is, moreover, dangerous nonsense, since it is widely believed by serious people, and is used as a guideline for social policy.

Problems of Society and the Scientist's Curiosity. Science, seen from one dimension, can be understood as a problem-solving apparatus, including a body of concepts that can assist in the organization of observation, a body of theories that may offer provisional explanations, a body of normative experiments that offer guidelines to practice, and a body of conveniently organized data that may be relevant in finding answers. But what sorts of problems will this apparatus be used to solve? Problems of two sorts.

Problems will be chosen because they are considered relevant to particular goals or purposes of society: finding a cure for cancer, putting a man on the moon, developing a source of low-cost atomic energy. *None* of such *social-problem oriented* research is included in the officially designated category "basic research." Social-problem oriented research is "applied." It falls in the category of Research and Development. The selection of its problems, necessarily, must be made by reference to goals and needs outside the domain of Academia.

Alternatively, problems will be selected because they relate to the prevailing interests, values, and preferences of Academia. Prestigious journals will publish their results, or they permit the scientist to demonstrate his research virtuosity to his peers, or they parallel the interest of established authorities, and hence to solve them would enhance the reputation of the problem-solver among those who wield power in Academia, or scientists simply find them intriguing. Such research is officially designated as "basic" not because it is intrinsically important but simply and specifically because it has no demonstrable practical importance and no discernable relevance to social problems or to human needs. Since the most general characteristic of such research is that it focuses on problems related to the prevailing interests of Academia, and since its results are judged by reference to the built-in values of Academia, it will be called here not "basic" but "academic."

Sometimes social-problem oriented research is difficult and challenging, sometimes its results are broadly valuable. More often, it would seem, social-problem oriented research (R & D) is repetitive and its results are of a narrow or trivial significance. Exactly the same can be said of academic research. Sometimes it is difficult and challenging. Sometimes its results are of wide interest. But most often academic research, like the research that is oriented toward social problems, is repetitive and its contributions are, by any standard, trivial.

The information or techniques or theories that emerge as a consequence of social-problem oriented research may be interesting to academic scientists. There is then a "spillover" from social-problem oriented to academic science. Sometimes the information or techniques or theories that emerge as a consequence of academic research are relevant to the problems of society and are useful to social-problem oriented research. There is then a "spill-over," from academic to social-problem oriented science. The spillover, in either direction, appears to be marginal.

In any case, a priori, insofar as choice and foresight count for anything, the results of a given investment of resources and effort in social-problem oriented research should have a greater relevance to social needs, while, alternatively, the results of that same investment in academic research should be intrinsically more intriguing to academic scientists. The one will be more useful, and the other will be more aesthetically satisfying.

And yet there are those, surely, who are confused and deceived by the terms currently in use. When they ask for more support for "basic research" they do not intend, as it turns out, merely that more support be given to academic studies whose only distinguishing characteristic is that they are without any discernable relevance to social problems or human need. Thus, the National Science Foundation, which provides the major government support for "basic research," disqualifies any research application even in the social sciences that can be shown to be of possible relevance to social problems or human needs. Rather the support of the nonacademic public for "basic research" is intended to promote a kind of science which is normatively, and not merely semantically, basic and fundamental. They are thinking of encouraging the kind of work that Einstein did (which was academic) and that Pasteur did (which was oriented toward social problems). What is it, then, that distinguishes Einstein's work from the mass of academic studies, or Pasteur's work from the mass of social-problem oriented studies? If the characteristic feature of such work can be identified, perhaps the sort of science that warrants public support can also be specified and an appropriate means of encouraging it can be devised.

Science Embellished and Science Transformed. At any given time, science can be understood as a problem-solving apparatus, composed of what Thomas Kuhn called "paradigms," [1] consisting of sets of related preconceptions, theories, techniques, normative experiments, and organized bodies of data.[2] All this, as a way of thought, is built into the value complex at the core of Academia. Nearly all research, whether academic or not, takes this problem-solving apparatus as given and applies it—with results that are sometimes useful or that are sometimes aesthetically satisfying. Such research, which is what nearly all scientists do all of the time, is called by Thomas Kuhn "normal science." It can perfect the problem-solving apparatus by eliminating certain apparent contradictions. It can apply the problem-solving apparatus and extend the body of data related to it, thereby facilitating future solutions. Such research in a word, embellishes science, but it cannot and does not transform the problem-solving

---

[1] Thomas Kuhn, *The Theory of Scientific Revolutions* (University of Chicago Press: 1962). The following excerpts from Kuhn, *The Theory of Scientific Revolutions,* are reprinted with the permission of the publisher.

[2] *Ibid.* "The activity in which most scientists inevitably spend almost all their time, is predicated on the assumption that the scientific community (already) knows what the world is like [p. 5] . . . . The commitments that govern normal science specify not only what sorts of entities the universe does contain but also, by implication, those that it does not" (p. 7). Certainly, the apparatus of problem-solving implies a notion as to what nature is like, what can and cannot be found in it, and what can and what cannot be asked concerning it.

apparatus. What was there before is now more fully realized—but the premises remain, the horizons are not changed.

Sometimes, very occasionally, research steps outside the given problem-solving apparatus, attacking questions that are beyond its scope, searching for relationships and phenomena that have no place in its world view, organizing observations under different conceptions, working from different premises. Such research, which implicitly rejects the given apparatus of science and subverts the way of thought at Academia's base, can, and very occasionally does, transform science.[3] When this happens successfully, the result is a differently premised, more powerful apparatus, which, whatever the source of the transformation, offers new potentialities for solving the problems of the academician, as well as those relating to social goals and human needs. Rather than accepting and embellishing science, Einstein and Pasteur, in a most revolutionary sense, transformed it. This revolutionary transformation of science is the valued characteristic of their work.

Those who clamor for more "basic research" presumably want to promote the pace of such transformation. They hope to accelerate scientific revolutions. That is indeed the problem: promoting scientific revolutions.

Academic Research to Promote Scientific Revolutions. Why should society support academic research that is without relevance to its needs and problems rather than supporting research that is demonstrably relevant to its needs and problems? It is not simply a matter of conceding a value to Academia's aesthetic criterion of *science pour la science* (which may be an important consideration), and being bamboozled by value-loaded symbols (which, no doubt have their impact). A rational case can be made that the pace of scientific revolutions accelerates as the support of academic research is increased. As a consequence, the transformed science will offer a continuously more powerful apparatus for solving the problems of society and satisfying the needs of men. It is, presumably, this expectation that has impelled a vast increase in the public support of academic research in the United States in recent years. Figure 23 below shows an increase in expenditures on "basic research" in the United States of more than 400 percent in the decade between 1953 and 1963, most of it paid for by the Federal Government and performed in colleges and universities.

[3] "Science repeatedly goes astray. And when it does—when, that is, the profession can no longer evade anomalies that subvert the existing tradition of scientific practice—then begin the extraordinary investigations that lead the profession at last to a new set of commitments, a new basis for the practice of science. The extraordinary episodes in which that shift of professional commitment occurs are known in this essay as scientific revolutions. They are the tradition-shattering complement to the tradition-bound activity of normal science." (*Ibid.*, p. 6).

FIGURE 23
Expenditures on Basic Research

	(*In millions of dollars*)			
	1953		1963	
Total Funds Used for Basic Research	$ 412		$1,815	
Performed by Federal Government	45		275	
Use of Federal Funds		45		275
Performed by Industry	151		500	
Use of Federal Funds		19		150
Use of Industry Funds		132		350
Performed by Colleges and Universities *	190		840	
Use of Federal Funds		110		530
Use of Industry Funds		10		30
Use of College and University Funds †		57		220
Use of other Nonprofit Institution Funds †		13		60
Performed by other Nonprofit Institutions *	26		200	
Use of Federal Funds		10		105
Use of Industry Funds		4		20
Use of other Nonprofit Institution Funds †		12		75

From the National Science Foundation, *Reviews of Data on Science Resources*, Vol. I, No. 4 (Washington, D.C., May 1965).

* Includes expenditures of Federal contract centers administered by organizations in this sector.

† Includes State and local government funds received by these institutions and used for research.

How successful has this great increase in the support to academic research been in promoting the transformation of the problem-solving apparatus of science?

The Failure to Produce Scientific Revolutions. The comparative magnitude of current academic research is suggested by the estimate of J. de Solla Price (based on an analysis of the number of papers published in scientific journals—and therefore, in a general way referring to academic research) that 90 percent of all the scientists that have ever lived are alive and are at work today.[4]

No matter how it is measured, there has been an enormous increase in academic research in the United States; the academic scientist in America has been permitted a level of experimental facilities and of instrumentation that is without parallel. This has been under the aegis of public and private grant-giving agencies. What has been the result?

Academic science has been vastly embellished. Great numbers of scientists in more learned journal articles than can be read have staked out their proofs of analytic competence. A mountain of data has been ac-

[4] J. A. de Solla Price, *Science Since Babylon* (New Haven: Yale University Press, 1961), p. 107.

cumulated, so that, surveying it, Robert Oppenheimer could say, "We need new knowledge like we need a hole in the head."

Spillovers of these academic embellishments and accumulations into solutions of problems afflicting the enterprise economy or relevant to the goals of the political economy are marginal. Significant examples are hard to find. But what about scientific revolutions, where a real payoff might be expected?

A quite famous physicist, the head of a major U.S. laboratory supported by government grants, said to me recently that since World War II there has been no progress in science. What he meant was that there had been no scientific revolutions. Large numbers of problems had been solved but the problem-solving apparatus remains essentially the same. If there is an exception, it is in the field of molecular biology, and that transformation came about in a British workshed, completely outside the big science massively supported by grant-giving agencies.

Sociologists P. Sorokin and L. Darmstadter have canvassed "scientific opinion" to tabulate the "important discoveries" of the past and the present and have recorded a rate of increase in the numbers of such "important" discoveries *not* in accord with the increase in scientific activity, or the expenditures on research, but rather a rate of increase that merely parallels the growth in the "size of the population, economic wealth, activity in the arts." [5] Even this modest claim must be drastically discounted in the light of the strong bias, necessarily built into "scientific opinion," to overvalue the more recent achievement by judging discoveries of the past in terms of their contribution or relevance to current theories and concepts. [6]

Certainly there is not the slightest evidence of an acceleration in the pace of scientific revolutions corresponding to the unparalleled expansion in the magnitude of academic research. An enormous increase in academic research, if anything, is to be correlated with a slowdown in the transformations of science.

The failure needs to be explained.

The Pitfalls of Affluence. Academic science prospers. The number of its researchers and the output of its learned journals have immensely increased. It has been given extraordinarily costly and complex facilities

[5] *Ibid.*, p. 118.
[6] Kuhn, "For reasons that are both obvious and functional, science textbooks (and too many of the older histories of science) refer only to that part of the work of the past that can easily be viewed as contributions to the statements and solutions of the texts' paradigm problems. Partly by selection and partly by distortion, scientists in earlier ages are implicitly represented as having worked upon the same set of fixed canons that the most recent revolution in scientific theory has made to seem scientific" (p. 137).

with which to work. Its skills command a high price; "big money" passes through its coffers. All this has obvious advantages. But it also poses problems. For any institution, affluence has a dangerous side.

When the academic community is small, and its published outputs are manageable, it is possible for each of the individuals who compose the community to know the performance, the intellectual capacities, and the character of the others. Then the autonomous emergence of a leadership could be based on the direct evaluation of personal qualities. It would be then possible for the community to choose a leadership rationally through man to man confrontation and the normal exchange of ideas.

But given the vast increase in numbers of researchers and the enormous increase in the published outputs of such research, interpersonal knowledge and evaluation ceases to be possible. Authority is no longer based on direct and personal evaluations, but is the synthetic product of the politics of organization. Leadership no longer inheres in an intellectual prowess that dominates the assembly, but in the obscure manipulation of distant cliques. The great man now is an abstraction, a public image. Academia is no longer a "natural" community. It becomes rather a mass that must be organized and controlled. The control powers of organizations increase, and the power of the privately held idea of the unique individual to influence the community correspondingly diminishes.

Today academic science offers rich rewards, not only in the satisfactions of research achievement, but also solid comfort, even wealth, and political power. There is "big money" to be had, in grants, contracts, and fees for those who can get it. Naturally, some will be drawn into academic science who are not concerned only, or indeed who are not concerned at all, with the joys of pure science, but who are attracted by the other, more tangible rewards. These may be men of great ability. The abilities they have and the skills they develop will be used, however, to promote themselves, and to climb the echelons of organization into the safe seats of status and the well-paid seats of authority. They will be more likely to take control over the academic organization than others not so preoccupied, and consequently their values and not those of the dedicated will tend to dominate the organization of an affluent Academia. But, without a powerful dedication to the values built into its core, Academia is without purpose and ceases to have any motivation to positive achievement.

Academia as a Change-Generating and as a Change-Resisting Institution.

The activities of Academia are motivated by a value built into the institutional core. But these values are diverse and in one important instance are contradictory. On the one hand, science postulates the revolutionizing of science as the highest end of the scientist. The heroes and the martyrs of science are its revolutionaries. The supreme achievement of the scientist is conceived to be the refutation of established laws and theories, the destruction and elimination of the existing structure and its replacement by a new, more powerful problem-solving apparatus. Inasmuch as it indoctrinates the competent and creative individual with this value as an end-in-itself, and inasmuch as it provides him the means of freely pursuing his own direction in his own way, Academia is a change-generating institution, and the support of academic research is a reasonable way of provoking the transformation of science.

On the other hand, the very apparatus of science (its world outlook, its concepts, its accepted techniques, and its normative experiments, its theories and its data-arrangements) is also valued as a way of life, as a way of thought, and as the stock in trade of the practicing scientist.

"Authority" in science is based upon a mastery of the established apparatus. Whatever erodes or subverts that apparatus also subverts authority and casts doubt on the values or validity of its whole previous structure of achievement. Consequently, whatever the past achievement or occasional revolutionary proclivities of individuals who stand high in the ranks of honor and influence, the norm and consensus of "authority" is always conservative, and always resists the threat or challenge to its established canons.[7] Academic authority will oppose the transformation of science. Since academic authority necessarily controls academic organization, the force of academic organization also will be used to crush incipient scientific revolutions.

In sum, whatever extends the research freedom of the creative individual is likely to foster the transformation of science. Conversely, whatever strengthens the hand of academic authority and increases the power of academic organization will tend to prevent the transformation of science. In the light of this, consider the *method* for the support of academic research in the United States.

Support Through the Grant-Giving Agency. As was shown in Figure 23, most academic research is performed in colleges and universities, and its costs are covered by grants from the federal government. Whether funds come from the federal government, from state or local governments, or from private donations, and wherever the research is performed, a grant-giving agency decides what research projects should be supported and,

[7] *Ibid.* "Normal science . . . often surpasses fundamental novelties because they are necessarily subversive of its basic commitments . . . [p. 5]. New theory implies a change in the rules governing the prior practice of normal science. Inevitably therefore it reflects upon much scientific work they have already completed . . . [p. 7]. No part of the aim of normal science is to call forth new sorts of phenomena; indeed those that do not fit the box are often not seen at all. Nor do scientists normally aim to invent new theories; and they are often intolerant of those invented by others. Instead normal scientific research is directed towards the articulation of those phenomena and theories that the paradigm already supplies" (p. 24).

hence, which scientists should or should not be supported, and the extent and terms of such support. The most important of the grant-giving agencies supporting academic research, with its procedures more or less parallel to those of the others, is the National Science Foundation.

Though the National Science Foundation is a government department, it is not, in fact, an instrument of the political economy. Rather it represents the interests of academic science and speaks with the voice of academic authority. Its task is to mediate between Congress, which appropriates the funds, and Academia, which performs the research.

At its lower echelon, the National Science Foundation is divided into a number of sections, each dealing with research proposals from a particular subbranch of scientific activity. There proposals are processed, approved, or disapproved, and passed upward for approval and further processing at the higher, narrowing echelons of authority, each higher level representing a broader, more general field of research activity. At the apex, distinguished spokesmen appeal for funds to Congress and for support from the public, all in the name of Science. Funds received from Congress are, in turn, divided downward between the broad fields of science, then subdivided between increasingly more narrowly specialized fields of research activity and, finally, between the alternative research projects that have been proposed. The budgeting, reporting, administering, selecting, negotiating, and pleading involved in this process absorb the time and the energy, determine the orientation, and shape the skills of the agency's staff. And, at each level, the agency official relies for support and for guidance upon "advisory committees" drawn from Academia.

The National Science Foundation gets money from Congress and distributes that money. It operates under no policy guideline, except that the research it supports must be "basic," which it interprets to mean, simply and specifically, having no conceivable practical relevance. The determination as to what researcher is to do what research is made by academic bureaucrats, in the persons of agency officials, together with academic authorities, in the persons of the "advisory committees."

The Choice of Research Paths. The National Science Foundation supports *projects* described in *proposals*. Proposals are not submitted by individual scientists, but by the authorities of "responsible" organizations: colleges, universities, corporations, research foundations, etc. Hence the initial request must pass the muster of the organizational authority.

Characteristically the agency official, charged with processing research proposals, is an ex-scientist who has given up the ghost. His job is a professional *cul de sac.* His activities are quasi-clerical. The skills he requires to survive are those of the bureaucrat and organizational politician, pleasing the powers-that-be in academic organizations and avoiding giving offense to academic authority. Nothing in his work would satisfy the vigorous, attract the dedicated, or arouse the curious. It is, therefore, highly unlikely that he has the capacity to evaluate research for its academic quality or researchers for the competence and skill of their performance, let alone to recognize the value of an original idea, or of a creative mind, or of an unprecedented proposal. Nor has this academic bureaucrat any *self-interest* in the excellence of the research he chooses to support, much less in encouraging that which might lead to revolutionary achievement. He neither receives credit for the success of the supported research, nor answers for its fumblings and futilities. As long as he observes the conventions and recommends only what falls within accustomed norms, he is safe. His only concern must be not to flaunt the consensus nor to offend established authority. If self-interest motivates him at all in the proposals he processes, it is to lend a helping hand to friends, ex-colleagues, or those who at some future time might be useful to him. Being the man he is, he will probably want a quiet life and will try to achieve a nice balance in his distribution of grants among yeomen scientists who propose minor variations of highly precedented research.

The quality of the "advisory committee" is not something entirely apart from the agency official it advises. The committee he forms (or the committee that will work with him) is likely to be scaled to his own level. And, of course, the official will decide what advice to take, and what to disregard.

The advisory committee may be selected from outside the grant-giving agency (chosen, for example, by the National Academy of Sciences) or selected by his superiors in the agency and imposed on the administering official. And it may exercise decisive control, with the agency official as mere secretary and clerk, preparing its agenda and forwarding its decisions.

The membership of such an advisory committee will be even less motivated than the agency official by self-interest in the success or by private accountability for the failure of the research it decides to support. The "advisory committee" is neither responsible for what occurs nor answerable for what fails to occur. Its membership makes no commitments—neither of career, of money, nor of reputation.

Such a committee may be peopled by men of many sorts, great men and small men, variously motivated: research scientists, academic politicians, organizational executives, science administrators, those absorbed in the exigencies and crisis of the instant, and those who judge from the detached and benevolent conditions of quasi-retirement, egoists habituated to the possession of power and aspirants on-the-make, eager to echo the views of their betters. But whatever their differences, the members of such a committee are likely to have this in common: they are in a hurry.

Their jobs, their ambitions, their responsibilities hardly center in the tasks of the committee. The work of the committee is part time, very part time, to be done in between, on the run. Its members in their judgments will bring to bear what they already know—but what they already know will not suffice to evaluate research that departs from precedented paths. They will not have time for the concentrated effort and the patient receptivity required to absorb an original vision. They will not have time for a deep study of the individual qualities or past achievements of those who seek research support. The words of Zacharias and White, written in a different context, are relevant:

Nothing is more dangerous to an operation of this sort than the "advisor.". . . Since he is neither in touch with the day-to-day operations, nor responsible for the finished product, his contribution is likely to be neither at the level of his own abilities nor at the level of the program's real needs. The sole involvement that makes sense is a continuing and deep involvement. . . . These are hard terms, but they must be faced.[8]

The members of the committee will probably differ in their opinions. This member will favor one deviation from the norm, that member will be tolerant of another—but the norm will be a common denominator on which they can all agree—the "sound," the proven, the familiar, and hence the conventional, the time-tested, the average.

And finally, the committee will embody and will speak for academic authority. It will represent a consensus of academic science. That, after all, is its *raison d'être*. But the consensus is the natural enemy of revolution, and the established authority will always resist the transformation of science.

A Design to Frustrate Scientific Revolution. The system for the support of academic research in practice in the United States today would seem perfectly designed to frustrate and prevent scientific revolution. And if that were the intention, one could concede that it had succeeded magnificently, for an enormous and historically unprecedented effort in academic research has resulted in no significant transformation in the problem-solving apparatus of science. Out of the vast, grant-supported activity have come no scientific revolutions. One might expect as much in a system that subordinates individual choice to the control of academic organization and places the power over organization firmly in the hands of established academic authority.

A Design to Foment Scientific Revolutions. The present system for the support of academic research in the United States is perfectly designed to reinforce resistances to the transformation of science. Yet the transforma-

[8] Zacharias and White.

tion of science is the rational justification for social support to academic research inasmuch as such support is premised on the expectation of eventual benefits to society. Suppose, then, the intention to design a system for the support of academic research, which would not frustrate but would, on the contrary, foment scientific revolutions. What would be the requisites of such a system?

It is first necessary to be clear about *what* is to be supported (and, evidently, to be rid of the nonsensical and pernicious notion that there is some inherent value in a research "purified" of practical relevance). If the objective is to accelerate the pace of scientific revolutions, then what should be supported is "free research," that is, the free choice of research direction by the individual scientists, according to their own lights, with neither subordination to external demands nor imposition of academic authorities. This assumes that if the scientist is permitted to follow his own bent, he will choose the path along which he is personally equipped to make a significant contribution, and that, at least in a sufficient number of cases, he will be motivated to confront the canons of science and to assert and prove his own vision in a challenge to the established apparatus.

Academia has produced scientific revolutions through the freedom of individuals to confront and to overcome the resistance of academic organization and the vested power of academic authority. Scientific revolutions will be fomented by extending and reinforcing the free research choice of the individual within Academia.

If this position is accepted, then the system would seek to find and support not the right projects, but the right scientists. The task would be to bring the right men into academic research and to keep the wrong ones out. Once in, they would be free to choose their own direction of research. The qualities to be sought in the "right scientist" would be (1) intellectual capacity and research competence, (2) creativity, and (3) dedication. Intellectual capacity and research competence can be objectively tested. It does not seem that creativity, at present, can be effectively identified or measured until it has proven itself in performance. Hence, it would probably be necessary to act on the assumption that, hopefully, a sufficient number of those who qualify by their intellectual capacity and research skills have the creative fire also. Nor can the quality of dedication be effectively identified and measured, but the conditions of Academia can be designed which will attract only the dedicated.

A Concrete Proposal for the Support of Free Research. This proposal envisions neither more nor less support for academic research but a change in the system of support, from one that relies on academic organization and strengthens the hand of academic authority to one that would underwrite the self-directed choice of the individual scientist and thus strengthen the force of free inquiry vis à vis the institutional authority. It would appear, nevertheless, that the *system* to be proposed would be cheaper, so that the same financing could support more research activity.

The grant-giving agencies, mediating between taxpayer and research scientist with layer upon layer of officials and clerks and advisory committees, with budgeting, pleading, negotiating, rationalizing, supervising, with salesmen, science promoters, and project brokers who feed proposals into the research-supporting machine; this whole bureaucratic complex would be entirely dispensed with. Instead, the government, on behalf of society, would in effect offer the individual a contract. If the individual could demonstrate by examination or otherwise the required level of competence in science and was willing to live an austere but secure life, accepting remuneration from no other source, he would be given ample experimental facilities and publication outlets, an unlimited and continuous access to educational facilities, and support for pursuing the research of his choice, in his own way, at his own pace, for his full working life. He would be offered security and opportunity for scientific achievement and for honor among scientists—but no opportunity for wealth, and no opportunity for power.

Nothing should prevent those who enter, but who find they have not the vocation for an austere life of freely chosen research, or who want to make more money, or who weary of it for whatever reason from leaving. Nor should those who have left be prevented from returning again, to take up their work at their own discretion. Nor should anything prevent those who have established their science competence and creativity late in their careers from joining the community of free research. Such cross-movements could facilitate the dissemination of idea and technique. The numbers of those thus supported by society would be controlled by the level of the required qualifications for entry.

This is a conservative proposal. It harks back to the system that prevailed for centuries in the Academies of Europe. There scientists who had established their competence by hard and objective test were, as dons, fellows, readers, and professors, henceforth granted lifetime security in the pursuit of the research objectives of their own choosing. And, all things considered, that small number of academic men operating with meager resources produced a prodigious number of scientific revolutions. The difference is that this proposal would open the research community to the talent of the whole society and would avoid university parochialism and the theocratic domination of the professorial "chair."

Summary: *Towards the Reorganization of Academic Science.* The term "basic research" is a misnomer. The research that, in fact, is covered by the term need not be in any normative sense "basic" or "fundamental." It is simply the research done by academic scientists, whose distinguishing characteristic is that it need have no discernable relevance to social objectives or human needs. Such research has been termed here "academic."

A priori society can expect to gain more from research oriented toward social problems than from academic research, which is without any direct or intended relevance to human needs. Nevertheless, during recent decades in the United States, there has been an increase in the public support given to academic research of a magnitude unprecedented in history. Behind such support is the expectation that such research will, ultimately, prove to be not only aesthetically pleasing to Academia but also beneficial to society.

There is only one reason why support to academic research per se might be expected to yield greater benefits to society than the same sums invested in social-problem-oriented research: namely through the acceleration of those scientific revolutions that transform the problem-solving apparatus of science—so that a more powerful apparatus, subsequently, can be used to solve problems that relate to social need, as well as those that have no practical relevance.

Support to academic research, particularly, might accelerate the pace of scientific revolutions *not* because such research is without practical relevance. Some of the greatest of scientific revolutions have derived from research that had highly utilitarian objectives. And it is *not* because such research is academic. On the contrary, academic organization is a major barrier to the transformation of science, and academic authority is always hostile to scientific revolutions. Academic research is likely to lead to scientific revolutions only because and to the extent that it allows the scientist freedom to choose his own research direction, freedom from the demands of any external paymaster looking for a fast return, and freedom from an academic authority that demands conformity with established canon; indeed, freedom precisely to defy academic authority and to throw all of his efforts into upsetting the academic applecart.

The massive support now being given to academic research in the United States is perfectly designed to frustrate the impetus to scientific revolution. It operates through grant-giving agencies. Proposals are submitted by the authorities of responsible organizations. Grants are made by bureaucrats who must kowtow to academic authority, or by advisory committees who represent academic authority. The effect is to subordinate individual scientific freedom to academic authority and to strengthen all the change-resisting forces of Academia. As a consequence, the unprecedented support to academic research in the United States has resulted in no transformations of science. There has been a slowdown in the pace of scientific revolutions.

Alternatively, a system to support academic research could be designed which would foment scientific revolutions. Such a system, above all, would extend and reinforce the freedom of the scientist's choice of a research direction. Society would underwrite, not research proposals, but research scientist. Those who had established their competence would henceforth be supported in work of their own choosing.

Chapter 28

The Household Economy

The Household Economy in the United States. The household economy here means the organization of production or consumption by families or family-like units and by solitary individuals, when production or consumption is for the sake of consuming or producing entity.

The great bulk of consumption in the United States is organized by households, numbering 54.7 million in 1962 in the United States.[1] Out of a gross national product of $553.9 million in 1962, a total income of $382.0 million was available for the disposition of households, and $356.7 million was spent by households.

It is, moreover, the efforts of households to save, that is, to distribute their consumption expenditures over time, which is the most important determinant of the magnitude of the GNP and the prime cause of fluctuations in aggregate expenditures.

The household economy not only organizes consumption. It also organizes production, and on a considerable scale. It is the primary agency for the care and training of children and for the provision of domestic comfort and recreation. Its capacity to provide these services, which is subject to wide variations within a society and between national societies, is an important intrinsic determinant of economic welfare.

When the mother or daughter shops or cooks or bakes or cleans or sews; when the father or son mows the lawn, tends the vegetable garden, washes the car, mends the roof; when the parent tutors the child; when the family throws a party—in each case goods or services are being produced that have, indubitably, a value to consumers and that, under alternative forms of organization, would be bought or sold on the market. But, as significant as these outputs are, their variation in gross magnitude and quality are difficult to measure and they are completely left out of account in current statistical indices of production and consumption. Hence what appears as an increase (or a decrease) in the GNP sometimes connotes a shift in production from the household to the enterprise economy; for example, when wives leave their homes in order to work in factories, the product of their labor in the factories appears as a net addition to the GNP, with no account taken of the services sacrificed in the home.

[1] *Statistical Abstract 1963,* p. 40.

The household economy is the prime organizer of consumption in every national economy in the world. In the organization of production, the household economy is also important, more important in rural than in industrial sectors, and preeminent in technically primitive economies.

The Theory of Decentralized Purchasing. In conventional economics, the household is considered simply as the rational, satisfaction-seeking purchaser and consumer of goods and services. In the limits of this conception, it is possible to analyze the advantages and defects of the household economy as a system of decentralized purchasing by entities directly concerned in end-product consumption. The theory was developed in Part I. The essential virtues of decentralized purchasing are (1) that it is supremely sensitive to the values of the consumers of final products, and (2) that it provides a spontaneous motivation to utilize purchased goods and services efficiently to satisfy consumer values. The system of decentralized purchasing has also its defects which create difficulties and crises. These, in turn, bring about ameliorative social adaptations. Households may voluntarily associate or delegate their prerogatives of independent choice to the management of a "cooperative" or some other agent or agency. In this case, some benefits of decentralization will be sacrificed, and certain of the defects of decentralization will be reduced. Certain problems inherent in the decentralized organization of consumption by households and the reciprocal social adaptations in the United States are briefly recalled below.

Externalities in Household Purchasing and Consumption. The decision to purchase and consume may affect, beneficially or detrimentally, others than the decision-maker. Such externalization of costs and benefits will increase to the degree that choice is decentralized. And in the household economy where choice is infinitely decentralized, the distortions of consumption due to externalities will be maximized. In response, American federal and local governments have sought (1) to reduce external diseconomies by regulating household choice, for example, in zoning laws, in safety requirements for automobiles, in building codes, in restrictions on the use of sooty fuels, etc., and (2) to organize consumption under political direction as a substitute for household choice where a disproportionate ratio of external economies unduly inhibit an optimal pattern of consumption, for example, in the procurement of roads, pavements, fire and police protection, and child education.

Economies of Scale. There are likely to be important economies of scale in concentrating choice vis à vis its decentralization among households. There are two sources of such economies: first, the cost of disseminating the information needed for choice, which must increase as a function of the number of independent decision-makers, and second, the costs of analyzing and evaluating available information as a basis for choice.

For example, the $4.7 billion spent in 1960 for advertising by the wholesale and retail trade represents a cost of disseminating information where consumer choice is highly decentralized (in contrast to the $5.2 billion of largely "image-building" advertising expenditures by the manufacturing sector).[2] In a sense, the $74 billion of expenditures in 1962 by the wholesale and retail trade represent a *cost* of distribution, and that cost, presumably, could have been less to the extent that purchasing was concentrated.

The evaluation of information (or indeed, the procurement of relevant information through test and experiment) as a basis for choice among complex products—chemicals, paints, medicines, foods, materials, automobiles, and other mechanical products—may be difficult and expensive. A single evaluation may suffice for the consumption of an unlimited number of a given product offering. There thus may be significant economies of scale in the concentration of the consumption choice. Where choice is decentralized, and each household evaluates on its own, these economies cannot be realized.

As a partial offset to this disadvantage of decentralized choice, the American government sometimes requires that manufacturers (or its own inspection sources) report information that would ease the task of decentralized choice. These requirements include the grading of meats, the specification of the ingredients of prepared foods, and the standard financial reports of corporations with shares on sale on the open market. Government agencies and professional associations have evaluated products, in lieu of households. This has been of particular importance in the instance of medicines and drugs. There have also evolved numerous consumer counseling agencies, such as the Consumer's Union. Nevertheless, the problem remains. Most household choice is made on the basis of a most amateur knowledge of the qualities and characteristics of alternative product offerings. In the prevailing haze, the household is subject to the influence of advertising that promotes choice based on emotional impulse, unrelated to knowledgeable discrimination.

Instabilities and Uncertainties. Costly uncertainties and functionless instabilities in price are also a consequence of the decentralized choice of households. This is painfully evident in the buying and selling of bonds, common stocks, and real estate in the efforts of households to protect the values of their asset-holdings. Erratic choice and group stampede lead to boom-and-bust in real estate values, and to extreme vertical movements in stock market price levels, which are transmitted via variations in con-

[2] *Ibid.*, p. 849.

sumption into the magnitude of the GNP and into employment levels and commodity prices. Such inflation and deflation in the values of possessions and the wild windfalls of gain and loss, and the random redistribution of wealth that they bring about, are not the consequence of changes in "real" output or in consumer wants or in profits, but rather are caused by erratic variation in the patterns of household choice.

Boundaries of the Conventional Premises. Conventionally, in dealing with the role of the household, economics has assumed: (1) that the cognitive action of the household is limited to the choice and purchase of end-products, (2) that the household is (or can be understood as the equivalent of) the solitary self-seeking individual, (3) that the values and purposes underlying household choice are given and are neutral to the task of explaining household choice, and (4) that the household is rational in the pursuit of its given values and purposes.

These premises assume away some of the most interesting and important questions concerning the household economy. The sections below will (simply) raise some of these questions.

The Technology of Household Production and Consumption. The cognitive action of households is not limited to the choice of end products. Both household production and consumption are complex and varied processes that require plans and organization, that use tools, that require technique, that can progress or regress. Washing machines, drying machines, lawnmowers, hedge trimmers, sewing machines, vacuum cleaners, garbage dispose-alls, and quick freeze units (and automobiles and supermarkets) are inventions integrated into household processes of production. In each instance, they were a part of the transformation of those processes. A house has been called a "machine for living," and it is, indeed, a complex instrument that makes possible an organized process of consumption. In these terms a house may be evaluated for its efficiency, serviceability, workability. The distribution and utilization of leisure time, the balancing of work and recreation, constitute difficult issues and problems of organization for the individual household and for the household economy. So, similarly, are the selection and balancing of asset-holdings, that is, the adjustment of security portfolios and the distribution of consumption through time. In support of the latter, there have evolved agencies and instruments for "saving" and for consumer credit: mortgages, household loans, and installment buying.

Evidently, the household is not simply an agency of choice. It is also an organizing agency, and the same questions can be asked of it as are asked of the agencies of the enterprise, of the political, and of the institutional economies. What are (1) its efficiency in the use of resources, (2) its capacity, through invention, innovation, and transformation, for progressive development, and (3) its intrinsic value as a way of life? In the organization of the household economy, this last consideration is of the greatest importance. The answer to these questions must be sought in an analysis of the structure and motivational force of the household.

The Structure of Internal Relationships. The household, ordinarily, is not an isolated, self-seeking individual. It is a family, or family-like entity, a kinship group that in some cultures can be quite large and distantly extended. It embodies and serves to perpetuate a traditional distribution of power and reciprocal obligation and systems of evaluation and choice. The choices made and the action taken by or through this group are of another order than those of the solitary, self-seeking individual (with an indifference map, allegedly engraved in his mind). The inappropriateness of the traditional premise is illustrated by reference to what are, perhaps, the household's most important consumption decisions (important not only intrinsically, but also in relationship to social organization and economic progress), namely, those which relate to the education of children. Such decisions are not made by the child in its own self-interest, nor by the father in his self-interest. They are made by the parent, or parents, *for* the child, by reference to some conception of roles, responsibilities, and "family" values.

The characteristic "family" distribution of power and responsibility is ordinarily supported by convention and reinforced by the law. In Western society, property and inheritance are the household's primary legal supports, and the substantive differences of property and inheritance laws in different societies reflect the wide variance in forms of household organization. In the essentially egalitarian, mobile American family, property laws convey no special status on husband or wife. In Latin societies, the legal prerogatives of family ownership reflect the dominance of the male head. Primogeniture among the British nobility reflected the effort to maintain a constant relationship between a particular set of possessions, powers, and responsibilities, where the household was a key component in the structure of political authority. In the traditional, extended Chinese family, property was communal, with interfamilial power attaching to traditional roles, which in turn, were supported in the law. In the traditional Mexican *ejido*, property is the inalienable possession of the tribal, village community.

Nonrational Components. If the intention is to understand the choice and behavior of households and the variations of such behavior, then the pattern of motivating values cannot be ignored. They are likely to be the key to the explanation, and, rightfully, of central interest.

Values are not given. They change, they are changed, and forces are perpetually working to change them. This process of change must be comprehended if the dynamics of household behavior are to be understood. And the problem of *how* to change household values is a perennial social issue.

Nor does it suffice to assume that choice is "sufficiently" rational or "tends to be" rational, if one seeks to explain variations in household organization and behavior. Here the objective should be, rather, to identify the sources of irrationality, and the irrational elements, that is, the taboos, the effective symbols, the habitual, tradition-based practices. This identification will suggest the existing limits of rational choice.

Questions Without Answers. The objectives of this chapter have been relatively modest. It has drawn the broad contours of the household economy and has suggested its magnitude and the significance of its functions, in contrast to those of the enterprise economy, the political economy, and the institutional economy in the United States. It has described certain of the problems of this economy, considered as a system of decentralized purchasing. And it has raised certain key questions required for the analysis of the organization of production and consumption by households, when analysis goes beyond the classical assumptions concerning the household as an economic entity.

Chapter 29

The Halfway House

The Economy as a Diversity of Systems. Each national economy is a half-way house, consisting not of a single one, but of a number of different systems for the organization of production and consumption. These systems, or "economies," in turn, are composed of diverse forms of organization. Each part of this economic complex contains its own inherent contradictions, generates its peculiar problems, and provokes correspondingly particular social responses. In these terms, the American national economy has been described, and some of its problems have been explained.

There are advantages in having a half-way house. There are also disadvantages. There are problems that are the consequence of the diversity itself, contradictions that are not endemic to any given system or form of organization, but that arise in their interactions.

The values of this diversity and the problems which are its consequence will be examined in this chapter.

Different Tools for Different Tasks. The tasks of the economy are not homogeneous. The production of a ton of steel and the raising of a bushel of corn, the consumption of a gross of stockings and the use of a radar defense unit, the education of manpower and the organization of basic research are alike tasks for the economy. But the optimal size of the operating entity and other technical prerequisites of efficiency will differ. The instrument appropriate to the expression of the relevant (individual, group, or collective) values and purposes will differ. The significance of market evaluations, the possibilities of effective market competition and of centralized supervision all will differ. Correspondingly, different operating systems and forms of organization will be appropriate. A diversity of systems and of forms of organization is required if the tools of choice and action are to be suited to the tasks.

Diversity as a Source of Flexibility. The needs and values that the national economy serves and the context of science and technology within which the national economy functions are not static. They change perpetually and in unpredictable ways. The economic mobilization in the United States for World War II and the subsequent postwar readjustment, the realization of the opportunities of the Common Market in

Europe, and, in the whole Western world, the new effort to gear organized science into technological transformation in the planned attempt to promote economic growth—all these exemplify unforeseen needs for structural change in the economies of nations.

Inasmuch as rapid and unpredictable structural changes are likely to be required, the sheer capacity for such change, that is, structural flexibility, is correspondingly advantageous. Diversity imparts flexibility. Each of the "economies" and each component form of organization provides a nucleus of experience and technical expertise around which structural change can be organized in much the same way as the cadre of military professionals provides the core around which civilian armies can be quickly created.

The Wider Choice of a Way of Life. Each system and form of economic organization requires particular sets of talents and values, and tends to promote those values and to develop those talents among the participants. But the individual is never simply the creature of an economic function. His values and attitudes are shaped by a variety of other influences. His abilities and proclivities, as a genetic heritage or as the consequence of a long cultural evolution, are to some extent independent of current modes of organization. Indeed, every social group includes a range of human types, some fit and others more or less unfit for the organizational requirements of the functional systems in which they are engaged.

To the degree that the national economy includes a diversity of systems and forms of economic organization, there will be more room for the individual to choose an environment and a way of life compatible with his values, and to find an appropriate outlet for his abilities. The range (and in that sense, the freedom) of choice is thereby extended, and a better use can probably be made of the diversity of talents that exist in society.

Cross-Supporting Forms of Economic Organization. Each form of economic organization that is present in the American national economy supports and supplements the activities of the others, performing *for* others the tasks it is peculiarly equipped to handle. The political economy provides research and extension services in support of decentralized price-directed agriculture. Large autonomous enterprise turns to universities for research, to small enterprises for services, and to contractors for the performance of particular work. The political economy massively "procures" from enterprise.

It is not only in the performance of tasks and in the rendering of services that the different forms of organization support each other. Each system and each form of economic organization promotes values and skills appropriate to itself. Yet, for its optimal operation, that system or form of economic organization will to some degree need men with skills and attitudes that are not promoted—but rather are discouraged by the environment of that system. The military establishment, for example, sometimes needs a Secretary McNamara, whose capacities and drives are shaped by a quite different universe of experience.

The environment of autonomous enterprise thus favors the development of the organizational man. But, to a significant extent, it is the experience on the farm or in small enterprise that feeds into the autonomous enterprise the rugged, creative individualism sometimes needed at the upper echelons of control. The politician and the civil servant may bring to the autonomous corporation the sense of its social role in the broad context of public affairs. The business executive may bring to the university the sense of its servicing obligations and its interdependence with the other parts of the society. The academician brings to government a capacity for abstraction, dedication, and disinterested analysis. The logic and objectivity of the scientist infiltrates business organization. The rationality of the factory organization and of the engineering blueprint infiltrates the operation of the farm. The interchange of ideas, talents, and proclivities fostered through the experience of one form of organization, supports and strengthens the operation of the others.

Dominance of a Single System, with Its Derivative Values. Though all national economies are composed of a diversity of systems and forms of economic organization, a single system and its derivative values tend to dominate the social outlook. In the United States, the outlook and values that dominate are those appropriate to the enterprise economy, and within that economy, increasingly those that are specifically appropriate to the autonomous, market-negotiating form of economic organization.

The tendency for a dominant set of derivative values and conceptions to arise out of the diversity of organizational experience has, probably, several causes. It may happen because one of the forms of organization is so much larger and more encompassing than the others that in fact it represents the characteristic experience. It may be because the achievements of a particular form of organization are relatively great and are generally admired. It may work the other way around. The normative form of organization may be the derivative of a pre-existing ideology. In the Soviet Union, the values, outlook, and image of socialism came first and dragged the actual forms of economic organization slowly in their train. Laissez-faire liberalism in the United States continued as the norm long after the decentralized market-direction, from which it derived, had ceased to be the major component of the national economy. Probably, a single form of organization and outlook also tends to dominate, because that simplification corresponds to the convenience of the individual and to the needs of society. To accept a mélange of co-existing values and outlooks appropriate to the diverse experience in different forms of organized activity is confusing. The individual ordinarily prefers a norm, where he can anchor his thought securely and in terms of which he can view and judge the multiple worlds of his experience, albeit inadequately. And a society, for the sake of its internal cohesion, may require a common outlook and shared values, even though, here and there, that outlook and those values are not suited to the requisites of operation and organization.

Whatever its cause, a dominant outlook will not ipso facto be appropriate for control of or choice within all the forms of economic organization that compose the economy. It will prevail where it does not belong. The infiltration of the businessman's philosophy into the ordering of higher education, the reliance on commercial criteria in the formulation of strategic choice, and the projection of the commonplaces of business experience onto the larger screen of public policy have been a source of persisting error and distortion in the United States. Two instances will illustrate this.

It is easy to prove that the public debt cannot be equated with a private debt, and that (whatever its genuine defects) an internally held public debt, no matter its size, cannot lead to national bankruptcy as a private debt can lead to private bankruptcy. Yet not only do the political jeremiads equating public debt with private debt and demanding a balanced budget as the sole means of preventing national bankruptcy continue as they have for nearly half a century, but these considerations remain basic in the formulation of public policy (in Eisenhower's Administration they were its central tenet). One can only account for this (or for the persistence of the gold standard) because these notions are so eminently reasonable in the context of business experience, because they are entirely compatible with a culture and cognition that works well for the businessman in the enterprise economy. The commonplaces of company management and the truisms of commercial choice are thus transmuted into canons for social policy.

Another example of the distortion that arises when an outlook, proper to the enterprise economy, dominates where it does not belong is the crucial choice in 1942 of a technique for the production of synthetic rubber by the American government, after natural rubber supplies had been cut off by the Japanese in Malaya.

A supreme military crisis in which the supply of rubber might be of key importance seemed to be approaching. The issue was between two sets of processes, those that would produce the essential ingredient, butadiene, from alcohol, and those that would produce it from derivatives of petroleum. Those who supported the adoption of the latter processes were large, powerful oil companies. They argued that butadiene could be made from petroleum derivatives more cheaply than in any other way.

The supporters of the alcohol-based processes (Chaim Weizmann, for example, then science emissary from Great Britain) argued that the petroleum derivatives used to produce butadiene were needed also to produce high-octane aviation fuel for which, in the pending crisis, there would also be a limitless demand. Alcohol, on the other hand, could be produced from surplus grain, stored in public warehouses, for which there was no critical, competitive need. Alcohol could be produced in capacity diverted from whisky distilleries, whereas petroleum-based processes would require the diversion of the highest priority equipment and materials. Finally, the alcohol processes were simple and proven in practice, while the petroleum processes were complex and untried and therefore to depend on them would be to risk the loss of all-precious time.

The government officials who exercised control, approached the issue like bankers intent on getting the highest return on the government's money. The promise of low money costs sufficed. They turned virtually the whole (700,000 ton) program over to the oil companies.

This decision caused a Congressional revolt, led by the "farm bloc" senators. In response, officials were forced, as a kind of bone thrown to howling political dogs, to assign 242,000 tons of scheduled butadiene capacity to alcohol-based processes.

In terms of the commercial criteria to which they adhered, and which the government officials accepted, the oil companies were right. The money cost of the petroleum-based processes was ultimately the lowest, and these processes are now the basis of a thriving privately owned industry in the United States. But in terms of strategic criteria, the government officials were entirely wrong. Alcohol-based processes supplied some 80 percent of the synthetic rubber produced during the critical war years, through August 1944. All that had been forewarned concerning the perils of butadiene-based production came to pass: the conflict with the aviation fuel program for the essential petroleum derivatives, the drain of highest priority materials and components, breakdowns, experimental trials, failures, and delays. Substantial quantities of petroleum-based butadiene were not produced until the closing months of 1944, after the crucial phases of the war were behind. As far as a war effort was concerned, the petroleum-based program was a flat failure and a tragic and useless drain on critical manpower and materials. It was a failure that came about because public officials thought like private bankers, and used commercial criteria as a basis for strategic judgments.

Not only does the dominant outlook impose itself upon forms of organization where it does not belong. But also, inasmuch as it becomes an ideology, it sets itself in opposition to, and probably seeks to suppress any value or system of thought other than its own and sometimes to eradicate forms of organization considered either ideologically heretical or favorable to views that run counter to those which the dominant outlook embodies. This pressure for ideological purity, more than merely giving comfort to zealots, may be required for the effective operation of those forms of organization in which built-in values are a motivating element or effectiveness requires a doctrinally unified dedicated elite. In the Soviet Union, and in all communist countries, a successful, prospering decentralized market-directed sector cannot be indefinitely tolerated. For this reason farming will be collectivized even though collectivization may be a relatively inefficient way of organizing agriculture. In societies where the dominant form is other than centralized political-direction, doctrinal impurity remains a threat to cultural unity. The American Civil War bears witness that in market economies also the diversity of outlook and values created by co-existent forms of economic organization may prove culturally and politically intolerable. In the economy of the United States today there are prejudices and pressures against any deviation from the organizational norm and resistance to operations that are not encompassed by the dominant ideology. The extension and development of the Tennessee Valley Administration was halted by the fear of "creeping socialism." Similarly, the peculiarly American development of price-regulated public utilities represents a compromise between a competitively unworkable market form and an ideologically obnoxious political control.

Incompatibilities. The forms of economic organization that coexist in a given national economy may not be compatible. They may act parasitically, the one exploiting or destroying the other. The one may thrive not because it is inherently more efficient or has a greater capacity to develop progressively, but simply through its great power to preempt a larger share of a jointly produced output. For example, the chain store may thrive in competition with the small retailer because, by threatening the withdrawal of its mass purchasing or by threatening backward integration into manufacturing, it is able to induce sellers to discriminate in its favor. Here it is discrimination, not price concessions, that counts. Any concession remains valuable only so long as others are prevented from also securing it. The mass buyer may prosper and grow, not because he is large, but because he is larger, that is, not because there are economies of scale, but because his relative size enables him to manipulate the price at which he buys. The mass buyer then benefits, not because he forces prices down, but only because he forces a discrimination in his own favor. If, instead of being a large unit in a universe of small entities, the buyer were a large business among large businesses, the "economies" on which it thrived need not exist. Conceivably, the power of large organizations to gain discriminatory treatment can destroy and supplant a particular universe of small enterprise, even though efficiency and progressiveness are thereby reduced and prices (reflecting costs) are higher than they would have been in the decentralized market-directed economy. Some have alleged that this is not merely conceivable, but that it frequently occurs. It is this danger that the Robinson-Patman Act is intended to counteract.

A similar dynamic governs the relationship between those members of the work force who negotiate with employers collectively through their trade unions vis-à-vis those who bargain individually in the decentralized market. This was the case, formerly, in the United States, where the skilled workers were combined in the craft unions of the old AFL, while semiskilled and unskilled were not organized in trade unions. When one part of the labor force is thus organized in trade unions and the other is not, it has been contended that the unions will indeed drive up the real and the money wages of their membership. They will do this by restricting the membership of the unionized sector to the (smaller) number whose greater marginal-revenue-productivity is equal to the higher wage. With fewer workers therefore employed in the unionized trades than would otherwise have been the case, consequently more are left to search for work in the nonunionized sectors. This greater availability lowers the marginal-revenue-productivity of labor outside the unionized sector and causes wages there to decline. Hence, it was argued, the *partial* organization of labor raised the real wages of the organized sector, but only at the expense of the real wages of the unorganized sector. There is, surely, another side to the case. Nevertheless, the argument suffices to illustrate another possible instance where one form of economic organization (unionized labor) benefits parasitically from another (nonunionized labor).

Full Employment Policy in the United States: A Study in Incompatibilities. A uniform social policy is not likely to be compatible with (or workable for) a multiplicity of coexisting forms of economic organization, since each of the various forms of economic organization will respond differently to the same regulation or to the same stimulus. This poses problems for social control. It is this incompatibility between a uniform social policy and a diversity of economic forms that has, so far, prevented the development of a policy that could effectively maintain full employment and stable prices in the United States.

Consider the parts of the American enterprise economy: on the one hand the decentralized market-directed, and the decentralized market-segmented (call these, for the purpose of this discussion, price-competitive enterprise), and on the other hand, the organizational market-negotiating (call this, price-determining enterprise). For price-determining enterprise, product prices are set by companies as a matter of policy, and wages are set by trade unions as a matter of policy. For price-competitive enterprise, price is a function of output, and output is a function of available resources. Resources flow with relative freedom, into or out from price-competitive enterprise.

Certain other postulates are required in order to explain the problem of controlling underemployment and price instability.

1. Population is growing, and the forces of economic progress are raising productivity. On both counts, the resources available for use (measured by their potential contribution to output values) are increasing. Resources, in the first instance, will be considered as manpower, that is, labor force times productivity per capita.

2. The secular increase in demand, as a consequence of the changing size, consumption proclivities, and normal income sources of the household economy, is not sufficient *at constant product prices* to employ all the continually increasing resources available for use. *The resources which cannot be employed at constant product prices are called here "surplus" resources.* An "adequate" secular increase in demand would be one that absorbed into employment, at constant prices, all increments of resources accumulating as a consequence of larger population and of technical progress. Secular increase in demand is therefore deemed "inadequate."

3. Price-determining enterprise sets product prices as a matter of policy, and trade unions set wages as a matter of policy. But what is the policy of trade unions with respect to wages, and of enterprise with respect to product prices? It will be assumed in the first instance that companies seek to maintain stable product prices or stable mark-up margins on product outputs so long as profits per unit will not thereby be reduced. And it will be assumed that trade unions seek to obtain stable real wages for their members—and hence that unions will force an increase in money wages to offset inflationary rises in the cost of living. Other company price and trade union wage policies are possible. Nevertheless the assumed wage-price policies appear consistent with the behavior of trade union wages and the behavior of prices in industries dominated by the large, autonomous corporation for considerable periods of time.

In sum, the following is postulated: (1) that there are two forms of organization in the enterprise economy, price-competitive enterprise where price is a function of output and output is a function of available resources, and price-determining enterprise where companies maintain constant product prices and trade unions are committed to maintaining the constant real value of wages; and (2) that manpower resources (productivity times population) are constantly increasing, and (3) that the secular growth in demand is not sufficient fully to absorb the incremental manpower into full employment. Surplus manpower therefore accumulates.

Depressive Effect of Surplus Manpower. The surplus manpower cannot be absorbed into price-determining enterprise, since product prices are held constant. Hence, in these industries surplus manpower may take the form of unemployment or underemployment.

Alternatively, surplus manpower can enter price-competitive industries. To the extent that it does, output in those industries will increase, product prices will decline, and wages will decline also, relative to equivalent wages and prices in price-determining enterprise. By the criterion of optimum distribution, there will be underemployment in price-determining enterprise and *overemployment* in price-competitive enterprise. Between the two, there will be a growing disparity in the remuneration to equivalent manpower, including the return to managerial or entrepreneurial skills.

Surplus Investment And Excess Capacity in Price-Determining Industries. Wages and profits will be relatively high in the price-determining industries, since the influx of surplus manpower by expanding output, forces a relative decline in the prices, the wages and the profits of the price-competitive industries. Price-determining industries will accordingly be attractive to both labor and investment. Surplus labor is kept out, however, by the refusal of companies to hire more manpower than they plan to use in increasing output. But surplus investment, in the sense of investment beyond that which is required to support the increase of output at constant prices, cannot be excluded. Seeking its share of the higher profits, it infiltrates, serving merely to expand the margin of excess capacity and to spread profit return over a wider equity base.[1]

Effects of the Increase in Aggregate Demand. Suppose that the government, confronted with a growing margin of unemployment at the periphery of price-determining industries, undertakes, through fiscal and monetary measures, to expand the magnitude of aggregate demand in order to absorb those resources into full employment. Consider the impact of this on the two forms of economic organization.

There will be a greater demand for the output of price-determining industries. This will cause employment and production to increase, while, in the first instance prices remain constant. Companies will be able to increase their production over a considerable range, at constant or declining unit costs and constant or increasing unit profits because (1) the previous influx of surplus investment has created in those industries a margin of excess capacity, and (2) there exists high-quality manpower unemployed, or employed at a low rate of remuneration in the price-

[1] Edward Chamberlin, *The Theory of Monopolistic Competition* (Cambridge: Harvard University Press, 1942). Chaps. IV, V, VI, and VII give an example of this process in his differentiated products case.

competitive industries, and anxious to work at the higher established wages and salaries of price-determining industries.

A greater aggregate demand must also cause a rising demand for the products of price-competitive industries. Simultaneously, their manpower will withdraw, attracted by employment opportunities at higher wages elsewhere. The greater demand for its outputs and the withdrawal of a part of its manpower resource must result in higher prices for the products of price-competitive industries.

Cost-Push Inflation.. Higher prices in the price-competitive industries raise raw material and other costs in price-determining industries and augment the cost-of-living, and hence lower real wages in price-determining industries. Following a policy of maintaining their real wage level, trade unions would force up wage rates. Rising wages and raw material prices result eventually in a rise in company costs per unit of output and a decline in profits per unit of output. Under this pressure, price-determining industries will raise the prices of their outputs. With the prices rising in both parts of the economy, the cost-push inflation is in train.

A Dilemma for Social Control. This general upward movement of price in both price-competitive and price-determining industry is likely to occur while substantial pools of unemployed or underemployed manpower remain. Higher prices check the power of a given increase in the level of aggregate demand to absorb unemployed resources. If government continues to raise the level of aggregate demand in order to force the absorption of the remaining surplus manpower into employment, the same cost-price sequence is repeated, and inflation is accelerated. On the other hand, the inflationary pressure may cease if the government does not offset the rise in prices in the price-determining industries by a further increase in the level of aggregate demand; but then surplus manpower will remain and will continue to accumulate, overemployed and underpaid in the price-competitive sector, and unemployed or underemployed in the price-determining sector. Because the two forms of organization respond differently to increments of available manpower and of investment in the first instance, and differently to the induced increase in aggregate demand in the second instance, the measures used to maintain full employment are not compatible with general price stability. This is the dilemma of social control.

Resource Maldistribution. Small, price-competitive enterprise is not the villain of this piece. It is true that prices rise first there; but this is partly because price-competitive enterprise has been the passive recipient of surplus manpower forced into relatively unproductive and unremunerative employment as a consequence of the price and output inflexibility in price-determining enterprise.

The manpower surplus is the consequence of an inadequate rise of secular demand in the face of the policies of price-determining enterprise. This surplus shows itself as unemployment in the one form of economic organization and as overemployment in the other. One case involves a waste of the resource; the other, a maldistribution of the resource. An induced increase in aggregate demand acts to correct both the waste and the maldistribution. Unemployed resources are absorbed into employment. Maldistributed resources are drawn into more remunerative work. A proper balance would require that for price-competitive industries resources continue to diminish and prices continue to rise until incomes and profits in these industries are on a par with those of price-determining enterprise. But this is precisely what the autonomous corporation and trade union will not allow to happen. They will use their price-determining power to reopen and preserve the gap. And government, seeing as a consequence of its program a rise of prices, rather than a reabsorption of the unemployed into increased production, ceases to promote the expansion of aggregate demand.

The problems of social control are rendered even more complex when stability is not the prime objective of trade union wage and company price policy. If the corporation's policy and strategy is continually to increase its profit margins, and the trade union's is continually to raise the level of real wage remuneration, new difficulties frustrate effective social control.

Summary. Every national economy is composed of a variety of forms of economic organization. This is a technical imperative. The tasks of the economy are varied, and different tasks require different tools. Diversity per se has advantages. The greater the diversity, the wider will be the opportunity for the individual to find a way of life that pleases him and a chance to make the best use of his particular talents. Further, with their different functional capacities, the various forms of economic organization provide services for each other. And each form of organization promotes skills and values among its participants that may, in important ways, support the activities of the others. Finally, the diversity of forms gives flexibility to a national economy, better permitting it to adapt or evolve in the face of unforeseeable crises and unpredictable needs.

The multiplicity of forms of organization poses difficulties also. The system of thought that tends to become dominant in a culture will be appropriate for one, but not for all the coexisting forms of economic organization, and its imposition on the others will lead to distorted choice.

Inasmuch as the dominant system of thought is also an ideology, and the particular form of economic organization to which it relates becomes idealized, ideological pressure will handicap or prevent the operation of other forms.

Different forms of organization may be functionally incompatible. One may thrive through a parasitical relationship upon another. Tensions and contradictions growing out of their interaction may greatly complicate the problem of social control. An example of this is the effort in the United States to devise a policy that will at once maintain full employment and stable prices.

PART III

SOCIAL SYSTEMS AND ECONOMIC DEVELOPMENT

Chapter 30

Functional, Cognitive, and Cultural Systems

A Conceptual Framework to Suit the Problem. Every problem needs a conceptual framework where hypotheses can be formulated embodying all of those elements that are considered relevant to a solution. For example, to explain a change in the price of coal compared to the price of petroleum, or in the price of both of these fuels compared to the price of meat and wine, one requires a conception of markets and of exchange, of the mechanism of market competition, of marginal costs, of the patterns of private preferences, and of the motivations of entrepreneur or manager and consumer. One turns, in other words, to the conceptual structure of microeconomics, which evolved in dealing with precisely these problems of relative price.

But when we are concerned rather with general inflation and deflation, with depression and mass unemployment, then the conceptions of microeconomics do not suffice. Marginal costs, consumer preferences, the mechanism of competition are no longer relevant. One approaches the problems of inflation, depression, or mass unemployment with a different set of conceptions: those of national income, of aggregate demand, of consumption propensities, of credit expansibility, of built-in resistances against the upward or downward movement of the general price level—in a word, with the conceptual frame of macroeconomics.

It may seem obvious today that the neoclassical concepts cannot encompass the phenomena of mass unemployment and depression. But this inadequacy was not at all evident to the economists who first confronted those problems. It took ten years of world depression finally to drive Western economics from the brain-grooves of microtheory. Even after Keynes came marching out with his hands held high, it took another decade to develop a consensus. It has been precisely this stepping from one conceptual structure to another that has constituted the "crises" of all the social and natural sciences.

Today, again, economics confronts phenomena of an unfamiliar sort. Using their established conceptual apparatus, economists attempt to deal with the new problems of growth and development, but neither microeconomics nor macroeconomics will do. A new framework must be devised.

Economic Growth and Economic Development. "Economic growth" and "economic development" both refer to the rate of increase in productivity. Hence both must be concerned with the invention of new industrial and agricultural techniques, with their practical application, and with their efficient utilization. Yet between economic growth and economic development there is a fundamental difference. The problem of "economic growth" is one of maintaining or accelerating a rate of increase in productivity in a society that has demonstrated its capacity to achieve the heights of modern technology. The problem of "economic development" is rather the failure of a particular society to scale those heights. Why has it not yet industrialized, why has it failed, and why does it continue to fail to avail itself of the opportunities offered by world science, or to respond to the stimuli of technical revolutions elsewhere? Why has this society, unlike others, been unable to break free from the bounds of tradition? Why does it seem unable to mobilize its forces for the coherent pursuit of its social goals? Why can it not take advantage of paths already broken, even of highways opened?

An analogy to illustrate the difference between the problem of economic growth and that of economic development is to be found, perhaps, in the task of teaching children to read. In a class where children read with normal variations around an accustomed norm, the creative teacher tries to find ways of teaching all of the students to learn more easily and more rapidly. This is a matter of improving classroom techniques, with the learning capacity of the children taken as given. But what about the task of teaching children who are in other ways intelligent but who cannot learn to read at all, who are for some reason blocked in connecting the printed word with the spoken? These pose a problem of another order. They fall outside that pedagogical competence which takes a certain intact learning capacity as given. Now, not the classroom technique, but the "whole" child, becomes a focal problem; everything that motivates or conditions the child, his psychology, his physiology, his nutrition, his home environment, his familial relationships, is open to inquiry. The analysis of economic growth can be compared to research on classroom techniques for children of normal learning capacities. The analysis of economic development is like a study designed to comprehend and aid the child who cannot take that initial step in the learning process.

The analysis of economic growth, conceivably, can be confined to a limited set of "economic" activities, taking the rest of society (its political organization, its motivational base, indeed, its capacity for effective social control and coherent social action) as given. Not so for economic development. At issue in economic development is an incapacity for effective, coherent social action. Anything that relates to that incapacity must be opened to inquiry.

In confronting the problem of economic development, the economist must try to discover why some societies thrust themselves forward while others lag, why some societies achieve revolutionary changes and others remain inert. The economist needs a conceptual framework that will encompass the whole of a society, enabling him to take into systematic account the diverse elements relevant to the organization of coherent, effective social action and (hence) fundamental economic change. What follows will propose such a framework.

Functional Systems. Society takes a practical meaning in the organization of the efforts of numbers of individuals (1) where the activities themselves are valued, for example, in recreation, or (2) where it is the external effects of the activities that are valued, for example, in the production of goods for sale. Such organized activities are called here "social functions." The production and the consumption of goods and services were described earlier as "economic" functions. There are social functions other than the economic: the waging of war, worship, the acculturation of new generations, the administration of justice, and so on.

The means by which social functions are organized are called here *functional systems.* Four broadly conceived functional systems are possible. Whatever the social function is, it will be organized according to one or some combination of these four functional systems. These are described below as (1) market systems, (2) political systems, (3) institutional systems, and (4) familial systems.

Market Systems. In market systems activity is organized through exchange. Power over resources resides in property or in money as a claim on property. Choice is significantly decentralized and autonomous. Price is an index of scarcity. Agencies of production depend, for survival, on the "profit" margin between operation costs and sales income.

Many human activities can be and, in different societies, have been wholly or partially organized through market systems, even including marriage, military aggression and defense, education, recreation, and religion.

Political Systems. Political systems organize activity through the actual or potential exercise of coercive force. To the degree that the exercise of coercive force is regularized and accepted, political authority is "legitimate." Political systems provide the means for the exercise of collective choice. Collective choice normally takes precedence over the particular interest within its orbit, that is, it is sovereign. Sovereignty is ordinarily exercised through a political system. In today's world, the sovereign systems of primary importance are nation states, with supranational political systems evolving.

Institutional Systems. Institutional systems organize activities around the commitment of participants to intrinsically valued goals. Institutional systems are the direct expression of accepted sets of values. The Catholic Church, or any church or religious society, is an institutional system. So is the Communist Party. So are most armies. So are the Boy Scouts. So are charities, universities, and research foundations.

In order to be effective, an institutional system must be based on a particular set of values to which its partisans and participants are dedicated. For the coherent organization of its activities, institutional systems always require a framework of cognition in terms of which those built-in values can be expressed.

Familial Systems. Activities are sometimes organized through families or family-like groups, bound by the force of convention or by the ties of love, affection, respect, and emotional need. Power in familial systems resides in status. Dominant patterns of reciprocal responsibilities and codes of behavior (different for kin, for stranger, for neighbor) are passed on as tradition. In all societies a wide range of functional activities are organized through familial systems, for example, recreation and the rearing and acculturation of children. In primitive societies, virtually all social functions are organized through familial (tribal) systems.

Functional Systems and Economic Activities. Any social function is likely to be organized by several of these functional systems concurrently; Part Two described the United States economy as an activity organized through all four of these functional systems. The enterprise economy includes variants of market systems; the political economy, variants of political systems; the institutional economy (for example, in the production of educated manpower and outputs of "fundamental" research), variants of institutional systems; and the household economy, a variant of familial systems.

Functional Systems and the Social Sciences. Neoclassical (micro) economics has dealt almost exclusively with the operation of a particular variant of market systems. Political science and law have been mostly concerned with aspects of the operation of political systems. Sociology recently has begun to study institutional systems, but hitherto has been concerned with variants of familial systems in complex modern societies. Anthropology has studied the broader range of activities organized primarily through familial systems in primitive societies.

Combinations and Permutations of Functional Systems. These four functional systems account for the organization of all social functions. There are, of course, many variants of political systems, of market systems, of institutional systems, and of familial systems. For example, as

Part II showed, variations in market systems in the United States range from that of the small farm, run by a single individual, that follows the dictate of market-determined price to the vast industrial corporation employing tens of thousands, setting its prices as a matter of policy, and embodying in its control mechanism a diversity of interests and wills.

Functional systems, moreover, are variously related and combined. Markets are sometimes controlled through political systems. Political systems are sometimes controlled through institutional systems, perhaps through a Communist Party, an Army, a Church. In the monarchical form, a political system is controlled through a superimposed familial system.

The Organization of Evaluation, and the Organization of Thought. Functional systems constitute the means of organizing action for its valued effects or for its intrinsic values. In the process of functional organization, problems must be solved and questions must be answered. In order to solve problems and to answer questions, it is necessary to collect and to classify information, to observe and to record observations, to process what has been recorded, to theorize, to criticize, to test the theory or the information. In other words, implicit in the organization of functional activities is the organization of thought.

Moreover, the organization of functional activities often requires that policies be formulated or choices made on the grounds of value-judgments. Hence, implicit in the organization of functional activities is the organization of evaluation.

These two, the organization of thought in the processes of problem-solving and the organization of evaluation in the process of choice, while related to functional activities, cannot be understood simply as parts of functional systems. They have, rather, an independent and integral existence. Within the given frame of functional organization, whether a family, a government, or a university, different systems for the organization of thought in problem-solving and different systems for the organization of values and evaluation in choice may be equally admissable. Algebra, calculus, computers, or other techniques for the organization of thought are used in many functional activities, but nevertheless they have an independent logic of organization and a dialectic of development apart from any of the functional activities in which they are used.

Cultural and Cognitive Systems. There are, then, systems for the organization of values and evaluation in the process of individual and group choice, and systems for the organization of information, observation and thought in the process of individual and group problem-solving. The former are called here *cultural systems.* The latter are called *cognitive systems.* Though related to functional organization, cognitive and cultural systems possess a rationale, a *modus operandi*, a coherence and a continuity that is independent of functional activities.

More specifically, a *cognitive system* is defined as a coherent set of ideas, including possibly concepts, theories, analytic techniques and systematized bodies of information interdependent and related as a process of problem-solving.

A *cultural system* is defined as a coherent set of interdependent values related together as a way of evaluation and choice, including the means of their expression and communication, and possibly including a means for the challenge, the establishment, and the disestablishment of values.

Interdependence of Systems. The effectiveness of functional systems [1] will always depend on the skills and motivation, that is, on the cognitive and cultural systems of participants. Conversely, the experience of functional activities feeds back into the development of culture and cognition. But the culture and cognition that evolves in the response to the problems of a particular social function cannot be confined to that set of functional activities alone. The values of a culture and the skills of cognition belong not to a particular functional system. They are a part of the individual, who participates in many functional systems and who spreads his outlook and his knowledge among other individuals, and who applies them in different functional activities.

The individual has a psychological need for coherence in his values and his ideas. Where the values he accepts, derived perhaps from the experience of divers systems, are in conflict, where the information he uses is incongruous, where the ideas he accepts are contradictory, then inner tensions tend to develop, pressuring the individual to find the means to integrate and to harmonize the diversity of the cognitive and cultural systems to which he is exposed.

Cognition and Cognitive Systems. Philosophers (who have their own peculiar systems of cognition) frequently philosophize on the nature of cognition. Here is one, for example, suggesting some of its possible dimensions.

A sense of spatial immensity, in its greatness and its smallness, disarticulating and spacing out, within a sphere of indefinite radius, the orbits and objects that press around us;

[1] A young wag suggests that since this chapter introduces a very considerable new vocabulary, there should be appended as a memory device the following table of examples:

SOCIAL GOAL:	A Chicken in Every Pot.
SOCIAL TASK:	Growing chickens.
FUNCTIONAL SYSTEM:	Modern, all electric, free-enterprise chicken farm.
CULTURAL SYSTEM:	Antivegetarianism.
COGNITIVE SYSTEM:	Poultry-breeding manual.

A sense of depth, pushing back laboriously through endless chains of events and measureless distances in time which a sort of sluggishness of mind tends continually to condense for us in a thin layer of the past;

A sense of number, discovering and grasping unflinchingly the bewildering multitude of material or living elements involved in the slightest change in the universe;

A sense of proportion, realizing as best we can the difference of physical scale which separates, both in rhythm and dimension, the atom from the nebula, the infinitesimal from the immense;

A sense of quality, or of novelty, enabling us to distinguish in nature certain absolute stages of perfection and growth, without upsetting the physical unity of the world;

A sense of movement, capable of perceiving the irresistible developments hidden in extreme slowness—extreme agitation concealed beneath a veil of immobility—the entirely new insinuating itself into the heart of the monotonous repetition of the same things;

A sense, lastly, of the organic, discovering physical links and structural unity under the superficial juxtaposition of successions and collectivities.[2]

Our concern is not so much with the nature or dimensions of cognition, but with its organization in relation to social action. The following brief examination of "science" is intended to illustrate what is meant by cognitive systems, and what is at issue in the analysis of their organization.

The Cognitive Systems of Science. Science can be understood as a problem-solving apparatus, but the nature of that apparatus will vary radically depending on the sort of problems to be solved and the universe from which the problem is drawn.

In some instances the problem is logical, and the solution is tautological. Objective conditions of the external world have nothing to do with correctness. Proof or disproof can relate only to internal consistency. The solutions to such problems may, nevertheless, be illuminating and subsequently useful in exploring the implications of observed phenomena. Such problems and solutions are characteristic of mathematics, but are found in all the sciences.

In some instances, the problem of science is drawn from a universe where relationships are sufficiently uniform and continuous that statements concerning it can be tested and, conceivably, refuted by derivative predictions. For this to happen, statements must be sufficiently precise, and phenomena must be reduced to quantifiable relationships in order to permit experimental prediction. Such is characteristically the case in

[2] Teilhard de Chardin, *The Phenomenon of Man* (New York: Harper & Row, 1961), pp. 33–34.

physics; but not even in physics are all relationships conceivably subject to prediction.

In some instances the problem is drawn from a universe of unique entities, where generalization must refer to phenomena that are merely analogous to each other, where relationships are discontinuous and beset by the element of creativity. The credibility of statements concerning such a universe cannot be established through derivative prediction but must rely on the observer's judgment. To facilitate this weighing of evidence by the observer (1) the statement to be evaluated should be comprehensible and its implications made clear, so that the statement and its implications can be contrasted with the phenomenon it purports to explain, and (2) the evidence pro and con should be systematically and objectively presented. Problems and statements of this sort are characteristic of sociology, history, and economics.

Science is augmented (horizontally) through the systematic accumulation of information, problem-solutions, and the consequent evolution of theories. Science advances (vertically) through the discontinuous reconstruction of its conceptual framework.

The problems of science are sometimes those of functional activity: for example, of agriculture, of fisheries, of metallurgy, of geology, of health and disease, and of war and defense. Confronting these problems augments and advances science, but the consequent accumulations and advances of science do not "belong" to any particular functional system, that is, need not be relevant only to the problems of the functional system or organization from which they derived.

Science is also augmented and advanced through the confrontation of problems that have no functional locus but which are raised by the scientist's "curiosity" and the predilections of Academia. Those advances or accumulations of science that are the consequence of such "fundamental" and "basic" research may eventually bear on the problems of functional activities.

The store of scientific information is augmented, the concepts of science are advanced and the problem-solving apparatus of science is applied through the related and interdependent work of great numbers of individuals spread over the whole world, weaving together strands through long periods of time. This requires communication—hence the techniques and instrumentalities of communication. It requires authority, and the means to establish and exercise authority. It requires that records be kept, verified, stored, disseminated. It requires that oncoming generations be indoctrinated and trained, and hence, that changes in the cognitive system be included in education. In this sense the science cognition depends upon functional organization.

The cognitive systems of science rest on value structures: science has its cultural base. Values are required in the choice of its problems, whether this choice follows the goals of functional organizations or the curiosity of academicians. Moreover, the activities of science are costly, involving complex equipment and facilities and engaging the efforts of men of high ability. These costs must be paid. Hence, the science cognition must be valued not only by those who perform the research, but also by the outsiders who pay the bill. Emphasis on publication, criteria in evaluating achievement, probity in communication, the glorification of scientific revolutions: all are the expression of a cultural system.

To recapitulate:

1. Depending on the universe of relationships from which problems are drawn, the cognitive systems of science will differ in analytic techniques, in their method of establishing credibility, and in their mode of expression.

2. Science accumulates and advances through its confrontation with problems. These problems are set by reference to the needs and goals of functional organizations external to science, or to the intrinsically valued goals of academic science.

3. The accumulation, advancement, and application of science is a group activity, which requires functional organization.

4. Choice between alternative avenues of scientific inquiry, the public or private support of scientific activities, the code that governs the behavior of the individual scientist and his relations with his group are all the expressions of a cultural system.

The Practical and the Traditional Cognitions. How do the "sciences" compare with those "practical" cognitions that have come to be taught as engineering, business administration, home economics, scientific farming, stenography, etc.? These latter cognitions, of course, vary enormously in their complexity and significance. But generally, compared to the cognitive systems of science, they are (1) more closely integrated with and specifically dependent for their development upon functional activities, (2) less oriented than science toward the development of a problem-solving apparatus as an objective of intrinsic worth, and (3) more oriented than science toward the assimilation and mastery of established practices.

Frequently these practical cognitions do not go beyond the continuous assimilation and consequent perpetuation of established practice. Systems of cognition designed only to perpetuate themselves intact will be called here "traditional."

Patterns of Culture and Choice. It is not possible to answer the question *What ought to be?* or *What should be done?* without explicitly or implicitly relying on a value premise. "Ought" is a statement of purpose, and purpose asserts a value. That which should be done can be set apart from that which should not be done only by recourse to a table of values. It is not possible to choose without value judgment.

If values are given, then, conceivably, the scientist can discover the way to their optimal realization through logical analysis and through the empirical comparison of hypothesis with observation. When, however, there is not an accepted table of values from which to start, but where the problem is to formulate a table of values or to choose between alternative paths indicated by different values, then the apparatus of science becomes irrelevant. The sum and substance of scientific cognition—statements consistent with the phenomena they purport to explain—provide no means to answer the questions: What is good? What is best? What is worth doing? This fact is perennially troublesome to social scientists who would like to guide social policy without transgressing the clear secure lines of scientific cognition. Alas, we cannot.

Our task, at this juncture, is not to formulate a table of values but simply to understand value structures and the process of choice as these exist.

Everywhere around us, policies are formulated and choices are made that imply some scale of values. Such choice cannot be understood as the result of a random distribution of psychological proclivities and reasoning capacities. There are marked patterns in the configuration of choice that vary from community to community, from social class to social class, from nation to nation. The long continuity of these variations in the patterns of value-related activities can be explained only as the reflex of cultural systems that are inculcated and perpetuated among groups from generation to generation. Preference map and consumption propensity are not the hard-core ultimates of social choice. They are themselves expressions of cultural systems that remain to be explored and explained.

The Interdependence of Culture and Cognition. If values are to be expressed as goals, if goals are to be supported by policies, strategies, and action, this must be done in terms of some conception of men and of society and, sometimes, of the physical universe. Therefore, the systematic articulation, propagation, and perpetuation of any cultural system necessitates the association of that cultural system with some cognitive system. Only within the cognitive frame can there be deduced the implications for behavior and policy of the postulated values. Only within a cognitive frame can the consequences of such behavior and policy be anticipated and a strategy of value-based action be designed.

Often the value basis of individual behavior, of group activity, and of national policy can only be inferred. Sometimes, however, a cultural system is laboriously elaborated and perpetuated by an institutional organization. When this occurs, the association of the cultural and the cognitive is made explicit. For instance, in order to express a system of values as a strategy of revolutionary action, Marxism formulates a cognition of historical process, of group motivation, and of comparative economic and political organizations. Classical economics expresses the value system of utilitarianism in the form of an apologia for status and of *laissez faire* through a cognitive frame subsuming economic organization, individual motivation and the determinants of personal satisfaction. Christianity has formulated (or evolved within) a cognition of history, of the human spirit, of the cosmos, and within that frame has articulated not only articles of faith but also codes of behavior.

Demonstrably, there is an interdependence of the cognitive and the cultural. Values must always be expressed through a system of cognition. And to apply any cognitive system requires a cultural substructure.

The Inertial Force of Culture. The cognitive systems of the individual, whereby he organizes his observations and resolves his problems, are based for the most part on the acceptance of authority. As a general rule, he does not independently formulate a conceptual framework for the organization of his observations. Rather he accepts the authority of the conceptual framework, and, for the most part, the "factual" content of that framework, as these are passed on to him. He does not resolve his problems as much by independent inquiry as by seeking out authoritative guidelines and precedent. So also the cultural choices of the individual are usually based neither on genuine evaluation on his own part nor even on his consciousness of values, but rather on the inertia of social habit and the acceptance of precedent. While all social behavior and private action are expressions of values, the individual, and, for that matter, the group or the society, rarely make a true value judgment. In selecting his breakfast, in picking his clothes, in deferring to his wife, in supporting a mistress, in sending his children to college, in attending the naval reserve, in his effort to "get ahead," in the church he attends and the vote he casts, the individual is likely to be reflecting the values with which he has been inculcated. In this sense, his choice is nominal. It is rather a conditioned reflex to a culture embedded below the surface of consciousness.

How a Culture Changes. Yet, occasionally, individuals or groups are forced, always under conditions of stress and tension, to make a genuine choice of values. As a consequence, cultural systems change. This may happen for various reasons.

1. Different values or different systems of value which imply contradictory responses may coexist, for instance, Christianity and Nationalism. These contradictions generate conflicts within a community and tensions within the private psyche that can be severe enough to expose the value substructure to conscious choice and reformulation.

2. While values cannot be disproven by logical demonstration or by reference to observed phenomena, the cognitive system with which the value structure is associated, and through which values are expressed in social choice and in imperatives for personal behavior, can be challenged as illogical or as inconsistent with observed phenomena and event. Sometimes the cognitive framework coupled with a given cultural system comes to appear so incongruous in the light of social experience, and so much in conflict with other established cognitive systems, for example, science vs. the traditional religions, that the disparity forces the cultural system along with its cognitive framework into the light of conscious reexamination and choice. The result may be the abandonment of values or the reinterpretation of given values in the frame of a transformed cognition.

3. Functional systems have their cultural base. Prevailing values provide the motivation for functional activity, define the prerogatives of functional authority, and determine the form of interpersonal behavior between the participants of functional organizations. When those functional systems work badly (when wars are lost, when national power diminishes, when economic growth lags and poverty is endemic), dissatisfaction and tension may mount as a consequence, finally forcing a conscious examination of the cultural content of functional organization and thereby permitting a restructuring of values.

Cultural-Cognitive-Functional Unities. Where individuals are engaged in the same functional activities and participate in the same functional organizations, their values and their cognition will have been shaped in the same universe of experience. Conversely, the existence of a community of culture and cognition provides a basis for integral functional organizations and for the development of functional links since goals are shared and communication and association are facilitated. Hence, there is a tendency for functional interdependence to parallel the ties of culture and of cognition, or rather functional interdependencies tend to produce and to be produced by a common culture and the shared cognition.

Cultural-Cognitive-Functional Disparities. Cultural-cognitive uniformity need not coincide with functional interdependence. Disparate cultures and cognitive systems may exist at the same functional nexus. Indeed, disparate and conflicting cultures and cognitive systems may be the product of the same functional activity. This will be so *when* the various roles implicit in the given functional organization impose upon those who play those roles a distinct and different universe of experience, *and when* groups are fixed and immobile in those roles. Then those groups set apart in different roles in the same functional system must, as a condition of the individual's success or survival, come to acquire a distinctive outlook, skills, knowledge, and values. Thus Marx found a conflicting culture and cognition dominating proletariat and bourgeoisie, reflecting their different roles in a given functional system. According to Marx, this cultural disparity between proletariat and bourgeoisie must eventually be resolved through a change in the form of functional organization.

Where cultural divergency develops through the experience of different roles in a given functional organization, for example, the gulf between officers and men, between landowners and tenants, between husbands and wives, the consequent interdependence of culturally diverse groups creates the danger of "domination" by one over the others. This "domination" means something other than exploitation. It means rather that the policies that control functional activities in which different groups are associated, and the direction that such activities are given, are in accord with the values and outlook of some but not all participating groups. The problem of domination between functionally related groups is likely to be particularly acute when cultural divergence is not only the consequence of differences in roles, but reflects also a different conditioning by history and physical environment. Such is the domination associated with "colonialism."

Society as a Nexus of Systems. Through the common participation in a functional system, individuals interrelate and depend upon each other in the achievement of private or of shared purposes—as members of families and neighbors, as politicians and citizens, as professors and students, as priests and worshippers, as officers and soldiers, as buyers and sellers. These functional ties can be more or less intense, more or less extended. They can be fixed and permanent (as they are in certain political systems) or fluctuating and short-lived. *Society will be understood here as the condition of functional interdependence.*

It is not only functional systems that link individuals. They are also bound together by their shared systems for the organization of thought and of choice inasmuch as these facilitate communication and produce a sense of community. Hence, the "condition" of society is also created through sharing elements of cultural and cognitive systems. Like those of functional interdependence, the binding elements of culture and cognition are more or less numerous, more or less intense, affording multiple layers of communication and community.

Society is a condition of functional interdependence, supported by uniformities or similarities of culture and cognition. Society, therefore, is a matter of degree; there can be more or less of society, depending on the density and intensity of cultural, cognitive, and functional ties.

Imagine a huge sheet of paper showing the distribution of the world's population, as it exists in space. On that paper lines are drawn from individual to individual, thicker and darker depending on the intensity of their relationship, marking interconnections in functional systems and the sharing of the elements of culture and cognition. Every functional organization would impose its web, layer upon layer, until the network covered the world. Parts of the great chart would be almost white in the absence of functional interconnections. Other spaces would be various shades of grey. Here and there the lines of relationship would be so numerous and intense that they seem to be shapes of solid black. A topography thus drawn would show the various degrees of intensity in which the condition of "society" exists. The darker configurations might be marked out as "societies."

Given the dense functional relations of a "society," where individuals are subject to the same pattern of influences and are shaped by the same universe of experience, there would tend to arise, as a characteristic of that particular society, a dominant system of culture and cognition integrating or encompassing subordinate systems. This dominant culture-cognition, acting so to speak as the language of the realm, evolves as a consequence of the need of the rational individual for a psychological equilibrium. Rational beings, associating at the various functional levels of the school, the family, the factory, and the church, and confronted with the diverse value and cognitive requisites of these different functional systems, have the need to "set things straight" for themselves. They try to do this by such synthesis and selection as might harmonize the values and render consistent the cognitive elements on which their minds have fastened. Moreover, an outlook and a set of values that dominate a society provide that society with important functional advantages, in the common points of reference and criteria for choice required for effective communication and harmonious social behavior. Presumably therefore there tends to emerge a dominant cultural and cognitive system under the pressure of social forces also, which are generated by this need for social harmony and ease of communication.

Inasmuch as all men are functionally interdependent and share elements of cognition and culture, there is an all-inclusive or world society. Within the world society there is a European society. Within the European society there is a French society. Each successive society is in this instance marked by denser functional interdependence and a greater uniformity of culture and cognition, and hence constitutes a closer approximation to the condition of "society."

The Changing Topography of Society. A true topography of society would not be static, but rather would be a picture in motion. Functional organizations are created and vanish, extend or contract. The configuration of functional interconnections correspondingly changes. Ideas are born, evolve, and spread, drawing individuals into new communities of cognition. Values are preached, accepted, rejected, relating or separating man and man by the ties of cultural systems. Where roles are differentiated and social immobility prevails, participation in the same functional system may give rise to different and conflicting cultures and cognitions. The stress and tension of these differences, breaking the bonds of domination, may result in the dissolution of functional ties, and the re-creation of functional systems. All this would change the configurations of functional, cultural, and cognitive interdependence and hence, the topography of society.

The topography of society is thus to be drawn in terms of the relationships of functional, cultural, and cognitive systems. The three are related. One may draw the others in its train, but always with leads and lags. And each expands or contracts on its own impetus, following its own dialectic, flowing in a peculiar course. Revolutionary changes in the configuration of society may be spearheaded by a change in functional systems, for example, the opening of markets or political conquests; or by change in cognitive systems, for example, the spread of Western science; or by change in cultural systems, for example, the onset of Christianity, the Renaissance, the French "Enlightenment," or what now goes by the name of "Americanization."

A Schematic Résumé Purposeful social activities are always organized in some variation or combination of four basic "functional systems," each with a distinct *modus operandi.*

FIGURE 24

Functional Systems

						For example—the organization of:
Functional	Market Political Institutional Familial	System	To Perform	Social Tasks		Production Consumption Recreation Military Defense Military Aggression Adjudication of Claims and Disputes, etc.

Related to these functional systems, necessary for their operation, but having an integral existence apart from functional activity, and capable of developing independently of functional organizations, are (1) *cultural systems* for evaluation and choice, and (2) *cognitive systems* for the provision of information and for the resolution of problems within parameters of accepted values or value-based choice.

FIGURE 25

Social Systems

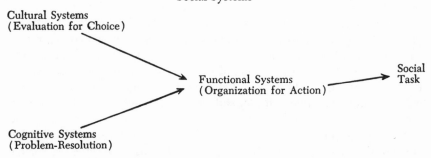

A given functional system will be more or less appropriate for the particular social task. Efficiency in waging war, rearing and acculturating children, growing wheat, or producing steel will each probably require different functional systems.

Not *any* cultural system serves to motivate and activate the efficient and progressive operation of a given functional organization. Not *any* cognitive system would serve to solve the problems implicit in a given functional organization. There can be no random assortment of social systems and social tasks. Cultural, cognitive, and functional systems and social tasks will be more or less compatible; only certain combinations will "work."

The individual and the designated group of individuals are involved in a complex of different tasks, participate in different functional systems, adhere to different cultural and cognitive systems, and seek various goals. These co-existing goals, tasks, and systems will be more or less compatible. The incompatibility of the various cultural and cognitive systems which may be concurrently accepted and used by the same individual or group constitutes a perennial source of tension, conflict, and social change.

A culture, that is, the complex of cultural systems operative for any designated group, affects that group's choice of goals and supplies its motivation for functional activity. The configuration of culture may be a source of conflict or a basis of effective communication. In these ways the culture influences the efficacy of functional organization. The relationships between culture and functional activities are illustrated in Figure 26.

Cognition, that is, the complex of cognitive systems operative for any designated group, relates to the specifics of the social task, say, tropical agriculture, and also to the capacity to organize decision-making and action in a particular sort of functional system, say, centralized planning. Cognition to a very significant degree determines the range open to social

FIGURE 26

Culture and Functional Activity

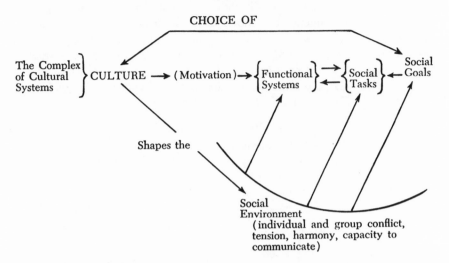

choice and hence influences the choice of goals, tasks, and functional systems. For example, the advance of a certain science cognition opened the way to a range of choices related to atomic warfare and to the peaceful use of atomic energy. These relationships between cognition and functional activity are illustrated in Figure 27.

FIGURE 27

Cognition, Social Tasks and Goals

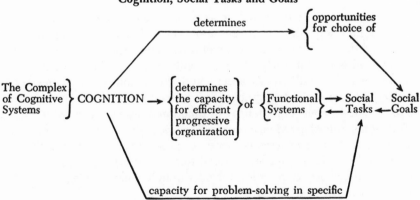

The components of social action are interdependent and instrumental in shaping or creating each other. Objective circumstances create the range of opportunity; social opportunity relates to the choice of goals; goals define tasks; tasks lead to the development of functional systems. Existing functional systems partly determine the range of social opportunities, and hence influence the choice of goals and the selection of tasks: in this way a strong army provides the opportunity for military aggression. A culture and a cognition may be required for the effective operation of particular functional organizations, and the experience in a given functional organization promotes particular values and knowledge. These "inputs and feedbacks" are illustrated in Figure 28.

FIGURE 28

Inputs and Feedbacks in Social Systems

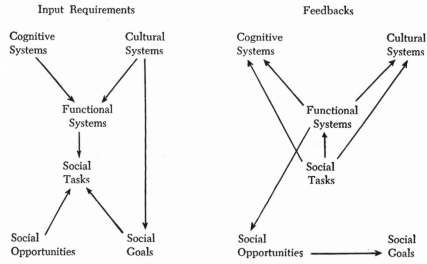

A *society* cannot be delimited as an object. It is rather a condition of functional interdependence between individuals. Such interdependence is established through the participation of individuals in the same functional systems, and is reinforced by the uniformity or compatibility of the cultural systems that individuals accept and the cognitive capacities they have acquired. A social topography could therefore be drawn in terms of the relative frequency and intensity of functional ties between individuals.

Functional interdependence, subjecting individuals to the same universe of activity and experience, tends to generate common elements of culture and cognition. Hence the condition of society, created by functional interdependence, reinforces itself through a community of culture and the sharing of a cognition.

Given the dense interdependence of a society, with individuals interrelating at numerous levels, there would tend to arise out of the diversity of cultural and cognitive systems some integral culture and cognition or, at least, some dominant cultural and cognitive system. The pressure of the individual's need to find a personal psychological and moral equilibrium and of the group's need to find a basis for communication, discipline, and collective action would militate for the establishment of one dominant system.

However, the feedback from functional organization to culture and cognition need not give rise to integral and harmonious systems. When social arrangements tend to confine generations of individuals to the performance of fixed roles in a given functional organization, the same functional system may generate different and conflicting cultural and cognitive systems. These cultural and cognitive differences will reinforce the social immobility that created them. The participation of culturally and cognitively distinct groups in the same functional system will produce the phenomenon of *domination* (not necessarily related to "exploitation") in the choice of social goals, tasks, and organizational means. This is illustrated in Figure 29.

FIGURE 29

Role Differentiation, Cultural Conflict, Domination

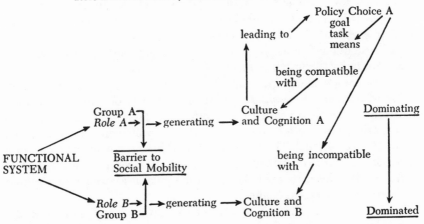

Chapter 31

Economic Revolution as a Revolution in Cognition

The Authoritative as an Element of Cognition. For each of us there are relationships, explanations, institutions, and values that are excluded from critical disputation and reason-based analysis but which, rather, are accepted as authoritative. Conversely, there are relationships, institutions, and values that the individual considers as open to question, to critical analysis, and to reasoned, deliberated change. What is and is not considered subject to choice and change will vary from person to person, depending on his social role. What the professor considers as subject to doubt and query, his students accept as authoritative. What the scientist questions, the doctor accepts; what the doctor holds open to question, his patient accepts, etc.

And also for a society as a whole, there will be those elements of cognition, culture, and functional organization that are accepted as authoritative, insulated from critical evaluation, and set outside the possibilities of systematic challenge or systematic change either by individuals, by groups, or by the instruments of collective choice.

Those values, conceptions, relationships, and forms of functional organization which, for a society, are set beyond the pale of critical evaluation or reasoned change are called here *traditional*. Those that are considered open to critical evaluation and are systematically challenged and changed will be termed *rational*. The term as it is used here is not synonymous with "scientific." What is described here as "rational" need not be planned or controlled. It suffices that it falls within the pale of reasoned inquiry and systematic, reason-based change.

For every society there is a zone of the rational and a zone of the traditional. What is contained in the zone of the rational vis à vis the zone of the traditional is of fundamental importance in determining the capacity of a society for economic development.

In the United States, for example, religion and its values or marriage and its obligations fall into the zone of the traditional. They are among the "givens" of life, accepted authoritatively, and set beyond the pale of challenge or reasoned evaluation or change. For the individual these are the "rules." Whether he decides to play fairly by the rules or not, the rules remain and he does not dispute them as such.

376

On the other hand, most Americans consider any machine or mechanism, any technique or process of production, or any business organization to be properly subject to critical evaluation, to reasoned study, to purposeful change. In the light of this rational cognition of mechanism, of technical process, and of business organization, Americans have developed the ways and means of subjecting these to systematic analysis, evaluation, and change. For some other societies, and particularly for the "developing" ones, the cognition of mechanism, of process, and of business organization fall within the zone of the traditional. They are then parameters, outside the scope of systematic challenge or change.

The Craft Economy and the Traditional Society. Insofar as the prevailing cognition serves simply to assimilate and to perpetuate established practice, the society itself is understood as a traditional society. The medieval societies of Europe were, in this sense, traditional societies. Baron, squire, bishop, priest, clerk, guildmaster, journeyman, apprentice, yeoman, villain, serf; what each did, where he did it, how he did it, his obligations and his privileges were fixed and immutable, bound into a social structure, sanctioned and sanctified by the Church, and defended as a hierarchy of privilege and a way of life.

Production was organized in the tradition of the *craft*. In the craft economy, the apprentice, taken in as a boy, was shown the position of his legs and his arms and his back, the posture and the rhythm; with hands strapped, and through a thousand repetitions, activity was driven into habit, until his fingers acquired the prescribed dexterity with the needle or with the awl. In the craft economy, a complex series of movements are mastered, skill and a feel for the work are acquired without cognition of cause and effect. The peasant, following in the ancient and venerable practices of his forefathers, observes and absorbs a way to pray and a way to plough, a way to marry and a way to harvest, a way to avoid the evil eye and a way to reap the grain and press the grape: all of a piece, mysteries are learned that he might survive, and, in turn, passed intact to his sons that they might survive.

In a traditional society such as that of medieval Europe, techniques and processes are integrated into a way of life and a structure of privilege, and are preserved and defended as such. Precisely those who have command over resources, and who could conceivably organize change, are the ones whose interests are vested in the preservation of status and whose values incline them to defend the traditional.

In order to exercise control over the craft economy it is not necessary to comprehend its processes and to master its techniques. The craft economy does not have to be managed in order to be exploited. It manages itself, following its beaten paths, moving by an ancient clockwork that has been driven into the instincts of the individual and into the habits of the group. Its rulers have only to keep each in his place and to take their due. In the medieval economy, the soldier baron and the aristocrat, possessing the temporal power, applied their reason to the strategies of war or to the affairs of State or the delights of the body or, possibly, to the salvation of the soul. Of the detail of the barnyard and the humble paths of the crafts, they remained oblivious. When those who control economic resources do not comprehend the techniques and processes for the organization of those resources, then they themselves cannot manage change in technique or in process nor will they be inclined to allow it.

The Culture of Individualism and the Shop Economy. The Industrial Revolution has been associated, naïvely, with the introduction of steam-driven machinery, but the use of a particular sort of machinery does not constitute an economic revolution. Steam-driven machinery existed as a curio in ancient Greece, and the use of steam-driven machinery in India and China for more than a century brought no economic revolution to their pre-World War II economies. On the other hand the farmer on the Israeli Kibbutz or the New Zealand sheepman, working without such machinery has long passed the threshold of the Industrial Revolution. Indeed, when economic revolution occurred in Britain, in Germany, in Japan, and in Russia it always involved quite different technologies.

Simply to use a technology is not to comprehend it, any more than to switch on or off an electric light (which, precisely, is to use a complex modern technology) means to comprehend the phenomenon of electricity. Today a workman or an engineer can and often does master a complex technique of modern technology—for instance, the programming and operation of computers—in exactly the same way as the medieval craftsman mastered his craft, by imitation, by assimilation, by rote, taking the technology as given, without acquiring either the motivation or competence to open that technology to challenge and question or to subject it to reason-based change. In such a case, no matter what degree of perfection the workman or engineer attains, his cognition remains traditional and his mastery can never be the basis for technical progress.

Certainly every economic revolution is characterized by the use of new techniques, but new techniques and technologies do not appear by magic. Techniques and technologies have themselves to be created, adapted, developed. The essential of every economic revolution is a new capacity to create, adapt, and develop new techniques and technologies. The only change that can explain the development of such capacity is a change in cognition and culture.

The classical Industrial Revolution is to be explained by a change in the system of cognition and culture. Like any significant change in the system of culture and cognition, the effects of this one were not confined to the economy but permeated all of social activity. The Industrial Revolution was part of a general assault on the traditional society by the individual in the rational pursuit of his self-interest. The values and cognition of self-aggressive individualism, defending the private right, imposing the private will, sceptical of authority and tradition, infiltrated every sphere of thought and activity: religion, science, art, politics, and economic organization, What, after all, is Protestantism other than the assertion of the individual's right to commune directly with his God; or democracy than the political means for agglomerating and reconciling individual wills and interests; or Renaissance art than the glorification of man as the individual; or the new science than a cognition that based credibility not on revealed authority but on proof acceptable to the sense and reason of any individual.

The traditional society, where the way of life and the norms of behavior were inherited and where rite and convention enveloped all activity, was transformed into a society where each was on his own, out for himself, free within the scope of his personal powers to inquire, to manipulate, to change the world for the sake of personal advantage. The sealed-in traditional system was fragmented into its atomic particles. Societies exploded with the breaking loose of individual ambitions, imagination, and reason.

The values of self-seeking individualism came to be expressed in the forms of functional organization. The economy was organized in an infinite number of discrete operations. Each was the instrument of the will and self-interest of a single individual. Each was subject to that individual's free, rational, self-interested inquiry. Each operation, and consequently the whole economy, was driven by the open-ended desire of the single individual for more for himself, more to consume, more to possess, more to display, more as a mark of worth and success. The "craft economy" of artisan and peasant became the "shop economy" of the technician-inventor and the free-wheeling entrepreneur: "shop economy" in the sense that the individual ran his own business or "shop" in his own way for his own purposes, under the imperative of market competition.

The Industrial Revolution was the change from the traditional cognition of the craft economy to the rational cognition of the shop economy. This is not to say that convention ceased to have force, or that the authority of tradition vanished. Rationality might be the rule, but many a banker and builder, farmer and philosopher, priest and politician continued to absorb the complexities of their roles by imitation; their activities continued to be ritualistic, their choices remained symbolic and traditional. Nevertheless, now the individual, rational and responsible in the domain of his shop and within the bounds of the market, spearheaded change. The watchwords in the shop economy were not authority but efficiency, not continuity but progress, not status but success. Processes lost their intrinsic value and were understood simply as the means to acquire possessions. The ancient rhythms of the crafts were stop-watched, manipulated, speeded, divided into parts, analyzed, redesigned. What had once been performed as a ritual was now broken down into its time and motion components, written out, rearranged, bargained over, standardized, communicated by blueprint and mathematical notation. Cash became the universal denominator. All activities were drawn through the market nexus. Every effort was measured and evaluated, with money costs set in perpetual balance against money gains thereby to maximize profits, to minimize costs, to acquire property.

The Industrial Revolution was thus a part of the overthrow of traditional society under the assault of a self-seeking individualism. The classical Industrial Revolution is associated with the bourgeoisie, a class of self-seekers, outside the old hierarchies of aristocrat, cleric, artisan, and peasant. In Western Europe it was indeed this class that tumbled the traditional society, and led the way to an immense reconstruction of economic organization and technology—led the way as the most aggressive, least encumbered element of a society already permeated from top to bottom with the values and outlook of rational individualism. Simply the existence of a class of self-seekers detached from the hierarchies of power and divorced from tradition-based processes is itself no guarantee of industrial revolution. Whether the self-seeking of such a class will contribute to economic progress will depend on the options that are open to it and on the orientation and cognition which it acquires.

The Industrial Revolution was manifested politically in Europe in a struggle against the feudal aristocracy that was the temporal stronghold of the traditional cognition, and against the Church that was the spiritual support of the traditional cognition. But where those who fought against the feudal power or the clerical authority did not also usher in an outlook of rational individualism (as they did not, for example, in Mexico) then, in spite of any change in functional organization, there was no Industrial Revolution. The class of bourgeois self-seekers in the economically backward societies, rather than being the advanced expression of a general social movement, is more often culturally isolated and unrooted. Faced with the antipathy of those in possession, and the apathy, primitive technical cognitions and rigid values of the mass, they are likely to find easier ways up the ladder of affluence than via the path of invention, innovation, transformation. Rather they become buyers-sellers, wheeler-dealers, monopolizers, influence-peddlers, concessionaires, speculators. When they have achieved wealth, they buy land and ape their betters, and educate their children to be lawyers, or priests, or otherwise to be comfortably placed among the hierarchs. Bourgeoisie or not, the cognition of technology remains for them among the mysteries. Economic processes stay outside the zone of the rational.

With the Industrial Revolution, rationality infiltrated the economy through the activities of the man-sized enterprise. All that went on within his factory or shop was submitted to the critical inquiry and creative imagination of the owner-entrepreneur. But what of the interaction of his shop with all the myriad of others? What of the interrelations of those who bought, sold, produced independently? These interactions were not brought within the zone of the rational. What occurred in the market vortex was not subjected to critical analysis or reasoned, deliberated change. Market coordination was accepted on faith. *Laissez faire* was the new commandment. What went on within the shop was rationally organized. All that did not fall within the reasoned inquiry of the individual in the domain of his private self-seeking was left to some beneficent but forever "invisible hand."

The Organizational Revolution. The shop economy extended the zone of the rational to activities within the scope of individual control and private self-interest, but there was no rational organization of the interaction of the vast numbers of these individually controlled entities. Another fundamental change in the scope of the rational cognition is now occurring. In the name of economic planning, or of political direction, or through the development of autonomous corporations that encompass a vast number of complex activities, the rational cognition is being extended beyond the scope of individual supervision and of private self-interest. Virtually all economic relationships are being opened to inquiry, to analysis, and to the possibility of control and systematic change. This has been called the Organizational Revolution. As its consequence, vast numbers of activities that previously were or would have been separately and independently operated are brought under an integral direction where the interaction of the parts is rationally controlled. The individual has been enveloped into the group. The characteristic entity of action, no longer the shop, is the large organization: hence, Organizational Economy.

The Organizational Revolution should not be confused with socialism or with any particular form of economic organization. In the past there have been centrally directed, politically controlled activities, such as the economies of ancient Egypt or of ancient China or of mercantilist France. In such economies, economic organization has been locked in tradition rather than opened to rational inquiry. In fact, this extension of the rational cognition is coming about in many ways and has been expressed in a variety of functional organizations. In Russia and China it is being engineered from the top downward with the rationality introduced first in the control of general relationships and in reference to collective goals. In the United States and Western Europe, emerging out of the rationality of small entities, it is occurring in the correlary growth of the large corporation and the extension of political responsibility.

The Organizational Revolution represents the extension of the rational cognition to economic activities and effects that were before left outside of it. But that they are open to inquiry does not mean that all significant phenomena are understood or even recognized and taken into account. Far from it. We are only on the periphery of a comprehension of the ways in which scientific activity relates to economic growth. Creative invention and creative activity generally remain a mystery. There is still no rational accounting of the values of economic organization as a way of life, or the impact of economic organization on culture and cognition, or the balance between preferred patterns of private consumption vis à vis preferred patterns of social activity. There remains the need to go beyond the question of what individuals want to consume, to the question of how a society wants to live. Yet, what does seem clear is that neither articles of faith nor institutional barriers set any body of economic phenomena beyond reasoned inquiry. And the efforts to extend the rational cognition have brought immensely complex relationships within the scope of rational control and of systematic change.

Hence, economic revolutions appear as the successive extension of the zone of rational cognition. Each extension has signaled an increase in the power to mobilize resources for selected objectives (and in the range of objectives for which resources can be mobilized). Each extension has served to accelerate the rate of economic progress.

Organizational Techniques and the Organizational Man. The organizational economy brings vastly more complex phenomena within the scope of systematic control. Controlling these, calls for new systems of cognition, including concepts, theories and techniques related to measurement, to the processing of data and the preparation of information, to supervision and control, to communication, to decision-taking. For example, Research and Development is specific to large organization. So, similarly, are the electronic computer, input-output analysis, linear programming. All these evolved within the context of the organizational economy, and are only practicable where complex activities beyond the supervisory capacities of the individual are brought within the scope of rational control.

The economy of large organizations needs not only new cognitions. It needs a new cultural system also. It requires different values as its motivational base. In the shop economy, where the efficiency of an operation and the progressiveness of its technology automatically generated personal gain for the entrepreneur who controlled it, entrepreneurial self-interest and aggressive profit-seeking might suffice as the universal motivating force. But when key decisions are made by government officials and by the executives of great corporations, then profit-seeking can no longer provide the motivation required to insure efficiency or progress. When each is on his own in the perpetual tension and combat of the competitive market, then the code of the rugged individualist might be appropriate. Not so when the man-to-man relationship is in the nature of continuing associations, when individuals work as teams, fitted into the slots of large private or public organizations. Then, for the sake of personal adjustment and as an imperative of effective operation, a different ("other-directed") code of behavior, a different set of motivating values, a different source of discipline are required.

Implications of the Changing Culture. The organizational revolution not only brings vast numbers of hitherto autonomous activities under an integral direction, but also, in so doing, generates new systems of culture and cognition. The derivative change in cognition and culture activates new changes in functional organization. The very abandonment of the former faith that autonomous forces working within the market frame must be relied upon to serve the collective welfare has had immense consequences. It means that social goals must be articulated and that social performance must be measured against those goals. The question is now asked: what is technically feasible? and then, what has been achieved? The consciousness of the feasible has caused a rise in mass expectations. The political force of rising mass expectations has resulted in virtually a world commitment to economic growth. In the light of this commitment, political authorities take a new view of their resources. Only today has Western Europe come to consider intolerable the virtual exclusion of its laboring majorities from the advantages of advanced education, and hence, the deprivation of the societies of Western Europe of the value of the latent talents and creative initiatives of the mass of their peoples. The effort to harness those latent energies and abilities to the goals of economic growth confronts the traditional imperatives of status and hierarchy. Under new pressures, the old forms give way and the old institutions are reshaped; consequently the well-ordered societies of Western Europe are breaking out of their former "closed," self-renewing structures to become open-ended. They take on an unprecedented dynamism. In other parts of the world, an even more explosive change has been triggered.

Summary. Within the framework of Chapter 30, which conceived of society as the interaction of interdependent functional, cultural and cognitive systems, this chapter explains economic revolutions as the consequence of cultural and cognitive change. Prior to the Industrial Revolution, a traditional cognition assimilated and perpetuated processes and techniques. A traditional culture perpetuated the structures of roles, powers, and privileges as authoritative, beyond tampering by reason and intrinsically valued as a way of life. The Industrial Revolution transformed all this. The culture became centered upon the values of private gain and individual self-fulfillment. The craft economy was displaced by the shop economy where all that fell within the scope of the individual self-seeker's control was opened to reasoned challenge and systematic change. But in the shop economy interactions between self-seeking individuals, coordinated in the market vortex, were excluded from the zone of the rational. Bringing whole processes of production and distribution, including the interaction of man-sized operations, within the scope of critical challenge and control constituted the organizational revolution. The characteristic entity of choice and action becomes a large organization, beyond the scope of self-interested control by any single individual.

The cultural-cognitional change that underlies an economic revolution will necessarily be expressed in other functional activities as well. Economic revolution will be accompanied by a correlary change in other functional systems, and by a general transformation of the social environment.

Chapter 32

The Revolutionary Leadership

Elites. By an elite is meant a group participating or attempting to participate in some functional system, differentiated from other participants by
a culture and cognition that orient it toward and prepare it for the role of
leadership or domination in that system. There are various elites, shaped
by values and competencies to dominate or control churches, armies,
businesses. Here the term will refer to those conditioned to dominate or
control political systems: *political* elites.

An elite need not be morally or intellectually superior. It is simply set
apart from the others and is united within itself by a particular culture
and cognition that prepare it for and orient it toward the assumption of
leadership and the exercise of control in some functional system. Not all
those who govern belong to elites. When governors and governed have
the same culture and cognition, so that the governors are a representative
body from among the governed, then they do *not* constitute an elite. Most
of those who have occupied the leading positions in the United States
government or in its political bureaucracy have not belonged to an elite.
The political systems of England, France, or Germany have, on the other
hand, to a considerable degree been controlled by political elites.

Political Elites and Economic Change. The purposes for which an elite
will exercise power will depend on the values to which it is committed,
that is, on its unifying culture. History suggests that political elites usually
have been committed to maintaining intact a closed social structure, to
perpetuating the form of given functional organizations, and to preserving or extending a political domain. Generally, political elites have not
been interested in the organization of economic progress, or in any sort of
social change: the brahmin caste of precolonial India, the mandarins of
the Chinese Empire, the "mandarins" of prewar France, the British Establishment never savored innovation.

There have also been *revolutionary elites,* committed not only to
achieve control of a functional system but also to use such control in order
to effectuate fundamental social change. Such change has usually been
conceived as a single, once-and-for-all transformation; so disposed were
the Federalists, Free-Masons, Jacobins, Fabians, Communists, Fascists.
Nor are revolutionary elites always political. For example, the Jesuits in

their time sought to reconstruct Catholic society, and in early Hispanic America they set in motion an abortive economic revolution among the Indians.

The Culture of the Governed. The capacity of an elite to organize change depends not only on their own values and competencies, but also on the culture of those whom they govern or through whom they govern.

Even the exercise of coercion depends on the values of those who constitute the instrument of coercion. In 1917 the ancient edifice of the Czarist State vanished—and in an instant. The soldier refused to obey orders, and instead raised his gun and shot his officer. Many the dictator who has come to power with grandiose schemes for social betterment at the head of a victorious army that kills and destroys at his command, but, alas, will not cease to kill, loot, and destroy because he commands it to. Nor can that army be used to teach in the schools, build factories, run hospitals, or eradicate disease. The army turns out to be an enormous parasite that cannot change itself and cannot be used to change anything else. The dictator's life and death power over his subjects turns out to be no more than the power to stay on the top of the heap and to take the first and biggest bite for himself.

A leadership may formulate policies, but policies must be executed. Policies will evolve in substance and in clarity through the process of their application, or they will be distorted through the venality and ineptitude of those who are charged with their execution. What in fact will occur will depend on culture-based capacities to execute policy, to respond to authority, or to resist authority. The enormous and ominous solidarity and order of the German crowd and the self-discipline of the British are cultural proclivities that determine the scope and power of their leadership.

There are functional ties other than those which bind individuals within a political system. There are cultural and cognitive ties extraneous to political systems. These nonpolitical links shape a complex of loyalties and allegiances and determine the powers to resist a political authority. Extra-political ties among the governed will determine their capacity and inclination to resist political authority and hence will set limits within which political authority can be exercised.

External Ties of the Elite. Elites also have a variety of ties with other groups than those they govern. These may be decisive in shaping their political choice. The British, French, Portuguese, Spanish, Dutch, and Belgian administrators who, for centuries, ruled vast colonial territories and populations in Asia, India, and Latin America were bound not only to those they governed. They were also tied by functional dependence and culture and cognition to their "home" society. These prior ties and obligations handicapped them in their capacity to promote economic development in the societies they governed. Communist elites, controlling national political systems, are tied functionally and by a shared cognition and culture to international Communism. During Stalin's regime particularly, they were painfully drawn by this relationship along paths other than those they would have followed as national leaders. Quite aside from functional interdependence, the elites of developing countries have been strongly bound to the values and outlook of foreign societies because their education was dominated by the culture and cognition of those societies. For example, the revolutionary elite of Latin America in the nineteenth century were dominated by the thought of Western European philosophers and economists. They saw the world through the eyes of Comte, Locke, Adam Smith, and Bentham. With a cognition and values derived from the specific circumstances and experience of Western Europe and North America, they often failed to see the realities at home. Benito Juarez exemplified the tragic consequence of this in Mexico, and his case will be examined later. The same holds true for the elites of Africa, Asia, and Latin America who conceive their societies through the cognitive frame of Marx-Leninism, or of Keynes and his disciples.

Governors and Governed. Whatever the culture and cognition of those who govern, and whatever the culture and cognition of those who are governed, the capacity for social change will also depend on the rapport between the two. This, in turn, will depend on the following:

1. *The acceptability to the governed of the goals to which a leadership is committed.* It may be possible to terrorize a population into obedience; but obedience may not be enough. When fundamental reconstruction requires creative effort on a broad front as it ordinarily must for economic development, it is then necessary to tap the enthusiasm and support of a substantial part of the population.

2. *The viability of the dialogue between leaders and led.* In order that leaders and led may communicate effectively they must share a cognition that gives their words a common meaning and their experience a common frame of reference. A dialogue between leaders and led needs positive motivation and an absence of the fears, deferences, resentments, and considerations of status that stand in the way of conversation. A distinguished American sociologist, after years of work in rural India, analyzed the cause of the failures of Indian development in a phrase: "They don't speak up." He meant that subordinate Indian officials didn't answer their superiors back. They took orders and kept silent. Then how would the superior ever learn from the experience of the subordinate? If the word moves one way only, as an order, from top downward, from center outward, then the cognition of those who formulate the rules cannot be regenerated, extended, and adapted to the needs and the real circum-

stances of action through the experiences of those who apply the rules and who (alone) can know their weakness and incompleteness. Only if there is such a dialogue can there be a feedback of experience. And only if there is a feedback of experience can doctrine become a working and, eventually, a workable hypothesis that changes, adapts, evolves.

3. *The extrapolitical ties between leadership and led.* The lines of political allegiance and loyalty will depend on shared values and on functional ties between leaders and led. These ties may transcend those of the political system and its objectives: the ties of "nationalism" bind leaders and led in a variety of political systems and circumstances. The strength of extrapolitical ties may depend on the manner by which a leadership is recruited. Sometimes, as in communist governments and in the Catholic Church, those who govern are to a considerable extent recruited from among the governed. In the colonial administrations, the leadership elites were recruited from another community entirely. Under condition of caste and class, a political elite tends to be drawn only from a select group with a fixed place in the social hierarchy.

The acceptability of the goals of leadership, the viability of the dialogue between leadership and led, and the strength of the extrapolitical ties between them: these three conditions for an effective leadership will be most fully satisfied when government is *not* by an elite but rather by governors recruited from among the ranks of the governed who represent and are representative of the governed, and where the political dialogue is reinforced through periodic election. Such government rests on the social consensus; hence the permissible scope of change must be within the limits of that consensus. Revolutionary change, in these circumstances, must come about through a prior basic reorientation of the consensus. The source of such a reorientation is likely to be outside the political system entirely.

Economic Development as a Social Revolution. Prior to the Industrial Revolution, the outlook and ideology of rational individualism had permeated Western Europe and eroded the traditional cognition and culture of feudalism. In developing societies this need not have happened. In the Industrial Revolution, the bourgeoisie of Western Europe manifested in the organization of enterprise that rational individualism which pervaded their societies. They grew politically strong and rich through the industry they created. With that strength they restructured society, reformulated the dominant culture and cognition, and struck down the feudal elite to gain for themselves full freedom to recreate the industrial technology. But in developing countries, a bourgeoisie, equipped by ambition and cognition to generate progress and growth, need not exist.

The communist revolutions of Russia and China were in effect struggles between elites for the control of a political system. These were not class struggles, but palace coups. In each instance, the sought-for prize was control of a political system that had shown itself over centuries capable of sustained, energetic, and coherent action in response to the directives of the centralized political authority. In developing economies, however, the task is not to capture the driver's seat of a political system. What use to capture the driver's seat when the wheel is detached, the crankshaft broken, and the motor dead? The task is to build the vehicle. In those societies, the system of centralized direction works badly. It sometimes doesn't seem to work at all. Directives from the center are disobeyed, muddled, or relegated to bureaucratic limbo. Communication fails. The collective purpose sinks into the collective apathy.

In the past, revolutionary elites went into battle with the cry of "liberty" or "justice." There is certainly injustice in developing economies, but these inequities are drowned in a vast and general impoverishment that reflects the sheer technical-social incapacity to produce. Under the yoke of such poverty, the values of individual liberty are dubious. The central objective, less moral, more practical, is to achieve a capacity for coherent social action and progressive functional organization.

In the past, social revolutionaries faced disciplined and conscious opposition on the part of the vested powers within their society, and the emnity of powerful nations outside it. In the case of developing countries, the opposition to the revolution of development is equivocal, and those who seek fundamental change may even hope for support and assistance from the great powers outside. Rather than the opposition of vested powers, the new revolutionary faces the incongruities of a cultural-cognitive patchwork, apathy, and traditional values and outlook that, while held in low repute in those societies, are nevertheless pervasive and powerfully inert. Pressing for development, as a raw force seeking its outlet, is a rise in mass expectations of a richer, more human life.

Revolutionary Elites and Economic Development. Does the revolution of economic development require a revolutionary elite? Economic revolution may occur autonomously, generated by individual self-seeking. But failure of such autonomous revolutions to occur hitherto suggests that in these societies appropriate conditions must be created before any economic revolution can occur autonomously. Or, otherwise, development must rely on the collective force of centralized political-direction. Either remaking culture, cognition, and functional organization to permit development to occur through spontaneous private initiatives or organizing development from the political center requires basic social reconstruction. Who will perform that task of social reconstruction?

For each developing society, the circumstances are unique. The problems implicit in the achievement of a social and economic revolution are always new and complex. The cognition required to conceive and to formulate these problems and to find the means of solving them cannot arise through the performance of established social roles. That cognition will evolve only if it is sought for in the deliberate pursuit of fundamental change. There must be those who pursue such change, marked off from the rest both by their dedication and by the cognition that they acquire in consequence of their effort. In order to achieve a revolution, those who seek it must find the means to act coherently and cohesively as a political force. Dedication to the goals of development, a cognition shaped to the tasks of development, and a capacity for unified political action are precisely the ingredients of a revolutionary elite.

The revolutionary elite may develop within the established political structure, as it did in Japan; but more often those who exercise political power in traditional systems are committed to the status quo and will resist change. Possibly a revolutionary elite can be supported by majorities, as perhaps it could be today in India. More often, there is no outlet for the expression of a public opinion, nor any sufficiently conscious and articulated social consensus upon which to base a coherent policy of social change. Then it may become one of the tasks of social reconstruction to develop the democratic outlet and to articulate and orient the consensus.

In any case, leadership is probably required for economic development. Those who undertake this fundamental reconstruction can hardly represent existing interests and current opinion. They must be differentiated from the rest by their commitment, and in consequence of that commitment by their acquired cognition of ways and means. In this sense the revolutionary leadership must be exercised by an elite. If it is to be effective as a political force, that elite must be unified and organized as an instrument of practical action.

The Destiny of a Revolutionary Elite. Consider the prospect of the one who commits himself to the achievement of social revolution, and, especially, in the early and critical days, before change has been set in motion, before success is in sight. Probably he will be isolated from his society since he cannot support that society as it is, but he serves rather a distant vision of what society should become. Despite his gentle manner and intention that all should benefit, he will certainly encounter resistance and hatred. Significant change always discomforts some, and it is precisely the richest and most powerful who have least to gain and who are most threatened by economic development and its requisites. But also, throughout society, for all those who possess a petty privilege or have a vested interest in status, the dangers of change are clear and its threat direct, while its benefits are as vague and nebulous as are all promises of things not yet known.

Poverty, danger, and frustration are the likely lot of those who set out on the path of economic revolution. Exhausted and empty-handed, they will probably be destroyed by the enemies of revolution or by the revolution itself, or else be cast aside and forgotten when the tides move through the breach they helped to make.

The Prophetic Vision. What is required to induce the individual to put aside self-interest and take upon himself this long, difficult, materially unrewarding task of social revolution? And what is required in order to unite the one with others into an effective revolutionary elite? There is needed, first, the common goal, a vision of what is sought for. That vision must strike sufficiently deep moral or emotional chords to incite men's dedication. Without the sense of a goal and without the emotional attachment to that goal, there can be no revolutionary elite.

Value-based, the goal of revolution carries an implicit system of evaluation. The revolutionary elite needs a shared system of values as a basis for unified choice.

Given its goal, the elite needs a conception of how to reach that goal. The vision of the world to come must be framed in a cognition of the world that is, since, in order to act, it is necessary to understand the field of action and the forces arrayed in that field and the way to mobilize support and to avoid defeat. This means that there is needed some common understanding of human motivation, of group interest, of social organization.

The revolutionary follows an uncharted path; his end is out of sight. Each turning may be the wrong one. The way ahead is long, stumbling, full of failures. Goals and anticipations have a way of growing insubstantial, the hope of change and betterment has a way of fading, against the persisting, omnipresent solid reality of a society as it is. In this long blind struggle, in its trials of frustration and failure, the revolutionary elite needs hope. It needs faith. It will better hold to its path if it believes that ahead there is a promised land; it will be sustained in its efforts if it is convinced that, in spite of the temporal powers who stand against it, God or Science or History or Humanity or some other named force is on its side.

A moral vision, a conception of the world within which that vision is to be made concrete, a faith: who can give these but the prophet? Perhaps every revolution needs its prophets, and revolutionaries need a sort of religion.

The Purifying Fires of Zeal. There are many prophets we choose to call false prophets, whose visions we find abominable. And there are also revolutionary visions we abhor. But, for all religions and for all revolutionary movements, no matter how lofty their aims and how exalted their values, dedication nevertheless may become fanaticism. Cognition may rigidify into dogma. Independent thought and human sympathy, all doubt of the faith, every concept that does not fit into the accepted cognition, indeed, everything that does not move as the automata of doctrine may be burned out with the purifying fires of zeal. When and whether this happens will depend on the prior intermingled cognitions and cultures upon which the new faith has been implanted. It will also depend on tensions and fears, deriving from fissures within the movement or from enemies without. Such threats drive the revolutionary ranks together in the discipline of the cornered and besieged.

Communism and Nationalism as Credos of Economic Development. But if, indeed, economic development needs its revolutionary elite and if that elite needs its faith and vision, what faith and vision are offered? *Nationalism* and *Communism:* almost nothing else.

Nationalism is more a passion than a vision of what should be or a cognition of what is. Of itself it provides no guidelines to the achievement of economic development, and it offers as much diversion from as incentive to the tasks of social revolution. As a credo, it adds to those blind, collective egoisms that are already a curse of modern civilization. Yet it may succeed in mobilizing the efforts of a society to end domination by those of an alien culture and after that, in inducing the efforts to render the nation prestigious and powerful vis à vis the others.

Communism provides a ready-made strategy for the seizure of political power and even for the organization of economic development. It contains a prophetic vision and a revolutionary faith. It offers the revolutionary a solidarity with like-minded, similarly dedicated men throughout the world. On the other hand, the classical Marxist cognition, conceiving a colossal struggle between a revolutionary bourgeoisie and an established aristocracy on the field of an obsolete feudalism or between a disciplined proletariat and an established bourgeoisie on the field of an overripe capitalism, could scarcely be more irrelevant to the problems and realities of developing societies. The acceptance of the communist credo involves the revolutionary elite in the dangerous and costly struggle between the great powers, and in the debilitating tensions of an ideological conflict that is quite irrelevant to its task of economic development or its achievement of social change.

Summary. The so-called "developing societies" are those that have not demonstrated a capacity for a normal rate of technological progress and economic growth, and that, presumably, do not yet possess that capacity, either through spontaneous individual choice and action or collective political direction. It is conceivable in some instances that a chance event, for example, decolonization, may remove barriers that previously blocked the processes of economic growth. More likely, progress requires a fundamental reconstruction of the functional, cultural, and cognitive systems that constitute the developing society. It cannot be assumed that the existing consensus is in any way relevant as a guide to this task, nor that those who currently possess political or economic power are or can be motivated to promote that reconstruction.

In its external circumstances and as a complex of cultural, cognitive, and functional systems, each developing society is unique. Therefore it cannot be known a priori what the barriers or significant problems for its development are, or how to counteract them. But this much, certainly, can be known: (1) no particular society's problems for development will be understood unless there are those who, confronting existing circumstances, seek to understand them; (2) a solution to those problems will not be found unless by those who, having understood what the problems are, try to solve them; (3) these solutions will not be applied unless there are those who, having seen the way to act, organize themselves to formulate and to implement policy.

The problem will not be solved without a problem solver, which is to say that revolutionary transformation of the economy will not take place without a revolutionary elite. A revolutionary elite is the first requisite for economic development. The revolutionary elite, in their difficult, lonely, and materially unrewarding task, require a vision that can inspire and unify, a cognition of the field of action, and a faith in the rightness and final vindication of their cause. The first concern of those who would support economic development should be with the existence, strength, goals, and cognition of the revolutionary elite.

Chapter 33

Economic Revolution in Russia

Russia's Economic Revolution. It must be repeated that by economic revolution is not meant violent upheaval, purge, the seizure of control of the political system or a change in the form of functional organization. These may or may not be incidental to economic revolution. Economic revolution here means fundamental change in the social capacity to organize economic processes. In this sense Russia has had an economic revolution. Russia has acquired the capacity to organize highly complex technical-industrial processes efficiently and to raise productivity continuously.

Undeniably, Russia continues to have severe economic problems, in agriculture for example. Perhaps economic revolution might have been achieved, as some say, without the Communist seizure of power, without the pain and cost of bloodshed, purge, and violence. Whatever might have been, in fact the Communist elite seized power and transformed the social capacity to organize economic processes. Hence the Russian experience can illuminate the relation of a revolutionary elite to the society upon which it acts.

Revolution, According to Marx. Karl Marx and his followers developed a certain cognition of revolution:

1. Economic and social revolution moves in a fixed sequence of two successive social transformations.

2. Each involves a struggle between a dominant and a revolutionary class for control of the State, that is, for control of the political system.

3. At the onset of the transformation, the dominant class controls the political system. It exercises control in order to preserve an existing form of economic organization in which it has a favored role.

4. Technical progress and the attendant social changes make the existing form of economic organization obsolete and anachronistic. Hence the dominant class is eventually committed to resist the transformation to a new form of economic organization that is more productive or internally more harmonious.

5. That functional group which knows it will be particularly advantaged by the new and more productive form of economic organization constitutes the revolutionary class. The revolutionary class seeks to control

the State, so that through such control it can forward the transformation of the economy in accord with its "class" interest.

6. The first of the two transformations is the industrialization of the craft economy. This transformation requires the individual initiatives and the hivelike private activity of bourgeois entrepreneurs. Hence the bourgeoisie, constituting the first revolutionary class, struggles against a dominant feudal aristocracy for control of the State. Since the bourgeoisie's accumulated cognition and competence is the key to national wealth and power, they must eventually win their struggle. The bourgeoisie becomes the dominant class and clears away the anachronistic policies, privileges, and economic organization of feudalism.

7. As industrialization proceeds, the proletariat or wage laborers working in the factories of the bourgeoisie become more numerous. Eventually they constitute a majority of the population.

8. Once the economy has been industrialized the constructive task of the bourgeoisie is complete. Thereafter they exercise their power no longer to transform the economy but to exploit the proletariat who work in the factories.

9. The power of the aristocracy was based on inherited feudal privileges. These privileges were protected through the coercive force of a State controlled by aristocrats. The power of the bourgeoisie is vested in the rights of property. These rights are protected through the coercive force of a State controlled by the bourgeoisie.

10. Through the advantages that inhere in property, that is, through the ownership of the means of production, or, "capital," the bourgeoisie is able to appropriate for itself the "surplus product," (the whole value of economic output over and above what is needed to sustain and motivate the proletariat).

11. The proletariat comes to realize that if the factories were owned by the State rather than by the bourgeoisie, and if they, the workers, controlled the State, then they could take for themselves the whole product of their labors, including the lion's share presently going to the capitalist bourgeoisie.

12. Conscious of their common interest in transforming the capitalist economy into one where economic control is exercised through State planning, and where the State is controlled by themselves, the proletariat becomes the new revolutionary class.

13. Moreover, capitalism gives rise to insoluble contradictions. Extreme inequalities of wealth produce an ever-widening disparity between the capacity to produce and the propensity to consume. This causes crisis and depression. The effort to escape the dilemma of unemployment and of unused industrial capacity leads to the competition of nations for protected market outlets in the form of colonies. This brings imperialist wars

and the suppression and exploitation of colonial peoples. Nor, given the extreme decentralization of economic choice among the owners of property, can production and consumption ever be brought into rational accord. The "contradictions of capitalism" cannot be resolved except through centralized State planning, which is not compatible with capitalism.

14. Because the economic function of the proletariat is essential while that of the capitalist has ceased to be, because of the widening preponderance of the industrial workers as a proportion of the population, and because the bourgeoisie struggles to preserve an anachronistic form of economic organization subject to deepening crisis and ever more insupportable contradictions, the revolutionary proletariat must triumph in its struggle against the dominant bourgeoisie.

15. The workers would then take control of the State. The State would take control of industry, and the economy would be organized in the workers' interest. Socialism would thus be realized. Socialism, by eliminating the capitalist contradictions, would make for a less wasteful, hence, more productive economy. It would also bring "fair shares" in the distribution of income, and more harmonious human relationships. It is not, however, presumed that it would result in higher productivity or in any acceleration in the pace of technological advance.

16. At this final stage in the revolutionary sequence, all would participate as workers, and all would share fairly in the economic output. Since there was no longer a dominant class, the State would cease to be an instrument for the support of the interests of one class against that of others.

Given this Marxist cognition of economic and social revolution, it could be predicted that (1) socialism must await and follow a successful industrial revolution by the bourgeoisie; (2) that the socialist revolution requires a powerful, highly organized proletariat, conscious of its class interest; (3) that the socialist revolution could only come where capitalism was "ripe," in highly industrialized, proletarianized economies, reacting against the bitter experience of capitalistic contradictions.

Dedication or Self-Interest as the Revolutionary's Motive? Marxism, like the economics of liberalism, postulated material self-interest as the motive force of social action. Individual self-interest was identified, however, with the interest of the class to which that individual belonged. Marxist revolutionaries were a living disproof of (or an exception to) this postulate. Their way of life (dangerous, thankless, impoverished, scorned, in every way deprived) ran counter to their personal self-interest in material gain, and, since they were bourgeois almost to the man, it ran counter also to what they conceived as the interest of the class of their origin. They were not materialistic self-seekers, but dedicated men. Marx was their prophet, and his vision was as a holy revelation which they served as an end in itself.

Whatever the revolutionary fervor and ferment Marx's writings may have generated, Marx was himself a product of a time of revolutionary fervor and ferment. He was of the generation that had witnessed the great technical achievement of the Industrial Revolution, and the failure of society to realize the opportunity to provide more harmonious and comfortable lives for most men. His generation had seen the unfolding of the bourgeois power, the peak of bourgeois affluence, and a vast proletariat at the nadir of its misery. They had known the capricious impoverishment of financial panics and depression. All this produced an atmosphere of unrest and frustration and a readiness for revolutionary change throughout Europe. Marxism gave to those ready for revolutionary change a coherent and purposeful outlet. It gave them a unifying culture and a cognitive base for association and communication, a frame for the resolution of their private differences and for the formulation of a common strategy—made them, indeed, into a revolutionary elite.

Marxism put itself forward as "scientific," based not on values and sentiments, but on the hard facts, the inexorable laws of history. With these laws it claimed to comprehend the past and to predict the future. In fact, like liberal economics, Marxism was based foursquare on a value system. It discovered no inexorable laws of history. As will be seen, its most basic predictions failed.

Aside from its validity as an apparatus of analysis and social forecasting, Marxism worked wonderfully well as the cognition and culture of a revolutionary elite, supporting that elite with a sense of absolute rightness and ultimate vindication, ranging science and history on their side. The revolutionaries, coming from every country of Europe and from every corner of the world, found in Marxism a common standard, a common language, a basis for unified action.

The Russian Revolutionaries. Those who, in the late nineteenth and early twentieth centuries grouped themselves under the banner of Marxism, came from many nations and included men of many sorts. They divided themselves into sects and factions. When they went into action in their own societies—French Socialists, British Fabians, German Worker's Parties—their theories changed and their tactics varied in response to particular circumstances.

Among these European Marxists were the Russians. They were peculiarly shaped and given a distinct character by reason of the intellectual's role within and his relation to Russian society. Russia was a vast closed empire, enveloped in a religious and political orthodoxy that opposed itself to the impure and corrupted ways of the West. Yet the Russian State needed technicians and specialists, and these had to be trained in Western Europe or in Westernized institutions. So, the Russian government sponsored the education of its "intelligentsia." "No sooner," wrote one of them, "had the young elements of the old estates . . . entered into the sunlit zones of European ideology, than they broke away irresistibly, almost without inner hesitation from feudalism and inherited orthodoxy." [1]

The West European cognition and culture derived from a different universe of experience, and was related to a different universe of action than the Russians'. Just as intellectuals from the less-developed countries today are often alienated from their society by a North American or European education, so similarly then was the Russian alienated from Russian society by his European education. The French, English, Swedish, Dutch, German, or Italian intellectual was part of his society. He expressed its diverse currents of culture and cognition. But the Russian who had absorbed the culture and cognition of Western Europe saw no more with the same eyes as his people did, nor could he empathize with their outlook or share their expectations. Within or outside of Russia, the intelligentsia was a group apart, isolated yet capable of an extraordinary science and art, and of an absolute commitment to social change.

In educating an intelligentsia, the Russian government knew it was creating an opposition to itself. Hence the intellectual was suspect, was kept under continuous police surveillance and was disciplined by prison and exile. Since all political opposition was limited and harried, those who sought significant social change were driven underground. Whether its objective was free enterprise and constitutional monarchy or land redistribution or socialism, significant political opposition had to take the form of a secret conspiracy. Russian Marxism was organized, of necessity, as a conspiracy. The Marxist lived as a conspirator, hunted or driven into exile. Cut off from contact with the people, without a functional role, culturally alienated, the revolutionary intelligentsia nevertheless accepted a total and absolute responsibility for Russian society. They lived "in a terrible moral tension, in a concentrated asceticism." [2] They did not express the interests or will of any substantial segment of the Russian people, but spoke in proxy for the imagined interest of imagined classes. The Decembrists of 1825 acted in the interest of a still unborn bourgeoisie. The *Narodnicks* sought to rouse and speak for the peasantry who remained, nevertheless, mute and dumb. And now the Marxists undertook to represent a Russian proletariat who, as yet, barely existed.

[1] Leon Trotsky, quoted by Isaac Deutscher, *The Prophet Armed* (New York: Oxford University Press, 1954), p. 189.
[2] *Ibid.*, p. 189.

Marxism and the Revolutionary Intelligentsia. Marxism was alien to the Russian situation and the Russian experience. Its strategy assumed an industrial revolution which, in Russia, had never taken place. It centered on the conflict between proletariat and capitalist, when in Russia neither one was significant. But that the Marxian cognition was irrelevant to practical policy or to revolutionary tactics in Russia hardly mattered to these idealists and malcontents. Exiles, without practical responsibilities, without a public opinion as their guide, the immediate danger to their effectiveness as a revolutionary elite was that each might drift along his private path of fantasy, and their voices dissolve into a babel. To offset disintegration they needed a common vision. It mattered little what they believed so long as they shared their belief and, fanatically, undeviatingly, adhered to it. They needed common values. They needed a cognitive mechanism to grind out uniform answers to their queries and to guide them in their perplexity. They needed an absolute belief to offset all that their lives lacked of the concrete and the specific. They needed discipline. All this, Marxism gave to them. Unified in sects, they worked out their strategies for overthrowing the Czar.

After the Czar? When Czarism was overthrown? No true Marxist had a notion that socialism would then come to Russia. Socialism could only be achieved where capitalism was well-advanced, ripe and overripe with contradictions exposed, and where the proletariat was a well-organized majority or, at least, a massive minority. Socialism might come in Germany, or in England, or in France, but in Russia it could not come for a very long time. Socialism was at the end of the line. Russia was only at the beginning. That was perfectly clear, according to the inexorable laws discovered by Marx.

According to the Marxist cognition, in a preindustrial society such as Russia the State must be controlled by an aristocracy. That aristocracy would use the State to perpetuate its feudal privileges. However, industry was beginning in Russia. Hence the capitalist bourgeoisie, at the helm of the new industry, must constitute a new revolutionary class. The next step in the revolutionary sequence would be the industrialization of the Russian economy through the hivelike activities of a creative bourgeoisie. For this to happen there must be a struggle, overt or covert, between the bourgeoisie and the feudal class for the control of the Russian State. In that struggle it would be the duty of the communists to support the bourgeoisie, thus to accelerate industrial revolution and hurry things along the winding path toward a distant socialism. All this was according to the inexorable laws discovered by Marx. For many decades no Russian Marxist, Bolshevik or Menshevik, thought to doubt it.

Trotsky's Prognosis of Revolution in Russia. We mean to suggest that not the relative ripeness of capitalism but the topography of culture and cognition has determined the course of socialist revolution in Europe and Asia. Rather than by any retrospective interpretation, this point can best be established by a prognosis and prediction made more than a decade before the start of the Russian Revolution by a Marxist in the teeth of his own doctrine.

Leon Trotsky had taken a leading role in the abortive Russian revolt of 1905. The uprising was crushed. Trotsky, who was then twenty-six years old, was imprisoned to stand trial for his part in the rebellion. While he waited in the Peter and Paul fortress in Petrograd for the trial that must send him to Siberian exile or to death, he re-examined and attempted virtually to reformulate the Marxist cognition. Consider only his prognosis of revolution in Russia.

In the Marxist conception, the first phase of the revolution must be the struggle between a dominant feudal aristocracy and a revolutionary bourgeoisie for the control of the State. But in Russia, Trotsky argued, this could not happen. In Russia there was no independent aristocracy that controlled the State, and there was no revolutionary bourgeoisie that could contend for it.

Russia had no equivalent to the independent aristocracy of Western Europe, with its sense of noblesse, its unity, its habituated privilege. The Russian aristocracy was a creature of the State, with no power or roots outside of it.

What had given the bourgeoisie of Western Europe the capacity to force the aristocracy from their established positions and to recreate society was a cognition and a culture slowly wrought through the centuries, shaped, for example, in the long struggle of the individual to assert the independence of the soul in relation to its God. But of that "purifying experience" of the Reformation, or of the "crafts, guilds, municipalities, and disputes" where "crystallized the precious habit of self-government," [3] Russia had no inkling. Bourgeois capabilities in Western Europe had been formed out of the concentration of crafts and commerce in towns that became great cities. But in Russia there had never been such concentrations. The few cities and towns of Russia were not centers of manufacture or commerce but were forts, barracks, arms depots, or administrative centers of government. The crafts, under the sponsorship of the police, were scattered thinly through the villages and in the peasant cottages. There were rich men, owners of large properties in Russia, but nowhere was there a unified, creative bourgeoisie capable of revolutionary leadership.

According to the Marxist conception, the State was the creation and the

[3] *Ibid.*, p. 151.

instrument of an economic class. In Russia, said Trotsky, the State was not the creation or instrument of a class. The Russian State was a self-sufficing, self-perpetuating institution embodying values, commanding loyalties in its own right. This institution dominated all the rest. It was arbiter of thought, censor of faith, dispenser of religion. It was the mechanism of change. The State was not controlled by any class. Rather the classes were its instruments, created and fashioned to accomodate its needs. The *boyar* was its agent. The peasant was its servant. The intellectual was its scrivener. The crafts were promoted by the police. Even "capitalism appeared as the child of the State." [4]

Who Would Topple the Czarist State? All the resources and the energies of Russia had been drained by the self-sufficient, self-perpetuating institutions of the State. Yet the Czarist State had become anachronistic. Time had eroded its foundations. It could no longer perform its tasks. The Czarist State was ready to fall, but who would topple it and rule in its place?

It would not, Trotsky argued, be the Russian bourgeoisie. If they owned Russian industry, in a more basic sense it was not theirs for they had not created it. It had been designed by foreigners, introduced by foreigners with State support under State protection. The Russian bourgeoisie were not innovators and organizers but the coupon-clippers and dividend receivers. Their aim was not to open the way for a more vigorous industrialization. Security was their objective, and Czarism was their bulwark. They would not revolt, and when the State collapsed, they would not have the capacity to exercise the governing authority.

Nor could the peasants destroy the Czarist authority and rule in its stead. They were too widely dispersed to be effectively organized for the seizure and exercise of political power. Moreover, their political objectives did not go beyond appropriating the land they worked.

There remained the new-born proletariat, very few in number but highly concentrated and strategically placed, cohesive in their isolation and full of grievances. They would respond to a doctrine that expressed their unbounded discontents with the whole established order. In the name of revolutionary socialism they would support the Communist seizure of power. The Russian proletariat, Trotsky predicted, would topple the Czarist State and would provide the under-pinning of revolutionary change.

Such was his prognosis: the tiny proletariat working in the incipient industry of feudal Russia would strike down the old regime and would bring the socialists into power. The communists would first triumph not in the ripe capitalisms of Germany or England or France, but in preindus-

[4] *Ibid.*, p. 151.

trial Russia. And so it came to pass. Under the stress of war and defeat Czarism tottered. An insurrection of the industrial workers collapsed the ramshackle structure of the State. The party of the capitalist was first to inherit the political authority. Rootless, they vanished in an instant. Next came the Mensheviks, committed to eventual socialism, but, in accord with the Marxist formula, supporting a bourgeois economy and a constitutional democracy as the necessary prelude. They too were sent into quick oblivion. The Bolsheviks rode with the tide. With the support of the industrial workers, they took and they held control of the political system.

The ripe and overripe capitalisms of the West, also under the stress of war and, sometimes, of defeat, did not fall under the assault of their organized class-conscious proletariats. Marx's inexorable laws didn't work then, nor have they worked since. In Russia, the change came precisely as Trotsky had predicted, and Trotsky's prognosis was based on the unique configuration of the Russian culture and cognition.

The Power of Centralized Direction. The peculiar path of revolution taken in Russia is to be accounted for by the established primacy of the political system. Since the centralized power of the political system stood in lieu of the interests and initiatives of functional classes, revolutionary change proceeded not through class war but through the struggle of ideologies to gain possession of the seat of central power.

Through the centuries, Russia had demonstrated a prodigious capacity for collective action. That capacity endured in spite of the ineptitude or tyranny of those who exercised authority. A culture and cognition shaped to support the unconditional submission to and acceptance of the unbounded authority of the State has been explained as the consequence of historical necessity. From time immemorial the Russians have lived on the high road of conquerors, on a great plain where nature offered no natural defense, neither sea, nor channel, nor mountain range to shield the people from attack. No other Western nation was so vulnerable. From the North came the conquering Goths. From the South came Byzantium, and conquered. From the East came the Hun under Attila; came the conquering Avars; came the conquering Bolgars; came the conquering Kahzars; came the conquering Pechenegs. From the North the Vikings came and conquered. From the East came the Golden Horde of Ghengis Khan, of Tamerlane, Mongol and Tartar, conquering. From the West came the Teutonic Knights and conquered. From the South came the Turk. From the West came the French of Napoleon. And, in our time, the plains of Russia again were the scene of invasions, of endless battlefields, the world's charnel house. Russia has lasted. It is said that her survival has required the concentration of her energies and the submission of all efforts and powers to a central will.

A story that reappears in different forms in the ancient chronicles has it that the Russians rebelled under the harsh rule of the Vikings and drove their conquerors from the land. After a number of years, a delegation of Russians came to the Baltic stronghold of their ousted tyrant with the plea "Our country is large and rich. But there is no order in it. Return and rule over us." The tale is apocryphal; but whether or not it relates an event that in fact occurred, it surely tells of a self-appraisal, a self-conception, a sense of the necessity for a supreme central power, above the will and beyond the volition of those who are ruled.

The Viking conquest led to the establishment of the Kingdom of Kiev which, via the river trade with Constantinople, introduced the culture of Byzantium with its fabled autocracy. The Kingdom of Kiev existed from 840 until 1240, when it fell to the Tartars. Thence, for two centuries, Russia served the Mongol, supplying tribute in goods and gold and offering her people as slaves. During this dark age Russia was ruled by its own princes on sufferance of the Khanate. For its servility to the Khan and for its ruthlessness with its own, the House of Muscovy was made chief among the Russian princes. But when the Mongol weakened, the Prince of Moscow led the Russians against the Khan and gathered the power of the Tartar overlord around himself. So the Russian State secured itself under Ivan, called the Terrible. This schizophrenic of amazing mind and will destroyed two successive aristocracies and subordinated all classes to the crown. The whole temporal and spiritual authority was concentrated in the State and the authority of the State was possessed by the Czar.

This pattern, the collective power unbounded, the central will supreme and the energies of all the people as a tool in its hand, strengthened itself in the habit of centuries. Nothing counterbalanced the central power, neither church nor aristocracy nor the constraints of tradition. In a manner without analogy in Europe, the State power was independent and absolute. In Russia the feudal lord did not make the crown, the crown decreed feudalism and, centuries later, the crown decreed the end of feudalism. Elsewhere the power of the monarchs derived from the upsurgent vigors of the nation. In Russia, it seemed the converse. When the crown was weak, the whole people retrogressed, and the nation sank. When the monarch was strong and vigorous, the whole vast people was whipped into prodigies of achievement. Where else is to be found the equivalent of Peter the Great? By his single will he changed the mores of the people, commanded away their conventions and their manners. He marched his serf battalions into the factories and the mines and built from nothing an industry that was, at the time, second to none. Within decades, he made a landbound people into a great naval power.

The Cultural System. What was the cultural system that gave enduring force to the centralization of power in Russia? Some have suggested that it is a system wherein the individual seeks coherence in his image of the

whole, and where he demands (and hence accepts) an absolute judge
and an absolute criterion for private conduct and for collective purpose.
The absolute judge carries absolute authority. Those who demand the
absolute judgment must correspondingly will themselves to absolute
submission, and must admit an unbounded claim upon their faith and
dedication. Such a scheme of values and outlook could support neither
the partial, segmented allegiances and reciprocal limited loyalties of
Western feudalism nor rule by a consensus and the systematic compromise of individual interests that is the essence of representative
government.

Whatever the inner structure of Russian culture, it suffices here simply
to observe its demonstrated consequences: the concentration of power in
the hands of a central authority, the extraordinary capacity of the people
to respond to the demands of the central authority, and their tragic inability to resist the tyranny and depredations of that authority.

In Place of the Czar. The Czar and his agents were overthrown by the
Communists and their agents. The central authority had a new name. But
this did not alter the peoples' conception of authority, or their capacity to
resist authority, or their will to obedience. They still looked in the same
direction for the signal to collective action. There had been a great coup
in the palace; the faces of those in the Kremlin had changed. There was a
change also in those whom the new rulers favored and those whom they
persecuted. Palace coups had occurred before, and would again. But
always this going and coming of rulers had remained beyond the ken of
Everyman. In place of the old áutocrat stood a new autocrat. For the old
ritual and religion, a new ritual and religion. One iconography for another. But authority made the same unbounded claims for obedience, for
faith, for belief. Submission and patience continued as the order of the
ordinary life. Whatever it was before that shaped the response to the
Czar, shaped now the response to the commissar. The central power of
the Russian State remained the hub of thought and action.

In the Marxist cognition the proletariat was no mere insurrectionary
force but a revolutionary class. It was supposed that the socialist power
would have to be based on the support of that class. The proletariat
would not only upset the old government, but, subsequently, the proletariat would dictate. Alas, the Russian proletariat dictated over nothing,
but was dictated to and driven. The Russian giant, wounded and dis-
traught, danced again to the whip of the central power. This time the
Communist elite, the surviving cult of the revolutionary intelligentsia,
called the tune. In Russia, the Communist State no more than the Czarist
State needed to base itself on the support of a particular functional class.
Once its authority was established, its power could rest (as it had under

Czarism) on the recongealed structure of the Russian outlook, on the centripetal force of the Russian culture concentrating power in the political center, and on the dedication to an ideology that the State embodied and ministered.

Cognition and Culture of the New Ruling Elite. If (as has been suggested here) the organization of the political system after the Communist seizure of power retained the form it had had under the Czar; and if social and economic initiative continued to rest with the political system as it had under the Czar; and if the configuration of culture and cognition of the mass of the people did not change; and if the tradition-based agriculture of the vast peasant economy, constituting the base of Russian society, remained—then what had been achieved by the Communist seizure? Simply this: the rulers had changed, and not merely the rulers, but the cognition and culture of those who ruled. In Russia where the centralized power was, demonstratably, capable of prodigious achievement, the assumption of power by an elite with a radically different value commitment could be of supreme importance. The Communist elite were not scientists but they idealized science. They were not technicians but they idealized technology. They were absolutely committed to the industrialization of Russia and to the organization of progressive technological change. They were committed also to the moral goals of socialism: fair shares, universal education, and an egalitarian society.

There were also similarities between the outlook and values of the old and the new occupants of the seats of Russian authority.

The revolutionaries had been conditioned by their years of conspiratorial opposition. Generations of persecution had shaped them into the inverse image of their persecutors. They were Slavophile Czarists turned inside out. They had learned the tricks of their trade from the Russian police. Against terror and violence they set violence and terror. Against the absolutes of the Czarist orthodoxy they posed the absolutes of a Communist orthodoxy, dogma against dogma, zealots alike, religious zealots, fanatics of the word, disciplined to the creed.

Revolutionaries or not, they were also Russian, conditioned by its history. At the moment of crisis, in their expectations of leadership and in their self-expectations, they would turn to the Russian mythos of greatness and take their models from among such strange and tainted heroes of the Russian pantheon as Ivan the Terrible or Peter the Great.

In one sense the revolutionaries were superbly conditioned and in another they were completely unequipped for their task of leadership. They were powerfully motivated; their dedication was hardened by martyrdom and weeded of weakness by the long years of exile and of underground struggle. They were disciplined. Under the most adverse conditions, they had evolved a system of decision-taking and unified action. They had a sense of history and a sensitivity to world forces. They came with a Book, a Truth, and a will to convert by fire and sword: and if the Russians were not willing converts, they were a people in search of faith and conditioned by centuries to the role of true believers. These were their advantages. To their disadvantage, the new elite had been led by an environment of betrayal and inquisition to "fanaticism in ideas. . . distrust and suspicion," and they brought this habituated environment into the place of established power. They remained conspirators even in the exercise of the legitimate authority. Their Marxist doctrine, their "Book," was entirely irrelevant to the realities of Russia or to the problems it faced. Their dialectical brilliance, their eloquence, their priestly vocation, their conspiratorial skills fitted them not at all for the tasks of engineering, of economic planning, of technical organization, of political administration, or for the other undertakings needed in order to govern, and to transform Russian society.

The Task of Economic Revolution. According to the Marxist sequence Communism was the last phase of economic revolution. Half a century of socialist strategy had been geared to taking over powerful industrial organizations and advanced technologies matured under capitalism. In Russia there was no such structure of machines, methods, disciplines, and cumulated skills. In Russia there were no massive echelons of disciplined workers. Technicians and engineers were lacking. It had been socialism's justification that it would divide equitably the large surpluses of a highly productive economy, but in Russia the economy was primitive with no surplus worth speaking of. Socialism was to be at the end of the line, but Russia was just at the beginning. Could this first crossing the threshold into an economy of high productivity industrialization be achieved under socialism?

Industrialization had never occurred under socialism. Its achievement under socialism had not even been contemplated. Always before, industrialization, starting with a mass of technically skilled craftsmen, had been brought about through the effort and initiative of self-seeking, technically creative individuals in the free market. Perhaps it could happen in no other way. Even if industrialization through centralized political-direction was conceivable, the new rulers in Russia had none of the competencies relevant to that task. Moreover, to judge from European experience, industrialization could only be achieved at a cost of great suffering by the people. The mass must be displaced from their lands, driven to work in factories, disciplined by fear, kept at starvation wages in order to accumulate the surplus needed to cover the costs of transformation. Would not the imposition of these privations and the ruthless disciplining presumably required for industrialization alienate the people from their leadership, and alienate the leadership from the values of socialism? The task would be even harder in Russia, since Communist Russia was largely barred by the enmity of her Western neighbors from the advantages of trade or borrowing. Surrounded by declared enemies, she must prepare to defend herself. Costs of defense would conflict with the costs of economic transformation. Yet that transformation was itself necessary for the defense of an isolated Russia.

Some Communists believed that the task of economic revolution was beyond their unaided capacities. On this account Trotsky staked his career (and lost it) in the effort to support revolution in Germany. He would have Russia serve as the springboard for the Communist seizure of power in the countries of Western Europe which already possessed a powerful and productive industry and a disciplined, politically sophisticated working class. Then, he supposed, joined with a socialized West, Russia could eventually assimilate the cultural and cognitive basis needed for industrialization and in due time be drawn into the European industrial complex. In fact, history gave the Communist leadership no choice but to industrialize Russia independently and in isolation. It was sink or swim.

By the balance of economic advantages, the possibility of creating a viable industrial economy under socialism was infinitely less in Russia than it might have been, say, in England, France, Germany, or the United States. But, compared to those other societies, Russia had another, decisive advantage, left out of account in any calculus of technological and economic assets and debits.

The form of the socialist economy is, essentially, that of centralized political-direction. For its effective functioning this form of economy requires the social capacity to respond to the central political power and to work effectively as a collective whole. For this Russia's culture and cognition and its accustomed organization for social action was supremely suited. Some societies might have slipped into socialism with a minimal change of technology. Russia made the transition with a minimal change in culture; a new driver but the same driving seat; a new goal but the same vehicle.

The peripheral property power of Russian capitalism, the facade of feudal privilege and medieval ritualism were thrust aside. The gigantic force of the State, of political authority at the hub of choice and action was laid bare. Attuned for a thousand years to a collective response to central direction, Russia awaited the new command, the new directive, the new program. Lenin is said to have defined Russian Communism as "Soviets plus electricity," by which he implied a socialism with the additional task of industrializing the economy. He might also have described

Russian Communism as "Czarism plus science" or perhaps as the "self-sufficing theocratic State plus universal education."

War Communism: The Initiation into Power. Power fell into the hands of the Communists in Russia at a moment of compounded crisis. The Russian armies were thoroughly beaten. Enormous manpower losses had been sustained. The transport system had broken down, and a large part of the capital structure was too depleted to be of any use. Disordered and undisciplined, millions of troops remained at the front awaiting new blows. Armies disintegrated in anticipation of Lenin's promise of "Bread, Land, and Peace." Trotsky was sent to bargain with the Germans, but the victor was making no bargains. In the "peace" of Brest-Litovsk, the Germans took possession of Russia's richest grain and ore lands, then turned their armies westward. By the time an Allied victory had removed the German threat, civil war had begun in Russia with "White" armies of the Old Regime moving in from Asia, from the Crimea, from the Baltic, serviced and supported with arms and troops of the British, the French, the Japanese, and the Americans. Simultaneously, the Poles, the Czechs, the Ukranians, the Finns, the Estonians, the Latvians, and the Lithuanians, raising the banners of nationalism, brought arms to bear against Soviet Russians.

Yet Red Russia managed to survive. She was aided, it is true, by the ineptitude of her enemies, the war weariness of the Allies and the antagonism of the peasants towards White Armies that stood for the return of the landlords. It is, nevertheless, remarkable that a new government and a new policy could have been born under this compounded adversity. The greatest handicap to the founding of the new society remains to be mentioned. This was the incompetence of the new incumbents. They were men without experience of government, without experience of administration, without experience of economic organization, without knowledge or experience of military strategy—who intended to reshape society from its roots. They were not engineers; they were not technicians; they were not soldiers. They were priests of planning, not planners. They were quasi-philosophers, quasi-theologians. They were experts in an esoteric doctrine, up-to-date scholastics able to settle the issues of centuries past and centuries yet to come with the roll of a dialectic. They were the living witnesses that what is required to achieve power need not be the same as what is needed for its effective exercise.

On assuming power in 1918, in the very middle of a sea of troubles, the Communists declared utopia by law. All land was nationalized and declared the possession of the State. To this the peasants paid no attention and continued to work the land as their own. All business was nationalized; large and small enterprises were taken over and run through the state bureaucracy. By 1920, some 37,000 enterprises had been expropriated by the State, including 5000 firms with only one employee. The banks were nationalized and Red Army guards marched in to see to it that the capitalists left the money in the vaults. The money remained in the vaults, but the banking function stopped. Credit vanished. Revenues ceased. The printing presses turned out rubles until the value of the incremental money was less than the costs of printing new paper. Marvelous benefits were conferred by decree upon the toiling masses: wage raises, pensions, vacations, medical benefits, protections. Full control of industry was vested in the workers, and the workers appropriated for personal use what, after all, belonged to them personally. The market was virtually eliminated. Resources were allocated by the central power. Consumption goods were rationed. Grain and foodstuffs were requisitioned. Prices were decreed. No incentive system replaced the quest for profits. No scarcity index replaced that of market price. The economy, of course, broke down.

Production dropped catastrophically. By the Gosplan Index, the output of large-scale industry dropped from 116.1 in 1916 to 12.8 in 1920. The output of small-scale industry dropped from 109.4 in 1916 to 20.4 in 1920.[5] Since money was worthless and nothing to buy was being produced, the peasant ceased offering his crops for sale. The Communists sent troops and labor gangs to the farms to seize the grain. The peasant consequently reduced his planting and slaughtered his livestock, and what he had left, he hid. By 1921, the output of grain was less than half what it had been during the years between 1909 and 1913. Because the chance of surviving was greater where a little could be scratched from the soil and private possessions could be traded for food, populations poured out of the cities. Moscow lost half its people. Petrograd lost two thirds. All the paper rights and benefits that had been conferred on "the toilers" were put aside and labor armies were drafted to work under the shadow of the gun. Along the Volga, even in the rich Ukraine, there was a great famine. This was the end of *War Communism*. In 1921 under Lenin, the Communists reversed their field. The New Economic Policy was inaugurated.

The New Economic Policy: A Return to Decentralized Choice. N.E.P. was a reluctant, expedient, hedged-in *laissez faire*, a *laissez faire* of the last resort. The Communists would rely on free exchange, a free market in which all enterprise, public and private would be engaged. The whole vast apparatus of the economy had come almost to a halt. Now self-interest and profit motivation would be allowed to draw producers back

---

[5] Alexander Baykov, *The Development of the Soviet Economic System* (Cambridge: Cambridge University Press, 1947), p. 8.

to their places and to set the apparatus of production and distribution again in motion. But this surrender to Mammon was to be only temporary. The Communists, holding the "commanding heights" waited for the time when they could put an end to it.

Under these circumstances, with entrepreneurial activity foredoomed before it started, there could hardly be any significant, long-range private investment or planned innovation.

Those who entered as bargainers into the new market arrangement included the peasantry, private traders, small enterprises returned to private ownership, large government-owned firms run by government-appointed managers, syndicates acting as trading agents for the state-owned enterprises, and cooperative procurement agencies for the peasant and other consumers. "Of the 165,781 enterprises . . . 147,471, or 88.5 percent were [returned and/or leased into] the hands of private persons, 13,697 or 8.5 percent were State enterprises, and 4,613 or 3.1 percent were cooperative enterprises. . . . State-owned industries accounting for only 8.5 percent of the total number of enterprises, employed 84.1 percent of all employed workers." [6]

State enterprises, concentrated in "trusts," were ordered to maximize profits through trade, and were allowed to retain a proportion of the profits as an inducement for so doing. The fiscal and monetary apparatus was resurrected. The State budget was balanced. The ruble was stabilized.

The recovery of industry and agriculture under N.E.P. was very rapid, but, of course, it was a recovery made from very low initial levels. During the seven years under N.E.P. a viable economy was recreated, able to produce nearly as much as had been produced in 1913. Per capita output remained less than in prewar Russia.

Russian Class Structure at the Period of N.E.P. Understanding a class to mean a group with a particular function in social organization and with distinctive values and outlook, Russian society at the period of N.E.P. can perhaps be divided into the following classes:

1. *The peasants,* constituting the mass of the Russian population, lived mostly in the *mir,* that is, in autonomous village communities with the land parceled out in strips among families and worked according to traditional practices.

2. *The kulaks,* who had left the *mir* to become relatively successful private farmers, worked their own land, sometimes possessed livestock and implements, and sometimes hired farm workers. These were certainly the most ambitious and aggressive of the rural community, presumably the most individualistic, and the best farmers. They were envied and resented by the members of the *mir.*

[6] *Ibid.,* p. 107.

3. *The N.E.P. men* included private traders, speculators, organizers of small enterprise. These were a marginal, fluid class.

4. *The proletariat,* politically favored, strongly indoctrinated, were a main source for the recruitment to Party cadres. The real wages of the industrial worker had been pushed well above the prewar level, but not until 1926-27 did his productivity approach that of 1913.

5. *Industry management,* qualified engineers and experienced technicians were mostly a remnant of the possessing classes of the old regime. Told by the State to organize monopolized industry as profit-seeking enterprise, their motivations and their criteria of choice became akin to those of management in Western Europe or the United States. They were distrusted by the Communists because of their social origins and because of the role they had been assigned. Hence their actions were under constant surveillance, and they were frequently denounced and punished at the initiative of Communist cells in their plants. In consequence, management avoided innovation that might be called sabotage if it failed. Correspondingly, the capacity for progressive change was impaired.

6. *The Old Guard Communists,* prerevolutionary bolsheviks, associates of Lenin, who had participated in the initial seizure of power peopled the upper ranks of the political system. They continued to be identified with international Communist movements. They were often visionaries, concerned with the ultimate goals of the revolution and sometimes with its humanist and socialist values. They were practiced pamphleteers, skilled debators, dialecticians, agitators, but their proven capacities and their acquired cognition and values were rarely related to the task of economic development. In that sense, they were supernumerary. They could neither abandon the habits of conspiracy nor unify against Stalin, who would destroy them one by one.

7. *The new technicians.* From the beginning the Communists placed the greatest emphasis on universal literacy, education, and science. Moreover, political turmoil and organizational flux opened opportunity to the tough and talented. These moved up, in the Party and in the Government. They were indoctrinated. Presumably they were dedicated. But, unlike the prerevolutionary intelligentsia, they accepted an established faith and not a revolutionary cult. They were functionaries and technicians rather than conspirators. They were engaged in crucial fields of concrete action, in confronting the knotty problems of electricity and the mines, of transportation and trade, of science and industry. Theirs were the specific tasks of economic revolution.

The End of N.E.P. Under N.E.P problems arose that were grotesque counterparts of those experienced in the West. Thus the so-called "scissors crisis" of 1923. Chapter 29 of Part II described parasitic relations that can exist between forms of economic organizations in the same national economy; in the United States, for example, fixing industrial prices as a matter of corporate policy while prices in agriculture and small enterprise move freely as a function of the availability of resources, has resulted in relatively low incomes for those in agriculture and small competitive industry, and underemployment of manpower and machines in the sector controlled by large corporate enterprise. Under N.E.P. precisely the same problems were experienced but in a more extreme form, since the Russian Trust was under continuous political pressure to raise wages and was without any competitive constraint on its power to raise prices. With industrial prices rising and agricultural prices falling, the prewar ratio was reached in 1921. Agricultural prices continued to fall, and industrial prices continued to rise, even though grain and foodstuffs were critically scarce and deliveries of grain were declining. By 1923 agricultural prices were 56 percent and industrial prices 190 percent of the prewar parity. The two price indices had thus moved apart like the two blades of a scissors. In agriculture, or wherever prices were competitively determined, factor income was correspondingly depressed. In industry, where prices and wages were fixed in accord with management and trade union policy, unemployment became a major Russian problem. By 1927 some two million or 20 percent of the industrial work force was unemployed.

By 1926-27, the N.E.P. was drawing to the end of its road. It had enabled the country to make a rapid recovery, but was quite unable to transform the technical base of the Russian economy. This was to be expected. None of those who participated could look beyond the expediencies of the moment. There could be no long-range planning and investment. Nor was there opportunity for spontaneous innovation, or any provision for a planned organization of economic progress. Productivity never quite reached the levels of 1913, either in industry or agriculture. In 1928, the first of the five-year plans was launched.

The Capacity for Industrialization under Centralized Political-Direction. Why was it possible to plan production and the transformation of the economy, and to organize complex industrial processes from the political center, in 1928 and not previously? Simply because leadership had acquired a cognition of technology and of practical organization that it had not had before. This had come about through the influx of a new generation of technicians into the ranks and through the experience gained by the Communist elite in facing the tasks of government. The Communists had now administered complex agencies. They had controlled vast territories and peoples. They had set up institutions of mass education. They had selected and dealt with the managers of State enterprises. They had organized and controlled central procurement systems. In the factories and in the cooperatives and in the trade unions their cells had acquired the know-how of production. They organized, operated or controlled credit and banking institutions. They had reorganized the transportation system. They had recreated and led armies. They had planned a vast program of electrification, and implemented that plan. They had maintained and operated a State monopoly of foreign trade. With the competencies thus acquired, they could now create a central planning agency to rough out the goals of national development and to devise general techniques of planning. The historic accomplishment of the N.E.P. period is not to be reckoned in production indices. It was, above all else, the time when the cognitive basis for an industrial revolution under centralized direction had been acquired.

The Collectivization of Agriculture. Planning was begun in an atmosphere of imminent national danger. The smell of a new war was in the air, and Russia was surrounded by declared enemies. In 1928 the gap between the Russian technology and that of its antagonists was greater even than it had been in 1913.

From the outset, the government faced this central dilemma. For a rapid and massive industrialization, it would be necessary (1) to import machines and skills and (2) to increase the numbers of industrial workers. Imported machines and skills must be paid for, and an increased industrial population had to be fed. It would be possible to feed masses of new industrial workers only by bringing in more grain from the countryside; and imported machines and skills could be paid for only by selling more grain abroad. The success of any plan would depend on the quantity of grain at the government's disposal.

The quantity of grain produced by the country slowly approached the prewar level, but of the grain produced, a much smaller proportion was marketed than before the war. Of an annual prewar output of five billion poods of grain, 1.3 billion, or 26 percent had been sold on the market. The rest went to feeding peasant households. Of the 4.75 billion poods produced in 1926-27, only 630 million or 13.3 percent was marketed. At approximately the same level of output, more than twice as much grain had been made available for export or for food for the urban worker before the war than in 1927. The share of total output consumed by peasant households had gone up from 74 percent to 87 percent. This was entirely as one might expect. Before the war, about 12 percent of the grain was produced by large landowners, about 38 percent was produced by kulaks, and about 50 percent was produced by the "poor and middle peasant." After the war, more than 80 percent of the output was by the "poor and middle peasant." The poor and middle peasants were at the level of life where the sale of their grain was at a sacrifice of food for themselves. Hence they ate a larger part, and sold, correspondingly, less of what they produced than had the landlord or the kulak. Moreover the real price of grain, in terms of the industrially produced goods offered in exchange, was much less than in 1913. Therefore, neither poor peasant nor kulak were willing to sell as large a proportion of their grain as they had before the war.

This was not a problem for technicians. It devolved upon the heads of government, upon the Party, upon the dictator; the solution bore Stalin's imprint. The problem was not conceived as one of increasing the output of grain, or even of strengthening the hand of the agencies of procurement. It was conceived, not in the frame of technology at all, but doctrinally, as a phase of class war, war between the traditional peasant mass in the *mir* and the kulak. Agitators were sent into the countryside. All the petty grievances that the poor peasant had against those who had prospered (having acquired a bit of land and a cow or two) and, above all, the poor peasant's envy for his neighbor's possessions, were whipped up. The troops came. The unfortunate kulak was dispossessed, killed, driven off to starve or to find some Siberian haven. The Class Enemy had been liquidated, and the rest of the peasantry were herded into giant collective farms.

This was not what Marx meant by a class war. But the liquidation of the kulak expressed what Marxism, debased by primitive fanatics, had then become. In quite the same way the auto-de-fe of the Spanish inquisition and the pogroms of Czarist Russia expressed a debased Christianity.

In one sense, collectivization achieved its objective. In the collective farm the peasant had no way of withholding his output for his own consumption. A much higher proportion of a considerably reduced agricultural production was collected by the State. There were also potential technical values in collectivization. Certainly in the United States there is a trend toward gigantic, mechanized, science-based agricultural operations. But Russian agriculture was collectivized before there were the tractors or mechanical equipment, or skills or chemicals and fertilizers to permit any science-based transformation. Collectivization began not as a technical innovation, but as a more effective system for rural policing.

Some of its effects were catastrophic. A million or more of the most rational and efficient farmers were eliminated. The greater part of the country's livestock and draft animals were voluntarily destroyed. Evidently the peasantry was profoundly alienated. When the Nazis invaded, the industrial worker resisted with an absolute heroism, and the defense of Leningrad is a marvel of history; but in the Ukraine the peasants first welcomed the invader. In some profound way, a psychological wound, a disaffection, a disidentification with the land, a loss of hope and energy among the rural Russians seems to have come about for which no cure has yet been found. Its evident manifestation is the stubborn lag in agricultural productivity, the greatest weakness of the Russian economy today.

The Russian Economic Revolution Today. In spite of the stress of a terrible war, and perhaps also because of it, Russia has made her economic revolution. The Russian leadership has absorbed a cognition of science, of technology, of process and practical organization, and has demonstrated a capacity to organize not only complex industrial processes, but also to organize the rapid and continuing progress of technology. Its leadership no longer rules as a cult apart converting by the sword, but rather, if not yet as representatives of a consensus, at least as the legitimate priests of an accepted faith.

The Marxist cognition gave the Russian revolutionary elite its unity and a direction. It also led them into costly errors. The achievement of economic revolution under political direction in Russia was based not on any guidelines given by Marxism, but rather on the prior culture and the preexisting capacity of Russian society to respond (and its incapacity to resist) the will of the central authority in a way not paralleled elsewhere *except* in China. In China also, for centuries, the pervading culture and cognition geared its people to a disciplined and total response to the will of central authority. Even the Confucianist religion, allegedly, was designed to support the centralized political system. In China, centralized political control was effectively maintained over a breadth of empire and for a length of time unmatched in history. It is precisely in China where once more industrialization is evidently being effectively achieved under centralized political-direction.

Chapter 34

The Cultural-Cognitive Basis for Economic Development

The Constituents of Economic Progress. Parts I and II examined at length the process of economic progress. It was shown that this process could be variously organized. No matter how organized, it involves three levels of activity: *invention, innovation, transformation.*

1. *Invention* constitutes the new idea, the discovery of relationships not before perceived, the notion of organizing differently or using in a different way what was known before. Inventions occur in every sphere of human activity, but here the term refers only to those which relate to economic outputs.

2. *Innovation* is the practical realization of an invention and its transmutation in practice. To iron out the bugs of a new process, to gain acceptance for a new product, and to establish the superiority of a new technique is likely to require a series of creative adaptations.

3. *Transformation* constitutes the changeover of existing processes and outputs to those which innovation has already shown to be technically superior or otherwise preferable.

Innovation and invention may yield a high reward to individuals, but for society the payoff in economic progress comes through the general transformation of industry and agriculture. In this transformation, a society may reap the benefits of inventions and innovations made elsewhere without having incurred the costs and risks of inventing or of innovating. Yet, the mark of the developing society is precisely the failure to transform to processes and products whose superiority has been established elsewhere. Why is this so?

If there is to be change, those who exercise power over resources must be motivated to organize change or to support it. Often they are not. A higher technology may require skills, a discipline, and a new orientation on the part of the population at large. These need not exist. Hence, economic development may require a building of the culture and cognitions needed for transformation.

THE COGNITIVE BASE

Relevant Cognitions. Cognition constitutes the essential ingredient of economic development. Particularly pertinent are (1) the cognition of mechanism, (2) the cognition of technical process, and (3) the cognition of politics and of association. A comparative lack of these three cognitions is characteristic of all developing countries. Indeed the so-called "under-developed economies" could be distinguished from the others by these three cognitive lacks alone.

Cognition of Mechanism. Development requires an appreciation on the part of the mass, hammered into their instincts, of how the machine works, of what makes it go, of what care the machine needs, and of the pace and discipline that it demands of its human partners. Culture also must be shaped to an appreciation of the machine as an extension of human power, as the instrument of a man's will. There needs to be a pride and a pleasure in the machine's inherent beauty, in its performance, in its perfection.

Out of this cognition of mechanism (and culture of the machine), innumerable specific skills can be shaped and reshaped. Given this cognition of mechanism, skills will spontaneously evolve and will adapt to the need and to the occasion. In technology as in every aspect of social organization, leadership only gives the signal. The group must respond to that signal. The cognition of mechanism gives the group its capacity to respond to the technological command and to adjust to technical innovation and transformation. The degree to which this cognition is absent limits the possibilities of successful innovation.

The Cognition of Technical Process. Machines, materials, human skills, and information do not operate as isolated segments, but must be geared together in *the process* of producing goods and services. A cognition of process is required: of its rationale and organization, its designs in blue-prints and specifications, of the communications linking together its parts, its rhythms, its dynamic, its implicit possibilities and boundaries for the shifting, adjusting and recombining of factors, its internal interests, and the contradictions and incipient conflicts of these. A cognition of process is needed in order to evaluate the rearrangement of factor inputs and product outputs and to translate each component element of the process, and of changes in the process into its cost (waste, savings, or profit) equivalent. The cognition of process is essential in organizing transformation, or in evaluating the applicability of invention or the acceptability of innovation.

The Cognition of Politics. Economic growth and economic development connote a succession of transformations in process and organization, not only in the activities and organization of the firm, but also of the family, courts of law, universities, and political agencies. Such transformation may require the reconciliation of conflicting interests. It may require that actions be undertaken simultaneously at different points under the impetus of diverse motivations. It may require that the support of numerous individuals or groups be mobilized and that resistances be met and overcome from many quarters. This ability shaped to the culture and the functional systems in which it operates, to incite action, to mobilize support, to guide the tides of opinion—this capacity to make groups move—requires the cognition of (call it) politics. The political cognition is expressed not only in the power of the individual to persuade but also in the capacity of the many to associate, and in the capacity of antagonists and opponents to converse rationally together. This cognition also is essential for development.

Cognition Matched to Role. The need is to cultivate those cognitions required for development and to organize them for use. The perennial task is to give those with functional responsibilities a cognition appropriate to their roles.

A society may fail to produce the cognitive capacities needed for its development. It may produce them and fail to put them to use. Scientists in developing countries, trained at great costs, may migrate because they are offered no outlet for the competencies they have acquired. Recruitment may fail to match the particular task or responsibility with its appropriate cognition. A deep cognition of process possessed by some will be wasted when innovation and transformation decisions are left to others with prerogatives based on inheritance, on family connections, on the privileges of caste, or to soldiers and professors, or to accountants, who have attained the decision-making power without reference to their cognition of process, and who are virtually without it.

Outlets for Creative Initiative. There is also the need to create outlets for creative initiatives, so that every relevant cognition may have its chance to contribute to innovations. This is quite another matter than recruiting the qualified individuals for given functional roles. It is one thing to determine the cognition that is required for given activities, but can one know beforehand the cognition that will be useful in inventing new patterns of activity? The cognition or competence able to produce significant invention need not be that appropriate to the management of the process after it has been transformed by the incorporation of that invention. It is not unlikely that the mechanic who repairs the cars or the machinist who produces some of the tools will have a deeper, more rational cognition of mechanism than will the President of the Company or its Chief Research Scientist. That cognition of mechanism can be the basis of important invention. Those with a deep cognition of mechanism who also have creative talent may contribute to economic growth not only through specific invention but also in the design of innovation—if they can make themselves articulate, if they will be listened to, if they have the opportunity to initiate change.

Henry Ford was a man who probably would never have gotten a B.A. in a good university. He was, in fact, uneducated, narrow, and bigoted. He lacked a cognition of science. In France he couldn't have qualified to teach in the primary schools or for the first rung of the administrative civil service. He was a mechanic who, in most societies, could never have gotten out of the garage. But he was a master mechanic with a sense of process and a touch of creative genius. In the fluid America of his day he had the opportunity to initiate change, and thereby he revolutionized industrial processes throughout the world. The status arrangements of all societies, particularly in traditional ones, serve to bar and check such initiatives "from the bottom."

The direction and relevance of creative inspiration need not run parallel to the lines of functional responsibility and authority. The academic scientist may have a contribution to make in transforming industry. An industrial scientist may have a contribution to make in transforming the university—provided there is the opportunity to initiate or the chance to be heard. The pigeonholing of specialists, the hierarchies of functional authority and divisions by disciplines, skills, and functional affiliation all serve to bar the criss-cross movement of creative initiative.

To a considerable extent, inventions arise and innovations take place through the readaptation and reapplication of experience acquired in an activity elsewhere. Indeed, the dialectic of progress lies in working out the implications of the new conception and in adapting the new idea in successive spheres of social activity. This requires that idea and concept flow between different sets of activities, disciplines, organizations, authorities; between biologist and physicist, between industrial and academic scientist, between industry and industry, between military and civilian research, etc. For the cross-flow of creative initiatives, there must be opportunity and motivation. The natural enemies of this cross-flow are the isolation of specialists, the jealousy of intellectual authority, the self-sufficiency of cognitive systems.

ORGANIZING SCIENCE AS AN INSTRUMENT OF DEVELOPMENT

Organization of the Science Cognition. The following section will consider some of the problems in organizing the science cognition as an instrument of economic development. It is hoped that the discussion will clarify the notion of *organizing* a cognition (of any sort) toward development.

The problems on which the efforts of scientists focus, it will be recalled, can be classified into those which are chosen (1) because they intrinsically interest academic researchers and (2) because they relate to the objectives of functional systems. The use of science to solve problems of the first sort is called here academic (rather than basic) research; the use of science to solve problems of the second sort is called here Research and Development or R & D.

Science as a cognitive system is uniquely capable of extending its own scope and of continuously improving its effectiveness as an instrument of problem-solving. Its published outputs appear in all of the world languages. It has numerous and proliferating disciplines, subdisciplines and interdisciplines, so specialized that communications concerning the research of each tend to be intelligible only to those who are themselves engaged in that research.

For academic research, and for some R & D without implications for weaponry or commercial strategy, for instance, pedology, hydrology, or preventive medicine, published outputs are universally available. At least there is no deliberate restrictions on their availability, and some efforts are made to disseminate essential findings. On the other hand, a substantial part of transmittable R & D outputs in fields such as geology, pharmaceutics, chemicals, and electronics, are deliberately withheld and kept secret. It is probably the enormous initial advantage in possessing these hidden stores of science data in synthetics, pharmaceuticals, and other chemistry-based fields that accounts for the comparative lag of newcomers like Russia and Japan in those industries. Perhaps most increments to R & D are not reported at all, but are embodied in processes and products or in the skills of individuals and teams. It requires trained scientists to evaluate the published outputs of science and, even more, to reconstruct the nature of unreported scientific advance which is embodied in some product or design of action. And this understanding of science must be coupled with a cognition of some fields of functional activity in order to discern the practical relevance of information produced through academic research or through R & D, or to use such information as a take-off point for invention or for the transformation of functional processes.

Science is a world activity which must be brought into local focus. This requires not only scientific skill coupled with the cognition of functional organizations. It also requires (which is quite another thing) an understanding of science as a functional system, subject to organization, administration, and control. The organizational task is to link the cognitions of science to the specifics of industrial and agricultural choice, to the provision of particular services or products, and to the formulation of development policy and to activation of development programs. What follows will consider the specifics of this organizational task, in linking science to development.

Components of the Science Infrastructure. Without implying any change in process or functional organization, science-based activities may be organized to provide managers, engineers, public officials, and policy-makers with a wider range of choice and a more precise basis for communication. "Modern crime detection," for example, uses "science"—chemical analysis, computers to process fingerprints, psychological testing, etc.—in order to give the police and the judiciary new information and more exact data on which to base their choice. Services of the same sort can be rendered through science for other functional activities, including any industry. Take the venerable tradition-based production of pottery and ceramics. What precisely are the mineral or organic components of the clays used? What are the relations between those mineral components and the behavior of the clay in the kiln, or to the qualities and the appearance of the finished pottery? What are the varieties of clay deposits available for use in a given geographical area? What are the kiln and processing requirements of each variety of clay? How can the qualities of the materials or the conditions that are relevant to their processing, such as plasticity and coloration, heat, vaporization, the dispersion of particles in liquids, etc., be precisely defined and measured so that control standards may be developed, specifications written, and information communicated exactly and unequivocally?

These are questions that can be answered through a research of sorts, and through the systematic organization of facts already known. The direct product of this category of science-based activity is neither invention nor innovation. Nor does it necessarily lead to invention and innovation or to any transformation in industrial or agricultural processes. Rather it supports a more accurate and rational choice by those engaged in agriculture or industry. By reducing the wastes through miscalculation, it serves to raise the level of productivity. Indeed, such support through science may be absolutely required for certain levels of business or social planning. By reducing uncertainty and by extending the range open to reasonable forecasting, science-based services of this kind may favor the acceptance of particular inventions, the undertaking of particular innovations, and the acceleration of transformations in industry and agriculture, which would not otherwise have been possible.

Thus, science-based services can contribute in providing farmers, managers, entrepreneurs, engineers, inventors, officials, policemen, soldiers, firemen, and also thieves, saboteurs, and spies, with a wider and more precise basis for communication and choice. Such science-based services would include the activities related to standards and standardization, to weights and measures, to materials testing, to soil analysis, to resource inventories (of forests, soils, waters, minerals), to weather prediction, to measuring the purity and pollution of water and of air, etc. Services of this sort involve (1) surveys and resource inventories including geological exploration and all forms of mapping, and inventories of forests, soils, minerals, animal, fish, insect, plants and human populations, of surface and underground water supplies, (2) studies to determine cyclical change or trends in the character of the natural environment, in climate, in river flows, in forest depletion or renewal, in soil erosion or fertilization, in wind movement, in the periodicity of hurricane, flood, tornado, insect plagues, water pollution, etc., (3) the analysis of the technical possibilities of utilizing resources or of the costs and benefits of their exploitation, (4) identification services for insect pests, plants, parasites, virus infections, (5) tests and analysis of mineral, soil, water, air, (6) experiments to determine the reactions of materials, processes, and equipment under characteristic environmental conditions, for example, weather resistance of paints, the durability of alternative road constructions, the corrosion rate of exposed materials, (7) documentation and administration services, that is, the systematization, synthesis, and presentation of such data, as is relevant to practical choice, to make it widely known, quickly available, and easily used. Documentation requires a cognition of science in classification, abstraction, and synthesis and also the contribution of data processors, editors, information officers, and librarians. These aggregated activities serving to provide a wider and more precise basis for functional communication and for choice, including the equipment and facilities they require and the institutions through which they operate, constitute the *science infrastructure.*

The Science Infrastructure: Efficiency and Transformation. Improvement in this infrastructure will serve to raise productivity, even though the processes and techniques of production remain exactly as before, by minimizing uncertainties and facilitating better-informed engineering and managerial or entrepreneurial choices. By widening the information base, by increasing the accuracy of specification, by facilitating precision in communication, by extending the range of reliable forecasting, the science infrastructure increases the invention potential, reduces the costs and risks of innovation, and eases transformation. For these reasons it can be understood as a component part of the complex of related industrial and agricultural processes and also as a part of the processes of invention-innovation-transformation. The services of the science infrastructure, moreover, are themselves subject to invention-innovation-transformation, correspondingly raising the level of industrial and agricultural productivity. Consider, for example, the use of aerial photography as a recently evolved component of the science infrastructure more or less specific to the needs of developing economies. Through a series of inventions and innovations airflight photography has been successively transformed. So have the techniques for interpreting the photographed image and the methods and organization for training, teaching, and servicing those engaged in this work. This has permitted the reduction in the cost of aerial surveys and in the successive application of a basic technology developed for topographical mapping to new spheres of functional activity, for example, to geophysical and geological surveys, to the surveying and inventorying of soils, of pasture lands, of forests, and even to the census of outlying populations. In consequence, information related to political or to business choice is provided more cheaply, and more information is made available than could otherwise be the case. This permits more accurate prediction and more efficient, less wasteful operations, and extends the feasible range of social and business planning. Furthermore, the way is opened to the transformation of economic processes, possibly through the opening of a new mine, or in the exploitation of forests or the reorganization of transportation.

The Science Infrastructure: Links to Operational Choice. The science infrastructure is a bridge between elements of world science cognition and a particular economy's need for information relevant to specific and localized choice. It is the channel through which information accumulated, and methods for test and survey developed throughout the world, can move into local practice.

The science infrastructure should be at once locally focused, with a point-by-point relationship to functional activities, and universal, bound into an evolving world science, since precisely its function is to select the relevant elements of scientific output throughout the world, to adapt these to serve local needs and to integrate them into the process of practical choice.

The science infrastructure may be integrated with practical choice through political dictate, for example, through public inspection and supervision, through building codes, sanitary codes, safety codes. Again, the organization of the science infrastructure and its integration with practical action may occur through the voluntary or quasi-voluntary associations of firms: in Great Britain, France, and Germany, industrial research associations supported partly by government and partly by industry provide a science infrastructure suited to the needs of a particular industry, and gear that infrastructure into practical industrial choice. In the Netherlands, the TNO, a government-initiated research agency, works for industry and for government under contract for the same purpose. Private consulting firms, information centers, and extension services link the science infrastructure to functional choice. Research and Development operations in large private companies create an infrastructure appropriate to the specific needs of the company with "antenna" receptive to relevant science-based services and developments throughout the world.

Choosing and Managing the Services of the Infrastructure. An infinite depth and range of information could conceivably be provided through the science infrastructure. But such services are expensive. To provide them involves the use of manpower which is everywhere scarce, and particularly so in developing countries. Hence society must choose the activities that should be supported and, conversely, those to be neglected.

Not only must a choice be made as to those infrastructural activities that will and will not be supported. It is also required, if the most is to be gained from the resources available, that the activities of the science infrastructure be efficiently organized and managed, minimizing waste of effort, and optimizing the dissemination and utilization of the information outputs. Ideally, the latter would require extending the services of the science infrastructure to all the functional activities to which its information outputs relate. The constraints of proprietary interests or political dominion will nearly always reduce the potential benefit of scientific information. For example, the contribution to productivity of information useful for tropical fruit growing would be greatest if that information were available to all ecological regions characterized by the given conditions of climate and soil rather than confined within a particular political boundary, or within particular proprietary control.

The science infrastructure is especially important where economic activities are centrally planned or are controlled through large organizations rather than through the independent choice of small, private owners. When operations are on a small scale and economic relations are between independent decision-makers, man-to-man communication in the process of exchange will generate a consensus on the meaning of terms and the acceptable level of standards even though terms are never precisely articulated or exactly defined. Such a common frame of reference cannot evolve organically through direct interpersonal dealings when a vast number of diversified tasks are assigned under a single plan and activities are integrated under a central direction. Then an external organization must deliberately formulate and provide precise specification, common standards, unequivocal terminology, based on exact measurement and quantification. Given centralized planning or control through large organization, the science infrastructure becomes essential for the efficient control or transformation of complex processes.

The Transfer of Science-Based Technologies. The services of a science infrastructure are only one of the important supports which organized science can give to economic development. A cognition of science is required in order to evaluate, organize, or control certain technologies and industrial processes. Atomic energy, plastics, synthetics and electronics, as technologies, are specifically the products of Research and Development. Consider the problem of transferring these science-based technologies to developing countries.

The establishment of science-based technologies in developing economies relies on the science cognition in four ways: first, in evaluating the costs and possible benefits of bringing such technologies into the economies of developing countries; second, in redesigning and adapting those technologies to the particular circumstances of the developing economy; third, in the organization of the processes incorporating those technologies; and fourth, in maintaining a competitive pace in the progressive improvements of the newly established technology through R & D.

The science cognition needed to introduce and establish science-based technologies must be indigenous if the initiative is to come from within the developing society. Only then will those who exercise the prerogatives of choice and formulate policy in the developing society have the capacity to weigh the technical feasibility and the economic or other benefits against the costs and risks of introducing the new technology. Even if specialists from the outside can be hired to test feasibilities, to recommend policies, and to set up new organization, it is still necessary that those who exercise the prerogatives of choice in the developing society possess cognition-based competence to hire the right experts, to ask them the right questions, and to evaluate their reports and recommendations.

If the initiatives for the key decisions are to be left to others outside the developing economy, then an indigenous science is not necessary in order to transfer a new science-based technology into a developing country. This would be the situation if IBM decided to open a data-processing operation in India based on its own continuing R & D in Europe and the United States. There are, however, dangers and drawbacks in a wholesale reliance on external initiatives based on the science cognition of others. The self-interest of those particular outsiders who possess that cognition need not coincide with the collective interest of the developing society, nor need those outsiders always be aware or be capable of discovering the local opportunities that actually exist relevant to the introduction of a new technology, or be equipped to organize operations effectively in the special milieu of that developing society.

Research Oriented to the Special Problems of Developing Regions. To some extent those who deal with the policies and problems of industry and agriculture in a developing society may turn for guidance to information accumulated through the studies and experiments of world science. Suppose, in some "developing" land, that the coffee crop is being destroyed by some unidentified blight. The plants would have to be examined, the leaves analyzed, and the blight identified. Then, by reference to reports of previous studies, a means of checking the spread of the disease and, perhaps, of saving some part of the infected crop might be prescribed. All this would be the role of the science infrastructure. But suppose the disease was unfamiliar, or that no technique of control or cure had yet been found? Then arises, as a research task for science, the need to seek out and develop a new method of cure, control, and prevention. Research and Development may focus on problems and phenomena that are particular to the natural environment or social conditions of a developing society for the purpose of providing new or superior practices and higher processes. This is something else again than the services of a science infrastructure, or the task of incorporating the science-based technologies of "advanced" societies into the developing economy.

The need for independent research focused on problems specific to developing economies parallels the divergence between the conditions characteristic of their natural environments and forms of social organization and those encountered in the technically advanced countries. Where there is such a divergence, the information gathered and concepts developed through the extensive researches in the technically advanced societies will be insufficient or inappropriate for the problems confronted in the developing economies. Such is the case, for example, inasmuch as a tropical climate is characteristic of developing economies and a temperate climate is characteristic of the advanced. The climatic variation creates a corresponding variation in soils, forests, plants, animal life, insects, and pests, and in animal, plant, and human disease. Correspondingly, different information and techniques—indeed quite another science and technology—in agriculture, horticulture, hydrology, forestry, animal husbandry, the exploitation of fish and wildlife, and medicine and public health are called for.

For an R & D intended to resolve the problems of industrial process and to produce technological innovations, systematic variations in the natural environment are significant—but even more important will be the distinctive characteristics of the social environment, including the differences in the prevailing cultural and cognitive systems, the structure of available skills, the social priorities, and forms of functional organization. For these reasons "world science," inasmuch as this is a complex of cognitive systems produced by and for the advanced countries, cannot be relied on to solve the problems or to evolve a technology appropriate to the needs of the developing societies. A development-oriented R & D focusing on the problems characteristic of developing societies and systematically evolving the cognition related to the special social conditions and peculiar natural circumstances of those societies is also needed.

Given a development-oriented science, organization is needed to link the outputs or the problem-solving potentialities of that science into practical choice and action. For this fusion of science-based method and science-produced data with functional activity, not only must information be offered; also, those engaged in functional activities or charged with their organization must be capable of understanding and motivated to use the information that is offered. In fact, such a dialogue often fails, because those engaged in research are indifferent to or incapable of understanding the real problems and needs of industry and agriculture, or because those engaged in industry and agriculture are incapable of comprehending the information that is offered, or because of the inability of those thus involved in functional operations to pose those problems that are susceptible to solution through science or to demand the information that they need. For example, one cause of the relative ineffectiveness of agricultural extension services in Africa and elsewhere in the developing world has been the passivity of farm communities and the lack of an effective collective pressure upon the agents and agencies designated to serve them. In these societies the individual farmer is not ordinarily capable of fusing together into a program for the practical transformation of his farm processes the diverse services and information profferred by extension specialists. Nor has he himself demanded from the extension specialists the information he needs to transform his farm operations successfully. Because the farmer is passive and does not exercise an effective demand through the medium of extension services upon the activities of the agricultural research station, research activities themselves drift away from the problems of practical application into the orbit of academic concerns.

Science Initiatives in Planning and Programing Development. The administrator, the lawyer, the politician, the banker, the economist, the businessman all have something to contribute to the progressive formulation of development policy. So has the scientist.

The politician, economist, public official, and administrator charged with programing economic development will have their ideas about what is needed, and these ideas, within the boundaries of their experience and capabilities, may be invaluable. Nevertheless, from the basis of his analytic capabilities and knowledge of a particular category of resources and techniques, the scientist is likely to see other possibilities for action and other paths for development that also would be of value. If those who are masters of science or technology are confronted with the circumstances of economic development, if they are engaged in its problems, if they share the responsibility for the solution of those problems and have the opportunity to take the initiative in development programing, they probably will see possibilities outside the conceptual ken of the administrator or public official. They will seek answers for questions that the administrator and public official would not have thought to ask, drawing their inspiration from another universe of cognition. The scientist can bring his particular experience and competence and turn of mind to bear in formulating development policy only if (1) he is confronted with the problems of promoting development, and with the responsibility for development programs, (2) he comes to understand the social context within which choices must be made, and (3) a way is opened for his independent initiatives. In fact, these conditions are rarely met, and the potential contribution of the scientist to the formulation of development policy has hardly been capitalized upon.

The I.R.H.O. as a Case Example of Development-Oriented Science. Scientific activity has been more fully and deliberately organized as an instrument of economic development by the French in their technical aid to French-speaking Africa than anywhere else in the world. Among its more important development-oriented scientific research organizations are six research institutes dealing with aspects of tropical agriculture.[1] The oldest of these, established in 1942, is the Institute de Recherche pour les Huiles et Oléogineaux (I.R.H.O.). Its activities illustrate the ways that the science cognition can be organized and used in support of economic development.

The I.R.H.O. has as its objectives to improve the yields and qualities of and to develop sales outlets for tropical oil-producing plants, like oil palms, coconut palms and peanuts, in Francophone territories. Its headquarters in Paris is a center for administration, liaison, documentation, and other technical services. There is also some headquarters' research. However, the bulk of its research is carried on in some twenty experimental stations and test plots in Africa and the Pacific. The I.R.H.O. has developed as (1) an element in the science infrastructure in French-speaking Africa and Oceania, (2) a research instrument specifically for the development of a science cognition shaped to a branch of tropical agriculture, and (3) as a participant in national development planning and programing.

An example of its service in providing a more informed basis for choice by the nonscientists who operate plantations or small farms in Africa is the I.R.H.O.'s system for continuously guiding fertilizer practices. Through the intermediary of field agents and experiment stations, hundreds of thousands of carefully marked leaf samples are sent to the Paris office. These leaves are submitted to a foliar analysis from which the

---

[1] Cf. ISEA (Institute d'Étude de Dévéloppement Économique et Social) "Recherches et Applications Techniques et Matière de Dévéloppement Économique et Social, et Repertoire d'Organismes Françaises," *Tiers Monde*, 1963.

nutritional needs of the plants are deduced. From the results of these tests, through the use of statistical sampling and computer techniques, soil conditions in specified areas are rapidly determined. On the basis of this determination, nutriment needs are diagnosed and an appropriate fertilizer formula for each area is prescribed. This is immediately forwarded to experimental stations and field agents to serve them in guiding local fertilizer practice. Through this science infrafunction, an information base is provided for more accurate agricultural choice. This service has so far been confined to French-speaking Africa.

The Research and Development activities of the I.R.H.O., through which it claims to have increased outputs in the regions it serves by a factor of from 2 to 10, exemplifies the contribution of the science cognition in solving problems specific to a developing economy. Its researches have been of the following sorts:

1. The control of plant diseases and pests—for example, the development of special varieties of peanuts resistant to viruses attacking the plant in those regions.

2. The development through selective breeding of more productive strains of oil palms. In 1964, the I.R.H.O was supplying about three and a half million seeds of hybrid varieties able to yield up to ten times the output of "natural" palm groves

3. The importation of adapted versions of technologies developed elsewhere, or the invention of techniques and processes and their incorporation into industrial practice. The I.R.H.O. developed and introduced, for example, mechanical shellers and low-priced ovens for uniform drying in the production of almonds. Palm oil factories and processes have been redesigned to increase yields and to reduce acidity.

4. The development or introduction of new products and byproducts of oil plants. These have included hardboard produced from palm stalks and groundnut shells, fatty acid derivatives for use as plasticizers, fungicides, insecticides, and detergents.

5. The development of a science focused on the phenomena of an ecological region. Research on regional phenomena has led to the modification and adaptation of scientific theories and science-based practices that evolved in temperate zones to the tropical environment and to the special needs and circumstances of oil crop cultivation in the tropics. For instance, the I.R.H.O. has been largely responsible for an important development in the use of mineral fertilizers for tropical soils. It appears that the nutritional needs of temperate and tropical soils are, in one sense, opposite. In temperate zones the soil sometimes needs mineral fertilizers, but a large proportion of such minerals are retained and, once "saturated," soils require only marginal renewals of mineral fertilizer. In these temperate zones, however, cultivation exhausts the organic component of

soils, and continual and relatively massive application of organic fertilizers is called for. In the tropics, on the other hand, the rapid spontaneous generation of organic matter virtually eliminates the need for organic fertilizer. But tropical soils for a variety of reasons (the soil structure, the concentration of rainfall, the very rate at which organic matter is spontaneously generated) are rapidly and continuously depleted of their mineral content. Hence tropical soils require massive and continual application of mineral fertilizers. This has been a key discovery in raising agricultural outputs in the tropics.

The relevance of the science cognition to national development programing and policy-making is illustrated by the I.R.H.O.'s role in developing an oil palm industry in the Ivory Coast. That country had chiefly concentrated on the production of cocoa and coffee. Consequently, it had been extremely vulnerable to fluctuations in the world prices of these two crops. As a means of achieving stability through a greater diversity of export crops, the I.R.H.O. formulated and recommended to the government a plan for expanding the production of oil palms and of developing the exportation of oil products. The plan, proposed in 1961, called for bringing 33,000 hectares of oil palm groves into cultivation by 1968, with 75,000 hectares of oil palm groves as the program's "medium-term" objective. The proposed program included a whole strategy of development, including the source of financing, the design of factories and of plantation blocks, and a system for training small farmers in the required agricultural methods. In 1962, the I.R.H.O. was asked by the government of the Ivory Coast to put its scheme into operation. Under the plan, factories are to be owned and operated by an agency of the Ivory Coast government. That public agency will also own and cultivate plantations in close proximity to each factory. The publicly owned plantations will provide the factories with oil nut supplies sufficient for "break-even" operations. However, the bulk of the production will eventually come from the private peasant holdings. The problem is to induce a section of the peasantry to convert its land into the production of oil palms where no yields can be expected for five years, and to train that peasantry in modern techniques of cultivation. To achieve this, a complex scheme of farm demonstrations, of loans conditional on the following of prescribed practices and of periodic inspections to assure the use of approved methods has been devised.

The activities of this single research agency illustrate the various levels at which the science cognition can be organized in support of economic development, through (1) a science infrastructure serving to support private choice and communication, (2) the incorporation of newly developed or adapted technologies into the industrial or agricultural practices of a developing economy, (3) Research and Development on particular problems of developing regions and the consequent development of a science cognition related to conditions characteristic of that economy, and (4) participation in the formulation and activation of development policy and programs.

The Place of Academic Research. It has been alleged that research carried on in the scientific institutions of developing countries tends to place a greater emphasis on academic problems without discernable relation to functional objectives than do comparable research organizations in technically advanced countries. Academic (or basic) research has aesthetic and symbolic values. It may serve to enhance national prestige, but its contribution to economic development is dubious. This emphasis on the academic in countries where the practical needs of development are so overwhelming can be explained (1) by the academic bias built into the education of scientists and (2) by the environment of developing societies as a context for research.

Students from developing countries educated in foreign universities, or in their own universities that follow foreign models, absorb an academic bias that imputes some inherent superiority to "pure" and "fundamental" science and that downgrades functionally oriented research. Students from Western Europe and the United States absorb the same academic bias, but when they leave the cloistered halls they are usually drawn into functionally oriented R & D by the promise of material reward and by the positive opportunities for creative action which are offered there. For the scientist who leaves his studies to return to a developing society, there is no vital, progressive, and exuberant industry to lure him into the realm of the applied and the practical by the offer of a high salary or by the opportunity for creative action. If he is to make the concrete contributions his people desperately need, it will only be by his own initiatives and in the face of grave resistances. Alas, his education has not conditioned him for such practical initiatives. It has inclined him toward academic research and away from the functional. In academic research he can find recognition by his peers and plaudits from his teachers. Through that recognition he may hope to escape the intellectual isolation and frequently difficult environment in which he finds himself.

THE CULTURAL BASE

The Need for an Integrating Culture. So far in this chapter emphasis has been on the cognitive requisites of development. There are also cultural requisites that need to be considered.

In any community there are diverse cultural systems. In any cultural system there are elements that set individuals apart and others that unify and integrate. A high degree of integration is always needed for purposeful social action. A culture that unifies is a prime requisite for economic revolution, for the following reasons.

Whenever directive or command must be passed along and interpreted in a variety of circumstances, the capacity for effective communication is needed. In order that the experience and hypotheses proceeding from a given source may be of service elsewhere in shaping decision, policy, and a consensus, a capacity for effective communication is needed. Cultural unity is a basis for effective communication. Communication needs a common language that, in the broad sense of language, functions through and embodies reference to shared experience, outlook, values, traditions, conventions.

Social organizations can be toppled by external pressure or dissolved into chaos by internal discontents. Their destruction requires no unifying culture. To construct social organizations anew needs a continuing, persisting, broad-fronted endeavor, and behind that endeavor the unremitting support of many. A great social innovation adapts as it develops. It grows organically, evolving at innumerable points. At each of these points, encountering the unforeseen, it is reshaped and remade through the initiative of those immediately engaged. To enlist the voluntary effort and imagination of those engaged along the whole periphery of change, participants must share a common commitment and vision. This is so when the change follows some grand design formulated at a political center. It is also the case when change relies on the spontaneous decen- ˙ tralized choices made by individuals independently. Individuals need not be directed, but, if their society is to be transformed, they must share a direction. This unifying vision generates the force and sets the goals of social change, provides a common conception of what is sought, of what ought to be.

The vision at the apex and the integrating culture at the base are interdependent. For a revolution to succeed, the two must fit, or be made to fit together. Whether the guiding idea guides, whether the vision can be made manifest will depend on whether it complements or can be tailored to suit the prevailing culture and cognition, or on whether culture and cognition can be reshaped in the ferment of revolution by the catalytic force of the guiding idea.

The Culture of Individualism. When De Tocqueville visited and studied the United States in the nineteenth century and wrote his great treatise on America, he noted with alarm the prevailing cult of "individualism." He considered that selfishness and self-seeking had been postulated as a principle and sanctified as the touchstone of prosperity. Certainly the utilitarian philosophy which was then dominant in England and the United States did idealize a rational, aggressively self-seeking individual. The epitome of the Darwinian or Spencerian evolution was a pleasure-seeking automaton whose whole aim was to maximize the satisfactions of increased consumption and simultaneously to minimize the dissatisfactions of the effort of acquisition. The dominant philosophical system was at once complex and shallow, optimistic and tragic. It conceived a world within a world. In an inner sphere, aggressive, rational satisfaction-maximizers in their blind, competitive self-seeking on the market progressively created a more productive technology, accumulated personal wealth, and enjoyed the greater "happiness" of more consumption. In an outer sphere human masses in their blind surrender to sexual lust were foredoomed to eternal Malthusian misery. This double vision had its counterpart in reality. The rising bourgeoisie of Western Europe and the United States were among the elect. The laboring class of Europe and the conquered, colonized peoples of Asia, Africa, India, South America composed the endless ranks of the damned.

Western Europe and the United States had, in fact, been carried over the threshold of the Industrial Revolution by the thrust of individual efforts in the pursuit of private ambitions. It was in Western Europe and the United States peculiarly, and not in the rest of the world, that the industrial revolution took place autonomously, under the spur of individual choice. Yet this phenomenon can hardly be explained simply as the consequence of Economic Man's aggressive self-seeking and his rational calculus of pleasure/pain. Western Europeans or North Americans have no peculiar cognitive competence in rationally balancing the satisfactions and pleasures of possession and consumption against the dissatisfactions of labor. Selfishness and self-seeking are qualities widespread among all human populations. Allegedly, nowhere can there be found a more aggressively individualistic, nor a more rationally self-seeking people than those in Latin America. There, too, they have made a cult of individualism called "personalissimo." Yet the economic revolutions have still to come in Latin America.

The Industrial Revolution also required collective actions and individual and group dedication. It needed its Pilgrims, and its Roundhead armies. It had its rebellion and uprising, its share of bloodshed, its martyrs, and its soldiers. If the French Revolution ushered in "economic liberty" for the self-interested pursuit of private gain, it also enunciated the rights of man. None of this can be comprehended in terms of the self-seeking automaton of classical economics. In fact, those countries that witnessed the autonomous Industrial Revolution were characterized by a remarkable degree of internal political stability and social discipline. They were marked by the capacity of individuals and groups to articulate opinions, to discuss differences, and to associate for common purposes. Nor are these proclivities and capacities inherent in the nature of things.

Rather they were specific to that particular culture that underlay the Industrial Revolution.

Puritan Individualism and Personalissimo. Max Weber and Tawney were nearer the truth than the economists when they traced the rise of capitalism (and the Industrial Revolution) to the spread of the Puritan ethic. And nothing is further from the Puritan ethic than the logic of the economic man for whom the perfect existence must be an existence without labor, where all effort is reckoned as a dissatisfaction, and where the ideal life is one where the dissatisfactions of work are nil, and where consumption, with its pleasures, is infinitely extended. The Puritan rather was a man of sobriety, of responsibility, for whom it was duty to labor and for whom work was a way of life. Contrast, for example, the individualism of the Puritan with the *personalissimo* of Latin America.

Puritan individualism builds a wall around each person or around each household. The person or the head of the household bears full responsibility for what occurs within those walls; for that, he stands entirely accountable. And he is responsible also, though to a lesser degree, for what occurs outside the walls. Within, he has certain rights, and above all the right to privacy, in his worship and in his thought. Outside, he has certain rights also, above all the right to seek undisturbed to achieve his private ends within the confines of the law. None may transgress his privacy, nor he theirs. His rights and theirs, his privacy and theirs are partly embodied in property and are defined and protected by the laws of property. Puritan individualism is implicitly a system of reciprocal rights, guarantees and obligations, a complex form of social organization built on the privacy and particularity of anonymous individuals.

In contrast *personalissimo* is not a code of reciprocal rights, guarantees, and obligations. It connotes no social arrangement. It is simply an emotional imperative. It does not seek to limit the collective power in order to safeguard the private domain of the individual. Rather it denies limitations of any sort upon the aggressions of the individual will or upon the prerogatives of the unique personality. It does not ask for a system of uniform rights for all, but asks all rights for the one. It only values and recognizes the particularity and the uniqueness of I, and of him. Person relates intensely to person, but they do not arrange themselves into a community. Individualism is built around the right of privacy. *Personalissimo* denies the right of privacy, for it asserts the right of the one to gather all unto himself. The individual is anonymous, the personality is not. The personality orates. It needs an audience. It needs applause. Its unbounded will demands submission. If individualism is the code of the Puritan, *personalissimo* is the code of Don Juan. For Puritan individualism, the orderly organization of society is prior to, and is a prerequisite for, the exercise of private choice. *Personalissimo* conflicts with any orderly organization of society. Puritan individualism complements democratic procedure and is entirely compatible with political association and cooperation. Conspiracy may be the one political association of which *personalissimo* is capable, with its proper form of government in the benevolence or tyranny of the most powerful person—the dictator.

Puritan individualism provided a cultural base for private effort and for social organization, for individual dedication, and for collective action. But the culture of *personalissimo* provides the cultural base neither for autonomous economic revolution through the market, nor for an economic revolution under political direction. Yet, oddly, it is not Puritan individualism, but *personalissimo* that suits the economic "calculus" and fits the description of self-seeking, satisfaction-maximizing Economic Man.

Variables in the Culture of Individualism. Not all of the businessmen who contributed to the Industrial Revolution subscribed to Puritan values. Other cultural systems than that of Puritan individualism are compatible with the autonomous economic revolution. But whatever the cultural system, it must motivate individual endeavor and also must provide some basis for group association or collective action. And, moreover, whatever the cultural system it must be coupled with the cognitions of mechanism and of process. The slickest and most aggressive entrepreneurial class, competing together in their financial skills and bargaining prowess, wheeling and dealing, hedging and speculating, influence peddling, and tax shading, will not add an iota to economic progress and certainly will generate no industrial revolution when they are without cognition of process and take technology as given.

The individual may be motivated, let us say, to maximize his profits, but for what purpose? What does he intend to do with his profits, with his wages, with his higher income? That matters also in the long haul of economic revolution. If he follows the calculus of classical economic theory, balancing the diminishing satisfactions of incremental gain against the rising dissatisfaction of incremental effort, his interest in his work, his willingness to labor, his concern for his business will diminish in proportion as he rises on the ladder of economic leadership, and as his wealth increases. If his cultural system idealizes the aristocrat, he will struggle upward only to escape the sordid world of trade and to enable himself or his heirs to lead a life of gentlemanly idleness, or to find an honorable profession in politics, the church, or the army; correspondingly the force for progressive economic change will be depleted. It is, surely, one great strength of American enterprise that the American culture seems to value wealth and income not so much for the pleasures they can purchase or the life they can provide, but rather as symbols of success in a business game where the joy is in the winning. This is a strength of the system because the goals of action are open-ended and never fulfilled. The drives of economic leadership do not peter out. The force of business motivation need not diminish as a consequence of the changing level of wealth, income, and power.

Voluntary Association and the Organizational Revolution. As long as operations remain within the scope of one-man control, a culture orienting ambition toward ownership and independence and a cognition built around the know-how of the "boss" may suffice for the efficient and progressive organization of economic activity. When, however, choice is made by public officials, or when it is exercised by corporate officials in companies where the scale and complexity of operations transcend one-man control, other values and another kind of knowledge are necessary.

One cultural-cognitive system that could support an organizational economy combines the dedication of an elite that plans and leads with the discipline and obedience of those that follow. Earlier, the culture requisites of leadership-followership were examined. A culture of discipline and obedience, the capacity for mass response to the distant signal, magnifies the power of an elite. Armies and military organizations are representative examples. But discipline and obedience neither enlist the initiative and creative capacities of the multitude, nor facilitate that "conversation" through which lessons gained in operating experience can feed back into the cognition of decision-makers. For this there must be integrating ties, proceeding perhaps from the wills, enthusiasms, needs, interests, shared vision, and objectives of the many who participate.

Latent capacities for voluntary association are often powerfully revealed in war or natural catastrophe, where common crisis forces the realization of interdependence. But aside from external crisis or even any sense of common goals, there are values inherent in association and psychological propensities that support it.

Association can be a way of life and an end in itself, built upon those same proclivities that lead children to form themselves into teams to play games or into gangs to wage gang wars, that brings the football squad (stars, scrubs, and the waterboy) to the long hard afternoons in the winter cold and mud, to spring training and to summer practice—in immense efforts for trumped-up purposes where reward inheres in the satisfactions of participating together.

De Tocqueville despaired of America's cult of individualism, but he believed that a peculiar capacity for voluntary association compensated for it. He saw voluntary associations springing up anywhere, for any purpose, or for no purpose. Whether or not this capacity and propensity for voluntary association has, as De Tocqueville predicted, safeguarded America against political tyranny, it did serve in ushering in an organizational revolution.

The culture of voluntary association with its emphasis on the group, on togetherness, on the team, contrasts with Puritan individualism and its emphasis on the privacy and isolated responsibility of the individual. The culture of voluntary association is the culture of the "other directed," of the "company man." It has its seamy side. The value of the culture of voluntary association is not simply that it provides the possibility of spontaneously organizing activities of a scale beyond the scope of one-man control. When an activity could conceivably be run by one man, it may be considered preferable that it be organized through voluntary association. Through such an association the creative initiative of subordinates can be most easily enlisted and their experience tapped. One-man leadership, moreover, requires a very particular sort of man, a jack-of-all-choice, a rare specimen. The requisites of decision-making and of recruiting and training an economic leadership become easier to meet when responsibility can be shared among specialists who have the ability to associate, rather than when concentrated in one individual.

Attitudes conducive to the effective control of one-man enterprise may conflict with the cultural requirement of voluntary association and, hence, may stand in the way of the achievement of organizational revolution. In French private industry today, the dominant culture and cognition reserves control to a single chief, the "grand patron." This propensity accounts for the failure of French enterprises to evolve into world corporations, and hence, beyond a certain point, for French enterprise to hold its own in international competition. It is one reason also for the relative importance of government-sponsored cooperative planning in French industry, since activities that cannot be organized on a sufficient scale by the private company must be organized under the direction of the State. It is rather in his participation in the formulation of the French Plan than in his work in his own company that the industry expert and company official finds himself an associate rather than a servant, with an outlet for independent, creative initiative.

This chapter has explored certain of the cultural and cognitive requisites of development. With reference to these requisites, the next chapter will consider the problems and failures of development in Mexico.

Chapter 35

Development that Failed: The Case of Mexico

Can We Learn From Failure? Mexico is a country of great natural resources. Its energetic people are the inheritors of two ancient civilizations. It has revolutionized its economy and its government. For more than a century it has sought development, yet it remains in the ranks of the impoverished and technically backward. What can be learned from this long Mexican effort to cross the threshold of modern, high-productivity technology?

A REVIEW OF MEXICAN HISTORY

Mexico Before the Conquest. Before the Spaniards came, some ten million Indians inhabited Mexico. They were of many different tribes, religions, languages, customs. In the dry rugged North they were wandering hunters. In the densely populated South they were peasant farmers. They were without the cow or pig or sheep or ox. They had no beasts of burden, no plow. They had never discovered the wheel.

Principally the peasant lived by raising corn. For this he burned the ground clean for planting. He dug a hole in the earth with a stick and built a mound of soil around the seed with his fingers. Kneeling women pounded the ripened corn, stone on stone, moulded the flour into *tamales* or *tortillas,* and cooked them over charcoal embers. As it was done then, so it is done now.

Among the great Indian peoples were the Mayans in the Yucatan, the Zapotecs and the Toltecs in Southern and Central Mexico, and the conquering Nahuas who had come out of the mountains in the North. Among the Nahuas, the fiercest tribe was the Aztec. The Aztecs occupied Anahauac, the "Valley of Mexico," a high fertile tableland, well-watered and temperate. By the time of the Spanish conquest, the Aztecs had extended their domain over nearly the whole of the civilized peoples of Mexico, exacting tribute for the beautification of their great city and prisoners for sacrifice to Huitzilopochtli, their insatiable God of War.

The tribal systems were theocratic. Warriors and *caciques* merged into the priesthood. The priests were the magicians, the astronomers, the architects, the scientists. They alone possessed a consciousness of history and of social purpose. They had invented a system of hieroglyphics, of numbers, an extraordinary calendar. But their greatest invention was the gods, for in them were articulated the values of a people and a conception of the universe. The tribe itself was shaped in the image of its deity. It was a singular tragedy that the Aztec war god, Huitzilopochtli, destroyer, insatiable in his demands for human blood, gained ascendancy over the Toltec's beneficent Quetzalcoatl, god of the morning star and the rippling stream.

Mexican Cultures After the Conquest (*1535-1759*). Through the Spanish conquest one political authority came to rule over Mexico. Nevertheless, there was never a single, integral Mexican society. Rather there were four and then five different and distinct "societies."

There was the society of the Indian.

. . . patient rather than aggressive, given to a stoical endurance rather than to conflict. In their intercourse with each other cheerfulness and good humor were the dominating note, and courtesy became a ritual. . . . Never having developed any strong sense of personal individuality, they rated human life very cheaply. For them the individual counted for little, and the welfare of the tribe was everything. When they submitted to conquest their resistance would usually be silent and passive but more stubborn and tenacious than that of other races. . . . Their loyalty was not to the abstractions of society and the state but to the neighbors and kinsfolk who comprised their tribe and to the chieftains who embodied it.[1]

The Conquest had wiped out the Indian's priesthood and thus tore out the people's tongue and robbed it of its memory.

The Conquest, as if by design, had destroyed all the leaders of Mexico, all of its wise men, all of its priests, all of those who had carried in them the accumulated wisdom of a strange and heroic people. Spiritually the cataclysm was complete, as if the head had been severed but the body by some miracle was permitted to wriggle in the dust.[2]

There was the society of the creoles—white settlers, American-born descendants of the *conquistadores* and their soldiers and those who had followed from Spain. They came from a nation of lords and serfs. They intended to be lords of the New Spain and to make the Indians their serfs.

There was the *gachupine* society. These were Spaniards who came from Spain, returned to Spain, and remained part of the Spanish world. A caste apart, they included the viceroys, the merchants, all the higher and most of the lower crown officials. They exercised all political authority.

---

[1] Henry Bamford Parkes, *A History of Mexico* (3rd ed., Boston: Houghton Mifflin, 1960), pp. 5–6. This and the following excerpts from Parkes, *A History of Mexico*, are reprinted with the permission of the publisher.

[2] Frank Tannenbaum, *Mexico: Struggle for Peace and Bread* (New York: Alfred A. Knopf, 1950), p. 29. This and the following excerpts from Tannenbaum, *Mexico: Struggle for Peace and Bread*, are reprinted with the permission of the publisher.

There was the society of the Mexican Church, powerful and multifunctional. During the eighteenth century, it included from ten to fifteen thousand priests and members of holy orders. It had built 12,000 churches. It had its own missions, its own schools and colleges, its own laws and courts of justice. It was by all odds the most important economic organization in Mexico.

Lucas Alaman, a good member of the Church, and the intellectual leader of the Church party in his day, estimated that at the end of the colonial period "not less than half of the real property and capital of the country belonged to the Church. Most of the remainder was controlled by the Church through mortgages. The Church was the landlord, the banker, and the trustee of the period." [3]

And there was, or came to be, the society of the *mestizo* or mixed blood. There was, of course, Spanish blood in the village Indian, and Indian blood in the town creole. What distinguished the *mestizo* was nonmembership in any of the structured communities bound together by functional interdependence or a common culture. He had left the village and cut himself off from the tribe. He was excluded from the world of the creole. He was the street rabble, beggar, itinerant laborer, muleteer, independent ranchero, bandit, city *lepero*. He was on his own, looking for a crack or a crevice in all the walls around him. He was the first to feel himself Mexican.

The Interests of the Spanish Crown. The *gachupine* elite in New Spain served the Spanish Crown, but the interest of the Crown was equivocal.

In the first instance the Crown sought to raise the conquered Indians to the status of loyal, productive, Catholic subjects.

The Spanish kings tried to give all the immunities and protections to the Indians that redounded to the Spaniards, they tried a thousand laws and ordinances to protect them and mold them into good Catholics, workers protected and paid in honest coin. . . . Perhaps no more generous effort was ever made by a conquering power to cast the mantle of protective justice over a defeated people.[4]

They believed also that the conquest of America was legitimate only if it proved beneficial to the races who had been conquered. No imperialist government in history has shown a more genuine concern for the welfare of a conquered race.[5]

The early viceregal officials limited and eventually abolished slavery

---

[3] Frank Tannenbaum, *Peace by Revolution* (New York: Columbia University Press, 1933), p. 54. Reprinted with the permission of the publisher.
[4] Tannenbaum, *Struggle for Peace*, p. 30.
[5] Parkes, p. 88.

and the system of *encomiendas* that turned the Indians into serfs. In 1567 they granted each Indian village a square league of communal land in perpetuity, thus safeguarding the communal village or *ejido*. For three hundred years—until the triumph of "liberalism"—the *ejido*, protected under Spanish law, was to be the Indian's only bulwark of dignity and independence. High Church officials and viceregal governors began a system of education for the Indian that included institutions of higher learning. They introduced the Indian to the cultivation of wheat, fruit and the grape, as well as mulberrys for raising silkworms in addition to his corn and *maguey*. They taught him European crafts and techniques. They brought in new industries for the production of wool, silk, leather, furniture, ironwork, and wines.

There was another interest of the Spanish Crown: to increase the economic and military power of Spain. Following the doctrines of mercantilism, it sought to do this by increasing the inflow of gold into the King's treasury through a favorable balance of trade. To this end, the law required that virtually all trade be with Spain or move through Spanish ports.

The merchants demanded more. In the name of mercantilism, they wanted to erase all the economic development that the viceregal officials and high churchmen had introduced in order to protect and to raise the living standards of the Indian, since such development weakened their export monopolies. The creole also opposed the policies of development since these might shield the Indian from creole exploitation.

Economic development and the protection of the Indian, or mercantilism, monopoly, and exploitation of the Indian? The issue was resolved by the weakening of the Spanish Crown itself. The royal line decayed finally into imbecility, dragging down the character of the colonial administration and its capacity to resist the interest of the merchant monopolist and the creole landowner.

The industrial development of New Spain was halted. The manufacture of silk was prohibited. Mulberry trees raised by the Indian to feed the silkworm were cut down. Vineyards were torn up. Wine presses were destroyed. All exports from New Spain were forbidden except minerals and a few dyestuffs.

The Indian was denied the right to plant European crops. He was forbidden from acquiring European plants, or animals, or instruments. He was excluded from the crafts and from all the professions. He was kept out of any official position. The schools that the old churchmen and the viceroys had built for him were taken away. He was denied any education. About a third of the indigenous people came to labor as serfs on the creole haciendas that covered most of the fertile Valley of Mexico.

Before the Conquest, the Indian had been ten million strong. By 1815, decimated by exactions, brutalities, and European disease, they numbered four and a half million.

The accession of Charles III to the throne of Spain in 1759 infused the Spanish colonial administration with vigor, reflecting the "new liberalism," antitraditional, anticlerical, antifeudal, which then excited the minds of Europe. Emphasis was on free trade, on individual initiative, on professional administration in government. Mercantilist doctrine was shelved. Science and education were encouraged. The period was one of unprecedented prosperity and progress. After 1788, Charles' successors abandoned his reforms. A corrupt and incompetent administration returned. But the past was not so easily regained.

New notions had infiltrated: rationality in political choice, equality before the law, natural rights, a free market. These were particularly important for the *mestizos,* who were outside the established orders and who were therefore in search of a culture and a cognition. Liberalism would become a *mestizo* creed.

The Collapse of Empire. In spite of the decadence of the Crown and the weakness of the colonial administration, and in spite of the divergence between the policies of mercantilism and the economic interest of the colonies, Spain maintained control over the vast territories of Hispanic America for centuries. This is to be explained partly by the Spaniard's monopoly of the political cognition, by the divisive pulls of five societies existing in counterbalancing antagonism, and by the power of legitimacy in societies where traditionalism is pre-eminent and all power is vested in hierarchies of privilege. The Crown's authority was the keystone of the tradition-based arch of the whole structure of established privileges and powers. When the armies of Napoleon overran Spain and deposed the King, the keystone was driven from the arch. Loyalty had never been due to Spain but to the King of Spain. Now the King was gone. Spanish officials lacked the authority of the Royal command and the support of Spanish arms. Uprisings began. The creoles expelled the Spaniards and assumed political control throughout Hispanic America—except in Mexico. In Mexico the struggle took a radically different turn.

Slave Uprising. It was in 1810 in the little Mexican town of Queretaro. A creole uprising against the Spaniard was in the air. The local social and literary club had hatched a scheme of military rebellion. The plotters included the local *corregidor* and his wife, some army officers, and one Miguel Hidalgo y Costillo, the parish priest from the nearby town of Dolores. Hidalgo, then nearly sixty, was a man of learning, influenced by the French rationalists and suspected by the Inquisition. In violation of the law he had taught the Indians of his parish to manufacture pottery and leather and to plant olive and mulberry trees. Recently the police had come to Dolores and had torn down the vines and destroyed the trees.

On September 13th, the Spanish authorities were informed of the plot in Queretaro. Warrants were issued for the arrest of the conspirators. Told that the police were coming and that he must flee or wait to surrender, Hidalgo, instead, followed a strange impulse He went to the church and rang the bells. When his Indian parishioners assembled, he told them that the time had come to overthrow the Spanish oppressor. He led a tiny procession of Indians carrying sharpened sticks and machetes and images of the Virgin into the countryside, and they marched. From everywhere the Indians joined them. Within weeks the little band had become a horde of fifty thousand. Under the banner of Hidalgo's rebellion, armies rose in the north and the south, spontaneously, armies of peons, of *leperos*, of brigands, armies that would stand up to cannon fire with their slings and that were able to envelop regiments of soldiers in their mass. This was not the palace coup that the creole had envisaged. It was a slave uprising.

The *gachupine*, the creole, and the clergy put aside their differences and united against this movement from the depths. Creole officers deserted Hidalgo's ranks. The Church excommunicated him. Nevertheless his armies reached the heights above Mexico City and stood ready to enter the gates of victory. There Hidalgo lost heart. A slave uprising is a terrible, vengeful, uncontrollable force. Instead of unleashing it, Hidalgo turned his armies back from the city. They disintegrated. They were caught and slaughtered. Hidalgo was captured. His severed head was displayed on a stake in the city square. The rebellion was crushed, but its impact was irrevocable. A blind and wrathful giant stood revealed, listening for the voice that would lead him. None could doubt his strength. And many would claim to speak for him.

The uprising disintegrated into a series of guerrilla wars. By 1818 it had exhausted itself. With the threat of social revolution gone, creole and *mestizo* united to rid themselves of the *gachupine* authority.

The Spaniards were expelled. With them went the only group in Mexico skilled in public administration and government. Ancient allegiances had been dissolved and the adhesive force of legitimacy was shattered.

With the Spanish gone, there were two contenders for power: the creole and the *mestizo*. The creoles had wealth, a habit of authority, and military skill. Through these, they took possession of the political system.

The Failure of Creole Rule. The greatest figure and the most persistent power during the whole period of creole domination was Antonio Lopez Santa Anna.

Though Santa Anna looked like a philosopher and talked like a disillusioned patriot, his hero . . . was Napoleon. . . . It was not, however, by any Napoleonic will to power but by traits more typical of Spanish America that Santa Anna succeeded in becoming, for thirty years, the curse of his native country. With his talent for composing plans and *pronunciamentos,* his taste for pageantry and personal display, his love for fine appearances and his blindness to realities, his frivolity and his dishonesty, his overweening pretensions and his amazing ignorance, he was an epitome of all those vices to which Mexican politicians were most apt to succumb. Representing nothing but the greed of generals and *agiotistas* and treacherous to every cause which he adopted. . . .[6]

Santa Anna epitomizes creole rule and explains its failure. He was demagogue and magician, immensely skilled in the art of landing on his feet and treading his way to the top of any heap. He was the romantic poseur, the pseudo-philosopher, but with no values other than self-glorification, no goal beyond the sheer possession and exercise of power. Of complex social problems, he had no cognition. So the creoles; for the problems of political anarchy and economic decay, they had no answer. Theirs was the heroic gesture. Their purpose was self-aggrandizement. At best they reincarnated the ancestral *conquistadore,* but now there were no Indies to be conquered, no treasure to be seized. The task was to govern, or rather to create a nation that could be governed. This was beyond their ken. The sense of political legitimacy, the culture of obedience and respect, the apparatus of political authority had all broken down. The creole could not resurrect them.

In every province there was guerrilla warfare and banditry. The silver mines were flooded and closed. Power was divided among the numerous *caciques.* The Yucatan seceded. The Americans took Texas and the whole great territory above the Rio Grande. American armies sacked Mexico City.

Creoles relied on the bayonets of the army, and armies must be paid. To pay the army, each succeeding regime borrowed from the *agiotistas* and from the foreigner, pledging the national credit and tax revenues. In the end, to fend off the *mestizo,* the clergy and the creole sought foreign intervention. In 1864, Napoleon III of France installed the Austrian Prince Maximilian as the new Emperor of Mexico. The Prince had the highest intentions—but he had no instrument of executive administration and no disciplined, obedient people to respond to his rule. He could accomplish nothing.

Maximilian was accustomed to the Hapsburg bureaucracy, with the habits of obedience which had been developed through six hundred years. He never realized that in Mexico there had always been a plethora of admirable laws

[6] Parkes, pp. 198–199.

and constitutions, but that since the sixteenth century it had been rare for a single one of them to be obeyed.[7]

The creoles' political system could not be maintained. Neither the guns of the French nor the leadership of the Prince could save it.

The Triumph and Tragedy of Liberalism (1867-1910). The patron and the father of *mestizo* liberalism was Benito Juarez. By chance and by charity he had been taken as a child from the ignorance of the Indian village. He had been educated. He became a lawyer and a professor of law, then a local politician and a successful provincial administrator. He finally led the *mestizo* liberals against the creole oligarchy in the war against Maximilian. In 1867 he became President and held that office until his death in 1872.

Juarez was a man of powerful character, of remorseless persistence, of integrity and dedication. But he also was a provincial lawyer in a distant corner of a backward society. He was a poor Indian who had learned all that he knew, and all that gave him status and power, by reading books of European law. His ideas and theories were derived from the culture and circumstances of other, far-away peoples. He relied, like those around him on the politics of *The Federalist*, on the laissez-faire liberalism of Adam Smith and his followers, on the logical positivism of Auguste Comte, as these filtered down through interpretation and hearsay.

Juarez was a rationalist and an individualist. He wanted a free-market economy and a political authority that confined itself to the maintenance of order and security. He wanted a government that was democratically elected, with political power delineated in a written constitution and divided between the central authority and the states.

His enemy was the Church, because the Church had chosen to be his enemy—fighting him with all the power and treasure at its command—and also because the Church was the antithesis of his liberal, nationalist credo. The Church was an independent government outside the national authority. The Church was an economic organization outside the free-enterprise economy. The Church was the bastion of traditional values in opposition to those of rational individualism.

Juarez sought full freedom of trade. This was to be achieved by sweeping away mercantile checks and aristocratic privileges, by eliminating regional trade barriers and vested monopolies, by obliging the Church to disgorge itself of its landholdings, and, also, by turning the communal *ejido* of the Indian village into the property of freeholders. It was supposed that once this had been done, the released initiative of the individual and his rational self-interest, operating under the free competition

[7] Parkes, p. 264.

of the market, would provide the motor force for economic development. *Ley Juarez* and *Ley Lerdo* were intended to achieve these objectives. *Ley Lerdo* required the public sale of all communally or corporately owned agricultural property.

Nothing turned out as Juarez anticipated. The Church was indeed forced to sell its land. But the village Indian could not buy it. The small holder was frightened by the anathemas of the clergy from bidding upon it. Instead it was bought up cheaply by the rich creoles and new *mestizo* oligarchs and served further to swell the wealth and the power of the great *hacendados*. Worse, in the days that followed, those laws would be used to break up the village common and to force the Indian off his *ejido* into peonage on the great estate.

Following the wisdom of *The Federalist*, the Mexican Constitution dispersed the political power among the provinces. This was conceived as a protection against tyranny from the center. But each province was in the fist of a *caudillo*, who consolidated his position through local economic monopoly. Without an overriding central power, there could be no integral economy. Without any national *cacique* there was no nation.

Nor did enterprise flourish under *laissez faire*. To get a railroad built between Mexico City and the Coast, Juarez was obliged to bring in and to subsidize the foreigner. After the death of Juarez, the mantle of laissez-faire liberalism fell on Porfirio Diaz, who was to rule Mexico as dictator for thirty-seven years.

The Dictatorship of Diaz. Don Porfirio Diaz, during the nearly four decades of his dictatorship, was respected and admired throughout the world. He was the darling of the American State Department and of the European Foreign offices. He gave full support to free enterprise. He believed in sound money and a balanced budget. He created conditions to attract foreign investment. He followed the advice of expert "economists." The profits of the *hacendados* were protected and their privileges were extended. The laws against the Church were not enforced. And Don Porfirio was very reasonable, willing to make a deal with anybody. Bandits, brigands, rebel chiefs, and their troops were brought into the regular army, and their looting was institutionalized. To each was given according to his power.

Every accommodation was made to attract foreign investment: low wages, no unions, few taxes, special privileges, even a separate law for the foreigner. In response, foreign investment poured in. From 1897 to 1911, there was more than a billion dollars of foreign investment in Mexico, mostly by Americans, first to build railroads, then to develop mines and smelters, then to develop an export trade in cattle and hides and cotton and chick-peas and sugar and chicle and henequen.

The lands in the public domain were opened to purchase and procurement. The last protections for the Indian *ejido* were withdrawn. Between 1877 and 1910 title to over 100,000,000 acres of land in Mexico changed hands, mostly under duress. A few acquired immense holdings. One family in Chihuahua had an estate of 33,000,000 acres. All the crop land was held by a few thousand *hacendados*. Half of the rural families lived and worked as peons on those haciendas. And peonage, as John Dewey wrote, was "in fact a slavery as effective as that of the Negroes in the United States before the Civil War." [8] Of the rural population, some 97 percent were landless.

By the statistics, by the measures of national income, of cash accumulation, of exports, of car loadings, etc., Mexico was a land of miracles, of amazing progress and great prospects. But how much filtered down as benefits to the people? Consider oil: pumped by foreign technicians with foreign equipment for use by foreign consumers. What was left for the Mexican? The empty earth.

The development of the Mexican oil industry was chiefly the work of Edward L. Doheny, who acquired in 1900, at a price of not much more than a dollar an acre, enormous oil fields in the neighborhood of Tampico. Other fields were afterwards acquired by the Rockefeller interests and by the British firm of Pearson and Son, headed by Lord Cowdray. Some of these wells could produce, without pressure or pumps, up to fifty thousand barrels a day. Yet apart from a negligible stamp duty the owners of Mexican oil paid no taxes and could export it freely. Mexico did not even benefit by low prices; for in spite of heavy taxation the price of oil in the United States was no higher than it was in Mexico.[9]

Something of course was gained by the Mexicans. Enough to rebuild Mexico City. Enough to support corruption and luxury in high places. There were the 15,000 miles of railroad grid, as a prerequisite to the national market. Something certainly had been gained. But measured against the suffering of the Mexicans and the loss of their resources, the gain was little enough.

In the name of Progress, the *Ley Lerdo* was enforced to the hilt. The Indian was entirely dispossessed. When he resisted he was shot or transported. "In Hidalgo some of them were buried up to their necks in the land which they had attempted to defend, after which a party of *Rurales* galloped over them." [10] In 1901 Victoriano Huerta completed the conquest of the Yucatan and reduced 100,000 Mayan Indians to the status of slaves,

[8] John Dewey, *Impressions of Soviet Russia and the Revolutionary World* (New York: New Republic, Inc., 1929), p. 172.
[9] Parkes, p. 310.
[10] *Ibid.*, p. 295.

to labor and die on the plantations of fifty creoles in the production of "henequen for sale to the American cordage trust and of chicle to satisfy the American appetite for chewing gum." [11] So also with the Yaquis who farmed the fertile valley lands of Sonora. They were driven off their farms into the mountains, subjugated through starvation and sold at 75 pesos a head to the plantations of Quintana Roo. There they died off, laboring in the torrid sun. Their lands became creole haciendas.

The statistics transmogrified it all to progress. All the gains made by *mestizo* and creole oligarchs appeared on the profit side of the commercial ledger. But of the degradation of men and the decline in the standards of human life, as these occurred in the self-sustaining economy of the Indian village and the hacienda, there was no record and no measure.

The Mexican agricultural laborers existed, during the Diaz regime, in a condition of sodden and brutish misery probably unmatched by the proletariat of any other country. Corn, chiles, and *frijoles* were still almost their only food. They still slept in small huts of wood or piled stones, and spread their straw *petates* on the bare ground. The prevalence of enteric, due to impure food and drinking water, of pneumonia, due to lack of shelter, and of venereal disease was as great as anywhere else in the world. . . . Such had been the lives of the peons since the colonial period, but under Diaz the *hacienda* system had spread throughout the entire country and the misery of its victims had been intensified.[12]

The hacienda system was inefficient. Its techniques had scarcely changed in three centuries. Its owners were gentlefolk living in Mexico City or Paris. Control was left with stewards who beat and tortured the peons and exercised feudal rights over their wives and daughters.

For this hacienda, this all-embracing institution, was neither creative nor enterprising. It was constructed for security and not for progress—not even for increasing profit. Its owners, at least toward the end of the nineteenth century, left the management of the estates to hired administrators . . . until the poor *aparecero* or *mediero*, species of sharecroppers who supported the entire load, was barely able to eke out the poorest sort of subsistence.[13]

It is no accident that Mexican agriculture remained stationary or declined. Fertility fell steadily all through the nineteenth century, prices of agricultural products increased greatly, and the hacienda system was saved from complete bankruptcy by a tariff on agricultural products.[14]

As on the land, so in the new factory, labor was extorted from the

[11] *Ibid.*, p. 296.
[12] *Ibid.*, p. 307.
[13] Tannenbaum, *Struggle for Peace*, p. 142.
[14] *Ibid.*, p. 146.

Indian through the whip and the gun. Unarmed workers in disputes with their employers were shot down by the hundreds.

Real wages declined steadily. The money wage of the peon remained what it had been for centuries, twenty-five to forty centavos a day, but prices doubled, tripled, quadrupled. A laborer in 1910 could buy with his wage a quarter of the corn that he could have bought in 1880.

The mountainsides had been stripped of their forest cover. The rivers dried, and the land eroded. Each year the fertility of the soil diminished and the yield in crops declined. Following the observations of Von Humboldt, it has been estimated that the average wheat yield in Mexico in the 1940's was 20 percent of what it had been in 1803. Indeed before the Spanish conquest, the Mexican Indian, without a horse, without a plough, with nothing but a corn seed and a stick, had fed a population of some 10,000,000 and had supported besides the edifices of mighty civilizations and the wastes of their wars.[15] Yet at the turn of the twentieth century, Mexico could not feed its ten million people. Hunger was endemic. Some starved, in spite of large imports of food.

In the political heights around the dictator, there had developed a new governing elite, the *Cientificos*. These were trained economists and financial experts, educated and aloof, who spoke the language of diplomacy and of Wall Street and the universities. They enunciated a new rationale of liberalism. In Mexico, amid the mighty ruins of the Mayan, the Aztec, and the Toltec civilizations, where Juarez, the father of liberalism, was a pure-blooded Indian, and where the dictator himself, Don Porifirio, had but a sprinkling of Spanish blood—in that Mexico it was promulgated as official doctrine and as established truth that the Indian was genetically inferior. The natural law, therefore, justified the Indian's serving his racial superiors until, under the beneficent laws of evolution, he was eventually decimated and replaced by a higher strain of man.

Mexico was ready for new convulsions. In 1910 the dictatorship collapsed.

Revolution and Its Aftermath (1910-1940). Gentle, inept Gustavo Madero came to power on the crest of a great wave of enthusiasm. The enthusiasm was not for Madero's triumph but for the defeat of Diaz. The reins were pulled from palsied hands. Mexico shed the dictatorship like a dead skin and exulted at the first free breath of air.

[15] This is Parkes' evidently very conservative estimate. J. H. Elliott in his article "The Spanish Heritage," *Encounter*, Vol. 25 (September 1965), basing himself on S. F. Cook and L. B. Simpson, *The Population of Central Mexico in the 16th Century* (1948) and "later studies in the same California series of Ibero-Americana" states that "Out of a pre-conquest indigenous population *of more than twenty million in central Mexico,* under three million remained by the end of the 16th century." (My italics.)

The system of political authority had tumbled, but those who had shared in the spoils remained. The *jefe politicos* were there, and those who lived by serving them, and those who schemed to fill their shoes. So were the provincial *caudillos* and their armies, and the Church, resurrected and powerful, and the creole *cientificos*, and the *hacendados*, and the foreign corporations backed by their embassies. It was, in fact, the American ambassador, Henry Lane Wilson, who underwrote the conspiracy and the treachery that destroyed Madero's government. Victoriano Huerta captured and murdered his chief. A great struggle began, a chaos of conflict and destruction that blanketed the land for nearly twenty years and killed a million people.

Out of this chaos there emerged the changes called the "Mexican Revolution." Its grand manifesto was the Constitution of 1917. It was expressed more concretely in the extension of educational opportunity. Thousands of new missionaries, this time preaching Mexican Nationhood, went into the villages to teach the Indian. It was expressed under the socialist administration of Lazaro Cardenas, from 1934 to 1940, in a massive redistribution of property and power. Under Cardenas some 45,000,000 acres of land were repossessed and returned to the Indian *ejido*. In 1910 more than 95 percent of the agricultural population had been landless. By the early 1940s half of the rural population and more than half the nation's crop land belonged to the *ejido*. The ejidoist was armed; a peasant militia was created. The ejidoist and the small holder were organized politically and were represented at every level of government. Industrial labor was organized into trade unions. The trade unions were incorporated into the political system. The temporal power of the Catholic Church was greatly reduced. The army ceased to be an independent institution and was also absorbed into the government. The foreign corporations were humbled, and the foreign-owned oil properties were expropriated.

Nevertheless, no more than before was there an integral or integrating culture. There was not one society, but several subsocieties, each with its distinctive values and outlook. For each of these, there was a separate law. Each (except the foreign corporation) had its independent representation in government. There was not and there could not be a democracy based on universal suffrage and majority rule. The rationale of majority rule is that it expresses the "general will," that is, the cultural-cognitional norm. But such a norm exists only for a substantially homogeneous group which shares a common cognition and culture. When, as in Mexico (or the United Nations) the community to be governed consists of distinct groups, each with a distinct system of values, conceptions, and interests, there is no cultural-cognitive norm that can be expressed as a general will through majority rule. Rather than following the general will, since there is none, democratic procedure would seek the consensus, the common denominator of the acceptable. The Mexican political system is based on the continual search for such a consensus.

Political power is, in the Mexican political system, exercised by a single party. The President and his entourage select their own succession. The term of the President is limited following postrevolutionary convention. Within the party structure, each cultural-cognitive group has a place. Each is organized to have a distinct political voice: the *ejidos*, the industrial worker, the Church, the "populars" (including the civil service, the army, and independent professionals), and each branch of business and industry. Opposition parties are allowed to wage election campaigns, but are not allowed to assume political office. Such campaigns help define the national consensus.

Political and all other functional relationships are intensely personal, in the pattern of the family. Political authority, concentrated in the office of the President, is akin to the authority of the father. The members of the paternalistic family argue together, making claim and counterclaim. They petition. They complain. They threaten. They cajole. The father listens. He refers to the tradition. He interprets the consensus. He decides. Similarly *El Presidente* presides over the party and the people. In office, he labors mightily to maintain direct and personal contact with every constituent group. His task is to sense the rising and falling intensity of demands, to comprehend the changing weight of social forces and to act responsively. On his capacity to do this, the power and the stability of the political system depends.

Political Developments and Economic Development (1940-1960). Statistics suggest important improvements in the Mexican economy in the two decades from 1940 to 1960. Land under cultivation and rural population have increased by about 90 percent, while the value of farm output increased by some 224 percent. This increase was concentrated in commercially produced crops such as wheat, beans, and tobacco. Corn yields nearly doubled, though the average yield of 14.9 bushels per acre remained very low in comparison to other countries.

World War II had created unprecedented opportunities for local manufacturing enterprise. It closed off imports from Europe and the United States, and opened Latin American markets to Mexican exports. It brought an influx into Mexico of refugee cash and skills. It induced U.S. financing of Mexican manufacturing development as an aid to the American war effort. In response to these opportunities a new class of Mexican entrepreneurs came into being, allegedly more inclined to technical innovation.[16] Certainly the older industrialists had lacked the cognition of

16 S. A. Mosk, *Industrial Revolution in Mexico* (Berkeley: University of California Press, 1950), p. 21.

mechanism and of process and had resisted technical change. For example, a 1942 study of the cotton textile industry found that three-quarters of the looms in use were installed between 1898 and 1910.

Between 1940 and 1960, GNP in Mexico has grown at the rate of about 2.5 percent per annum on a per capita basis. During this period, for example, iron and steel production increased from 238,000 to 1,600,000 tons, paved roads increased from 5,000 to 30,000 miles, electrical generating capacity from 681,000 to 2,740,000 installed kilowatts. The statistical record is impressive.[17] The degree to which it measures an amelioration of social conditions remains equivocal.

Mexico is a land of great facades. On the surface the record of the Diaz regime was striking. Behind its facade festered profound distress. In the days of Santa Anna, Mexico City was called the Paris of the New World, and the rulers of Europe looked upon the land as a treasure store. When the French king put his hands into the coffers, he found no treasure. And now?

Behind tariff walls, great fortunes have been accumulated, grounded in high prices and low wages. Who pays the high prices, and who gets the low wages? Throughout these years of rising productivity, real wages in industry and in agriculture appear actually to have declined. The value of corn the ejidoist sells has not risen with the rapidity of the prices of the goods he buys. In 1942, 1943, 1944, riots and hunger marches signaled extreme distress. It nevertheless seems probable that some part of the gain in output has filtered down into the hands of the mass. There are many more factory workers, and even if the lot of the factory worker has not improved it is better to be a factory worker than to be a field hand. There have been extensive welfare measures in social security and in medical care. Regardless of the price at which he sells his corn, insofar as he produces for his own consumption, higher productivity must raise the farmer's level of life.

With all her gains, and in spite of her gains, Mexico remains a "developing country," deeply impoverished, technically backward, relatively unproductive. In the prerevolutionary era of rugged individualism under a regime of balanced budgets and enormous inflow of foreign investment, Mexico failed to develop into a high-productivity economy. It failed similarly in the sphere of public ownership in an epoch of public control. Its agriculture remained static and primitive when the land was held in vast private estates; and its agriculture remained primitive and static when the land was turned over to the village *ejido*. It failed to develop under the democratic liberal leadership of Juarez, and, equally, under the

[17] Cf. Raymond Vernon, *The Dilemma of Mexico's Development* (Cambridge, Mass.: Harvard University Press, 1963), for a summary of development from the revolution to 1960.

Marxian socialist leadership of Cardenas. What are the barriers which have checked or have limited development over the centuries?

THE BARRIERS TO MEXICAN DEVELOPMENT

Traditional Cognition. In order that the native genius of a people may generate technical change, that people must understand technology and the organization of economic activity as a variable subject to rational evaluation and choice, rather than as a parameter of existence, fixed, immutable, unsubjected to question and challenge. In Mexico, the cognition of the mass has been traditional. Mechanism and process have remained outside the zone of rational choice and change. The Indian has lived and lives in a traditional society where the way of producing is handed down generation to generation, as part of a way of life.

Throughout these six thousand years the cultivation and preparation of the maize, and the lives of the peasant populations who depend upon it, have scarcely changed. The stone *metates* for grinding the seed which are unearthed by archaeologists are almost identical with those on sale today in Mexican markets.[18]

For the rural folk the economy represents an ancient design upon which modern innovations have made little impression. Most of the people live much as they did at the time of the Conquest; they use primitive tools, till the soil in a manner little changed in hundreds of years, grow corn as they always have, live in adobe or reed huts without windows, furniture, or covered flooring, and subsist on the rim of the modern world.[19]

The Indian knows himself as *los naturales.* The others are *gente de razon* (reasoning people). He, the Indian, does not conceive himself as capable of abstraction, generalization, and analysis. He follows an ancient path along the edge of survival, and he hardly dares deviate. To hold to the traditional way has been his sole protection. Every time he has ventured into the world of the stranger, he has been beaten, robbed, degraded. Nor is it only the Indian's fears that turn him inward. It has also been the habituated attitudes of the others toward him. For centuries it was the policy of his masters to keep him in ignorance. He was denied all access to the European's knowledge. He was forbidden to practice the European's skills.

The *hacienda* also was a stronghold of the traditional cognition. The *hacendado* had the means of educating himself or his children, but his role, his prerogatives, his exactions were grooved in tradition, and were supported by the habit of centuries. His self-interest and the values of his

18 Parkes, pp. 11–12.
19 Tannenbaum, *Struggle for Peace*, p. 174.

caste wedded him to support all the complex rituals and hierarchies upon which his own high status was based.

The hacienda had been inherited. . . . It represented no investment by its current owners. It yielded an income, but not a profit. It paid few or no taxes. It expended as little as possible on its internal operations. . . .

The blacksmith, carpenter, mason, and woodcarver would, by ancient rote, do all the building. They would make the primitive tools. . . .

But these villagers supplied their labor in return, not for money, but for a piece of land to till. . . .

In return the hacienda received a fourth, a third, a half of the yield from each little plot, depending upon the prevailing custom and the crop under consideration. The operation was by rote and a kind of local common law known to all concerned. The peons lived in a world of their own and considered themselves part of the hacienda. The owner was a beneficent or malevolent spirit, depending upon time, temper, and circumstance. The church, if there was one, stood by the big house. A school, if there was one, was by the church. The hacienda had its own jail and stocks and administered a kind of rude and accepted justice traditional upon the place.[20]

The Cognition of Mechanism and of Process. The *Latino* of the town, whatever his aggressive rationality, seems to have lacked that cognition of mechanism and process that is essential for economic development. This also is to be accounted for by the conditioning of history. The North American colonist had to master a hard natural environment and put its resources to skillful use, or perish. For the Spaniard, another, and, in the short run, an easier path was open: to conquer the Indian, to replace the Indian rulers, and to live on what could be taken from the Indian peasant. The culture of the warrior-aristocrat scorned matters of mechanism and process and the calculus and connivance of business.

Over the centuries of colonial rule, the policies of Spanish mercantilism forbade industry in New Spain. The creole and the *mestizo* could not assimilate the industrial technology emerging elsewhere for they were denied contact with it. Hence they did not acquire the dimension of rationality on which that new technology was based. And, as time passed and the technical cognition continued to advance, it became increasingly difficult to assimilate. From the self-interested point of view of the individual buyer or user it became cumulatively more advantageous to rely on the technical competence of the foreigner and to import the complex outputs of foreign industry rather than attempt to develop local production.

Mercantilism spawned monopoly. Established monopolies honeycombed the economy. The merchants who sold to the Mexican consumer and those who exported the goods produced in Mexico did so under

[20] Tannenbaum, *Struggle for Peace*, pp. 143–145.

Crown grants of monopoly. Even the craftsmen brought by the early viceroys to train the Indians in European skills refused to teach once they reached New Spain lest thereby they dilute the value of their monopolized techniques. The universe of petty monopolies was antithetical to the cross-flow of information. The struggle for special privilege which became the normal objective of rational economic endeavor dissipated men's efforts and ingenuities in an activity which could not yield technical progress.

Cultural Primacy of the Familial System. The dominant functional system in Mexico has been the familial, perhaps as a heritage of the Indian tribe perpetuated in the *ejido,* and of the Spanish patriarchy continued in the *hacienda.* Moreover, the genetically perpetuated blood ties of family or tribe are likely to be of consummate importance in a universe of such boundless strife and bottomless insecurity. As a consequence, the organization of political and economic activities has tended to take the form and *modus operandi* of the patriarchal family. All relationships are given an intensely personal cast, where submissiveness and loyalty from below are traded for recognition and protection from above. In the *hacienda*

the *patron* was the father or the godfather of his people. From him all blessings came, and from him favors could be asked with hat in hand, and from him protection could be expected.[21]

In the political system, at the apex of authority, *El Presidente* is father among fathers.

In a subtle sense the mass of the rural population, Indian or *mestizo,* illiterate or schooled, expects the President of the country to play the part of the great father. There is an instinctive submissiveness—a bending of the head, an attitude of acceptance, and compliance—which unconsciously forces upon the President the exercise of arbitrary power. Like a father he must rule personally and cannot delegate his authority. If he does, he will risk losing it. Men, big and little, sit for weeks in the antechamber to be received and heard over an unimportant detail that any clerk might have disposed of. But a clerk is a poor shadow of the great father, and so is any member of the Cabinet. The personality of the President must be part of every minor transaction between the rural folk and their government. Time matters not at all. Years may be spent in securing an audience just to have judgment come from the only source whose authority is not only political but also moral. It is in this situation that administration breaks down. . . . there is no alternative between personal government and revolution. Inefficiency, corruption, cruelty—if they be personal—are all acceptable. What is not acceptable is a cold, impersonal, efficient government.[22]

21 Tannenbaum, *Struggle for Peace,* p. 143.
22 Tannenbaum, *Peace by Revolution* (New York: Columbia University Press, 1933), pp. 96–97. Reprinted with the permission of the publisher.

An emphasis on personality and the personalization of all functional relationships must profoundly handicap the organization of complex operations. Efficient organization may require that the impersonal logic of mechanism, of process, and of science prevail. It may require that evaluation and recruitment be according to objective criteria. It may require that the activities of large numbers be geared into an impersonal plan and guided by general rules.

The Culture and Cognition of Elites. The culture and cognition of political elites in Mexico has been extraordinarily equivocal. Those who sought political power have been capable of the highest dedication and of an absolute corruption. From the earliest viceregal governments and the religious orders that served the needs of the Indian in the wilderness, through all the years of chaos to the present, the capacity for self-sacrifice and for dedication has been evident. So also graft (literally *morida*—the "bite") has been an immense and continuous drag on the capacity for effective government and economic progress.

The Mexican intellectual and with him the incipient revolutionary elite were indoctrinated into a European culture and cognition. Their conceptions were not evolved out of any process of problem-solving in Mexico. Their science, philosophy, economics, sociology were shaped elsewhere, reflecting a pattern of circumstances and responses often different and distant from that appropriate for Mexico. For the great part of their history, Mexican intellectuals have constituted a lonely outpost of European or American thought. When their borrowed doctrines came to be applied, the consequences were sometimes tragic.

Lack of a Unifying Culture and Cognition. The task of economic development requires the capacity for coherent unified action on the part of groups and a capacity for cohesive endeavor by society as a whole. Prior to leadership, there must be this capacity to respond to the signals of leadership. For this a degree of unity in culture and cognition is required (1) in order that there may be a common response to crisis and need, (2) in order that the leaders may communicate with the led, and (3) in order to enlist the spontaneous efforts and initiatives of the mass behind collective goals.

Mexico has lacked this unifying culture and cognition. Its constituent groups, rather, have been marked by distinct values and systems of thought, which could only be marginally related. As a consequence, nearly all functional organizations involving numbers of Mexicans, including the organization of political activities, have had either to be *dominated* by one group, imposing its outlook and values on the others, or operated within the limits of a consensus. During the long centuries of colonial rule, the political system was dominated by the Spanish official.

The creole *hacendado* dominated rural organization. The *gachupine* dominated commerce. The *gringo* came to dominate industry. The Church dominated finance and education. Today, collective choice operates more within a consensus. But either domination, or action through a consensus of highly diversified groups, gravely limits the possibility of social transformation. The capacity to dominate may depend on the weakness of the dominated. Then those who dominate will have a self-interest in perpetuating that weakness by promoting and maintaining divisions, tensions, and offsetting antagonisms among the dominated. This, in turn, reduces the possibility of purposeful change or of any effective social action. Or the capacity of one group to dominate others may be based on the acceptance of a tradition of which the role of the dominating group is an integral part. Where this is so the power of those who dominate will depend on the general acceptance of the traditional structure. Hence those who exercise power will have a self-interest in promoting and preserving the tradition though the traditional cultures are antithetical to social transformation. Either way—promoting divisions and antagonism among the dominated or protecting a traditional culture—the self-interest of the dominating group conflicts with the requisites of progressive change. Domination, moreover, paralyzes the enthusiasm and creative contribution of the dominated and hampers a dialogue between those who control and those who are controlled.

Choice through a consensus of diverse groups also limits the possibilities of creative transformation, for every complex undertaking will be plagued by multiple vetoes. Every new proposal will be required to justify itself in terms of the interests and outlook of each of the different groups. And every change, no matter its intrinsic or general value, must confront the pervasive fear that it might disturb the balance between groups and the structure of power.

In Mexico, the extreme cultural-cognitive diversity has allowed no alternative to rule by domination, or through such a consensus. In either case the capacity to organize progressive change is gravely handicapped.

Division as a Heritage of the Conquest. Mexico is thus divided into culturally and cognitively distinct entities, in part as a heritage of the Conquest. In North America, elements of an English society more unified in their culture and cognition than were the English people as a whole came to a wilderness inhabited by a few primitive hunters. And those who followed later were absorbed into an open society characterized by an extraordinarily homogeneous culture. But the Spaniards in Mexico came upon a vast and rich Empire, which they conquered and upon which they imposed themselves as a caste apart. *Gachupine*, creole, and ecclesiastic were separate societies, co-existing with the many tribes of the conquered Indians. Rule by domination stratified and perpetuated these differences. When *mestizo* or *gringo* moved onto the scene there was no common or open culture into which they could be absorbed.

Division as an Accident of Geography. The geography of Mexico has imposed formidable physical barriers to communication, to transportation, and to the effective exercise of political authority. It also has been a source of division. The arable valleys are cut in the criss-cross of great mountain ranges. There are few navigable rivers. Not until the end of the nineteenth century did a railroad link the capital city with the sea. The single seaport, Vera Cruz, was for centuries isolated by a belt of jungle and swamp and by malaria and yellow fever. The Yucatan, without a land route linking it to the rest of Mexico, was not finally conquered until the turn of the twentieth century. Conversely, throughout history, from Ur and ancient Egypt to the United States of America, integral societies having a unified cultural base have taken form almost exclusively in areas marked by ease of physical access.

Even before the Conquest, there was no cultural unity among the tribes and no political unity either, except that of domination. After the Conquest the Indian remained "thirty different tribes, intensely self-centered, jealous of their autonomy, prizing isolation." [23]

The Lack of Functional Interdependence. An integral society and a unifying culture tend to be created through the density of functional ties and functional interdependence. Through most of Mexican history there have been few ties of functional interdependence (aside from the parasitical relation of thief and victim) tying together individuals and groups throughout Mexico.

The economy of the Indian village has been isolated, self-contained, related to the outside chiefly by the demands for tax and tribute.

Most of the little villages scattered over the width and length of the land have mainly a non-pecuniary economy and remain almost completely outside the national market. The villagers construct the little furniture they use, in many instances make or weave their own clothes, and satisfy the few needs that they cannot provide for within their own village in the parochial market from products made in neighboring towns. The modern national market has little inner connection with the parochial one.[24]

Not only the Indian village but also the hacienda was self-contained, economically, politically, socially sealed in, a world unto itself. In order to maintain its hold over the peon, it sought isolation, opposing the establishment of other activities, for example, mining, in its vicinity.

[23] Dewey, *Impressions*, pp. 156–157.
[24] Tannenbaum, *Struggle for Peace*, p. 175.

The hacienda was so large that (the peon) could not trade anywhere else even if he wanted to. His token coin would not have been acceptable in any other place, and he was not permitted to leave the hacienda if he was in debt. [He] . . . was in fact living on credit . . . beyond his means even at his low level of subsistence, and the hacienda store carried him on its books for his whole life, and his children after him. . . . These folk huddled in little miserable huts about the big house of the hacienda, a castle built of stone, with narrow windows, and slits in the walls for defense against marauding bands or revolutions, guarded by armed men, and surrounded by a high wall with strong gates. . . . It was not just a house; it was a fort. From this fort emanated the rule that governed.[25]

As it was with the hacienda, so also it was with the missions of the orders, and with the estates of the Church.

Neither interrelationships of trade and exchange, nor the organization of production and distribution tied Mexican together with Mexican. Rather the functional interdependence through trade and exchange drew economic activity in Mexico into the orbit of other, distant societies. During the centuries of Spanish mercantilism, virtually all trade had to be with Spain. Even commerce with the neighboring provinces of New Spain was funneled through Spanish ports under the control of Spanish merchants. Local industries to satisfy local needs were forbidden in order to safeguard the vested rights of the Spanish export monopolies. Mexican producers produced for Spain and shipped to Spain, and Mexican consumers depended upon goods imported from Spain or smuggled in from elsewhere—nothing in all these relationships of production and exchange related Mexican to Mexican. After the Spaniards had gone the pattern was as before. Under Spanish rule gold and silver had been hauled from the mines, carried muleback to the ports and shipped to Spain. After Spanish rule, gold and silver and in addition lead, zinc, antimony and oil were taken from the earth, transported to the ports, and shipped to Europe and to the United States. But for the great part of Mexican history, trade was not an integrative force drawing Mexican elements into a cohesive society.

Development of a Unifying Culture and Cognition. Whatever the differences that have thwarted Mexican development, there surely also has been a strong and persistent search for unity. Spanish Catholicism, *Mestizo* Liberalism, and Mexican Nationalism have attempted to shape a common and unifying culture and cognition.

Spanish Catholicism. From the early days of the Conquest, the high clergy and the Catholic orders sought to indoctrinate the Indian with the values of Catholicism. The Indian was converted. He became a believer,

[25] *Ibid.*, pp. 143–145.

capable of intense devotion. A common religious faith was something of a bridge between tribe and tribe, and man and man. Nevertheless, Catholicism did not unify Indian and Spaniard, nor did it draw the Indian into a universal community. Rather it enabled the Indian to continue his former mystic immolation and passionate communion with the supernatural. Except that now the new dispensation was purer, less sullied with old cruelties and barbarism, and its imagery was more remote from the universe of native experience. It was higher no doubt but nevertheless a continuation, fulfilling a need of the indigenous culture without greatly changing it. The need was there and the need was fulfilled, with or without the village priest, with or without the echelons of the hierarchy. When the Church and the government came into conflict, and the priest was forbidden by order of the Church or of the State to say the Mass or to minister to the faithful, devotion and ritual continued in the villages under the ministry of the elders. The hierarchs in Mexico City, the Pope in Rome, the universal domain of the Church, Catholic brotherhood, and the rest evidently became no part of the Indian's cognition.

Liberalism. One appeal of "Liberalism" to Juarez and his followers was that it seemed a means of creating a common culture and a rational cognition. Wipe away the superstition, unloose the grip of mystical doctrine, of piety, of faith in the word of the priest, allow enlightened reason to emerge. Eliminate the parochialism and particularist barriers of feudal privilege, of village communalism, of local protectionism and established monopoly—and allow the free competitive market to perform its task. Then, according to the teachings of European liberalism, people would be released from class, tribe, and dogma. Then there could be communication and community. The interactions of the competitive market would unite its parts in an integral economy.

There was force in the liberal vision. Unfortunately, when the ancient walls were shattered, enlightened and rational individuals did not stride out of the shadows; rather the wolves came in through the breaches of the walls to prey on those within. The policies of liberalism, in the first instance, became an instrument of exploitation.

Nationalism. The Indian who had drifted out of village, the disinherited creole, those wandering in the wake of destroying armies, soldiers, escaped peons, village peasants, rancheros, desert savages, swept in the ebb and swirl of civil strife, scattered in defeat, fixing themselves into new niches in victory: from all these there has come another race, mixed, residual, *mestizo*, Mexican because it is nothing else. At first marginal, later pre-eminent, the *mestizo* provided an avenue of integration. His need for identification, his search for values was the basis of nationhood.

Whatever their inner divisions, the Mexicans have an experience which is their own, and which sets them off from all others. It is in contrast with others that they have felt their identity. Common hatred, the brotherhood of resistance has been their cement. In their hatred of the established power, the peon, the *leperos*, the bandit, the village Indian united in Hidalgo's army. In their hatred of the *gachupine*, the creole and *mestizo* found union. Against the creole, the *mestizo* and the Indian could unite. Against the American armies of Zach Taylor and Scott, against the French armies under Bazaine, against the rule of an Austrian Prince, against the power of foreign oil companies, Mexico took arms as a nation. And the sense of nationhood once awakened has its own continuing force. This Mexican nationalism has its credo, its sense of destiny, its dream of destination. Its disciples find their roots in an Indian past. Its teachers have gone into the villages. Its artists seek a Mexican image. Its heroes belong to the whole people. Given the stability of the political system, given the considerable social and economic mobility which today exists, given the values of nationhood, given the *mestizo* community growing in size and power and open to influx, a more homogeneous, unified society must continue to emerge.

Technology and time reduce the geographical barriers that once divided the people. Roads, railroads, airlines, telephone and telegraph, the extension of electrical power, the elimination of sectional monopolies and provincial protectionism open the way to internal trade and interdependence. Functional interrelationships also weave an integral Mexican society.

Chapter 36

The World Environment of Economic Development

Economic development is not simply a function of the organization of internal forces. Development occurs in a world context and may be promoted or checked by forces external to a society. In this chapter, some of these external variables conditioning development will be considered.

The Extraordinary Phenomenon of Economic Aid. It is an extraordinary phenomenon of our time, inconceivable before World War II, that the rich and technically advanced countries of the world offer to assist in the economic development of the poor and technically backward. Even more extraordinary, such assistance by former governing powers to those whom they once had governed has often followed immediately upon bitter struggles and bloody upheavals that forced the colonial powers out of countries under their rule.

Such assistance is mostly bilateral, from one country directly to another. Sometimes it is organized through a consortium of donor countries, sometimes through international organizations such as the agencies of the United Nations to which both donors and recipients belong. Assistance is sometimes given through regional organizations including donors and recipients, such as the Organization of American States, or through regional organizations consisting exclusively of donors, like the "six" of the European Common Market. There are international financial institutions which make "soft" loans for development-related projects.

When economic aid is in the form of grants or low interest loans made bilaterally, it is ordinarily "tied," which is to say restricted to purchases from the donor country. Aid may be in the form of grants in kind, for instance, food from American farm support programs, scholarships and fellowships, or in the help of experts, technicians, or peace corpsmen. Frequently donor countries commit themselves to specific technical undertakings, perhaps the building of a dam for irrigation and for the supply of electric power, or the erection of a steelworks, or the draining of swamp areas.

In any case, the effort of wealthy and technically progressive nations to assist the economic development of the technically backward and impoverished has become quite suddenly a massive undertaking.

Aid as an Expression of Cultural Values. What is "behind" this new willingness of the rich and technically advanced to "aid" the poor and technically backward? Surely one reason is the sense of human solidarity, man's compassion for man. Without that sentiment it could not have happened.

This sentiment of human solidarity is perhaps peculiarly important at this juncture. Societies throughout history (or at least the marginal groups that give societies their goals and dynamism) have always needed an outlet for dedication and imagination. The outlet for dedication has varied as the culture has changed. When men believed in the salvation of souls, missionaries traversed the ends of the earth. When the highest value was defense of the faith, the chivalries of Europe and its tattered rabble rode and walked towards the Holy Land to free Jerusalem from the infidel. When nationhood was the prime value of cultural systems, patriots found their outlet in nationalist unifications, nationalist revolutions, nationalist expansions, conquests, manifest destinies, and empire. Today the old idealisms no longer suffice. Religion ("old time" religion) has become largely a matter of private conscience and personal indifference. The Nation appears to many as simply a system of political action, sometimes useful and sometimes dangerous but no "end all" for their aspirations. Latent social energies seeking a new dedication sometimes find an outlet in this commitment to development.

Whatever solidarity and compassion there might be, before such sentiment was made manifest in national policies, it had first to be established that aid was a feasible undertaking. An innovation that seemed to lead the way was the Marshall Plan, forced by the economic destitution of Europe and the exigencies of the cold war. The United States contributed a vast sum for the economic reconstruction of Europe and seemed none the worse off for having done so. If economic aid could support the rapid and successful reconstruction of Europe, then why not such programs to support development in Latin America, Africa, India, Asia? The precedent was established; experts and agencies were ready.

Even when technical assistance simply manifests compassion for others, there remains the question of who should be helped to have what. That question will be answered differently, depending on the cultural-cognitional lens through which the donor sees. In general, aid programs not only support development, but also promote the values built into the cultural systems of the donor countries. If there are incongruities and conflicts in the objectives of aid programs, it is partly because of incongruities and conflicts in the cultural systems of aid-giving societies. For example, the United States has proposed that those who receive aid should undertake to equalize wealth and to achieve a more equitable distribution of income through land reform and otherwise. Public sentiment will not condone using the American taxpayer's "hard-earned" dollar to make the very wealthy minorities in developing countries richer still with the poor and miserable remaining as poor and as miserable as before. But while we demand reform, our aid is used to support stand-patters who resist all reform against those who militantly demand it for fear that the reformers would subvert free enterprise and usher in communism.

Aid for Social Tranquillity. Aid may bring certain objective benefits to those who give it. By satisfying the expectations of the impoverished peoples for progressive change, those frustrations and tensions that lead to upheaval may be avoided. Aid might thus serve in lieu of the coercive force formerly imposed by colonial administrations to maintain vast areas and large populations in a condition of "law and order," and to reduce the international dangers arising from local conflagrations.

Aid and the Cold War. Aid has also been an instrument of the cold war. It has been used by the grand opponents to proselytize uncommitted people and range them on "their side" in an ideological or, if need be, military struggle. This intermingling of moral aims and strategic policy, of human sympathy and ideological zeal, has had tragic consequences. It has greatly strengthened the hand of military dictators and of those vested interests in developing countries most resistant to change. It has fomented bloody civil wars. It has subordinated aid policy to the manipulations of diplomats and the calculations of professional soldiers and undercover agents. It has not added an iota to anyone's security, but has kept the world close to the brink of atomic war. It has degraded the image of the great powers.

Economic Benefits to the Donor. Are there any concrete material benefits to be gained by the American citizen through the use of his tax money to support educational programs *in the United States* or to support economic development in some laggard region or industry in his own country? There are benefits that he can expect though he does not live in the laggard regions, or work in the failing industries, or go to the sup-ported schools. And these are precisely the same benefits that can be expected by donor countries (or by ourselves as citizens of donor coun-tries) from aid to the developing world. The objective of aid is to raise productivity in developing countries. Given trade and competition, the benefits of a rise in productivity will normally be spread in the form of higher incomes for producers in developing countries and in the form of lower prices for consumers in donor countries. Higher productivity, whether it takes place in the United States or in any donor country or in any developing country, also creates problems. It alters the structure of comparative advantage. It requires an upward adjustment in the propensity to consume to offset the greater capacity to produce. These problems of plenty are surely to be preferred to the alternative problems of scarcity.

A further consequence of successful development would be to raise the cognitive level of many millions to a point where they are able to make a contribution to science, technology, and art in accordance with their inherent energies and creativity. That contribution is never an exclusively national possession. Given normal intercourse and communication (which aid itself promotes), all societies will share in increments to science, technology, and art, whatever their source. Whenever the creative energy, talent, and genius of a substantial number of people is suffocated by poverty, ignorance, and the rigidity of traditional cultures, their consequent failure to contribute to art and to the advance of science and technology is at the expense of the whole world.

There are also particularistic commercial interests that seek their own under the cover of economic aid. The self-seeking of particular commercial interest is virtually never a motivating force for the extension of economic aid, but such commercial self-seeking often limits and distorts aid programs. It is to be expected that politicians, nudged by their constituents, should ask this question: If we give grants or make loans, why shouldn't those who receive that aid use the money to buy from our industrialists and farmers? If there are to be profits, let them accrue to our own businesses. Hence laws are passed requiring that those who receive grants and loans in aid confine the use of these grants or loans to purchases from the donor country. Grants and loans thus are "tied" to purchases in the donor country. This has led to a situation where each large donor country ties its grants and loans so that the recipient cannot procure from those producers, sellers, or experts who are best able to meet its needs, but must divide its expenditures according to the sources and distribution of its aid funds. The net result must be a less effective use of aid. Resources are badly allocated. Competition between firms serving developing regions is dampened and monopoly is protected No particular advantage accrues to any donor country since the restrictions imposed by one in its imagined self-interest balances out against the restrictions imposed by others in their alleged self-interest. In the eyes of the recipient, aid becomes less an expression of human solidarity than a manifestation of commercial greed.

Cultural Disintegration. For the first time in history, the masses of all societies have been reached by the notion that through social organization it is possible significantly to improve their condition of life. This is the beginning of a revolution in cognition. It brings into question the whole complex of the social system and it fissures traditional cultures.

It is a mistake to think that prevailing cultural values are necessarily "valued" by the societies where they prevail. They are, rather, learned and accepted, followed by habit, by imitation, without any conception of alternatives. Private choice, for the most part, follows paths tramped out by former generations. For the individual, in any society, freedom in the choice of his values is marginal. He does not choose his culture but is born into it. Within a cultural system, it is hard for him to escape from conforming even if he is of a mind to, since his choices are conditioned and limited by the choices of others. His individual freedom never implies the option of living in accord with another value system, but only of living in disaccord with an existing one. Hence each culture has great inertial power to perpetuate itself, even though it conforms less and less with the private beliefs, volitions, and inclinations of the individuals who act in its frame.

Yet that disassociation of the individuals' faith, belief, volition, and inclination from a prevailing culture empties the system of its vitality. It becomes a mask for a void.

The experience of centuries has served to alienate the people of developing societies from their cultural heritage. The old cultural systems are associated with subordination, servility, failure. Those with the power or wealth to do so have been educated in Europe or America and have absorbed foreign ways so that the old culture remains most dense and solid among the poor and ignorant. Hence, among the people of the developing society itself, their native culture is associated with poverty and ignorance. That cultural heritage, moreover, is likely to be incongruous with the science in which individuals are trained, with the technical process into which they are integrated, with the machines they come to master.

Within the shell of the old culture and cognition, the people of developing societies are readied for the new. Through contacts of all sorts, through education, through all the media of communication, new elements infiltrate and are absorbed, helter-skelter.

Rising Expectations. What can be the result of this repudiation of old cultural and cognitional systems, the ready imitation, assimilation, absorption of that which infiltrates from the outside; conjoined with a prevailing sense that a basic reconstruction of society is possible? In the first instance, the impact is a rise in mass expectations, vague but powerful expectations of betterment, of power, of being as the others, of having more, of doing less. And because these expectations are not automatically matched by any corresponding rise in functional capacities or by the spontaneous development of a basis for social action, they will increase discontents and frustration and bring pressure for change and a willingness to run risks for change's sake. Then? Then, perhaps there will be turmoil without end. Or perhaps there will be a fruitful economic revolution. The form of economic revolution, should it be brought about, will depend upon the cognition and culture that has been absorbed from the outside or hammered from within the developing society.

The Sacrifice of Old Values. Individuals are not able to choose the culture into which they are born. Nor are they, in the torrent of economic revolution, ordinarily able to choose the culture into which they are flung. Whatever the benefits, or, indeed, whatever the imperative of the change, it is likely that through such change something that corresponds to human needs, inclinations, and capacities will be lost. Some of those who live in the new age will miss the old, and with reason. Consider, for example, the lament of Charles Péguy, writing in 1913 of the France he knew before the "modern revolution."

Can we be believed?—and once more this amounts to the same—we have known workmen who really wanted to work. No one thought of anything but work. We have known workmen who in the morning thought of nothing but work. They got up in the morning (and at what an hour), and they sang at the idea that they were going off to work. At eleven o'clock they sang on going off to eat their soup. Work for them was joy itself and the deep root of their being. And the reason of their being. There was an incredible honor in work, the most beautiful of all honors, the most Christian, perhaps the only one which stands of itself. . .

We have known an honor of work exactly similar to that which in the Middle Ages ruled hand and heart. The same honor had been preserved intact underneath. We have known this care carried to perfection, a perfect whole, perfect to the last infinitesimal detail. We have known this devotion to *l'ouvrage bien faite,* to the good job, carried and maintained to its most exacting claims. During all my childhood I saw chairs being caned exactly with the same spirit, with the same hand and heart as those with which this same people fashioned its cathedrals. . . .

Towards this fine honor of a trade converged all the finest, all the most noble sentiments—dignity, pride. *Never ask anything of anyone* they used to say. . . . For to ask for work was not to ask. The most natural, the most normal thing in the world to claim, not even to claim, was to take one's place in a work-room, in a working city, quietly to take one's place before the work which awaited one. . . .

Those bygone workmen did not serve, they worked. They had an absolute honor, which is honor proper. A chair rung had to be made well. That was an understood thing. That was the first thing. It wasn't that the chair rung had to be well made for the salary or on account of the pay. It wasn't that it had to be well made to satisfy the boss, or to please the connoisseurs, or to satisfy the buyers. It had to be well made in itself, for itself, in its very self. A tradition coming, springing from deep within the race, a history, an absolute, an honor, demanded that this chair rung be well made. Every part of the chair which could not be seen was just as perfectly made as the parts that could be seen. This was the self-same principle of the cathedrals. . . .

For them in their homes there was not the shadow of a doubt. The work was there. One worked well.

There was no question of being seen or not being seen. It was the innate being of work which needed to be well done. . . .

All the honors converged towards that honor. A decency and a delicacy of speech. A respect for home. A sense of respect, all the respects, of respect itself. A constant ceremony as it were. Besides home was still very often identified with the work-room and the honor of home and the honor of the work-room were the same honor. It was the honor of the same place. It was the honor of the same hearth. What has become of all this? Everything was a rhythm and a rite and a ceremony from the moment of rising in the early morning. Everything was an event; a sacred event. Everything was a tradition, a lesson, everything was bequeathed, everything was a most saintly habit. Everything was an inner elevation and a prayer. All day long, sleep and wake; work and short rest, bed and board, soup and beef, house and garden, door and street, courtyard and threshold, and the plates on the table.

Laughing, they used to say, and that to annoy the priests, *to work is to pray* and little did they know how true it was.

So much of their work was a prayer, and the work-room an oratory.[1]

. . . In those days, one earned nothing, so to speak. No one can have an idea today how low the pay was then. Yet there was enough to eat. In the humblest homes there was a kind of ease, of which we have lost the memory. At bottom no one calculated, no one reckoned. There was nothing to reckon about. Children could be raised. They were raised. The economic strangulation that year by year tightens its grip on us did not exist. One earned nothing. One spent nothing. And everybody lived.[2]

Péguy echoes the words of Genesis. There also the departure from the certainties of the instinctual and the peace of the settled and traditional way for the hard, turbulent, unsure world of rational self-seeking and calculation, was to leave Eden.

And in the United States those who today bereave the passing of the rugged, self-reliant, inner-directed individual also mourn a casualty of another economic revolution.

In Chapter 31, the course of economic revolutions was conceived as the extension of rationality successively to more complex and inclusive spheres of choice. It will be the achievement of another economic revolu-

[1] Charles Péguy, *Basic Verities* (New York: Pantheon, 1943), pp. 80–87. Quotations from *Basic Verities* (Copyright 1943 by Pantheon books) are translated into English by permission of Random House, Inc.
[2] *Ibid.*, pp. 78–79.

tion to take rational account of the social environment and the human relationships implicit in forms of economic organization, so that these too are the objective of deliberated choice, of invention, of innovation, of transformation.

The Pains of Transition. For each of us there are incongruities between the different goals we pursue, the different things we want, in what we each judge right or wrong, ugly or beautiful, attractive or repulsive; incongruities, that is, in our own system of values, in our personal culture. Such incongruities are a source of inner conflict and tension. And not only are there conflicts in the individual's values. There are incongruities also in the way the individual thinks about things, in the concepts he uses to structure observations, in the way in which he answers questions and accepts or rejects information. The great Isaac Newton, whose synthesis dominated physics until Einstein, wrote a book in which he claimed to establish the exact age of the world to the day and the hour, by reference to biblical revelations. Evidently he accepted two cognitive systems, and these two were not congruous.

The individual is pressed by the discomfort and dilemma of these conflicts and incongruities to find a synthesis, a harmony in the elements of his cognition and culture—hence, to be "mature," "balanced." Therefore, through the needs of those who compose it, a society is pressed somehow to eliminate the incongruities of the prevailing culture and cognition. A society in transition is necessarily a society that suffers, massively, from such incongruities. This is particularly so where transition is initiated through the infiltration and assimilation of ideas and values from elsewhere—as is the general case in developing countries. For then the new idea does not evolve as a continuum of the old. It need not arise out of some common experience or functional need. Rather, new ideas, concepts, and values, and new forms, new patterns of activity, newly accepted knowledge, newly concluded beliefs, new manners and modes all drift in piecemeal, without explicit connections, to mingle with the elements of the old.

These difficulties are compounded since what is observed and assimilated, indeed, what is systematically propagated and taught because it is valid and proven elsewhere, may be irrelevant and useless—worse, may be a positive source of misconception and error in the transitional society. The sociology, the political science, the economics that is taught at Columbia, Harvard, Oxford or Heidelberg, or Paris, and alas also the economics, sociology and political science that is taught in faithful imitation in Accra, Karachi, Mexico City, and Dakar is not drawn from the experience, nor related to the realities, nor focused on the problems of the developing countries. It is, therefore, only of partial or marginal relevance for these societies and their needs. Through such indoctrination the intellectuals of the developing society are weaned to take a distorted view of their native universe or to close their eyes to the realities of that universe entirely. The student, for whom the test of truth is success in an examination, faithfully learning his lessons, trying to please his teacher, cannot discriminate between that which is and that which is not relevant for and valid in his society. He learns; only later and painfully may he learn to discard what he has learned.

Nor is this blatant incongruity between the taught cognition and the realities of the transitional society only to be found where the body of thought and knowledge is *about* society. It will exist in all of the applied arts and sciences, in agronomy and pedology, in business administration and engineering, in social psychology and psychiatry, in architecture, even in medicine, since the doctor learns not only about disease but also how to organize his activities in a particular social context.

These are the contradictions and confusions and incongruities that inhere whenever the change of culture and cognition is through imitation and assimilation. The syndromes of the consequent stress and tension may be an apathy before a universe that escapes the conceptual grasp, an incomplete personality, a schizoid cognition.

There are other sources of social pain and stress inherent in the condition of transition and social revolution. The established cycles wherein realization meets expectation are shattered. What people anticipate, does not occur; what they have prepared themselves to do, is not required; and what they have not prepared for, is demanded. Social problems proliferate more rapidly than social policy can adjust. The new generation, less encumbered, adjusts more easily to the successive waves of change, so that either the authority of the older is thrown into disrepute, or youth is crushed between its submission to the obsolete parental demands and its own need to confront the realities of change.

These discontinuities and incongruities, and their attendant tensions and conflicts, are the painful lot of developing societies. They are not to be escaped, but they can be recognized and understood, so that they can be dealt with rationally—rather than suffered blindly.

Chapter 37

Economic Development in Puerto Rico

Puerto Rico is a small, densely populated island, the end of a chain that reaches a thousand miles or so from the tip of Florida through the Caribbean, curving outward into the Atlantic. A hundred miles long, thirty miles wide, it has a mountainous center surrounded by a narrow and fertile strip of coastal plain. Columbus praised its beauty. Its first governor was Ponce de Leon, whose fortified mansion still stands.

It had at long last achieved political autonomy under the Spanish Crown, in the very year of the Spanish-American War. The Americans conquered it, reduced it to an abject colonial status, almost forgot it, the "poorhouse of the Caribbean." Always too poor to have supported an aristocracy or any enclaves of great wealth and power, it evolved a multi-racial society, with a quality of civilization that is unremarked but rather remarkable. It has a tradition of reason in politics and tolerance in social affairs. Its 450 years of history have not been marred by civil war or minority persecution: a record which would be difficult to match in any other political entity in North or South or Central America.

Background for a Revolution. Economic development in Puerto Rico starts in 1940. Puerto Rico then was a land of despair. During the late 1920s and the 30s, two hurricanes and the Depression brought its people nearly to starvation. In 1940, thanks largely to federal relief expenditures, it had an annual per capita income of $121.00. The men chopped sugar cane under the sun, and in their huts the women and children stitched and embroidered. Raising sugar was the dominant industry, accounting for half of the island's agricultural and manufacturing income and over two-thirds of its exports. Sugar technology was static. The vast sugar estates were in the hands of large corporations, mostly U.S. owned.

The economy was hopeless, and there was no hope in politics either. Puerto Rico was the butt of American colonialism at its worst: which is to say the colonialism of complete indifference. Its governorship was the end of the line for a series of political hacks and military favorites. Its local politics was a study in impotence, with poets arguing about the priority of their dreams at the summit, and corrupt favor-seekers grabbing for the minor spoils at the bottom. The issue that divided the two parties was the issue of status. Should Puerto Rico be independent or should Puerto Rico

471

be a State of the Union? This was a matter of dignity, *dignitad*. Should
Puerto Rico strike out, brave, small, single, alone, proud, on the great
sea of independence? Or should it merge its history and find its identity in
the mighty power of the United States?

The Reformulation of Goals. The change began when Luis Munoz Marin
broke away from the party of Independence and formed the new Popular
Democratic Party. The issue, he said, was not political but economic,
not whether to be independent or to be a State but how to get rid of
poverty. While men labored in the cane fields for 15 cents an hour and in
the tobacco fields for 6 cents an hour, and while thousands squatted in
homeless destitution, *dignitad* could wait. Dignity could be found in an
honest vote; there was dignity in hope. With his followers, Munoz went
into the hills to the peasant farmer and landless worker with the message:
"Don't sell your vote, use it." The victorious banner of the Populars was a
white rag, centered in red with the crude profile of a countryman, and
around that profile the words *Pan* (bread)—*Tierra* (land)— and *Libertad*.
Influenced no doubt by the fervor, idealism, optimism of Roosevelt's
New Deal and the tensions of the Civil War in Spain and all the
reverberations of moral crisis in Europe, Munoz Marin and those around
him enunciated new goals and forced a consciousness of the possibilities of changing, through concrete political action, the level of life and
the range of opportunities for Everyman. They sought to remake the
relationship between governors and governed. Instead of humility and
pleading from below and patronage or abuse from above, there would be
a dialogue of responsibility and response. This conscious effort to reshape
the Puerto Rican outlook and values has not ceased. To this day the art
and the artists of Puerto Rico are mobilized to that end. In the old
farmers' market in San Juan, painters, writers, movie makers are now at
work seeking to evoke a consciousness of the Puerto Rican past and to
invoke the questions of its future. Agents are sent into the hills to live in
the villages, *not* to represent the government, but to stimulate the people's
political demands upon government, to suggest the potential benefits of
self-assertion and collective action, thus to combat lassitude and *humil-
idad*.

Shaping an Arm of Political Administration. Rexford Tugwell served as
Governor of Puerto Rico from 1941 to 1946. Tugwell was an experienced
administrator and a sophisticated politician who deeply identified himself
with the aspirations of Puerto Rico. He brought Puerto Ricans of intelligence and dedication into his administration and formed them into an
effective instrument of administrative action. Munoz Marin focused the
powers and formulated the purpose of the Puerto Rican people. Tugwell

shaped an effective administrative arm. There now occurred another stroke of fortune.

The Abortive Effort to Achieve a Socialist Economy. Under the special circumstances of the war years, sales of rum from Puerto Rico sky-rocketed. Between 1941 and 1946 there was remitted 160,000,000 in taxes to the Government of Puerto Rico from the sale of rum in the United States. This was invested in nine public corporations. These corporations had three general purposes: (1) to provide an industrial infrastructure of public utilities, (2) to develop cooperative farming, and (3) to build and operate a variety of industrial plants. The long-term goal evidently was a socialist commonwealth, with a cooperative agriculture and government-owned, centrally planned industry.

The effort to provide public utilities (including urban transportation, ports and airports, electric power, irrigation, water supply, and sewerage disposal) was conspicuously successful. Cooperative agriculture never developed in spite of an investment of $34,000,000.

A government-owned-and-operated industry came into being, but its values were equivocal. There were difficulties in management. Some operations made money; others lost it. The role of the public official as an employer with the task of minimizing costs conflicted with his role as a political representative of free labor. Political suspicions infiltrated commercial relationships. More essentially, to realize the benefits of socialism requires the government-planned disposition of all economic resources. In fact, the powers of the Puerto Rican Government were too limited for such a task. It could not create money, nor, on its own account, pledge its credit and borrow, expropriate property, nor dictate the disposition of the island's resources or the distribution of its economic output. Sovereignty rested elsewhere. Moreover, even if the government of Puerto Rico had been sovereign, it would still have controlled only a trivial fraction of the resources and activities upon which its economic welfare depended, for the economy of Puerto Rico was inextricably bound to that of the United States. Perforce "socialism" in Puerto Rico consisted of setting up commercial entities, run by public officials who were caught in the buffeting of the United States market system.

In 1947, after five years of driving effort and the investment of nearly $20,000,000, the Puerto Rico Industrial Development Company (PRIDCO) owned and operated five factories—a cement plant, a glass container plant, a paperboard mill, a shoe factory, and a plant making structural clay products and sanitary ware. The commitment of funds and scarce executive talents had created less than 2,000 new factory jobs. It was decided to liquidate the program. Instead of publicly owned industry the government would "foment" private enterprise.

Why Puerto Rico Failed to Develop Spontaneously. Puerto Ricans have the same Constitutional protections and the same degree of public security as the citizens of the United States. There are no constraints upon the movement of people or goods to or from the continental United States. These conditions were essential to the program for the economic development of Puerto Rico. Yet those conditions existed long before there was such a program. Why during all those prior decades was there no spontaneous economic development? With the same access to markets and resources, why didn't Puerto Rico develop spontaneously on its own steam, as Florida or California or New Jersey did? Characteristically this difference has been explained as a consequence of Puerto Rico's (1) lack of natural resources, (2) lack of "capital," and (3) overpopulation. In fact, none of these accounts for the failure.

Consider "natural resources." For the organization of production, it matters not at all that there are mineral resources underfoot. What matters is whether resources can be procured and the price at which they can be procured. Coal, oil, steel, lumber, or any other resources were as available to producers in Puerto Rico as they were to producers elsewhere in the geographical domain of the American political system. The producer in, say, Boston or San Francisco or Minneapolis bought his coal or steel or petroleum or lumber with the same coin and under the same political constraints as a producer in San Juan or Ponce. The producer in Puerto Rico pays more or less for these goods and raw materials than producers located elsewhere in the United States depending on relative costs of transportation. From this point of view, Puerto Rico is very advantageously placed at the juncture of intersecting low-cost sea routes (and now of air routes). The transportation costs of both imported resources and exported products puts the producer at a relative cost advantage in Puerto Rico compared to most locations in the United States.

Or consider "overpopulation." If, in fact, the density of population was a key disadvantage, the population was free to move elsewhere, anywhere in the United States. Before the epoch of development, it did not move. During the period of development there was a considerable movement of the work force to higher paying job opportunities on the continent. But those who left Puerto Rico generally settled on another island, Manhattan, which was more densely populated than any place in Puerto Rico. Population density did not stop the economic development of New York City. New York was part of the land-rich American economy. So was Puerto Rico. Nevertheless, Puerto Rico remained impoverished and hungry even though it was part of an economy that suffered not land scarcity but perennial food and land surpluses.

Or consider the "lack of capital." Regardless of the source of savings, nothing prevented banks or private investors from putting their money into enterprise in Puerto Rico, rather than Detroit or Los Angeles or Philadelphia or elsewhere. The money went where profits were anticipated, and profits were anticipated where individuals and companies showed themselves capable of organizing economic activities successfully. The lack of capital was a consequence, not a cause, of the failure to develop.

In fact, business organizations did not move spontaneously from the United States to Puerto Rico, American finance did not flow into Puerto Rico, and Puerto Ricans did not avail themselves of the business or work opportunities in the United States. But the barriers were not political and geographical. The barriers actually lay in the differences of culture and cognition. The lack of a unifying culture and cognition blocked communication and prevented the easy interaction of individuals and functional organizations in the United States and in Puerto Rico It was its peculiar cultural system and its structure of acquired cognitions that accounted for the lack of initiatives from the Puerto Rican side and the failure of individual Puerto Ricans to organize progressive economic change in their island.

Transforming the Structure of Cultural and Cognitive Systems. Development required that cultural and cognitive systems be transformed. The first step was the evolution of a political elite, disciplined and dedicated to the achievement of that economic revolution. The second step was the creation of a more aggressive electorate, aware of its power with lines of responsibility and answerability between leadership and led. The third step was the inculcation of the revolutionary elite with the cognition of administration and of politics and later of business organization and technology. This it acquired under an enlightened American tutelage and in the abortive effort to create a socialist commonwealth. As a consequence of that foredoomed effort Puerto Rican leadership had developed and managed new industries. They had promoted sales. They had recruited and organized a work force in the factory. They had faced the labor unions across the bargaining table. They had borne the brunt of strikes and production failures. They had handled technical, financial, legal, and political problems of some complexity. They were thus transformed from enthusiasts and ideologues into technicians and administrators capable of organized basic economic change.

Their goal was to transform the economy through self-interested private efforts on the market. This required yet another component in the Puerto Rican structure of culture and cognition: aggressive individualism coupled with a cognition of technical processes and business practice. Such cognition did not sufficiently exist in Puerto Rico. The governing elite chose to import it. It became the objective of the political system to induce those who could organize private industry to come to Puerto Rico from the continental United States.

Operation Bootstraps. By the close of the 1940s, having abandoned the goal of a socialist economy, the Puerto Rican government set about promoting the in-migration of entrepreneurship from the United States. This was the task of the Economic Development Administration, called *Fomento,* with Teodoro Moscoso at its head.

Puerto Rico and its bona fide residents pay no taxes to the federal government of the United States. Fomento offered firms setting up new industries in Puerto Rico a ten-year exemption from *all* taxes, federal and local. No other locality in the U.S. political domain could offer this advantage.

Puerto Rican wage rates were low compared to those of the United States. Its geographical position as a trade center had many advantages. Moreover, Fomento undertook to arrange all sorts of services and aids for in-migrating industries. It made loans and equity investments in new enterprise. It constructed factory buildings and had them ready for lease or for sale. It helped in the recruitment and in the training of workers and supervisors. It offered subsidies to start enterprises considered particularly important for economic growth. In order to ease cultural transition and thereby to encourage the in-migration of American management, it financed private English-speaking schools. It encouraged housing developments. To accommodate business visitors, it built the Caribe Hilton. It made San Juan a leading musical center and brought in an English-speaking theater—at the same time promoting Puerto Rico as a vacation resort and vaunting its climate as another inducement to attract American entrepreneurs.

Fomento's promotional effort, in spite of the unique advantages it offered, might never have succeeded except for the war in Korea. Puerto Rico had a labor surplus. The Korean War created a very tight labor market in the United States. From 1950 to 1954, employment in Fomento plants in Puerto Rico increased from 5,000 to 22,000 and nearly 100,000 Puerto Rican workers migrated to the continental United States.

Profits of Fomento firms in Puerto Rico, before taxes, have been running about twice as high in relation to equity investment and about three times as high in relation to sales as those of companies in the same asset size class in the United States. For tax-exempt Fomento plants, this means profits about four times as high in relation to equity and five times as high in relation to sales as their U.S. counterparts. Nevertheless, U.S. companies have established plants in Puerto Rico only under hard sales pressure. The barriers of culture and cognition remain; to the American businessman, the continental United States is home. Moreover, those who came were mostly the small entrepreneurs from the soft goods trades. The large autonomous corporation seemed indifferent to the opportunities of a tax holiday and of low-wage labor; for more than a decade, it has remained deaf to Fomento's blandishments.

Economic development has proceeded under certain constraints, which have proven at once a handicap and an advantage. American trade unions to protect their membership from "unfair" competition of low wages tried to unionize labor in Puerto Rico and periodically pressured Congress to impose higher minimum wages in Puerto Rico. Congress, in response, has raised minimum wages in Puerto Rico more rapidly than a promotion-minded Puerto Rican government would ever have done on its own. This has insured that a substantial part of the increased value of output went to labor and was diffused through the Puerto Rican society. On the other hand, the rise in minimum wages killed the hand needlework trades, which were the major employer of labor as late as 1954. Throughout the period of development, more than 10 percent of the work force in Puerto Rico has been continually unemployed.

The development program has been an unquestionable success. Per capita income in Puerto Rico rose from $121 for fiscal 1940 and from $272 for fiscal 1949 to about $600 in 1961, without concentrating benefits at the top. In *real* terms per capita gross product rose from $269 in 1939–49 to $673 in 1960-61, and continues to grow at an accelerated pace. By 1961 some 730 new plants had been established providing more than 54,000 high wage industrial jobs. Puerto Rico seems to have crossed the threshold of industrial revolution.

The American Enclave. A dilemma remains. As the means to its economic revolution, Puerto Rico "imported" American entrepreneurship. The *Americano* constitutes a separate enclave. It is the *Americanos* who run the economy. The values of the *Americano* must be catered to in order to bring them in and to induce them to stay. Hence the American culture strongly imposes itself, creating conflict and tension. The dilemma seems to offer a choice of three paths for Puerto Rican policy, and each path is represented by a political party.

There are those who fear that Puerto Rican identity, the Puerto Rican "soul," will be drowned by the culture of the *Americano*, that the uniqueness of San Juan will be lost in the neon-lighted monotony of another Miami Beach, that Puerto Ricans will be strangers in their own land. This fear is felt, to some degree, by all Puerto Rican intellectuals. For a few it is obsessive. They would reject the *Americano*, break free of all political ties, minimize economic interdependence, go it alone at any cost as a sovereign independent state. These constitute the now very small party of the *Independentistas*.

There are those who want to be American. They "feel" American as much or more than those who have come in recent generations to the United States from Europe. They want to learn and assimilate, and to get ahead in American society by acquiring its cognition and accepting its values as quickly as they can. They include many of the rich, and particularly those who have risen on the recent waves of affluence and who have been educated or educated their sons at the Wharton School of Business, or Cornell, or Miami University. They include many of the poor and recently poor, for whom the Puerto Rican past is not of Ponce de Leon and the *conquistadores* but of poverty in a hut in the hills, under the hard hand of a Spanish *patron*. Swept in the back-and-forward movement of labor to and from the United States, these have family and friends on the continent as well as on the island. For them the objective is to remove the differences, and perhaps the stigma of Puerto Rico, once and for all, to become Americans exactly as the others. To this end, a great many want Puerto Rico to become a State of the Union, to vote for the President, to have their representatives in Congress and the Senate, even if this will mean (as it must) that federal taxes will have to be paid, and therefore that Fomento will lose its major instrument for promoting new industry on the island. This point of view is represented by the Statehood Party, the second party in Puerto Rico. It is the party that, discounting personal and party loyalty, probably represents the sentiment of the majority.

The *Populars,* in power since the early 1940s, stand for a mid-course between separation from and assimilation into the United States. They would "associate." They are more concerned with increasing local political autonomy than with seeking representation in the U.S. Congress. They would like to retain the advantages of functional interdependence with the United States and yet to foster a separate cultural identity. To this end they have sought to develop *Commonwealth Status.*

In 1946 Puerto Rico's first native-born Governor was appointed by President Truman. In 1947 Congress passed the Elective Governor Act. Under that act, in 1948, Munoz Marin was elected to the Governorship by a large majority. In 1950 Public Law 600 granted Puerto Rico the right to its own Constitution. With the adoption of that Constitution in 1952, which provides for local autonomy within the context of the federal law, the Puerto Ricans considered that Commonwealth Status had been achieved.

But, of course, Commonwealth Status no more than statehood could resolve the essential issue: will Puerto Rico remain functionally integrated and culturally apart from the United States? That will be settled by forces about which we still know little: the capacity of the established values to perpetuate themselves, the Puerto Rican propensity to assimilate, the power of the North American culture and cognition to take root.

Chapter 38

Policy and Strategy

Part III has suggested a conceptual frame to encompass the elements that constitute a society and in that frame has analyzed aspects of economic development. This final chapter touches upon questions of policy and strategy in assisting the process of economic development, particularly from the point of view of the United States.

A REVOLUTIONARY LEADERSHIP

A Revolution Needs Revolutionaries. Economic development is feasible, but economic development is not compatible with the maintenance of status or even with social continuity. It requires profound and discontinuous change. It requires the reorganization of functional systems, and of cultural and cognitive systems; it means a sortie deep into the unknown that, if successful, can raise up many, but that also is likely to tumble some down. Economic development means revolution, and revolution needs revolutionaries.

Economic development must work from within. It is not something that happens to a society but is, rather, something that a society does with itself. Nevertheless, though led from within, its leaders can be influenced, can be taught, can be helped and conditioned from the outside. And in the past those who have led social revolutions have been inspired and taught by others, distant from their societies in time and space. It is, however, only in our epoch that the established governments of the world's most powerful nations have undertaken to encourage and support economic revolution among the poor and weak.

The West, particularly the United States, has preferred to conceive this problem of aid to economic development as one of diplomatic persuasion and goodwill, of sound banking and of capital accumulation, of engineering and of anticommunism. It has moved in with resounding slogans, boatloads of goods and guns, of diplomats, of consultants, of engineers with portfolios of project-blueprints, of generals, of CIA agents, of economists and bankers with big checks. But a dedicated and determined leadership in the developing societies, united in purpose and cognition, upon which an aid program could be effectively based, has been lacking, and no attempt has been made to find or to develop that leadership.

Therefore American aid has failed, spectacularly, in Korea, in all of Latin America, in Vietnam, and elsewhere.

The Failure to Develop a Leadership for the Development Revolution. The first problem for aid is to support the evolution of a leadership that can guide the revolution of economic development, a leadership whose values are in accord with our own and whose cognition is viable for its long, slow, and painful tasks.

Who could constitute such a leadership? Not the political toadies who do the bidding of the State Department or the CIA for a price. Not the established elites whose power, wealth, and privileges are based on the continuation of status. That leadership is to be found among those who are dedicated or could be dedicated to the goals of development. They must be ready for responsibility and power and united in a vision of what should be.

The basic need is for a revolutionary leadership. The long run, but essential task of aid is to foster, influence, and support the evolution of a revolutionary leadership, not as a conspiratorial claque, but as a movement of thousands in the ranks and up from the ranks, in every level of social activity.

A REVOLUTIONARY COGNITION

Communisim and a Development Elite. As Western aid has failed, the Communist East, providing relatively minuscule quantities of arms and material support, has been comparatively successful in giving to developing societies its own revolutionary direction. This success has been wholly due to their recognition of the prior and essential role of a revolutionary elite. The ideology of Communism has given those ready for dedication a unifying vision, values, a cognition related to the achievement of revolutionary change. To those ready for a dedication to the goals of development, the Communists have offered association and solidarity with like-minded men through the thick and thin of the revolutionary effort. The West offers an emergent leadership no coherent cognition or value system, nor any organization designed to meet the needs of revolutionary change.

What does it matter to us that those who attempt to lead the development revolution find their unity in Communist doctrine?

There are two sorts of benefit that, conceivably, might accrue to Americans or to other Western peoples from economic development. First, we might share in the increased output which is the consequence of higher productivity. But, in fact, inasmuch as there is trade, we will share in this increase of output, whether economic development comes about through

Communist leadership or otherwise. Second, we might enjoy the benefits of the contribution to science, technology, and the arts made by the peoples of those societies whose talents and creativities have, up until now, been straightjacketed by tradition and suffocated by extreme poverty. But, in fact, inasmuch as there is communication, we will enjoy these benefits whether economic development comes about through Communist leadership or otherwise. Of course, if Communist-led revolution breeds doctrinal bitterness and builds barriers against communication and trade, these important benefits will to some degree be denied us. This suggests our interests will best be served by a revolutionary leadership not identified with an ideological antagonist, but disposed to trade and to communicate with us.

The much vaunted issue of national security is a false issue. In spite of the costly and troublesome game played by generals, diplomats, and intelligence agencies, there seems to be neither past nor prospective benefits to American security to be had through ranging the nations of the developing world in military alliances on "our side." The present accumulation of nuclear warheads and missiles enables the great powers to blow each other and anyone else between into bits quite nicely without help from third parties. Nevertheless, given the terrible game played by generals, diplomats, and spies, and given traditional fears and traditional strategies, economic development under the banner of Communism in territories that were formerly satellites or colonies of the Western powers is likely to provoke fear, tension, and trouble. The Western interest, indeed, the interest of the Soviet Union and above all the interest of the people of the developing world is that those societies should develop "trouble free" and not spawn new conflicts. This would best be served if developing societies were committed to neither ideology.

Hence the American interest, the Western interest, and the world interest in trade, community, and security against war will best be served where economic development is achieved neither under the banner of Communism nor of anti-Communism.

Marxism as a Cognition for Development. History suggests that the verisimilitude of doctrine has little to do with its capacity to arouse fervor or even to provide a basis for unified action. Gideon's army, after all, consists precisely of those who can believe the unbelievable. Nevertheless the verities and relevance of doctrine do matter, because doctrine sets its imprint on the particulars of policy and on the patterns of action. And Marxist doctrine has precious little to offer in comprehending the realities of developing societies or in resolving their problems of economic development. Armageddon, with bourgeoisie ranged against proletariat, will not be fought on the fields of developing societies, and to try and play out that drama in those societies will lead to purposeless suffering and frustration of the humanist impetus to change. In these societies the essential issue is not who dominates whom, but the incapacity to organize coherent purposeful action.

Communism and anti-Communism confuse a functional system with the moral order. They give centralized political-direction a symbolic and absolute value for good or evil. Actually, every advanced "communist" or "capitalist" society, confronting real problems beyond the doctrinal pale, evolves a variety of economic forms suited to a variety of economic tasks. The sanctification of a single (politically directed or decentralized market) form of functional organization fixes blinders on the revolutionary elite.

It is, therefore, in the interest of the developing societies and in the American interest that the Marxist cognition be rejected as irrelevant, and that the leadership of the development revolution find its unity and base its policy on an alternative system of culture and cognition, a system at once operational and neutral with respect to the tensions and antagonism between the great powers. But can such an alternative be offered to a revolutionary elite? Alas, though many of its elements have been conceived, no alternative vision and approach has yet been forged. Nor are we in the United States necessarily best equipped to create it. Yet we can be aware of the need for it. We can search, and support others in their search for it. We can contribute what is relevant from our experience, cognition, and culture.

EDUCATION FOR ECONOMIC REVOLUTION

Education as an Instrument of Development. Education has many purposes. Some of the most important of these are not related to economic development. For example, education may open men's minds to an intrinsically valuable heritage, in philosophy, history, science, and art, enriching their lives, or enhancing communication with their fellows, or providing entrée into select circles, or distinguishing them as the members of a class or caste. Some such intrinsically valued teaching is surely necessary among developing societies or among any civilized people, but worthy as it is, it will not concern us here. Here concern will be only for education that prepares individuals to perform some role in, or which otherwise furthers, economic development.

Economic development needs a dedicated leadership with a cognition of politics. It needs managers with a cognition of process. It needs scientists to solve a continuum of problems and to provide certain key services, and it needs science-trained engineers and specialists of many sorts. But all of these are elites whose task it is to give direction, to give signals. Someone must respond to the signal. Also at issue is the capacity of the community at large, of its own volition, to respond to the goals, ideas, directions of elites, to adapt, to adjust, to give momentum to the engineering scheme, to fulfill the management objective. The mass capacity to respond to the signals of its leadership has been and may be taken for granted in the United States and Western Europe. In the developing societies, it cannot be taken for granted. To shape it is the essential task.

At the apex of any industrialized, technically progressive society there must be a certain number of scientists, technically sophisticated managers, and science-trained engineers. Below that peak there must be a relatively much larger number of skilled mechanics and technicians. And finally permeating the community as a whole there must be the cognition of mechanism. There is required at base a mass understanding of the machine as subject to rational manipulation and control, a recognition of the demands it makes on man, and a sense of its value for the individual and the group.

In the United States and Western Europe virtually the whole system of education, inasmuch as it geared into the process of economic growth or development, has been designed to produce those elites at the apex. The middle mass of mechanics and technicians and the technological orientation and cognition of mechanism on the part of the community as a whole were taken for granted. This was feasible since in Western Europe and the United States the people are technically oriented through their day-to-day experience in an industrial environment, and since the skill of mechanic and technician are acquired outside the formal system of education through observations on the job, through apprenticeships, through family indoctrination, or through ad hoc training in the store or in the factory.

Developing societies lack not only the apex of science-trained elites. They lack even more the middle mass of mechanics and technicians and the base of a community-wide cognition of mechanism. Nor, in developing societies, can that middle mass or that base be acquired in a reasonable period or possibly at all except through a planned system of indoctrination and training. In developing societies no industrial environment spontaneously provides a technological orientation. Nor is there a self-perpetuating nucleus of mechanical and technical skills able to expand in response to the stimulus of need and opportunity. Hence a planned system of education becomes the necessary means of providing not only the scientists and the science-based engineers and specialists, but also the large number of technicians and mechanics, and the mass cognition and culture of the machine.

Changing the Learning Sequence. In the educational sequence of Western Europe and North America, followed generally throughout the world, the student is first given his literary, historical, aesthetic "foundation." He then proceeds to learn science in its most general (academic or fundamental) form. Finally he may be taught the general principles of some selected sphere of technology. Characteristically only outside the school system does he develop the specific skills of application. The Western system of formal education thus tends to exclude from its scope the managerial cognition of process, technical and mechanical skills, and the mass cognition of mechanism. Since these necessary cognitions cannot be acquired in a developing society except through formal education, the characteristic learning sequence needs to be changed.

Education might begin with a universal indoctrination into the logic of the machine and the rationale of its control. A substantial fraction of those so indoctrinated might then be further trained in mechanical skills and special techniques. The most able of these would then be taught the principles and practices of engineering and industrial management. Among these, those who had established their capacity and inclination would subsequently be trained in science and higher mathematics. In such a sequence, the whole population first would be introduced to the cognition of mechanism and the values of a machine-based culture. Then those with the capacity for it would be educated into a progressively more profound cognition of technology and science. Perhaps in this way formal education might produce not only the apex, but the whole pyramid of competencies required in an industrialized, technically progressive society.

A Mass Cognition of Mechanism. It is of particular importance that the mass of the population acquires a rational cognition of the machine and is culturally adapted to coexist with the machine. But how is this culture and cognition to be instilled among the adult population of a pre-industrial society without everyday experience in an industrial environment? Unconventional methods of training are surely needed: traveling fairs, demonstration centers, the use of mass advertising techniques.

There has been, for example, an enormous exposition of "industry and agriculture" in full swing in Moscow since the mid-1930s. The tourist who wanders into that exposition will find it replete with socialist realism and Stalinesque gingerbread. Heroic statues of noble workers and of broad-beamed peasant women in babushkas stand on every corner and gaze at distant horizons. Thousands of Russians visit it daily. They come from collective farms, village workshops, factories—from every Republic of the Soviet Union. They see the "latest" in textile weaving and shoemaking, sewing and machine tooling, grape pressing and wine making, etc. They watch the instructors and try out the machines themselves. They talk over their back-home problems with the experts. The exposition serves the same purpose that the country fair did in an older rural America: it gives the ordinary Russian, still outside of daily contact with industry, a deeper sense of mechanism. This has been, in part, the purpose of the American demonstration farm and of rural extension services. Even in highly industrialized and technically sophisticated societies, unconventional approaches to technical training and to the mass indoctrination in the potentialities of new science-based technologies may be required, and they have been used as a stimulus to economic growth. For example, after World War II the TNO (Netherlands Organization for Applied Research) introduced pilot plants for the processing of plastics. These were opened to the general public for demonstrations. They were turned over to companies or individuals for experimental use. The cognition of a new process was thus established. As a direct result plastics became the basis for major new industries in Holland. Similarly, Rotterdam's unique Building Center exemplifies an unconventional method for a continuing education in technique and process. The Center maintains a permanent exposition of virtually all kinds of construction materials and equipment and household appliances. It demonstrates significant innovations in construction, in architecture, or in household organization. Its high-powered research staff and documentation center is available to anyone, at the cost of a guilder (about 20 cents) per inquiry. It responds to some 40,000 inquiries a year, servicing builders, architects, engineers, public officials, consumers, householders, housewives, and do-it-yourselfers.

Such unconventional techniques on an unprecedentedly vast scale are required to transform the mass cognition of developing societies.

A Role for the Large International Corporation. The large industrial corporation, operating in both advanced and technically backward societies, has often in the past been a thorn in the side of colonial peoples and dominated nations. It has exploited their natural resources and organized their human resources for the benefit of others elsewhere. It has corrupted their politicians and has used its influence to secure the intervention of the great powers, sometimes in the form of military force, on its own behalf. Nevertheless, the international corporation (which stands as a bridge between the science and advanced technologies of Western Europe and the United States, and the organization of functional activity in developing societies, and which has as its peculiar competence the capacity to adapt and to transfer techniques and processes between highly diverse social organizations and national environments) has an enormous potential value as an instrument for the promotion of development (1) in inculcating the science cognition in the developing economy, (2) in carrying out development-oriented R & D, (3) in introducing advanced techniques and in planning the transformation of processes, and (4) *particularly* in producing managerial elites in developing economies who have a cognition of process and mechanism.

Whether international industrial corporations will make a significant contribution to economic development will depend on their policies, particularly with respect to the recruitment and training of technicians and managers. Governments of both the advanced and developing societies can influence corporate policy toward an accommodation to the needs and interests of economic development, particularly in regard to the systematic recruitment and training of technicians and managers from among the indigenous peoples of developing societies.

The Content of Higher Education. Scientists, managers, engineers, doctors, experts, and professionals of every sort are needed for the tasks of economic development. How many are needed? In what specialties? How and where should they be trained? These are knotty problems. But the knottiest and perhaps the most basic problem of all involves what any given specialists are to be taught—the subject matter itself. Teach them to be doctors. But is the existing body of medical knowledge and techniques suitable for their needs? Train them to be agronomists. But is the present knowledge of agronomy sufficient to their tasks? Train them to be economists. But will teaching them the existing corpus of economic concept and information be of use to them in understanding their own economies or in formulating their policies of economic development? Of course there can be no absolute answer to these questions, but certainly the body of science and sociology as it is taught is incomparably more relevant to the practical needs and current problems of the advanced societies than of the developing ones.

Thousands of students from developing countries are trained in the colleges and universities of the United States, France, England, Germany, Holland, etc. They are taught a science and a technology that have focused on the phenomena and have reflected the needs of Western societies. They are indoctrinated along with Western students into a culture appropriate to the circumstances of Western societies and to the demands made by those societies upon their professionals and specialists.

This issue transcends educational policy. Educational policy can decide to teach B rather than A and can devise the means of teaching B. But here the B that needs to be taught does not yet exist. The problem is for science to develop in teachable form a body of knowledge that focuses on the phenomena and relates to the needs of developing societies.

Development-Oriented Science. Some verities of science have a validity and a utility that transcend differences in regions or in social systems. There is hardly any regional connotation, for example, in higher mathematics or physics. But universality is no test of relevance and much of the knowledge and understanding that is most significant for the needs of developing economies is specific and particular.

A body of science that explains the natural phenomena and ecologies characteristic of a particular region will be only partly relevant and sometimes wholly misleading in relation to the natural phenomena and ecologies characteristic of other regions. Hitherto the focus of scientific inquiry has been on the natural and social phenomena and ecologies that characterize the environment or are otherwise important to the rich and technically advanced societies of the world, who have had the competence to undertake the research and the wherewithal to pay for it. Conversely, characteristic phenomena and ecologies of poor and underdeveloped societies—for example, the tropics—have been relatively neglected, and the teachable body of "science" and technology related to the advance of agriculture, horticulture, forestry, animal husbandry, fisheries, medicine, and public health, for those regions, remains to be created.

Nor is the need only to develop bodies of science related to regional variations in natural phenomena. Even more the social sciences have evolved in response to the particular problems and peculiar phenomena of Western societies. In developing societies, problems are of another order and forms of social organization are radically different. Correspondingly, social sciences as the product of Western problem-solving will be inadequate or inapplicable to their needs.

The task of creating the subject matter to be taught must precede that of teaching it. This requires a development-oriented natural and social science continuously and cumulatively producing bodies of relevant knowledge. It requires R & D, with practical problems of developing societies as its focus, to shape the technologies that are to be taught.

SHARING THE GAINS OF DEVELOPMENT

When Productivity Increases? Assume that programs of economic development have been undertaken and that they have succeeded; as a consequence there would be a rapid rise in productivity. Since the developing economies are largely agricultural, agricultural output would rise correspondingly. There would be an increase in the production of coffee, rice, sugar, cotton, palm oil, natural rubber, peanuts, pineapples, cocoa. What then? Who would benefit? Given the inelasticity of demand for these products, prices could drop so precipitously that, in spite of the increase in output, the producer's net income would decline. Producers might even be worse off than before. Virtually the whole benefit of development would accrue to consumers in rich, technically advanced societies in the form of lower food and raw material prices. Such a prospect could discourage development.

The experience of American agriculture is somewhat analogous. It was only after the farmer was guaranteed through a system of agricultural price supports a substantial share of the gains achieved through higher productivity that the rapid progress of American agriculture occurred, benefiting farmers and consumers alike. For tropical agriculture in developing regions, an analogous series of international commodity agreements should guarantee minimum prices for an agreed output of the traded products in order to support development and to ensure equitable division of the gains of rising productivity between producers and consumers. This guaranteed price should be allowed to decline year by year as a ratio of the projected increase in productivity. For example, with an anticipated increase in productivity of 3 percent per annum, the guaranteed price (at a constant price level) might decline at, say, 1.5 percent per annum.

The problem is not only securing an equitable sharing of the benefits of higher productivity between producers in developing economies and consumers throughout the world; it is equally important to ensure that producers equitably divide the gains of higher productivity between those who own and those who labor. Such a sharing might be guaranteed by tying minimum wage conditions to whatever commodity agreements or tariff or import quota concessions are made in support of economic development.

Index

Abramovitz, Moses, 92
Academia
    conservatism of, 315, 316, 318–319,
        321, 328–329
    defined, 308
    external demands on, 309–311, 319–
        321
    in closed, class-structured societies,
        310, 312–313, 320–321
    in liberal, democratized societies, 310–
        311, 313–315, 320–321
    innovation in
        imposed, 319–321
        internal, 315–319, 320–321, 328–329
    as an institutional system, 308–309,
        320
    and organizational revolution, 311
    and technology, 311
    value commitment in, 309, 327–329
    as a way-of-life, 309, 315, 328–329
    See also Education, Science
Advertising, institutional cost in autono-
    mous enterprise, 77, 78
Agriculture
    in the American enterprise economy,
        208–209, 218–221, 244–248, 259–
        260
    employment in, 223, (chart, 223)
    extension services, 246, 427
    internal uncertainties in, 49–50
    Mexican
        decline of productivity, 449
        foreign land ownership, 446–448
        hacienda, 447, 448, 454, 458–459
        land redistribution, 450
        peonage, 447, 448, 454
        preconquest, 438, 449
    parity pricing and output controls, 221
    price trends in industry and, 219, 220
        (chart, 220)
    progress, economic, in, 221, 244–248,
        259–260
    public supports of, 270, 271
    Soviet collectivization of, 62, 348, 413–
        415

transformation in India, 109
tropical, 426–427, 428–430
See also Ejido
Alaman, Lucas, 440
Amory, Cleveland, 179
Anti-trust
    and autonomous enterprise, 228, 255–
        256
    conditions for conspiracy, 212–213,
        226–227
    and innovation, 164–166
    inter-enterprise conspiracy, 232–233
    laws, 227
    policy, 227, 228
Atomic Energy Commission. See Infor-
    mation
Autonomous organizations
    and anti-trust policy, 228, 255–256
    choices within exemplified, 29–31
    as a community, 18, 196, 198–201
    contract renegotiation, 229
    and economies of scale, 76
    excess capacity in, 351
    as a government, 18–19
    individual choice within, 20–21
    and minimum wage, 229
    planning, internal to, 72, 73, 87, 237–
        238
    policy problems of
        arbitrary power, exercise of, 80–83,
            228–231, 255–257
        full employment, 84–85, 221–225,
            349–354
        inter-enterprise competition, 232–233
        investment incentives, 231
        monopoly and invention, 255–256,
            261
        price control, 233–234
        recruitment in, 229–231
        research and development concen-
            tration, 252
        sequestering science, 163–164, 256–
            257, 261
        wage bargaining, 233–234
    power in, 19, 73, 74, 80, 81, 82, 83,
        87, 228–239

and science infrastructure, 424
taxation of, 229
See also Corporate enterprise, Organizational market-negotiating form
Aztecs, 438, 439

Babage, Homer D., 295
Bacon, Sir Francis, 117
Baykov, Alexander, 409
Bazaine Marshal, 461
"Bell Report," 282, 283, 284, 285, 286, 290, 291, 297
Bell Telephone Laboratories, and transistor technology, 82, 83
Bentham, Jeremy, 24, 387
Blough, Roger, 20
Böhm-Bawerk, Eugen, and the capital-accumulation theory of productivity, 94, 96
Borrowed doctrines, 386–387, 445, 456, 469–470
Boulding, Kenneth Ewart, 37, 172
Bouwcentrum (Building Center), in Rotterdam, 485
Brandeis, Louis, 228, 236
Brest-Litovsk, treaty of, 408
Bureaucracy, culture of, 186–187, 196
Bush, Vannevar, 128, 250

Capital
  Böhm-Bawerk's antidote to Marxism, 94
  as an immobilized resource, 94, 95
  measurement of, 92, 93
  and normal replacement, 104–105
  and productivity, 90, 91–100
    relationship tested, 92
    roundaboutness as a source of, 96–100
    theoretical contradictions, 93–94
Capitalist contradictions, in Marxian theory, 395–396
Cardenas, Lazaro, 450, 452–453
Centralized political-direction
  allocation of resources under, 58–67, 70–71
  characteristics of, 7–12, 58
  in China, historically dominant, 415
  and cognition, 191–192, 195, 297–298
  consumption under, 67–69, 70–71
  cultural-cognitive system, complementary to, 401, 402–404, 407, 415
  cultural values in, 190, 194–195
  and economic revolution, 406–415
  economies of scale in, 61–62, 71
  education in
    formal 149, 158–159
    self-taught, 148–149, 158

experimental opportunities under, 149–153, 158–159, 318–319
"ideologically-directed" man of, 192–193, 199, 201
income distribution under, 69–71
invention under, 148–150, 158–159
  dissemination of, 153, 159, 297–300
invention-innovation (research and development), investment in, 150–151, 158–159
norm of choice, 32, 60
and progress, economic, 148–159, 292–301
in Puerto Rico, 473
receptivity to information under, 153–154, 159
the "religious core" of, 59–60, 71, 187–189
and research and development, 151–152, 159, 292–301
in Russia, historically dominant, 400–405, 415
science, investment in, 150–151, 159
as a social environment, 186–195
speed of transformation under, 153–159
Chamberlin, E. H., 212, 351
Chardin, Teilhard de, 363
Charles III, of Spain, 442
China
  capacity for collective action, 415
  elites, recruitment of, 36
  revolution, 388–389
Choice
  authoritative
    analogy to the United States Supreme Court, 22–28
    characteristics of, 21, 32
    culture of, 191–192
    merits and defects of, 23, 24
  authoritative and composite, *see* Cultural systems
  composite
    analogy to the United States Congress, 22–28
    characteristics of, 21, 32
    merits and defects of, 23, 24
  engineering, 111, 112
  entrepreneurial, 17–18
  household, 337–340
  individual, 20–21, 29–31
  individualized
    characteristics, 32
    and classical economics, 32
    and progress, economic, 125–127, 129–130
  managerial, 111

operating, and a science infrastructure, 245–246, 260, 421–422
organizational, 17–18
of research and development alternatives, 296–297
transformation, 113
and values, cultural, 365–366
Christianity, as a cultural-cognitive system, 366–367
Church, Catholic
and cultural integration, 459–460
as an institutional system, 304–306, 360
in Mexico, 440, 443, 445–446, 450, 457
Científico, 449, 450
Clarke, J. M., 212
Class struggle
in Marxian theory, 394–396
and property, 37, 394–396
Classical economics, as a cultural-cognitive system, 366–367
See also Liberalism, laissez-faire
Cobweb Theorem, 50
Cognitive systems
and centralized-direction, 191–192, 195
dominating, 368–369
in the United States economy, 345
and economic revolution, 122–130, 406–409, 480–485
Marxist, 394–397, 481–482
mechanism, cognition of, 417, 435, 454–455, 482–486
nature of, 362–363
in organizational market-negotiating form, 200
and organizational revolution, 382–384
politics, cognition of, 417–418, 451, 455–456, 482
practical, 365
process, cognition of, 417, 435, 454–455, 482–486
rational, 376–377, 379–381
relation to function, 363–365, 418–419
traditional, 122–124, 365, 376–378, 381, 438–439, 453–454
See also Cultural-cognitive system
Colonialism
mercantilism, in Mexico, 440–442, 454–455, 459
and political elites, 386–387, 388
and technical assistance, 462, 464
of United States in Puerto Rico, 417–472
Columbus, Christopher, 471
Commodity agreements, 487–488

Communication
and association, 436
costs of, 142, 147
cross-disciplinary, 419
and cultural integration, 431–432
governors and governed, 387–388
and monopoly, 455
organization of, 297, 298
and a science infrastructure, 421–422
and transformation, 118–120, 153–156
Communism
as credo of economic development, 392, 480–482
war, 408–409
Communist Party, as an institutional system, 304–306, 360
Competition
imperfect, 212–213, *see also* Decentralized market-segmented form
monopolistic, 212–213, 351
pure, *see* Decentralized market-direction
Comte, Auguste, 387, 445
Congress of the United States
and composite choice, 22–28
and social reform, 26, 28
Consumer sovereignty
consumer dethroned, 67–68
consumer reshaped, 85–86
Cook, S. F., 449
Corporate enterprise
and choice, organizational, 17
influence, political, 85, 86
transformation power, locus of, 109–110
See also Autonomous organizations
Cowdray, Lord, 447
Craft economy. *See* Traditional societies
Creativity
barriers to initiatives, 419
outlets for, 152–153, 418–419
population, a quality of, 115, 132–134
See also Invention
"Creeping Socialism," 348
Creole, in Mexico, 439, 442, 443–445, 454, 457
Cultural change
causes, 170–173, 174, 189, 197–198, 367–368, 382–383, 442, 465–467
consequences, 173, 310–315, 371, 383, 444–449, 467–470
costs, 467–470, 477–478
process of, 465–466, 472, 476
Cultural-cognitive system
centralized-direction, complementary to, 402–404, 407, 415
Christianity, as a, 366–367

classical economics, as a, 366–367
and Communist revolution, 400–406, 412–413, 414, 415
for elites, revolutionary, 396–398, 405–406, 408–409, 412–413, 414, 415
of enterprise, American, imported into Puerto Rico, 475–476
Marxism, as a, 366–367
Cultural-cognitive-functional systems
interdependence, 172–174, 362, 366–367, 372–373
in change, 371–375, 442–443
and conflict, 368–369, 445–446
and domination, 369, 375
in economic development, 416–437
and homogenization, 368, 370
workable combinations, 372
Cultural incompatibilities
and economic development, 432–435
of economic organizations, 180
with democracy, 180–181, 185, 194, 201–202, 433–435
with nationalism, 182–184, 185
with political freedom, 181–182, 185
with political liberties, 193, 202
with Protestantism, 182–184
Cultural systems
of Academia, 308–309, 327, 329
advertising, formed by, 77, 78, 238–239
of bureaucracies, 186–187, 196
change, caused by
cultural contradiction, 367–368, 466
functional failure, 368, 466
and change, economic
direction of, 173
stimulus to, 371, 442–443, 445–446
and choice
authoritative, 22, 24, 31–32
composite, 31–32
in conflict
American Civil War, as, 348
"creeping socialism" and the TVA, 348
literary and scientific, 31
in Mexico, 439–441, 443, 445–446, 456–458
in Puerto Rico, 477–478
in Soviet collectivization, 348, 414–415
and technical assistance, 464
disintegration of, 465–466
dominant, 369, 370
conflict with functional need, 346–348, 414–415, 455–456
in Mexico, 455–457
in United States, 345

and economic development, 431–437
economy as a source of, 170–173, 174
for elite, revolutionary, 391–392, 405–406
in enterprise
American, 210, 435–437
French, 210, 437
Mexican, 454–455
of the governed, 386, 406, 442, 451, 455
in household organization, 341–342
for individual and collective evaluation, 52, 68, 69
of individualism, 432–437
in decentralized market-direction, 178–179, 378–381
and invention, 127–128, 137–138, 144–146, 147
personalissimo, 434–435, 456
Puritan, 434
and science, 126, 137–138, 144–146, 147
De Tocqueville's view, 179, 432, 436–437
in traditional societies, 380–381, 388, 432–437, 445–446
and utilitarian philosophy, 432–433
integrating, 180, 345–346, 431–432, 450–451, 456–461
inertial force of, **367**
of liberalism, 24–25, 387, 445–446
in Mexico, 439–440, 451, 454–461
clerical, 440, 445–446,
creole, 439, 441, 443–444, 457
gachupine, 439, 440–442, 456–458
Indian, 438–439, 441, 453, 455, 457–458
mestizo, 440, 442, 445–446, 455–456, 460–461
nature of, 361–362, 366
and organizational revolution, 382–384
in Puerto Rico, 472, 475
Russian, 403–406
of science, 303, 328–329, 364–365
and technical assistance, 463
of voluntary association, 436–437
See also Cultural incompatibilities, Cultural-cognitive systems, Values, cultural

Darmstadter, L., 327
Darwin, Charles, 432–433
Decembrists, 398
Decentralized market-direction
and American agriculture, 208–209, 221, 244–248

antithesis to centralized political-direction, 58
characteristics of, 4–7, 207–208
consumption under, 50–53, 56–57
and economies of scale, 38–39
education, self-acquired in, 135–136, 146, 237
and experimental opportunity, 137, 147, 244–245, 318–319
income distribution in, 53–54, 57
"inner-directed" man of, 199
institutional costs of, 38–40, 237–239
and invention, 135–141, 147, 244
  dissemination of, 141–144, 147
investment in transformation, 138
and motivation, economic, 136–137, 146, 147
natural resources, depletion of, 225, 226
norm of choice, 32
and progress, economic, 127, 129–130, 135–147, 244–248
public participation in, 219–221, 244–248, 270–271
receptivity to information in, 142–143, 153–154, 245–246
reform, implications of, 55–56
and research and development, 140–141, 237, 244–245
resource allocation in, 34–53, 56–57
role of government in, 7, 245–246, 339
as a social environment, 175–185
transformation in, speed of, 141–144, 147, 245–246
and uncertainties, economic, 47–50
values in, cultural, 178–179, 184–185, 190–191
Decentralized market-segmented form
and anti-trust policy, 226–228
the "Brain Drain" from, 258–259
characteristics of, 211–212
and imperfect competition, 212–213, 226–227
importance in the United States economy, 213–214
inventions in, 257–258
Decision-making. *See* Choice
Democracy, 180–181, 194, 201–202, 379
limitations of the consensus, 388, 451, 456–457
See also Cultural incompatibilities
Department of Defense. *See* Information, Military establishment
Department of Scientific and Industrial Research (DSIR), 258
Desegregation, role of the United States Supreme Court, 28

Deutscher, Isaac, 398, 400, 401
Dewey, John, 311, 447
Diaz, Porfirio, 446–449
Discrimination, racial and religious, in autonomous organization, 229–231, 232
Dobb, Maurice, 7, 9
Doheny, Edward L., 447
Domination
and colonialism, 369
of a cultural-cognitive-functional system, 345–348, 354, 369, 370, 375, 456–457, 458
of political government by autonomous organization, 234
Dubridge, Lee, 288

Economic development
agriculture
  extension service, 427
  transformation of, 108–109, 487–488
  tropical, 425–427, 429–430
alienation of intellectual, 398, 431
barriers to, 389, 454–461,
and borrowed doctrines, 386–387, 445, 456
and capital scarcity, in Puerto Rico, 474–475
case study of,
  Mexico, 438–461
  Puerto Rico, 471–478
cognitions, relevant for
  Marxist, 481–482
  mechanism, 417, 454–455, 482–485
  of politics, 417–418, 451, 482
  preconditions of, 416–419, 482–483
  of process, 417, 454–455, 482–483
and the Cold War, 392, 480–482
and commodity agreements, 487–488
communism as credo for, 392, 480–482
conceptual framework needed for, 357–359, 482
consensus, based on, 388, 390, 450–451, 456
costs of transition, 467–470
creative initiatives for, 418–419
cultural integration for, 431–432, 439–440, 450, 456–461
cultural requisites of, 431–437, 459–461
economic growth, compared to, 358
education for, 431, 469–470, 482–487
external influences on, 462–467
foreign aid and, 462–465, 479–488, *see also* Technical assistance

household economy in, primacy of, 338, 455
incapacity for coherent social action, to overcome, 389, 392–393
individualism and, 380–381
and international corporations, 229–231, 485–486
leadership for, 385–393, 479–482, *see also* Elites (for revolution of economic development)
in Mexico, 380–381, 451–452, 453–461
and monopoly, 454–455
nationalism as credo for, 392, 450, 460–461
of natural resources, and Puerto Rico, 474–475
and overpopulation, alleged, 131–134, 474–475
progress, economic, in traditional societies, 122–124, 129–130, 377–381
and recruitment for function, 418
and research, academic, 431
and rising expectations, 383, 389, 465–467
science
  and infrastructure in, 421–424, 428–429
  organized for, 425–431
as social revolution, 388–389
technology, receptivity to, 424–425, 429, 454–455
Economic Development Administration of Puerto Rico (*Fomento*) 476
Economic growth, compared to development, 358
Economic organizations
as decision-taking systems, 3
incompatibilities
  cultural, 180
  political forms and institutions, 174
See also Centralized political-direction, Decentralized market-direction, Organizational market-negotiating form, Price-regulated public utilities form
Economic revolution
and cognitive systems, 122–130, 376–384
and cultural integration, 431–432
See also Industrial Revolution, Organizational revolution
Economic stimuli
adjustment-time to, 40
sensitivity
  in autonomous enterprise, 78, 79, 87

under centralized political-direction, 62–64
under market-direction, 40–42
under market-direction, in consumption, 52, 337–338
and transmission distance, 62–64
types of, 40–41
Economy, defined, 205
See also National economy
Education
and autonomous organization, 160–161, 237, 248–249
under centralized political-direction, 148–149, 158–159
communist commitment to, 405, 408, 411
continuous, technical, in France, 316
for economic development
  aims of, 482–483
  alienation of intellectual, 398, 431, 469–470
  irrelevance of curriculum, 469–470, 486–487
  the learning sequence, reform of, 483–484
European
  crisis in quantity, 312–313
  philosophy of, 310
in the institutional economy, 302, 306–307, 308–321
and invention, 115–116, 120, 148–149, 151–152, 158–159, 160–161, 244, 246
political participation in, 271–272
or population increase, 134
reform of
  under decentralized control, 318–319
  innovation from within, 316–319
  resistances to, 315, 316
  secondary school physics, 316, 318–319
science manpower, conflicting demand for, 293–296
self-education through small firm, 135–136, 146, 237, 248
in United States, 306–307
  crisis in quality, 313–315
  philosophy of, 310–311
  and Sputnik, 316
See also Academia
Efficiency, criterion for evaluation of economy, 15, 53
Einstein, Albert, 324, 325, 469
Eisenhower, Dwight, 27

Ejido
destruction under "liberalism," 446–449
protection under Spanish crown, 440–441
revived under Cardenas, 450
self-contained economically, 458
traditional cognition, 453
Elites
Catholic
recruitment of, 388
revolutionary, 385–386
Communist, 385
cognition for task, 406, 408
external ties, 386–387
recruitment of, 388
and Russian revolution, 394, 401–402, 404–406, 408
for economic development, 389–390, 479–480
cultural system of, 390–393
in Puerto Rico, 472–473, 475
external influences on, 386–387
managerial, 197, 248–250
planning
in autonomous enterprise, 75–76, *see also* Planning, economic
cultural system of, 59–60, 187–189, 191
political, 385–386
Chinese, 36
external ties of, 386–387
and the governed, 386–388, 406
Mexican, 439, 440–442, 443, 456
and nationalism, 388, 392, 450
recruitment of
in autonomous organization, 74–75
under centralized political-direction 58–59, 285–286
under decentralized market-direction, 35–38
and research and development, 152, 248–250
revolutionary, 385
Marxism as a cultural-cognitive system of, 396–399, 406
motivation of, 396–397
"religious core," 391–393, 397, 405–406
tribulations of, 390–391
Elliott, J. H., 449
Employment, full. See Full employment policy
Enarson, Harold D., 295, 296
Enterprise. *See* Autonomous organizations, Corporate enterprise

Enterprise economy, 205, 206, 207–264 (chart, 216)
characteristics, 207
importance in national economy, 207
income, transfers into, 267–268
production and distribution in, problems of, 218–243 (chart, 240–243)
progress, economic, in, 224–264 (chart, 262–264)
public participation in, 270–271
research and development in, 250–255, 260–261
structural changes, 218, 236–238
See also Decentralized market-form, Decentralized market-segmented form, Organizational market-negotiating form, Price-regulated public utilities form
European Common Market, 462
Experimental opportunities
under centralized political-direction, 149–153, 158–159
in decentralized market-direction, 137, 147, 168
in decentralized market-segmented form, 257–258
in organizational market-negotiating form, 160, 168
in Soviet Union, 152–153
External economies and diseconomies
caused by, 43–44
under centralized political-direction, 64–65, 68
under decentralized market-directed choice, 42–45, 52, 338
and innovation, 103, 138–140, 150–151
the "invisible hand," 42
and natural resource depletion, 225, 226
nature of, 42–43
with organizational market-negotiation, 79, 80
and progress, economic, under market-direction, 138–139
and science, investment in, 138–140
in transformation, 103

Fair Employment Practices Act, 231
Fair return
"prudent investment" criterion of, 236
in public utilities, 214
"reproduction costs" criterion of, 235
Familial systems
characteristics, 341, 360

dominant in Mexico, 455–456
household economy, 205, 206, 337–342
Federalist, The, 24, 445, 446
Ford, Henry, 419
France
  cultural system, 210, 437
  economic planning, 10, 168, 231, 437
  technical aid, 428–431
Freedom, political, 181–182, 185
Friedman, Milton, 320
Full employment policy, 224, 225, 349–354
Functional systems
  combinations, permutations of, 360, 361, 372
  defined, 359, 371
  diversity, benefits of, 343–345
  dominant, 345–348, 354, 400–401, 402–405, 455–457
  explained by social sciences, 360
  incompatibilities of, 348–354, 411–412, 413–415
  interactions
    institutional-market, 303–306, 309–311, 312–315, 319–320
    political-familial, 268, 270, 339, 455–456
    political-institutional, 267–268, 271–272, 294–296, 303–304, 306, 309–311, 319–320
    political-market, 270–271, 289–292
  interdependence of
    as the condition of society, 369–370 374
    and unity, cultural, 458–459, 461
  See also Familial systems, Institutional systems, Market systems, Political systems)

Gachupine, 439, 440–442, 443, 456, 457, 461
Galbraith, John Kenneth, 290
Geography
  and cultural disunity, 458
  of Puerto Rico, 471
Goal creation. *See* Invention, Research and development
Goldwater, Barry, 27
Government
  and household purchasing, 339
  power, nature of, 18–19
  research and development, procurement by, 252, 255
  role
    in decentralized market-direction, 7, 219, 221, 226, 227–228

  in organizational market-negotiating form, 14–15, 74, 78, 83, 84, 87, 166–168, 169, 202, 228–234
  in progress of agriculture, 245–248
  See also Centralized political-direction, Political economy
Grant-giving agency
  academic authority, 330–332
  advisory committees, 331–332
  research, support of, 329–332
Greenwalt, Crawford, 19–20

Halifax, Marquis of, 126
Harris, Seymour, 313
Harrod, Roy, 91
Hayek, Frederich August von, 8
Hicks, J. R., 14
Hidalgo y Costillo, Miguel, 442–443
Hierarchy, culture of, 191
Hill, Christopher, 126
Household economy, 205, 206, 337–342
  consumption, organization of, 337–338
  importance in national economy, 337–338
  income, transfers into, 267–268
  production outputs, unmeasured, 337
  and property, 341
  technology of, 340–341
  See also Familial systems
Howard, Frank, 165–166
Huerta, Victoriano, 447, 450
Huitzilopochtli, 438, 439
Humboldt, Alexander von, 449

Image
  Boulding's, 172
  private, 172
  projected, 173
  shared, 172
Imperialism, in Marxian theory, 395–396
Indian, Mexican, 438–439, 442–443, 446–449, 453, 455–456, 458
  degraded, 439, 441, 446–449, 453
  decimated, 441–442, 447–448, 449
  racism concerning, 449
Individualism
  and collectivism, 190–191
  era of
    economic progress in, 124–128, 129–130, 378–381
    emergence, 124–125, 378–379
    and science, 125–127, 129–130, 379
    shop economy in, 379–380
  and the Industrial Revolution, 127–128, 379–381, 383–384
  and the organizational revolution, 238–239

See also Choice (individualized), Cultural systems

Industrial research associations, 168, 258, 423

Industrial Revolution, 136, 379–381, 388, 477
  as cognitive change, 379–380

Industrialization
  communist commitment, 405, 407
  in Marxian theory, 395
  United States, impact on, 25

Inflation, cost-push, 352

Information
  optimal use of, 154–156
  planned dissemination of, 293
  research and development, dissemination of, 297–301
    by Atomic Energy Commission, 298–299
    by Department of Defense, 299–300
    "need to know," 300
  sequestered, 163–164, 256–257, 261
  See also Communication

Inheritance
  and malrecruitment, 37–38
  and motivation, economic, 35

Innovation, 103
  in agriculture, support for, 247–248
  under centralized-political-direction, 150–151, 158–159
  costs, 114
  development contracts in the U. K., 168
  and economic development, 416
  and externalities, 103, 138–140
  and individualism, 127, 144–146, 147
  in institutional systems, 306, 315–321
  and monopoly, 164–166, 255–256
  resistances to, 116, 120, 138–139, 143, 144, 147, 156–157, 164–167, 169, 245, 255–256, 258, 260, 315, 316, 318–319, 328–329, 330–332, 419
  systematically organized, 151
  transformation, as phase of, 114, 120
  uncertainties of, 103, 138–140

Instabilities, economic
  under centralized political-direction, 66
  of employment and production
    in autonomous enterprise, 84, 87, 221–224 (chart, 222, 223)
    with price stability, 225, 349–353
  exogenous, 45
  in household economy, 339–340
  of price level
    under decentralized market-direction, 45–47, 219 (chart, 220), 221

  and full employment, 225, 349–353
  and the social environment, 175–176

Instabilities, political, 66

Institute d'Étude de Dévéloppement Économique et Social (ISEA), 428

Institute de Recherche pour les Huiles et Oleogineaux (I.R.H.O.), 428–431

Institutional costs
  under centralized political-direction, 60–62
  under decentralized market-direction, 38–40 (in consumption), 51–52
  under organizational market negotiation, 76–78, 87

Institutional economy, 205, 206, 302–307, 308–321
  and education, 302, 306–307, 308–321
  external influences, 303, 304, 305, 306
  income, transfers into, 267–268
  See also Institutional systems

Institutional systems
  characteristics of, 302–305, 328–329, 360
  degeneration of, 327–328
  resistances
    to external control, 806
    to innovation, 306, 315, 318–319, 321, 328–329
  transformation of, 306, 315–321
  value commitment in, 302–305, 328–329
    congruency of, 304–305
    as "way-of life," 305–306, 315
  See also Institutional economy

Invention
  in autonomous organization, 161–164, 248, 249–250, 252, 255–257, 261
  under centralized political-direction, 148, 150–151, 158–159
  costs, 116, 120
  under decentralized market-direction, 135, 244–245
  dissemination of, 118, 120, 141–144, 147, 153–157, 158–159, 163–164, 245–246, 255–256
  education for, 115–116, 120–121, 160–161, 244
  as an individual activity, 114–115
  and individualism, 137–138, 144–146, 147
  knowledge as a parameter, 116, 120
  receptivity to, 116, 120–121, 153–154, 162, 164–166
  resistances to, 138–139, 156–157, 164–166
  and science, 117, 150–152, 162–163, 256–257, **261**

social preconditions, 115–117, 120–121
in traditional societies, 123–124, 129–130
transformation, as phase of, 114, 416
See also Creativity, Patents
Investment
in education, 149, 158–159, 161, 169, 237, 248–249
and household saving, 337–340
incentives, 231
in research and development, 150–151, 158–159 (chart, 253–254), 277–278
in science, 138–140, 150–151, 159, 161, 162, 237 (chart, 253–254, 326)
in transformation, 138
Ivan the Terrible, 403, 405

Juarez, Benito, 387, 445–446, 452, 460
Justice, in income distribution
under centralized political-direction, 69–70, 86
criterion for evaluation of economy, 15, 53
equality as a measure of, 53–54
equity as a measure of, 54
under market-direction, 53–55, 86
in organizational market-negotiating form, 86–87

Kendrick, John, 247
Keynes, John Maynard, 4, 27, 98, 224, 357, 387
Knight, Frank, 50, 212
Korea, economic development in, 480
Korean War, 476
Kuhn, Thomas, 127, 324, 325, 327, 329

Landrum-Griffin Act, 232
Latin America, economic development of, 480
Lenin, Nikolai, 407, 408, 409
Ley Juarez, 446
Ley Lerdo, 446, 447
Liberalism, laissez-faire
choice, conception of norm in, 32
as a dominant cultural system, 24, 25, 381
as *mestizo* creed, 442, 445–446, 460
Liberties, political, 193
Locke, John, 387

Madero, Gustavo, 449, 450
Malthus, Thomas, 131–132
Malthusian theory, 131–132, 433
failure of prediction, 132
in open societies, 131

Man
and economic relationships, 171–172
"ideologically directed," 199
"inner directed," 199, 201, 468
as integrator of cultures, 173–174, 180, 362, 368, 469
"other-directed" (organizational), 199–200, 201, 382–383, 437
shaped by economic environment, 170–171, 382–383
the social being, 192–193
Manufacturing, in American enterprise economy, 210, 211 (chart, 222–223)
Market systems, operational characteristics, 359
See also Functional systems
Marshall, Alfred, 4, 24
Marshall Plan, 463
Marx-Leninism, 387
Marxism
and capital, 94
choice, conception of norm in, 32–33
and conflict of cultural-cognitive systems, 368–369
as a cultural-cognitive system, 366–367
for revolutionary elites, 396–398
debased, 414
and economic development, 392
cognition for, 481–482
"laws," failure of, 396–397, 399–402
and Russian intelligentsia, 397–398
as theory of revolution, 394–396, 399–402
Mason, Edward S., 3, 8
Massel, B. F., 92
Maximilian, Emperor of Mexico, 444–445, 461
Mayans, 438, 447, 449
Mercantilism, Spanish colonial, 441
Mestizo, in Mexico, 440, 443, 445–446, 458
Methodology
conceptual framework
for economic development, 357–359
macroeconomic, 224, 357
microeconomic, 224, 357
of science, 363–365
Mexico
agriculture, *see* Agriculture (Mexican)
borrowed doctrines, 386–387, 445, 456
cognitions in
of mechanism 451–452, 454–455
of politics, 443–444, 445, 450–451, 455–456

of process, 451–452, 454–455
traditional, 438–439, 453, 454
Constitution of 1917, 450
cultural disunity, 439–440, 456–461
and functional interdependence, lack of, 458–459
and geographical divisions, 458
and heritage, historical, 457–458
cultural unification
and functional interdependence, emerging, 461
and liberalism, 460
and nationalism, 445, 450, 460–461
and catholicism, 459–460
economic developments, recent, 451–453
enterprise in, 451–452, 454–455
familial system dominant, 455–456
history of
before the Conquest, 438–439
creole rule, 443–445
Diaz dictatorship, 446–449
liberalism, triumph of, 445–446
revolution, the, 449–451
slave uprising, 442–443
Spanish rule, 440–442, 454–455, 459
individualism, sterility in, 380–381, 456
political system, 450–451, 455–457
and the United States, 444, 446–448, 451
See also Cultural systems (in Mexico)
Military establishment
innovations, sources of, 289
as institutional systems, 303–304
research and development
dissemination, 299–300
management, 286–288, 301
Mitchell, Billy, 113
Monopoly
and economic development, 454–455
innovation, as barrier to, 144, 164–165, 169
in Mexico, 454–455
regulated, 214–217
and research and development concentration, 252
and utilization of leadership talent, 36–37
Monopsany, 348–349
Morida, 456
Morison, Elting, 113–114
Mort, Paul, 315
Moscoso, Teodoro, 476
Moscow Exposition of Industry and Agriculture, 484
Mosk, S. A., 451

Motivation, economic
in American enterprise, 435–436
in autonomous organization, 74–76, 87, 160
under centralized political-direction, 58
under "cost-plus" contract, 283, 284
and economic development, 434–436
in household purchasing, 51, 338
to invent and innovate
in autonomous organizations, 160, 255–256
under centralized political-direction, 148, 158
under market-direction, 147
under market-direction, 34–35, 147
patents and dissemination, 141
in political economy, 289–290
under profit regulation, 236
and rents, 35
to self-education under market-direction, 136–137, 146
to transform, 113
Munoz Marin, Luis, 472, 478

Nahuas, 438
Napoleon, Bonaparte, 442
Napoleon III, 444
Narodnicks, 398
National economy
cultural-functional incongruities
commercial criteria and strategic choice, 346–347
public debt, 346
TVA, 348
dominant cultural system, 345–348, 354
functional diversities, 3, 205, 343
complementarities, 344–345, 353
greater flexibility, 343–344, 353
individual opportunities, 344, 353
functional incompatibilities
and full employment, 349–354
monopsany, 348–349, 353–354
price-competitive and price-determining enterprise, 349–354
unionized and nonunionized labor, 349, 354
See also Enterprise economy, Household economy, Institutional economy, Political economy
National Labor Relations Board, 232
National Science Foundation
organization of, 330
support to academic research, 324
See also Grant-giving agency
Nationalism, 182–184, 185, 388, 450, 460–461

credo of revolution, 392, 445, 450
an integrating force, 388, 460–461
Natural resources
conservation of, 225, 226
and economic development in Puerto Rico, 474
Netherlands Organization for Applied Research (TNO), 423, 485
New Economic Policy, 409–412
Newton, Isaac, 469

Oil, Mexican, 447, 450
"Operation Bootstraps," 476–477
Oppenheimer, Robert, 327
Organization, the age of. *See* Organizational revolution, Research and development
Organization of American States, 462
Organizational market-negotiating form
in allocation of resources, 72–85, 87
arbitrary power, and control of, 228–234
characteristics of, 12–15, 209
choice, norm of, 33, 72
cognitive system in, 200
conflicts of interest in, 196–197
consumption under, 85–86
education
self-acquired, 160, 237, 248
support to, 161, 169, 237, 248–249
government, role in, 14–15, 74, 78, 83, 84, 87, 228–233, 256–257
importance in national economy, 210–211
and income distribution, 86–87
instability of production and employment, 221–225
institutional costs, 76–78, 237–239
and invention, 161–164, 255–256
and "other-directed" man, 199–201
progress, economic, in, 160–169, 249–257, 260–261
receptivity to information, 162
and research and development, 161–162, 164, 249–252, 260–261
science, investment in, 161, 162, 237, 253, 254
as social environment, 196–202
values in, 198–201, 202
voluntary association under, 196
See also Autonomous organizations, Organizational revolution
Organizational revolution, 17, 128, 236–239, 381–384
and cognitive systems, 382–384
and cultural system, 382–384, 436–437

and education, 248–249, 260–261, 311
and progress, economic, 248, 382
and research and development, 249–250, 261, 382
Orlans, Harold, 295
Orthodoxy, and innovation, 116, 144, 147, 156–157, 315, 318–319, 329–330

Pareto, Vilfredo, 55
Parkes, Henry Bramford, 439, 440, 444, 445, 447, 448, 449, 453
Passinetti, Luigi, 92
Pasteur, Louis, 324, 325
Patents
in autonomous organization, 163–166, 167, 169, 255–257, 261
and economic motivation, 141, 255
and monopoly, 255–256
and research and development per capita, 258–259
under socialism, 152
See also Property
Péguy, Charles, 467–468
Perroux, Francois, 234
Personalissimo, 380, 433–434,
Peter the Great, 403, 405
Planning, economic
in American political economy, 275–276
in autonomous organization, 19, 72–73, 74, 75, 87, 168
and centralization, 8
in centralized political-direction, 58–60, 71
costs, 60–62
cultural values, impact on, 186–187, 189, 191, 192, 194–195
elite in, 11–12
exclusions under, 65–66
in France, 10, 168, 231
the process of, 10–11
"the religious core," 59–60, 187–189, 391–392, 393, 397, 405–406
science-based initiative in, 427–428
and the science infrastructure, 424
technology of, 66, 424
and transformation, 109–110
Political economy, 205, 206
consumption in, 265–270
for collective purposes, 265–267
defined, 265
education, impact of research and development procurement on, 294–296
elites, science-trained, need for, 285–286, 290–292, 301
participation of, in production

in enterprise economy 270–271
in institutional economy, 271–272, 325–326
production in, 270–275
and redistribution of income, 268, 270
residual tasks of, 270, 276
transfer of income by
to enterprise economy 267–268
to household economy, 267–268
to institutional economy, 267–268, 325–326
Political economy, research and development in, 252, 255, 274, 275, 277–301
alternative choices of, 296–297
dissemination of R & D information, 297–301
"in-house"
military management of, 286–288, 301
elite, for recruitment of, 290–292
planning
to allocate resources 293–294
to eliminate duplication, 293–294, 297–301
control fragmented, 277–281, 292
to minimize uncertainty, 293–294
possibilities, 292–294
possibilities of international collaboration, 297
procurement of
agencies of, 277–281
deficiencies of system, 283–292
domination by private contractor, 289–292
organization of, 281
subordination to strategy, 288–289
Political systems
characteristics, 359
Mexican, 450–451, 456–457
Ponce de Leon, 471
Population increase
and creative talent, pool of, 132–133
and investment in education, 134
Malthusian prognosis, 131–132
and productivity, 90, 132–134
in Puerto Rico, 474
Power, economic
arbitrary, in autonomous organization, 14, 81, 82, 83, 84, 166–167, 196–197, 198, 228–231
and government, 18–19
under market-direction, 81
anonymity of, 176
of planning elites, 11, 187
public opinion, to form, 197–198

to transform, 109–110
See also Property
Price
control of, in autonomous organization, 233–234
and cultural values, 177
as economic regulator, 4
Price, Don K., 294
Price, J. A. de Solla, 326, 327
Price-regulated public utilities form
characteristics, 214–215
importance in the United States economy, 215–217
policy problems
of motivation, managerial, 236
regulator, subversion of, 234, 235
Process
described, 101
"higher," 101, 102
transformation of, 102, 103, 106–110
See also Transformation
Productivity, measurement of, 89
Profits, uncertainty, function of, 50, 212
Progress, economic
in agriculture, American, 221, 244–248, 259–260
and centralized political-direction, 148–159, 292–301
criterion in evaluation of forms of economic organization, 53, 88
under decentralized market-direction, 135–147
defined, 88
economic growth, contrasted with, 88–89
in households, technology of, 340–341
individualism, in era of, 124–127, 129–130
notation on, 102–103
and the organizational market-negotiating form, 160–169
preconditions, cognitive, 416–419
and science, 128–130, 244–246, 249–250, 419–420
and technical assistance, 464–465
in traditional societies, 122–124, 129–130, 377–381
See also Productivity, Transformation
Progress, idea of, 124
Property
and class barriers, 37
costs of adjudication and contract, 39–40, 238
and cultural values, 178
and economic motivation, 34
in the household economy, 341

information as, 138–139, 141–142, 154–156
  institutional aspect of, 303, 304
  in Marxian theory, 395
  and nepotism, 37
  patents as, 142, 154–155
  as a power locus, 6
Protestantism, 182–184, 379
Public debt
  interest on, 269–270
  tabu, ideological as, 346
Puerto Rico
  Commonwealth status, 478
  cultural-cognitive systems
    conflicts of, 477–478
    economic development in, barrier to, 472, 474–475, 476
    reformulated, 472, 475
    of U. S. enterprise, imported, 475–477
  geography of, 471
  Independentistas, 477
  "Operation Bootstraps," 476–477
  political system, 475–476
  Popular Democratic Party (*Populars*), 472, 478
  socialism, abortive, 473
  Statehood Party, 478
  United States, relation with, 471–472, 476, 477–478
Puerto Rico Industrial Development Corporation (PRIDCO), 473
Pusey, Nathan, 295, 296

Queretaro, 442
Quetzalcoatl, 439

Rand, Ayn, 27
Reisman, David, 199
Renaissance, 124–125, 379
Research, academic
  and economic development, 431
  ideology of, 328–329
  and practical objectives, 323–324, 334
  and scientific freedom, 333–334, 335–336
  and scientific revolutions
    contra academic authority, 328–329, 330–332, 335
    design to frustrate, 332, 333
    failure to produce, 326–327
    program to foment, 332–333, 335–336
  support through grant-giving agency, 329–332, 335

Research, applied, 80
  See also Research and development
Research, basic. *See* Research, fundamental
Research and development
  and academic research, 322–323
  and American agriculture, 245–246
  in autonomous organization, 128–129, 161–163, 164, 237, 249–250, 261
  under centralized political-direction, 151–152, 159, 292–301
  competition in, 164, 169
  under decentralized market-direction, precluded, 140–141, 244–245
  in decentralized market-segmented enterprise, 257
  for developing regions, 425–427, 486–487
  dissemination of information, 297–301
  duplication, 156–159, 164, 293, 297–301
  elites, function in, 152
  in the enterprise economy, 250 (chart, 250), 252, 255
  expenditures on, 277 (chart, 278)
  "goal creation," 102
  historical development, 128–130, 249–255, 260–261, 382
  in the institutional economy (chart, 250)
  in a military environment, 286–288
  and the organizational revolution, 249–250, 382
  and patents per capita, 258–259
  and the patent system, 255–256
  in the political economy (chart, 250), 252, 255, 274, 275, 277–301
  preconditions of, 249–250
  research alternatives
    choice of, 296–297
    cost-benefit analysis, 296–297
    international collaboration in determining, 297
  and science, receptivity to, 153–154, 162–163
  as "social-problem oriented," 322–323
  source of funds (chart, 253–254)
  See also Political economy, research and development in, procurement of
Research, fundamental, 80
  in the institutional economy, 302, 306–307
  myth of, 322–324
  source of funds (chart, 253–254), 326

See also Science, Research, academic
Research, pure. *See* Research, fundamental
Resource, natural. *See* Natural resources
Revolution
    autonomous, 389
    Chinese, as palace coup, 388–389
    of economic development, 388–389
    Marxist theory of, 394–396, 399–402
    Mexican, 449–451
    Russian, *see* Russian revolution
    under representative government, 388
    See also Economic revolution, Industrial revolution
Robinson, Joan, 91, 92, 93, 212
Roosevelt, Franklin D., 472
Roosevelt, Theodore, 113–114
Rosenzweig, Robert M., 295
Rural Electrification Administration, 248
Russia
    collective action, capacity for, 401, 402–405, 407, 415
    invasions of, 402, 407
Russian Civil War, 408
Russian intelligentsia
    cultural alienation, 398
    in Holy Russia, 297–298
Russian revolution, 386, 397–407
    and cultural-cognitive systems
        incapacities built in, 406, 408–409
        shaping history, 401–406, 407
        transformation of, 410–413
    as economic transformation, 394
    and New Economic Policy, 409–412
    as palace coup, 388–389, 404
    peasantry, alienation of, 413–415
    proletariat, role in, 401–402, 404–405
    war communism, 408–409

Santa Anna, Antonio Lopez, 443–444
Scale, economies of
    for autonomous enterprise, 76
    under centralized-direction, 61–62, 71
    in household purchasing, 338–339
    under market-direction, 38–39, (in consumption) 51–52
    for transformation, 107–109
Schmitz, Herman, 165
Schon, Donald A., 118
Schumpeter, Joseph, 106, 107–108
Science
    under centralized political-direction, 150–151, 159
    cognitive systems of, 363–365
    development-oriented, 425–426, 429–430, 486–487

    and economic development, 419–431, 482, 485, 486–487
    and externalities, 138–140
    and individualism, culture of, 137–138, 144–146, 147
    and infrastructure, 245–246, 421–422
    initiatives, 427–428, 430–431
    innovations, technical, integrated into, 128–130, 244–246, 249–250, 420, 423–425
    as an institutional system, 302, 303
    and invention, 117, 163–164, 426–427, 429
    investment in (chart, 253–254), 324–326
    manpower, conflicting demands for, 293–296
    methodology, 363–365
    myth of basic research, 322–324
    "normal," 324
    "paradigms" of, 324
    pitfalls
        of affluence, 327–328
        of bigness, 327–328
    political participation in, 271–272
    a "problem-solving apparatus," 324
    and research and development, 153–154, 162–163
    revolutions in, 325–327
    sequestered, 163–164, 256–257, 261, 420
    subordinated to strategy, 286, 288–289
    technically oriented, 151–152, 322–324, 425–427
    in De Tocqueville's America, 145–147
    transformed, 325
    and uncertainties, 138–140
    See also Research, academic, Research and development, Research, fundamental
"Scissor's Crisis" in Russia, 411–412
Scott, Winfield, 461
Secrecy, industrial, 119, 141
Security classification, 119
Security Exchange Commission, 232
Simpson, L. B., 449
Smith, Adam, 24, 171, 387, 445
Snow, Sir Charles, 31
Social environment
    autonomous organization, as a, 196–202
    centralized political-direction, as a, 186–195

decentralized market-direction, as a, 175–185
economy, as a, 170–174
Social sciences, explaining functional systems, 360
Socialism
  Marxian requisites for, 396
  in Marxian theory, 395–396
Society
  conceptions of, 176–177, 186
  functional interdependence, as a condition of, 369, 374
  furies of, 190–191
  topography of, 369–371, 374
  traditional, *see* Traditional societies
  as value locus under political-direction, 186, 190
  See also Individualism (era of)
Societies, Mexican, 439–440, 450–451
Solo, Robert A., 320
Solow, Robert, 92
Sorokin, P., 327
Soviet Union
  agricultural collectivization, 62, 348, 413–415
  dominant cultural system, 345
  experimental opportunity, 152–153
  revolution, Russian, *see* Russian Revolution
Spanish-American War, 471
Spencer, Herbert, 24, 433
Sputnik, 316
Stagnation thesis, 93–94
Stalin, Joseph, 26, 387
  and collectivization of agriculture, 62, 413–415
State
  in Marxian theory, 394–396
  Russian, 400–405
Steffens, Lincoln, 235
Stevenson, Earl, 117
Supreme Court of the United States
  and authoritative choice, 22–28
  changing role of, 22–28
  and desegregation, 28
  and reapportionment, 28
Synthetic rubber, strategic choice in, 346–347

Taft-Hartley Act, 232
Tannenbaum, Frank, 439, 440, 448, 453, 454, 455, 458, 459
Tawney, R. H., 434
Taylor, Zach, 461
Technical assistance, 462–465
  benefits to donor, 464–465, 480–481
  and the Cold War, 464, 479–482
  and commodity agreements, 487–488
  cultural values, underlying, 463–464
  through international organizations, 462
  for international tranquillity, 464
  loans
    "soft," 462
    tied, 462, 465
  Marshall Plan, as precedent, 463
  project aid, 462
Technology
  household, 340–341
  inter-industry transmission of, 252, 419
  receptivity to, 141, 423–425, 427, 429
  science based, 128–129, 151–152, 244–245, 424–425
  in De Tocqueville's America, 145–147
  transmission of
    Bell Labs and transistor, 82–83
    in traditional societies, 122
Tennessee Valley Administration, 348
Tocqueville, Alex de, 126, 144–147, 171, 179, 432, 436–437
  and voluntary associations, 436–437
Toltec, 439
Trade unions
  grievance procedures, 232
  internal relationships, 232
  support of, 229
  wage bargaining exemplified, 29–31, 78
  wage policy, 233–234
  See also Autonomous organizations
Trade, wholesale and retail in American enterprise economy, 213, 214, 223 (chart, 222, 223)
Traditional societies
  characteristics, 122
  cognitive systems in, 122–124, 376–378
  and craft economy, 122, 377–378
  individualism in, 380, 388
  invention in, 123–124
  technology
    achievement in, 122–123
    transmitted, 122
Transformation
  of agriculture in India, 109
  choice, 113
  costs of, 103, 104, 105, 106, 110, 114, 157–158
    opportunity and capital stock, 105
  "distance," 103
  and economic development, 416
  economies of scale in, 107–109

goals, 102, 106, 110
piecemeal, 105
power for, 109–110, 157–158, 473
  and income inequalities, 109–110
of processes, 101, 102, 110, 416
and science infrastructure, 422–423
speed under
  centralized political-direction, 153–159
  decentralized market-direction, 141–144, 147
  organizational market-negotiating form, 163–166
strategy of, 106, 166–167
supported, U. S. agricultural, 247–248
Trotsky, Leon, 398
  at Brest-Litovsk, 408
  Russian revolution, prognosis of, 400–402
  and world revolution, 407
Truman, Harry, 478
Tugwell, Rexford, 472

Uncertainty, economic
  in autonomous organization, 85
  caused by, 48–49
  under centralized political-direction, 66–67, 68
  in decentralized market-direction, 47–50, 52–53, 138–139, 339–340
  exogenous, 47
  and innovation, 103, 138–140
  profits, a source of, 50
  in transformation, 103
Uncertainty, political, spill-overs into economy, 67, 85
United Nations and technical assistance, 462
United States Congress. *See* Congress of the United States
United States national economy. *See* National economy
United States Steel Company, 81, 82
United States Supreme Court. *See* Supreme Court of the United States

Universities. *See* Academia, Education

Values, cultural
  and centralized political-direction, 189–190, 194–195
  and decentralized market-direction, 177–179, 184–185, 190–191
  derived and inculcated, 189, 197–198
  in the organizational market-negotiating form, 198–201, 202
Vanderbilt, Commodore, 179
Vera Cruz, 458
Vernon, Raymond, 452
Vietnam, 480

War communism, 408–409
Way-of-life
  in Academia, 309
  anti-trust policy, objective of, 228
  in centralized political-direction, 186–189
  choice of, 344
  as criterion in economic evaluations, 53
  in decentralized market-direction, 175–177
  and household economy, 341
  in institutional systems, 305–306, 315
  in organizational market-negotiating form, 196–198
  See also Social environment
Weber, Max, 434
Weizmann, Chaim, 346
White, Stephen, 317, 332
Wilson, Henry Lane, 450
Windfalls
  and economic motivation, 35
  and malrecruitment, 37–38
Wolfe, Dael, 248

Yaquis, 448
Yucatan, 438, 447, 458

Zacharias, Jerrold R., 316–317, 332